PRODUCT PLANNING AND MANAGEMENT

DESIGNING AND DELIVERING VALUE

McGraw-Hill Series in Marketing

Allen, Spohn, and Wilson: *Selling Dynamics*
Anderson, Hair, and Bush: *Professional Sales Management*
Baier: *Direct Marketing*
Berkman and Gilson: *Advertising*
Bovee and Thill: *Marketing*
Bowersox and Cooper: *Strategic Marketing Channel Management*
Britt, Boyd, Davis, and Larreche: *Marketing Management and Administrative Action*
Buell: *Marketing Management: A Strategic Planning Approach*
Buskirk and Buskirk: *Selling: Principles and Practices*
Corey, Lovelock, and Ward: *Problems in Marketing*
Dobler, Burt, and Lee: *Purchasing and Materials Management: Text and Cases*
Guiltinan and Paul: *Cases in Marketing Management*
Guiltinan and Paul: *Marketing Management: Strategies and Programs*
Guiltinan and Paul: *Readings in Marketing Strategies and Programs*
Johnson, Kurtz, and Scheuing: *Sales Management: Concepts, Practices, and Cases*
Kinnear and Taylor: *Marketing Research: An Applied Approach*
Loudon and Della Bitta: *Consumer Behavior: Concepts and Applications*
Lovelock and Weinberg: *Marketing Challenges: Cases and Exercises*
Monroe: *Pricing: Making Profitable Decisions*
Moore and Pessemier: *Product Planning and Management: Designing and Delivering Value*
Rossiter and Percy: *Advertising and Promotion Management*
Shapiro: *Sales Program Management: Formulation and Implementation*
Stanton, Etzel, and Walker: *Fundamentals of Marketing*

)

PRODUCT PLANNING AND MANAGEMENT

DESIGNING AND DELIVERING VALUE

William L. Moore
University of Utah

Edgar A. Pessemier
University of Virginia

McGRAW-HILL, INC.

New York   St. Louis   San Francisco   Auckland   Bogotá   Caracas
Lisbon   London   Madrid   Mexico   Milan   Montreal
New Delhi   Paris   San Juan   Singapore   Sydney   Tokyo   Toronto

PRODUCT PLANNING AND MANAGEMENT
Designing and Delivering Value

1 2 3 4 5 6 7 8 9 0   HAL   HAL   9 0 9 8 7 6 5 4 3 2

ISBN 0-07-043046-2

This book was set in Palatino by The Clarinda Company.
The editors were Bonnie K. Binkert and Bernadette Boylan;
the production supervisor was Denise L. Puryear.
The cover was designed by John Hite.
Arcata Graphics/Halliday was printer and binder.

Library of Congress Cataloging-in-Publication Data

Moore, William L. (William Loyd), (date).
    Product planning and management: designing and delivering value /
  William L. Moore, Edgar A. Pessemier.
      p.   cm. — (McGraw-Hill series in marketing)
    Includes bibliographical references and index.
    ISBN 0-07-043046-2
    1. New products—Management.   I. Pessemier, Edgar A., (date).
  II. Title.   III. Series.
  HF5415.153.M66   1993
    658.5'74—dc20   92-13522

ABOUT THE AUTHORS

WILLIAM L. MOORE is Professor of Marketing and the Lawrence R. Knowles Faculty Scholar at the David Eccles School of Business, University of Utah, Salt Lake City, UT. He received his B.S. (1968) and M.B.A. (1970) from Oklahoma State University and his Ph.D. (1976) from the Krannert Graduate School at Purdue University. Prior to coming to the University of Utah, Professor Moore was on the faculty at the Graduate School of Business, Columbia University in New York City. He has published articles in leading academic journals such as *Journal of Marketing Research, Journal of Consumer Research, Marketing Science, Journal of Marketing, Journal of Product Innovation Management,* and *Sloan Management Review* and serves on the editorial review boards of *Journal of Marketing Research* and *Marketing Letters.* Additionally, he is co-editor of *Readings in the Management of Innovation.*

EDGAR A. PESSEMIER is the C. Stewart Sheppard Professor of Business Administration Emeritus at the Darden Graduate School of the University of Virginia. He received a B.S. from the University of Notre Dame, an M.S. From New York University, and a D.B.A. from Harvard University. He has served on the faculties at Purdue University and Washington State University, and was active in the doctoral program at Purdue and Virginia.

Professor Pessemier's research interests have centered on modeling consumer and market behavior, particularly as these topics relate to problems in product design and management. His publications include five books, two research monographs and numerous articles and papers.

CONTENTS

PREFACE

Coping with change is one of the most persistent problems facing a firm. The firm's capacity to exploit evolving technical and market conditions is best reflected in the strength of its product line. These products determine what it sells, to whom it sells, with whom it must compete, and the human and capital resources that are required to succeed. This text is designed to help decision-makers effectively analyze, plan, and manage the product function.

The text examines the process by which attractive new and improved products are developed and successfully introduced. A broad perspective has been adopted that includes coverage of products and services aimed at both consumer and industrial targets. A strong managerial approach is taken to the conceptual and analytical framework that is used to analyze product strategy, development, and marketing. The source of data, the methods of analysis, and the interpretation of results are presented in enough detail to permit one to be an informed user.

The text's emphasis on planning and value is not accidental. Planning is the process for determining the most desirable results and actions needed to achieve these results. Enhancing the value of a firm's products and services should be a central objective of its long-range plan. The value received by buyers and users can be best examined by dividing it into two parts: the value of the offer and the value delivered by marketing.

The value of the offer flows from the actual product or service, its positioning and communications message, and its price. The value created by marketing support is represented by consumer knowledge and ready availability. Consideration of these latter elements leads to the analysis of marketing budgets and their allocation to the various elements in supporting marketing activities. The text's companion computer programs present analytical methods for developing effective marketing budgets for both new and maturing products.

The text is divided into five major sections that are listed below:

Finding desirable product opportunities: Identifying product opportunities that fit the firm's business strategy. Successfully managing the development process.

Develping a successful offer: Techniques for designing desirable new and improved products and services, as well as determining prices that are based on value to the consumer. Four applications illustrate the methods that are presented.

Testing the offer's value: Approaches to testing concepts prior to full development as well as to forecasting sales prior to full-scale market introduction.

Marketing delivers value—product introduction: This section expands on the model of market behavior introduced in the previous sections and applies a spreadsheet model and companion computer program to develop the best strategy and budget for a new product introduction. A detailed illustration is included.

Marketing delivers value—the maturing product: A computerized marketing response model is presented that is suitable for maturing products. It helps one determine the best size marketing budget and its allocation to individual activities or marketing mix elements. Illustrative applications are included.

Depending on an instructor's course objectives, the text can be used in a one quarter or one semester offering that either does or does not use the computer programs. By adding case material, computer exercises, and planning assignments, multi-quarter or multi-semester offerings can be developed. An instructor's manual contains course outlines, case suggestions, and some sample cases. The speed with which the material is covered will be influenced by course objectives and students' academic background and applied experience. Classroom tests of the text with undergraduate students, MBA students, and executive MBA students indicate that the analytical and computer work is well within their grasp.

A number of activities and methods related to completing a marketing plan are not covered in the book. These subjects include most aspects of developing general background information, sales forecasting techniques, and standard marketing research methods. These topics are adequately covered by marketing research texts.

The work on this book and the associated computer programs has extended over a number of years and has benefited from assistance offered by many individuals and organizations. Very early in the process, the Marketing Science Institute provided support. The Darden Graduate School of Business Administation's support was substantial and enduring. Generous donations from Ezekiel R. and Katherine Dumke, Jr., and Lawrence R. and Marilyn E. Knowles provided release time during the writing phase. Frank Bass and John Gwin kindly

permitted us to use their classes to test the text with MBA and undergraduate students. Robert Carraway, Cornelis de Kluyver, Paul Farris, Philip Pferfer, James Olver, and H. Paul Root offered encouragement and useful comments as did a number of our other professional colleagues and doctoral students. Dave Brady added color and graphics to the LMIXMENU programs. Although they must remain anonymous, the group of professional managers who applied the MARMIX program and offered constructive suggests deserve special thanks. Finally, we would like to thank the following, academic reviewers: Sucheta Ahlawat, Baruch College, CUNY; Arthur Allaway, University of Alabama; C. Anthony di Benedetto, Temple University; Michael J. Houston, University of Minnesota; Thomas Hustad, Indiana University; Dipak Jain, Northwestern Universilty; and Akshay Rao, University of Minnesota. We hope to continue to receive feedback from practitioners and our academic colleagues.

Thanks also go to Scott Smith for providing PC versions of a number of the computer programs that are discussed in Chapter 5. We also thank Richard Johnson for kindly offering copies of Saw Tooth Software's Adaptive PC programs for our use and reference.

Finally, we would like to thank our families who have provided support and encouragement.

William L. Moore
Edgar A. Pessemier

PRODUCT PLANNING AND MANAGEMENT
DESIGNING AND DELIVERING VALUE

INTRODUCTION

INTRODUCTORY ISSUES

Before describing the text, we will discuss three specific areas briefly in order to provide a better understanding of the organization and structure of this text. These areas are the need for continuous innovation, the division of the marketing mix into the value created by the offer and marketing support, and the relevance of marketing models to managers.

This book emphasizes the need for continual improvement of products and services. In contrast to many books on product management, this text covers the planning and management of both new and existing products.[1] Many students are interested only in revolutionary innovations. However, most innovations are incremental changes to either the product or the process used to make it. Furthermore, the cumulative impact of these incremental innovations can be greater than the original, more radical innovation. Therefore product development and improvement must be an ongoing process.

One cannot develop a new product and forget about subsequent improvements. For example, although the original IBM PC introduced in 1981 was a very successful product, without continuous improvement IBM's line of PCs would have long ago ceased to be a factor in the industry. Similarly, the success of many companies such as Honda, Compaq, and SAS is based on programs of continual improvement.

This need for continual improvement of existing products has several implications for this text. First, it requires a focus on the planning and management of both new and existing products, not just new products. Second, many of the issues discussed in conjunction with new products are just as applicable to the improvement of existing products. Finally, most new products are introduced by companies that have experience with similar products. Therefore, the

---

[1]To avoid the more cumbersome "products and services," this book will use the term "product" to encompass both products and services.

1

firm's current offerings (and the skills needed to produce and market them) need to be considered when developing the new product.

A basic philosophy behind the book is that marketing mix decisions are best made by breaking the mix into two parts that are partially independent of each other: the offer and marketing support. The offer is composed of the product and/or service, the message sent to intermediaries and customers, and the price charged. The purpose of the offer is to create a positioning, i.e., an image of the product or service in the mind of the potential customer differentiating it from the competition. Positioning includes both prepurchase anticipation and postpurchase satisfaction. The development of the offer is referred to as "creating value," where value means worth in the mind of the customer. Much of this activity is performed by people outside of the marketing group, such as R&D and operations. Furthermore, much of the expense of creating value may not show up in the marketing budget. This part of the marketing mix can be researched by using a number of techniques covered in this book, including multidimensional scaling, conjoint analysis, concept tests, and product tests.

The second half of the mix is marketing support. This is composed of the spending and activities that get the word out and make the product available for purchase, i.e., spending to gain awareness and distribution. This is sometimes referred to as "delivering value" or "creating value by marketing." Most of the marketing budget is usually spent on marketing support. Several approaches to determining the proper level and allocation of support are discussed in the text.

The idea of value is one of the cornerstones of the book. To be successful a firm needs to provide greater net value—that is, benefits minus total price—than the competition. This can be achieved either by providing comparable benefit at a lower price or providing superior benefits. Value is created through a combination of elements. First, value can be created by the physical product (for example, by providing greater durability, reliability, performance, and/or special features). It can also be created by the service, either through its outcome (such as a better interest rate, consulting report, or haircut) or through its process (friendlier, closer, or more responsive). Value can also be created by speed of response. In many cases, the consumer has to be educated about the value of a product or service, so ready knowledge and availability also create value. Finally, price is used to capture as well as signal value.

Value Creation Is a Four-Step Process

1. *Value Opportunity Found*   Economics, marketing, and management research

2. *Value Opportunity Developed*   R&D, marketing, operations, and management

The activities in 1 and 2 are predominantly intellectual and managerial. They are characterized by word pairs like information and research, perception and insight, creation and integration, and planning and control. *They define what is to be done to create value.*

3. *Value Produced*   Operations

4. *Value Added by Marketing*   Marketing support

The activities in 3 and 4 execute the work defined in 1 and 2.

5. *Value Retained*   Rewards for stakeholders

Each of the top four activities can yield more or less value than the cost of performing that activity. The more effectively and efficiently each activity is performed, the more value the stakeholders (management, employees, and investors) will retain. The above constructs are represented graphically in Figure 1.

FIGURE 1 Value-creating components: costs and revenues.

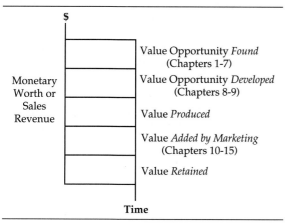

As this figure indicates, the text concentrates on the first, second, and fourth steps in the process. Purchased materials and services must be netted out of each activity's value to obtain a measure of the "value added" by the firm. The degree of value added by the firms in an industry can help measure the industry's attractiveness. The larger the value added, the greater is the scope for exercising managerial effectiveness and retaining value.

The final comment is about the analytical nature of the text. While the book is reasonably analytical, its purpose is not to make the reader a marketing researcher or a specialist in marketing models. Rather it is to teach the reader enough about these methods to enable him or her to be an intelligent consumer of marketing research with regard to new and improved products. In many cases, the biggest problems with marketing research are that the wrong questions were investigated or improper use was made of the research. Similarly, in many instances, managerial inputs to models have a greater impact on the model's predictive power than the inputs from marketing research. Therefore, it is imperative for the manager to properly specify what questions should be

answered and realize the limitations of various approaches.

In spite of the primary focus on being an intelligent consumer of research, enough information is usually given to allow the reader to conduct relatively simple studies on his or her own without the help of an outside supplier.

The text is analytical, but it is not as complex as it appears at first glance. Many of the analytical portions are based on tools that most business students and many managers already possess: spreadsheets and regression models. A small number of new models are introduced, but they are covered in considerable detail. And much of the apparent complexity is due to detail, especially in the spreadsheet portions of the text.

For example, the number of people who try a product is a function of the number of people who would be interested in the product given awareness and distribution, the number who are aware of it, and the number of people who can find it. Although it would be easier to attempt to forecast trial without explicitly considering intention to purchase, awareness, and distribution, this more complex approach provides valuable diagnostic information. If trial is lower than expected but concept tests indicate many people are interested in trying the product, the problem may be that the levels of awareness or distribution are too low rather than that there are any problems with the product itself. On the other hand, if people are aware of the product and initial distribution levels are satisfactory, the problem may be that people do not want the product. Overall trial levels may be similar in both cases, but the corrective action would be quite different for each.

The actions needed to make final buyers favorably aware of a product are usually referred to as "pull" marketing effort. The actions devoted to obtaining effective support from resellers are usually referred to as "push" marketing effort. Because the audience and objectives for each activity are different, budgets will be analyzed in terms of how well they serve these separate needs. The joint effect of pull and push actions is to increase the number of people who will consider trying or rebuying a brand; people who know about it and have it available at the time of purchase.

Once customers have tried a brand, attention shifts to customer satisfaction and the relative frequency with which they repurchase that brand. Two repurchase statistics deserve attention: the proportion of the purchasers of the firm's brand on the last occasion who buy it again on the next occasion and the portion who purchased a competing brand last occasion but buy the firm's brand on the next occasion. Because the actions best suited to retaining customers are often different from those best suited to attracting buyers of competing brands, these two statistics have important diagnostic value.

The text treatment of marketing support makes extensive use of the above concepts, particularly with regard to measurement and modeling. Three primary managerial purposes are served by this approach: defining the goals of the firm's marketing activities, determining the total amount that should be spent to add value by marketing, and allocating these funds to specific marketing tasks. In each case, a serious effort is made to integrate managerial knowhow with available marketing research and marketing data bases. The following section concerning the book's organization provides further insight into how these matters will be treated.

ORGANIZATION OF THE BOOK

The book is broken into five major parts. The first part contains three chapters and sets the stage for what follows. The first chapter discusses product strategy and planning: the importance of delivering superior value to the customer, the role of planning in accomplishing that objective, and the tasks that are part of the marketing planning process. The second chapter

discusses product-market evolution. This provides a framework for understanding change and highlights the fact that new product development and modification must be a continuing process. The third chapter deals with product development. After discussing the reasons for new product success and failure, the chapter presents a new product development process as a way to reduce the risk of failure.

The second major part focuses on finding and creating value: designing, pricing, and positioning a product or service. This part contains four chapters. The first chapter deals with ways to search for new product ideas. The next covers two ways of understanding what the consumers desire and their satisfaction with current offerings—multidimensional scaling and conjoint analysis. This is followed by a chapter on pricing. The final chapter in this part gives a number of illustrations of techniques discussed here.

The first chapter in the third part of the book outlines a general model that can be used with the results of concept tests, product tests, or test markets to forecast new product sales. Then a way of testing consumer response to new product ideas (or concepts) called concept testing is introduced. The last section of this chapter covers ways of testing consumer response to the product or prototype after it has been developed; it is called product testing. This chapter shows how to use the results of concept and product testing to forecast new product sales. The second chapter in this part discusses ways of testing the overall marketing mix, using simulated test markets and test markets.

The fourth part contains three chapters that treat strategy and budgets for new products being introduced into established product categories. The first chapter discusses a general spreadsheet methodology for analyzing the tasks that create value for new or modified products. The second chapter contains an illustration of how this spreadsheet might be used and the type of information that is gained. The final chapter in this part discusses how to forecast awareness and distribution and how to allocate a budget to specific strategic tasks, using a decision calculus model.

The final three-chapter part deals with the development of an annual strategy/budget that add value to an established product. Like the model in the foregoing chapter, this part contains a decision calculus model. It uses the manager's assumptions about the market reaction to various marketing mix variables and calculates an optimal budget and allocation on the basis of these assumptions. The first chapter explains the model and gives a number of illustrations of its use. The second chapter gives detailed instructions for developing input to the model.

The focus in both the third and fourth parts is on effectively creating and delivering value through marketing support. The final chapter in the fourth part extends the discussion of a number of the topics treated earlier, presents approaches to effectively integrate the allocation of marketing dollars across products and/or market areas, and concludes with an outline for a product fact book and an annual marketing plan.

The text covers many product planning and management problems in detail. Furthermore, it adopts a general perspective that includes industrial and consumer offerings as well as both goods and services. For these reasons, the approaches advocated here can be tailored to specific contexts. Readers who have such a context in mind should try to build an efficient adaptation of the planning system as they go through the book and experiment with the associated computer programs.

NOTICE

Several specialized computer programs can be made available by your instructor. The programs implement models described in the text. The conceptual framework on which these models are based can be appreciated without hands-on use of the programs. Nevertheless, those who are at ease with a computer can sharpen their appreciation of marketing planning by completing a set of related computer analyses. A commercial extension of the programs may be available at a later date.

These computer programs are for the recipient's personal use on one computer at a time. They may not be copied for any other purpose. Program support is not offered by the publisher or the authors, but the authors welcome written suggestions about program improvements.

Although the programs have been extensively tested, they are reasonably complex and probably contain some bugs. Therefore, the programs are not warranted to be fit for any purpose. All risks of use and any damages that might result therefrom are the sole responsibility of the user. Use of the programs constitutes acceptance of these terms.

A User's Guide appears as an appendix to the last chapter and additional instructions can be found at suitable places in the text.

PART 1

SETTING THE STAGE

PRODUCT STRATEGY AND PLANNING

PRODUCT AND MARKET EVOLUTION

SUCCESSFUL PRODUCT DEVELOPMENT

—

1

PRODUCT STRATEGY AND PLANNING

Marketplace success is achieved by continually delivering superior value to customers. Here, *value* is defined as the difference between total benefits received (both functional and emotional) and total cost incurred (including purchase price, life cycle cost, and acquisition cost) by the consumer. See Lanning and Michaels (1987). A company can provide superior value either by offering benefits whose superiority outweighs any difference in cost to the customer or by offering equivalent benefits at a lower cost to the customer. Of these two, the approach of providing greater benefits has generally proven to be more successful.

DELIVERING SUPERIOR VALUE

Other than companies in the resource extraction business, sixty-five of the seventy companies that Peters and Waterman studied for their book *In Search of Excellence* (1982) "focused on 'revenue line enhancement'—on quality, service, courtesy, customer listening, and nichemanship (Peters and Austin, 1985, p. 52)." This group of companies included Boeing, Delta, Frito-Lay, Johnson & Johnson, Maytag, Merck, 3M, and Walt Disney Productions.

Similarly, in their study of high-performing mid-sized companies, Cavanagh and Clifford (1983, p. 12) found that these companies

almost always compete by delivering products or services that provide superior value to customers rather than on price. . . . Midsized businesses producing products in the highest-quality category (as perceived by the manufacturer) achieved 4-year ROI levels that averaged 60 percent higher than those of companies whose products fell in the lowest value category.

Some of the better-known companies in this study include Loctite (anerobic adhesives), Sealed Air (plastic packaging material), Lenox (chinaware), A.T. Cross (writing instruments), and Dunkin' Donuts.

9

This difference is even greater for business units in the Profit Impact of Marketing Strategies (PIMS) data base. As shown in Figure 1-1, business units whose quality ranked in the top third have an average return on investment (ROI) that is twice as large as the average of those in the bottom third (Buzzell and Gale, 1987). The rewards of higher quality can be taken in the form of either higher prices or increases in market share.

Furthermore, when market share is held constant, there is little relationship between relative quality and relative cost. This seems to be true because many factors such as better product design, closer coordination between design and manufacturing, and better manufacturing practices lead both to higher quality and reduced rework, scrap, and service costs. Additionally, higher quality can lead to higher volume and economies of scale, which may also reduce costs. These savings can offset potentially higher costs of such items as better ingredients, materials, components, or service. Higher quality and lower costs were achieved by the Japanese automobile manufacturers during the decade of the 1980s when they were able to produce higher-quality products in terms of defects, reliability, fits, and technology, at lower costs than U.S. manufacturers.

FIGURE 1-1   Quality and ROI.

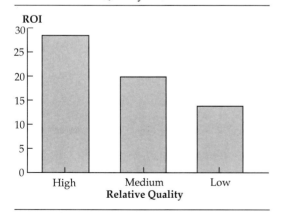

Source: Calculated from Buzzell and Gale (1987).

Value is created by providing a benefit, solving a problem, meeting a need, or helping a customer achieve a goal. In many instances, value is created by the *offer,* which consists of the physical product or service, the price, and the communications message offered to the customer. Value can also be added through *marketing support*—activities that make customers aware of the offer and make it conveniently available. Finally, value can also be created by providing the offer or support in a *more timely fashion.*

Distinctive Competence

The ability to provide superior value to customers on a continuous basis must be based on some unique capability the firm possesses. If not, any differences in benefits or prices can easily be copied. A set of unique capabilities that is not easily duplicated is called a "distinctive competence." One goal of strategy should be to provide the capability of offering greater value than the competition on a continuous basis.

Differences in the value competitors provide to the consumer are based on differences in skills and resources, business systems, and the management of business systems (Day, 1990). Skills are possessed by individuals or groups working for a firm. They could include special knowledge about technologies or markets, the ability of people from different functional areas to work together, or attitudes about the importance of the customer. Resources are usually more tangible assets, such as cash, plants, or distribution systems, but they may also include such items as brand name and company reputation.

A business system is that group of strategically relevant and distinct activities that a company performs to create, sell, and service what it makes (Gluck, 1980). Activities can be overlaid with the integrating functions, such as human resources management, technology development, information systems, and marketing. One example of a business system is given in Figure 1-2.

FIGURE 1-2 Business system.

These activities include:

Research and Development: marketing and technological activities involved in developing new products and services. Firms may differ in terms of such things as the amount and type of interaction between marketing and R&D functions, degree of desired innovativeness, supplier involvement, and the mix between basic and applied research.

Sourcing: inbound logistics. Firms may differ in terms of what components they make or buy and linkages with suppliers.

Operations: manufacturing or service delivery activities. Firms may differ in terms of scale, scope, and location of these activities, how quality is monitored, and level of automation.

Delivery: outbound logistics. Firms may differ in the use of intermediaries and linkages to buyers.

Sales and Promotion: how the word is spread. Firms may differ in the absolute level of expenditures as well as the mix and role among sales force, advertising, promotions, and publicity.

Service: including applications engineering, installation, and maintenance. Firms may differ in terms of who performs the service as well as level and type of service.

Value can be created at any point in the business system. For example, if minimal downtime is an important characteristic of a machine tool, there are several ways of providing this benefit.

One is to maintain a large service force, so every time a machine tool breaks down it will be repaired quickly (service). It is also possible to provide this benefit by designing machine tools that break down less frequently or are easier to repair (design and development). It may be possible to decrease the number of breakdowns by using better quality parts (sourcing) or through better assembly (operations). It may also be possible to train the purchasing company to make minor repairs and perform preventive maintenance on their own (delivery).

When looking for ways to increase customer value, one needs to examine those points in the business system that are capable of adding the most value as well as those that incur the largest portion of the costs. Typically, it is assumed that most of the value will be added through manufacturing. However, value derives from scarcity (the ability to do things that others cannot) and that can occur at any point in the business system. For example, Liz Claiborne has been one of the most successful makers of women's wear, but it does not do its own manufacturing and has no direct sales force. For another example, see the boxed insert.

Change and the Importance of Innovation

Because customer needs and desires as well as competitive offerings are constantly changing, the company needs to innovate continually just to stay even with competition.

This means the firm needs to search perpetually for new and improved products, services, and messages to give to the customer. Furthermore, it needs to improve its manufacturing or service delivery process continually. The company that loses its ability to innovate quickly falls behind.

Toshiba is the worldwide leader in laptops in part because of its rapid introduction of new product models. Hamel and Prahad (1991) point out that Toshiba has discontinued more models than some of their competitors have introduced

An illustration that value can come from any point in the business system is provided in a recent article by Rapport and Halevi (1991). They believe that the ultimate goal of computer and semiconductor companies should be to create value in computing rather than to manufacture computers or chips. Because computing power is beginning to outstrip our ability to use it in many applications, the real value added is not in creating more power, but in defining how it will be used. In many instances ninetieth percentile computing power is sufficient and enough firms are providing this level to make it almost a commodity.

Microsoft is arguably the most powerful computer company in the world today. It has achieved this position by doing a very good job of bridging the gap between computer power and utility as its proprietary system is able to take advantage of the advances of most hardware companies. This is evi-

denced by its $13 billion market value, which is second only to IBM in the industry. In contrast, Apple, which sets the industry standard for ease of use and graphics capability, has a market value of only $8 billion. The big advantage of the Macintosh has always been its operating system—its software. However, by pairing that operating system with proprietary hardware, it has cut itself off from the rest of the industry's R&D spending. As a result, technological progress has been much quicker for hardware associated with Windows than the Macintosh. It appears that Apple is attempting to change this situation through recent alliances with IBM and Sony.

Similarly, semiconductor manufacturing techniques have improved and diffused so much that many chips can be made with ninetieth percentile manufacturing capability, which is also close to being a commodity. In many applications, advances in manufacturing technology

have made design, rather than fabrication skill, the determining factor in what can be built. Semiconductor companies such as Altera, Chips & Technologies, Cirrus Logic, and Weitek focus on custom chips for niche markets. They have seen that most value can be added through design, sales, and service. Because adequate manufacturing capability is abundant, it adds little value, and they contract that out.

Although this strategy has been successful for these companies, there is some question as to whether they can continue to add design value without also participating in fabrication. The strategy is based on an assumption that ninetieth percentile technology will continue to be adequate for most applications (and plentiful). Recent price wars in both computers and semiconductor components provide support for these contentions.

in the last several years. However, sales of its U.S. subsidiary in late 1990 and early 1991 were down more than 35 percent from the previous six months. The reason for this drop was lack of new products: notebook computers, computers with 80386 chips, limited hard-disk capacity, and lack of new models with battery power. Compaq beat Toshiba to the market with a laptop with a hard disk in late 1989. Similarly, Compaq, AST, and Dell introduced 80386 laptops before Toshiba. Toshiba's recent slow response has been blamed on decision-making in Tokyo that misjudged the U.S. market (Armstrong and Gross, 1991).

However, change creates opportunities as well as threats. One of the most important factors behind changes in sales and market share is the introduction of new and improved products and services. This is illustrated in Figure 1-3, which comes from Hewlett-Packard's annual report for 1991. This graph shows that more than half of Hewlett-Packard's orders for both 1990 and 1991 were for products introduced during the past two years.

Ford's position as the most successful American car company in the late 1980s is also testament to the importance of new and improved products. Its sales rose 73 percent

FIGURE 1-3   HP product orders by year introduced.

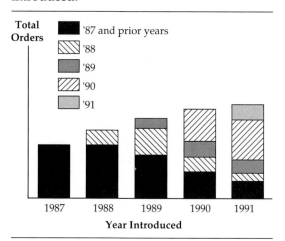

Source: Hewlett-Packard 1991 Annual Report.

from 1984 to 1989 (Taylor, 1989), largely due to the introduction of a string of successful new cars and models, such as Taurus, Lincoln Continental, Probe, Escort/EXP, and Thunderbird. Similarly, Honda's rapid model changes have made the Accord the best selling car in the United States in 1989, 1990 and 1991. After holding steady for eight years Jeep Cherokee's sales were off 21 percent in 1990 because of the introduction of the Ford Explorer, which was outselling Jeep two to one (Treece and Landler, 1991).

Following three years of flat sales in the United States, Reebok's 1991 sales are up 10 percent, due primarily to the introduction of a basketball shoe called the Blacktop. After hearing how fast shoes wear out on urban outdoor courts, Reebok designed the Blacktop with a tough sole and heavy leather uppers (Hammonds, 1991).

Patterns of Innovation

Most people tend to associate innovation with people in white laboratory coats and huge technological leaps. However, the vast majority of

innovations are incremental changes in either the product (or service) or the way it is manufactured. Furthermore, the cumulative impact of these incremental changes is often greater than that of revolutionary innovations. Most industries have a pattern of technological innovation in which continual evolutionary change is punctuated by infrequent revolutionary changes. Most new markets and industries are created out of revolutionary changes; for example, when Ford made the Model T a mass car, and when television and the microprocessor were invented. On the other hand, sustained success in any industry is the result of continuous evolutionary or incremental change.

Many revolutionary new products are paradigm breaking, they require that people do things in a very different way. When Hewlett-Packard (HP) set out to develop a better desktop printer in 1983, impact printers were affordable but produced disappointing quality print and the cheapest laser printers cost more than $100,000 and were used only with mainframes. They broke tradition by purchasing components from a number of companies, including Canon, Motorola, and Microsoft, rather than by self-manufacture. This allowed Hewlett-Packard to introduce a laser printer in little more than a year. Also, in contrast to its typical operating procedure, Hewlett-Packard designed the printer to be compatible with non–Hewlett-Packard products and sold it through other channels in addition to its traditional sales force (Huey, 1991).

When Hal Sperlich attempted to sell his idea for a minivan to the people at Ford in the mid-1970s it was rejected. One of the reasons for rejection was that he could not prove there was a market for the minivan because there was no historical segment for the vehicle. Chrysler has sold more than 2 million units since its introduction in the mid-1980s; it has become a mainstay of Chrysler's profits (Huey, 1991).

However, it is not enough to introduce a revolutionary innovation. Continued success in an industry requires a continuing stream of incremental innovations both in the product or service and in the manufacturing or service delivery process. While the original Hewlett-Packard laser printer was a hit at $3495, Hewlett-Packard has maintained a 50 percent share of the market by a constant stream of improved products and price cuts. A much better laser printer is currently available for under $1000 (Huey, 1991).

Possibly nowhere is the importance of continuous incremental innovation more evident than in the personal computer industry. The same inflation-adjusted amount of money that bought an IBM PC in 1981 would buy thirty-five times the processing power, 1200 times the storage capacity, much better reliability, a color monitor, and more in 1991 (Schlender, 1991). This need for continual improvement is seen even in mature product categories like automobiles. Holusha (1990) reports that the gas mileage of the best-selling car increased from 10 miles per gallon in 1974 (full-size Chevrolet) to an EPA mileage rating of twenty-four/thirty miles per gallon in 1990 (Honda Accord). Similarly, the quality of U.S. cars has improved from seven defects per car in 1981 to 1.5 now. However, the gap between American and Japanese cars has not competely closed; they reduced the defects per car from a little over two to 1.1 during the same period (Woodruff and Levine, 1991).

Management's Challenge[1]

First, firms must produce a continuing stream of new products and services in their current markets. However, because margins narrow and sources of growth dry up as industries mature, companies need to continually search for opportunities in related markets.

There are several problems managing innovation. First, businesses need to manage attention. People and organizations tend to concentrate on and protect existing practices rather than focus

on new ideas. Furthermore, the more successful an organization is, the harder it is to get its people to pay attention to new ideas.

People tend to seek new ways of doing things only in response to crises, dissatisfaction, or stress. Furthermore, gradually deteriorating conditions may result in accommodation rather than solution. There is an oft-told example that if a frog is dropped in a pot of boiling water he will jump out immediately, but if he is put in a pot of tepid water that is slowly heated, he will boil to death. This illustrates the way many people and organizations react to environmental change. Additionally, in groups the problems of conformity, inertia, and incompatible preferences may further exacerbate this situation.

Additionally, the more specialized, insulated, and stable an individual's job is, the less likely that person is to pay attention to new ideas. People need to experience personal confrontations with problems, opportunities, and threats. They need to come in contact with customers, especially problem customers. They need to come in contact with machines and systems that don't work. They also need time to work on these problems, as problems without time create stress and result in crisis decision-making and poor implementation.

A second problem is managing ideas into good currency; that is, getting the organization to adopt good ideas. This is the heart of the product champion's job. Typically, it involves building a coalition and gathering resources and support to bear on a problem. This process is easier if there is an appropriate level of funding to investigate potentially successful innovations.

A third problem is managing part-whole relationships. Innovation is usually not carried out by an individual, but by a group. Usually, innovation requires a complex and interdependent bundle of transactions. While complexity implies specialists and differentiation, interdependence points to integration. Traditionally, the new product development effort has been divided into sequential tasks, each of which is handled by specialists, and someone else is in

---

[1]Much of this section is based on Van de Ven (1986).

charge of integrating the specialized parts. This process has resulted in a lack of communication and misunderstanding among the specialists, causing delays and errors. The problem is caused by people with limited identifications.

Recently, a better solution seems to be using small autonomous teams, sometimes called "concurrent engineering." People on these teams need to develop an understanding of all the essential aspects of the innovation, not just the parts for which they are responsible. This allows team members to think globally while acting locally. In order to be self-contained, the team needs to possess knowledge of all critical dimensions of the environment.

MARKETING STRATEGY, PLANS, AND BUDGETS

To be successful, a firm needs to be able to sense change more quickly than its competition and to respond more quickly. A company might be able to succeed without plans or strategies if it is able to adapt faster than the environment changes. In a world of increased global competition, shortening product life cycles, technological change, blurring industry boundaries, deregulation, and changing sociopolitical systems, this is rarely possible. Therefore, plans and strategies help adapt to a changing environment. They can lay the groundwork for a stream of incremental changes in the current arena and point the way to extensions outside that arena. However, in a rapidly changing environment, plans quickly become outdated and must constantly be adapted.

Planning should be part of a continual search for ways to add value. At times, the planning process may be the primary engine for change. To play this role, planning must move from forecasting to creativity—from concentrating on what was to focusing on what is possible. In this case, one of the outputs of the planning process is a new strategy—an integrated set of activities that is designed to produce a sustainable advantage over competitors. This strategy, called a *deliberate strategy*, is a coherent plan to reach an objective.

However, in most cases strategies do not emerge directly from the planning process. They may come from experiments carried out by the organization, serendipity, or modifications to past strategies. As people continue to do what works and modify those aspects that don't, a pattern of behavior emerges over time. This unplanned pattern of behavior is called an *emergent strategy*. In the case of emergent strategies, planning may merely work out the implications of the strategy. Sometimes planning provides the background and hard data that are helpful in formulating a new strategy.

Neither of these types of strategy is sufficient by itself. A deliberate strategy precludes any learning; it is just an execution of a plan, no changes or improvements. An emergent strategy provides no control; it is just a series of trials. In a changing environment no one is smart enough to think of all contingencies, so a deliberate strategy is insufficient. On the other hand, some control is needed, as unmanaged growth is just as bad as stagnation. Regardless of whether a strategy is primarily deliberate or emergent, planning is important. It forces people to confront the future, requires the collection and analysis of certain data, and provides a vehicle for communication. Although plans are important, it should be remembered that the ultimate purpose of planning is not to produce plans, but to contibute to better decision-making.

Most companies regard marketing plans as fundamental to the management of both new and existing products.[2] Preliminary new product marketing plans are written early in the new product development process in order to get agreement among all participants and to obtain funding for product development work, tooling, and the plant costs that will follow. New product introductory plans are written to

---

[2]A reminder that in much of this book, the term "product" refers to both product and services.

ensure that major concerns are addressed and no important details are forgotten. After the introduction, a series of annual marketing plans are written in order to continually improve the product and its marketing support.

Strategic marketing plans that take a broader perspective also need to be prepared. They provide the rationale for the amount of money that should be devoted to various product categories and determine the allocation between new and existing products. Because most new products are introduced into existing product categories, strategic plans can be used to assess opportunities before new product activities are begun. In fact, most new products are improvements or extensions of products currently being produced by the firm. Marketing plans for existing products should point the way to unmet needs and form the base for new product activity.

To emphasize the importance of basing marketing plans and budgets on a well-defined strategy, the term "strategy/budget" is used frequently. Next, the planning and budgeting process is reviewed by looking at four major topics: doing a situation analysis, setting objectives, generating strategy/budgets, evaluating strategies and budgets, and implementing a strategy/budget. The last section of the chapter reviews a set of topics that play an important role in marketing planning. Finally, a brief outline of both an overall strategic market plan and an annual marketing plan can be found in the appendix.

Figure 1-4 highlights six elements of an integrated marketing plan. As one moves down the elements, methods for dealing with them have been relatively less well developed. Elements one and two, which deal with market analysis, are important, but they are adequately covered in other texts. Therefore, this book focuses primarily on the third, fourth, and fifth elements— finding, developing, and delivering value.[3]

----

[3]References dealing with the first, second, and sixth elements of the marketing plan will be given in the appropriate places in this chapter.

FIGURE 1-4   Elements of an integrated marketing plan.

A marketing plan is a written document that describes how the business and its product will compete successfully in the marketplace. It is the result of a thoughtful process by which marketing objectives are established along with effective means for their realization. It provides directions and gives guidance to those involved in marketing: product managers, advertising specialists, salespeople, marketing researchers, and so on. It also represents an agreement between the marketing manager and relevant others in the company in terms of objectives, activities, and resource commitments. At a minimum marketing plans should answer four questions:

1. *What is the current situation?* How is the brand doing? Who are the primary competitors? What are the major trends in the industry? What are the potential problems and opportunities?

2. *Where do we want to go?* What are the objectives for the brand? This should include general strategic direction as well as measurable goals for the short term.

3. *How can we get there?* What strategies will achieve these objectives? What activities are needed to implement the strategies?

4. *What will the result be?* How much money will be allocated to the various marketing activities? What are the expected results?

The key decisions influenced by the marketing plan include *the value to be created through the offer*—that combination of the product or service, price, and communications message that is presented to the customer—and *the amount of marketing money that will be spent enhancing and delivering value*—principally by making the customer aware of the product and creating availability. In turn, these decisions are related to decisions about *the customer target(s) chosen* and *the amount of money to be invested in these customers.*

THE PLANNING AND BUDGETING PROCESS

A general marketing planning process for both new and existing products is outlined in Figure 1-5. Although these activities will be discussed as if they form the linear process shown below, reality is more complicated. For example, the situation analysis may have to be repeated as new alternatives are evaluated or strategies may have to be changed because of implementation problems or lack of funds. Still, the framework is useful. Because of their commonality, the planning process for new and existing products will not be discussed separately. Usually it will be clear

FIGURE 1-5 The marketing planning process.

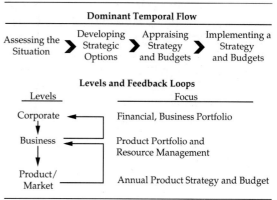

whether a comment pertains to one or both situations. For example, comments about past performance are usually relevant only for existing products.

The levels and feedback loops section of the above figure display a common set of planning interactions between levels of an organization. Marketing managers must negotiate goals and justify strategy/budget requests with corporate and business unit managers. Good general marketing planning references include Abell and Hammond (1979), Day (1984, 1990), Hopkins (1981), and McDonald (1986).

Situation Analysis[4]

The purpose of the situation analysis is to answer the question, "Where are we now?" The output of the situation analysis should be a list of problems facing the brand as well as opportunities for new and improved products.

The definition of the business The situation analysis should start with a definition of the boundaries of its competitive arena. The way a business is defined tells a manager where to

---

[4]See Lehmann and Winer (1987) for more detail on the situation analysis.

look for new sources of revenue. Businesses have traditionally been defined internally, in terms of the products or services provided (e.g., a bank or an automobile company), the technologies employed (e.g., an electronics or a chemical company), or the raw materials used (e.g., an oil company).

Levitt (1960) noted that these definitions are too narrow because they do not highlight threats coming from outside the industry and may unnecessarily limit the search for new products. He argued that businesses should define themselves externally in terms of the needs they are trying to satisfy. For example, railroad companies might have sensed the threats from interstate trucking more quickly if they had defined themselves as transportation companies. During the New Haven Railroad's last profitable year, it hauled material to build the Connecticut Turnpike, whose truck traffic ultimately drove the railroad into bankruptcy (Nulty, 1992). A broad definition of the business lessens the chance that it will be blindsided, although it can greatly increase the size of the arena to be analyzed.

The realization that internal definitions (an automobile company) can be too limiting, but external definitions (a communications company) can lead a business into unrelated areas where it has no expertise, has led to multidimensional business definitions which include (1) customer segments, (2) needs satisfied, benefits provided, or functions performed, (3) the product, technology, or materials that provide these benefits, and possibly (4) stage of fabrication (Abell, 1980; Buzzell, 1978; Day, 1984). One implementation of this approach uses a customer-technology-need grid to highlight attractive target segments. A business definition can be viewed as a series of choices along these dimensions. Some businesses concentrate on a single cell, whereas others are spread over a number of cells. An example of such a grid is given in Figure 1-6.

A multidimensional definition has several additional benefits. First, it forces an external orientation by requiring the business explicitly to consider its customers and their needs. Second, it leads the business to consider different ways of satisfying the same needs. Third, although it allows the business to look at all companies that are serving the same needs of its target segments, it highlights the most direct competitors—those serving the same needs with similar technologies or products. Finally, by comparing competitor success with business definition one can think about possible changes to one's own business definition, such as increasing the number of customer groups served, concentrating on a smaller number of technologies, or focusing on related needs. For example, recently retailers focusing on product lines and customer groups, such as Wal-Mart, IKEA, and Home Depot, have been more successful than their broad line competitors.

Usually, internal or supply-side considerations suggest bigger business units for economies of scale (e.g., in purchasing, sales force, or service network) and the creation of business units that are based on similarity of internal functions, such as manufacturing. External or demand-side considerations point to units that are more closely aligned with specific types of customers but may cut across several technologies.

The business definition puts some boundaries on which customers, competitors, technologies, and distribution systems should be analyzed in greatest depth.

Industry analysis   One of the determinants of whether a company should invest in a business or not is the attractiveness of the industry; that is, whether the industy's structural factors allow a good chance of earning a reasonable return on investment. Traditionally, industry attractiveness has been judged in terms of such factors as size, growth, current profitability, concentration, cyclicality, ability to maintain prices during downturns, base technology, and rate of technological change.

FIGURE 1-6 Characterizing product-market segments.

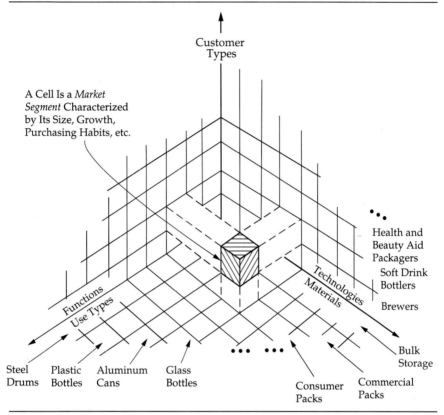

Source: Adapted from R. Buzzell, "Note on Market Definition and Segmentation," ICCH 9-579-083, Harvard Graduate School of Business, 1978, p. 7; used with permission.

Deciding whether or not to invest should start with an historical analysis that examines trends that influence the environment and projects them into the future. Examples of such trends include industry sales, improvements in technology, and changes in the population served by the industry. Identification of trends is more important than the specific forecasting technique; simple forecasting methods seem to work about as well as more complex ones (Armstrong, Brodie, and McIntyre, 1987).

An historical analysis of the appliance industry (Clark, Freeman, and Hanssens, 1984) forecast that penetration would not increase in the next ten years (until 1992) without a marked increase in disposable income. Similarly, replacement sales were forecast to come from new products that take advantage of changing demographics like smaller households, two-breadwinner households, and changes in the level of public services.

Porter (1980) argued that industry attractiveness (the ability to keep a large portion of the value created by the firms in an industry) is a function of the five competitive forces shown in Figure 1-7.

The first competitive force is the _intensity of rivalry_ among the firms in the industry. Competition tends to be more cutthroat when the industry is growing slowly or not at all,

FIGURE 1-7   Forces driving industry competition.

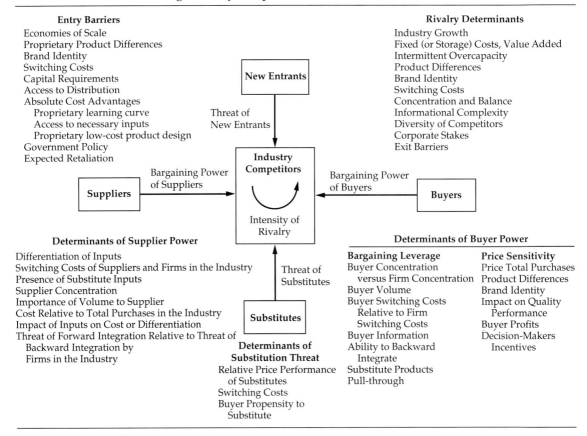

Entry Barriers
Economies of Scale
Proprietary Product Differences
Brand Identity
Switching Costs
Capital Requirements
Access to Distribution
Absolute Cost Advantages
    Proprietary learning curve
    Access to necessary inputs
    Proprietary low-cost product design
Government Policy
Expected Retaliation

Rivalry Determinants
Industry Growth
Fixed (or Storage) Costs, Value Added
Intermittent Overcapacity
Product Differences
Brand Identity
Switching Costs
Concentration and Balance
Informational Complexity
Diversity of Competitors
Corporate Stakes
Exit Barriers

Determinants of Supplier Power
Differentiation of Inputs
Switching Costs of Suppliers and Firms in the Industry
Presence of Substitute Inputs
Supplier Concentration
Importance of Volume to Supplier
Cost Relative to Total Purchases in the Industry
Impact of Inputs on Cost or Differentiation
Threat of Forward Integration Relative to Threat of
    Backward Integration by
    Firms in the Industry

Determinants of Buyer Power

Bargaining Leverage	Price Sensitivity
Buyer Concentration	Price Total Purchases
versus Firm Concentration	Product Differences
Buyer Volume	Brand Identity
Buyer Switching Costs	Impact on Quality
Relative to Firm	Performance
Switching Costs	Buyer Profits
Buyer Information	Decision-Makers
Ability to Backward	Incentives
Integrate	
Substitute Products	
Pull-through	

Determinants of Substitution Threat
Relative Price Performance
    of Substitutes
Switching Costs
Buyer Propensity to
    Substitute

Source: Porter (1985, p. 6).

because then increased sales must come from a competitor. Greater rivalry is also seen in industries that have numerous firms with equal sizes and resource levels than industries in which there are few firms or a clear leader. One of the most devastating kinds of competition—price competition—is more likely when there is little differentiation among offers or high fixed costs. Most of these factors, such as slower dollar sales growth, decreased product differentiation, and new entrants, have contributed to lower profits in the personal computer industry the last few years. High exit barriers, which keep firms from leaving an unattractive industry, lead to more intense rivalry and generally depressed profits.

Second, industry attractiveness is related to the potential *threat of new entrants*. The likelihood of entry is related to the existence of entry barriers and the expected reaction from existing competitors. Economies of scale act as a barrier if new firms need to enter on a large scale to be competitive. In recent years, economies of scale in various areas have had an impact on profitability in pharmaceuticals (R&D), semiconductor chips (manufacturing), mainframe computers (sales and service), and soft drinks and beer (advertising and promotion). Lack of access to distribution channels constitutes an entry barrier in many industries, such as packaged goods and stereo equipment. Strong brand image constitutes an entry barrier when new entrants must spend heavily to overcome loyalties. This has been reflected in the large number of package goods company acquisitions in the late 1980s, when many firms thought it was more economical to buy a brand name than to build one.

Although government actions are becoming less of a factor in some countries, they still constitute an entry barrier in many cases, like the restrictions by most European governments on imports of Japanese automobiles. High switching costs, which are one-time costs associated with switching from one supplier to another create entry barriers in some industries like mainframe computers. Finally, cost advantages that are independent of scale, like experience curve effects, can limit entry if they can be kept proprietary. In addition to entry barriers, firms will be less likely to enter if existing firms have a history of vigorous retaliation and are committed to the industry.

Third, industry attractiveness is constrained by the *existence of substitute products,* which may put a ceiling on the prices that can be charged by the industry. Cable TV and the Fox network have limited the amount that the major networks can charge for advertising time. The existence of potential substitutes typically leads the participants in an industry to attempt to improve the performance of their product rather than participate in the substitute industry (Cooper and Schendel, 1976).

The last two forces, the *bargaining power of buyers and suppliers* are mirror images of each other. In either situation, the power of the buyer or supplier is a function of the relative importance of the product to each party. For example, a buyer's power is reduced if a product is a large part of its total purchases but not a large part of the seller's output. This has led some companies with many brands to consolidate their media buying within one advertising agency to gain additional clout with the networks. Similarly, when the product represents a large part of the seller's output, the seller is tied to the fortunes of the purchasing industry and may need to pro-

tect it through cooperation. On the other hand, if the product is differentiated and is important to the buyer, the supplier will have considerably more power. Currently Intel is in this enviable position with respect to microprocessors. Finally, the potential for forward or backward integration may shift the relative balance of power.

An industry analysis should consider both the current and future impact of these forces. For example, as industry growth slows, industry profitability may decrease because of increased rivalry within the industry or increased power of buyers. On the other hand, an industry may become more profitable if entry barriers are raised or if potential substitutes fail to materialize. Lack of knowledge may be the greatest entry barrier early in an industry's life cycle. Later, it may become economies of scale or product differentiation.

A systematic analysis of competitive forces has several advantages over traditional industry analyses. First, it is a disciplined way of analyzing an industry. Second, forecasts of industry structure provide more useful insights than a static analysis. Finally, it leads one to think about ways to insulate a business from competitive forces, such as erecting entry barriers or curbing supplier power.

Customer analysis   Once a potentially attractive industry has been uncovered, attention should shift to finding ways of offering greater value than the competition. While value is measured relative to competition, the primary focus of strategizing should be on customers. The first step in strategy formulation should be an assessment of the needs, goals, problems, and desires of both intermediaries and final customers as they relate to the product category at hand. Additionally, the importance of various benefits and the extent to which each competitor is supplying the desired level must be assessed.

First, the appropriate consumer decision-making unit should be *identified.* For most consumer nondurables such as soft drinks and many durables such as clothes, individual consumers make the purchase decisions. For many durables (e.g., automobiles and refrigerators) and some nondurables such as catsup, the decision-making unit is frequently the family. The appropriate decision-making unit for industrial goods also differs across purchases. Usually, the increased risk imposed by higher purchase prices, innovative products, and unfamiliar suppliers increases the size of the decision-making unit or raises its level in the organization. Some decisions, such as the choice of a hospital for obstetrical services, are influenced by multiple parties: the family, the physician, the health care choice of the firm employing the husband or wife, and so on.

Next, a *basic analysis* of these decision-making units must be conducted to determine what they purchase, why they made those purchases, and what else they may want. A combination of qualitative and quantitative methods should be used to answer the following questions. What benefits do they want or what problems are they trying to solve with these products? What brands do they like best and which do they like least? How do they think the various brands compare; which are the best quality, the least expensive, the most popular, and so on? How can these people or companies be described in terms of demographic and other enduring characteristics? How do they buy? Who in the decision-making unit actually makes the decision and who influences them? How much do they buy? Are purchases made on a seasonal or cyclical basis? In brief, what do customers value and how valuable are these customers to the firm?

Next, individual decision-making units should be combined into *market segments;* groups of potential customers who are expected to respond in a similar manner to a company's actions. Strategic market plans may stop at the level of strategic market segments (Garda, 1981), where each segment is served by a very different marketing mix, such as Original Equipment Manufacturer (OEM) and retail segments for tire

manufacturers. Annual plans may subdivide strategic segments into smaller, more homogeneous groups, like retail segments that want different price-performance combinations of tires.

There are two fundamentally different approaches to segmentation. In the first approach, potential customers are grouped on the basis of relatively *enduring characteristics*. Then these groups are compared to see if they differ in their response to marketing variables. Probably more companies identify segments by using demographic and socioeconomic factors than any other factors. Consumer companies use variables like age, income, sex, region of the country, and occupation. Industrial companies use such variables as industry [usually based on Standard Industrial Classification (SIC) codes], region of country, and size of firm.

This type of segmentation is useful when there are substantial differences across demographic groups in terms of products or brands used, price sensitivity, level of consumption, or benefits sought from the product class. For example, firms in different industries may use the same product in very different ways. Teenagers consume different products than their parents. Another benefit of demographic segmentation is the considerable amount of secondary information that is available in this format. This information, which includes census data, Nielsen television ratings, county business data, and Dun and Bradstreet reports, makes it easier to measure and project the size of these segments.

A second popular group of enduring characteristics used by consumer marketers consists of psychographic or life-style variables. Industrial customers can be segmented in terms of corporate culture or the dominant functional area. As with demographic segments, one needs to relate differences in life style or corporate culture to differences in purchasing patterns, needs, and/or benefits sought.

In the other major approach to segmentation, potential customers are grouped into segments that are homogeneous with respect to *a variable of interest*, such as benefits sought, purchase quantities, price sensitivity, or brands purchased. (The most widely used of these approaches is benefit segmentation.) Then these segments are examined for differences in terms of demographic or other enduring characteristics. People desiring the latest fashions may have a different demographic profile than those looking for longer-lasting value.

In Chapter 5, joint space analysis is discussed as a way to portray the desires of the market, the perceptions of competitive offerings, and the locations of opportunities. Conjoint analysis is a technique to determine which attributes or characteristics are most important when forming preferences or making choices among these products. Both techniques can be used to form benefit segments.

Using either approach, segments must be compared to see if they warrant different treatment in a marketing strategy/budget. If two or more segments are expected to respond similarly to a given offer, they can be treated as a single segment. Changes in segment sizes should be forecast. Small segments are generally pooled or dropped but any segment with a promising future should be retained. Finally, one or more segments should be chosen as the focus of marketing efforts.

Competitor and internal analysis[5]   Once the benefits various competitors are offering and the costs customers are incurring to obtain those benefits are known, the firm needs to do a competitor analysis. The heart of a competitor analysis should be a comparison of costs, capabilities, methods, and strategies. In many cases it is based on quantitative factors such as the size of the sales force, plant capacity, price, and performance. Additionally, the various steps in the business system need to be compared to see how they are providing a certain level of value. Generally this analysis will suggest areas the

firm can copy or improve upon; however, it is important to keep focused on the factors that are most important to consumers.

This information can come from a number of sources including published documents such as annual reports, 10K reports, security analysts reports, news stories, sales brochures, and statements by key people. Additionally, one can reverse engineer competitive products, consume services, check prices, analyze communications messages, and question intermediaries and final customers.

The end result of a competitor analysis should be a response profile for each competitor, that is, a forecast of future strategic moves and expected responses to the actions of other firms. See Figure 1-8.

Construction of a competitive response profile requires an assessment of the competitor's *current strategy*. This assessment should be based

FIGURE 1-8   Major influences on competitor actions and reactions.

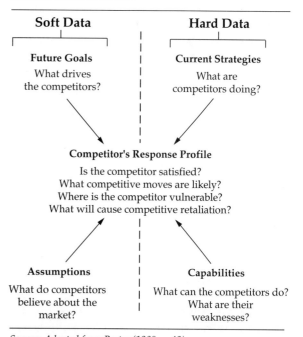

Source: Adapted from Porter (1980, p. 49).

---

[5]See Porter (1980) and Rothschile (1978) for more detail.

on the following dimensions: customer targets, market share of each major segment, positioning, strong and weak points of the offer, and expenditure patterns and levels.

The second step is a detailed analysis of the competitor's *capabilities,* both strengths and weaknesses. This should include an analysis of the entire business system: product development, manufacturing processes and technologies, how technology is incorporated into its products, cost structure, and effectiveness of its marketing and sales efforts. Other pertinent information such as financial condition, should also be gathered.

Third, some assessment should be made of each competitor's *future goals.* Here, one should consider whether it is trying to grow, maintain, or harvest its business, whether it is satisfied with its current level of growth and profitability, its success relative to other parts of the company, and the success of the company as a whole.

Finally, one should determine if any assumptions have been made about the industry (e.g., future growth or technology trends) or what it takes to be successful in this industry (e.g., that they must carry a full line to be successful) that might be used against them.

Rod Canion, former CEO of Compaq Computer Corporation, cites two examples where going against conventional wisdom was beneficial (Weber, 1990). When Compaq introduced its first notebook-sized computer, none of its competitors had a model with a hard disk; everyone "knew" that a hard disk could not be put in a computer of that size. Compaq decided not to introduce a computer without a hard disk and figured out how to include one. Similarly, before the introduction of 386-based computers, industry wisdom was that the rest of the industry had to wait for IBM to introduce a new generation in order to ensure compatibility. However, by knowing which areas it could change without affecting compatibility and which it could not, Compaq was able to introduce the first 386-based personal computer.

The results of these analyses can be displayed visually by showing price points, quality levels, market shares, etc., of the various competitors. Additionally, these results can be combined with role playing to help predict future strategies (what has worked in the past), ability to implement chosen strategies (what its capabilities are), and reactions to moves by other firms (firms with a goal of growth will react very differently than firms that are concentrating on current profitability). In particular, competitive reactions to the company's marketing plans should be forecast.

A *new product diagnostic audit* (Kuczmarski, 1988) can be used to evaluate the relative success of all new products introduced in the last five years. First, these products are classified by type of new product; e.g., new to the world, new to the company, or line extension. Then development costs, revenues, profits, payback period, and development cycle time are calculated for each product. These results are compared to the forecast results generated during the new product development process to assess the level of success for each product. Finally, the causes of success or failure for each product are assessed. Individual product findings can be aggregated to determine the success for each type of product (e.g., new to the world, new to the company, or line extension).

The audit should uncover problems the company has had with each kind of product. For example, the audit might discover a lack of new product objectives, inadequate marketing research and product testing, or a lack of marketing support during introduction. A comparison with competitors' new product records shows how the company stacks up against others in the industry.

Summary   The result of this data gathering and analysis activity should be a picture of the current position of the business and likely environmental changes. Furthermore, it should highlight a number of problems and opportunities.

These results lay the foundation for the development of a sound marketing plan.

A situation analysis of existing products should suggest a number of new product possibilities, including line extensions, needed improvements in current products, and new products that could be used to block competition.

Furthermore, this same type of analysis should be done for any product category the firm is considering entering. The main differences are in terms of internal analysis. Here, the key question is how current strengths transfer over to the new industry.

The following nongraphic implementation uses tables to lay out the key dimensions, summarize the attractiveness of various product/ market combinations, and outline the firm's present and planned participation.

Figure 1-9a displays some essential features of the fastener industry, which makes products to fasten or attach two or more items. Each cell can have five mutually exclusive states. If a cell is crossed out, it is not applicable (for example, drug chains do not stock rivets). If a cell is blank, the firm does not currently offer the product or plan to offer it in the future. If the firm offers the product to a segment and no significant change is planned, a check mark appears in the cell. A planned increase in emphasis is indicated by a plus sign and a decrease in emphasis is indicated by a minus sign.

This coding scheme permits a manager to see *at a glance* the firm's strategic position in each segment. Opportunities for increased penetration can be seen by examining the columns for each product offered by the firm. Opportunities

FIGURE 1-9a Fastener industry.

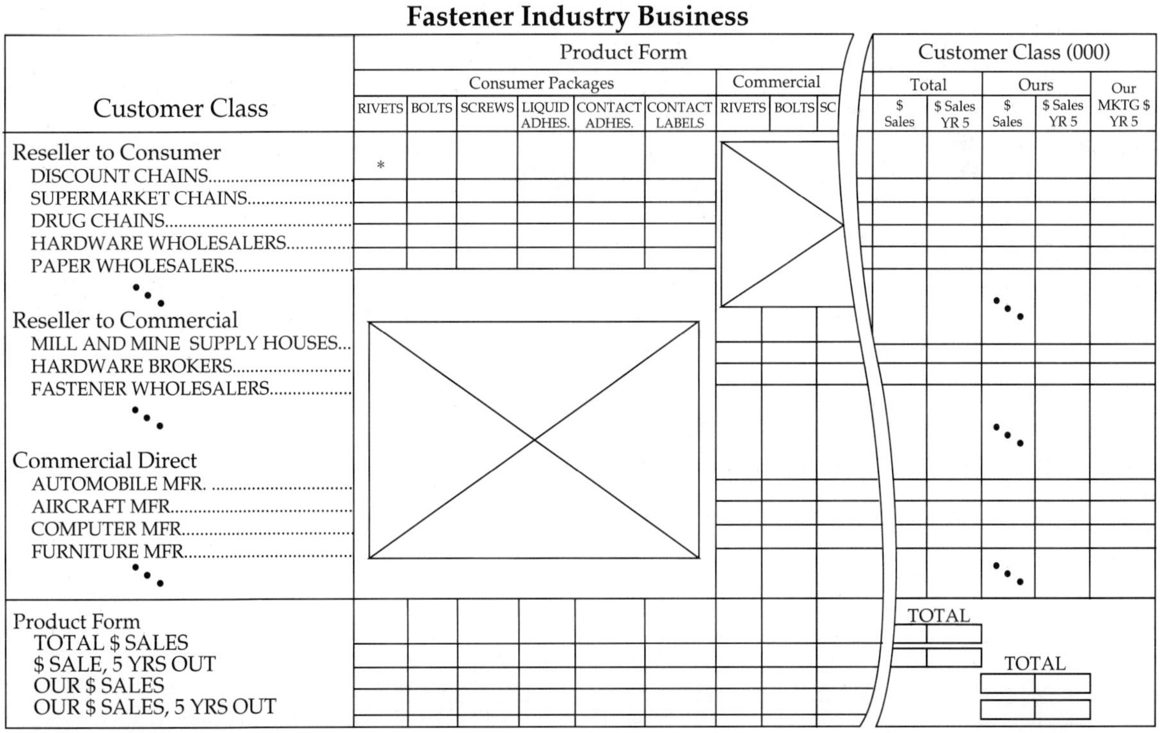

Fastener Industry Business

* See the text definitions of cell entries.

to strengthen sales to a market segment are uncovered by examining the row for each segment served by the firm. Opportunities for changing a product offering are found by comparing the total dollar sales produced by each product with total dollar sales realized by the firm. To think about segment development, the firm compares total sales produced by a customer segment with the total sales realized by the firm. These comparison values are developed and recorded on the table's row and column stubs. In addition to current totals, estimated future total and firm sales are shown in the right and bottom stubs of the table. These last two types of entries are especially useful in identifying opportunities to introduce new products and finding markets that are attractive to enter.

Figure 1-9b summarizes the resources needed to support each product properly. The cell entries use the same symbols described for Figure 1-9a. However, a check mark means that the current resources are adequate and will not require significant change. A plus sign indicates that significant increases are needed, and a minus sign indicates that significant reductions or eliminations can be made. The row stubs on the right of the table are the same as the column stubs at the foot of Figure 1-9a. The table's column stubs at the foot are numerical fractions. The first row of these entries indicates how well a class of resource meets current needs. The second row indicates how much a resource needs to change in order to meet the needs at the end of the planning period.

These two tables can be elaborated in various ways. For example, a table with rows for cus-

FIGURE 1-9b   Fastener industry.

Product Form	Skills and Resources Required							Product Forms (000)				
	METAL STAMP-ING	METAL MACH-INING	LIQUID COM-POUNDING	COATING OPER.	PRINTING OPER.	DIE CUTTING OPER.		PACK-AGING OPER.	TOTAL $ SALES	TOTAL $ SALES YR 5	OUR $ SALES	OUR $ SALES YR 5
Consumer Forms	*											
RIVETS...............................												
BOLTS.................................												
SCREWS..............................												
LIQUID ADHESIVES...........................												
CONTACT ADHESIVES.....................												
ADHESIVE TAPES..........................												
CONTACT LABELS............................												
•.•.				•.•.						•.•.		
Commercial Forms												
RIVETS												
CLIPS AND FASTENERS												
BOLTS.................................												
SCREWS												
LIQUID ADHESIVES												
CONTACT ADHESIVES												
ADHESIVE TAPES												
CONTACT LABELS												
•.•.				•.•.						•.•.		
Required Abilities												
CURRENT FRACTION OF REQ.												
(REQ. YR 5)/ (CURRENT LEVEL)												

(Fastener Industry/Business)

* See the text definitions of cell entries.

tomer segments and columns for needs, benefits desired, or functions performed can help identify gaps in the firm's coverage of each customer segment. A table with rows for product forms and columns for needs satisfied, benefits provided, or functions performed can help identify gaps in the firm's product line. Additional table layouts may increase one's understanding of the current position and future possibilities of a business.

The externally generated numerical data found in the stubs of the above tables are best developed by analyzing each multidimensional cell or category (for example, liquid adhesives sold to consumers). The narrowness of the breakdown (for example, rubber cement sold to consumers through art supply stores) depends on the importance and actionability of the category. For each qualified combination of customer class and product form, the following data would be available:

1. Description of each customer type: number, economic characteristics, etc., definitions of the product, and statement of the required skills and resources

2. Current and projected levels of sales and contribution margin of the major suppliers of the product to the customer type

3. The firm's current and projected levels of sales and contribution margins for the product sold to each customer type

4. Description of the competitive environment and how the firm is competing or plans to compete

5. Description of the firm's capacity to compete

6. Planned changes in the resource commitments

Setting Objectives

Objectives   Strategic objectives define the primary results to be achieved in the planning peri-od. They specify whether a marketing manager should attempt to grow an existing business at the expense of current profits, maintain its position, or harvest it. Similarly, objectives state how aggressively a new product should be supported. It is rarely possible to maximize growth and profits simultaneously. Growing a business usually requires investment in new products, better service, lower prices, or greater marketing support that will not be recouped immediately. Therefore, strategic objectives must outline the permissible trade-offs. When AT&T introduced its "free for life" Universal card, which included a 10 percent discount on long distance calls, in March 1990, it was clearly looking for growth rather than short-term profits. On the other hand, Campbell Soup, after coming off an overly aggressive new product push, appears to be more interested in current profits; it cut its work force, decreased new product introductions, and raised prices recently.

Operational objectives restate the strategic objectives in measurable terms that are applicable to the current planning period. For example, a strategic objective of maximum growth subject to minimal cash flows over the next five years might be operationalized as increasing market share to 25 percent by the end of 1997 while maintaining a minimum annual cash flow of $2 million.

Factors to consider   Not all businesses have equally bright futures, deserve equal levels of investment, or should be held to the same objectives. The choice of a strategic objective (such as growth, maintenance, or harvest for an existing product), or, equivalently, the amount one is willing to invest in a business should be based on the attractiveness of the investment opportunity and the ability of the business to take advantage of that opportunity. One should invest money in those areas in which the firm can provide superior value and reap appropriate rewards for doing so. The information to make this decision should have been gathered in the situation analysis.

Generally, growth industries are considered to be attractive places to invest money. Many feel it is easier to gain (or lose) market share in a higher-growth market than in a lower-growth market. Additionally, investments in growing industries should yield higher dividends. However, industry attractiveness is also related to other factors, such as size, profitability, and pricing strength. More recently, Porter's competitive factors have been used to measure industry attractiveness.

Ability to provide superior value is based on the ability to offer greater benefits at an equal cost or equivalent benefits at a lower cost. In turn, this is based on the possession of certain skills, resources, and knowledge. Customer analysis can tell which factors customers think are most important and which they are most dissatisfied with. However, it does not directly address how a business might go about satisfying these needs better than the competition. On the other hand, competitor and internal analysis tends to focus on general strengths and weaknesses and may not look specifically at those related to important customer benefits. Therefore, a combination of customer and competitor analysis is needed to determine the company's relative standing in terms of important skills, resources, and knowledge.

Rather than look directly at skills, resources, and knowledge, which may be very hard to judge, many companies have looked at past success as an indicator of strength in an area.

Market share is widely recognized as one measure of business strength; higher-share businesses are generally more profitable. There is a strong relationship between market share and profitability, but it is useful to keep Jacobsen's (1988, p. 78) comment about the cause-and-effect relationship in mind when setting market share targets:

Both market share and ROI are joint outcomes of successful strategies that managers implement by design or chance. Strategies based on the assumption of market share influencing, rather than reflecting, profitability may be inappropriate and detrimental.

Business strength can also be measured in terms of market share in attractive segments and leadership in areas such as image, quality, and technology. Ultimately, competitive strength comes from the ability to deliver greater value than the competition.

Although there is some disagreement about how to measure attractiveness and ability to deliver superior value (or business strength), most people agree that one should invest more in potentially strong businesses in attractive markets. This general strategic approach also provides managers with the rationale for eliminating weaker businesses and increasing investments in more promising ones. It also points out that as a product moves through the life cycle, objectives will generally change. Early in the life cycle, growth may be more important than current profitability, but later in the life cycle this situation would be reversed.

Over the past several years General Electric (GE) has said that it wants to be number one or number two in every industry in which it competes. The 1989 GE report to shareholders discussed the major lines of business that hold leading or important positions in their industries. These are displayed in Table 1-1. Lines of business that GE has withdrawn from when it did not hold strong positions include mainframe computers and consumer electronics (including RCA TV). In commenting on its past actions and current (1989) performance, the company stated,

In 1981 we were a $28 billion company of 350 business or product lines. . . . Today we are a $54 billion company with 13 world-leading enterprises. . . . Over a decade, earnings per share have grown 12% a year. . . .

A top-down, bottom-up perspective   Setting objectives needs to be a combined top-down,

TABLE 1-1   RANKING OF A DOZEN GE BUSINESSES

LINE OF BUSINESS	IN THE UNITED STATES	IN THE WORLD
Aircraft Engines	1	1
Broadcasting (NBC)	1	Not Applicable
Circuit Breakers	1	1
	Tied with 2	Tied with 3
Defense Electronics	2	2
Electric Motors	1	1
Engineered Plastics	1	1
Factory Automation (joint with Fanuc)	2	3
Industrial Power Systems	1	1
Lighting	1	2
Locomotives	1	1
		Tied with 1
Major Appliances	2	2
		Tied with 1
Medical Diagnostic Imaging	1	1

Source: Fortune, *March 27, 1989.*

bottom-up process. In order to make resource allocation decisions and set performance standards, people at the corporate level need to take a top-down view. In doing so, they should review the opportunities facing various businesses within the corporation and the funds available at different interest rates. Their decisions usually lead to trade-offs across different business units and to the consideration of major external investment opportunities.

The people running each of the businesses have the greatest knowledge of that business and its market environment. They are the logical ones to assess the attractiveness of the industry and the potential for their company to develop a strong position in it. The bottom-up perspective is also important to motivate the people running the business. They need a level of participation that will gain their whole-hearted commitment to longer-term objectives. Once these objectives have been negotiated, they must be broken down into a number of shorter-term guideposts to make sure that the business is on track as it moves forward.

Strategic alternatives   Next, one must think about ways of achieving those objectives. Strategic alternatives describe in general terms how the objectives will be reached. Consider the following model of return on investment:

ROI = (unit sales) × (margins)/(investment).

One can increase ROI through some combination of growth (increasing the number of units sold) and increased productivity (keeping the number of units sold relatively constant but raising margins or lowering investment).

Growth must come from some combination of three sources: people or organizations that are not currently using this product category, customers that are using other brands, and increased usage by current customers. Early in a product's life cycle, nonusers may represent the most attractive target. This was the case for CD players in the 1980s. This is called market development.

Attracting customers of other brands may involve attacking new segments for the company. Examples of attacking new segments include

Nordstrom's geographic expansion to the East Coast from its traditional West Coast base, Apple's movement from the educational and home markets into the business computer market, and Johnson & Johnson's repositioning of its baby shampoo into a shampoo for all people. Alternatively, growth may be gained at the expense of current rivals (think of the head-to-head competition between Ford and Chevrolet trucks, Diet Pepsi and Diet Coke, or Dell and Compaq).

Finally, sales can be increased by increasing the usage of the current users of the brand. This may be done with line extensions (e.g., portable TVs), new uses (e.g., baking soda to deodorize the refrigerator), or new usage occasions (e.g., "orange juice is not just for breakfast").

In addition to growth, profitability can be increased by either increasing margins or lowering investment. Margins can be improved by lowering costs through better manufacturing practices or raising prices (possibly by selling more at full price, cutting sales promotions, or offering additional benefits such as better warranties). Margins can also be improved by changing the product mix. Many chemical companies (e.g., Dow and Monsanto) are moving from commodity to specialty chemicals. Bringing out new and improved products is another route to better margins. The upscale Japanese cars and Gillette's Sensor shaving system are two examples.

Similarly, there are several different ways to lower investment. Just-in-time manufacturing systems are able to cut inventories. Also, many companies have reduced the ranks of middle management in an effort to reduce fixed costs.

These alternative paths to objective accomplishment are not equally attractive. Furthermore, their relative attractiveness changes over time. For example, long-run profitability might best be accomplished through an emphasis on growth early in the life cycle. Later a volume-maintenance profit-increasing program of cost cutting may be preferred.

Pursuing different strategic alternatives requires different marketing strategies and possibly different products. For example, increasing margins may require dropping low-margin products, adding higher-margin products, or making some changes to existing products so they can command higher margins. Similarly, taking business from a competitor may require modification of the product, increased advertising, or a lower price.

Generation of a Strategy and Budget

A strategy is a general plan to reach the chosen objectives. For example, it would tell how to attack a certain segment, or what steps to take in order to raise prices. A marketing strategy statement for a new or existing product should include the positioning to be achieved, the way it will be embodied in marketing actions, the total level of marketing expenditures, and the allocation of the total across the various mix elements.

Positioning   Positioning refers to the image that customers and potential customers have of a product or business relative to the competition. Typically, positioning is concerned with an individual brand, but it can refer to the company as a whole. In a number of package goods companies like Procter and Gamble, brands are not directly linked to the corporate name and virtually all the emphasis is on positioning individual brands. In other cases, "brands" may be denoted by numbers, such as Dell's System 320LT laptop, and the primary positioning emphasis is on the company or division. Companies for whom company or divisional positioning is important include Intel, IBM, and General Electric's major appliance division. General Motors is an example where both the brand and corporate positionings are important. Although most of the following discussion is on brand positioning, when corporate positioning is important, it should come first.

McKenna (1986) says that products in high-tech markets should be positioned on the basis of more intangible attributes, such as quality, performance, reliability, or service, instead of narrow performance specifications or low price. There are two reasons for his recommendations. First, technical leads on any given dimension are often short lived. Second, most customers rely more on overall feelings of quality or performance than they do on technical details. His advice probably holds in most markets.

A consistent positioning strategy is desirable, but evolving markets require change. The faster the environment changes, the more often the positioning has to be modified. Even if the basic positioning of outstanding service, performance, or quality remains the same, the product or service that delivers this bundle of benefits must be improved continually. Similarly, the execution of the general message usually needs to be refreshed periodically.

Because positioning concerns how a manager wants the market to view the product relative to the competition, the starting point in this process should be a detailed understanding of the market and the competition. First, customer targets should be chosen.

Second, competitive efforts should be considered. Just as a given offer will not be equally attractive to all customers, it will not affect all competitors equally, so one needs to decide which rivals to compete with most closely. It may be possible to choose the most vulnerable competitor, then work out a plan to take its customers. For example, when Norton saw that Carborundum was having quality problems with its grinding wheels, it was able to take away a large number of Carborundum's distributors.

Finally, the business needs to develop a core strategy and an offer. The core strategy is the concept that ties all of the pieces together. It should provide a reason for customers to purchase the firm's product and define the way the business is going to compete. In this sense, a core strategy is similar to the term "Unique Selling Proposition" (USP) coined by the Ted Bates advertising agency a number of years ago. However, it is broader in that it not only looks outward to determine how to compete, but also looks inward and describes what is needed from each organizational unit. This decision cannot be made until customer and competitor targets have been chosen, since different segments require different core strategies.

Several authors (e.g., Porter, 1980; Hall, 1980) have suggested that there are two basic core strategies. The first is offering the lowest price along with acceptable quality. The other is providing the highest quality or most differentiated offer. The judgment of quality or differentiation must be from the standpoint of the customer, but the points of differentiation may be in some combination of the physical product, service and closeness to the customer, and speed of delivery. Furthermore, product quality can be defined in various ways, including durability, reliability, performance, and inclusion of innovative features.[6]

Hall (1980) has shown that companies in mature industries achieving one or both of these positions perform better than companies without a clear focus. Porter (1980) points out a number of instances in which trying to achieve both of these positions simultaneously is not possible. He presents a number of theoretical and empirical arguments to show why companies that focus on one of these approaches do better than firms that lack this focus. There are cases, however, when a firm starts out to capture one of these positions and ends up capturing both. This can happen when a high-quality approach brings a large market share, which results in lower costs through economies of scale. Similarly, actions taken to reduce costs some-

---

[6]When quality is measured in terms of reliability or percentage of defects, "quality is free." In many cases higher-quality products end up being less costly because of better design, being built right the first time, or requiring less service once they are in the field. When quality is measured in terms of performance, innovative features, or product variety, there may be a quality versus cost trade-off. This discussion refers to the latter situation.

times lead to higher-quality products, or volume gained through low costs and prices may allow a firm to improve product performance.

Recent analysis of the PIMS data base indicates that relative product quality is the most important determinant of profitability as measured by ROI. The most profitable combination of price and quality appears to be highest quality and premium price, but it is closely followed by a combination of highest quality and parity price (Buzzell and Gale, 1987).

Offer: creating value   Historically, marketing literature has focused on separate marketing functions that can be characterized by a phrase like "The Four Ps: Product, Price, Promotion, and Place." This approach is satisfactory for some purposes, but managers need an approach that more nearly parallels the way markets, marketing organizations, and marketing budgets are structured. A better approach is to separate the planning and decision-making activities of marketing managers into two principal domains. The first is the offer. It consists of product, service, price, and communications message. The second is the marketing support activities that enhance and deliver the offer, making it an attractive purchase among both resellers and final consumers.

A convenient way to think about developing the offer is to recognize that it includes those activities that create the desired image or positioning. A manager's activities on behalf of the offer should favorably answer the question, *"How can I make my product more appealing among current and potential customers who know about my product and competing products and who have ready access to these products?"* Practitioners can use a number of analytical methods to help determine the offer. Chapters 2 through 9 cover many of the aids to help find product opportunities and specify a product design, price, and positioning.

Decisions about the offer should be based on an understanding of how attributes or features of the product are related to perceived benefits, preferences, and choice. For automobiles, important attributes may include such factors as seating capacity, head and foot room, styling, price, acceleration, handling, reliability, durability, and the location and quality of service facilities. Similarly, important attributes for a bank might include services offered, interest rates paid on deposits, interest rates charged on loans (including credit cards), location of branches, and the availability and location of ATMs.

Positioning messages should be defined in terms of the adopted strategy and the customers who will receive the message. If different messages need to be sent to different groups, such as intermediaries and final consumers, or if different media are employed, the positioning message should be specified for each group or medium. For example, a credit card could be positioned in terms of prestige to final customers and in terms of the type of customers and incremental volume that the card would bring to retailers. Finally, the price charged has a large impact on the perception of the product and needs to be considered along with the product, service, and message. A separate chapter is devoted to pricing.

In spite of the importance of the offer, its items do not usually appear as expense categories in the typical marketing manager's budget. R&D expenses are usually included in overhead; they may not be allocated to individual products. Furthermore, the R&D organization is rarely under the direct control of marketing managers. This managerial separation diffuses accountability.

Although price is a major determinant of sales volume and contribution to profit, it does not appear directly in a marketing budget. Also, many marketing managers may have less latitude on pricing decisions, except short-term promotions, than they have with their marketing budget. In many cases, the planning price is a planning assumption, like unit cost. Corporate policies about product and service quality as well as pricing can seriously constrain a manager's flexibility.

Decisions about the communications message typically have little direct monetary impact. Image depends more on what is said in the message about a product or service than on the level of media spending that is employed on its behalf. Nevertheless, positioning has an influence on important elements like distribution outlets, advertising, and the operations of a sales force. For this reason, it is normally necessary to develop a positioning strategy and offer before making final decisions about marketing support spending.

Marketing support: enhancing and delivering value Support activities include all of the manager's efforts to present the offer favorably to current and potential buyers and users; that is, to enhance and deliver the offer's value. The expense of the main support activities such as advertising media and sales force is the major part of a marketing budget. With few exceptions, all support items are under the control of the marketing manager. Short-term adjustments are usually possible and the effects may be visible quickly.

A principal problem for marketing management is determining the right level of total support spending and its allocation among the constituent line items in a budget. During this process, the two principal purposes of support spending ("push" and "pull" effects) must be kept in mind. First, support spending must give buyers the information they need to become favorably aware of the offer. Few, if any, buyers will choose an unknown product. Second, support spending must encourage wide availability of the product through cooperative channels of distribution. Potential buyers cannot purchase a product that is unavailable.

These twin goals of favorable awareness and availability give marketing spending both direction and a way to measure what spending accomplishes. First, the marketing support elements that create buyer awareness and convenient availability must be defined. These can include natural categories like advertising, personal selling, promotions, and public relations, but other breakdowns may be more useful. Four rules for choosing spending categories or marketing support elements should be followed when using the MARMIX model associated with this text.

1. Include only those elements that are going to produce a market response.

2. Include only elements that are under the manager's control. For example, even if corporate-level public relations and image campaigns have an impact on a brand's sales, it is not appropriate to include them if the marketing manager cannot control them.

3. Breakdowns should be such that each one contributes to a distinct response. For example, if some sales force time is devoted to account maintenance and some to opening new accounts, these two activities need to be planned, budgeted, and accounted for separately.

4. The elements should be chosen with a view to parsimony. The analysis can get needlessly complicated when unimportant support elements have been included.

Second, an appraisal must be made of the way awareness, distribution, and sales will respond to distinct expenditure levels for each marketing support element. Finally, an appropriate total budget and allocation among elements should be chosen. The analytical methods that can be used to plan effective support spending have not been well developed. For this reason, an assortment of computer-based aids to various aspects of this problem are covered in Chapters 10 through 15. The accompanying computer disk contains these programs.

Integration and coordination A manager's offer and support spending plans must come together as an effective whole. When they do, the overall marketing plan has taken shape. As noted earlier, this plan can best be described as an integrated strategy/budget. The strategy elements deal principally with questions of what is to be accomplished and the budget elements spell out the overall resource commitment and how these resources will be deployed. An overview of the above philosophy of planning and budgeting is displayed in Figure 1-10.

At a minimum, an integrated marketing strategy means that the elements of the marketing mix do not work at cross purposes with each other. Advertising that stresses high quality while the distribution channels suggest lower quality, or inferior service provided for a high-price, high-quality product illustrate dysfunctional conflicts. Ideally, the different parts of a strategy should reinforce each other. For exam-

ple, the package might be shown in advertisements and some of the advertising message might be repeated on the package. Similarly, advertising and the sales force might be used in a complementary fashion. Advertising can introduce the company or give the sales force added credibility, while the sales force might use advertising to convince resellers that their customers will be aware of the product.

In addition to being integrated, the elements of the marketing strategy should have a common degree of efficiency. This means that an additional dollar spent on any element of the marketing mix should produce the same return. Under these circumstances, it will not be possible to increase sales by a reallocation of the existing budget.

Finally, the notion of an integrated mix points to the fact that a strategy should be built

FIGURE 1-10   Principal components of a marketing strategy.

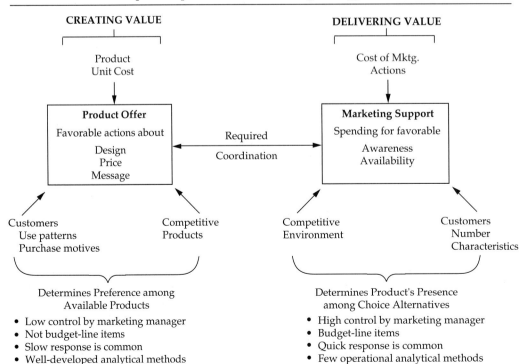

around a common theme—a core strategy. Brand positioning should implement this theme, conveying a positive image to customers and potential customers. All the other elements of a strategy should key to this common theme or positioning.

A related issue is the degree to which a strategy and its implementation must be coordinated with other product lines within the business unit, and more generally, with the company's other business units. How an industrial firm markets equipment that is predominantly sold direct to large customers may have to coordinate this effort with the marketing of other equipment that is sold through distributors to smaller customers. In a similar manner, a consumer goods company with separate product lines sold respectively through exclusive and mass retail outlets needs to coordinate marketing activities to preserve its reputation in each market.

Implementation

Marketing actions   Next, marketing actions that are best suited to implement the chosen strategy should be chosen. For example, if the strategy is to increase sales by attracting a certain group of nonbuyers with a general positioning of higher quality, possible actions include gaining trial by advertising to this group of customers with a quality and value message delivered by a specific number of media insertions. If an increased rate of repurchase is part of the strategy, coupons might be packed with the product or sales might be backed up with improved after-sale service.

Strategies describe in general terms how objectives will be reached. Planned marketing actions spell these out in greater detail. Some actions, such as an R&D program to improve the quality of a product, may not be part of a marketing budget, but marketing needs to provide appropriate input. Marketing support actions like promotion or sales force programs are clearly the marketing manager's responsibility and

usually appear in the product's budget. Since several possible sets of actions can implement most strategies, the selection of a set of actions and its budget should follow careful analysis. One of the purposes of the NEWSTRAT and MARMIX computer programs discussed in Chapters 12 to 15 is to help a manager look at the desirability of alternative strategies and budgets.

Budgets   *A marketing budget is the quantitative representation of the actions called for by a marketing plan. The principal purpose of a budget is to facilitate implementation of strategies through planning and control.* Budgets are integrally related to a product's characteristics and, more importantly, to the supporting marketing effort planned on its behalf. The budget relates costs to actions. Even after a strategic direction and offer have been chosen, there are multiple combinations of marketing support elements that could implement that strategy. Budgets are central to the evaluation of various strategies; a company needs to ask what it will cost to reach an objective.

Budgeting consists of two related elements: the size of the total budget and the allocation of the budget across different expense categories. At different budget levels the percent spent on various categories should change unless each of them has the very same response function, which is highly unlikely.

Although budgets can be set in a number of ways, all are at least implicitly based on the notion of marketing response functions. A marketing response function describes the relationship between changes in a budget item and sales or market share. Theoretically, the best way of setting a budget is the objective and task method. First, an objective is set for a particular budgeting element. For example, the objective could be the increase in trial purchases for a product by an advertising campaign. Then a budget is chosen that is believed to be large enough to accomplish this task. This budget may be chosen on the basis of experience with other brands, competitive spending, or intuition, but there is always an implied relationship between the number of advertising dollars spent and product trial.

Sometimes budgets are chosen with an eye toward maximizing short-term profits. In this situation, profit is assumed to be a function of one or more marketing mix elements. If the function is well defined, the level of spending which will maximize profit may be mathematically determined. Although a manager seldom knows the functions well enough to proceed in this manner, formally considering market response to spending can guide budget decisions. Related to this approach is the marginal or break-even approach to budgeting. An increment or decrement to a budget is proposed and one must decide whether the change in profit is expected to offset the budgetary change.

Sometimes budgets are set on the basis of competitive parity. Doing so can mean either matching the budget of competition or choosing a budget so the business' fraction of total industry spending is equal to the desired market share. This procedure assumes that every competitor's expenditures have the same response function, even if that function is unknown. A closely related approach is the practice of setting expenditures equal to a certain percentage of sales. These two approaches have obvious theoretical shortcomings, but they may provide a good starting point and are useful reality checks.

Budgeting is very difficult because the response functions for spending categories are rarely known. Even in the few instances when statistical studies have been carried out to determine these relationships, changes in the environment render them less satisfactory over time. Therefore, a manager must observe the market carefully, study historical performance, and, when feasible, conduct market experiments to determine the effectiveness of various budget categories.

NEWSTRAT is a decision-support model that can help a manager determine the size and strategic allocation of marketing dollars during the initial years of a new product's market life. MARMIX is a decision-support model that can help a marketing manager determine the appropriate size of the marketing support budget and the proper allocation of that budget across the various elements for a more mature product. Detailed discussion appears in later chapters. The appendix to this chapter contains the outlines of both a sample strategic market plan and a short-term marketing plan.

Strategy/Budget Evaluation

Strategy generation and evaluation are separated so that undue early criticism does not prematurely choke off the search for innovative strategies. Still, strategies should be generated with an eye on how the results will be judged.

Because many strategies are poorly implemented and results fall short of those promised, many companies are less than satisfied with strategic planning. Day (1984) suggests that some of the dissatisfaction may be due to inappropriate methods for evaluating strategies. Strategies should be evaluated along the following dimensions:

Consistency The strategy needs to create a common theme. All parts of the strategy have to hang together. Conflict between the various elements of the strategy should be minimized. It cannot force the business to try to be all things to all people, but needs to specify which elements are most important and which are less so.

Competitiveness The strategy has to take the competition into account. The business should offer something that the competitors cannot. This factor requires the strategy to remain appropriate in the face of change (for example, it cannot be a strategy whose success is based on low petroleum prices), and to offer some basis for future advantage, something that competitors cannot easily match or leapfrog.

Validity The assumptions underlying changes in major variables such as profits or sales need to be questioned. For example, if sales are forecast to increase because of a price cut, one should look at the results of previous price cuts. An assumption that sales will be more responsive to price cuts than in the past should be questioned.

Feasibility The business needs to possess the required skills, resources, and commitment. Additionally, it must have access to markets, technology, and servicing capabilities.

Financial desirability The strategy should create sufficient economic value. The expected gain should exceed the risks associated with the strategy in order to enhance the value of the business.

In many cases, strategies are evaluated primarily in terms of financial desirability. If the strategy does not pass these other tests, it should probably be rejected regardless of what the numbers say.

SOME KEY CONSIDERATIONS

Basic Structural Elements

The following discussion concerns several areas that either need emphasis or that should be introduced at this point. Their importance to formulating marketing plans is noted here, but each topic will be discussed in greater detail later in the book.

Trial and repeat When one is trying to analyze the success or failure of a brand at an early stage in its life cycle, one needs to look beyond aggregate sales and analyze trial purchases and repeat or replacement purchases separately. For example, the same overall sales pattern could be caused by either of two very different situations. First, it could be caused by a very large number of people trying the product once (because it promises to solve a problem that they have) and few of them repurchasing it (because the product or service fails to live up to its claims). The same sales pattern could also be caused by few initial purchases (either because few people know about it, because few can find it, or because few have the problem that this product promises to solve), followed by a large number of repeat purchases (because the triers were quite satisfied). These two situations call for very different corrective actions. This situation is illustrated in Figure 1-11, which shows hypothetical sales graphs for two frequently purchased products in the same industry. These two products have equal sales, as shown by the height of the bars. Based only on that information, one would think they have equally bright futures. However, the distribution of sales between trial and repeat is dramatically different. Product *A* has achieved a high level of trial sales, but few people are repurchasing it. Once everyone has tried it, its sales will probably drop off sharply. Product *B* has had fewer triers, but has developed a core of repeat purchasers. Its future looks much brighter.

In other situations, companies may buy a small quantity of a product like personal com-

FIGURE 1-11a Quarterly sales for Product A.

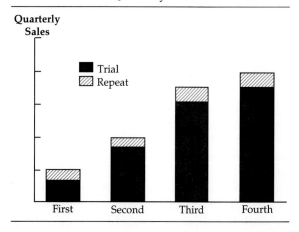

FIGURE 1-11b   Quarterly sales for Product B.

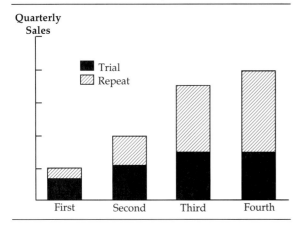

puters or machine tools to try them out. These initial purchases could be made because of the benefits promised. However, larger quantities will be purchased only if the product performs well in early tests. These subsequent purchases constitute a different kind of "repeat" sale.

At a later point in the product life cycle, purchases will be almost entirely repeat or replacement purchases and this distinction will become less important. However, when this distinction is important, a separate analysis of trial and repeat sales should be conducted.

Intervening variables—preference, satisfaction, awareness, and distribution   While the ultimate focus of marketing efforts should be on sales and profits, consideration needs to be given to the effect that marketing mix elements have on a number of intervening variables. First, the customer must be aware of the product. Next, the customer must prefer the product—believe that it offers greater value than alternatives. Finally, the customer must have it made available. If the activities associated with these intermediate variables are performed inadequately, the sales of the product will suffer. So, these intermediate variables provide valuable diagnostic information as well as goals for marketing programs.

Repeat or replacement purchases are caused in large part by satisfaction with the product or service. With frequently purchased items, the consumer may have to be reminded of the brand and must be able to find the product. The latter two variables have been mentioned previously, but satisfaction is a new intervening variable. It provides particularly useful diagnostic information about why some products enjoy a higher repeat purchase rate than others do. A target level of satisfaction should be set for most products and related services.

In considering the above intervening variables, one should keep in mind the motives that drive purchase and use. Some products such as scratch pads and motor oil provide value directly through use and are *non–ego-intensive* if failure is unimportant or highly unlikely. Some products like health care items and insurance can be *personally ego-intensive* if their performance strongly affects the consumer's welfare but they are socially inconspicuous. Finally, other products are *socially ego-intensive;* they affect an individual's sense of self-worth and social well-being. Automobiles, most apparel, and jewelry are examples.

The less ego-intensive a product is, the harder it will be to create awareness and preference and the greater the need will be for convenient availability. The more ego-intensive a product is, the greater the emphasis the seller must place on the psychosocial benefits it conveys. For personally ego-intensive products, the advice of experts and personal satisfaction are more important, whereas the attitudes of peers and superiors are more important for socially ego-intensive products. For many ego-intensive products, distribution is an essential component of its image.

Demand analysis—segments and subsegments   At the most basic level, one must identify the decision-making units. These units can be aggregated into segments only if they exhibit sufficiently common characteristics. The common majority fallacy arises when the product desired by the "average" consumer is actually favored by few if any individual customers. An example of this situation would occur if half the people really wanted large cars and half really wanted small cars, yet no one wanted a medium-sized car. If averages are examined, one would come to the conclusion either that size was not important or that the average person wanted a mid-sized car. This problem points to the need for analyzing the market at the level of individual customers and placing customers in segments only when there is sufficient homogeneity.

The economics   A major result of the planning and budgeting process is an assessment of how much it will cost to attain some objective. Managers must continually ask whether the predicted results are worth the cost. In addition, managers need to give serious thought to increasing the efficiency of marketing activities. Substantial parts of Chapters 14 and 15 are devoted to the topic of how profits can be increased by reducing resource commitments or increasing contribution revenue.

New Versus Established Products

There are several important differences between new and established products. One of the most important differences is the amount of information that the customer possesses. This fact is reflected in potential customers' inability to provide informed judgments about new products and to predict future purchases. Furthermore, until a product has been on the market for some time, purchase data provide only modest help. Therefore, concept testing and conjoint analysis may do a much better job of predicting trial. The criteria by which consumers judge products are also likely to change more with a new product than with an established product. As a result, forecast quality is lower early in a product's life cycle. Similarly, a manager's judgments about the response to marketing spending will tend to be subject to greater error with new products than with established ones.

Another large difference concerns the way that managers think about the effects of marketing variables. With new products, some actions are going to be used to generate consumer trial while others will focus mainly on generating repeat or replacement purchases. The type of actions that generate first purchases may be quite different from the type of actions that generate repeat purchases. However, when a product becomes established, most of the purchases will come from existing customers and the separate analysis of first versus later purchases is less valuable.

Consumer Versus Industrial Products

Important differences are usually found between new and established and between frequently and infrequently purchased products. Similar degrees of difference are common between consumer and industrial products. Industrial purchases are usually based upon somewhat different criteria than consumer purchases, and the importance of many industrial purchases results in a more intensive evaluation of alternatives. Even so, industrial and consumer decision processes can be fairly similar. People that make industrial purchasing decisions also make personal purchases and they are probably no more rational in one case than in the other. In many consumer situations, decisions (especially those involving more money or longer-lasting consequences) are made by more than one person, just as many industrial purchases may involve influential individuals.

Nevertheless, marketing mix elements and the allocation of marketing funds tend to vary in important ways between consumer and industrial markets. For example, advertising and wide distribution may be more important for consumer products than for industrial products, while sales calls may be more important in industrial settings. However, similar differences can exist among various consumer goods or various industrial goods. When suitably adapted, the concepts and methods discussed in this book are applicable to either case, as well as to the differences found within each classification. The central problem remains linking spending to the desired marketing results.

Decentralized Versus Global Planning and Budgeting

The degree of centralization is often manifest in the way a firm handles regional and national or product and business strategies and budgets. The key difference is the impact that actions in one area have on other areas. Are they tied together solely by an overall budget constraint or are the ties more direct?

In a decentralized planning system, each business unit, product, or geographic area has its own objectives, strategies and budget, and may even be funded by its own revenue. Financial allocations across business units are typically made with the aid of a portfolio approach, and may be concerned chiefly with approving capital requests that are not directly part of an annual marketing budget. Additional funds are given to businesses that have more attractive prospects. Discretionary money is not allocated to areas that show less promise. The amounts allocated are primarily determined by corporate objectives.

On the other hand, "global" planning and budgeting refers to the situation where one business plan is written for a number of businesses (for example, more than one geographic area or more than one model or product in a product line). The budget allocation process may be more formal and have a stronger top-down flavor. If response functions are generated for each region (country or product), the optimal allocation can be determined in a way that is similar to the way in which the optimal allocation across the mix elements is determined for an individual product. For this scheme to be applicable, products or other primary units of analysis must have similar objectives, such as increasing annu-

al profits. A computer aid for consolidated budgeting is described in Chapter 15.

Present Versus Future

One of the hardest business decisions involves balancing the needs of the present with those of the future. It is difficult enough to estimate the response to marketing mix elements in the near future (for example, if advertising is increased by $2 million, how much will market share go up this year?), but it is even more difficult to forecast the longer-term impact. Even if it were possible to determine the future value of a current increase in market share, changes in the environment could make those general forecasts wrong. Still, when making short-term planning and budgeting decisions, the company must consider their long-term impact. In the case of the MARMIX computerized decision aid, the user is able to specify the amount of carryover that current actions have. This is a simple but crude solution, although the uncertainty of future events may make it a useful approach.

Changing Information Technology and Modeling Capabilities

There have been numerous advances in information technology over the last two decades and the pace of change is unlikely to slacken in the near future. The purpose of this section is to comment briefly on some of the changes that are occurring. See McCann (1986) for further details.

The first change is the increase in the type, quality, and timeliness of data that are available to marketing managers. The most visible example of these trends is UPC (universal product code) scanner data in the packaged goods industry. Retail-level scanner data are beginning to augment traditional market-tracking data now, and this process is expected to accelerate as scanner data become available more frequently (once a week rather than bimonthly) and on smaller geographic regions than current store audit or warehouse withdrawal data. Similarly, consumer-level scanner data are replacing traditional purchase-panel data. A second source of additional data is expected to come from field salespeople who carry portable computers and gather such information on each sales call as volumes ordered, prices, retail facings, competitive prices, and out-of-stock conditions. It is quite likely that other currently lagging industries will also develop much more extensive data bases.

As more of these data become computerized, retrieval and analysis can be simplified. Increasing computerization has led some firms to combine different data bases, such as retail scanner data with MAJER'S retail advertising data or household scanner data with television viewing data. Other firms are providing higher-level analysis programs that combine data from several standard data bases collected by different suppliers.

Similarly, computerization has increased the user's ability to interact with these data bases using either terminals connected to mainframe computers or personal computers. For example, several analysis packages allow one to combine retail scanner data with factory shipment data for the analysis of inventory in the pipeline. Some packages are able to perform such tasks as measuring the efficiency of sales promotions by looking at the difference in volume between promotional and nonpromotional periods and areas, or econometric analyses of the relationship between sales volume and independent variables like price, consumer promotions, and advertising.

Additionally, several decision aids such as this book's MARMIX program allow one to use judgmental inputs to estimate the best allocation of a marketing budget. Although impressive progress has been made in the last ten years, there is substantial room for improvement. A larger volume of data coming at more frequent intervals will create a demand for more user-friendly analysis packages as well as advances in analysis and decision aid methodology. Also, user experience should cause these trends to

continue and accelerate. Many firms have computerized their manual tabulations, but have not added any new types of analysis. This will change with increased experience. Data that come regularly, such as retail scanner data, store audit data, or warehouse withdrawals, presently may be combined manually with data that come irregularly such as trade promotions. In the future, relational data base management systems will facilitate the computerization of these tasks.

CONCLUDING REMARKS

In spite of the fact that this book is about a value-based approach to marketing analysis and planning, it needs to be reemphasized that the end result of the planning process is not a written plan, but better decisions. In the case of both new and existing products, this involves two different sets of decisions. The first is a decision about the offer: the actual product or service, price, and messages to be directed at various targets. The second set of decisions is concerned with marketing support. This breakdown between the offer and support has been made for several reasons. Budgetary decisions concern the marketing expenses involved in marketing support, but decisions about the offer usually do not show up as expense items. Furthermore, decisions about the offer tend to be more long-term oriented even though every element may undergo continual evolutionary changes. The results of budgetary decisions are more observable in the short run.

These two decisions are the output of the marketing analysis and planning, but they are also part of a hierarchy of decisions. Before deciding on an offer, one must choose a core strategy and positioning. Here, one needs to specify customer and competitor targets as well as the image that the business should have in the eyes of potential customers. Similarly, before choosing a level of marketing support, one must decide on strategic objectives, as a growth objective is typically associated with a larger marketing budget than a harvesting objective.

Decisions about objectives and the core strategy are at the top of the decision hierarchy. In turn, they are a function of the threats and opportunities facing the business. Therefore, a starting point in the marketing planning process is the situation analysis. This includes an analysis of the industry, potential customers, and competitors, as well as an analysis of the strengths and weaknesses of the particular business.

REFERENCES

Abell, Derek F.: *Defining the Business: The Starting Point of Strategic Planning,* Englewood Cliffs, N.J.: Prentice-Hall, 1980.

_____ and John S. Hammond: *Strategic Market Planning: Problems and Analytical Approaches,* Englewood Cliffs, N.J.: Prentice-Hall, 1979.

Armstrong, J. Scott, Roderick J. Brodie, and Shelby H. McIntyre: "Forecasting Methods for Marketing," *International Journal of Forecasting,* 3, 1987, 355–376.

Armstrong, Larry, and Neil Gross: "Its a Shakier Perch for Toshiba's Laptops," *Business Week* (August 5, 1991), 62–64.

Buzzell, Robert D.: *Note on Market Definition and Segmentation 9-579-083,* Boston: Harvard Business School Publishing Division, 1978.

_____ and Bradley T. Gale: *The PIMS Principles: Linking Strategy to Performance,* New York: The Free Press, 1987.

Cavanagh, Richard E., and Donald K. Clifford, Jr.: "Lessons from America's Midsized Growth Companies," *McKinsey Quarterly* (Autumn, 1983), 2–24.

Clark, William A.V., Howard E. Freeman, and Dominique M. Hanssens: "Opportunities for Revitalizing Stagnant Markets: An Analysis of Household Appliances," *Journal of Product Innovation Management,* 1, December, 1984, 242–255.

Cohen, William A.: *Developing a Winning Marketing Plan,* New York: John Wiley & Sons, 1987.

Cooper, Arnold C., and Dan Schendel: "Strategic Responses to Technological Threats," *Business Horizons,* February 1976, 61–69.

Crawford, C. Merle: *New Products Management,* 2d ed., Homewood, Ill.: Richard D. Irwin, Inc., 1987.

Day, George S.: *Strategic Market Planning: The Pursuit of Competitive Advantage,* St. Paul, Minn.: West Publishing, 1984.

_____: *Analysis for Strategic Market Decisions,* St. Paul, Minn.: West Publishing, 1985.

_____: *Market Driven Strategy: Processes for Creating Value,* New York, The Free Press, 1990.

Garda, Robert A.: "Strategic Segmentation: How to Carve Niches for Growth in Industrial Markets," *Management Review,* 70, August 1981, 15–22.

Gluck, Fredrick W.: "Strategic Choice and Resource Allocation," *McKinsey Quarterly,* Winter 1980, 22–33.

Hall, William K.: "Survival Strategies in a Hostile Environment," *Harvard Business Review,* 58, September–October 1980, 75–85.

Hamel, Gary, and C.K. Prahad: " Corporate Imagination and Expeditionary Marketing," *Harvard Business Review,* July–August 1991, 81–92.

Hammonds, Keith H.: "The 'Blacktop' Is Paving Reebok's Road to Recovery," *Business Week,* August 12, 1991, 27.

Holusha, John: "The Love for Cars: A Quarter Century of Best Sellers," *New York Times,* November 18, 1990, F6.

Hopkins, David S.: *The Marketing Plan,* New York: The Conference Board, 1981.

Huey, John: "Nothing Is Impossible," *Fortune,* September 23, 1991, 135–140.

Jacobsen, Robert: "Distinguishing Among Competing Theories of Market Share Effect," *Journal of Marketing,* October 1988, 68–80.

Kucamarski, Thomas D.: *Managing New Products,* Englewood Cliffs, N.J.: Prentice-Hall, 1988.

Lanning, Michael J., and Edward G. Michaels: "A Business Is a Value Delivery System," working paper, McKinsey and Company, 1987.

Lehmann, Donald R., and Russell S. Winer: *Analysis for Marketing Planning,* Plano, Tex.: Business Publications, 1987.

Levitt, Theodore H.: "Marketing Myopia," *Harvard Business Review,* July–August 1960, 45–56.

McCann, John M.: *The Marketing Workbench: Using Computers for Better Performance,* Homewood, Ill.: Dow Jones-Irwin, 1986.

McDonald, Malcolm: *Marketing Plans,* New York: Franklin Watts, 1986.

McKenna, Regis: *The Regis Touch,* Reading, Mass.: Addison-Wesley, 1985.

Mintzberg, Henry: "Crafting Strategy," *Harvard Business Review,* July–August 1987.

Nulty, Peter: "Change with the Market or Die," *Fortune,* January 13, 1991, 62–63.

Ohmae, Kenichi : "The 'Strategic Triangle' and Business Unit Strategy," *McKinsey Quarterly,* Winter, 1983, 9–24.

Pessemier, Edgar A.: *Product Management: Strategy and Organization,* 2d ed., New York: John Wiley & Sons, 1982; Reprinted by Robert E. Krieger Publishing Co., Inc. Malabar, FL, 1988.

Peters, Tom, and Nancy Austin: *A Passion for Excellence,* New York: Random House, 1985.

_____ and Robert H. Waterman, Jr.: *In Search of Excellence: Lessons from America's Best-Run Companies,* New York: Harper and Row, 1982.

Porter, Michael E.: *Competitive Strategy: Techniques for Analyzing Industries and Competitors,* New York: The Free Press, 1980.

_____: *Competitive Advantage: Creating and Sustaining Superior Performance,* New York: The Free Press, 1985.

Quinn, James Brian: *Strategies for Change: Logical Incrementalism,* Homewood, Ill.: Richard D. Irwin, 1980.

_____, Henry Mintzberg, and Robert M. James: *The Strategy Process,* Englewood Cliffs, N.J.: Prentice-Hall, 1988.

Rapport, Andrew S., and Shmuel Halevi: "The Computerless Computer Company," *Harvard Business Review,* July–August 1991, 69–80.

Rothschild, William E.: *Putting It All Together: A Guide to Strategic Thinking,* New York: AMACOM, 1976.

Schlender, Brenton R.: "The Future of the PC," *Fortune,* August 26, 1991, 40–48.

Taylor, Alex: "Caution: Bumps Ahead for Ford," *Fortune,* December 18, 1989, 93–96.

Treece, James B., and Mark Landler: "Beep, Beep! There Goes Ford's Explorer," *Business Week,* January 28, 1991, 60–61.

Tushman, Michael L., and William L. Moore, eds.: *Readings in the Management of Innovation,* 2d ed., Cambridge, Mass.: Ballinger Publishing Company, 1988.

Urban, Glen L., and John R. Hauser: *Design and Marketing New Products,* Englewood Cliffs, N.J.: Prentice-Hall, 1980.

Van de Ven, Andrew: Central Problems in the Management of Innovation," *Management Science,* 32 (6), 1986, 590–607.

Weber, Alan M.: "Consensus, Continuity, and Common Sense: An Interview with Compaq's Rod Canion," *Harvard Business Review,* 68, July–August, 1990, 114–125.

Woodruff, David, and Jonathan B. Levine: "Miles Traveled, More to Go," *Business Week, The Quality Imperative,* October 25, 1991, 70–73.

APPENDIX— BRIEF PLANNING OUTLINES

SHORT-TERM MARKETING PLAN

1. *Executive Summary* A one- to three-page synopsis of the plan.

2. *Situation Analysis* A several-page analysis of the current threats and opportunities facing the business.

   a. Industry Analysis

   b. Customer Analysis

   c. Competitor Analysis

   d. Internal Assessment

   e. Cost and Profit Analysis

   f. Summary and Planning Assumptions

3. *Marketing Objectives* A short statement of the strategic and operational objectives as well as the reasons they were chosen.

4. *Offer* A discussion of the core strategy, positioning and offer chosen to achieve the marketing objectives.

   a. Core Strategy

   b. Positioning

   c. Product and/or Service

   d. Price

   e. Communication Messages

5. *Marketing Support* A discussion of the marketing budget to implement the strategy.

   a. Advertising

   b. Promotion

   c. Sales Force

6. *Financial Documents*

7. *Monitors and Controls* Specific information to be collected during the planning period.

8. *Contingency Plans and Other Miscellaneous Documents*

   a. Contingency Plans

   b. Alternative Strategies Considered

   c. Miscellaneous

STRATEGIC MARKETING PLAN

1. *Executive Summary* A one- to three-page synopsis of the plan.

2. *Planning Situation* A short discussion of the competitive arena and the relationship to the rest of the corporation.

   a. Business Definition

   b. Recent Performance

   c. Corporate Guidelines

3. *Situation Analysis* A several-page analysis of the longer-term threats and opportunities facing the business.

   a. Customer Analysis

   b. Competitor Analysis

   c. Environmental Analysis

   d. Internal Capabilities and Current Position

e.   Cost and Profit Analysis

f.   Summary and Planning Assumptions

4. *Objectives and Strategies*   A several-page discussion of the   strategic direction of the business, proposed level of investment in the business, and the reasons for these choices.

a.   Strategic Objective

b.   Strategic Alternatives

c.   Core Strategy and Positioning

d.   Resource Requirements

e.   Key Programs

5. *Financial Documents*

6. *Contingency Plans and Other Miscellaneous Documents*

REVIEW QUESTIONS

Q1-1   What is a marketing plan?

Q1-2   What are the essential questions that a marketing plan should answer?

Q1-3   What are the main reasons for a marketing plan?

Q1-4   Describe the process by which a marketing plan is developed.

Q1-5   Describe the essential features of a situation analysis.

Q1-6   How and why should a market be segmented?

Q1-7   Why is the term "strategy/budget" an appropriate way to describe the resource allocations required by a marketing plan?

Q1-8   What are the advantages and limitations of a top-down, bottom-up planning cycle?

Q1-9   What criteria did Day (1984) offer for the evaluation of a strategy?

Q1-10 Discuss the rationale for dividing the planning work into those elements concerned with the offer and those elements concerned with marketing support.

Q1-11 For the following consumer products,

bread
carbonated soft drinks
running shoes
laptop personal computers
paper clips

discuss the relative importance of each component of the offer to a marketing manager.

Q1-12 For each of the above products, assume that you are charged with understanding each component of the offer as it applies to the major competing products. Concern centers on how design, price, and positioning influences purchases. What would you measure or analyze and how would you do it?

Q1-13 In the above cases, who is in charge of managing each component of the offer? How much time and what kind of resources are required to make a change in each component?

Q1-14 Discuss the importance of tracking trial and repeat purchases.

Q1-15 Discuss the importance of tracking preference, satisfaction, awareness, and distribution.

2

PRODUCT AND MARKET EVOLUTION

This chapter deals with the evolution of products and markets; the stages in product and market development, technological evolution, competitive evolution, the managerial implications of the product life cycle, and methods of forecasting change. One purpose of this chapter is to provide a framework for thinking about how markets evolve that should enable you to be more proactive when planning for new and existing products. A second purpose is to reinforce the need for continuous innovation. Chapter 3 examines the elements that lead to successful product development: the characteristics of new product success and failure, the development process, and managing product development.

The five chapters that make up the next part extend the discussion of value creation to specific decisions about the design of a product, its price, and positioning. Short of traditional demand analysis, which is not formally treated, the eight chapters in the first two parts constitute an integrated discussion of the product offer: how opportunities to create product value can be identified and developed.

PRODUCT LIFE CYCLES

One of the most pervasive, yet confusing and criticized concepts in marketing is that of the product life cycle (PLC). The PLC is based on the belief that most products go through a similar set of stages over their lives, much like living organisms. It suggests that many products will face common opportunities, problems, and challenges in a somewhat predictable pattern. In turn, this pattern points to several issues to which a manager should be alerted. Typically, the PLC is represented with a graph of sales over time. An idealized pattern is shown in Figure 2-1; it is divided into four major stages.

Introduction An initial period of slow growth. Marketing effort relative to sales may be quite high. Usually, this effort is

FIGURE 2–1   Pattern of sales over a product's life cycle.

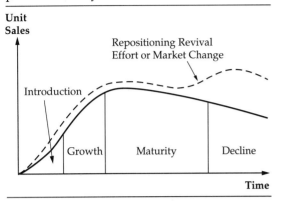

directed primarily toward creating awareness and gaining trial.

Growth   The period of rapid sales growth following introduction. It is driven primarily by new users, satisfaction, emulation, and repeat sales. This may be a period of strong but declining marketing support relative to sales.

Maturity   The period during which sales are high and stable. This may be a period of reduced marketing support and increased price competition. Various environmental changes and revival efforts can extend or reduce the length of this phase.

Decline   The period of the product's market life in which sales are significantly below their peak and are declining.

Part of the confusion about this concept arises because there are at least three different product life cycles, depending on the definition of the "product" (Capon, 1978). At the highest level of aggregation is a product class, industry, or category life cycle. This would be the life cycle for cigarettes, automobiles, microprocessors, or breakfast cereals. One level down would be the combined life cycle for a number of closely competing brands in a product category. This could

be the life cycle for plain filter cigarettes, nutritional cereals, thirty-two-bit microprocessors, or mid-sized cars, and is called a product form or subcategory life cycle. At the lowest level of aggregation is the brand or model life cycle. This would be the life cycle for Philip Morris plain filter cigarettes, Cheerios, Intel 80486 microprocessors, or the Ford Taurus. For an example of these three types of life cycles within the cigarette industry see Figure 2-2.

A manager is ultimately interested in the brand life cycle, but this chapter concentrates on the more aggregate levels of life cycles. For planning purposes and to understand the environment, product form and product class life cycles are more important, in part because there is a greater ability to generalize across product classes than across brands. For example, there are probably more parallels between the product class life cycles of computers and automobiles than there are between the brand life cycles of the Ford Model T and the Taurus. Second, these product class or product form life cycles are influenced to a greater extent by environmental conditions and less by the actions of individual managers than brand life cycles. Unless otherwise stated, the term "product life cycle" will refer to one of these more aggregate life cycles.

Several criticisms have been leveled at the product life cycle concept over the years. Some, such as those of Dhalla and Yuspeh (1976), have focused on the brand life cycle (as opposed to product class or product form life cycles) and have correctly pointed out that reducing support at the first sign of a sales decrease can result in a self-fulfilling prophesy.

More relevant to this discussion are a number of criticisms that relate to product form and product class life cycles. First, although the form shown in Figure 2-1 is more common than any other form, it is far from universal (Buzzell, 1966; Polli and Cook, 1969; Rink and Swan, 1979). Some products display a fad cycle that has no, or a very short, maturity stage. In addition to some fashions, toys such as video games, gifts such as pet rocks, and unique appliances

FIGURE 2–2 PLCs for a brand, product form, and product category.

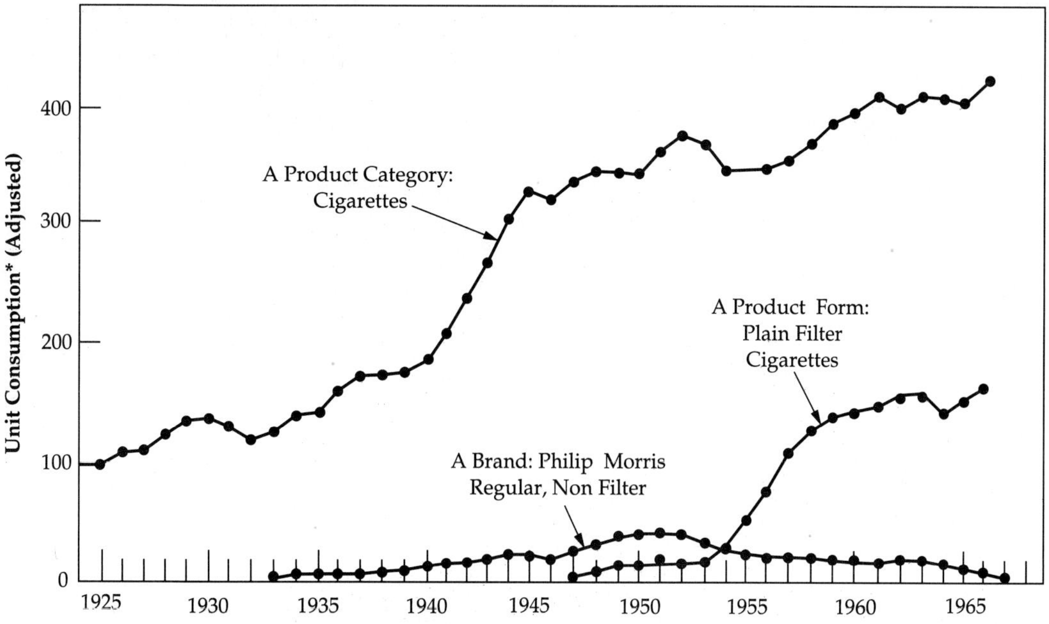

*Number of cigarettes per $100 of constant dollar nondurable consumption.

Source: *Polli and Cook (1969, p. 389).*

such as single-patty hamburger cookers might have similar life cycles.

Other products have life cycles that involve one or more recycles between the growth and maturity stage. This pattern could be caused by the introduction of new technology that creates additional uses, such as more powerful PCs, or by an increase in certain needs; for example, when increasing oil prices in the 1970s led to a resurgence in the sales of chain saws and wood-burning stoves. A third common form is a growth-decline-plateau cycle (Rink and Swan, 1979). Here, the growth period is immediately followed by a partial decline to a stable volume that is considerably lower than peak sales. This pattern is typically associated with goods having a long repurchase cycle. Here, the market is quickly saturated through a number of first purchases, but after this surge, sales are a function of replacement and new people entering the market. This form can also be observed in packaged goods that enjoy a rapid penetration but fewer repurchases.

A second criticism is that there are no agreed-upon definitions to separate product class from product form life cycles (Rink and Swan, 1979). For example, should minicomputers and microcomputers be considered new product classes or just new forms in an overall computer product class life cycle? When these two innovations were introduced, many people probably classified each of them as creating a separate product class, but now with the differences between mainframes, minis, and micros blurring, there may be more debate. Similarly, there are no agreed-upon definitions for what constitutes the various stages. For example, there is no agreement about the point at which the introductory phase ends and the growth phase begins. Furthermore, it is not possible to predict the length of any future stage given knowledge about previous stages.

Probably the most important criticism of the product life cycle is that it is too simple to capture the variation that occurs across different product classes. The product life cycle curve for a particular product class is a function of market, technological, and competitive factors (Lambkin and Day, 1989). These three forces are discussed in the next three sections. The topics are discussed separately, but it is clear that they interact; that events in one area affect the other two. It is this interaction that causes the shapes of life cycle curves to vary across product classes.

The following discussion will not attempt to settle any of the definitional disputes, but argues that general product life cycle or, more broadly, product and market evolution concepts have managerial value. Specifically, the product life cycle is a useful way to think of product and market development and to look at the factors that cause product life cycle curves to have different shapes and heights. Even if not all products follow the same life cycles, the manager has a framework for analysis. Use of these concepts forces a proactive rather than a reactive view. It is important to alert the manager to possible changes even if their timing and impact are uncertain.

MARKET EVOLUTION

Introductory Stage

This stage starts with the market introduction of the first brand in a product category or subcategory, and ends when sales start to increase rapidly. Many (even successful) products spend a long time in this phase (one example is frozen orange juice) and many failures never progress past this stage. These products could be creating a new product class life cycle the way the first mainframe computers or the original Xerox copiers did. On the other hand, they could be

launching a new product form, as when radial tires replaced bias-ply tires.

The key factors at this stage are uncertainty, lack of knowledge, and, in many cases, poor product performance. At this point, few consumers have direct experience with the product, so they may be uncertain about its usage and relative benefits. They may also have questions about durability, reliability, and likely changes in performance and price over time. In addition to facing many of these same questions, producers may also be uncertain about the best ways to market the product, the rules of competition, and the entry of other firms.

Rate of diffusion   The length of the introductory stage is a function of the rate of *diffusion,* or the speed with which the new product (innovation) spreads throughout the system. The rate of diffusion is positively related to several characteristics of the innovation (see, for example, Gatignon and Robertson, 1985; Rogers, 1963; 1983).

1. *Relative advantage:*   The degree to which it is superior to competitive products.

2. *Compatibility:*   The consistency of the innovation with the values and experiences of potential adopters.

3. *Divisibility:*   The degree to which it can be tried on a limited basis.

4. *Communicability:*   The relative ease of observing and describing the benefits to others.

Additionally, the rate of adoption is negatively related to two other factors.

1. *Complexity:*   The degree of difficulty in understanding or using the product.

2. *Perceived risk:*   The subjective estimate of the probability that something will go wrong and the cost of failure.

For any given new product, some of these factors may be fixed, but it is possible for the producer to influence many of them. Firms can increase the relative advantage of the product by conducting appropriate marketing research to determine what benefits customers desire, using concept and product tests to determine if the new product promises and delivers these benefits, and by communicating these advantages to the customer. Feedback from early users can be used to improve the product. Similarly, although many new products are inherently complex, certain steps can be taken to reduce this complexity, as was done with the mouse and pull-down menus introduced with the Macintosh computer and the computerized tutorials associated with many new software packages. Complexity can also be reduced through appropriate positioning and comparisons with existing products. Risks can be reduced through guarantees, warranties, leasing, and trial periods.

Other factors are only partly under the control of an individual producer. The value of one product may be a function of the availability of complementary products. The value of early automobiles was greatly enhanced by an increased number of gas stations and garages, better roads, and so on. An important determinant of the success of a new computer or operating system is the amount of software available. The value of a product may be decreased if there is uncertainty about compatibility or the lack of standards, such as in the 1970s when there was a question about whether Beta or VHS would be the dominant videotape format. Similarly, rapid progress in either improving product performance or decreasing costs may cause customers to wait for a better price–performance trade-off.

In addition to characteristics of the innovation, Robertson and Gatignon (1986) hypothesize that the rate of diffusion in industrial markets is related to various characteristics of the adopter and supplier industries. For example, the rate of diffusion is positively related to the competitive intensity of the supplier industry, the reputation of the supplier industry, and the vertical coordination between the supplier and adopter industries; however, the rate of diffusion will be highest when the level of competition and of heterogeneity within the adopter industry is at an intermediate level.

Adopter categories   In addition to differences in the rate with which different innovations diffuse through the population, some people or organizations tend to adopt innovations more quickly than others. Rogers (1963, 1983) classified adopters into five categories, depending on how soon they adopt an innovation. He calls the first 2.5 percent of the people or organizations to adopt[1] an innovation the innovators and the next 13.5 percent the early adopters.[2] The first people to adopt an innovation are typically younger, have higher incomes and more education, have greater social mobility, and are more venturesome, but there does not appear to be a general innovator that adopts many different products early. Instead, trends seem to be category specific; innovators and early adopters tend to be heavy users of related products and are interested in the new product. Rather than concentrating on the number of people or organizations in each adopter category, it is usually more important to focus on the differences between earlier and later adopters.

Similarly, organizations that are first to adopt an innovation tend to be the ones that expect to profit most from it. When the adoption requires a large capital outlay, large firms are more likely to adopt first.

In summary, the introductory stage lasts until

---

[1]Rogers defines adoption as when the consumer decides to make full and regular use of an innovation. In the case of durable goods, adoption is operationally defined as occurring when the first purchase is made.

[2]Mahajan, Muller, and Srivastava (1990) have developed another scheme for identifying adopter categories that is based on the Bass new product model, which is discussed later in this chapter.

sales start to grow rapidly. The length of this stage is due in part to the factors influencing the rate of diffusion. Some of these factors can be influenced by producers. The length of this stage may say little about the ultimate success of this product class or product form.

Growth Stage

This stage begins when sales start to increase rapidly and ends when growth slows to the approximate growth rate of the target market population. Rapid growth can be sparked by a number of factors. First may be the emergence of a "dominant design" (Abernathy and Utterback, 1978), i.e., a standard product that reduces market uncertainty. The IBM PC and the MS-DOS operating system performed this role in the personal computer industry.

Second, the value of the product may have increased sufficiently through improvements in the product's performance, introduction of associated products, accompanying service, reliability, or decreases in cost for many consumers to see a large relative advantage in adopting the new product.

Third, risk may have been reduced by posi-

tive word of mouth or by noting a sufficient number of satisfied users. The first two of Rogers' adopter categories, the innovators and early adopters, have already been mentioned. They are less influenced by other people who have adopted the product—although they may consciously try to be the first to adopt innovations in their areas of interest; for example, they may want to be among the first to see a new movie or try the latest new restaurant. The last three categories of adopters: early majority, late majority, and laggards (the next 34 percent, 34 percent, and 16 percent, respectively) are influenced more by seeing or hearing of others using this innovation. Therefore, adoption by these people requires a critical mass of past adopters. The growth stage may occur as this critical mass accumulates.

A graph of these adopter categories is generally shown as a bell-shaped curve. In this curve, the number of people or organizations that adopt the innovation in any time period is plotted against time. (In statistics, this is called a frequency curve.) An example appears in Figure 2-3. A different (but equivalent) way of representing this process is to plot the penetration (the number or percentage of people who have

FIGURE 2–3 Rogers' adopter categories.

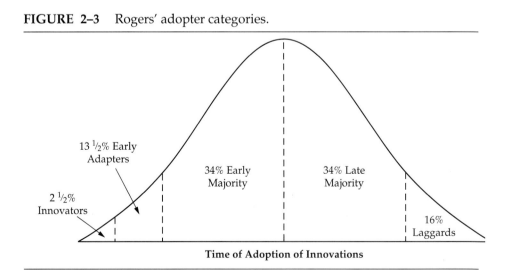

13 ½% Early Adapters

2 ½% Innovators

34% Early Majority

34% Late Majority

16% Laggards

Time of Adoption of Innovations

already adopted the innovation) against time. In this way of representing the same data, the penetration, or cumulative adoption curve, is S-shaped.

The growth period may be prolonged (or the rate of growth may be increased) through the introduction of new models that stimulate greater repeat, replacement, or additional purchases. For example, the introduction of solid state electronics in color TVs is believed to have led to replacement purchases before the original models had worn out. Similarly, the introduction of smaller TVs (for rooms in addition to the TV room), portable audiotape players, and laptop computers has led to additional purchases in these product categories.

Figure 2-4 shows the sales of U.S. color television sets over time. Total sales have been broken down into first purchases, replacement purchases, additional purchases, and institutional purchases. Several things should be noted from this figure. First, most first purchases have taken place well before the growth rate slows. In this example, many of the laggards (Rogers' last category of adopters) made purchases during the growth stage. After 1973 most first purchases were believed to be made by people entering the market because of new household formations. This figure also highlights the difference between the product life cycle curve (Figure 2-1 and represented as the total sales curve of Figure 2-4) and the adoption curve (Figure 2-3

FIGURE 2–4 U.S. color television sales.

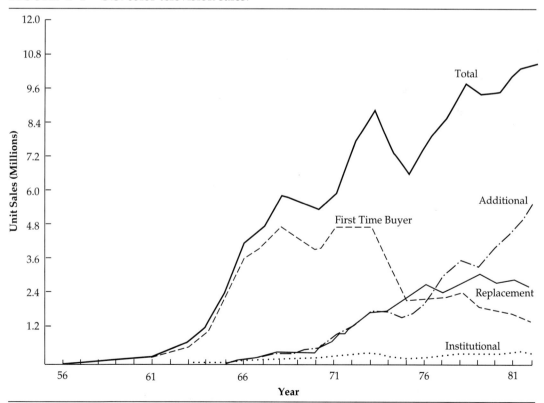

Source: *Bayus, Hong, and Labe (1989, p. 9).*

and represented as the first purchase curve in Figure 2-4). Finally, this curve shows the importance of replacement and additional purchases on sustaining growth.

Generally, the most important cause of increasing sales in the growth stage is the addition of new users. Therefore, the growth period will tend to continue until the product approaches its maximum penetration, that point at which nearly all of the target market has tried the product. After this, sales will be primarily replacement or repurchases, and new users entering the market may be approximately balanced by people ceasing to purchase the product.

The knowledge of the average customer usually increases during the growth period. People purchasing a product for the first time are able to consult an increasing pool of previous adopters. Also, producers and resellers will become more knowledgeable over time. People making repeat or replacement purchases will also be more knowledgeable than when they made their initial purchase. Finally, the emergence of a dominant design may lessen uncertainty about standards and best approaches. As knowledge of both producers and consumers increases, producers are able to introduce products aimed for specific segments or niches.

DeBruicker and Summe (1985) point out that organizational buyers tend to evolve from inexperienced generalists to experienced specialists. When a new product class is first introduced, the people responsible for purchasing decisions will be inexperienced. They will also tend to be generalists, people who are competent in traditional skills and are good at dealing with uncertainty. These could be general managers or design engineers who deal with introducing new technologies into their companies. Over time, as these companies become experienced, the responsibility for purchasing tends to be delegated to specialists—either functional specialists with detailed knowledge about the product or purchasing agents.

In sum, the growth stage is a period when there is rapid growth in sales, usually because

new customers are entering the market. However, for more frequently purchased products, repeat, replacement, and additional purchases can play a critical role. This period usually ends when the product approaches maximum penetration. The length of this period can be shortened by applying additional marketing resources or using a penetration pricing strategy. On the other hand, this period can be extended or the market expanded by introducing new and improved products that stimulate replacement and additional purchases.

Maturity Stage

This is the period when sales are fairly stable or are growing at the approximate rate of the target market population. During this stage, most purchases are repeat, replacement, or additional purchases. First purchases are made primarily by people entering the market; for example, those buying a first refrigerator soon after purchasing a first house.

It is possible that sales will increase after a period of stable sales because of changing tastes or new product capabilities. For example, the sales of both chain saws and wood-burning stoves increased dramatically during the 1970s as energy bills rose. Roller skates and skateboards have enjoyed a resurgence, partly because a new generation is using these products and partly because of substantial product improvements. These kinds of change "recycle" the growth stage, but do not invalidate an evolutionary model. They just require that an allowance be made for the new conditions when forecasting future product sales.

If uncertainty characterized the introductory stage, greater buyer knowledge characterizes the maturity state. At this time, few purchases are first purchases. Even if the product class has undergone substantial changes since the last purchase (as might be the case in industries with either long repurchase cycles or in industries enjoying rapid technological change), the buyer will tend to be much more knowledgeable than in earlier stages.

Also, there is a tendency for products serving a certain segment to become more similar over time. In part this is because many of the good ideas get copied and in part because the less successful products are forced off the market. The combination of greater buyer knowledge and greater product similarity tends to drive competition to be more price oriented.

The maturity stage continues until sales of the product start on a permanent decline, typically, for one of two reasons. First is a change in preference that renders the product less attractive. Examples of this include the decreased per-capita cigarette consumption caused by increased fears of cancer and the decreased purchases of hats for both men and women because of changing fashions.

The other reason would be the substitution of one product for another. For example, steam replaced sails as a power source for ocean transportation and transistors replaced vacuum tubes in electronic devices. Sales may also decline because of demographic changes. In the 1970s, a drop in the birth rate led to a decline in the sales of baby foods and related products. Rising incomes in developing countries could also lead to decreased purchases of inferior goods. Without changes in demographics, changes in basic needs, or the appearance of substitutes, a product class could remain in the maturity stage indefinitely. One might expect toothpaste, airplanes, and televisions to be around for a long time.

To summarize, the maturity stage is one of relatively stable sales. Purchases are made by knowledgeable buyers. In many cases, products appealing to certain segments become more like commodities and price competition tends to increase.

Decline Stage

This stage is typically caused by changes in taste, changes in demographics, or substitution. As with other stages, the decline stage can differ dramatically across product categories. The decrease in sales may be quite slow (coffee or cigarettes) or rapid (video games). The decline may continue until only a very small volume continues to be sold (vacuum tubes) or the decline may level off at a higher level and may even increase in the future (baby food).

As a result of these factors, the decline stage can be relatively profitable for some firms or it can be unprofitable for all. First, the decline stage is a much more attractive environment when the decline is relatively slow. The more predictable it is the easier it is to manage. Generally declines caused by changes in taste are less predictable. Second, the existence of niches that continue to demand the product also make this stage more attractive. Third, this stage is more attractive when the products are somewhat differentiated. Finally, low exit barriers can help reduce the intensity of competition.

Summary

In spite of the fact that the product life cycle is not deterministic, a number of generalizations can be made at this point. First, customers tend to become much more knowledgeable about the product class as the life cycle progresses. Second, product performance typically improves over the cycle and the relative differences in brands competing for the same segment decline as successful ideas are copied. This leads to increased competition based on price, image, service, durability, reliability, and other factors, and may result in increased value (benefits relative to costs) to the consumer. Finally, the source of sales changes over time. Early in the life cycle the only purchasers are people who have never used the product class. In the maturity stage, most sales come either from repeat purchases by previous customers or from competitors' customers. All of these changes require adjustments in the way the product is marketed.

TECHNOLOGICAL EVOLUTION

In many cases technology evolves through long periods of incremental change that are punctuated by technological discontinuities occurring in the product itself or in the process used to make it. These discontinuities trigger a period of technological ferment until a dominant design emerges as a synthesis of a number of proven concepts. The discontinuities can either be competence-enhancing or competence-destroying for the existing firms in the industry (Tushman and Anderson, 1986). Usually a new product class is formed through a major technological discontinuity. In many industries there is more than one technological discontinuity during a product class life cycle. However, these discontinuities are relatively rare and their effects generally decrease over successive discontinuities. This paradigm of a small number of radical, or revolutionary, innovations followed by a series of evolutionary innovations is closely related to the three patterns of innovation observed by Abernathy and Utterback (1978).

Fluid Pattern

The first pattern of innovation they observed is the fluid pattern. It is a pattern of major product innovations. A new product class life cycle is typically initiated by a radical or discontinuous product innovation. The first automobile, computer, or frozen food is illustrative. Radical innovations can lead to either a new product class life cycle or a technological discontinuity in an existing life cycle. For example, the invention of the automobile would probably be viewed as a new life cycle rather than a continuation of an existing life cycle for "personal transportation vehicles" that would include bicycles and buggies. However, radial tires would probably be considered a discontinuity in the evolution of automobile tires.

Typically, radical innovations come from an individual or a small firm. Examples of individuals or small firms include Edison (incandescent lights), Polaroid (instant photography), Carlson (Xerox), and Intel and Advanced Memory Systems (microprocessors). Large firms that have produced major innovations outside of their major area include Procter and Gamble (disposable diapers), General Motors (diesel locomotives), and EMI (cat scanner). Some consumer electronics firms such as Sony and JVC (VCRs) and Sony and Philips (compact disc players) are producing discontinuous innovations in their area. Similarly, Corning Glass produced major innovations in fiber optic waveguides. Generally, large size can hamper a firm's ability to innovate. When revolutionary innovation does occur in a large firm, the work is often done by the "wrong" part of the company. In fact, the members of the industry being supplanted typically either do not try to participate in the new industry or they fail (Cooper and Schendel, 1976).

The recognition of an unmet need stimulates an entrepreneur to search for a way to meet this need. For example, Chester Carlson worked in a patent office where twelve copies of many documents were needed and carbon paper worked for only three or four. The product initially introduced may be crude, costly, and unreliable; when General Foods developed the first freeze-dried coffee Maxim, it initially cost thirty-five dollars per ounce and was nicknamed "Black Gold."

The product usually begins by serving a specialized niche. Early transistors were expensive and had poor temperature stability and frequency response, but they were lightweight, rugged, and had low power requirements. Thus, they were ideal for missile guidance systems and hearing aids. The first use of a Xerox machine was to make printing plates for offset printing. Diesel locomotives were originally used only in switchyards.

Many times, the most important use of major product innovations is not the first one envisioned. Computers were originally thought to be only large-number crunching machines for scientific computations. Some early market forecasts envisioned the need for only twelve computers in the United States. Similarly, the early market research for Xerox assumed that all the copies would be made at the point of document origination—just like carbon copies—but by far the largest number is made after receipt. Ford developed the Model T as a car for rural people.

Because the most desired characteristics may not be known with certainty, wide product diversity is common early in the product class life cycle. Feedback from vendors and innovative users is used to improve the product. A lot of experimentation takes place and improvement may be rapid. For example, gasoline-powered cars were decidedly inferior to steam and electric cars prior to 1900, but by 1902 they had won their first race; by 1904 they were clearly dominant, and the Olds Motor Company produced 2,500 cars (Abernathy, 1978).

During the fluid pattern of innovation, competition is based primarily on product performance and product features because the product is not very good. Product deficiencies lead to a lot of experimentation to improve the product. This experimentation means that few units are made of any one model. For example, only one or two units were produced of 75 percent of the models of mainframe computers developed between 1944 and 1950 (Knight, 1963). Similarly, small volumes of VCRs were produced several times before their major introduction in 1975 (Rosenbloom and Cusumano, 1987).

However, if the technological and market uncertainties are low enough from the start, it is possible that the fluid pattern will be found only when building prototypes and performing product or market tests prior to introduction.

In sum, in the fluid pattern of innovation, the primary type of innovation is product innovation. Typically there is a significant amount of product diversity and few units of any model are produced. The manufacturing process needs to be flexible and may be organized as a job shop with general-purpose tools operated by highly skilled labor. The industry consists of one or more small organizations which usually have organic organizations. When large companies attempt to enter the market at this time, they may use "skunkworks" or separate organizational units to mimic entrepreneurial start-ups. Most of the organizations present during this stage fail.

Dominant Design

As a result of experimentation, a "dominant design" may emerge; it is an optimal product configuration that becomes a standard and does not undergo major change for some time. Usually, such designs are evolutionary. Most of its major features will have appeared in previous models, but this particular combination of features is new. For example, Ford's Model T contained a number of features that were embodied in virtually all cars between 1920 and 1970: longitudinally mounted engine in front connected to rear-wheel drive via torque tube, left-hand steering, "H" transmission, water-cooled engine, independent body and chassis design, and the essential driver controls of today (Abernathy, 1978). The Model T was not the first car with many of these innovations but it was one of the first to incorporate all of them. Based on a large number of experimental designs, this one proved to be optimal. Similarly, the DC-3 incorporated a number of important design changes, but the plane did evolve from the Boeing 247, the DC-1, and the DC-2. However, its design was so dominant that by the start of World War II, 80 percent of the airplanes in U.S. fleets were DC-3s.

Currently there are several competitors for a dominant design in high-definition television (HDTV). The only system on the market is the Hi-Vision system produced by a number of Japanese companies, including Matsushita and NEC. It is an analog system based on technology from the 1970s. At least four digital systems being tested by various U.S. companies are vying with the Japanese analog system for adoption by the FCC as the U.S. standard.

Dominant designs act as powerful guideposts for further technological developments and can be found across many technologies and industries. Other examples include the Smith Model 5 typewriter, IBM 360 Series computers, and the Fordson tractor. All of these shaped the evolution of their respective industries for more than twenty years.

Dominant designs can emerge for several reasons, including superior technology (DC-3), market acceptance (IBM PC), or a management decision to freeze the design in order to reduce costs (the Model T). In many cases the dominant design is the result of positive feedback, where success breeds success. Getting to the market first, having an early cost or design advantage, or obtaining a large order early in the product's life can give the product an insurmountable long-run advantage. For example, two technologies competed for market dominance in videocassette recorders, VHS and Beta. As VHS gained a small early-sales advantage, more stores were willing to stock and promote that format and more compatible tapes were recorded by leading artists. In turn, more people purchased VHS machines (and tapes), leading to further gains in experience and scale economies, and giving VHS producers the ability to price and promote more aggressively. In time, this feedback cycle forced the Beta format out of the market (Arthur, 1990).

Positive feedback does not necessarily lead to the survival of the best product. Rather, it favors the luckiest or most effective early entrant. Once a set of favorable feedbacks is operating, it is very difficult for less fortunate competitors to gain a major position in the market. Consider how IBM and Microsoft set the standards for personal-computer operating systems and Lotus 123® did the same for spreadsheets. Because switching costs can be high for users and resellers, dislodging such products usually requires a major shift in the technology or the market.

Similarly, Gould (1986) discusses the reason for the emergence of the QWERTY keyboard.

The origin was quite logical: If one typed too fast, the keys jammed. In the early typewriters, the keys struck the paper from the bottom, so key jams were not easily detectable and were therefore much more serious. The middle row of dfghjkl suggests that the first layout was alphabetic and certain letters were removed to slow the typist down. The QWERTY design survived because of contingency and incumbency—a series of chance happenings and the inertia that followed. In 1882, Longley founded the Shorthand and Typewriter Institute in Cincinnati and developed the eight-finger method of typing using the QWERTY system. When she was challenged to prove that her method was better than some other, Longley engaged Frank McGurrin to use her method. McGurrin had memorized the keyboard and used the touch typing method that most good typists use today. In a well-publicized match he beat the competition. This led lots of manufacturers and typing teachers to adapt the QWERTY keyboard, even though it probably had little to do with his victory. Once it gained the dominant share, it was never relinquished, in spite of the fact that the navy found that the cost of retraining all typists to the Dovark simplified keyboard could be recovered in ten days.

The emergence of a dominant design, coupled with increased knowledge of user requirements, may lead to the development of new products for specific segments or niches. These new products share a number of basic design features with the dominant design. Some examples of these niche innovations or product line extensions include different-sized cars, off-road vehicles, special steel alloys, and laptop PCs. As the product and market continue to evolve, different versions may continue to be introduced for new segments.

In many cases, this product proliferation is made possible because of an increased ability to achieve greater variation in product performance with smaller differences in physical products as the technology matures. The graph in Figure 2-5 of horsepower versus displacement

FIGURE 2–5 Evolution of engine size versus horsepower for the Ford engine line, 1903–1958.

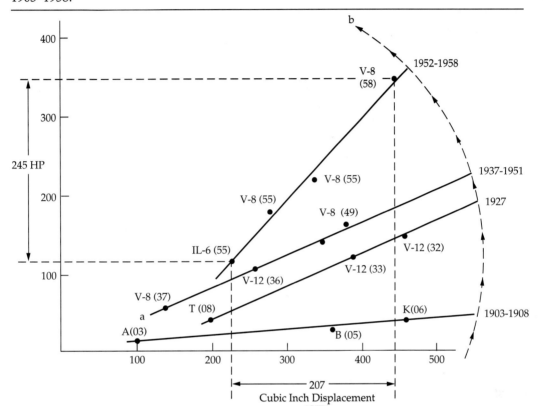

a. The number in parenthesis is the year in which the engine model was introduced.
b. Rotation (the dotted line) shows a decrease in the ratio of mechanical variety needed to deliver a given range of performance in horsepower from the 1903-1908 era to the 1952-1958 era.

Source: *Abernathy and Clark (1985, p. 17).*

of automobile engines illustrates this type of evolution. Similarly, consider the reasonably small differences between the way a personal computer with the older 8088 and a personal computer with the newer 80486 chip are manufactured.

Transition Pattern

The emergence of a dominant design leads producers to a decision that more is to be gained by decreasing the number of experiments on the product and by beginning to rationalize the production process. If the product becomes popular, companies may be forced into process innovation to meet demand. The use of special-purpose equipment and longer production runs become common. This leads to a time of major process innovation. It may also be a time of deskilling the labor task. An example of this kind of process innovation is Ford's utilization of an assembly line for the Model T.

As a result of these actions, the interdependence between the product and the process may begin to build up—decisions in one area start to have a more important effect on the other. As soon as a piece of special-purpose equipment has been installed, the range of product modifications that can be handled may be reduced. This interdependence (as well as the inability to discover major product innovations) leads to more incremental product changes. Furthermore, this process innovation usually makes the manufacturing process more capital intensive and may make small-volume manufacturing uneconomical. These two factors, as well as the different requirements for success, can lead to a shakeout.

The decision to standardize the product and start down the experience curve is important because it is only in retrospect that one knows which design will become dominant. For example, in the early days of semiconductors, the large corporations—RCA, GE, and Philco—focused on process innovations early in the life cycle while the new entrants—IBM, Texas Instruments (TI), and Fairchild—continued to pursue product innovations (Tilton, 1971). Apparently, there was more to be gained by continued product innovation, as the new entrants have been much more successful. Ironically, several years later TI guessed that the LED technology would be dominant for digital watches and built a huge plant to produce watches with LED displays. Shortly thereafter, innovations made the LCD technology far superior.

As products become more standardized and superior designs are copied, differences in terms of performance and features tend to diminish. This means that competition within a given segment will hinge more on price and differences in durability, reliability, image, distribution, and service. In turn, manufacturing skill in cost reduction and conformance with specifications may become more important than the ability to make new models. This pattern of major process innovation continues until there are few major process innovations to exploit. That point marks the start of the specific pattern.

Specific Pattern

If the dependence between the product and the process continues to build and if the product is able to attain a large enough volume to support such a production system, a pattern of incremental product and process innovation will emerge. This is called the specific pattern. This pattern is characterized by standardized products manufactured in high volumes with efficient techniques. It is a time when both product and process innovation are incremental. Still, the efficiency of the production process continues to increase as islands of automation emerge and are linked together through automatic work feeding, removal, and material-handling devices. Much of this innovation is based on informal changes that may not be designated as specific projects. In many cases, the sum of these incremental improvements can increase productivity as much as the original innovation (Enos, 1967; Hollander, 1965).

The stream of incremental innovation may cause the interdependence between product and process to become even greater. For example, at the beginning of the specific stage in the automobile industry (about 1950) most companies manufactured all car models in most assembly plants, but as the phase wore on, the plants became more rigid and assembled only one or at most a small number of closely related models (Abernathy, 1978). These changes make it much harder to shift production mixes quickly to keep up with changing consumer tastes.

In sum, this is a stage of incremental product and process innovation during which products are produced in high volumes in efficient plants. The organizational form tends to be more bureaucratic. Competition has shifted from performance to image, price, durability, reliability, and so on.

Lean Production[3]

This evolution from a job shop to a mass manufacturing process has been observed in a number of industries that began around the turn of this century. It was based on assumptions of a mature stage during which there is little environmental change, there is a limit to productivity and quality improvement, and the most efficient manufacturing process under these conditions is based on worker and equipment specialization, extensive (hard) automation, and long production runs.

In many cases, there are several unintended consequences of this phase. First, the only real engines of change are the "experts," as the line workers are required to learn a task but not change it. Second, mass production systems become "buffered." For example, high inventory levels act as a buffer against machine breakdowns or poor quality of upstream parts and huge repair areas are set aside to buffer against poor assembly quality. Third, there is an acceptable level of quality that does not need to be exceeded.

In spite of their efficiency, the rigidity and waste of mass production systems have led a number of people to question whether mass production should be the end of this evolutionary path. Led by Toyota, a number of companies are embracing "lean production systems." In these systems, the product is continually improved and anything that does not add value is minimized or eliminated. This is accomplished through a thorough understanding of the production process and a continual attempt to improve it. For example, work-in-process inventories do not add value but are needed if production equipment is unreliable, upstream parts are of inconsistent quality, or parts are manufactured in large batch sizes. These other problems

need to be solved before inventories can be cut. If large batch sizes are required because of long setup times, the setup process needs to be analyzed for ways of shortening it.

In 1950, Japanese output was 31,597 cars and trucks, less than a day's production for U.S. makers. In the United States, stamping presses were totally dedicated to stamping out one part; for example, a hood. The dies would remain in the press for the production life of the car and would take several days to change. This was an acceptable level of downtime if it occurred every few years. On the other hand, Toyota's volume did not allow it the luxury of dedicated presses. This forced the company to search for ways to change the presses more quickly. Over a ten-year period, it was able to reduce the time to change body stamping dies to fifteen minutes by using smaller presses, automating as much of the process as possible, doing preparations for the changeover while the presses were running, and training teams to specialize in rapid setup. It had to understand the process and figure out ways to change it.

Low volumes also forced Toyota to broaden worker jobs in order to keep the workers fully employed. First they were required to operate several machines, then perform their own maintenance, and finally inspect their own parts for quality. Surprisingly, Toyota found that each of these changes also improved productivity.

The visible success of certain firms that have adopted this system and the inherent drawbacks of the rigid specific phase have led a number of people to advocate this evolutionary pattern. In many ways the evolution to lean production is similar to the earlier observation of a pattern of innovation from major product to major process to incremental innovation. However, by aiming for a different combination of quality, productivity, and flexibility some proponents of lean production, like Toyota, have been able to do well on all three dimensions. Lean production is not a job shop as parts flow through the production system. It combines some of the hands-plus-

[3]Much of this section is based on Cusamano (1988), Krafcik (1988), and Womack, Jones, and Roos (1990).

mind philosophy of the job shop, but with standardization and an assembly line.

Other Patterns

For a number of reasons, these three patterns do not occur in the same order or have the same relative importance in all industries. This model is more appropriate for products that are manufactured as discrete parts than for liquids, gases, or solids whose output is measured by weight or volume rather than in physical units. Some of these latter products that are able to be manufactured in a continuous flow process (such as many chemicals) may proceed from the fluid to the specific phase without a real transition phase. Other liquids (for example, beer and wine) may be limited to a batch process because of the requirements of aging. In general, process innovations appear to be more important to these products, although one can think of important product innovations such as light beer and special steel alloys.

However, if the product does not achieve sufficient volume or technological and demand stability, a truncated pattern of innovation may occur in which one never reaches the specific phase. For example, the general printing process will probably always be batch or job shop. Moreover, recent advances in computer-aided manufacturing may enable some of these job-shop or batch operations to achieve many of the benefits of the specific pattern without the accompanying rigidity.

A Series of Dominant Designs

The pattern of incremental product and process innovations continues until there is another technological discontinuity. These subsequent discontinuities could be events that create new product class life cycles, such as when calculators replaced slide rules. Alternatively, they could lead to an industry shakeout in the same

product class life cycle, such as when integrated circuits replaced transistors in minicomputers.

Mainframe computers have been successively designed around four generations of components: vacuum tubes, transistors, integrated circuits, and large-scale integrated circuits. Each of these changes required changes in computer design. After each revolutionary innovation there was a period of consolidation in which a large number of minor changes followed the original innovation.

This pattern of revolutionary and evolutionary innovations can be seen in the commercial aircraft industry. After the DC-3 there were no major innovations until the jet in 1959. Then the next major innovation was the widebody jet in the 1970s. The impact of these changes on airline productivity is shown in Figure 2-6.

These improvements may look as if they came out of thin air (and to some of the competitors it probably seemed that way). However, Foster (1986) demonstrates that many times technological advances occur in a systematic fashion. Specifically, if the value on a performance parameter (such as speed, memory capacity, or strength) is plotted against cumulative effort, an S-shaped curve generally results. An idealized curve is shown in Figure 2-7. Progress is slow at the start of this process because a knowledge base must be built, lines of inquiry must be established, and unworkable approaches need to be discarded. After the groundwork has been laid, progress may be very rapid. However, at some point, physical limits constrain future development and growth slows again. This curve predicts that when the rate of technological progress is at its maximum, half of the potential is gone, and technical progress will start to slow down.

The slow pace of progress when a new technology is first investigated may lead outside observers, especially those working with the old technology, to dismiss it as being something that will never work. However, after a sufficient base has been built up, successful new technologies show rapid improvement. Furthermore, if the

FIGURE 2–6 Seat-miles-per-year capacity of the most capable plane flown by U.S. airlines 1930–1978.

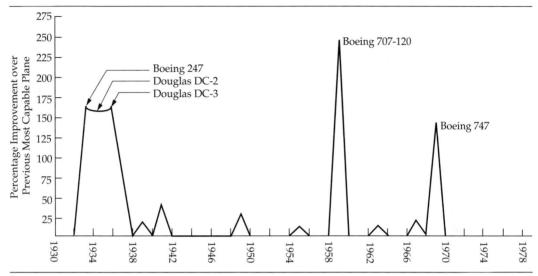

Source: *Tushman and Anderson (1986, p. 453).*

FIGURE 2–7 Foster's S-curve.

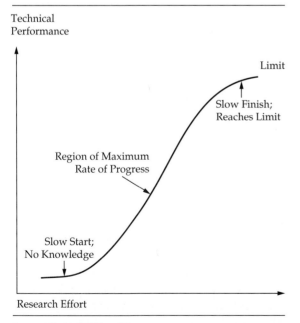

Source: *Foster (1986, p. 31).*

older technology is at the top of its S-curve, the new technology may quickly pass it in performance, appearing to have come from out of nowhere.

This rapid replacement pattern is shown in the middle of Figure 2-8, where nylon overtakes rayon in tire cord performance. While nylon's initial performance was much lower, its progress was more rapid. Additional R&D spending on rayon had little impact on its performance.

If the first innovation creates the industry, volume may build slowly. However, when subsequent innovations occur, companies may have to ramp up production more quickly. These discontinuous innovations can be competence enhancing by building on previous competences, such as replacing tubeless tires with tube tires. Alternatively, they can be competence destroying , as happened when diesels replaced steam locomotives. In either case, discontinuities are likely to lead to a reverse transition from the specific back to the transition pattern. This trend has been observed in automobiles over the last

FIGURE 2–8   S-curves in tire cord technology.

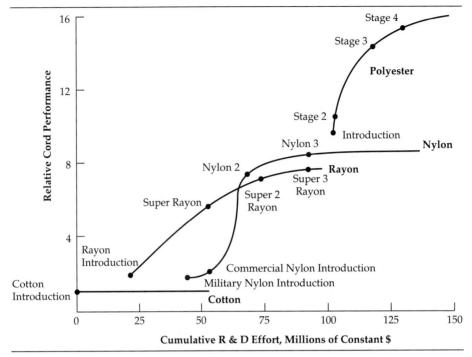

Source: *Foster (1986, p. 124).*

decade as there is more product design variation and manufacturing flexibility.

The impact of these evolutionary and revolutionary changes can be seen in Figure 2-9, which shows the increase in the precision with which machine tools can produce parts. There is a steady decline through the mechanical era, then a sharp drop between comparators and electric comparators, then another steady decline during the electronic era.

Model Changes

In addition to changes in dominant designs, many products go through a series of smaller changes which might be called model changes. Sometimes a new model is given a different name, such as Ford's Taurus or Chevrolet's Lumina; at other times the name may not be changed. For example, Honda's Accord has undergone a number of redesigns without a name change. At still other times, most of the name will remain the same, but the model number or name will change slightly, as with the IBM's PC, PC Jr., XT, and AT. The amount of the change can vary from quite large (e.g., Taurus) to relatively small (e.g., IBM XT).

Abernathy (1978) has shown that the market value of introducing an individual new model generally decreases over the product life cycle. This result may hold in many industries where products tend to become more similar over time. Still, the cumulative improvement from a series of incremental changes can be extremely important in maintaining or building market share. Furthermore, its importance is amplified when one competitor is doing much more of it than others.

FIGURE 2–9 Evolution in machine tool accuracy.

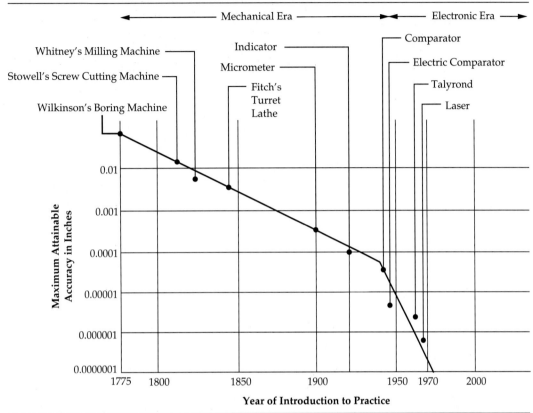

Source: *Adapted from Bright (1978), based on an earlier figure by Eugene Merchant.*

One of the important advantages that Japanese automakers enjoy over automakers in the United States is shorter model cycles from concept to the time the last car rolls off the line. On average the Japanese automakers produce the last unit of a model only seven and a half years after the concept is originated, in the United States, the average car rolls off the line thirteen to fifteen years after the concept. On average the Japanese always have newer models in the showroom.

Similarly, in residential air conditioners, Mitsubishi was able to make a number of changes between 1979 and 1985 that resulted in a very superior product. In 1979 Mitsubishi's three-horsepower air conditioners were similar technologically to those of a U.S. manufacturer. Whereas the U.S. firm made no major changes, Mitsubishi made the following: introduced integrated circuits (1980), introduced microprocessor controls (1981), added "quick connect" freon lines and high-efficiency rotary compressors (1982), added sensors to the unit and more computing power (1983), and introduced an inverter that increased the energy efficiency ratio (1984). In 1985 the U.S. company thought about adding integrated circuits, but when its development cycle would not allow an introduction before 1989 or 1990, it decided to source its air conditioners from Japan (Stalk, 1988).

Summary

First, there is a general and systematic change in the amount and type of innovation as a product class evolves. This is shown in Figure 2-10. A product class is formed with the introduction of a radical innovation. This triggers a period of product innovation in which a variety of product forms compete for dominance until a dominant design emerges as a synthesis of a number of proven concepts. Once a dominant design emerges, technological change shifts to process innovation. After major process innovations are in place most technological progress is driven by numerous incremental improvements. However, the cumulative impact of these changes on performance and cost can be great. This pattern of evolution is related to differences in the basis of competition, manufacturing process, and organizational form. It does not occur automatically, but must be managed.

Some industries face a more complicated evolutionary pattern. Rather than a single radical innovation followed by a dominant design and incremental changes, there may be several radical innovations, each of which is followed by a consolidation phase consisting of a series of evolutionary innovations. These radical innovations can occur either in the product itself, such as enclosed steel bodies, jet engines, and integrated circuits, or in the manufacturing process, such as iron and steel's transition from the Bessemer process to open hearth to basic oxygen to continuous casting, or the manufacture of flat glass

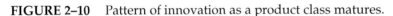

FIGURE 2–10   Pattern of innovation as a product class matures.

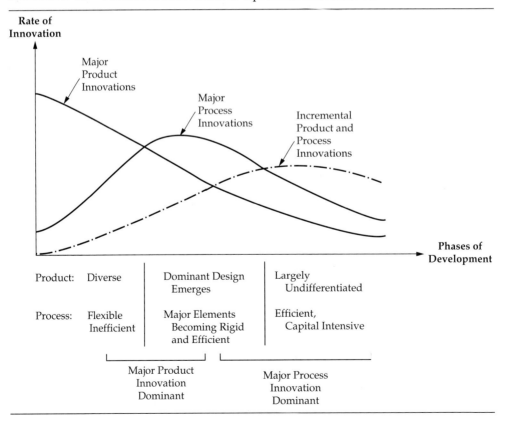

from continuous grinding to the float process. Typically such changes are followed by a consolidation phase that may be characterized as learning by doing.

When a technological discontinuity is accompanied by relatively little market uncertainty, it is possible to move from one high-volume process to another without the job-shop phase.

COMPETITIVE EVOLUTION

A third key factor is competitive evolution. Rather than following the path of evolution throughout this entire section a number of issues will be treated separately.

Population Ecology[4]

The population ecology perspective has been taken from biology. As the name suggests, it deals with the way that different populations of organisms (organizations in this case) adapt to the environment.

The first firms to enter an environment are termed r-strategists. They enter at a time of low population density and can therefore avoid direct competition. Each of these firms makes a decision about the number of niches it will enter; that is, the number of market segments it will serve. Those that attempt to serve a small number of segments are called specialists and those that attempt to serve a large number are generalists. Once this decision has been made a certain amount of structural inertia develops and it is more difficult for the firm to adapt to change. Environmental change provides an opportunity for new organizations to enter and serve emerging segments. Firms that enter later are termed K-strategists.

Early in the evolution of a product class there is a great amount of uncertainty. This leads to

substantial diversity in organizational approaches to the market. Some of the early entrants may be generalists, but most of them are small specialists whose lack of resources requires that they attack only a small number of segments. Low population density reduces direct competition. Most of these firms fail, but the specialists tend to have a higher survival rate than the generalists because of their focus on a single segment.

As the market begins to grow and the uncertainty declines, new firms are attracted. Typically these K-strategists are generalists that attempt to capitalize on the inefficiencies of the earlier entrants. However, some firms entering the market at this time attempt to exploit specialized niches and are termed K-specialists. This is usually the period of the greatest number of entrants. As the number of firms continues to grow relative to the size of the market, the population density increases until the population exceeds the carrying capacity of the environment (market) and there is a shakeout. Typically, the K-generalists are the most successful competitors at this stage.

The number of entrants is expected to decrease during the mature phase. Successful entrants are those that are able to exploit unrecognized niches or whose resources are especially suited to this environment (for example, low-cost manufacturers).

The findings of Romanelli's (1987) study of the minicomputer industry were generally consistent with population ecology theory. The majority of the entrants in the emergence stage were specialists, more firms entered the market during the rapid growth stage than any other, and firms entering the industry during the transition to the maturity phase were the least numerous and had the lowest survival rate. Also, when strategies were characterized in terms of being generalist-specialist or aggressive-conservative, most of the firms maintained the same strategy.

In spite of this type of consistency, firms were able to adapt by changing the segments on

[4]Much of this section is based on Hannan and Freeman (1977) and Lambkin and Day (1989).

which they focused and by continually introducing new products. Contrary to the theory, most of the entering firms during any period were specialists. Romanelli found that the three most successful firms were fast moving and aggressive, but when the survival rates of all firms were examined a lack of aggressiveness adversely affected only those firms with a generalist strategy.

Pioneering Advantages

There are obvious risks to being first, but there are also rewards for surviving pioneers. Several authors have found that surviving pioneers tend to have higher market shares than followers. Urban et al. (1986) studied twenty-four consumer goods categories (some appear to be product classes, like cat food and fabric softener, while others may be product forms within a product class, like instant soup and high-filtration cigarettes). All else being equal, the pioneer had a market share 1.4 times greater than the second entrant. The second firm's share was 1.2 times bigger than that of the third entrant, and so on. A superior position or greater advertising expenditures could counteract this advantage.

Using the PIMS data base across 371 mature consumer goods businesses, Robinson and Fornell (1985) found that "pioneers" had an average market share of 29 percent, "early followers" had shares of 17 percent, and "late entrants" had shares of 12 percent. In a similar study of 1,209 mature industrial businesses, Robinson (1988) found that "pioneers" had an average market share of 29 percent, "early followers" 21 percent, and "late entrants" 15 percent.

All of these studies analyzed only survivors. Furthermore, most of these businesses were a part of a large corporation. A causal link is not necessarily postulated. It is possible that a third variable—say, technical or marketing skill—is responsible for both early entry and continued success. Still, there is a positive relationship between early entry and higher market share. In some cases, this is related to positive feedback.

In his study of managerial enterprise in the United States, England, and Germany between 1880 and 1930, Chandler (1990) found that the dominant firms were aggressive first movers. They made early investments in plants, marketing, and people to take the lead in an industry. Most of them retained their industry leadership many years in the future. Similarly, in Corey et al.'s (1989) study of four industrial distribution networks, all of the market leaders enjoyed first-mover advantages. They had entered the market early with an innovative or technically superior product. In turn, this allowed them to establish a strong distribution system. It appeared that early leadership positions tended to be self-perpetuating. Early product superiority led to distribution strength and market leadership. The installed base led to spare part and service revenues for the distributors. In turn, this led to distributor strength and loyalty, giving the manufacturer the edge in maintaining product superiority through access to knowledge about product applications.

Looking at the other side of the coin, Biggadike (1979) examined the success of firms diversifying into existing markets. (By definition, these firms were not pioneers.) While entry into the growth versus maturity stage was not broken out, it is assumed that most of these firms entered growth markets. He found that it took eight years on average for these ventures to become profitable and an extrapolation of these results indicated that it would be ten to twelve years before the ventures reached the profitability of mature businesses. Furthermore, he found that an aggressive entry strategy produced better results over time even though early years' losses were greater.

Mobility Barriers[5]

The term "mobility barriers" will be used to refer to entry barriers to an industry, mobility barriers that inhibit entrance into certain strate-

---

[5]Much of this section is based on Porter, 1980.

gic groups, and exit barriers. Usually mobility barriers will change over time.

Early in its development the industry may be populated with a large number of small firms. This suggests that barriers will not be related to economies of scale. Typical entry barriers early in the product life cycle include lack of access to proprietary technology and key inputs, as well as insufficient, distant, and uncertain returns. The technology barrier could be a function of either the product design or the production process. Key inputs could be capital, raw materials, or skills.

As the industry starts to prosper, the importance of these mobility barriers decreases. If the reward is sufficient, it is possible for new entrants to obtain technology either by hiring people or reverse engineering. Similarly, as growth starts to take off, the size, distance, and uncertainty of future rewards become a much smaller barrier.

Over time the specific mobility barriers for many industries change and consolidation occurs in response to rising mobility barriers. As a dominant design emerges and firms shift to process innovation, economies of scale tend to become more of a mobility barrier as does the amount of capital needed to enter. The capital commitments could be needed either for plants or for marketing costs. As some brands become established their brand awareness will also constitute a mobility barrier.

Other barriers, such as access to distribution channels, may also change over time. It is possible that early in the life cycle distribution channel access is a barrier either because there are no distributors to handle the product or because the preferred intermediaries do not want to carry an unproven product. Later in the life cycle, many distributors may want to carry only one or a small number of brands and access to distribution channels again becomes a mobility barrier.

In a declining market, the relevant barriers are exit barriers, not entry barriers. Exit barriers tend to keep firms in an unattractive industry when they would otherwise choose to exit.

Examples of exit barriers include specialized assets, fixed costs of exit (such as labor settlements), and emotional barriers (based on an attachment to the business or a reluctance to admit failure).

MANAGERIAL RESPONSES TO PRODUCT AND MARKET EVOLUTION

The evolution of a product class is due to the interaction of a number of factors, including actions by competing producers, buyer behavior, and legal and social forces. Because changes in societal attitudes, producer actions, the appearance of substitute products, and new uses of the product cannot be predicted from past sales, the product life cycle is not deterministic. For example, one cannot predict the height of the curve from the length of the introductory period because eventual success has little to do with the speed of diffusion. Some products that diffuse fairly slowly become almost universal, such as automobiles in the United States. Other products diffuse more quickly and become universal, such as TVs in the United States. Other products spread quickly to a small portion of the population, such as certain fads or fashions.

However, realizing why these evolutionary changes take place and what impact they have on sales of a product category allows a manager to make more intelligent forecasts about the likely future of the particular industry. For example, changing attitudes about health have led to a per-capita decrease in cigarette and coffee consumption. Furthermore, some of these factors can be influenced by the companies selling the product. The rate of growth can be accelerated by continually improving the product, cutting price to give it a better value, or spending money on promotion to increase awareness. On the other hand, producers can create uncertainty and slow the rate of diffusion by failing to agree on standards.

Therefore, in spite of the problems caused by

different shapes of product life cycle curves, disagreements in terms of whether a given innovation is part of a new product class or product form, and an inability to perfectly predict the future on the basis of the past, the product life cycle can be a managerially useful concept.

Typical Patterns

Although sufficient data do not exist on all stages of market development, changes that tend to occur between the growth and maturity stages of the product life cycle have been found using PIMS data (Hambrick, MacMillan, and Day, 1982; Anderson and Zeithaml, 1984). As an industry grows and matures, the following tendencies have been found: A smaller percentage of sales comes from new products, the difference in relative product quality gets smaller, market shares become more stable, and the ratios of R&D, sales force, and promotional expenditures to sales drop. Somewhat surprisingly, the average ROI does not decline as the industry moves from the growth to the maturity stage. However, the ratio of cash flow to sales increases.

These statistical regularities suggest that one can forecast the way product attributes, demand, production, and competition will change as a product class matures even if the timing of these changes is uncertain. These evolving characteristics can be summarized in tabular form, one table for the market and marketing elements (Table 2-1), one for price, sales, and cost elements (Table 2-2), one for product and process elements (Table 2-3), and one for the strategic posture of the business (Table 2-4).

These guidelines are useful in that they form consistent packages. Nevertheless, they are based

TABLE 2-1 CHANGES IN THE MARKET AND MARKETING STRATEGIES OVER THE PRODUCT LIFE CYCLE

Element	PHASE OF PRODUCT LIFE CYCLE Introduction	Growth	Maturity	Decline
Customers	Innovators	Early imitators	Mass market	Laggards, special groups
Competitors	Few	Many (often small size)		Declining numbers (often larger size)
Selling approach	Product awareness, trial	Brand/ features	Brand/ value	Reliable specialist
Channels	Few and/or exclusive	Selective	Broadcast	Selective
Promotional emphasis	Prestige	Features	Price	Special applications
Service	Low	High	Moderate	Low
Marketing expenditures	Relatively large	Large	Moderate	Small

TABLE 2-2   CHANGES IN SALES, PRICES, AND COSTS OVER THE PRODUCT LIFE CYCLE

Element	Alternative Strategies	PHASE OF PRODUCT LIFE CYCLE			
		Introduction	Growth	Maturity	Decline
Market size	A*	Small	Growing	Large	Declining
	B*	Moderate	Rapid growth		
Sales growth rate	A	Low	High	Low	Low negative
	B	Moderate			
Unit price	A	High	Declining	Lowest	Rising
	B	Low	Low		
Unit cost	A	High	Declining	Lowest	Moderate
	B	Moderate	Low		
Unit margin	A	High	Declining	Lowest	Moderate
	B	Negative	Moderate		

*A and B indicate alternative strategies:
A. Skimming entry price, product strategy, and promotion.
B. Aggressive entry price, product strategy, and promotion.

on averages and no individual product class evolves in an average manner. Second, they do not take such factors as relative market share into consideration. Third, a marketing manager has considerable freedom to depart from the most common strategic patterns. For example, Table 2-2 shows two very different price-volume strategies that can be suitable for a given product class. The choice will depend on the firm's capabilities, its overall strategic posture, the likely behavior of competitors, and the degree of price sensitivity and segmentation that may exist among potential buyers.

Although the above framework contains a number of potentially useful strategic prescriptions, a knowledgeable manager may find good reason to reject or modify any or all of these guidelines. There is no substitute for an intimate knowledge of the firm, its markets, and the product class.

Introductory Stage

The primary characteristic of this stage is uncertainty and lack of knowledge by all parties. Producer uncertainties include, but are not limited to, target markets, marketing approaches, desired benefits, technical approaches, industry structure, and future price-performance improvements. This leads to extensive experimentation with different products and approaches.

It suggests that firms enter the product class as soon as possible, since *surviving* pioneers tend to benefit more from positive feedback and retain higher shares than later entrants. On the other hand, it is important to realize that the real pioneers are often casualties and are not remembered (Intel and Apple are much better known than Advanced Memory Systems and MITS computers). Furthermore, some pioneers such as Minnetonka in soft soaps have been

TABLE 2-3   CHANGES IN THE PRODUCT AND ITS MANUFACTURING PROCESS OVER THE PRODUCT LIFE CYCLE

Component	EXTENDED PHASES OF PRODUCT LIFE CYCLE				
	Product Development	Introduction	Growth	Maturity	Decline
Product design	Basic features	Unstable	Elaborated/improved	Segmented/superior	Basic
Product quality	—	Mixed	Better	Best	Declining
Product research	High: basic functions for new products	Moderate: design support	Low: design support	Low: new function, technology	Moderate: new function, technology
Product engineering	High: basic design	Moderate: redesign	Moderate: second-generation basic design	Moderate: redesign	Moderate: cost saving and new product design
Applications engineering	High: basic use tests	High: basic applications aid	Moderate: new applications aid	Moderate: customer service	Minimal: customer service

overtaken by larger companies such as Procter and Gamble and Jergens. Also, it is possible for a pioneer to focus on the wrong solution to a problem and be overtaken by others who learn from the pioneer's mistake(s). Still, there is no evidence that these failing pioneers would have been more successful if they had waited to enter the market.

Olleros (1986) feels that the two biggest causes of pioneer failure prior to the shakeout period are market uncertainty and technological uncertainty. Market uncertainty can result in a long embryonic state that stretches out the payback. Technological uncertainty may mean that other approaches become dominant or that second- and third-generation products may be vastly superior and incompatible with the first-generation products. A firm can lessen its chance of making a wrong decision by waiting; however,

it may lose other advantages. Olleros suggests that small firms attempt to save money by joint ventures, licensing, and subcontracting as much of the manufacturing as possible.

Porter (1980) points to several times when early entry may be risky. These include when the bases of competition and most important segments will change over time, when the costs of opening up the market are great, when early competition will be quite costly, and when technological changes will make early investments obsolete. If it is possible to forecast that one or more of these factors will occur, an early entry strategy can be modified. For example, if the most important segments will change over time, one can spend time with both segments—with the early segments to gain production experience and with the later segments to develop the best product for their needs. Similarly, more

TABLE 2-4 CHANGES IN STRATEGY OVER A PRODUCT'S LIFE CYCLE

Phase of Product Life Cycle

	Introduction	Growth	Maturity	Decline	Termination
Product Strategy	Aggressive		Holding	Harvesting	
Production Strategy	Flexible →	Sequential →	Integrated →	Intermittent	
Performance Focus	Improve Product Performance		Maximize Sales	Minimize Costs	
Investment Flows	Moderate	Large	Moderate	Minimum	None
Risk Sources	Product Technology, Demand Forecasts		Competitive Pressures, Process Rigidity	New Product-Types, New Consumer Tastes	
Normal Time Intervals	1 1/2 to 4 Years		2/3 of the Product Life	2 Years to a Decline	

Illustrative Marketing Sequence:

Induce Trial
Gain Distribution
Widen Acceptance
Promote New Features
Promote Lower Price
Emphasize Value and Reliability
Ensure Channel Support
Reposition

Illustrative Production Sequence:

Stabilize Quality
Expand Output
Modify Product or Process
Expand Output
Improve Quality
Expand Output
Lower Cost

uncertainty may warrant a less aggressive marketing program, so the early emphasis would be on learning, not sales.

At this point in the life cycle, producers need to concentrate on making desired improvements in the product. In turn, this means that the firm needs to identify early adopters and work with them to learn about desired product configurations and how to make them. Second, producers must worry about shaping the industry and properly positioning themselves for the future. They need to forecast how the industry structure might evolve and what they might do to influence it or adapt to it. Third, virtually all purchasers will be previous nonusers of the product class. Therefore, the selling task tends to be one of getting people to try the product class rather than getting them to choose a certain brand. This industry advocacy stance needs to become more self-serving over time.

Innovative, technologically based products and products whose utility increases with the number of units of the product in use usually experience positive feedback and can profit from special attention early in the life cycle. An aggressive pricing strategy is one approach. Redmond (1989) found that low pricing pioneers had better performance levels and enjoyed fewer competitors during the growth stage than pioneers that priced high. However, in many instances the effectiveness of a low price is limited by the capacity of competitors to cut their prices. More commonly, success is a matter of mounting a sound marketing strategy and taking advantage of good fortune. The introductory program in such cases must be forceful enough to gain a leading position. Subsequently, this market lead must be aggressively protected and expanded.

The feedback principle also operates in international trade, where early success and aggressive expansion can give a country's firms a significant competitive advantage. Industries in a country, like companies in an industry, gain greatly by establishing their product form as a standard and by developing the technical, manufacturing, and marketing skills that are not easily acquired later or by less determined entrants. Since World War II, Japanese and West German firms have dominated a number of technologically based industries. Their success demonstrates the effectiveness of purposeful policies that are supported by aggressive follow-up.

Growth Stage

This stage is characterized by less uncertainty but continued large changes. A dominant design or a smaller number of contending designs may emerge. Because the number of entrants is usually highest in this stage, firms should position themselves to survive the shakeout that commonly occurs at the end of this stage. To reach this latter objective, many firms attempt to gain market share in the growth stage. However, as Aaker and Day (1985) have pointed out, the wisdom of this action depends on several assumptions. It is usually assumed that it is easier to gain share in a high-growth market, that share gains are worth more, that there is less price pressure at that point, that it is easier to gain access to the technology if one enters the market early, and that an aggressive strategy will deter rivals. Many of these assumptions do not hold in certain situations. If any of these are violated significantly, increasing share may be an inappropriate goal.

For example, if most of the competing firms believe in the importance of market share, they will resist losing share at all points in the life cycle, not just after growth has stagnated. Similarly, in many industries firms engage in experience curve pricing to keep rivals out. If this happens, price pressure may be just as great in the growth stage as in the maturity stage. Also, pursuing this objective implies that the firm believes it can maintain the share it will gain in the growth period. Share gained through price cuts may not be sustainable. Also, it is likely that the requirements for success will change over the product life cycle.

In general, product innovation and stimulating trial are important early in the product life cycle. Over time manufacturing and distribution tend to become more important. Therefore, in order to maintain share, the firm has to build skills to compete as the industry matures. Hall (1980) found that the most successful firms in the mature stage were ones that were viewed as the most differentiated or had the lowest delivered cost. Firms should start working on these two elements during the growth stage.

Therefore, the firm needs to consider what its basis of competition—e.g., quality, low price, service, or wide selection—is going to be in the future. Then it needs to identify and acquire the key assets and skills that are required to achieve that position.

As consumers become more knowledgeable,

it will be possible to find segments or market niches that can be filled with specialized products. The firm should actively search for these segments and, when one is located, decide whether it warrants development. In addition to providing opportunities for growth, preempting a segment discourages the growth of competition. If a segment is not that desirable in and of itself, it may be worthwhile to keep potential competitors out. For example, IBM might have been better off to come out with a laptop computer and a work station earlier. In a similar manner, a steady stream of product improvements tends to keep competitors on the defensive.

Finally, companies need to keep up with changes in their current customers. As De-Bruicker and Summe (1985) note, just as buyers generally evolve from inexperienced generalists to experienced specialists, products tend to become more similar over time.

When new product classes are first introduced, significant differences in brand characteristics and the inexperience of buyers raise the need for applications and technical support. On the other hand, if there are only small differences in products inexperienced buyers will be interested in price as well as technical support and service.

As users become more experienced, the bases of their preference will depend on whether the product remains highly differentiated or not. If the product remains differentiated, experienced users will tend to be more interested in product performance and applications support. If the competing products are relatively undifferentiated, price along with acceptable quality may be most important.

Maturity Stage

While this is the period of greatest knowledge and stability, it should not be viewed as a period of stagnation. Sellers need to continually improve the price-performance characteristics of their products. It is hard to think of a mature industry that has not witnessed a number of technological changes during its mature stage. For example, the basic oxygen process, continuous casting, and mini mills have all been introduced during the mature stage of the steel industry. Large-screen TVs, watchman, and high-definition television are three innovations occurring in the mature television industry.

Changes in government regulation, the economy, or the demographic profile of the market provide opportunities for growth. Furthermore, model changes, even if they are relatively insignificant individually, can add up to major competitive changes. The discovery of new consumer needs or variations in them paves the way for new products. In a mature market many niches are larger than entire embryonic markets, making these niches quite attractive to the appropriate firm. Therefore, it is important for the firm to continue to learn from its environment and to exploit emerging opportunities.

Decline Stage[6]

Traditionally, firms have been advised to exit the industry during the decline stage. Research by Harrigan (1985) indicates that the appropriate end-game strategy is a function of the attractiveness of the declining market as well as of the firm's strength in that market. A declining industry is more attractive when the decline is slower and relatively predictable, when there are one or more enduring pockets of demand, when the products are differentiated, and when there are low exit barriers. Businesses with stronger positions are ones that have low manufacturing costs or products which have favorable performance, image, reliability, or service characteristics.

Firms with weak positions in unattractive industries are advised to get out as soon as possible or harvest the business. Raytheon (receiving tubes) and DuPont (rayon acetate) both followed this strategy. When high exit barriers are

---

[6]This section is drawn largely from Harrigan (1985).

present, reducing costs and gradually giving up market share is a possible strategy.

On the other hand, firms with strong positions in attractive situations might profit by maintaining their positions or even increasing their investment in the business. Investment is particularly attractive if the firm is well positioned to compete for a pocket of enduring demand. GTE Sylvania helped other receiving-tube manufacturers to exit the industry by buying their assets.

MODELS TO FORECAST CHANGE

When developing marketing plans and setting sales objectives for individual brands, marketers typically start by forecasting sales for the entire product class or product form. Then the market share of an individual brand is a function of its relative appeal and the marketing effort that is placed behind it.

People have looked at two related areas in an attempt to improve these industry, or product class, forecasts. First, economists and engineers (e.g., Fisher and Pry, 1971; Mansfield, 1968) have studied technological substitutions. Sociologists and marketers (e.g., Bass, 1969; Rogers, 1962, 1983) have studied the diffusion of innovations. These two areas are related, as many innovations are substitutes for products or processes that already exist in the market. The radical innovation may create a new product class such as electronic calculators (substituting for slide rules and mechanical calculators) or they may be a new product form in an existing class, such as ball point pens (substituting for fountain pens).

Second, people have used similar approaches to study each of these phenomena. However, substitution deals with relative preferences or purchases between two products and diffusion deals with sales of one product without direct reference to any other. The next two sections look at models developed to study these two processes.

Technological Substitution

Regularity of the substitution pattern   The pattern of substitution is remarkably similar across different types of products. If the penetration of a new product or technology is plotted against standardized time, the typical pattern is S-shaped. The early substitution occurs at a slow rate, but it increases with time. In the central part of the process, substitution occurs at a fairly rapid pace. In the final part of the cycle, the rate of substitution is modest and decreases with time.

Fisher and Pry (1971) standardized the time of substitution for a group of seventeen superior products and processes and plotted the change in penetration over time. Figure 2-11 shows the resulting graph. Virtually all of the points fall very close to the curve, indicating substantial similarity across various substitutions.

Typically a long time is required from the introduction of a superior product until it has replaced half of the uses of the inferior product. In one extensive study, the modal time was twelve to fifteen years, with 23 percent of the superior products requiring twenty-four to forty-seven years. See Martino, Chen, and Lenz (1978) and Linestone and Sahal (1978). The rate of substitution in a given situation is a function of the same factors that govern the rate of diffusion of an innovation (relative advantage, compatibility, communicability, trialability, perceived risk, and complexity). Additionally, increased switching costs will slow the speed of substitution. These could be due to past investments in learning to use the current product, complementary products that need to be purchased (such as software), or the amount of useful life left in the current product.

On the other hand, some substitutions occur quite rapidly, typically these are fads or are subject to fashion influences. Cabbage Patch® dolls and Batman® paraphernalia replacing more traditional types of toys illustrate the former. Apparel and home furnishing colors and auto-

FIGURE 2–11   Substitution percentage as a function of standardized time.

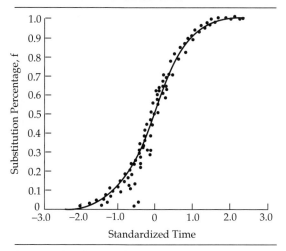

Source: *Adapted from Fisher and Pry (1971, p. 87).*

mobile styling changes illustrate the latter. Furthermore, the popularity of some items and features reoccurs in cycles. Hemlines in women's apparel and single- versus double-breasted suit jackets for men are examples.

When a product's "superiority" is largely psychosocial, the substitution (or adoption) curve can rise rapidly before it flattens out. In these product classes, the problem of predicting the maximum population of potential users or adopters is the most critical forecasting problem. Nevertheless, most major innovations take more than ten and less than forty years to reach the 90 percent, or takeover, level of replacement.

In most cases, the process moves slowly enough for an observant manager to be able to make estimates of the speed of substitution early enough to offer practical guidance about key decisions such as investments in plant and equipment and the probable sales, costs, prices, and profitability of both the new product and its inferior competition. However, management can be lulled into a false sense of security through the knowledge that most new technologies fail. Foster's (1986) S-shaped technological progress

curve in Figure 2-7 shows how the slow progress of a new technology can lead to complacency. Once the substitution curve starts to rise quickly, it may be too late for the producers of the existing products to react effectively. Both radial tires and electronic cash registers went from a 20 to an 80 percent market share in approximately four years (Foster, 1986).

The shape of the substitution curve is typically plotted as a penetration or a cumulative substitution curve. It is related to both the S-shaped cumulative adoption curve that is associated with the bell-shaped adoption curve shown in Figure 2-5 and the S-shaped technological progress function shown in Figure 2-7. The regularity of the substitution process is probably based on factors related to both technological progress and diffusion of innovations.

The following model has been used to study the process of substitution. The probability that a person who has not previously tried the product will do so in period t, P_t, is proportional to the number of previous triers, TT_t, as shown below:

$$P_t = b\,TT_t \qquad (2\text{-}1)$$

where b is a proportionality constant that determines how fast substitution occurs. Martino, Chen, and Lenz (1978) found four factors that explained about half of the variance in b among the cases that they examined.

The number of new triers in period t is T_t. It is equal to the product of the number of people that are left to try it, $M - TT_t$ (where M is the size of the market[7]) times the probability that they will try it during this period, $b\,TT_t$.

$$T_t = b\,TT_t\,(M - TT_t) \qquad (2\text{-}2)$$

---

[7] In most cases, a simplifying assumption is made that the size of the market, M, remains constant. When this assumption is not made, the size of the market will have a temporal subscript, M_t.

This process could be compared with the spread of a disease which requires both a victim and a carrier. Early in the process, there are lots of potential victims (nonadopters = $M - TT_t$), but few carriers (previous adopters = TT_t). So the disease spreads slowly at first. As these two groups become more equal the process speeds up; then it slows down as the number of carriers exceeds the number of potential victims.

The carriers could be viewed as spreading either word-of-mouth support or visual signals about the new technology's superiority. Alternatively, this model also holds if there are no social system effects but increased sales are related to increases in product performance or decreases in price. The size of b, the proportionality constant in Equations (2-1) and (2-2), is a function of both of these effects—the social system influences and better value.

When making forecasts with a model like the one described above, one should consider the factors that are influencing the substitution process. If the underlying factors change, so will the rate of substitution b. Twiss (1984) studied the substitution of oil-based man-made fibers for cellulosic fibers in western Europe. As the graph in Figure 2-12 demonstrates, the rate of substitution slowed significantly after 1973 because the increased price of oil raised the relative price of oil-based fibers. This discontinuity serves as a warning that substitution forecasts should not be made in a wholly mechanical fashion.

Fitting a substitution curve   The size of the market, M, typically includes only those applications where substitution can eventually take place. Take the substitution of scanner checkout equipment for regular cash registers in grocery stores. When this equipment was first introduced, it was assumed that smaller stores would not invest in the equipment. As equipment cost declined with accumulated experience, the store-size limit was reduced and the size of the potential market increased. In addition, the

FIGURE 2–12   Substitution of oil-based fiber for cellulosic fiber in western Europe.

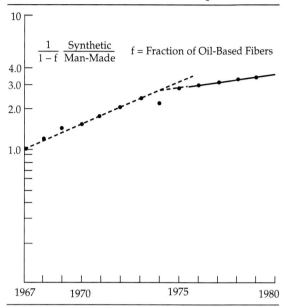

Source: *Twiss (1984, p. 24).*

number of food stores changed. Both of these factors led to an increase in M_t over time.

Adjustments may also need to be made in the particular uses where the new product will be substituted for the older inferior product. This may be a function of competitive response. As purchases of the older product decline, its producers may take steps to improve their product and lower its price. This action may reduce the number of situations in which the new product is superior. On the other hand, the new product may create new demand that is not linked to the older product. For example, transistors not only replaced vacuum tubes but they also opened up applications for which vacuum tubes were not appropriate, such as hearing aids and portable radios. Finally, the population of possible substitute applications of the new product can change because of a change in the population of users or application opportunities. Initially, nylon was principally a substitute for silk in women's hosiery. Over the years, many other uses were found for nylon as a substitute for other materials. It is possible that a different curve would be needed for each substitution.

After considerable algebra, the model in Equation (2-2)

$$T_t = b\,TT_t\,(M - TT_t)$$

can be restated as a logistic function of time:

$$\ln (TT_t/(M - TT_t)) = a + bt \qquad (2\text{-}3)$$

where $\ln (TT_t/(M - TT_t))$ is the natural logarithm of ratio of the penetration of the new product to that of the old product,[8] a is a constant that adjusts for the index on the year, b is

the rate of substitution, and t is the time period. The logarithm of the penetration ratio, which will be written as L_t for convenience, is a linear function of time.

$$L_t = \ln (TT_t/(M - TT_t)) = a + bt \qquad (2\text{-}4)$$

The first step in fitting a substitution curve to historical data is to compute the logarithm of the ratio formed by dividing the percentage of the new product by the percentage of the old product. Then either this ratio can be plotted against time or a regression can be run to determine the slope and the intercept of the line. The regression equation is

$$L_t = \hat{a} + \hat{b}\,t \qquad (2\text{-}5)$$

The slope of the line, $\hat{b}$ is the rate of substitution.

Table 2-5 shows the computations made for the substitution of diesel locomotives for steam

---

[8]$TT_t/(M - TT_t)$ can be stated either in terms of the ratio of the number of adopters to the number of adopters left or in terms of the ratio of the number of users of the new product to the number of those using the old.

TABLE 2-5   SUBSTITUTION DATA FOR DIESEL LOCOMOTIVES, 1931–1959

Year	No. of Diesel	No. of Steam	Total	% Diesel (D)	%Steam (S)	f= %D/%S	ln(f)
1931	80	57,820	57,900	.1	99.9	.001	−6.91
1933	85	53,302	53,387	.2	99.8	.002	−6.22
1935	130	48,477	48,607	.3	99.7	.003	−5.81
1937	293	46,342	46,635	.6	99.4	.006	−5.12
1939	639	43,604	44,243	1.4	98.6	.014	−4.27
1941	1,517	41,911	43,428	3.5	96.5	.036	−3.32
1943	2,476	41,983	44,459	5.6	94.4	.059	−2.83
1945	4,301	41,018	45,319	9.5	90.5	.105	−2.25
1947	6,495	36,942	43,437	15.0	85.0	.176	−1.74
1949	12,025	30,344	42,369	28.4	71.6	.397	−.92
1951	19,014	22,590	41,604	45.7	54.3	.842	−.17
1953	24,209	12,274	36,483	66.4	33.6	1.976	.68
1955	26,563	6,266	32,829	80.9	19.1	4.236	1.44
1957	29,137	2,608	31,745	91.8	8.2	11.195	2.42
1959	30,097	871	30,968	97.2	2.8	34.714	3.55

Source: Interstate Commerce Commission, Statistics of Railroads,1925-1960.

FIGURE 2–13   Logistic substitution ratio graph for diesel locomotives, 1931–1959.

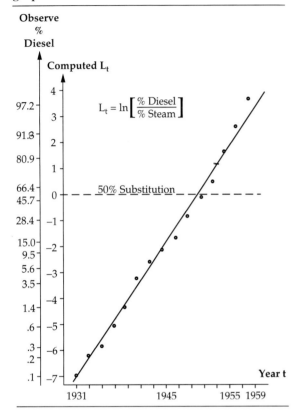

example, a prediction made in 1945 of the percentage substitution in 1955 would be made by reading L_{1955} from the chart and computing

$$\text{Fraction diesel} = e^L /(1 + e^L)$$
$$= 4.015/5.015 = .801$$

This forecast is about one percentage point lower than the observed figure of 80.9 percent.

With either the curve or the regression equation, one is able to estimate the percentage of locomotives that are diesel. This percentage can be converted to the number of diesels that would be in service by multiplying that percentage by M_t. In turn, M_t would have to be estimated by other means, say with the aid of an econometric model. In addition, the number of sales that are used in any year usually exclude established uses where the new product is unlikely to be competitive. Other cases may be excluded on more arbitrary grounds. In the locomotive example, exposition and analysis were simplified by excluding a small number of electric locomotives.

Sales Patterns

The discussion of technological substitution focused on the effect that a relative advantage between a new product and an established product has on the percentage of each product being sold or used. The discussion of forecasting industry sales begins with models of diffusion which generally do not explicitly consider any existing products. In addition to diffusion, which will be made operational through the initial purchases of a product, replacement, repeat, and additional purchases will also be covered.

Models of diffusion   One of the most popular diffusion models is the Bass (1969) model (see Mahajan, Muller, and Bass, 1990, for a recent review of research in this area). It is quite similar to the substitution model. In the Bass model, the probability that a person will try a product for

locomotives. Figure 2-13 displays the log ratio plotted against time for the period since the new product was introduced.

Several things should be noted about the locomotive data. First, the total number of locomotives in service is the basis for computing substitution. For shorter-lived products, sales data could be used. Second, the population in which substitution could take place—total locomotives in service—declined throughout the period from 1931 through 1955. Also note the possible lack of fit for the final two periods.

Once a straight line has been drawn through the points, forecasts can be made for any suitable time period by reading the predicted value for the future year of interest from the straight line fitted to the available observations. For

the first time at time t is

$$P_t = p + (q/M) \times TT_t \qquad (2\text{-}6)$$

where

p = probability of first purchase at $t = 0$, or the coefficient of innovation,

q = coefficient of imitation,

M = total number of potential adopters, and

TT_t = number of adoption purchases *by* the tth period.

The number of adopters *at* time t is calculated by multiplying the probability in Equation (2-6) by $(M - TT_t)$, the number of people that have not adopted the product yet:

$$\begin{aligned} T_t &= \{p + q/M \times TT_t\}\,(M - TT_t) \\ &= pM + (q - p)\,TT_t - (q/M)(TT_t)^2 \end{aligned} \qquad (2\text{-}7)$$

In these equations, p, the coefficient of innovation, measures the proportion of people that will purchase the product for the first time without the influence of previous purchasers. Sometimes this is called the coefficient of "external"

(outside the social system) influence. Similarly, q, the coefficient of imitation, can be called the coefficient of "internal" (inside the social system) influence. If p is equal to zero, this is equivalent to the substitution model of Equation (2-3) with q/M being equal to b.

The maximum number of adopters occurs at t^*:[9]

$$t^* = (1/(p + q))\ln(q/p) \qquad (2\text{-}8)$$

and the sales at the peak of adoption is:

$$T_{t^*} = [M_t(p + q)^2]/4q. \qquad (2\text{-}9)$$

This model has been tested successfully with a large number of new products (e.g., Bass, 1969; Heeler and Hustad, 1980; Nevers, 1972; Tigert and Farivar, 1981). Mansfield (1968) has tested a similar model with data on numerous technological innovations. Table 2-6 shows the results of fitting the Bass model to data on the adoption (first purchases) of color TV.

Bass's fit to earlier TV data and to ten other products was relatively good, but here the model's fit is not as good. In part, this result

---

[9]See Bass, 1969.

TABLE 2-6 FIT OF THE BASS ADOPTION MODEL TO COLOR TV DATA, 1962–1969*

Sales Period	Year	SALES (000) Est. Mfg's	SALES (000) Actual Mfg's
1	1962	473.25	438.00
2	1963	1,031.72	747.00
3	1964	2,128.31	1,404.00
4	1965	3,923.89	2,694.00
5	1966	5,908.43	5,012.00
6	1967	6,607.00	5,563.00
7	1968	5,311.69	5,981.00
8	1969	3,261.74	5,962.00

Source: Adopted from Nevers, 1970.

may be due to the inability to purge repurchases from total sales in later years (see Figure 2-4) and to the fact that color TVs were not as pure an innovation as black-and-white TV had been. Mixed adoption and substitution processes are common. Furthermore, the model presents some data and structural problems. Accurate estimates of M_t made by the model require a substantial number of observations.

In most applied cases, it is advisable to estimate M, the maximum number of adopters, using marketing research or econometric methods, and set $M_t = M$ for all t (Hustad and Heeler, 1980). When external estimates of M are available, the following substitutions are made in Equation (2-7):

$$T_t = a + b\,TT_t + c\,TT_t^2 \qquad (2\text{-}10)$$

and the coefficients a, b, and c can be estimated by regression. Then, estimates of the model's coefficients can be computed from

$$\hat{p} = \hat{a}\,/\,\hat{M} \text{ and } \hat{q} = -\,\hat{c}\,\hat{M} \qquad (2\text{-}11)$$

The coefficients in the equation for T_t should be estimated using at least five observations. If they are not, bias adjustments become important. See Bass (1969). The forecasts of T_t can be made recursively using Equation (2-10). The fit of these forecasts can be assessed by comparison to actual adoptions in period t.

This model forecasts a smooth curve of sales. In many cases, durable goods are strongly affected by economic conditions. Therefore, macroeconomic variables have been added in order to model some of these changes. Also, other studies have found that the diffusion rate is affected by pricing, advertising, and sales promotion decisions made by the sellers. These variables have also been incorporated in a number of instances (Mahajan, Muller, and Bass, 1990).

Whatever approach is used, the model recognizes innovative and imitative behavior in a sensible way and produces a unimodal adoption distribution. More importantly, the model emphasizes the fact that there is a finite pool of potential adopters and that rapidly growing early adoption will peak. The estimates that it provides of the timing and the size of the peak are managerially valuable.

Norton and Bass (1987, 1990) have examined the increasingly common situation where both adoption and substitution processes are operating on a single product type. They studied several generations of substitutions within twelve product categories, including dynamic random access memories, static access memories, pharmaceuticals, consumer recording media, and oil-drill bits. In each case, the generation attracts some but not all of the potential buyers. These potential buyers may be adopters of the old technology who make a substitution decision as well as potential adopters of the old technology who have not yet made an adoption decision. In addition, the new-generation product may enlarge the pool of potential users, creating new potential adopters of the latest product generation. If the time between generations becomes shorter, the adoption or substitution purchase distributions can overlap to a considerable degree. Finally, the relationship between succeeding generations in a product category is fundamentally the same in that good fits are obtained when using the same estimate of p and q for every generation in a product category. The predicted and observed results reported by Norton and Bass for DRAMS appears in Figure 2-14.

The above process is relatively common among both consumer and industrial goods. The movement of audio recording media from seventy-eight rpm to thirty-three and a third rpm to tapes to compact discs and the transition of TV sets from small black and white to larger-screen black and white to early color to high-definition color sets are examples from the consumer field. Increases in the size, range, and reliability of commercial aircraft and the growing accuracy of machine tools that have computer controls pose a similar mix of adoption and substitution pro-

FIGURE 2–14   Overlapping DRAM adoption/substitution curves.

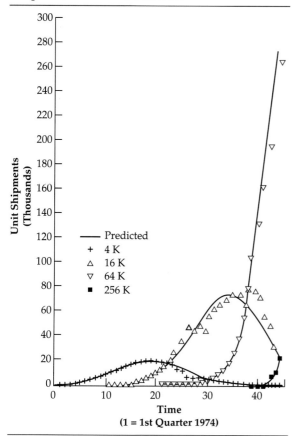

Source: *Adapted from Norton and Bass (1987, p. 1078).*

cesses in the industrial field. Under these circumstances, it is essential that producers keep track of the entire set of competing products. Managers must be sensitive to the life cycle stage that each successive product generation occupies at a point in time and to how each one is likely to behave in the coming months and years.

Later first purchases, replacement purchases, and additional purchases[10]   Researchers at

---

[10]Most of this section is based on Bayus, Hong, and Labe (1989).

RCA have been interested in forecasting more than first purchases early in the product life cycle and have added a number of techniques.

Later first purchases.   Looking at Figure 2-4, first purchases drop off significantly after 1972 and plateau in about 1976. By 1973, the diffusion process is complete as 70 percent of all households have color TVs. After 1972 most first purchases of color TVs were expected to be due to new household formations. They captured these sales with a model that made first purchases a function of lagged housing starts as a percentage of total households, percentage change in real GNP, and time. Parameters were estimated via linear regression, so forecasts of first purchases could be made by inserting forecast values for the independent variables into the following equation:

$$\ln(S_t) = 7.9 + 19.3\,\text{LHS}_t \\ + 2.4\,\text{PGNP}_t - .02\,t \qquad (2\text{-}12)$$

Here, S_t is first purchases in year t, LHS_t is lagged housing starts divided by total households in year t, and PGNP_t is the percentage of change in GNP between $t - 1$ and t.

Replacement purchases.   With an estimate of the average life of a product, one could assume that all products purchased in a certain year would be replaced at the same time. It is more realistic to assume that a certain percentage will be replaced at various periods before the average life is up and a certain percentage will be replaced at various periods after the average life is finished. In this case, the forecast life of a product would really be a probability distribution about an average life. Then, one could forecast replacement purchases by assuming that every product purchased in a particular year would be replaced according to this probability distribution.

Replacement purchases may occur if there are advances in the product even if the old model is not ready to be scrapped. Additionally, replacement purchases may be a function of economic conditions as changes in income might lead some people to replace a durable sooner or later than would otherwise be expected.

Bayus, Hong, and Labe (1989) used all of these factors to model the change in the number of sets being replaced. The first factor was based on the change in the number of old units that had worn out; the second was a dummy variable that indicated whether the time period was before or after 1976, as solid state technology became more prevalent in color TVs after this point; and the final factor was change in disposable income. The following equation was estimated on past quarterly data and was used to predict future changes in the number of sets being replaced.

$$DREPL_t = -165.3 + .9\ DSCRAP_t \\ + 8.7\ DYD_t - 466.5\ D_{1976} \quad (2\text{-}13)$$

where $DREPL_t$ is the change in the number of sets replaced between t and $t-1$, $DSCRAP$ is the change in the number of sets scrapped between t and $t-1$, DYD_t is the change in personal income between t and $t-1$, and D_{1976} is a dummy variable that is zero for times before 1976 and one for time periods after.

Additional sales.   Finally, they looked at additional sales that were not replacement sales. There was less theory to guide the modeling of these sales than there had been with replacement sales. However, econometric studies found that additional sales were correlated with purchasing power and total number of sets that had been in use at least five years. This resulted in the following equation to forecast the change in the number of additional sets purchased:

$$DADD_r = -130.9 + .1\ DSIU5_t \\ + 6.1\ DYD_t \quad (2\text{-}14)$$

where $DADD_t$ is the change in the number of additional units purchased between time t and $t-1$, $DSIU5_t$ is the change in the number of sets in use for at least five years between period t and $t-1$, and DYD_t is the change in disposable income between period t and period $t-1$.

CONCLUDING REMARKS

This chapter has examined the factors that affect the evolution of a product class. Although the PLC model is too simple to handle the complexity of product class evolution, it provides an organizing framework for three underlying factors: market, technological, and competitive evolution.

The section on market evolution emphasized the consumer behavior factors that help determine the shape of the PLC curve and the changes in consumer behavior associated with the evolution of a product class.

The section on technological evolution focused on the cycles of revolutionary and evolutionary innovations. It pointed out the need for a continuous stream of innovations over the entire product life cycle to improve the price-performance characteristics of the product. These innovations need to occur in both the product and its manufacturing process.

The section on competitive evolution focused on the importance of early aggressive action and the need to anticipate changing competitive conditions.

The final sections dealt with the implications of these evolutionary forces and provided some tools to forecast rates of substitution, adoption, and, more generally, product sales.

REFERENCES

Abernathy, William J.: *The Productivity Dilemma: Roadblock to Innovation in the Automobile Industry*, Baltimore: Johns Hopkins University Press, 1978.

_____ and Kim B. Clark: "Innovation: Mapping the Winds of Creative Destruction," *Research Policy*, 14, 1985, 3–22.

_____ and James M. Utterback: "Patterns of Industrial Innovation," *Technology Review*, 80, 1978, 41–47.

Anderson, Carl R., and Carl P. Zeithaml: "Stage of the Product Life Cycle, Business Strategy, and Business Performance," *Academy of Management Journal*, 27 (1), 1984, 5–24.

Arthur, Brian W.: "Positive Feedback in the Economy," *Scientific American*, February 1990, 92–99.

Bass, Frank M.: "A New Product Growth Model for Consumer Durables," *Management Science*, 15, 1969, 215–227.

Bayus, Barry L., Saman Hong, and Russell P. Labe, Jr.: "Developing and Using Forecasting Models of Consumer Durables: The Case of Color Television," *Journal of Product Innovation Management*, 6, 1989, 5–19.

Biggadike, Ralph: "The Risky Business of Diversification," *Harvard Business Review*, 57, May–June 1979, 103–111.

Bright, James R.: *Practical Technology Forecasting Concepts and Exercises*, Austin, Tex.: The Industrial Management Center, 1978.

Buzzell, Robert D.: "Competitive Behavior and Product Life Cycles," in *New Ideas for Successful Marketing*, John Wright and Jac Goldstrucker (eds.), Chicago: American Marketing Association, 1966.

Capon, Noel: "Product Life Cycle," HBS case 9-579-072, Boston: Harvard Business School, 1978.

Chandler, Alfred D.: "The Enduring Logic of Industrial Success," *Harvard Business Review*, 90, March–April 1990, 130–140.

Cooper, Arnold C., and Dan Schendel: "Strategic Responses to Technological Threats," *Business Horizons*, February 1976, 61–69.

Corey, E. Raymond, Frank V. Cespedes, and V. Kasturi Rangan: *Going to Market: Distribution Systems for Industrial Products*, Boston: Harvard Business School, 1989.

Cusamano, Michael A.: "Manufacturing Innovation: Lessons from the Japanese Auto Industry," *Sloan Management Review*, Fall 1988, 29–39.

Day, George S.: *Analysis for Strategic Market Decisions*, St. Paul, Minn.: West Publishing Co., 1986.

DeBruicker, F. Stewart, and Gregory L. Summe: "Make Sure Your Customers Keep Coming Back," *Harvard Business Review*, 63, January–February 1985, 92–98.

Dhalla, Nariman K. and Sonia Yuspeh: "Forget the Product Life Cycle," *Harvard Business Review*, 54 (1), 1976, 102–112.

Dertouzoa, Michael L., Richard K. Lester, and Robert M. Solow: *Made in America*, Cambridge, Mass.: M.I.T. Press, 1989.

Enos, J.: *Petroleum Progress and Profits*, Cambridge, Mass.: M.I.T. Press, 1967.

Fisher, J.C., and R.H. Pry: "A Simple Substitution Model of Technological Change," *Technological Forecasting and Social Change*, 3, 1971, 75–88.

Foster, Richard N.: *Innovation: The Attacker's Advantage*, New York: Summit Books, 1986.

Gatignon, Hubert, and Thomas S. Robertson: "A Propositional Inventory for New Diffusion Research," *Journal of Consumer Research*, 11, March 1985, 849–867.

Gould, Stephen Jay: "The Panda's Thumb of Technology," *Natural History*, 96 (1), 1986.

Hall, William K.: "Survival Strategies in a Hostile Environment," *Harvard Business Review*, 58, September–October 1980, 75–85.

Hambrick, Donald C., Ian C. MacMillan, and Diana L. Day: "Strategic Attributes and Performance in the BCG Matrix — A PIMS-Based Analysis of Industrial Product Businesses," *Academy of Management Journal*, 25 (3), 1982, 510–531.

Hannan, Michael T., and John Freeman: "The Population Ecology of Organizations," *American Journal of Sociology*, 82 (5), 1977, 929–964.

Heeler, Robert M., and Thomas P. Hustad: "Problems in Pretesting New Product Growth for Consumer Durables," *Management Science*, 26, October 1980, 1007–1020.

Hollander, Stanley: *The Sources of Increased Efficiency*, Cambridge, Mass.: M.I.T. Press, 1965.

Howard, John A., and William L. Moore: "Changes in Consumer Behavior Over the Product Life Cycle," in *Readings in the Management of Innovation*, 2d ed., Michael L. Tushman and William L. Moore (eds.), Ballinger Publishing Co., 1988, 343–351.

Knight, Kenneth E.: "A Study of Technological Innovation: The Evolution of Digital Computers," unpublished doctoral dissertation, Pittsburgh: Carnegie Institute of Technology, 1963.

Krafcik, John F.: "Triumph of the Lean Production System," *Sloan Management Review*, Fall 1988, 41–52.

Lambkin, Mary, and George S. Day: "Evolutionary Processes in Competitive Markets: Beyond the Product Life Cycle," *Journal of Marketing*, 53, July 1989, 4–20.

Linestone, Harold A., and Devendra Sahal: *Technological Substitution*, New York: American Elsevier, 1976.

Mahajan, Vijay, Eitan Muller, and Frank M. Bass: "New Product Diffusion Models in Marketing: A Review and Directions for Research," *Journal of Marketing*, 54, January 1990, 1–26.

_____, _____, and Rajendra K. Srivastava: "Determining Adopter Categories by Using Innovation Diffusion Models," *Journal of Marketing Research*, 27, February 1990, 37–50.

Mansfield, Edwin: *Industrial Research and Technological Innovation*, New York: W.W. Norton, 1968.

March, Artemis: "The Future of the U.S. Aircraft Industry," *Technology Review*, January 1990, 27–35.

Martino, Joseph P., Kuei-Lin Chen, and Ralph C. Lenz, Jr.: "Predicting the Diffusion Rate for Industrial Innovation," *NTIS*, PS-286 693, March 1978.

Mehta, Raj T.: *Diffusion of Innovations: A Segmentation Approach*, unpublished Ph.D. dissertation, University of Utah, 1991.

Nevers, John V.: "Extensions of a New Product Growth Model," *Sloan Management Review*, 13, Winter 1972, 78–89.

Norton, John A., and Frank M. Bass: "Diffusion Theory Model of Adoption and Substitution for Successive Generations of High Technology Products," *Management Science*, 33, September 1987, 1069–1101.

_____ and _____: "The Law of Capture: Substantive Findings of an Investigation of a Model of Diffusion and Technological Substitution," working paper Darden School, University of Virginia, 1990.

Olleros, Francisco-Javier: "Emerging Industries and the Burnout of Pioneers," *Journal of Product Innovation Management*, 3 (1), 1986, 5–18.

Pessemier, Edgar A.: *Product Management: Strategy and Organization*, 2d ed., New York: John Wiley, 1982; reprinted by Krieger, Robert E. Krieger Publishing Co., Inc., Malabar, FL, 1988.

Polli, Rolando, and Victor Cook: "Validity of the Product Life Cycle," *Journal of Business*, 42, 1969, 385–400.

Porter, Michael E.: *Competitive Strategy: Techniques for Analyzing Industries and Competitors*, New York: Free Press, 1980.

Redmond, William H.: "Effects of New Product Pricing on the Evolution of Market Structures," *Journal of Product Innovation Management*, 6 (2), 1989, 99–108.

Rink, David R., and John E. Swan: "Product Life Cycle Research: A Literature Review," *Journal of Business Research*, 78, September 1979, 219–242.

Robertson, Thomas S.: *Innovative Behavior and Communication*, New York: Holt, Rinehart and Winston, 1971, 249–294.

_____ and Hubert Gatignon: "Competitive Effects on Technology Diffusion," *Journal of Marketing*, 50, July 1986, 1–12.

Robinson, William T.: "Sources of Market Pioneer Advantages: The Case of Industrial Goods Industries," *Journal of Marketing Research*, 25, February 1988, 87–94.

_____ and Claes Fornell: "The Sources of Market Pioneer Advantages in Consumer Goods Industries," *Journal of Marketing Research*, 22, August 1985, 305–317.

Rogers, Everett M.: *Diffusion of Innovations*, New York: The Free Press, 1962; 3rd ed., 1983.

Romanelli, Elaine: "New Venture Strategies in the Minicomputer Industry," *California Management Review*, Fall 1987, 160–175.

Rosenbloom, Richard S., and Michael A. Cusumano: "Technological Pioneering and Competitive Advantage: The Birth of the VCR Industry," *California Management Review*, 29 (4), 1987,

Stalk, George: "Time—The Next Source of Competitive Advantage," *Harvard Business Review*, 66, July–August 1988, 41–51.

Tellis, Gerard J., and C. Merle Crawford: "An Evolutionary Approach to Product Growth Theory," *Journal of Marketing*, 45, Fall 1981, 125–132.

Tigert, Douglas, and Behrooz Farivar: "The Bass New Product Model: A Sensitivity Analysis for a High Technology Product," *Journal of Marketing*, 45, Fall 1981, 81–90.

Tilton, John B.: *International Diffusion of Technology: The Case of Semiconductors*, Washington, D.C.: Brookings Institution, 1971.

Tushman, Michael L., and Philip Anderson: "Technological Discontinuities and Organization Environments," *Administrative Science Quarterly*, Winter 1986, 439–465.

Twiss, Brian C.: "Forecasting Market Size and Growth Rates for New Products," *Journal of Product Innovation Management*, 1 (1), 1984, 19–29.

Urban, Glen L., Theresa Carter, Steven Gaskin, and Zofia Mucha: "Market Share Rewards to Pioneering Brands: An Empirical Analysis and Strategic Implications," *Management Science*, 32, June 1986, 645-659.

von Hippel, Eric A.: "Users as Innovators," *Technology Review*, January 1978, 31–39.

Wilton, Peter C., and Edgar A. Pessemier: "Forecasting the Ultimate Acceptance of an Innovation: The Effects of Innovation on Perceptions and Preferences of New Objects." *Journal of Consumer Research*, September 1981, 62–171.

Womack, James P., Daniel T. Jones, and Daniel Roos: *The Machine that Changed the World*, New York: Rawson Associates; 1990.

REVIEW QUESTIONS

Q2-1 Briefly describe each of the four main stages of the product life cycle.

Q2-2 Discuss the distinction between product class, product form, and brand as these terms apply to the product life cycle.

Q2-3 What conditions can extend or shorten the product life cycle?

Q2-4 What are the principal criticisms of the product life cycle as an operationally useful construct?

Q2-5 Characterize the market conditions during each of the principal stages of the product life cycle.

Q2-6 What factors lead to rapid diffusion of an innovation? Slow diffusion?

Q2-7 Describe the types of adopters and their market behavior.

Q2-8 What is known about the sources of technological innovation?

Q2-9 What is a dominant design and when is it most likely to appear during a product life cycle?

Q2-10 How do manufacturing methods and unit costs tend to behave during the product life cycle? Why?

Q2-11 What drives incremental product and process innovation? What are its drawbacks?

Q2-12 What features of technological change are illustrated by Figures 2-8 and 2-9?

Q2-13 What is the significance of periodic model changes to R&D, manufacturing, and marketing, respectively?

Q2-14 What does population ecology suggest about the pattern of competition over the product life cycle? What does it assume about the competitive climate? Is the observed pattern of behavior consistent with the theory?

Q2-15 What can be said about the merits and demerits of pioneering a product innovation?

Q2-16 Using Tables 2-1 through 2-4 as general guides, describe the behavior of one of the following firms with respect to the two stated product classes.

FIRM	*PRODUCT CLASS*
P&G	Disposable Diapers Pringles
IBM	Personal Computers Electric Typewriters
Kodak	35mm Color Film Copy Machines
Hewlett–Packard	Pocket Calculators Laser Printers

Q2-17 Discuss the forces driving the patterns of substitution displayed in Figure 2-11.

Q2-18 Choose a product class (other than locomotives), assemble the data, and fit a substitution curve in the manner (regression) shown in Table 2-5 and Figure 2-13.

Q2-19 Discuss the behavioral theories underlying the Bass adoption (first purchase) model.

Q2-20 Choose a product class (other than color TV), assemble the data, and fit an adoption curve in the manner (regression) described in the text. How did you estimate M?

Q2-21 What have you learned from the Norton-Bass results shown in Figure 2-14?

COMPUTER EXERCISES

SUBSTITUTION AND ADOPTION

1. Using the synthetic versus natural fiber data, run a logit regression for the years 1930–1965. Predict the fraction substitution for 1967 and 1990. Comment on your results.

SYNTHETIC VS. NATURAL FIBER SUBSTITUTION DATA*

DATE	FRACTION SYNTHETIC
1930	.04
1935	.08
1940	.10
1945	.14
1950	.22
1955	.28
1960	.29
1965	.43
1970	.47

*Adopted from Earl Stapleton: "The Normal Distribution as a Model of Technological Substitution," Technological Forecasting and Social Change, 8 (3), 1976.

2. Using data on the number of telephones per 1,000 people, fit the Bass adoption model. What coefficient values did your regression yield for p and q? In what year did the number of telephones increase most? What is the num-

ber per 1,000 people expected in 1975? Is your model appropriate for predicting the number in 1990? Comment on your results.

NUMBER OF TELEPHONES PER CAPITA*

DATE	FRACTION OF LIMIT[a]
1880	.002
1885	.003
1890	.005
1895	.007
1900	.025
1905	.070
1910	.118
1915	.149
1920	.177
1925	.208
1930	.233
1935	.196
1940	.237
1945	.284
1950	.403
1955	.484
1960	.585
1965	.686
1966	.716
1967	.744

[a] Limit is 696.9 phones per 1,000 people

*Adopted from Earl Stapleton: "The Normal Distribution as a Model of Technological Substitution," Technological Forecasting and Social Change, 8 (3), 1976.

3

SUCCESSFUL PRODUCT DEVELOPMENT

The first section of this chapter looks at the reasons for success and failure of both individual new products and overall new product programs. In large part, these failures are due to a lack of appropriate new product strategies, skipping or inadequately performing steps in the new product development process or managing this process poorly. The rest of the chapter covers the steps in a new product development process and ways to manage this process. New product strategies are covered in the next chapter.

DIMENSIONS OF NEW PRODUCT SUCCESS AND FAILURE

New Product Success Rate

Estimates of the new product failure rate have varied from a low of about 20 percent to a high of 90 percent. However, over the past twenty years, when a representative sample of people working for relatively large companies involved in new products have been asked, they typically said that about one-third of all new products their company introduced to the market fail to meet company objectives. For example, Booz-Allen (1982) found a new product failure rate of 35 percent across a wide variety of consumer and industrial products companies. In a survey of members of the Association of National Advertisers (primarily large packaged goods companies), Hoo and McDonald (1983) found that the failure rate differed according to the type of new product, with failure rates of 27 percent, 40 percent, and 46 percent for line extensions, new brands in a current category, and new brands in a new category, respectively.

On the other hand, when a third party makes an assessment, the failure rate tends to be higher. For example, Neilsen (1971) has found that only 47 percent of the products that enter test market are on the shelf one year later. RJR (*Advertising Age*, 1976) calculated that the cigarette industry had a failure rate of 61 percent during the early 1970s. Similarly, Hardin (1976) calculated a cereal new product failure rate of about two-thirds during both the 1951 to 1955 and the 1968 to 1972 periods. All of these studies are limited to certain product categories. Still, they suggest that failure rates may be somewhat higher than those found through direct questioning.

Success and Failure of Individual New Products

Researchers have compared pairs of successful and failing new products to determine the factors that were associated with each. For example, Davidson (1976) compared fifty pairs of new grocery products, Rothwell et al. (1974) reported the results of two studies totaling seventy-two pairs of chemical products and scientific instruments, Maidique and Zirger (1984) studied fifty-nine pairs in the electronics industry, Cooper (1981) studied ninety-three failures and 102 successes involving industrial products, and de Brentani (1989; Cooper and de Brentani, 1991) examined 150 successes and 126 failures involving industrial services.

Additionally, several researchers have studied the factors that are related to the failure of individual new products. For example, Cooper (1975) studied 114 industrial new product failures and Poole (1978) studied failures among twenty-four major packaged goods firms. Finally, a much smaller group has looked at the factors that relate to successful and failing new product programs. Despite the differences among the products studied, the conclusions are quite similar.

Superior value in the eyes of the customer
The most important factor seems to be the delivery of a product that the customer perceives to have a significant price-performance advantage over the competition. Furthermore, this is not based on luck, but on a superior understanding

of the customer. Davidson (1976) found that almost three-fourths of the successes were perceived to deliver better performance and 80 percent of the failures were perceived to deliver no better performance than existing products. Additionally, he found that 68 percent of the successes were viewed as "very different" or "dramatically different" from the competition, whereas 70 percent of the failures were viewed as "similar" or "marginally different" from existing products. Similarly, Cooper (1979, p. 100) said, "The single most important dimension leading to new product success is Product Uniqueness and Superiority." Furthermore, he found that market knowledge and marketing proficiency (in the market assessment and analysis stages as well as test marketing and market launch) were the next most important items in new product success.

Maidique and Zirger's (1984, p. 201) first conclusion about success factors was, "The developing organization, through in-depth understanding of the customers and the market place, introduces a product with a high performance-to-cost ratio." Similarly, de Brentani (1989) found that successful services were more likely to satisfy identified consumer needs and provide superior customer value in terms of solving previously unsolved problems and providing a more reliable or faster service.

Also the first difference between successful and failing products mentioned by Rothwell et al. (1974, p. 259) was, "Successful innovators were seen to have a much better understanding of user needs." And Davidson (1976), Cooper (1979), Maidique and Zirger (1984), and de Brentani (1989) found that being a pioneer was related to success of the new product.

An efficient development process   The second factor was an on-time and within-budget development process. Several of the primary findings of Rothwell et al. (1974, p. 259) help explain superior performance.

3) Successful innovators perform their development work more efficiently than failures but not necessarily more quickly.

4) Successful innovators make more use of outside technology and scientific advice, not necessarily in general but in the specific area concerned.

5) The responsible individuals in the successful attempts are usually more senior and have greater authority than their counterparts who fail.

Maidique and Zirger (1984, p. 201) came to similar conclusions:

3) The product provides a high contribution margin to the firm (and therefore has fewer organizational problems).

4) The R&D process is well planned and executed.

5) The create, make, and market functions are well interfaced and coordinated.

6) The markets and technologies of the new product benefit significantly from the existing strengths of the developing business unit.

7) There is a high level of management support for the product from the development stage through its launch to the market place.

Cooper (1979, p. 101) found that, "The third most important new product dimension which impacts on success/failure is a technical one, Technical and Production Synergy and Proficiency." The successful firms carried out the technical and production activities more proficiently than others. Similarly, Rubenstein et al. (1976) found that clarity of performance requirements and objectives, organizational cooperation, and cooperation within the project team and across departments bore a significant relationship to project success.

An efficient development was even more important to industrial services than products. Cooper and de Brentani (1991) found that synergistic financial services were more than four times as successful as those that lacked synergy.

Moreover, they found that projects exhibiting a dedication to marketing and the marketplace were three times as successful as those that lacked a marketing orientation. Companies with poor internal communication and without support from all functional areas had worse new-service records.

The relative importance of the service development process arises from two factors. First, the apparent ease of developing and modifying services has led many companies to pursue new-service development in a haphazard manner. Second, the importance of involving the front-line people, those who deliver the service, is often overlooked in the new-service process.

A well-directed and well-funded market launch Successful products are targeted to customers better, the message is more appropriate, and enough money is spent supporting the product. Rothwell et al. (1974, p. 259) found that "Successful innovators pay more attention to marketing and publicity." Maidique and Zirger (1984, p. 201) found, "The developing organization is proficient in marketing and commits a significant amount of its resources to selling and promoting the product." Similarly, Cooper and de Brentani (1991) found that financial services associated with a high-quality launch were over three times as successful as those without one. Finally, two studies involving the PIMS data base found that more aggressive introductory strategies were more successful (Biggadike, 1979; Swire, 1984).

Factors associated with failure In studying the failures of twenty-four large packaged goods companies, Poole (1978) found that 30 percent of the failures were based on a new product concept that met no unfilled need. They did not offer the consumer anything that was not being offered by the competition. Another 40 percent failed because the product did not live up to the concept. Finally, he found that the advertising had to stress the concept clearly, believably, and with authority.

Cooper (1975) studied 114 industrial new product failures. First he looked at the general reasons for failure (see Table 3-1) and found that the primary reason for new product failure was that anticipated sales never materialized. Then,

he looked at specific causes for each of the general reasons. See Table 3-1 for the specific causes of low sales. In most cases, the specific cause of low sales seemed to indicate the product was inferior: For example, customers would rather buy competitive products, not as many people bought it as expected, it was not worth the price

TABLE 3-1   REASONS FOR INDUSTRIAL NEW PRODUCT FAILURE

General Reasons for New Product Failure

GENERAL REASON	RATING*
Sales fell below expectations	70.7
Profit margins fell below expectations	33.0
Development costs exceeded expectations	29.9
Investment exceeded expectations	8.8

Latent Reasons for Low Sales

LATENT REASON	RATING
Entrenched competitors	43.2
Overestimated number of users	35.9
Price was too high	34.7
Technical/manufacturing problems	33.0
Misdirected selling/promotional efforts	27.9
A "me too" product	27.3
Did not meet customer needs	26.7
Inadequate sales/distribution efforts	25.0

Deficient Activities During New Product Process

ACTIVITY	RATING[†]
Preliminary assessment of market	74.0
Test marketing	58.1
Product launch	53.9
Detailed financial analysis	51.5
Prototype testing with customer	48.9
Preliminary market assessment	47.7
Prototype testing —in-house	38.3
Initial screening	36.7
Product development (R&D)	36.3
Pilot plant production	33.7
Production start-up	30.6
Preliminary technical assessment	30.2

* Rating is based on a weighted average of the percentage of the time this was the main factor (w = 1.0) and the percentage of the time it was a contributing factor (w = .5).

[†]This is a sum of the percentage of time this activity was judged to be either deficient or missing.

charged, or it was a "me too" product. A secondary reason appears to be misdirected or insufficient marketing efforts. A final major reason related to technical problems with the product. All of these findings corroborate the earlier findings regarding success and failure of new products.

Finally, Cooper looked at the latent reasons for these problems, the activities in the new product process that were either skipped or carried out inadequately. See Table 3-1. This table suggests that a number of marketing activities (e.g., market analysis, product testing, and test marketing) were deficient. Lesser problems occur in evaluating the product before launch (that is, in screening and financial analysis) and in the technical-production area (for example, product development, testing, and production start-up).

Success and Failure of New Product Programs

Not as many studies have looked at what makes for a successful new product program. Booz-Allen (1982) compared companies that had a batting average of more than 90 percent (more than 90 percent of the new products they introduced achieved company objectives) to those that had less than a 50 percent batting average. There were many similarities between these two groups—both spent about the same amount of money on new products, introduced about the same mix of new products, used a formal new product process, and spent about the same amount of time and money on each of the new product steps.

The more successful companies tended to have a greater commitment to growth through new products; they were more likely to have a strategic plan that mandated a certain percentage of growth from new products, they typically had their new product development process in place for a longer period of time, and they pre-screened new product ideas more thoroughly.

They also reported fewer obstacles—such as management's short-term focus and lack of a strategic plan—to new product development. Marketing and R&D were likely to have a greater influence on the new product process. New product executives had a longer job tenure and were more likely to tailor the process to the specific type of new product.

Cooper (1984a, b) analyzed the new product strategies of 122 industrial marketers. Each company rated its strategy on sixty-six variables that were classified into four groups: nature of the new products developed (e.g., level of innovativeness and fit with current product line), nature of the markets sought (e.g., size, growth, and fit with firm), nature of the technology employed (e.g., concentrated or diversified, degree of maturity, and fit with technology base), and orientation and nature of the new product process (e.g., offensive or defensive, proactive or reactive, and level of spending). The companies also rated the success of their new product program on ten dimensions, including percentage of sales made by new products, success rate, extent to which they met objectives, success of the program relative to competition, and an overall success rating.

In the first analysis of these data (1984a), Cooper factor-analyzed the ten dimensions of new product success and found there were three independent factors of new product success: *high success rate* (high batting average), *high impact* (high percentage of sales from new products and new products making an important contribution to sales and profits were two of the variables that rated high on this factor), and *high relative performance* (important contributor to sales and profits, high profitability, met objectives, high rating versus competitors, and high overall success rating measured high on this factor). Independence among these three factors means that doing well on one of these is unrelated to success on the other two. In particular, a high success rate on individual products is unrelated to doing well on the other two measures of success.

Firms with a high success rate employed a conservative strategy and stayed close to the markets and technology they were currently employing. The firms with a high-impact strategy were technologically oriented, spending large amounts on technically focused areas trying to provide products with a differential advantage. However, there was an absence of marketing synergy, in that they were more likely to enter markets that did not fit their marketing resources. The high relative performance strategy was also technologically aggressive, but it was better balanced with marketing than the high-impact strategy. It was a marketing-dominated strategy in which the marketing department was proactive in looking for new product opportunities. Furthermore, marketing as well as technological synergies were captured.

In the second analysis (1984b) Cooper clustered the firms into "gestalts" based on the elements of their strategies. He found the following clusters: technology driven (26.2 percent of the firms), balanced strategy (15.6 percent), defensive, focused, technologically deficient (15.6 percent), low-budget conservative (23.8 percent), and high-budget diverse (18.9 percent).

The balanced-strategy firms performed the best (by far) on nine of the ten success measures. These firms were strongly R&D oriented, employing state-of-the-art development and production technologies to produce highly innovative products with unique features. These firms and their new product process were market oriented; the process was dominated by the marketing group and new product ideas were market derived. They were also focused; they developed products that fit with the technological, production, marketing, and customer strengths of the company.

Summary

The determinants of individual new product success are quite similar for package goods, high-tech products, chemicals, and industrial services. By far the most important factor of success is a superior value in the eyes of the customer. Superior offers are based on a new product idea that meets the needs of the market and a product that lives up to the concept. These facts emphasize the importance of initial marketing research to identify unfilled needs or latent problems and the importance of developing a product that meets those needs.

The second major factor is an efficient development process, one that is on time and within budget. An efficient development process requires that new products fit with the company's marketing and technical capabilities, that the company has appropriate problem-solving and conflict-resolution skills, and that projects are appropriately organized.

Finally, there needs to be a well-directed and appropriately funded introduction. The proper target market and message need to be chosen and the company must invest in a sufficiently aggressive new product introduction.

Cooper's study of failures indicates the reason for most failures is that several marketing activities (e.g., detailed marketing study, product testing, and test marketing) are inadequately carried out. In a more recent study by Cooper and Kleinschmidt (1986), individual new product success was strongly related to the completeness of the new product development process and how well each of the steps was executed. Even though many managers said they had a systematic process in place, when individual new product projects were analyzed, many of these activities were either poorly performed or skipped. Deficiencies in preliminary market studies, initial screening, and detailed market analysis were cited most frequently.

Related to Cooper and Kleinschmidt's (1986) results are those of Hoo and McDonald (1983). They asked their respondents which activities needed more effort in order to improve the new product success rate. The most important activities were market analysis and opportunity identification (57 percent), strategy formulation (44 percent), concept and positioning development

(36 percent), basic R&D (36 percent), idea generation (32 percent), product development and testing (32 percent), pretest market sales estimation (26 percent), and concept tests (22 percent). In both of these studies, the most important omitted activities tend to be the ones at the start of the new product development process. Still, the general problem is that several steps are either missed or inadequately performed. Similarly, Calantone and di Bennedetto (1986) used a multiple-equation model to highlight the importance of all activities.

When the success of overall new product programs is studied, a sound strategy and consistent execution seem to be the most important factors. The strategy should guide development efforts into profitable areas for the company. Consistent execution does not imply the need to slavishly follow a detailed procedure manual, but it does mean that key steps cannot be skipped.

The next two sections deal with two of the three factors that have an impact on new product success: the new product development process and management of that process. The third factor, new product strategy, is covered in detail in the next chapter.

NEW PRODUCT DEVELOPMENT PROCESS

In their study of companies with successful new product records, Booz-Allen (1982) found that they were more likely to have a formal new product process in place for an extended period of time. The new product process should act as a road map, providing direction to new product efforts. It reminds people to go through the relevant steps in the proper order. The new product development process should specify a small number of clear approval points at which go/no-go decisions are made in a relatively rational and nonpolitical manner.

It should be possible to modify the product development process on the basis of the product's degree of newness to the company. However, the specific steps in the process should be agreed to at the start and not changed halfway through the process if the project falls behind schedule. Finally, the new product development process should help ensure adequate consumer testing.

The specific steps in the new product process can vary by company. Most new product processes have between four and twelve steps. The new product process shown in Figure 3-1 is similar to that proposed by Booz-Allen (1982).

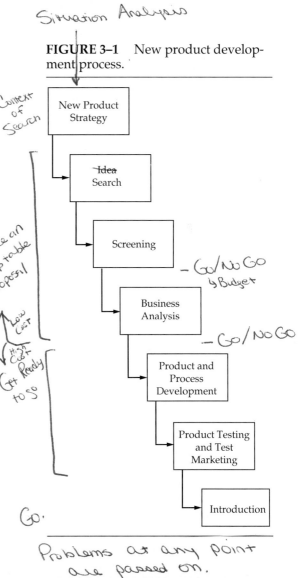

Situation Analysis

FIGURE 3–1 New product development process.

Content of Search

Produce an Acceptable Proposal

Low Cost / High Cost / Get Ready to Go

— Go/No Go by Budget

— Go/No Go

Go.

Problems at any point are passed on.

The first step—new product strategy—is not associated with a specific new product. However, it is included to emphasize the importance of a strategy for the new product effort. The next three steps—idea search, screening, and business analysis—are collectively referred to as the planning, problem-solving activities or concept investigation phase. The goal of this phase is to develop and agree upon a concept that the market wants and the company can produce. The product's performance, cost, and features are determined in this phase. It ends when development and preliminary marketing plans have been approved. Taking time to settle all disputes at this stage usually results in overall time savings.

This is a time of greatest uncertainty. The best approach is seldom known in advance—the problem may not even be well defined. As a result, this phase may be more loosely organized and structured than later phases. Furthermore, it is less subject to elaborate planning systems.

The next two stages—product and process development and product testing and test marketing—make up the development and testing phase. There should be less uncertainty in this phase and it can be managed in a more structured manner.

The final phase is introduction or launch.

New Product Strategy

A new product strategy is needed to focus the product development effort and tie it to business unit or corporate strategy. Its importance has been documented by both Cooper (1984a, b) and Booz-Allen (1982).

In spite of the importance of new products, top management has neither the time nor, in many cases, the expertise to search for new product ideas. Furthermore, new product ideas need to come from everyone in the company, not just top management. Still, management needs to be able to influence this process.

Typically, management attention is directed to those points in the new product development process at which most of the money is being spent, rather than where its input could have the greatest leverage. Figure 3-2 shows a graph of the way it is generally believed that top management spends its time on new products, contrasted with the time when it has the most leverage. In general, management has the greatest leverage early in the new product process, but spends most of its time at the end of the process when the expenses start to pile up.

A new product strategy provides a way for management to influence this process. First, the new product strategy should contain *new product objectives* which are needed to determine the size of the task, specify the amount of required resources, and define the way success will be judged. Second, it needs to provide guidance on *where to look* for new product ideas (i.e., specify the relationship between desired new products and the company or business unit's current product line). Finally, it should delineate the financial and nonfinancial *criteria used to judge* new product ideas.

Planning

Idea search   People need to look for new product ideas. While many ideas are not directly derived from a new product strategy, the strategy should be known to those people who are searching for ideas or are likely to encounter new product opportunities. That way, they know if the idea is in an area that management is considering. If they choose to pursue an idea outside this area, they know what they are up against. Furthermore, people who submit new product ideas should know the criteria that are used to judge them.

There are two different ways for the search process to occur. In one approach, a product category search is undertaken first. After an attractive category has been identified, the search

FIGURE 3–2 Activity profile of the chief executive during the new product development process.

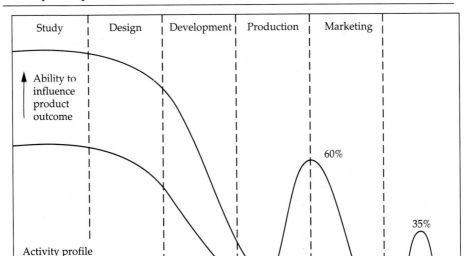

The expertise of a chief executive can most influence any new technology-based product development program in the program's early stages—during preliminary study, design, and development. But current research suggests to the author that chief executive officers actually devote only trivial amounts of their time and attention to these early stages of such new-product programs. Instead they typically have significant involvement only during production and marketing—when "it's too late to do anything that can influence the outcome." says Professor Roberts. (This illustrative figure comes from related work by Foster and Gluck of McKinsey and Co.)

Source: *Roberts (1977, p. 23). (Roberts credits Foster and Gluck of McKinsey for the original drawing.)*

shifts to a product within that category. This is the more typical procedure, because search tends to be problem or opportunity driven and the category is implicitly specified in many of those cases. Also, many new product ideas are line extensions introduced into areas of current business. In the other approach, new products are searched for directly. For example, applications of a new technology are usually not restricted to certain product categories.

New product search can also be characterized in terms of the extent to which the primary uncertainties are market oriented (i.e., whether the consumer wants this product) or are technically oriented (i.e., if this product can be made). In the former case, the search is more marketing driven and in the latter it is more technology driven.

There are numerous ways to search for new product ideas. These include both formal and informal marketing research, sales force contact with customers, direct customer feedback (e.g., complaints), brainstorming, analysis of competitive products, technological forecasting, and R&D work.

If a company wants new product ideas, it must emphasize the importance of new products, appropriately fund idea search, and reward good tries. Marketing research must be done, R&D must receive thoughtful direction and adequate funds, salespeople must be rewarded for their ideas, and engineers need to be put in the field to observe customer needs. These and related activities cost time and money. Furthermore, management must provide continuing interest and support.

Screening   Once a number of ideas have been generated, the bad ones need to be thrown out and the good ones need to be improved and pushed forward. This process can be likened to a series of ever-finer filters. The first filter should screen out ideas with serious flaws and ones that obviously do not fit with the company. Over time, the filters get finer and pass on only the best ideas. However, the goal of a new product program should not be a 100 percent success rate, as that typically requires the firm to be too conservative and causes it to reject a substantial number of products that would have been successful.

Before any formal screening takes place, the idea generator should informally review the idea with relevant people, including members of the screening committee. Not only will this review improve the idea, generate support, and anticipate problems, but it may also point out flaws that were overlooked.

Formal screening is a quick analysis to determine which ideas should be dropped because of fatal flaws and which have some merit and deserve more detailed study. This may involve a demonstration of technical and/or marketing feasibility. Therefore, screening may be preceded by some preliminary technical work or concept tests.

While screening is carried out informally by many companies (Cooper and Kleinschmidt, 1986), this activity should be based on a checklist in which the product is rated on a number of important criteria. The use of a standardized rating form helps ensure that nothing is overlooked. It also provides some uniformity of evaluation and indicates what criteria are considered to be important. This way the person presenting a new product idea for evaluation knows how it will be judged.

After a short amount of analysis and informal discussion, a screening proposal should be prepared. This is a short (one- to ten-page) description of the new product idea. At a minimum, it should discuss the four factors discussed in the next two paragraphs.

The criteria should be chosen by the company to reflect the factors that are considered to be more important. However, the criteria should include items from four areas: product factors, market factors, company factors, and financial factors. At this stage, the first three are more important. New product concepts should be screened on *product factors* such as: Does it fill an unfilled need or solve an important unsolved problem? Is it a new or unique idea, and is it a potentially superior product in the eyes of the customer? Also, concepts are screened on whether the product costs less or offers better value. Many industrial companies such as Boeing and Allen-Bradley will not let a product idea pass this stage unless a customer has agreed to participate in tests or joint development work.

Included in *market factors* are such factors as the size and growth of the market (both overall and by segments), strength of competition (including intensity of price competition, number of competitors, and number of recently introduced products), and current and predicted future profitability of the industry. The *company factors* include items like fit with current customers, distribution, manufacturing, and technical skills, ability to achieve a proprietary position (either through patents or through features that are hard to copy), and ability to service.

Finally, new products should be judged on a series of *financial factors*, including sales volume, margins, required investment, and discounted cash flow. These financial projections should be viewed with appropriate skepticism because of the lack of knowledge at this stage. Still, they can alert management to potential problems, such as the size of the investment.

Sometimes this checklist is converted into a scoring model in which the new product's rating on each criterion is multiplied by an importance weight associated with that criterion and summed to generate an overall score for the new product concept. In evaluating overall scores, one must remember that a product does not have to be shot, stabbed, and poisoned to be killed. One fatal weakness is enough. An example of a partial screening checklist is given in Figure 3-3.

Once it has been prepared and submitted, the proposal is sent to a screening committee. Such committees should have representatives from the principal areas involved in new product development; R&D, marketing, manufacturing, finance, and possibly legal. Their task is to carefully examine the proposal for flaws that could be fatal, suggest improvements, and decide on appropriate actions to be taken.

Many proposals can be rejected without the collection of additional information. When these rejections are well founded, time and effort is conserved. Other proposals present potentially interesting opportunities and deserve a commitment of the firm's resources. The commitment may be no more than funding a small concept test. In other instances, it may entail a costly examination of the technical feasibility of designing and manufacturing the product. Once the product passes this hurdle, a budget is approved and the product takes on a life of its own.

The screening process should be open so that the sponsor of a rejected project knows the reasons for rejection. In spite of the apparent formal nature of this process, the sponsor should generally learn the likely outcome through informal discussions prior to the official decision. In addition, the sponsor should be given an opportunity to appeal the screening committee's action by submitting additional information. If this is not done, the proceeding may be viewed as unfair and seriously ego threatening. In such an environment, too few people will risk the time, effort, and personal exposure required to bring forward a product proposal. If the new product screening committee does not encourage an adequate flow of high-quality ideas, it cannot sus-

FIGURE 3–3 Product factors segment of a new product screening checklist.

Product Factors	Not Appli-. cable	Do Not Know	Relation to Proposal: Very Impor-tant … Not Impor-tant	Effect on Proposal: Very Favor-able … Very Unfavor-able
1. Fills an unmet need	☐	☐		
2. Solves an unsolved problem	☐	☐		
3. Offers unique benefits	☐	☐		
4. Higher performance	☐	☐		
5. Lower price	☐	☐		
6. Better value	☐	☐		
7. New idea	☐	☐		
8. Potentially a superior product	☐	☐		

tain the competitive health of the firm's product line. This fact leads many firms to provide very positive encouragement to successful sponsors in the form of recognition and financial awards.

Business analysis   The next step is business analysis. Here the idea is expanded into a business proposition which should result in a preliminary new product marketing plan. Between the screening and business analysis checkpoints, a detailed market analysis and a concept test should be performed. The market analysis needs to cover the issues discussed in the situation analysis portion of Chapter 1. This includes an industry analysis to determine its attractiveness, a customer analysis to judge the size and growth of segments in the industry as well as satisfaction and problems with current products, a competitor analysis that anticipates reactions to a new product introduction, and an internal analysis that appraises the company's ability to compete in this market. Concept tests should examine buyer acceptance. Also, some preliminary development work, called "concept investigation" by Hayes, Wheelwright, and Clark (1988), should be conducted to investigate the design and manufacturing options.

Booz-Allen (1982) found that most companies felt business analysis was the most important step in the new product development process. This finding is consistent with Cooper's (1975) finding that the omission of a detailed market analysis is associated with new product failure.

The proposal resulting from the business analysis should contain five sections.

1. The first is a product specification. It is a detailed description of the product so that everyone agrees to what is being proposed. This includes its strategic role or objective, i.e., whether it is to be a line extension, a replacement, or a totally new product. The description should also contain a protocol (Crawford, 1984), which is an agreement between marketing and R&D about what will be produced. Marketing specifies benefits to be delivered or performance, but not design, specifications; R&D agrees to meet marketing's requests, but is not bound to deliver a particular design.

2. The proposal should contain the results of the studies conducted since screening: detailed market, competitor, and internal analyses; technical feasibility studies; concept or product tests; and product or process development efforts.

3. Engineering, design, and manufacturing should submit a development plan that includes the steps of product design, process design, product testing, pilot plant operation, and volume ramp up.

4. A preliminary marketing plan that includes customer and competitor targets, basic positioning, distribution plan, and spending levels should be developed.

5. A financial analysis of the proposal, including sales volume, margins, costs, and discounted cash flows, should be made.

Summary   The first three steps in this process—idea generation, screening, and business analysis—are relatively inexpensive, but the costs can climb quite rapidly during the next two steps of development and market introduction. Therefore, one wants to kill as many bad ideas at this point as possible. Booz-Allen (1982) found that companies are placing more emphasis on these first three "up front" or strategic phases. As a result, the percentage of funds that are spent on marketplace failures has dropped from 70 to 46 between 1968 and the 1980s. Hoo and McDonald (1983) also found that progress could be made in reducing the new product failure rate by additional emphasis on these strategic areas.

Although the success or failure of a new product is not known with certainty before development, the company should have an answer to the following four questions.

Is the consumer interested in the idea behind the product or service?

Is there a good chance that this company can build a product that will live up to the concept?

Does the venture represent a reasonable fit with the company's strengths?

Can the company afford to introduce it?

Additionally, there should be agreement on product specifications and performance relative to competition. This allows all groups to move ahead quickly.

Product Development and Testing

Development   Product development consists of several steps that start before the development phase begins. First, marketing and technological information are combined to develop a product concept; that is, a description of the product from the consumer's perspective. Successful concepts describe not only what the product is and does, but also to whom it is targeted and what it means for those customers.

Next, the product concept needs to be translated into a preliminary product design. This may require technical feasibility studies such as the construction of bench or breadboard models. These models are able to test the functions of the final product, but may not look anything like it. In some cases, these models are computer generated. This step may also entail the construction of mockups. These full- or limited-scale models of the product can be used to test aerodynamic properties (in the case of vehicles), test buyer reaction, or simply provide a visual

representation. The preliminary product design might include rough engineering drawings, size, general performance characteristics, component choices, and technologies to be incorporated.

After business analysis, a more detailed product design is created. This is usually a series of design-build-test cycles. First, drawings of the product are made and specifications are written both for the product and for its various components and subassemblies. After the drawings are released, they are converted into prototypes which look like finished products, but are not constructed with volume production tooling. Prototype testing usually results in revised engineering drawings.

Product designs are also converted into information about the manufacturing process through another series of design-build-test cycles. The first step may include the design of the overall plant, tooling, equipment, software, and worker skills and standard operating procedures. After equipment and tooling have been acquired or constructed, they are tested through the construction of a new generation of prototypes. These prototype tests may lead to new engineering drawings or to changes in the manufacturing process or tooling. Finally, pilot plant operations are initiated.

Product testing   Product testing can be conducted at several stages in the development process. Early in the process, mockups, clay models, or drawings can be used to gauge early buyer reaction. If the cost of prototypes is high, mockups may be used as sales tools. For example, Boeing has shown mockups of alternative passenger cabin configurations to airline executives to get feedback and book orders.

If the product is changed as it goes through the various prototype stages and pilot plant production, product tests should be repeated. In many cases, the process of development and testing needs to be iterative with the results of product tests used to improve the product at the next prototype stage.

Industrial companies perform "alpha" and "beta" tests. Alpha tests are conducted within the company developing the product. One purpose of alpha tests is to make sure the product works as designed. Many companies can use the product they make in their everyday operations. Such test sites can be useful if the risk of failure and favorable biases can be controlled. For example, Apple uses its computers not only in its offices, but also in its factories to control production processes.

Beta tests are performed by people working for other companies. The tests may be performed at the customer site. For example, Xerox tested over 1,200 prototypes of its Star workstation in a wide variety of environments, including the Carter White House. While this product was not a success, many of the features developed as a result of these product tests were incorporated into Apple's Lisa and Macintosh computers. At other times, companies ask their customers to bring sample applications into the facilities of the company developing the product where tests can be completed.

In consumer product tests a consumer may be given a single product or a pair of products and is instructed to use it (or rotate the use of the two products in a certain way). At the end of the usage period, the subject is asked to evaluate the product(s). Packaged goods companies also use laboratory test markets and sales waves experiments. Laboratory test markets expose consumers to advertisements for relevant brands in the category and allow them to make a purchase in a simulated store. This allows a company to test the power of the advertisement to stimulate trial of the new product. Sales waves experiments are used to simulate marketplace behavior over time. In this case, the consumer is periodically visited by someone from a research company and is allowed to choose one or more brands from a product category, with the new brand being one of the choices.

This is also a time to do name, packaging, and advertising tests. Finally, the preliminary marketing plan developed for the business analysis stage needs to be finalized. This would include the production of advertisements, sales brochures, and introductory promotions.

Test marketing and regional rollouts   Production for a test market or regional rollout may be done in a pilot plant or a full-sized plant. In either case, the plant must be constructed prior to the start of this phase.

There are three primary purposes of test markets. First is to provide the most realistic estimate of sales volume as well as marketing and operations costs. Second is to test the entire marketing mix. Third is to practice making, distributing, and selling the product.

Test markets are used primarily by companies producing frequently purchased products for the consumer market. However, many industrial marketers use pilot plants to produce sufficient quantities to conduct large-scale product tests for these same purposes.

In order to reach these objectives, the company needs a marketing plan that it intends to use during national rollout so the practice run and market forecasts are based on realistic conditions. (However, the results of the test market may persuade the company to change the original plan.) About 70 percent of the products that enter a test market are rolled out nationally, so this step tends to be less of a decision-making step than a practice run and an opportunity to fine-tune marketing plans. In addition to being the only place to test the entire marketing mix, this is also the only place to test such factors as trade resistance.

Production Ramp Up and Introduction

During this phase, the introductory marketing plan is finalized. Sales force and service people are trained. Advertisements and promotions are placed. Production volumes are increased. The product is introduced.

Summary

Regardless of the number of steps, Figure 3-1 and its accompanying description have made the process look very linear and orderly. In reality, it is usually quite messy. Furthermore, it may look as if one functional area works during part of the process and then hands its contribution off to the next group. However, an interfunctional group should be assigned to this project from start to finish. Preliminary marketing studies should be going on at the same time that preliminary technical work is being carried out. In

many respects, the Booz-Allen chart shown in Figure 3-4 is more consistent with this view in that there is continuous consumer testing and the manufacturing concept is being developed at the same time that the product is being developed.

MANAGING THE NEW PRODUCT PROCESS

When developing new products, companies need to focus on creating value (in the eyes of the customer), development cycle time, and development cost. Furthermore, it is more important to be on time than within budget in

FIGURE 3–4 New product development process.

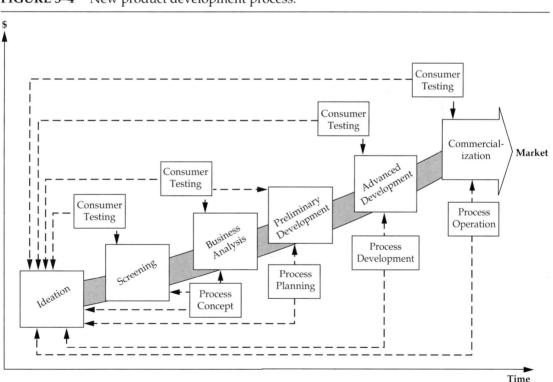

Source: *Sommers (1979, pp. 14–15).*

most instances. The consultants at McKinsey & Co. developed an economic model for fast-moving industries that shows if a new product is within budget but six months late, its profits over a five-year period will be down by 33 percent. On the other hand, if it is introduced on time but is 50 percent over budget, profits over five years may be off by only 4 percent (Dumaine, 1989a).

The purpose of this section is to discuss several issues that relate to managing the development process more effectively.

Accelerating the New Product Process

Many advantages are gained by decreasing new product development cycle time, hereafter called cycle time. Being first to market may allow a product to command a premium price. Additionally, higher volume from being first can lead to lower costs through experience curve effects and economies of scale. Products that are designed closer to the time they are introduced are less subject to technological and market changes. The time between concept generation and the financial break-even point is reduced. Many costs are correlated with the length of the development process, so shortening the process tends to lessen these costs. Finally, it is possible to introduce more generations of a product in a given amount of time. This results in having newer products on the market. It is especially important early in the product life cycle when market and technological uncertainty may necessitate more than one attempt to develop the best product.

There are several ways to reduce cycle time. Many of them are related, so changing one may have a positive impact on some of the other factors.

Stess the importance of speed   First, management must believe in and *communicate the importance of innovation and new products*. Most successful innovators are convinced of the need to innovate. They realize that standing still is the surest road to failure. Leslie Vadasz, then senior vice-president for planning at Intel, said, "Two things drive this business, technology and paranoia" (Sherman, 1984, p. 68). The people at Intel realize that competitive offerings can make their products obsolete overnight. Still, 42 percent of the respondents to a survey by Gupta and Wilemon (1990) indicated that lack of management support and lack of resources were major reasons for new product delays.

One of the ways that HP stresses the importance of new products is by including a graph of orders by year of introduction in its annual report every year (see Figure 1-3). Stories of successful innovators abound at 3M. Management must back up its talk by assigning experienced people to new products, providing an appropriate level of support, and not overly punishing good tries that fail. Pepsi-Cola president Craig Weatherup launched Diet Pepsi in Japan (where "diet" has a medicinal connotation) against the advice of his boss. When its failure cost $3 million, his boss told him to be more careful next time, but not to stop taking risks (Dumaine, 1989c).

Second, management must *make speed a priority*. Most project managers know exactly what it would cost to add one more engineer to the project, but few know what a delay of six months will cost. When the importance of speed has not been explicitly stated, managers may make trade-offs in ways that save money rather than time. For example, they may pursue policies that try to achieve maximum utilization of either people or equipment rather than maximizing speed of development.

Traditionally, Xerox used a centralized model shop to create prototypes for new products; however, it was split apart in the mid–1980s and people were assigned directly to specific new product development projects. While the cost per prototype probably increased due to lower utilization rates, it now takes one week to build a model versus eight to ten weeks in the early 1980s (Uttal, 1987).

Hewlett-Packard has indicated the importance of speed with its BET (break-even time) program in which CEO John Young challenged employees to cut the time between conception and profitability by half (Dumaine, 1989a). Similarly, Canon has benefited from its "50 percent down" program, which has a goal of halving both new product development time and cost. These very challenging goals require people to rethink the whole development process; these are goals that cannot be attained simply by working harder.

There should only be a small number of clear goals and checkpoints; however, they should be strictly adhered to. For example, when broadcast-quality videotape recorders were selling for $50,000, the co-founder of Sony, Masaru Ibuka, set a target price of $5,000, but did not suggest how to achieve it. When that goal was reached he reduced it to $500 (Rosenbloom and Cusumano, 1987).

Once there is agreement on product specs, time to market should be one of the goals. Silicon Graphics, maker of workstations, uses a rigorously scheduled process to develop and launch most of its breakthrough products in eighteen months. Tom Jermoluck, head of product development for Silicon Graphics, says, "Forget the incremental stuff. Go 95 percent of the way and launch it. If you wait until you get 100 percent of what you want you'll surely get beat to the market by the competition" (Dumaine, 1991). This process allowed the company to develop a replacement for a $75,000 computer that was just as fast and was under $10,000—in eighteen months.

Product specification should be frozen as early in the process as possible. Conflicts over specs should be surfaced early and resolved. Gupta and Wilemon (1990) found that the most frequently cited reason for new product delays (71 percent of respondents) was poor definition of product requirements. Lack of knowledge about customer desires, technology, suppliers, and competition led to frequent changes in the product. Closely related, were delays caused by

the evaluation of technologies which became available during development or by creeping elegance; that is, continual attempts to refine the product (cited by 58 percent of the respondents).

Not only do product modifications cause delays, but the later in the process a change is made the more costly it is. Dataquest estimated that if a change was made in a major electronics product during the design phase it would cost $1,000; during process planning the same change would cost $100,000; and during final production, $10 million (Port, Schiller, and King, 1990). Therefore, enough time needs to be spent in the planning stage to resolve all conflicts.

The development process can also be accelerated by *reducing the number of formal approvals.* Approvals slow the process for two reasons. First, managers who need to give their approvals are typically busy and are not able to study all projects quickly. Second, project personnel can spend a significant amount of their time preparing for presentations. One can imagine the delays that were absorbed by the company that had the set of formal linkages shown in Figure 3-5.

Contrast that diagram with the experience of AT&T. When the 4200 cordless phone was developed in 1988, the multifunctional development team had the authority to make every decision on design, manufacturing, and price. It was able to develop a lower-cost, higher-quality product in less than half the typical time (Dumaine, 1989a). At GE, researchers built a $1 million pilot plant without management approval when developing Ultem, a durable heat-resistant plastic with sales of more than $100 million (Labich, 1988).

Cycle time can also be reduced through *better planning.* First, strategic planning usually leads to greater new product focus and fewer resources being spent on products that ultimately fail. Second, adequate market, technology, and competitor analysis is needed early in the process to decide on product specifications, which leads to faster development. Finally, if subsequent generations are considered in the

FIGURE 3–5   New product sign-off.

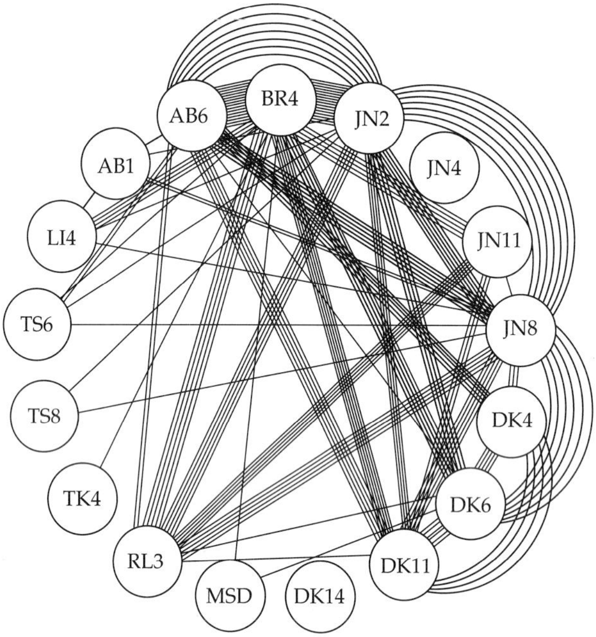

Source: *Peters and Waterman (1982, p. 18).*

initial plans development people are able to freeze the design and leave improvements for the next generation. Technological progress is usually faster when taken in small steps rather than in one giant leap. Small steps also increase reliability and decrease overall cost.

Balance problem-solving workload and problem-solving capacity   Product development can be characterized as a number of problem-solving cycles. For example, developing an optimal concept may involve trade-offs among performance, cost, size, and aesthetics. Once the desired features and performance specifications have been agreed to, problems have to be solved concerning the overall design as well as the design of each component. One must also solve problems concerning the best way to manufacture the product. Product quality is a function of

the quality of these interdependent individual solutions.

Cycle time is a function of the *problem-solving workload*, which is dependent on the project's *content* (i.e., the degree of innovation, complexity, and design sophistication) and *scope* (i.e., the number of new components that are developed in-house), as well as *problem-solving capacity*, which depends on *skill* in engineering, the *speed of prototyping*, the *organizational structure*, and *communication patterns.*

The amount of problem-solving within any specific new product project can be reduced by pursuing a strategy of *smaller, but more frequent, changes.* This was illustrated in Matushita's development of its air conditioners, as cited in Chapter 2. Similarly, Honda has benefited from introducing three product generations of the Accord since the Ford Taurus was introduced in 1985. At this point the technology in the Accord is about seven years newer than in the Taurus. On average, the life cycle of a Japanese automobile (the time from the development of the initial concept to when the last car rolls off the line) is 7.5 years versus fourteen to fifteen years for U.S. cars. The amount of required problem-solving can be further reduced if successive generations are considered when the current new product is being developed. Finally, problem-solving is reduced if known technology and standard components are used to the extent possible.

The second way to reduce the in-house problem-solving task is to *reduce project scope* by involving suppliers to a greater extent. One study of five very successful Japanese new products (Imai, Nonaka, and Takeuchi, 1988) found that the percentage of new components developed by suppliers ranged from 65 to 90, with a median of 70 percent. For this to substantially reduce the problem-solving workload, the suppliers need to be involved in the new product process early and treated like partners rather than independent third parties.

Cycle time can also be reduced by *improving problem-solving skills.* Some companies have better problem-solving skills than others. They can diagnose and solve problems more quickly and better than others because they have a higher level of technical competence, particularly at lower levels in the organization. For example, better-trained employees, special equipment such as CAD/CAM systems, and organizational arrangements such as prototype shops that are set up for speed rather than maximum resource utilization contribute to greater problem-solving capacity.

Improve linkages   Linkages among functional areas (e.g., between marketing and R&D) as well as between upstream and downstream activities (e.g., between product design and process design) need to be improved. These two sets of linkages are related because (1) different functional areas typically perform different activities in the new product development process, (2) the barriers between upstream and downstream activities are similar to those between functional areas, and (3) it is difficult to improve one of these linkages without improving the other.

Traditionally, development stages have been organized sequentially. Research or marketing develops a new concept and hands it to the people in design. They turn it into blueprints and a prototype. They throw the design "over the wall" to manufacturing engineering, which designs a process to make it. Then purchasing sends out requests for bids for components and equipment. Finally, manufacturing makes it and the sales force sells it. With this process, information flows in large chunks, mostly in one direction. The downstream group cannot start to work until the upstream work is completed.

This sequential approach was adopted because people thought the best way to perform a complex task was to break it into smaller pieces. This process was also viewed as a way to fully utilize scarce engineering talent. In that sense, it can be likened to a job shop that keeps talented people busy with a backlog of projects. The costs of this approach include the time a project sits in queues each time it is transferred downstream, a decreased manufacturability and serviceability of product designs, and the extra cost of making design changes late in the process.

A closely related topic is conflict between different functional areas. The reasons for conflicts include interdepartmental differences in the tasks of product development, and personality, sociocultural, and general goal differences (Gupta et al., 1986). However, a subtle problem is the presence of different thought worlds (Dougherty, 1989, 1990). Dougherty found little open conflict. None of the groups ignored or belittled the activities of others, nor were there arguments about relative priorities. Instead, each group had a qualitatively different view of the new product development process. Each group thought about the whole process from idea generation to commercialization, but it emphasized its own role. It tended to focus on the issues within its area and glossed over problems not directly in its purview.

As a result, none of the groups fully appreciated the complexity of the process. For example, R&D worried about the technical details, but figured if it got them right, the product would almost sell itself. The planners (product managers) thought in terms of new revenue streams, target markets, and positioning, placing the design and manufacturing problems in a decidedly secondary role. Salespeople thought what the market wanted was obvious; it was the sales task that was complicated.

Because people in each group felt they had a complete view of the process, these self-contained thought worlds tended to keep important new information out and make it much harder for the groups to work together.

Across several hundred development projects, Souder (1988) found some degree of conflict between marketing and R&D almost 60 percent of the time. Mild disharmony (20 percent of the projects), which may have been caused by different thought worlds, occurred when there was insufficient communication between R&D and marketing. Frequently, groups stopped communicating because management did not stress the importance of communication or because people in one group did not think the other group needed the information. Everybody concentrated on his or her own job. In a few cases, the two groups became so friendly that they did not want to contradict the other on issues where the other group should be the expert.

Severe disharmony (41 percent of the projects) was characterized by distrust or lack of confidence in the other group. This might occur if marketing had little success in reading the market or if R&D could not develop the desired product or did not care about real-world information. In this situation R&D might completely develop a product without any input from marketing. Then marketing would do its best to find a reason to kill the project.

Souder (1988) found a strong relationship between harmony and project success:[1]

RELATIVE PROJECT SUCCESS

States	Partial Success	Success	Failure
Harmony	52	35	13
Mild Disharmony	32	45	23
Severe Disharmony	11	21	68

When there was mild disharmony, some products failed to meet some important customer needs, were late, or did not perform as planned. When there was severe disharmony, many of the failures were catastrophic. Similarly, Dougherty found that the completeness of thought world held by all participants was strongly related to new product success.

In spite of its importance, it is hard to maintain harmony (or develop complete thought worlds) across several projects over time. Unless interaction is strongly encouraged, the different groups tend to drift apart, creating mild disharmony. Furthermore, unless controlled, mild disharmony can grow into severe disharmony. Once severe disharmony is present, it is very hard to eradicate, short of making personnel changes.

At a minimum, companies should form multifunctional teams from the start of each project. In addition to marketing, R&D, and manufacturing, these teams should include other groups, such as purchasing, packaging, and legal, as well as suppliers when appropriate.

However, forming teams is not enough. Dougherty found that the team needed to define the product in a way that was meaningful to all groups and allowed everyone to have the same understanding of the product and how it should fit into the market. For example, when develop-

---

[1]As with all survey research, the direction of causality needs to be considered.

ing the 1990 Accord, the team came up with the image of a "rugby player in a business suit," i.e., someone rugged but gentlemanly.

Additionally, one needs to build an unusually strong person-to-person relationship between people from different groups. Formal organizational contacts needed to be supplemented with informal interactions and participative forums. In one successful project the technical person referred to the marketer as his technical assistant, while the marketer called the other his marketing assistant. Sometimes these personal contacts were the result of such things as making joint customer calls, viewing focus groups together, and jointly analyzing market studies. Interfunctional cooperation also needs to be encouraged and rewarded.

Recently several techniques, such as design for manufacturability, quality function deployment, and return maps, have been developed that encourage interdepartmental coordination. Two of these are discussed in the last section of this chapter.

Harmonious relationships were less likely to form if the development process was sequential, as each group would emphasize its part of the process. Similarly, if one functional area dominated the development process, the concerns of other areas tended to get glossed over. Therefore, the project also needs to *overlap the upstream and downstream activities.* In order to start downstream activities before upstream ones are completed, downsteam people need to receive partial solutions and be able to guess what the final solution will look like. It requires a two-way flow of information and the downstream group must be able to influence the upstream decisions. Much of the information flow has to be informal.

While overlapping phases usually mean that the individual phases, especially, the upstream ones, get lengthened, the overall development cycle time is reduced. Furthermore, the improved two-way information flow about design changes and manufacturing requirements usual-

ly results in better designs. This is important, because in many industries 80 percent of the cost of the product is fixed at the design stage. Similarly, most product defects are designed in and are not the fault of manufacturing. When executed properly, overlapping development methods are faster and provide better, less expensive designs. These two methods are contrasted in Figure 3-6.

Even if teams and overlapping processes are encouraged, conflicts will still occur. Therefore, management has to promote good conflict resolution techniques to quickly identify and resolve conflicts at the lowest possible level through mutual accommodation. Also, interlocking task forces should be created to provide joint marketing-R&D representation at all levels.

Finally, Dougherty found that typical ways of developing and judging new products always need to be questioned. Not all standards applied to current products are appropriate for all new products. An unquestioning acceptance of these assumptions cuts down on creativity and learning.

FIGURE 3–6 Phased versus overlapping development approaches.

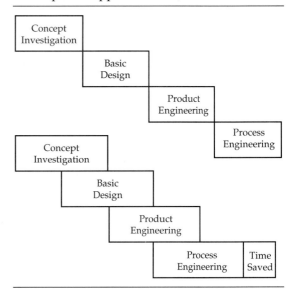

Clark and Fujimoto (1989, 1991) and Womack, Jones, and Roos (1990) have looked at differences in cycle time for Japanese and American car manufacturers. On average, the Japanese took seventeen fewer months (43.3 versus 60.3) and used 1.3 million fewer engineering hours (3 million versus 1.7 million).

They defined the new product development process in terms of two stages: planning and engineering. Planning included activities associated with concept investigation, styling, and overall design and performance specifications. The difference in planning lead time of 5.7 months (13.6 versus 19.3) was due primarily to problem-solving workload. The project scope for Japanese cars was lower; although there were fewer common parts, more of the design task was handled by suppliers (saving about five months). Second, the amount of major innovation was less on each Japanese car (saving an additional month); their strategy is to introduce models more frequently and incorporate fewer changes each time.

The engineering stage included the construction of detailed engineering drawings, prototypes, plant layouts, tool and equipment design, and the development or acquisition of production tools. The difference in engineering lead time of 7.5 months (32.2 versus 39.7)[2] was due to skills and greater overlap of upstream and downstream activities. The Japanese were able to produce product prototypes and dies for body panels much faster (saving 8.5 months). Also, the effect of more frequent but smaller changes was to save 1.6 months. Finally, smaller and simpler cars saved 1.9 months. Once these factors were held constant, the American companies could carry out the engineering phase more quickly.

An example of upstream and downstream overlap can be seen in the die-cutting operations of U.S. and Japanese automobile manufacturers. The large dies that are used to stamp body panels are produced by cutting a large block of metal to precise specifications, using computer-driven cutting machines. The U.S. companies have traditionally waited until they received precise specifications, then ordered all the blocks and cut them. In the Japanese companies, the die makers have greater informal contact with the designers. They order blocks based on preliminary design specifications and begin making rough cuts in the blocks before the car design is finalized.

This overlapping process requires the die cutters to understand the panel design process in order to anticipate the final solution. It also requires continuous communication between the two groups. The Japanese company will pay a cost penalty if the die cutter anticipates the wrong design (which happens infrequently), but is able to produce the final dies much more quickly.

---

[2]The difference between total lead time and the sum of planning and engineering lead time is due to overlaps or gaps between these two phases.

Summary Companies that have adopted these recommendations of emphasizing speed, forming small multifunctional teams from the start of the process, overlapping upstream and downstream activities, and emphasizing the project over functional departments have achieved considerable success. In one study, the National Institute of Standards & Technology (NIST) and Thomas Group found the following improvements: time to market, 20–90 percent less; engineering changes, 65–90 percent fewer; overall quality, 200–600 percent higher; dollar sales, 5–50 percent higher; and return on assets, 20–120 percent higher (Port, Schiller, and King, 1990).

It should be noted that quicker development means eliminating unnecessary delays, doing things right the first time, and sharing information with all concerned parties. It does not mean saving time by skipping steps such as internal or consumer testing or launching products without a well thought out manufacturing, distribution, and marketing plan. The preceding boxed insert discusses the impact these changes have had on Japanese automobile manufacturers.

Project Management

The way a new product development project is organized[3] can have a large impact on cycle time, quality, and cost. There are three major ways of organizing development projects: by functions, as a matrix, or as a project team.

When a development project is organized functionally, the people are grouped by discipline and the project is divided into segments which are assigned to these groups. The project is coordinated by functional and upper-level management with the aid of detailed specifications. The primary responsibility for the project passes sequentially from one function to another. A variation of this structure is a "lightweight" project manager (Hayes, Wheelwright, and Clark, 1988). Here, people reside in their functional areas with the exception of a project manager, who has the responsibility of coordinating the work through departmental liaisons but is given little authority.

At the other extreme is a project team organi-

zation, in which people from different functional areas are formally assigned and dedicated to a self-contained project team. A project manager has control over resources and rewards to team members. Typically, members leave their functional locations and move to a common area. The functional managers have no formal involvement. This form is also called a tiger team, venture team, or skunk works.

A matrix organization is a combination of these first two organizations that integrates the functional structure with a project structure. The project participants report simultaneously to both project and functional managers. The project manager has the responsibility of integrating the various disciplines in the development process. The functional managers have the responsibility of incorporating the latest disciplinary knowledge into the project and ensuring the technological integrity of the product to be developed. Project and functional managers have the joint power to make technical decisions regarding work activities, salaries and promotions, staffing, and assignment of personnel to particular project activities.

When the power and influence of the functional and project managers are nearly equal, it is called a balanced matrix. When the functional (project) managers have greater power, it is a (project) functional matrix (Larson and Gobeli, 1987). A matrix can also be described as a heavyweight project manager form when the project manager has authority over the people working on the project.

The most appropriate structure probably depends on the specific project. If technical considerations outweigh either cost or timing considerations (as in NASA), the functional organization may dominate. On the other hand, if the technological risk is low but speed is crucial (as for IBM's PC), a project organization is optimal. Finally, if both technological considerations and speed and marketing considerations are very important (as with new airplanes), a matrix form may be best.

However, looking across a wide range of

---

[3]These organizational forms deal only with the new product project itself and not with the larger organization. Any of these new product organizations could fit within a large number of oranizational designs. Furthermore, these new prodcut development structures are independent of the location of the new product function.

projects, Larson and Gobeli (1987, 1989) found that the most successful structures were generally the project team, the project matrix, and the balanced matrix. Hayes, Wheelwright, and Clark (1988) also found that heavyweight project manager and tiger team approaches produced better results than the lightweight project manager or the functional organization. This was because the latter two organizations did not give enough power and authority to the project manager. Furthermore, the heavyweight project manager and tiger team manager tended to be more experienced and credible. The combination of these two factors allowed the heavyweight project manager to communicate directly with the engineers on the project.

From their study of U.S. and Japanese automobile projects, Womack, Jones, and Roos (1990) also concluded that some type of a matrix structure was required. Engineers needed a tie to their functional areas because of substantial component overlap across programs (e.g., in transmissions) as well as their need to maintain contact with technological frontiers. On the other hand, some level of project coordination was required. The U.S. companies used a lightweight project manager to coordinate the development process. The manager did not have the power to resolve design conflicts. Engineers on the project were evaluated only by their functional bosses. Therefore, they made decisions consistent with what was best for their functional area (e.g., power trains) rather than what was best for the car. In contrast, the Japanese companies employ a very heavyweight project manager who is able to make decisions and evaluate the people working for him. These differences in project organization were viewed as another interrelated reason the Japanese development projects were more successful.

Integration Techniques

Several techniques have been introduced within the last few years in an attempt to integrate the functions involved in new product development.

Quality function deployment One of these processes is quality function deployment, or QFD (Griffin, 1990; Hauser and Clausing, 1988). The heart of this process is a matrix whose rows contain customer attributes (CAs) and columns contain engineering characteristics (ECs). See Figure 3-7 for a simplified example. The rows are used to list the desired attributes of the product from a customer point of view. Here economy and safety are two overarching characteristics. Economy is further broken down into low purchase price, low operating cost, high resale value, and long life. Typical applications may have more than 100 CAs.

The importance of each CA is listed in the first column. In this example economy is more important than safety and low price is the most important aspect of economy. The last column is a graph or perceptual map indicating how company *A* and its two major competitors, *B* and *C*, stand on each CA. The combination of importance and competitive standing suggests which attributes are most desirable to change. Company *A* would be most interested in improving purchase price and operating econo-

FIGURE 3–7 Quality function deployment.

ENGINEERING CHARACTERISTICS						
Customer Attributes	Importance	Weight	Engine Power	Antilock Brakes	Wheel Base	Customer Perceptions
Economy	8					Worst ⟶ Best
Low price	8	–	–	–		A C B
Low operating cost	5	–	–			A C B
High resale value	3		+	+		B C A
Long life	4			+		B CA
Safety	6					
Head-on crash	9	+				B C A
Collision avoidance	4	–	+		+	CAB
		1,000 lb.	hor. pow.	yes, no	in.	
Car A		3.2	160	yes	104	
Car B		2.8	125	no	98	
Car C		3.0	150	no	100	
Target		3.1	160	yes	104	

my, as these are two important attributes in which it rates low.

The columns in the middle of the chart list the engineering characteristics that have an impact on one or more CAs. For example, weight has an impact on purchase price, operating cost, safety in a head-on crash, and collision avoidance. The engineering characteristics are stated in terms that engineers can measure, such as pounds and inches. The units of measure are listed in the row following the CAs.

The intersections of the rows and columns indicate the amount and direction of impact that each engineering characteristic has on each customer attribute. Pluses indicate a positive impact, blanks indicate no impact, and minuses indicate a negative impact. Multiple pluses or minuses can be used to indicate stronger impacts. This figure indicates that increasing the weight of the car has a negative impact on purchase price, but makes it safer in a head-on crash.

The bottom of the matrix indicates the physical measurements for each of the three brands. This shows that car *A* is a large car with greater horsepower and antilock brakes. Engineering must consider what the customer wants in terms of CAs, then decide which ECs represent the best ways of making desired changes. The final line in the matrix indicates the target level of each EC for the new product. In this case, Company *A* has decided to reduce the weight slightly without changing the wheelbase. Also, it has decided to keep the current level of power and the antilock brakes for improved performance and safety.

The big benefit of this process is that it integrates engineering and marketing by forcing these two groups to make joint decisions early. They must set targets that are based on what customers say they want. This process requires a great deal of work. Anecdotal evidence concerning Japanese firms (Hauser and Clausing, 1988) indicates that it is well worth the effort. In Griffin's survey, 82 percent of the respondents using QFD believed that it provided definite strategic benefits in the long term, but they had observed fewer benefits to the project they were

currently working on. So it is a process that takes time to develop.

Return maps Hewlett-Packard has developed return maps as a way to integrate functional areas (House and Price, 1991). These maps are graphs with time (in a linear scale) on the horizontal axis and money (in a logarithmic scale) on the vertical axis. This allows the organization to plot cumulative investment, sales, and profits over time. The horizontal scale is broken into three phases: investigation (determination of features, costs, price, and timing), development (development of product and manufacturing process), and manufacturing-sales (the period after product introduction). Two of the key metrics they look at are time to market (TM), which is the length of the development cycle, and break-even time (BET), which is the time at which cumulative profits equal the investment. An example of a return map is given in Figure 3-8.

In this example, the investment in development is $3 million, about $500,000 of which is incurred during investigation. The product is introduced two years after investigation started and time to market is eighteen months. The product has sales of $10 million in the first year after introduction and $90 million the second year. Corresponding levels of profit are $0.8 million and $4.2 million. It breaks even forty-five months after the start of investigation.

The return map is generated by marketing, R&D, and manufacturing during the investigation phase. These initial estimates are used as a standard of comparison during the rest of the project. If new marketing or technical information is uncovered during the process, a new return map can be developed to determine the impact of any potential changes. After introduction, the whole process is reanalyzed to determine how the company could have made better forecasts and how the project could have been managed better.

Like QFD, this process forces different functional areas to work together. Return maps do

FIGURE 3–8   Return map.

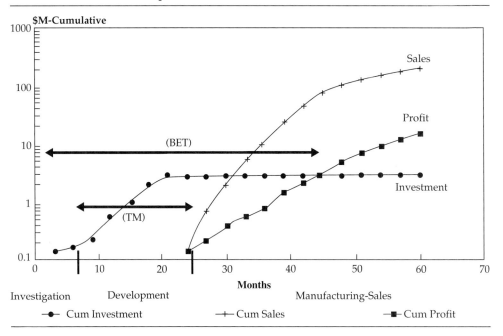

$M-Cumulative

Investigation   Development   Manufacturing-Sales

—●— Cum Investment   —+—Cum Sales   —■—Cum Profit

CONCLUDING REMARKS

This chapter has examined the reasons for the success and failure of both individual new products and new product programs. Factors associated with individual new product success include a superior value in the eyes of the customer, an efficient development process, and a well-directed and appropriately funded introduction. The primary factor associated with the success of a new product program is a strategy that directs the effort in productive areas.

The rest of the chapter covered areas that are related to success in product development. First was a description of a new product development process. Many new products have failed because several steps in the process were omitted or were not performed adequately. Following such a process helps to ensure that adequate market analysis and consumer testing take place. Second, it should encourage a small number of checkpoints at which the project is evaluated in an objective and nonpolitical fashion. Third, it points out the responsibility of the various parties.

The final section discussed a number of issues in the management of the new product development process. The first part discussed ways of accelerating the new product process. Then different project organizational forms were covered. Finally, ways to decrease interfunctional conflicts were discussed.

REFERENCES

Advertising Age: "RJR Monitors 105 New Brands," July 12, 1976, p. 3.

Biggadike, Ralph: "The Risky Business of Diversification," *Harvard Business Review,* 57, May 1979, 103–111.

Booz-Allen and Hamilton, Inc.: *New Product Management for the 1980s,* New York: Booz-Allen and Hamilton, Inc., 1982.

Calantone, Roger J., and C. Anthony di Benetetto: "An Integrative Model of the New Product Development Process: An Empirical Investigation," *Journal of Product Innovation Management,* 5 (3), 1988, 201–215.

Clark, Kim B., and T. Fujimoto: "Lead Time in Automobile Product Development—Explaining the Japanese Advantage," *Journal of Engineering and Technology Management,* 6 (1), 1989, 25–58.

_____ and _____: *Product Development Performance: Strategy, Organization, and Management in the World Auto Industry,* Boston: Harvard Business School Press, 1991.

Cooper, Robert G.: "Why New Industrial Products Fail," *Industrial Marketing Management,* 4, 1975, 315–326.

_____: "The Dimensions of Industrial New Product Success and Failure," *Journal of Marketing,* 43 (3), 1981, 93–103.

_____: "How New Product Strategies Impact on Performance," *Journal of Product Innovation Management,* 1 (1), 1984a, 5–18.

_____: "New Product Strategies: What Distinguishes the Top Performers," *Journal of Product Innovation Management,* 1 (3), 1984b, 151–164.

_____: "Defining the New Product Strategy," *IEEE Transactions on Engineering Management,* EM-34 (3), 1987, 184–193.

_____ and Ulricke de Brentani: "New Industrial Financial Services: What Distinguishes the Winners," *Journal of Product Innovation Management,* 8 (2), 1991, 75–91.

_____ and Elko J. Kleinschmidt: "An Investigation into the New Product Process: Steps, Deficiencies, and Impact," *Journal of Product Innovation Management,* 3 (2), 1986, 71–85.

Crawford, C. Merle: "Defining the Charter for Product Innovation," *Sloan Management Review,* Fall 1980, 3–12.

_____: "Protocol: New Tool for Product Innovation," *Journal of Product Innovation Management,* 1 (2), 1984, 85–91.

Davidson, Hugh J.: "Why Most New Consumer Brands Fail," *Harvard Business Review,* 54, March–April 1976, 117–122.

Data Development Corporation: *Sales Waves Experiments,* New York: Data Development Corporation, n. d.

DeBrentani, Ulrike: *Evaluation of New Industrial Product Ideas: An Empirical Study of the New Product-Screening Model and an Analysis of Managerial Screening Behavior,* unpublished Ph.D. dissertation, McGill University, 1983.

_____: "Success and Failure in New Industrial Services," *Journal of Product Innovation Management,* 6 (4), 1989, 239–258.

Dougherty, Deborah: "Interpretive Barriers to Successful Product Innovation," MSI working paper, Report No. 89–114, September 1989.

_____: "Understanding New Markets for New Products," *Strategic Management Journal,* 11, 1990, 59–78.

Dumaine, Brian: "How Managers Can Succeed Through Speed," *Fortune,* February 13, 1989a, 54–59.

_____: "P&G Rewrites the Marketing Rules," *Fortune,* November 6, 1989b, 34–48.

_____: "Those Highflying PepsiCo Managers," *Fortune,* April 10, 1989c, 78–86.

_____: "Closing the Innovation Gap," *Fortune,* December 2, 1991, 56–62.

Griffin, Abbie: "Functionally Integrating New Product Development," working paper, Graduate School of Business, University of Chicago, April 1990.

Gupta, Ashok, S.P. Raj, and David Wilemon: "A Model for Studying R&D-Marketing Interface in the Product Innovation Process," *Journal of Marketing,* 50 (2), 1986, 7–17.

_____ and David Wilemon: "Accelerating the Development of Technology-Based New Products, *California Management Review,* Winter 1990, 24–44.

Hardin, David K.: "The Final Decision: Are You Really Ready to Roll Out?" in *How to Develop and Market New Products . . . Better and Faster,* David Hoo (ed.), New York: Association of National Advertisers, 1985, 254–258.

Hauser, John R., and Don Clausing: "The House of Quality," *Harvard Business Review,* 66, May–June 1988, 63–73.

Hayes, Robert H., Steven C. Wheelwright, and Kim B. Clark: *Dynamic Manufacturing: Creating the Learning Organization,* New York: Free Press, 1988.

Hoo, David, and Bob McDonald: "Prescription for New Product Success," in *How to Develop and Market New Products . . . Better and Faster,* David Hoo (ed.), New York: Association of National Advertisers, 1985, 24–47.

House, Charles H., and Raymond L. Price: The Return Map: Tracking Product Teams, *Harvard Business Review,* 69, January–February 1991, 92–101.

Imai, Ken-ichi, Nonaka Ikurjiro, and Hirotaka Takeuchi: "Managing the New Product Development Process: How Japanese Companies Learn and Unlearn," in *Readings in the Management of Innovation* 2d ed., Michael L. Tushman and William L. Moore (eds.), Cambridge, Mass., Ballinger Publishing Company, 1988.

Johne, Frederick A.: "How Experienced Product Innovators Organize," *Journal of Product Innovation Management,* 1 (4), 1984, 210–223.

Katz, Ralph, and Thomas J. Allen: "Project Performance and the Locus of Influence in the R&D Matrix," *Academy of Management Journal,* 28 (1), 1985, 67–87.

Labich, Kenneth: "The Innovators," *Fortune,* June 6, 1988, 49–64.

Larson, Erik W., and David H. Gobeli: "Matrix Management: Contradictions and Insights," *California Management Review,* 24 (4), 1987, 126–138.

_____ and _____: "Significance of Project Management Structure on Development Success," *IEEE Transactions on Engineering Management,* 36 (2), 1989, 119–125.

Maidique, Modesto A.: "Entrepreneurs, Champions, and Technological Innovation," *Sloan Management Review,* Winter 1980, 59–76.

_____ and Robert H. Hayes: "The Art of High Technology Management," *Sloan Management Review,* Winter 1984, 17–31.

_____ and Billie Jo Zirger: "A Study of Success and Failure in Product Innovation: The Case of the U.S. Electronics Industry," *IEEE Transactions on Engineering Management,* EM-31, November 1984, 193–203.

Neilsen, A.C., Co.: New Product Success Ratio, *Neilsen Researcher,* No. 5, 1971, 1–10.

Pessemier, Edgar A.: *Product Management: Strategy and Organization,* 2d ed., New York: John Wiley, 1982; reprinted by Krieger, 1988, Robert E. Krieger Publishing Co., Inc., Malabar, FL.

Peters, Thomas J., and Robert H. Waterman, Jr.: *In Search of Excellence: Lessons from America's Best-Run Companies,* New York: Harper and Row, 1982.

Port, Otis, Zachary Schiller, and Resa W. King: A Smarter Way to Manufacture," *Business Week,* April 30, 1990, 110–117.

Roberts, Edward B.: Generating Effective Corporate Innovation," *Technology Review,* October/November 1977, 33.

Rosenbloom, Richard S., and Michael A. Cusumano: "Technological Pioneering and Competitive Advantage: The Birth of the VCR Industry," *California Management Review,* 29 (4), 1987, 51–76.

Rothwell, Roy, C. Freeman, A. Horsley, V.T.P. Jervis, A.B. Robertson, and J. Townsend: "SAPPHO updated—project SAPPHO phase II," *Research Policy,* 3, 1974, 258–291.

Rubenstein, A.H., A.K. Chakrabarti, R.D. O'Keefe, W.E. Souder, and H.C. Young: "Factors Influencing Innovation Success at the Project Level," *Research Management,* May 1976, 15–20.

Smith, Lee: The Lures and Limits of Innovation," *Fortune,* October 20, 1980, 84–94.

Sommers, William P.: *Product Development: New Approaches in the 1980s,* New York: Booz-Allen and Hamilton, Inc., 1979.

Souder, William E.: "Managing Relations Between R&D and Marketing in New Product Development Projects," *Journal of Product Innovation Management,* 5 (1), 1988, 6–19.

Swire, Donald: "Evidence on What Drives New Venture Success: The PIMS Experience," paper presented at the Conference on New Product Success in Business/Industrial Markets, sponsored by Institute for the Study of Business Markets, Pennsylvania State University, June 1984.

Tauber, Edward M.: "Brand Franchise Extension: New Products from Existing Brand Names," in *How to Develop and Market New Products Better and Faster,* David Hoo (ed.), New York: Association of National Advertisers, 1985, 152–161.

Uttal, Bro: "Speeding New Ideas to Market," *Fortune,* March 2, 1987, 62–66.

von Hippel, Eric: "Successful Industrial Products from Customer Ideas," *Journal of Marketing,* January 1978, 39–49.

_____: "Lead Users: A Source of Novel New Product Concepts," *Management Science,* 32, July 1986, 791-805.

REVIEW QUESTIONS

Q3-1 How should product success be measured? What is the observed new product success rate?

Q3-2 What contributes to new product success? Failure?

Q3-3 Discuss the extent to which a firm's new product program can have a success rate that is too high.

Q3-4 Discuss the problem of effectively searching for product opportunities. Distinguish between technologically based opportunities and opportunities produced by idea search.

Q3-5 Discuss the risk-reward profile of each cell in Figure 3-2.

Q3-6 Out of every 100 submitted product ideas, what percentage are rejected at each step in the process?

Q3-7 In Figure 3-4, what percentage of the out-of-pocket expenses is incurred at each step in the process?

Q3-8 Discuss two principal objectives of the screening process.

Q3-9 How does business analysis differ from screening?

Q3-10 How can new product projects be managed to deal with the cultural differences between research, development, manufacturing, and marketing organizations?

Q3-11 Discuss how desirable it is to minimize the time required to bring a sound product idea to market.

PART 2

FINDING AND CREATING VALUE: THE OFFER

4

SEARCH FOR NEW PRODUCT IDEAS

The last chapter stressed the importance of a new product development process; however, the end result of the development process can be no better than the ideas that go into the process. The focus of the next two chapters is on generating new product ideas. This process should begin with a new product strategy, something that gives some guidance on where to look for new product ideas and how to judge them once they have been found.

NEW PRODUCT STRATEGY

While innovation and growth seem to be resistant to formal planning, decisions about which markets to serve and which products to develop and introduce are so important that they must be influenced by corporate or business unit top management. For example, given the risks and potential rewards, Sony's top management needed to be involved in the decision to work on VCRs, Mavica cameras, Walkmans, and workstations. Similarly, RCA spent $2 billion on the ill-fated development of video disc players. These decisions needed top management approval. Both Cooper (1984a, b) and Booz-Allen (1982) found that a new product strategy was a major predictor of the success of a new product program. A new product strategy is important because it ties the new product program to business unit or corporate strategy.

Top management cannot carry out the search for new product ideas, but it can use a new product strategy to help focus the activities of others without straitjacketing potential champions excessively. Furthermore, the creation of a new product strategy allows top management to intervene at the point at which it has the greatest amount of leverage. A new product strategy or a product innovation charter (Crawford, 1980) should give some guidance on where to look for new products and how to judge the ideas once they have been found.

New Product Objectives

The first part of a new product strategy is a statement of new product objectives—what one wants to accomplish from the new product program. This is important, because it designates the desired role of new products and indicates the amount of financial and human resources that need to be devoted to new products. It also indicates what management thinks will constitute a successful new product program. Booz-Allen (1982) found that companies with more successful new product programs have an explicit objective for new products (e.g., 20 percent of sales should come from products that are less than five years old).

The most common new product objective is growth. When the strategic plan indicates a revenue or profit shortfall in future years, it is typically projected to be made up with increased sales of existing products, acquisitions, and new products. It is much better to set a new product objective as a consistent percentage of sales rather than attempt to increase new product activity quickly when profits decrease and slack off when profits are acceptable.

Growth is not the only objective desired of new products. Another typical new product objective is to lessen one's dependence on a certain market. For example, Sony wants to have 50 percent of its revenue come from industrial customers, up from about 20 percent in the late 1980s. Similarly, with changing East-West relations, many defense contractors need to lessen their dependence on the military market. McDonald's offered breakfast menus in an attempt to utilize their facilities better. Recently they test-marketed pizza to increase dinnertime traffic. Ski resorts have attempted a number of things to build summer business. Many service businesses have added new services in an attempt to lessen swings in demand. Stability of sales can be more important than their absolute level.

New products may be introduced to fill out a product line even if they do not contribute much to corporate profits. General Motors needs to produce smaller cars to meet CAFE gas mileage requirements as well as to attract first-time buyers whom they hope to retain over time. Similarly, companies may produce a top-of-the-line or technologically advanced product for prestige or to maintain a reputation as a technological leader even if it does not make much of a direct contribution to profit.

Companies may also bring out new products to fight competition rather than make profits. Several U.S. small cars have been dubbed "import fighters." Similarly, Gillette introduced its Good News disposable razors to combat BIC even though disposable razors generate a lower margin than shavers and blades.

Products may also be introduced to utilize excess capacity, by-products, or intermediate products. Reportedly, one of the reasons that General Foods introduced Cycle Dog Food was the existence of an idle canning plant in Wichita (Homichael, 1980).

As an example of how new product objectives can highlight the required size of the new product program, consider the following example. A $500 million company that is in an industry that is growing at approximately 7 percent annually will have revenue from its core business of about $700 million in five years. An objective that 10 percent of sales must come from products less than five years old means that products launched during this period have to generate $70 million in sales that year. A new product audit revealed that line extensions and flankers typically have annual sales of $5 million–$15 million (with an average of $10 million), while new-to-the-company products have annual sales in the range of $20 million–$80 million (average $50 million). To achieve this new product objective the company must have seven successful line extensions, two successful new-to-the-company products, or some combination of them in the next three or four years.

On the other hand, if the company objective dictated that 25 percent of its sales come from products less than five years old, a $230 million revenue gap would result. Most likely this would have to be made up with three or four new-to-the-company products and a good number of line extensions. By looking at the investment requirements, marketing costs, and failure rates of past new products, a good estimate of the size of the task can be made.

Although objectives provide valuable information about the size of the task, they may not give enough guidance on where to look for new products. That is the role of the next element of the new product strategy.

Search Criteria

Areas for new product search   Next, the new product strategy must delineate which are possible areas for new products and which are out of bounds. This is closely related to the company's or business unit's definition of its business. (See Chapter 1.) Many companies define themselves in terms of the products they produce, the technologies they use, or the natural resources they consume. Levitt (1960) suggested that companies define themselves in terms of the needs they served; for example, as an energy company instead of an oil company. This broader definition allows one to see threats more easily and allows the company to evolve with its customers. However, this definition may be too wide because an improper interpretation would see automobiles and snowmobiles as competitors. Furthermore, it does not consider the company's strengths and weaknesses.

These criticisms led people to consider multidimensional business definitions. Booz-Allen (Johnson and Jones, 1957) and Ansoff (1965) defined businesses in terms of customers and products (or technologies). This results in a two-dimensional matrix where each row represents a different customer group (existing, related, and new) and each column represents the relationship to present technology or products (existing, related, and new). One version of this type of matrix is shown in Figure 4-1.

FIGURE 4–1   Product-market scope.

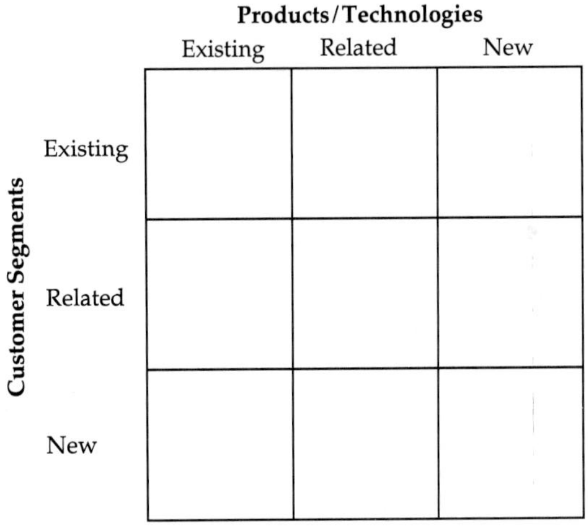

The company's current product-market scope is made up of that group of product-market combinations in which it currently does business; that is, the various groups of customers it has chosen to serve and the products with which it is attempting to serve them. In most cases, the current product-market scope includes several product-market combinations. For example, Canon produces copiers for the business office market and cameras for the consumer market.

Once the company has defined its current business scope, a growth vector can be used to designate the direction of growth from this base. The exact definitions of existing, related, and new may be open to debate in a given situation, but growth can be described in the following terms.

Growing within the current product-market scope is called *market penetration*. IBM has traditionally attempted to "hold and grow" its customer base by moving the customers to larger systems as their needs grow. Coca-Cola's reintroduction of New Coke as Coke II is another attempt at market penetration.

Growth by moving down the matrix is called *market development* and is achieved by selling current products or technology to new customers. Such a move could include attacking new segments (Apple selling its computers to larger companies) or new geographic areas (Nordstrom opening stores on the East Coast out of its traditional West Coast area). This path has also been chosen by 3M as it attempts to apply its coating and bonding technology to a wide variety of customer needs. Similarly, most of Canon's businesses are based on its competences in precision mechanics, optics, and micro-electronics. Realizing the need for products to flow from its core competencies—from what it does best—Rubbermaid encourages its people to look at processes and technologies across the entire company. This led a manager to adapt technology from cooler plants to make an inexpensive durable line of office furniture. The WorkManager System now accounts for 60 percent of its furniture division sales (Dumaine, 1991).

Product development occurs when one moves across the matrix by developing new products for its current customers. Depending upon the relationship between the new and old products these could be complements (Epson PCs to go with their printers), substitutes (most of the leading fiber optics companies in Japan were originally metal wire companies), product line expansions (Toyota's introduction of the Lexus model) or new product lines (Honda's introduction of lawn mowers and snow blowers).

Finally, a change in both customers and products results in *diversification*. Many times these movements are the result of acquisitions rather than a new product program, such as Mobil Oil's entry into the retailing business through the acquisition of Marcor. However, internal diversification programs such as IBM's entry into robotics and analytical instruments or Sony's entry into the noodle shop industry are also possible. Currently Motorola is attempting to leverage its quality and customer service skills, gained in cellular phone, semiconductor, and paging device businesses, to enter the electronic ballasts market.

Most movements are going to require some

changes in both customers and technologies. The degree of customer change (whether a group of customers is considered to be existing, related, or new) depends both on the company's knowledge of the customer and on the customer's perception of that company as an appropriate source for the new product. For example, Seiko offers microcomputers through its Epson subsidiary. It is possible that the target markets for their watches and computers are similar. Therefore, Seiko may understand these people. However, if the customer does not see the connection, the customer might be classified as related.

Similarly, the degree of technological newness is a function of the difference in knowledge and skills that is required by the new product. While the introduction of a VCR was a big step for both Sony and Ampex (the maker of the first broadcast video tape recorder), it was a bigger leap for Ampex (Rosenbloom and Cusamano, 1987). Even though Ampex had the technology to make high-quality broadcast tape recorders, apparently it did not have the high-volume manufacturing skills required nor the engineering capability to simplify and reduce the cost of the product.

There is considerable evidence that companies that stay close to a core technology but diversify slightly are more successful than companies that diversify more widely (e.g., Rumelt, 1974). This basic finding is echoed by Maidique and Hayes (1984), who found that successful high-technology businesses are highly focused. They get the great bulk of their sales from a single product line or a closely related set of product lines.

Furthermore, there may be some evidence that it is more important to stay close to customers than to the technology. A.T. Kearney, Inc. (1974) cites the following probabilities of new product success: an improved product into the present market—.75; a new product with unrelated technology in the present market—.50; an existing product into a new market—.25; and an external diversification—.05. Similarly,

Meyer and Roberts (1986) found that more successful small technology-based firms stayed closer to their original customer base and core technology than did similar but less successful firms. Furthermore, they found that staying close to customers was more important than staying with technology. However, Pavia (1990) found no difference between sticking with customers or sticking with technology in the success of small high-technology firms. Cooper (1984a, b) found that successful new product strategies were built on strengths in marketing and technology. All of these findings are echoed in the advice of Peters and Waterman (1982) to stay "close to the customer" and "stick to the knitting."

This suggests that after a business unit has identified its product-market scope, it should first search for opportunities within that area. Then it should consider existing and improved products for its current and related customers before looking further afield.

Competitive timing   A third factor to be considered is competitive timing of entry. This decision is closely related to the company's technology strategy (see, e.g., Ansoff and Stewart, 1967; Maidique and Patch, 1978). This is an important decision for two reasons. First, the requirements for success change as the product matures. Early in the life cycle the basis of competition tends to be on product performance. Successful companies need to quickly introduce superior products. Over time, as successful designs are copied, differences in product performance may decrease, causing the basis of competition to shift toward manufacturing and distribution strengths.

Second, the requirements for being a technological leader differ from those of a follower along a number of important dimensions. Few companies do much basic research, but there are several differences between applied research and development (Ansoff and Stewart, 1967). In a research-oriented environment, the problem is

understood but the solution is unknown. Therefore, the task is to discover and evaluate alternative solutions. In a development-oriented environment, the general solution has been agreed to, so the central task is determining the most efficient design.

This difference between indefinite and well-defined design specifications has several implications. As the design freedom increases (with indefinite specifications), so does the need for individual initiative and creativity. Increasing design freedom also allows many people to work in parallel. As design freedom decreases, supervision becomes more highly directive and design work must be coordinated. Research involves finding alternative solutions, and a key management task is to recognize commercially significant results. The management of design and development is more concerned with efficiency. Because of these differences, few firms are equally skilled in both research and development.

Firms that spend a high percentage of sales on R&D relative to the industry tend to be closer to the technological state of the art than firms that spend less. There are several reasons operations become less stable as companies operate closer to the state of the art. Typically, these companies are trying for rapid and significant advances which may disrupt their operations. Second, as they get closer to the state of the art, predictability decreases because researchers are working in areas of partial knowledge. Similarly, precedent is sparse near the state of the art, which means that managerial mistakes are more likely to be made. All of these problems are magnified when products are experiencing short life cycles and rapid technological change. Finally, firms that are more research intensive and spend more than the industry average on R&D tend to use more internally developed technology and acquire less by licensing.

The above factors suggest that a firm's technology policy has an important impact on the types of new product opportunities that it should expect. Four competitive timing options are available.

The first of these is the *pioneer* or *first-to-market* strategy. It entails a research-intensive R&D group, a level of funding that is higher than industry average, and work that is closer to the state of the art. Large potential payoffs coupled with uncertainty make this a high-risk, high-reward strategy.

This timing option requires continuous funding of R&D, time allocated to individual creative work, and a management that is willing to live with the risks. A top executive of 3M in the late 1970s presided over two failures and three large successes on his way up. It requires engineers to have a "good enough" philosophy to get the product out quickly and make improvements as they learn with the market. Finally, a company needs a good patent department. Corning Glass has spent most of the last twelve years battling patents on its wave guides for fiber optics (Magaziner and Patinkin, 1989). Marketing emphasis is on building primary demand, getting customers to consider this product class.

Successful pioneering companies include Intel, Hewlett-Packard, 3M, Sony, and Corning Glass. HP and 3M are viewed as archetypical entrepreneurial companies. Intel is well known for its refusal to decrease R&D spending during economic downturns. Corning has been involved in a number of important innovations: electric light bulbs, TV picture tubes, Corning Ware, and fiber optic wave guides. Sony is one of the most innovative companies around, with products including Beta-format VCR, transistor radio, Trinitron TV, Walkman, Watchman, and the Mavica camera.

A second competitive timing strategy is *fast second,* or *follow the leader.* This approach implies entry about the time growth starts to accelerate or at the time the dominant design emerges. It might also mean a quick imitation of the pioneer as opposed to a totally independent development effort. Components of this strategy include a slightly lower R&D-to-sales ratio than the pioneer and a greater allocation to development than applied or basic research relative to the pio-

neer. To imitate the pioneer quickly, a fast second needs to be fairly close to the technological state of the art, and nimble.

It must quickly recognize dominant designs, possess fast development cycle time, and have the ability to get distribution quickly. Because it can learn from the pioneer's mistakes the desire for speed should not lead to the introduction of simple me-too products.

Although IBM is a technological leader in the laboratory, it is not always the first to incorporate new technology into its products. A good example of a follower strategy was its introduction of the IBM PC. Frequently large companies allow smaller ones to compete on innovation, but after an innovation has proven to be popular, larger companies attempt to compete on quality and marketing strength. For whatever reasons, Caterpillar let Deere introduce a reticulated grader first and followed several years later. The major U.S. automobile companies let Mazda pioneer the Wankel rotary engine, but did not follow. The major microcomputer companies introduced RISC-based computers and workstations only after they had been pioneered by others.

The third timing-of-entry strategy is that of the *specialist.* These companies attempt to serve niches with special applications of the basic technology. They are usually not pioneers, but may enter the life cycle at any time after that. Probably the most typical time of entry is in the early growth stage. This strategy requires applied engineering and flexible manufacturing as well as close customer contact in order to fashion products for niches. The ratio of R&D expenditures to sales may be close to that of pioneers and fast seconds. Because they do not produce large volumes, cost control is important for this strategy.

The final competitive timing strategy is *late to market* or *me-too.* These companies might be viewed as manufacturing specialists. Generally, they are more process oriented than product oriented. They may have cost advantages that are hard to duplicate, such as low wage rates, access to raw materials or power, or government subsidies. They would be more likely than the earlier groups to license rather than develop their own product technology. These companies might also have a flair for value engineering—determining the components on the basis of a trade-off between cost and the value delivered to the customer. This results in the use of standardized components and modular construction to gain economies of scale. Many times these companies can be characterized as "running a tight ship" with no first-class travel, vending machines rather than a company cafeteria, and so on.

Examples of these manufacturing specialists include National Semiconductor and White Consolidated. There is a very good description of Samsung's late entry into the microwave market in Magaziner and Patinkin (1989).

Screening Criteria

In addition to providing guidance about where to search for new products, a new product strategy should indicate how new product ideas are judged. These guidelines should be closely related to the screening criteria the company uses during the new product development process.

Financial criteria Financial results are probably the most commonly used criteria to judge new product ideas. In its best-practices study, Booz-Allen (1982) found that the most typical guidelines were sales, return on investment, profit contribution, market share, payback, and internal rate of return. Furthermore, it suggests that the financial hurdle should be a function of the strategic role and risk of the new product. For example, products entering a new category or involving special risk factors should receive a higher hurdle rate than a new product designed simply to use existing skills and capacity. However, these higher-risk projects may also be allowed a longer-term payback.

The use of financial criteria is clearly necessary, but there are several problems with strict reliance on financial criteria. First, it is hard to put a value on many new product development efforts. For example, estimates of how much money P&G might make from olestra (the fake fat undergoing FDA testing) range from several hundred million dollars to over a billion (Dumaine, 1989). Second, estimates of financial results are based on large numbers of assumptions and the final numbers tend to be remembered more clearly than the assumptions on which they are based. Third, as typically applied, these criteria tend to favor more conservative projects. Fourth, the value of doing nothing is typically overstated, making change relatively less attractive. Finally, there is a certain amount of game playing. In addition to helping make decisions, people often use financial estimates to justify the decision they have already made. (However, this problem is not limited to financial criteria!)

Some of the problems associated with the use of financial criteria can be alleviated by using a new product diagnostic audit (see Chapter 1) to track the results of past forecasts. Also, financial theory should be properly applied. For example, if a company makes an initial investment in a new area and future investments depend on its outcome, the initial investment should be evaluated as a call option and not in discounted cash flow (DCF) terms (Myers, 1984). That is, the cost of establishing a foothold may generate a negative net present value (NPV) for a project. However, if a successful initial project gives the firm the option of making a second profitable investment and the present value of this option offsets the first-stage negative NPV, the initial investment should be made.

In general, the track record of financial forecasting is not very good. Tull (1967) studied sixty-three new product introductions from twenty-four financially successful companies. A comparison was made between the forecast and actual levels of sales and profits. The primary measure of forecasting error was the absolute relative error (ARE), which was defined as:

$$\text{ARE} = \left| \frac{F_i - A_i}{A_i} \right| \times 100 \qquad (4\text{-}1)$$

where F_i is the forecast outcome and A_i is the actual outcome of the ith new product. The results are given in Table 4-1. There is a consistent upward bias in the forecasts; the bias appears to be greater for industrial than for consumer products and greater for profits than for sales. Surprisingly, the errors are slightly greater for "adaptive" products than they are for "innovative" products.

At a minimum, these results suggest that financial criteria should not be the sole criteria for judging the likely success of new products. Furthermore, appropriate financial analyses should be made and differences from strategic analyses should be reconciled.

Attractiveness of the industry   A second screening criterion is industry attractiveness. This raises the question of whether the industry or product class is worthy of investment or if products introduced into that industry are likely to return a reasonable profit. Typical dimensions used to assess industry attractiveness include size, growth, current profitability, level of competition, cyclicality, and rate of technological change.

Porter (1980) argued that the average profitability of an industry is a function of five competitive factors (see the discussion in Chapter 1). His approach forces one to take a systematic look at the industry and these underlying factors. In performing this analysis, the important question is not what the current levels of these factors are, but what the future levels will be. By forecasting the changes in these competitive forces, it is possible to do a better job of forecasting future industry profitability.

When considering the attractiveness of the industry for purposes of entry, one of the most important factors is that of entry barriers. A study of entry barriers indicates not only what factors may cause the entrant's costs to be greater than those of entrenched competitors, but they may also indicate what retaliatory moves the competitors may make. For example, if there are economies from shared operations, it may be cheaper for some firms to enter an industry than others. Similarly, entry barriers may make it more advantageous for entrenched competitors to employ fixed rather than variable cost strategies.

Fit with company strengths   Not only should the opportunity be in an attractive industry, but it should also be a good one for the company conducting the analysis. The opportunity needs to fit with this company's strengths. In order to succeed in the long term, one must be able to offer customers a differential advantage; that is,

TABLE 4-1   COMPARISON OF ACTUAL TO FORECAST SALES AND PROFITS

TYPE OF PRODUCT	MEAN ARE*	MEDIAN ARE	PERCENT F>A
Sales			
Consumer	49	23	63
Industrial	85	37	70
Profits			
Consumer	78	26	66
Industrial	225	73	89

* ARE is absolute relative error.

provide the customer with something the customer wants but cannot get elsewhere. To do this, the company needs suitable facilities and core competencies. Furthermore, the company needs to be at least adequate on other dimensions that matter in the industry.

One way of thinking about the company's ability to produce a product with greater benefits or lower costs than its competition is with a value chain (Porter, 1985). The value chain groups the activities of the firm into the steps needed to design, produce, deliver, sell, and service the product as well as the supporting activities such as procurement, human resources management, and technology management. An example of a generic value chain is given in Figure 4-2. Typically only those activities where most of the value is added or most of the costs are incurred are analyzed in detail. The firm needs to compare its ability to perform these activities with the ability of the most successful companies presently in the industry.

The company should first determine what the various segments want; that is, what trade-offs members of these segments are willing to make. Then it has to decide which operations of the business are related to these customer desires. For example, a segment may be very interested in minimal downtime. This could be achieved through some combination of more reliable

products or quicker service once they break down. Reliability can be improved through better designs, components with fewer defects, or better manufacturing practices. Faster service can be achieved through some combination of modular designs that allow the bad part to be replaced on the spot or a service operation employing a large number of trained technicians. An entering company can analyze its ability to achieve minimal downtime to that of the firms presently in the industry by using the value chain.

Superior performance can be achieved by performing activities better than the competition or by reconfiguring the value chain. Lexus decided it could offer comparable performance to Mercedes and BMW through superior designs and manufacturing skills. Savin attempted to equal Xerox's service, not by duplicating its service network, but by offering modular designs that were much easier to repair or replace on the spot.

Similarly, low costs may be achieved in a number of ways. Two important drivers of costs are economies of scale and experience curve effects. Still, a new firm may achieve lower costs because it has a more modern plant, a design that is easier to manufacture, better manufacturing practices, or low input costs (e.g., raw materials, power, or labor).

Analysis of competitive strengths and weaknesses is not easy. Like other people, managers usually find it difficult to be objective about what their firm is good at and what it is not. Pride attributes strengths to areas that have only average capabilities. Strengths in one area can falsely suggest strength in other areas. Similarly, a company's reputation does not carry over as much as many managers are prone to believe.

In determining strengths, one might look at the company's standing in its industry. Past successes and failures can be examined. Customers, intermediaries, and suppliers can be surveyed. It is also possible to poll the sales force. Much of this analysis can be centered on the components of the value chain.

FIGURE 4–2 A generic value chain.

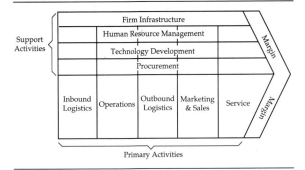

Source: *Porter (1985, p. 37).*

Viability of the offer   Management needs sufficient evidence that there is a need for the product being proposed. With new technologies, customers may not recognize all benefits of the product and may be reluctant to deal with a new technology. In this case, traditional concept tests may be misleading. For example, traditional marketing research techniques might have shown that people did not want electric refrigerators when they were first introduced. Furthermore, potential customers may not have recognized the convenience of once-a-week shopping. However, they would have been able to identify a large number of drawbacks of their current product. This latter approach would have suggested that a new product might be successful, but could not have foretold that electric refrigerators were the best solution.

Similarly, Polaroid came out with an instant movie camera, Polavision®, because Edwin Land believed consumers wanted to take moving pictures and see them quickly. As the success of camcorders demonstrated, the need was waiting to be filled, but Polavision® was not the solution.

When 3M developed Post-It notes, concept tests and test markets indicated that there was no interest. However, the people at 3M who used them became addicted. They attempted to duplicate this process in other companies by mailing free samples to the executive secretaries of Fortune 500 CEOs. As these examples indicate, product tests may be more appropriate than concept tests in some cases. Judging the viability of radical innovations is difficult. However, most innovations are more evolutionary.

People   The final criterion concerns the people in back of the project. Venture capitalists routinely put more weight on the people proposing a new venture than their financial forecasts. Peters and Waterman (1982) cite a number of examples of the importance of committed product champions; in a study of fifty new product introductions, Texas Instrument found that every failure lacked a volunteer champion; similarly, when GE studied twenty-four business initiatives, it found that fourteen of fifteen successes had a clear champion and six of the nine failures lacked one. Quinn (1979, p. 20) said "It was, in fact, difficult to find any successful major IBM innovation that derived directly from formal product planning rather than this championship process." People at 3M have joked that every project needs to get killed at least twice just to see if the people are committed.

Summary

A new product strategy is needed to focus on new product development (NPD) efforts. It gives management a way to influence the search for new products without carrying out the search personally. A new product strategy should specify objectives to set the scope of the task, directions on where to look for new products, and criteria by which they should be judged.

IDEA SEARCH

People need to continually look for improvements in current products as well as opportunities in new and related markets. The people searching for new product ideas should be familiar with the new product strategy. That way they will have an idea both about what management is looking for and how potential ideas will be judged.

Baker et al. (1967) found that 94 percent of the ideas generated in an R&D lab were in response to organizational needs, problems, or opportunities. Also, it appears that the ideas behind most successful new products start with communication about a need, which is followed by a search for technical possibilities to meet it (Utterback, 1974). However, idea generation is more complicated than this. Information is continually generated both in terms of what the market wants and what is technologically feasible, so the original source of a new product idea is often forgotten (see, e.g., DeBrentani, 1983). In many cases, it takes a trigger event, such as a visit by the president of a key customer, an invitation to be part of a jointly funded research project, or a competitive entry, for these ideas to come to light (Conway and McGuinness, 1986). Last, the initial search appears to be an individual task, but the idea must be refined through communication with other members of the firm.

Typically, people search for a product category before looking for a specific product. This occurs because search is usually problem or opportunity driven. Also, when new product ideas are generated from competitor and customer analysis connected with existing products, the product category becomes an implicit decision. However, sometimes, such as when searching for an application of a new technology, ideas are not necessarily restricted to certain product categories.

Most of this section focuses on product search in which the primary uncertainties are market oriented (Does the consumer want this product?) rather than technically oriented (Can this product be made?). Therefore, it covers determining what the customer wants or possible applications for a technological discovery rather than searching for the best technological solution to a problem of known demand.

Category Search

Category search usually involves secondary data; that is, data collected for some other purpose. Information can be gathered from annual reports, financial analyst reports, and the trade press. Additionally, several firms collect industry-specific data. Both A.C. Neilsen and IRI collect data on sales from grocery stores. IMS surveys physicians to collect information on prescriptions. Trendex surveys consumers on their purchases of major durables. Intelliquest and Yankee Group survey users of high-technology products. These data typically provide

information on such things as industry sales, sales by brand, and purchase price. Data from grocery stores also cover purchase quantity, which brands were being promoted, and which brands were stocked. Durable goods purchase data may also contain information on other brands owned, brands traded in or discarded, and satisfaction with previous brands.

Companies use these data to look for product categories that are growing rapidly, are currently profitable, and have only fragmented competition. Additionally, one should consider such things as whether growth in dollar sales is due to increasing units or prices, whether growth is coming from new or existing products, the relationship between product improvements and growth, the cost of new product introductions, and the new product mortality rate.

It is also possible to analyze social trends and think of industries that might be affected by them. Important trends might include such factors as the aging population, two-career families, single-parent families, concern with the environment, corporate delayering, and interest in the quality of purchases.

Informal Marketing Research

This includes less formal and more qualitative contact with intermediaries and customers. For example, salespeople, engineers, or manufacturing people can talk to customers about features they would like to see in a new product or problems they are having with products currently on the market. When he was working for the family garden supply store, Dick Duke learned of all the problems and unanswered questions that people had about lawn care. This knowledge, plus his knowledge of agricultural use of liquid fertilizers, led him to form ChemLawn (Nayak and Ketteringham, 1986).

Other companies come up with new products in a more systematic way, by hiring anthropologists to study people and the way that various products fit into their lives. Nissan has sent a team of anthropologists with a video camera to interview people in their homes and film their surroundings. A greater understanding of consumer life styles resulted in such things as a better-balanced trunk lid that could be opened and closed more easily by a person juggling children and groceries. Ichirou Suzuki, the chief engineer for the Lexus, spent weeks interviewing U.S. consumers, chatting about hobbies and values. Struck by how conservative they were, he decided to produce the LS 400's interior with a soft and comfortable feel (Woodruff et al., 1990).

Ohmae (1990) reports how one Japanese camera company analyzed 18,000 pictures to see why some pictures did not turn out very well. Common problems included poor focus and lack of light. In total they came up with more than 200 ideas for improvement, including a built-in flash and automatic focus.

User-generated innovation (where the end user provides both the need or problem and its solution, possibly in the form of drawings, prototypes, or finished products) is an important source of new product ideas in many industries. Von Hipple (1978) found that 82 percent of the major improvements and 70 percent of the minor improvements in four types of scientific instruments were made initially by customers. Similarly, in semiconductor and electronic sub-assembly process innovations, all major advances were user developed, as were 63 percent of the major improvements.

The power of informal marketing research was documented by Peters and Austin (1985, p. 25). General Electric sent one marketer and three engineers out to hold workshops on the premises of their principal customers for railroad locomotives. There they lined the walls of a room with butcher paper and drew up lists of desired features. Then they divided them into features that GE would try to provide and ones that the customer could do best. The products that resulted from this activity allowed GE to increase its position in the market from that of a distant second to a commanding number one between 1980 and 1984.

Some companies collect information primarily from "lead users," consumers who have certain needs in advance of the general market. In consumer goods these people would be thought of as fashion or trend setters. Because many automotive trends start in California, several car companies have located design studios there. In many computer applications, government, university, and industrial labs discover needed capabilities long before typical users. It may be possible to anticipate the market by locating lead users.

Von Hippel (1986) suggests a four-step process for locating lead users. First, one needs to identify important trends in the market. These could be societal, technological, or attitudinal. Then people or firms that are on the leading edge of these trends in terms of product needs and expected benefits are identified. Next these lead users' needs must be assessed. Finally, these solutions have to be projected back to the rest of the market.

Focus groups   Companies have found that focus group interviews with small groups of current or prospective customers can also be an important source of product ideas. In focus group interviews, several people (usually six to twelve) engage in an open, in-depth discussion which is led by a moderator. The moderator's job is to generate a nondirective, free-flowing discussion that is focused on experiences with the relevant product class and on problems related to purchasing and using the product. This allows complaints and desired features that are not easily uncovered by more structured methods to surface.

Discussions should start out wide and become narrower over time. After a round of self-introductions, the general area should be introduced.[1] The first question should deal with general problems and unmet needs with the

---

[1]See McQuarrie and McIntyre (1986).

product class. However, it should not be limited to the product; for example, the focus should be on oral hygiene rather than toothpaste. This can be followed up with more specific questions: What do you hate most about going to the dentist? What do you dislike most about brushing your teeth? What improvements do you wish they would make in toothpastes?

The group can also be asked things like (Langer, 1982):

1. What if the product category did not exist?

2. What are the current attitudes and behaviors of group members in the product category?

3. What product attributes and benefits do they want?

4. What are their dissatisfactions, problems, and unfilled needs?

5. What changes are occurring in their life styles that are relevant to the category?

After the groups have been probed for potential ideas, the company can present any new product ideas it has developed. The new product concept should be presented in a written statement. After any clarifying questions have been answered, the participants should be asked to evaluate the concept. After a general discussion of the concept, the moderator should probe for responses to certain features. Finally, the participants should be questioned about any modifications that might be made. For example, they can be asked (Goldberg, 1978):

1. What can be added or subtracted from the product or service?

2. Can there be more or less of some of the ingredients?

3. Can it be made bigger or smaller?

4. Can the elements be combined differently?

5. Can the flavor, form, packaging, or color be changed?

In many cases, focus groups are held in rooms with one-way mirrors, so managers can view the entire session. Moreover, most focus groups are videotaped and a complete transcription of the session is made. Additionally, the moderator provides an analysis of the focus group, including major themes, a number of verbatim responses, the moderator's interpretation of the interview, and specific new product ideas.

When running focus groups, it is often helpful to have groups that represent different market segments: heavy versus light users, physicians versus nurses, coaches versus players, foremen versus machine operators, and so on. Doing so often provides a wider range of attitudes, desires, and behaviors, since each group has common interests and perspectives which can vary greatly from those of other groups.

Focus groups can generate insights that are not possible through other methods. Additionally, they provide an opportunity to view real customers. Furthermore, focus group studies can usually be conducted more quickly and at less cost than quantitative studies. On the other hand, they are only as good as the skill of the moderator allows. There may be a greater tendency to remember only the parts that agree with previous notions ("Remember what the woman in the yellow dress said?"); however, selective perception is a problem with all research. The sample sizes are small and the respondents may be unrepresentative. Finally, the group may be unduly influenced by certain participants who are forceful or articulate. Still, when properly used, they can provide very useful input.

Formal Marketing Research

Attitude and usage surveys. Qualitative research should be supplemented by more formal quantitative surveys. One method is to use attitude and awareness surveys that deal with knowledge, satisfaction, problems, and purchase intentions for all (major) brands currently on the market. This information can be combined with demographic, psychographic, or purchase behavior information about the consumer to identify various market segments.

Attitude and awareness surveys usually contain the following types of information:

1. Aided and unaided awareness of major brands

2. Brands in the consideration set

3. Brands currently owned (for durables) or brands purchased last or most frequently (for frequently purchased goods)

4. Brands used in certain situations

5. The importance of product attributes

6. Ratings of each brand on important attributes

7. The likelihood of purchasing a brand in that category in the near future (for durables)

8. Purchase likelihood or expected purchase quantity for each brand.

These surveys can answer questions like the following. What brands, sizes, and/or models are purchased by various market segments? What brands are most consumers aware of? Who are the heavy purchasers, light purchasers, and nonpurchasers, and how do they differ in the way they purchase and use the product? In what contexts and in what manners are different products used? How satisfied is each class of user with the various products when each product is used in the different contexts? What activities are associated with the use of the different brands and models? Which brands and products are viewed as the safest, most effective, best value, and so on?

Survey responses to the above kinds of questions recorded across a number of time periods can help management to identify product opportunities. Furthermore, answers to these ques-

tions can be combined with changes in consumer demographics, attitudes, and life styles to predict new product opportunities.

Chapter 5 covers ways to display the results of attitude surveys and ways of learning what characteristics or features consumers most desire in certain products.

Quadrant analysis   Quadrant analysis can be performed either as part of an attitude and awareness survey or as a separate study. Here people are given a list of attributes and are asked which ones are most important or most desirable. Then they are asked to rate their satisfaction with their current brand on that attribute. When these responses are averaged over people for a brand, the results for that brand can be displayed as shown in Figure 4-3.

Those attributes in quadrant A are important to the respondent, and the respondent is quite satisfied with them. Quadrants B and C are for unimportant attributes, and D contains the attributes that the respondents feel are important, but with which they are not satisfied. One tries to find attributes or groups of attributes in Quadrant D that the company can provide.

FIGURE 4–3   A matrix for quadrant analysis.

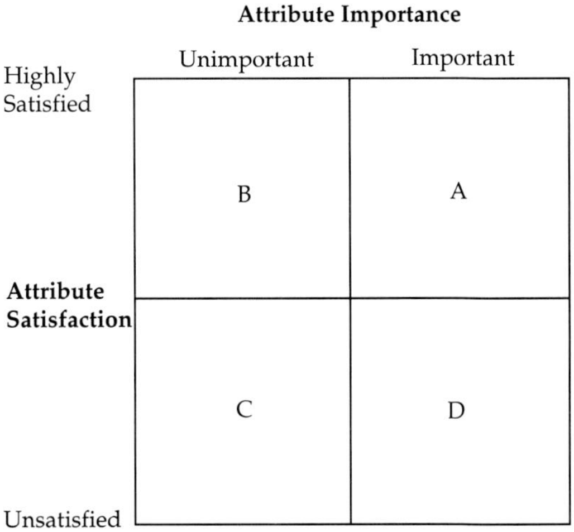

Problem detection studies A related approach is the problem detection study. It is based on the assumption that there is just as much to be gained by eliminating problems as by providing new benefits. Typically, small group interviews are used to generate a list of problems; however, it is possible to use past complaints or managerial insights for this purpose. If focus groups are used, the discussion should not be limited just to the product itself (shampoo), but should be expanded to include a general discussion of that part of a person's life (e.g., problems with hair).

Next, a larger-scale survey asks a different group of respondents how frequently each problem occurs and how big a problem it is when it does occur. Finding solutions to big problems that occur frequently can lead to successful new products.

Brand franchise extensions Tauber (1979) proposed the idea of brand franchise extensions as a way to develop new products in a new category from existing brand names. A two-step procedure is used to identify appropriate categories for an extension. First, a focus group is used to generate meanings and associations for the brand. This is done by probing for product features, benefits, uses, associations, and so on. For example, people might make the following associations with Minute Maid frozen orange juice: frozen, healthful, natural, liquid refreshment, orange flavor, and pure.

In the second identification step, consumers are asked to identify categories that are related to each association. For example, frozen might be associated with frozen vegetables, ice cream, and pizza, and liquid refreshment might be associated with soft drinks, milk, and beer. Then these product categories are evaluated along three dimensions: perceptual fit, competitive leverage, and benefit transfer. First, consumers are asked to evaluate how likely the following products would be: Minute Maid frozen peas, Minute Maid ice cream, and Minute Maid soft drinks. Then consumers name other brands in each category and evaluate the ways that Minute Maid would be better or not as good as those brands. Finally, they are asked if there are any benefits or advantages that the parent product has that might be transferred to the extension. These benefits might include tastier orange sherbet or orange soft drinks, healthier soft drinks, or other attributes.

Direct Customer Feedback

Many firms provide a channel for direct customer feedback. One important approach is a telephone-answering center that offers product information, hears complaints, and assists customers who need help with the company's products. G.E.'s Answering Center has handled more than 20 million calls since 1981. Its toll-free lines are served by more than 200 trained representatives and it operates twenty-four hours a day the year round. WordPerfect and some other software producers run similar services, as do many other firms.

When properly operated, these centers greatly improve customer relations and provide a wealth of useful information to product development and marketing personnel. The primary benefit of this information tends to be improvement of existing products rather than new ones. For example, in the early 1980s Sony modified some models of TVs so they would be easier to hook up to computers, GE modified their driers so owners could turn off the buzzer at the end of the drying cycle, and Procter and Gamble put high-altitude recipes on its Duncan Hines brownie mixes. The centers also provide an early detection system for product problems due to the failure of certain components, which could also lead to improved products.

Analysis of Competitive Products

One can also examine competitive products to decide what features to offer. This can be done with marketing research by asking customers what they like about competitive products or the company can do it. For example, Ford looked at forty cars in the same basic class as the Taurus and Sable when they were being designed. They found 400 features that they attempted to build into these new models (Waterman, 1987).

Similarly, when there is a technical question, many companies reverse engineer competitive products. Here, products are taken completely apart, parts lists are prepared, manufacturing techniques are guessed at, and costs are estimated. In the 1970s Xerox reverse-engineered Savin copiers and found them to be made with a much higher proportion of common parts than comparable Xerox machines. This allowed Savin to attain lower costs even though it did not have the volume that Xerox did. By reverse-engineering a number of cars, including Mercedes and Jaguar, Toyota decided that the Lexus could match them on performance and reliability. Many PC clone makers got started through a less rigorous form of reverse-engineering when they opened up an IBM PC and decided they could make something like that.

When analyzing competitors, it is imperative to keep the needs of the customer in mind. In discussing a consulting experience with a manufacturer of coffee makers, Ohmae (1990) noted that if it had focused on competitors it would have looked at existing features and would have proposed shortening the brewing cycle or cutting energy consumption. Instead the company asked why people drank coffee and what benefits they wanted. If good taste was the primary benefit, the company looked into what factors had the greatest influence on taste. The most important was water quality; another was the length of time between grinding the beans and brewing. This led to a coffee maker with a built-in dechlorinating function and a built-in grinder.

Technological Change

One can examine technological trends. For the last twenty years, the density of chips, in terms of number of transistors that can fit on their surface, has quadrupled every three years (Corcoran, 1991). Technological improvement allows one to do things that were not possible before. For example, graphical interfaces, voice and handwriting recognition, in microcomputers are becoming more feasible due to increased chip density. In the future, these developments will open new applications. Similarly, the invention of Aspertame® has allowed the creation of a number of good-tasting diet products. Some of these technological advances are made by the company itself.

Preproject Technical Work

New products can also be the direct result of the firm's R&D efforts. In many industries, 30 to 60 percent of all technical work is carried out prior to formal project initiation (Roberts and Fusfeld, 1981). Here, technical people are engaged in problem-solving work to advance their areas of specialization or to look for ways to solve certain consumer problems. For example, researchers at 3M came up with a synthetic nonwoven fabric. After failed efforts in disposable diapers and seamless cups for bras, it has found success as a material for surgical masks (Smith, 1980). Similarly, the adhesive that was later used in Post-It note pads was discovered by Spence Silver in the course of a four-year "Polymers for Adhesives" research program carried out in the 1960s (Nayak and Ketteringham, 1986).

Brainstorming and Introspection

This is the last section on idea search, not because it is least important, but because it should be performed after the previous steps have been carried out. In many cases, the best new product ideas do not come *directly* from customer, competitor, or technology analysis, but from careful and creative thinking about the implications of these data. Really new product ideas need to lead consumers, not just provide what they say they currently want. Still, this step needs to be based on a deep understanding of consumers, their desired benefits, pressing problems, reasons for using the product class, and new options that would really excite them.

Additionally, people can generate new product ideas by thinking about what they would like. The idea generator can get too close to the product to be objective, but many people and companies use the products they make and are capable of thinking about desired changes. Chester Carlson worked in a patent office and tired of the number of errors that occurred because documents could not be duplicated. His concern eventually led to the invention of plain paper copiers. Similarly, as an athlete and later as the track coach at the University of Oregon, Bill Bowerman saw the problems that poorly designed shoes gave athletes. Rejection of his designs by leading American sporting goods companies led him eventually to found Nike.

Brainstorming   In many cases a person will seek the help of others in solving certain problems. Brainstorming (Osborn, 1953) is used to increase the creativity of a group of people trying to generate a solution to a particular problem, such as applications for a new technology, product modifications, technical solutions to a problem, or product categories to consider for entry.

Most people have experienced a "Eureka" sensation when they have thought unsuccessfully about a solution to a problem for some time, but an answer comes when they are no longer consciously thinking about it. To increase the chances of this occurrence, a briefing document that defines the problem and includes relevant information should be disseminated to the participants a week or so in advance, so they can think about the problem before the session. However, people should not be given too much information on what has failed in the past, as it may inhibit creativity.

This briefing document might contain some exercises to enhance creativity or stimulate thoughts about the problem. IdeaScope provided brainstormers from a manufacturer of laundry detergent with an "experience kit." It contained samples of competitive products, a diary for recording their family's laundry activities, the address of a local laundry to visit, and a badly soiled shirt which had to be washed and worn to the brainstorming session (Mattimore, 1991). Many of the participants came to the session with a whole new perspective, in spite of the fact that they had spent ten years managing detergent brands.

In many cases a creative solution is based on a new combination of ideas that were already known. Consequently, brainstorming sessions should include people from diverse backgrounds in order to bring different perspectives to bear on the problem. This can be accomplished by including people from different functional areas within the company, but the group may also contain people from outside the company. Also, the assumptions about the problem and information given to the participants should be questioned to generate new perspectives.

In order for the group to benefit from different perspectives, each of the participants needs to be viewed as having something important to contribute. If people from different organizations are brought together the introductions should include reasons why everyone was selected. If people from different levels within the same company participate in the brainstorming session, it needs to be clear that all opinions are valued equally.

One of the biggest blocks to creativity is the fear of negative judgment, sometimes called the Voice Of Judgment, or VOJ (Ray and Meyers, 1986). In order to eliminate VOJ, not only does it have to be emphasized that no one can criticize anyone's ideas, but each person needs to feel free to express his or her ideas. In many cases, the biggest VOJ comes from within each person, who is afraid of what others think regardless of what they say. Also to reduce VOJ, participants are encouraged to come up with the wildest ideas possible, and quantity is valued over quality. Groups have used "superheroes" to reduce problems of VOJ (Mattimore, 1991). Some of the participants take on the role of such characters as Superman or Wonder Woman when making suggestions.

Some people feel that these sessions should be held off-site, not only to minimize interruptions, but also to get away from surroundings that indicate rank within the company. Others feel that tables should be round so that all seats are equally prominent. People should not sit next to their best friends, because their communication may indicate judgment and stop new perspectives.

A moderator is needed to prepare a problem statement and disseminate the relevant information, see that all ideas are viewed as valuable, and make sure that assumptions are challenged. Furthermore, the moderator usually has the job of recording the ideas and promoting cross-stimulation as much as possible.

In spite of all this effort, people may not be able to think creatively without some other stimulation. Therefore, several creativity tools may be incorporated into a brainstorming session. For example, one can use *attribute listing.* Here a product is broken down into its attributes. Then a subset of these attributes is chosen and each is changed in some way, but the rest of the product remains the same. For example, a tape recorder could be broken into power source, recording mechanism, playback mechanism, speaker, and case. Then one or more attributes can be selected and the group can think about how those attributes might be changed to improve the product. The Walkman was invented when the traditional speakers were replaced with headphones and the recording mechanism was deleted to save space. The same kind of changes to attributes that were suggested in focus groups can be used here (e.g., can it be made bigger or smaller, something added or subtracted, can the ingredients be changed?).

A related technique is *morphological analysis.* Here, all the variations of each attribute are generated, then all combinations are considered. For example, in the case of tape recorders, there are several possible power sources: solar, batteries, and AC power. Similarly, different speaker forms include built-in speaker, detachable speakers, and headphones. Looking at these two attributes gives us nine possible combinations to examine. A solar-powered tape player with headphones might be useful to backpackers, but a tape player with detachable speakers may require too much power to be solar powered. Serious consideration of unlikely combinations may release a creative spark.

Another vehicle is a *creative vacation.* After people seem to wear out, the moderator can get them to put the problem out of their minds and think about something very different. For example, imagine the world's best meal. After several have been listed, one or more are discussed. After ten or fifteen minutes, the moderator returns the group to the original problem and uses seemingly unrelated comments about the vacation topic to explore the problem at hand. For example, "We talked about the contradiction between taste and being fat-free. How could we make a fat-free tape recorder?"

At the end of the session, the ideas are reviewed by one or more people. The best ideas at this stage can be subjected to additional analysis, like attribute listing, to see if further improvements can be found.

Summary

If a company wants new product ideas, it must emphasize the importance of new products, appropriately fund idea search, and reward good tries. Marketing research must be done, R&D must receive thoughtful direction and adequate funds, salespeople must be rewarded for their ideas, and engineers need to be put in the field to observe customer needs. These and related activities cost time and money. Furthermore, management must provide continuing interest and support.

ENCOURAGING PRODUCT CHAMPIONS

The section on new product strategy emphasized the importance of product champions or entrepreneurs. This finding is echoed by Schon (quoted in Maidique, 1980), who found "the new idea either finds a champion or dies . . . no ordinary involvement with a new idea provides the energy required to cope with the indifference and resistance that major technical change provokes." Similarly, Roberts and Fusfeld (1981) found that when few new product ideas are being proposed, many companies wrongly believe that it is the result of having too few idea generators. Usually, the problem is one of having too few product champions.

Much of the new product process is a team effort, but idea generation is individually motivated. Therefore, a company has to encourage individuals to search for new product ideas. In many cases, a general problem (e.g., declining market share or slow response to customers) or objective (e.g., increase the percentage of sales from new products by 30 percent) may be known. There are several ways of solving most problems or reaching most objectives. As a first step, one or more ideas must be generated. Although certain people may be assigned this task, everyone should be encouraged to search for new product ideas. For this to happen, people must have appropriate problem-solving skills and access to the required information (both technical and political). It is possible for the idea generator and product champion to be the same person, but they need not be. See Morrison (1988) for an interesting example.

Three important characteristics of a product champion are commitment, knowledge of the area, and leadership ability. Drucker (1979) said

"Whenever anything is being accomplished, it is being done, I have observed, by a monomaniac with a mission." Quinn (1985) characterizes many successful entrepreneurs as "experts and fanatics." In his study of technological innovations, he found innovators were "tinkers" who had a good feel for what was possible. On the other hand, Kanter (1982) said that innovating middle managers did not seem to be particularly unusual except that they shared the following traits: comfort with change, clarity of direction and a long-term focus, thoroughness, good organizational insights, participative management style, persuasiveness, persistence, and discretion.

Some companies are able to produce a much greater number of product champions than others. To do this, people must be given confidence, they must be provided with access to support (they need to know to whom to talk), they must have the interpersonal skills to get others to join them, and they must be provided with a sense that it will all be worthwhile.

Potential innovators must know what problems are important to the organization. One way of providing this information is through the planning process. Several people who have studied innovative companies (e.g., Kanter, 1982; Peters and Austin, 1987; and Quinn, 1986) agree that strategic planning should provide general goals, broad long-term actions, and flexible programs. Top management should control most of the funding, require that the money spent produce meaningful results, and balance centralization and decentralization.

Innovative companies are convinced of the need to innovate and let their people know that innovation is viewed as mainstream. One thing that keeps Apple innovating is the recognition of IBM's market power. Stories about people who have produced successful innovations should be an important part of a company's culture.

Companies that are innovative are overwhelmingly marketing oriented, not in terms of large advertising and sales promotion budgets, but in terms of being genuinely interested in their customers and their problems. Innovative companies are much more proactive in searching out problems with their current products.

Important cross-functional communication can be fostered by lateral job rotations, company training programs, and smaller organizational units. There is some disagreement about whether entrepreneurs should be rewarded as well as they would be on the outside, but there is unanimous agreement that people should not be punished for good efforts. Finally, a pool of uncommitted funds should be available to keep promising ideas alive. In this way a single "yes" can get a project started, but a single "no" cannot kill it.

A key player who helps the product champion is the sponsor or executive champion (Maidique, 1978; Roberts and Fusfeld, 1981). Such a person has been through the process before, probably several times, and understands the risks and rewards. In some form, the role of the sponsor should extend all the way up the management hierarchy. Sponsors should be comfortable with change and familiar enough with the products and technology to be able to make intelligent trade-offs. Like the role of

champion, the role of a sponsor needs to be a volunteer role; it cannot be formalized or legislated. One of management's jobs is to encourage people to take this role and not punish people who sponsor potentially productive but losing causes.

The sponsor's role is demanding. Sponsors must spend time with champions. They may have to listen to a large number of ideas to see which deserve support, help shape these ideas into workable concepts, and run interference for the sponsored projects. Effective sponsorship deserves special recognition.

CONCLUDING REMARKS

A company's new product program can be no better than the quality of ideas generated. To get good new product ideas, the company needs a new product strategy to indicate where to look for new products and what criteria should be used to judge them. Then it has to conduct a thorough search process. It has to encourage product champions to generate new product ideas and step forward to push them through the rest of the development process.

REFERENCES

Ansoff, Igor H.: *Corporate Strategy*, New York: McGraw-Hill, 1965.

_____ and John M. Stewart: "Strategies for a Technology-Based Business," *Harvard Business Review*, November/December 45 (6), 1967, 71–83.

Baker , Norman R., Jack Seigman, and Albert H. Rubenstein: "The effects of perceived needs and means on the generation of ideas for industrial research and development projects," *IEEE Transactions on Engineering Management*, EM-14, December 1967, 156–163.

Biggadike, Ralph: "The Risky Business of Diversification," *Harvard Business Review*, 57, May 1979,

Booz-Allen and Hamilton, Inc.: *New Product Management for the 1980s*, New York: Booz-Allen and Hamilton, Inc., 1982.

Conway, H. Allan, and Norman W. McGuinness: "Idea Generation in Technology-Based Firms," *Journal of Product Innovation Management*, 3 (4), 1986, 276–291.

Corcorn, Elizabeth: "A Chip-making Plan to Leapfrog Japan," *Scientific American*, July 1991, 110.

Crawford, C. Merle: "Defining the Charter for Product Innovation," *Sloan Management Review*, Fall 1980, 3–12.

_____: "Protocol: New Tool for Product Innovation," *Journal of Product Innovation Management*, 1 (2), 1984, 85–91.

Day, George S.: "A Strategic Perspective on Product Planning," *Journal of Contemporary Business*, Spring 1975, 1–34.

Dumaine, Brian: "Closing the Innovation Gap," *Fortune*, December 2, 1991, 56–62.

Goldberg, Alice: "The Generation and Screening of New Product Ideas," talk presented at A.N.A. Workshop on New Product Marketing, November 8, 1978.

Johnson, Samuel C., and Conrad Jones: "How to Organize for New Products," *Harvard Business Review*, May/June 35 (3), 1957, 49–62.

Kearney, A. T., Inc.: "Analyzing New Product Risk," *Marketing for Sales Executives*, New York: The Research Institute of America, 1974.

Kuzmarski, Thomas D.: *Managing New Products: Competing Through Excellence*, Englewood Cliffs, N.J.: Prentice-Hall, 1988.

Langer, Judith: "When Using Qualitative Research to Generate New Product Ideas, Ask These Five Questions," *Marketing News*, May 14, 1982, 15.

Levitt, Theodore: "Marketing Myopia," *Harvard Business Review*, July/August 38 (4), 1960, 45-56.

Maidique, Modesto A.: "Entrepreneurs, Champions, and Technological Innovation," *Sloan Management Review*, Winter 1980, 59–76.

_____ and Robert H. Hayes: "The Art of High Technology Management," *Sloan Management Review*, Winter 1984, 17–31.

_____ and Peter Patch: "Corporate Strategy and Technology Policy," Harvard Business School Case 9-679-033, 1978.

Magaziner, Ira C., and Mark Patinkin: *The Silent War: Inside the Global Business Battles Shaping America's Future*, New York: Random House, 1989.

Mattimore, Bryan W.: "Brain-Stormers' Boot Camp," *Success*, October 1991, 60–61.

McQuarrie, Edward F., and Shelby H. McIntyre: "Focus Groups and the Development of New Products by Technologically Driven Companies: Some Guidelines," *Journal of Product Innovation Management*, 3, March 1986, 40–48.

Meyer, Marc H., and Edward B. Roberts: "New Product Strategy in Small Technology-Based Firms," *Management Science*, 32 (7), 1986, 806–821.

Morrison, Elting: "Gunfire at Sea: A Case Study of Innovation," in *Readings in the Management of Innovation*, 2d ed., Michael L. Tushman and William L. Moore (eds.), Cambridge, Mass.: Ballinger Publishing Company, 1988.

Myers, Stewart C.: "Finance Theory and Financial Strategy," *Interfaces*, 14, January–February 1984, 126–137.

Nayak, P. Ranganath, and John M. Ketteringham: *Breakthroughs!* New York: Rawson Associates; 1986.

Ohmae, Kenichi: *The Borderless World: Power and Strategy in the Interlinked Economy*, New York: HarperBusiness, 1990.

Osborn, Alex: *Applied Imagination*, New York: Charles Scribner's Sons, 1953.

Pavia, Teresa M.: "Product Growth Strategies in Young High-Technology Firms," *Journal of Product Innovation Management*, 7, December 1990.

Pessemier, Edgar A.: *Product Management: Strategy and Organization*, 2d ed., New York: John Wiley; reprinted by Robert E. Krieger Publishing Co. Inc., Malabar, FL, 1988.

Peters, Thomas J., and Nancy Austin: *Passion for Excellence*, New York: Random House, 1985.

_____ and Robert H. Waterman, Jr.: *In Search of Excellence: Lessons from America's Best-Run Companies*, New York: Harper and Row, 1982.

Porter, Michael E.: *Competitive Strategy: Techniques for Analyzing Industries and Competitors*, New York: Free Press, 1980.

_____: *Competitive Advantage: Creating and Sustaining Superior Performance*, New York: Free Press, 1985.

Quinn, James Brian: "Technological Innovation, Entrepreneurship, and Strategy," *Sloan Management Review*, Spring 1979,

Ray, Michael, and Rochelle Myers: *Creativity in Business*, Garden City, New York: Doubleday & Co., 1986.

Roberts, Edward B.: Generating Effective Corporate Innovation," *Technology Review*, October/November 1977, 33.

_____ and Alan R. Fusfeld: "Staffing the Innovative Technology-Based Organization," *Sloan Management Review*, Spring 1981, 19–34.

Rosenbloom, Richard S., and Michael A. Cusumano: "Technological Pioneering and Competitive Advantage: The Birth of the VCR Industry," *California Management Review*, 29 (4), 1987, 51–76.

Rumelt, Richard: *Strategy, Structure, and Economic Performance*, Boston, Mass.: Division of Research, Harvard Business School, 1974.

Smith, Lee: The Lures and Limits of Innovation," Fortune, October 20, 1980, 84–94.

Tauber, Edward M.: "Brand Franchise Extension: New Products from Existing Brand Names," in *How to Develop and Market New Products Better and Faster*, David Hoo (ed.), New York: Association of National Advertisers, 1985, 152–161.

Tull, Donald S.: "The Relationship of Actual and Predicted Sales and Profits in new product Introductions," *Journal of Business*, 40 (3), 1967, 233–250.

Utterback, James M.: "Innovation in Industry and the Diffusion of Technology," *Science*, 183, February 1974, 658–662.

von Hippel, Eric: "Successful Industrial Products from Customer Ideas," *Journal of Marketing*, January 1978, 39–49.

_____: "Lead Users: A Source of Novel New Product Concepts," *Management Science*, 32, July 1986, 791–805.

Woodruff, David, Karen Lowery Miller, Larry Armstrong, and Thane Peterson: "A New Era for Auto Quality," *Business Week*, October 22, 1990, 84–96.

REVIEW QUESTIONS

Q4-1 Discuss the problem of effectively searching for product opportunities. Distinguish between technologically based opportunities and opportunities produced by idea search.

Q4-2 Should a company have a new product strategy? Is it likely to miss out on some opportunities because of the constraints caused by the new product strategy?

Q4-3 Are there times when a company should not look for new product opportunities close to home?

Q4-4 Discuss the risk-reward profile of each cell in Figure 4-1.

Q4-5 Should companies use financial criteria to judge new product opportunities at an early stage? What if the judgment based on financial criteria differs from other assessments?

Q4-6 What action should be taken if the product champion believes there is a real need for a product, but early consumer tests indicate no need?

Q4-7 Discuss the trade-offs between getting lots of people to submit new product ideas and the company's need to remain relatively focused in its product-market scope.

5

DESIGNING THE OFFER

The purpose of this chapter is to discuss two marketing research techniques. These methods—perceptual mapping and conjoint analysis—are used to find product and service opportunities, as well as to specify the product or service's features, price, and communications message.

Perceptual mapping (PM), including multidimensional scaling (MDS), and the related joint space analysis is covered first. The primary purpose of PM is to understand the market and the competition as they currently exist. It is typically used during the idea search phase, which was discussed in the last chapter. PM can suggest changes that the company might make, but it may be better to test the effect of these changes either through traditional marketing research techniques such as concept testing, product testing, and test marketing, or through conjoint analysis.

The second major topic is conjoint analysis. In conjoint analysis, consumers are asked to react to a number of hypothetical concepts, or product (or service) descriptions. This information is used to determine which concepts different segments would like best and whether a new concept is preferred over descriptions of products that are currently on the market. It is also used to determine the importance of various attributes, including price.

THE PROCESS OF DESIGNING THE OFFER

Once a positioning has been determined, it is generally desirable to develop the rest of the offer before addressing the marketing support elements. Since design, price, and communications message are so closely related to one another, decisions about each must be made either simultaneously or with full allowance given to prior decisions about any of the other components. Together, the elements of the product or service, price, and communications message determine preferences for the brand among consumers and, indirectly, among resellers.

Since it is very difficult to make all the decisions about a marketing plan simultaneously, decisions about the offer and the marketing support are somewhat uncoupled. After the offer is relatively well defined, the supporting marketing activities are developed and the budget is prepared. Although this procedure means that product design, price, and message content are usually developed first, one must remember that the marketing plan needs to be a carefully integrated whole.

JOINT SPACE ANALYSIS OF THE OFFER

Perceptual mapping has been a popular way to represent what people believe about choice objects. These "objects" can be brands in a product class, services, people—such as candidates for office—or ideas. (The term "brands" will usually be used when referring to any of these objects.) All perceptual mapping methods yield a spatial representation of how individuals perceive the various brands. In a perceptual space, brands that are perceived to be similar are located close to each other and brands that are perceived to be dissimilar are further apart. A joint space displays both brand perceptions and consumer preferences in a single map. Stated differently, a joint space or market map contains representations of both brands and people.

Joint space studies attempt to answer three questions that are of considerable importance in the design of new products and the improvement of existing products (Johnson, 1971):

1. How are the various brands in the market perceived by consumers?

2. What do consumers want and how satisfied are they with what is currently being offered to them?

3. How can these findings be integrated strategically; that is, how can one determine the

greatest opportunities for new brands or the best way to modify an existing product?

Interpretation

Perceptual spaces The basic concepts of perceptual spaces are illustrated in Figure 5-1. The brands are shown as points on a map spanned, or defined, by two (or more) dimensions. These dimensions usually appear at right angles to each other and represent distinct general properties of the brands. The similarity between brands is inversely proportional to the distance between them. For example, in this market Miller Lite and Coors Light are perceived to be more like each other than either is to Budweiser.

If the dimensions of the space have been interpreted, it is possible to infer the rationale behind these perceptual judgments. Here, the first, or horizontal, axis is labeled Premium-Budget and the second, or vertical, axis is labeled Heavy-Light. The location of a brand relative to each axis indicates whether it is perceived to be more of a premium or budget beer

FIGURE 5-1 Perceptual map of a beer market.

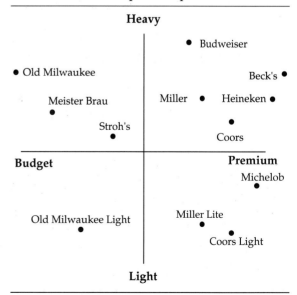

and whether it is perceived to be heavier or lighter than average. For example, Beck's and Heineken are both perceived to be premium beers, as they lie to the right of the origin (center of the space), and Meister Brau is viewed as a budget beer. Also, Michelob is perceived to be a lighter beer and Budweiser is perceived to be heavier. Old Milwaukee and Meister Brau are perceived to be similar because both are heavier budget beers. They differ from Miller more in terms of the premium-budget dimension than they do on the lightness-heaviness dimension.

Joint spaces   Joint spaces are constructed from perceptual spaces by including some measure of preference or likelihood of purchase in the space. This can be done by using either ideal points or preference vectors. In Figure 5-2, preferences are represented by ideal points.

An ideal point represents a consumer's ideal, or most preferred combination of the attributes defining the space. People are assumed to prefer

brands that are located closer to their ideal points over those that are located further away. In this particular example, these are segment ideal points that represent the swarm of the ideal points of the people in that segment. The people in the first segment judge a heavier fairly premium beer to be ideal and one would expect them to like Budweiser and Miller best and Old Milwaukee Light least. The people in the second segment prefer a light fairly premium beer and probably like Michelob, Coors Light, and Miller Lite best.

A second way of representing a consumer's preferences is with a preference vector, which is a vector passing through the origin indicating a direction of increasing preference. Vector representations of preference imply that preference continually increases with movement in the direction implied by the vector; that is, that person wants as much as possible of those attributes. Preference for an individual brand can be related to a preference vector by drawing a line from that brand's location to the vector in such a way that the line is perpendicular to the vector. The point at which this line intersects the preference vector is called that brand's "projection" onto that vector. Brands that project closer to the head (arrow end) of the vector are assumed to be more preferred than those projecting closer to the tail. This is illustrated with the preference vector for one hypothetical person in Figure 5-3.

The projections onto this vector can be drawn to aid the interpretation. Old Milwaukee projects furthest out in a positive direction, so it is the most preferred, and Michelob projects furthest in a negative direction, so it is the least preferred. This preference vector implies that the person's preference for a brand is increased by making it less expensive and/or heavier; that is, moving it in a northwest direction. Because this preference vector lies closer to the horizontal than the vertical axis, price is more important than heaviness in determining preference.

FIGURE 5-2   Ideal point joint space.

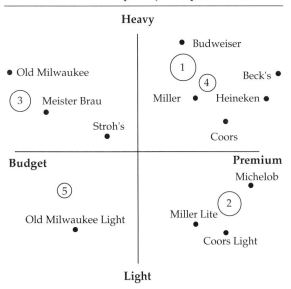

FIGURE 5-3   Vector joint space.

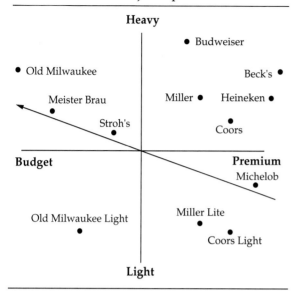

Summary   Joint spaces provide a lot of important information; furthermore, the visual format makes it much easier to digest the essential features of a market than if the same information were presented in tabular form. The locations of the brands in the joint space show how the various brands are perceived, both in terms of similarity to other brands and in terms of possession of the general attributes represented by the axes. This perceptual mapping is important because choices are based on perceptions rather than objective product specifications.

Longitudinal analyses conducted at regular intervals over the product life cycle can help reveal how perceptions and preferences change over time. As consumers gain experience with a product class, one would expect that not only would the image of some of the brands change, but that the perceptual variability of most brands would also tend to decrease. Similarly, the dimensions that best differentiate the brands and the most desired characteristics would probably change. Furthermore, these studies can also monitor the effect that specific changes in the product, service, or communication program have on brand images and on market shares. (See Moore and Winer, 1987, for an example.)

Second, complete joint spaces show how well the various customers are satisfied (how close each ideal point is to any brands or where each brand projects onto each of the preference vectors). These locations also indicate how well each brand is positioned relative to the competition. Many joint space models also provide a measure of the relative importance of the dimensions (general attributes) to a person or segment in determining brand preferences.

In most cases, managers are more interested in the behavior of market segments than in individual buyers. If it is possible to cluster people into homogeneous segments with respect to brand purchases, brand preferences, or desired product benefits, ideal points can be developed for each segment. In this case, the perceptions and predicted market behavior of each segment can be examined. As a final step, one can determine how these segments differ in terms of background variables. See Ginter and Pessemier (1978) for an example of this type of analysis.

These spaces also give some information on how the sales of existing brands can be improved and how new products could be positioned to maximize sales. Sales of an existing brand can be improved in a number of ways (see, for example, Boyd, Ray, and Strong, 1973).

1. One can attempt to change the perception of a brand and reposition it closer to one or more ideal points and away from the competition. Usually, changing perceptions requires a change in the physical product or associated services, but in some cases, it may be accomplished by emphasizing different attributes in promotions. For example, the makers of Coors might try to reposition the brand so it is perceived to be heavier in order to attract more business from segments one and three.

2. One can attempt to move people's ideal points closer to the brand—educate them to prefer a different level of a given attribute than they currently do. For example, Coors might encourage people to drink a lighter beer.

3. If a brand is favorably positioned with respect to one or more attributes, an effort can be made to increase the importance of those attributes when forming preferences. For a particularly safe vehicle, it could be advantageous to emphasize the importance of safety.

4. Sales might be improved by introducing attributes not currently represented in the space into the evaluation process. For beer, a seller might introduce beechwood aging, fire brewing, or the inclusion of a new ingredient.

A joint space can also indicate the most appropriate ways to position new entries. For example, a new brand can be introduced into areas that have ideal points but few brands (such as around the fifth ideal point) or it can be introduced close to competitive brands in order to disrupt their activities.

However, it is not possible to study the effect of changing variables on which the brands do not currently differ with joint space analysis. For example it is not possible to infer the preference for a nonalcoholic beer from the joint spaces in this illustration, because all the beers contain alcohol.

These joint spaces can be produced either with some special software or with standard multivariate statistical packages, such as SAS, BMDP, SYSTAT and SPSSX, that have both discriminant analysis and regression subroutines.

Perceptual Space Construction

This section deals with two issues that are related to the construction of perceptual spaces.

They are the method of building the space and the determination of which brands and attributes should be included in the space. The solution of these issues requires the assistance of marketing researchers, managers, R&D personnel, customers, and possibly research suppliers.

Composition and decomposition methods of constructing perceptual spaces There are two general methods of constructing perceptual spaces: *decomposition* and *composition*. Decomposition or similarity scaling methods require the rated similarity of each pair of brands (or at least many of the pairs). These ratings can be obtained by presenting a respondent with a suitable set of brand pairs and asking the respondent to rate the similarity of each pair on a one to nine scale, where one means very similar and nine means very dissimilar. If the respondents' perceptions are assumed to be homogeneous, it is possible to have different people rate different subsets of the pairs. These judgments of overall similarity can be used to estimate the distances between brands in a space of two or more dimensions. Any of a number of MDS programs will perform this decomposition (Green, Carmone, and Smith, 1989; Green and Rao, 1972; Smith, 1988).

The above method of constructing perceptual maps is favored by a number of researchers because it is useful in exploratory work, where the most important attributes are not known or cannot be easily expressed verbally. On the other hand, it suffers from two drawbacks. First, the respondent must be familiar with a relatively large number of brands to provide enough information to obtain a map in two or more dimensions. Second, the interpretation of the dimensions must be made either on the basis of managerial judgment or by collecting additional information about the attributes that each of the brands is perceived to possess. (In the example of brands of beer, a researcher would need to ask the respondents to rate each of the brands on a number of attributes, such as body, flavor, mildness, and popularity.) Unfortunately, a manager's judgments may be quite different from those of consumers, and additional data collection can be costly.

In the composition approach, consumers must rate each of the brands on a number of attributes, usually using a five- to ten-point scale. For example, a beer-drinking respondent might be asked to rate each beer on popularity, where one means extremely unpopular with my friends and ten means very popular with my friends. This task is the same as one might use to gather the information to interpret a decompositional space, so less data in total are required. With these data, it is possible to locate the brands in a space that has one dimension for each attribute, but doing so can result in far too many dimensions. Therefore, a method of reducing the spatial dimensions is normally employed to combine related attributes into a smaller number of more general dimensions. This can be done with either discriminant analysis or principal components analysis, but for a number of reasons discriminant analysis is preferable.

It is also possible to collect contingency data—data that indicate only whether a brand possesses an attribute or not instead of requiring a rating on that attribute. For example, a respondent can be asked to check each car that gets good gas mileage or each beer that is full bodied. The obvious benefit of this response mode is the speed of data collection and the ability to collect data over the telephone. If such data are collected, they can be analyzed with correspondence analysis (Hoffman and Franke, 1986; Smith, 1988). A brief illustration of the technique appears later in this section.

Determining the appropriate brands and attributes Regardless of the method a researcher uses to construct a space, a decision must be made about the brands to be included in the study. In general, the boundaries of the competitive set are a function of the objectives of the study. More strategically oriented studies generally require broader definitions of the competitive set (and more brands). Given the analysis set of brands, a researcher must decide which attributes should be used to produce the space. Mistakes about the brand and attribute sets are serious since they cannot be corrected without redoing the entire study. Within reason, it is better to err on the side of including too many brands and attributes than omitting a critical one.

Two criteria should be considered when choosing the brands of the space. They should be relatively familiar to most of the respondents and they should collectively span the range of possible attribute values in the choice set. For example, if one were studying the entire automobile market, both large and small cars would need to be included, as would expensive and inexpensive and foreign and domestic cars. On the other hand, if the researcher wanted to study perceptions of compact cars, the brands chosen would have to span the range of possible values for compact cars. In many cases the competitive set has a big influence on the resulting perceptual dimensions. Size may be one of the most important ways that people differentiate automobiles, but if only compact cars are considered, size differences may appear to be unimportant.

In many cases, competition will not be contained in a well-defined product category, so the brands included in a study do not need to come from the same product class (Day, Shocker, and Srivastava, 1979). For example, one could include juices, milk, soft drinks, coffee, tea, beer, wine, and mixed drinks as possible beverage accompaniments to a meal. The objectives of a study have a major impact on how widely competition should be considered (in some cases a business trip, phone call, and letter may compete with each other), but there is also the need to look at what consumers view as competing alternatives. Consumers need to be questioned about what they would use in certain situations or how they would solve certain problems.

The attributes included in a study should be determinant; that is, they should both be related to preference (relative value) and differ across brands. The color of a soft drink can is a possible attribute, but if few people consider it when choosing among brands of soft drinks, it should not be included. Similarly, although safety is a primary concern in air travel, if most airlines are perceived to be about equally safe, this attribute should not be included either. There is some debate over whether the list of attributes should consist only of cognitive attributes (believing) or whether affective attributes (liking) should also be included. Preferences generally should not be included when developing a perceptual map since this space will be used to determine what attributes are associated with preference. However, affective attributes such as rich flavor, mature style, and flattering appearance influence preference and should be included. Furthermore, attributes such as price and value for the money provide much information and can also be included.

A number of methods can be used to elicit both the set of brands and attributes. First, managers should be questioned about important competitive brands and the attributes that they think influence preferences and choices. These individuals know the market, and their involvement increases the probability that the results of the research will be utilized. Second, consumers can be polled in a number of semistructured ways, using either focus groups or individual interviews. Brand names can be elicited through aided and unaided recall questions and consumers can be asked what brands or general products they would consider using in certain situations. Attributes can be generated by directly asking what the respondent considers to be important when making purchase or consumption decisions. Alternatively, consumers can be presented with a series of brand pairs and be asked to describe how the brands are similar and different (and/or which they would choose and why), or they can be given brand triples and asked which two are most similar and why and how these brands differ from the

FIGURE 5-4 Abbreviated questionnaire example.

1. Circle the number that best represents your perception of the GAS MILEAGE of each of the following brands.

	Very Low Gas Mileage							Very High Gas Mileage
Ford Escort	1	2	3	4	5	6	7	8	9
Buick Riviera	1	2	3	4	5	6	7	8	9
Nissan Sentra	1	2	3	4	5	6	7	8	9

2. Circle the number that best represents your feelings about the PRICE of each of the following brands.

	Very Inexpensive							Very Expensive
Ford Escort	1	2	3	4	5	6	7	8	9
Buick Riviera	1	2	3	4	5	6	7	8	9
Nissan Sentra	1	2	3	4	5	6	7	8	9

third brand. Finally, consumers can be asked what their favorite brand is and why. Do they choose other brands sometimes; if so, why, and so on.

The resulting lists, which may contain thirty brands and 100 attributes, usually need to be reduced. Obviously, managerial judgment is needed about the appropriate competitive set and which attributes are important and different. It is also possible to let a small group of consumers (say, fifty) rate a number of brands on these attributes. These responses can then be analyzed with principal components to determine which attributes are really different and which are restatements of others.

Once the brands and attributes have been chosen, a questionnaire should be constructed. Figure 5-4 provides an example of what such a questionnaire might look like. A pretest should be performed to make sure that wording is appropriate.

Discriminant analysis The idea of discriminant analysis is best understood by first discussing the concept of an F ratio. An F ratio is the amount of between (or among) brand variance divided by the amount of within brand variance. For a single attribute, between brand variation is a measure of how much the average ratings of one brand differ from those of another brand. For example, looking only at the brands Ford Escort and Buick Riviera, if most people think a Ford Escort gets very good gas mileage and a Buick Riviera gets relatively poor gas mileage, there would be high between brand variation. On the other hand, if the average perceived gas mileage ratings of these two cars were quite similar, there would be little between brand variation.

Within brand variation refers to the amount of variation in the ratings of a particular brand on that attribute. It is a measure of the amount of the disagreement the respondents have concerning that brand's ratings on an attribute. If most people agree that a Ford Escort gets good gas mileage, there would be little within brand variation, but if some people think it gets good gas mileage and another sizable group thinks it gets poor mileage, there would be a large amount of within brand variation.

An F ratio for a given attribute will be *high* if:

1. Brands are perceived to differ on that attribute (i.e., high between brand variation), and

2. There is agreement on how much of that attribute each brand possesses (i.e., low within brand variation)

With a large F ratio it is easier to differentiate the brands on the basis of that attribute. If F ratios were computed for each attribute, the one with the highest F ratio would be the one on which the products differed most dramatically.

If two attributes measure related dimensions of a product, such as top speed (TS) and engine size (ES), it might be possible to do an even better job of differentiating among various brands by taking an average of these two measures. This would occur if some of the random errors cancel each other out so the average provides a better discrimination between brands.

$$D_1 = .5\, R_{TS} + .5\, R_{ES} \qquad (5\text{-}1)$$

where D_1 is the average rating and R_{TS} and R_{ES} are the respondent's ratings of an automobile on top speed and engine size.

Carrying this argument one step further, it might be better to form a weighted average of the two ratings where the attribute that is able to provide the greater discriminating power is weighted more heavily.

$$D_1 = d_{11}\, R_{TS} + d_{12}\, R_{ES} \qquad (5\text{-}2)$$

where D_1 is the weighted average of the ratings of top speed and engine size, d_{11} and d_{12} are the weights, and the other two variables are defined as in Equation (5-1).

This is the basic idea of discriminant analysis. It finds that weighted combination of all the attributes that best differentiates among the brands as measured by an F ratio. That is, it finds a linear combination (i.e., a weighted sum) of the attribute ratings such that the ratio of the among to within brand variance is a maximum. Again, this is a linear combination on which the average values of the brands differ most relative to the disagreement about each brand. It is the combination for which there is both minimum disagreement about each brand and the biggest difference across brands.

It should be noted that some, or all, of these weights can be negative. Engine size and gas mileage are typically negatively correlated (i.e., larger engines are usually associated with lower gas mileage). If they were both good discriminators, a linear combination would include one positive and one negative weight.

This best discriminating linear combination is called the first discriminant function. If there were m attributes it could be written as:

$$D_{1j} = \sum_{i=1}^{m} d_{1i} R_{ij} \qquad (5\text{-}3)$$

where D_{1j} is the value of the first discriminant function for the jth brand, d_{1i} is the weight assigned to the ith variable in the first discriminant function, and R_{ij} is the rating of the jth brand on the ith attribute.

Once this best discriminating linear combination of attributes is found, discriminant analysis finds the second best linear combination, subject to the constraint that it is unrelated (or uncorrelated) to the first linear combination:

$$D_{2j} = \sum_{i=1}^{m} d_{2i} R_{ij} \qquad (5\text{-}4)$$

where the terms are defined for the second discriminant function in a way that is analogous to the first function.

In the case of automobiles, the first linear combination might be primarily a function of gas mileage, top speed, engine size, and so on (i.e., the weights associated with these attributes would be the largest in absolute size). The second linear combination might be primarily a function of reliability, ability to maintain resale value, general quality, and so on.

Discriminant analysis continues to extract linear combinations, or dimensions, in this same fashion; that is, the next dimension chosen is the one with the maximum F ratio subject to the constraint that it is uncorrelated with each of the previous linear combinations. This process continues until the number of discriminant functions equals the number of attributes or one less than the number of brands, whichever is smaller. Once the discriminant functions have been extracted, the brands are located in the perceptual space by forming linear combinations of the average attribute ratings of each brand. For example, the location of the jth brand on the first dimension, X_{1j}, would be formed by:

$$X_{1j} = \sum_{i=1}^{m} d_{1i} \overline{R}_{ij} \qquad (5\text{-}5)$$

where X_{1j} is the location of the jth brand on the first dimension, d_{1i} is the weight of the ith attribute on the first dimension, and $\overline{R}_{ij}$ is the average rating of the jth brand on the ith attribute.

The weights in the discriminant functions can be used to interpret the dimensions. The dimensions are best characterized in terms of attributes that have relatively large (in absolute value) weights on that discriminant function.

Once the brands have been positioned in the space, attribute vectors (locations) can also be incorporated in the space to aid interpretation. There are several ways to do this. First, one can correlate each attribute with the linear combination that defines each dimension. These correlations serve as the coordinates of the heads of attribute vectors emanating from the origin. Second, this can be done using PROFIT, which is a property-fitting program (Green and Rao, 1972; Smith, 1988). Alternatively, it is possible to fit these attribute (or property) vectors by using a regression program. A different regression is run for each attribute. The dependent variable is the brand's average rating—that is, $\overline{R}_{ij}$ of Equation (5-5)—on the attribute that is being fitted into the space and the independent variables are the brand's coordinates on each of the dimensions of the space—i.e., the X_{kj}'s of Equation (5-5). Assuming there are two dimensions in the space, the following regression would be run for each of the attributes used to define the space:

$$\overline{R}_{ij} = \hat{a} + \hat{b}_1 X_{1j} + \hat{b}_2 X_{2j} + e_{ij} \qquad (5\text{-}6)$$

where $\overline{R}_{ij}$ is the average rating of the jth brand on the ith attribute, X_{1j} and X_{2j} are the coordinates of the jth brand on the first and second dimensions, $\hat{a}$, $\hat{b}_1$, and $\hat{b}_2$ are the estimated regression weights, and e_{ij} is an error term.

The two regression weights can be used to plot the direction cosines of the attribute vector in the perceptual space. The direction cosine (which measures the angle) of the attribute vector with the first axis, DC_1, is given by:

$$DC_1 = \hat{b}_1 / (\hat{b}_1{}^2 + \hat{b}_2{}^2)^{1/2} \qquad (5\text{-}7)$$

The direction cosine with the second dimension is found by transposing the dimension subscripts in Equation (5-7).

These concepts are illustrated in Figure 5-5, which shows the directions of the attribute vectors for thirteen of the attributes on which twelve brands were rated. The location of these vectors indicates that the first discriminant function had large positive weights on attributes such as premium, special occasions, dining out, and popular with both men and women; large negative weights on attributes like on a budget and good value. Attributes like pale color and full bodied had weights close to zero on the first discriminant function.

The second discriminant function had large positive weights on attributes whose vectors point almost straight up and large negative weights on those that point almost straight down. The closer a vector lies to an axis, the more it contributes to interpretation of that dimension.

When many of the vectors lie approximately midway between two of the axes, it is possible to alter the orientation of the discriminant functions. This rotation of the space will improve interpretation of the resulting map. When this step is taken, three or more discriminant functions may have important marketing meaning. In the case of automobiles, a final set of discriminant dimensions might be labeled: operating characteristics, maker or dealer reputation, value

FIGURE 5-5   Perceptual map of a beer market.

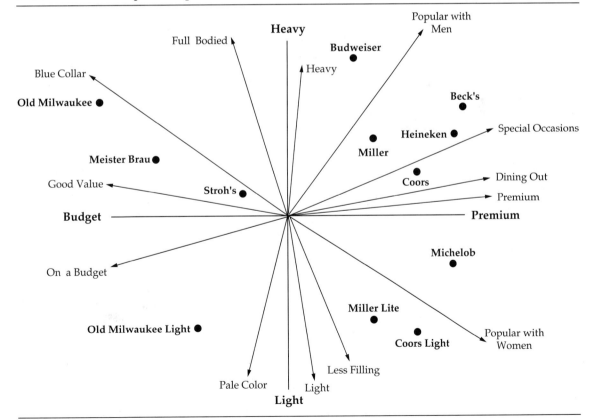

and economy, and pleasing appearance. The amount of detail in the final perceptual map will depend on the nature and variety of the analyzed brands and the richness of the set of attributes the respondents judged.

It is also possible to construct perceptual spaces using principal components or factor analysis. In this case, the dimensions would be defined in terms of linear combinations that maximize the sum of the within brand variance (disagreement about the brand) plus the among brand variance (differences across brands). Although maximizing explained variance is usually a good property, it does not seem logical that one would want a linear combination that maximized the within brand variance, since it is a measure of confusion. Furthermore, the discriminant analysis solution is usually less sensitive than principal components or factor analysis solutions to the addition or deletion of a few of the independent variables. See Pilon (1989) for an extended discussion of a number of issues regarding the construction of perceptual spaces with these techniques.

However, from a practical standpoint, the among brand variance is usually much larger than the within brand variance, so the two procedures give similar answers in many cases. Still, discriminant analysis seems to offer a conceptually superior approach.

Correspondence analysis Another way to construct perceptual spaces is by using correspondence analysis. This technique requires only contingency (yes/no) data and is thus much easier to collect. In the application of correspondence analysis to perceptual mapping, respondents would be questioned about which brands have certain features. For example, one might question people about which brands of beer are popular with men, popular with women, full bodied, and so on, or which brands of automobiles get good gas mileage, are of high quality, handle well, and so on.

The result is a contingency table of the associations between the *m* brands and the *r* features

(or attributes). The typical entry in the table gives the number of people who thought a certain brand possessed a specific attribute. Usually a second column is added for each attribute that indicates the number of people who thought a brand did not possess that attribute.[1] At this point the *m* brands can be located in an *r* dimensional attribute space where the location of a brand on any attribute dimension is equal to the number of people saying that brand possessed the attribute. Correspondingly, the *r* attributes can be represented in an *m* dimensional brand space where the location of an attribute on any brand dimension would be equal to the number of people who said that attribute was possessed by the brand.

Like discriminant analysis or principal components, the objective of correspondence analysis is to find a lower dimensional representation of these brands and attributes that retains as much information as possible.

The technical details and issues concerning the interpretation of distances are beyond the scope of this chapter, but here is a brief illustration. In the Harvard Business School case Vicks Health Care Division: Project Scorpio (A) (Williams and Yip, 1981), the results of an awareness and usage study were reported in which 761 people were asked which ingredients they believed were contained in five popular cold remedies. An interpretation of these results is given in Table 5-1.

Using the original numerical percentages, we can describe the five brands in a six-dimensional ingredient space by plotting each brand based on what percentage of the people think that brand has each ingredient. A two-dimensional representation of the brands and ingredients (which contains 98 percent of the information in Table 5-1) is given in Figure 5-6. This space con-

---

[1]If a subject does not say whether a product has or does not have an attribute, it indicates that the subject does not know if the brand has the attribute. The percentage of do not know responses for an attribute is a measure of perceptual confusion. This percentage should be examined both cross-sectionally and longitudinally.

TABLE 5-1   PERCEIVED INGREDIENTS IN SPECIFIC COLD REMEDIES

Brand	Total Aware*	Fever Reducer	Conjestion Reliever	Cough Reliever	Sneeze Reducer	Sleep Inducer	Ache/Pain Reliever
Comptrex	432	55%	75%	56%	52%	27%	63%
Contac	745	42	79	23	65	34	58
DayCare	486	40	70	72	48	13	57
Dristan	723	45	76	17	67	20	54
NyQuil	735	41	68	77	39	84	52

*Out of a base population of 761.

Source: *Vicks Health Care Division: Project Scorpio (A) HBS case 9-582-039, 1982.*

tains the locations of both the ingredients present and the ingredients not present (i.e., the location corresponding to not having a certain ingredient).

Several observations can be made about this space. The ingredients fever reducer, congestion reliever, and ingredients to relieve aches and pains are close to the origin, indicating that the brands are not perceived to differ much on those ingredients. The two best differentiating ingredients are ones to induce sleep (which only Nyquil has) and a cough suppressant (which are perceived to be contained in Nyquil, DayCare, and Comptrex). Additionally, both Dristan and Contac are perceived to be better at reducing sneezing than the other brands. Looking at the ingredients not present, DayCare is the least associated with ingredients to induce sleep. Dristan and Contac are least associated with relief of coughs. At the time of the survey, Comptrex was relatively new, so its image was not as clear as the others, and it is positioned closer to the origin than the others. [This particular analysis was performed with the CORAN program, which is part of Smith's (1988) PC-MDS software.]

Construction of Joint Spaces

Once a perceptual space has been constructed, there are two fundamentally different ways to represent preferences for the various brands: ideal points and preference vectors.

Information to place these preference measures in the space can be gathered in two ways: explicitly and implicitly. Consumers can be asked to explicitly state their most preferred level on each of the attributes. This information can be gathered in the same part of the questionnaire as the attribute data by labeling one of the brands as the ideal. Once the discriminant functions have been calculated (based only on the real brands), these most-preferred levels are inserted into the discriminant functions to locate the ideal brand just as the average brand ratings were inserted into the discriminant functions to locate the brands in the space. For example, after the discriminant function of Equation (5-5) has been calculated, the location of the ideal point on the first dimension, Y_1, is a function of the ratings of the ideal product on each of the m attributes, R_{i1}

$$Y_1 = \sum_{i=1}^{m} d_{1i} R_{i1} \qquad (5-8)$$

When an implicit procedure is used, consumers are asked to state their preference or likelihood of purchase for each of the brands they rated on the attributes. If the prices of the competing alternatives vary substantially, rating

FIGURE 5-6   Correspondence space perceptual map of the cold remedy market showing twelve defining attribute vectors.

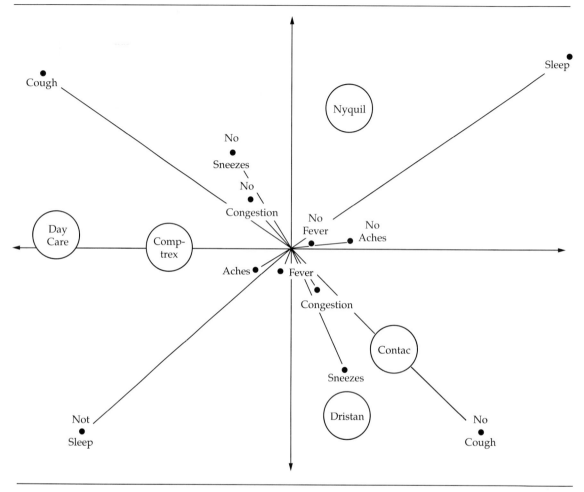

brands on the likelihood of purchase rather than preference should be considered. It is possible that lots of people who *prefer* Mercedes Benz automobiles are more likely to *purchase* Chevrolets. These preference values, P_j's can be used as the dependent variable in a regression with the brand locations, X_{1j} and X_{2j}, as the independent variables to produce either ideal points or preference vectors. PREFMAP (Carroll, 1972) is a computer program that will produce a joint space from these two sets of variables. It is also possible to do this analysis with a standard

regression program. This latter procedure will be discussed for the simplest of the PREFMAP ideal point models.

Ideal points   This formulation assumes that the squared distance between a brand and an ideal point is inversely related to preference for the brand. In the following example, it is assumed that preferences apply to a single person. However, it is possible to average the preference ratings of all of the people in a given segment to form an average ideal point for that segment. (Also, it is assumed that larger preference ratings indicate greater preference.)

The following equation models preference for a given brand as a linear function of the squared distance from the ideal point in a two-dimensional perceptual space:

$$P_j = \hat{a} - \hat{b}\, d_j^2 + e_j \qquad (5\text{-}9)$$

or

$$P_j = \hat{a} - \hat{b} \sum_{i=1}^{2} \left(Y_i - X_{ij}\right)^2 + e_j \qquad (5\text{-}10)$$

where P_j is the preference for the jth object, Y_1 and Y_2 are the coordinates of the ideal point which must be estimated, X_{1j} and X_{2j} are the coordinates of the jth brand, and $\hat{a}$ and $\hat{b}$ are regression weights to be estimated.

After some rearranging, Equation (5-10) can be rewritten as:

$$P_j = \hat{c} + \hat{B}_0 \left(\sum_{i=1}^{2} X_{ij}^2\right) + \hat{B}_1\, X_{1j} + \hat{B}_2\, X_{2j} + e_j \quad (5\text{-}11)$$

where $c = \hat{a} - \hat{b}\sum_{i=1}^{2} Y_i^2$, $\hat{B}_0 = -\hat{b}$, and $\hat{B}_i = 2\hat{b}Y_i$.

Therefore, the location of the ideal point on the ith dimension, Y_i, is given by:

$$Y_i = -\hat{B}_i / (2\hat{B}_0). \qquad (5\text{-}12)$$

Summarizing, it is possible to run a regression where P_j is the dependent variable and $X_{1j}^2 + X_{2j}^2$, X_{1j}, and X_{2j} are the three independent variables. The location of the ideal point is given by Equation (5-12). The number of observations in this regression is equal to the number of brands in the space. There are two more parameters (including the intercept) than there are dimensions in the space. If eight brands were scaled in a two-dimensional space, this ideal

point model of preference would require that four parameters be estimated from these eight observations.

Preference vectors   One can use the same procedure to locate a preference vector for this individual in the space by running a regression that is analogous to the property-fitting regression. The only difference is that a brand preference rating replaces the attribute rating. This is shown in the next equation:

$$P_j = \hat{B}_0 + \hat{B}_1\, X_{1j} + \hat{B}_2\, X_{2j} + e_j \qquad (5\text{-}13)$$

The direction cosines for the preference vector are found in the same manner as the direction cosines for the attribute vector in Equation (5-7). In this case, there is one more parameter to be estimated than dimensions in the space.

Prediction   Joint space models can be used to predict preferences and choices for a new brand or the change in preference for a brand that has been repositioned. Considering the case of ideal points, the first step is to locate the brand in the space. This is done by assessing (or forecasting) that brand's ratings on the various attributes and inserting those ratings into the appropriate discriminant functions [just as an explicitly rated ideal point was fit into the space using Equation (5-8)]. Then the preference for that brand is estimated by using its forecast location with Equation (5-11). The brand with the highest predicted preference rating is usually the one that is predicted to be chosen by that person or segment; however, it is also possible to make brand choice a probabilistic function of the preferences. (This will be discussed in the section on conjoint analysis.)

Similarly, if preference is modeled with a vector representation, the first step is to locate the brand in the joint space. Then its preference rating can be predicted using Equation (5-13). Again, usually the brand that projects farthest toward the head of the vector is the one that is predicted to be chosen, but a probabilistic function can also be used.

Designing for minimum cost   In a composition joint space, the position of an object on each component dimension is a linear function of the levels of the underlying attributes, principally those that lie close to each component dimension. See Equation (5-5). This means that more than one configuration of attribute levels (designs) can yield the *same* location, and there is more than one way to change the configuration (design) in order to move an object to *any* new location.

The above design freedom raises the question, "How can a desired perceptual location be attained at minimum cost?" If the causal link between attribute levels and perceptual positioning is clear and the cost of changing a judged level of each attribute is known, linear programming methods can be used to determine the minimum cost configuration of each location in the perceptual space.

Since a joint space allows one to forecast a product's sales for any position it might occupy in the perceptual space, it is possible to compute the maximum contribution to profit implied by each possible position. One does so by using the product's unit sales forecast, its unit price, and the unit cost of the most efficient design.

Although it is worthwhile recognizing the above positioning and design facts, the limitations of both the joint space model's predictive power and the absence of adequate cost data prevent the formal application of this approach in many cases. Nevertheless, managers should use the information provided by a composition joint space to favorably redesign and/or reposition an offer.

Summary   Each of these methods of representing preferences has certain strengths and weaknesses. When ideal points are explicitly rated, consumers tend to want the highest quality and the lowest price. Looking at Figure 5-4, we see that expensive is highly correlated

(closely related) with popular. If the person wants a very popular but inexpensive beer, the ideal point may be nearer to the center of the space than that person really wants. Also, with an explicit rating methodology, consumers tend to understate the importance of some attributes, such as product popularity or product status.

The practice of using preferences for existing products as an input to a regression program also has certain disadvantages. It is possible that a person does not like any of the products very much. The program will locate the subject's ideal point closest to the brand for which the person has the highest preference, even if it is not highly preferred. This regression also requires that quite a few brands be in the space for the regression weights to be estimated with much efficiency. Although many product classes appear to be better modeled by ideal points than by preference vectors, the vector model seems to give better preference predictions in many cases.

In either case, it is a good idea to validate the joint space either by comparing the brands that each person is forecast to choose with the brands that the person has recently chosen or by comparing the market shares predicted by the joint space with actual market shares.

Operational Aspects

First this section will discuss ways of creating joint spaces with standard statistical packages such as SAS, SYSTAT SPSS, and BMDP. Then a number of specialized programs will be mentioned. Before discussing any particular programs, several points need to be made about the number of brands and attributes that are used in the analysis. First, a typical respondent can provide about twelve paper-and-pencil attribute ratings per minute (McLauchlan, 1987) or 120 ratings in a ten-minute interview. These ratings could be for eleven attributes on eleven brands (including an ideal brand). Therefore the number of brands and attributes is constrained by respondent fatigue. The number of brands is also constrained by the need to have enough brands to do property fitting or preference regressions. For a two-dimensional space, one would like to have a minimum of eight brands; ten to twelve is a better number. This requirement has to be traded off against the number of brands that the respondents are familiar with. In many product classes, most respondents are familiar with a smaller number of brands. It is possible to have respondents rate only the brands they know about, but doing so raises questions about how to interpret the perceptual spaces.

SAS, SYSTAT SPSS, BMDP Perceptual spaces and the associated joint spaces can be created with any standard multivariate statistical package that has discriminant analysis and regression subroutines. Smith's PC-MDS (1988) also contains PC versions of both discriminant analysis and regression subroutines. When the perceptual space is created with discriminant analysis, the brands are called "groups" and the attributes are the "variables." Each respondent provides a set of independent variables (attribute ratings) on each group (or brand), so the number of observations on each variable in the discriminant analysis is equal to the number of respondents times the number of brands.

The input data that have been gathered in a questionnaire format like the one shown in Figure 5-3 need to be converted into a form that is appropriate for the discriminant analysis subroutine. The converted data should be in the form of a matrix, where the number of rows is equal to the product of the number of respondents times the number of brands; each combination of a brand and a person is a separate observation or record. The first column of the matrix should be an integer that identifies the brand and the remaining columns contain that person's attribute ratings of that brand.

When viewing the output, the "group centroids" are the brand locations in the perceptual space, the "group means" of the variables are the average attribute ratings for each brand, and

the discriminant functions are the linear combinations that define the space. Most computer packages provide a graphical display of group centroids as an option, so the space can be produced by the computer. The coordinates of the group centroids are always printed out and can be plotted by hand if desired.

With most discriminant analysis programs, a separate regression must be run to locate each attribute vector in the space. In these regressions, the dependent variable is the group mean of that attribute for a given brand, and the independent variables are the coordinates of the brands (group centroids). Each brand provides one observation in this regression. The dimensions should be interpreted by those attributes that lie closest to the axis and those regressions that have the highest R^2s. Some judgment is needed in this step.

Adaptive perceptual mapping Sawtooth Software, Inc., offers a microcomputer-based system, Adaptive Perceptual Mapping (APM) for producing joint spaces. It is a combination questionnaire design, data collection, and analysis system. The perceptual space is constructed using discriminant analysis, and explicitly rated ideal points are used to represent preferences. It differs from the above-mentioned procedure in a number of important ways. First, the data are collected by computer. Once the desired brands and attributes have been determined, the computer manages the data collection and analysis task. Second, each respondent is asked how familiar she or he is with each brand and how important each attribute is. Once this is done, there is an option of questioning the respondents only about the brands with which they are most familiar and on the most important attributes. Third, in addition to the aggregate level discriminant analysis perceptual space, individual perceptual spaces are generated with principal components analysis. In an individual level analysis, there is only one observation per brand-attribute combination, so there is no within brand variance. Therefore the attribute combinations that maximize the between brand variance are found using principal components. An individual perceptual space is used to predict a person's reaction either to a new brand or to repositioning of an existing brand. With this method, each person's preference is a function of his or her own brand perceptions rather than average perceptions of the brands.

In sum, APM appears to be a user-friendly way of generating joint spaces. The primary drawback is that the spaces can be generated in only one manner. One is not able to build perceptual spaces with principal components and is not able to build preference representations using vectors, nor is the researcher able to use anything except self-explicated ideal points. This program is also more expensive than the others to be reviewed. If these limitations are not important, it is a good alternative.

MDS programs   This set of options includes the mainframe tape from Bell Labs and PC-MDS by Smith. Both of these packages contain a number of analysis programs that deal primarily with decomposition or similarity-based perceptual spaces and do not have questionnaire generation phases.

Both packages contain two of the most popular decomposition algorithms: KYST and INDSCAL. If one is interested in collecting and analyzing similarity data, these programs are among the best alternatives. Additionally, both packages contain PROFIT to fit attribute or property vectors into the perceptual space if attribute as well as similarity data have been collected. Furthermore, both packages contain PREFMAP, a program that has several models for fitting ideal points or preference vectors into a perceptual space using preferences for existing products. Finally, both packages contain one or more clustering algorithms, including Howard-Harris, which uses attribute data, if one wishes to cluster people into preference segments. PC-MDS also contains a correspondence analysis program. Also see Green, Carmone, and Smith (1989).

Both of these MDS packages are priced under $500 and have a large number of programs. The main difference is whether one wishes to perform the analysis in a mainframe or a PC environment.

MAPPING PHYSICAL ATTRIBUTES

A product's objective characteristics can be used to display competitive relationships and the temporal changes in a manner that is similar in appearance to a perceptual map. Usually these displays are based on readily available data. Figure 5-7 shows the range and seating capacity of the aircraft produced by two of the world's leading airframe builders, Airbus and Boeing. The relationship of capacity to range stands out, as does the relative coverage provided by each manufacturer's fleet.

Figure 5-7 can be elaborated in a number of ways. Price, operating cost, date of first delivery, and total number delivered and on order can be included for each model. The delivered and on-order figures could be further broken down by airline. In brief, there are numerous ways in which objective market maps and related graphic displays can contribute insight into current and prospective product offerings. For example, consider the competitive impact on Airbus of the positioning of Boeing's new 777 and 777ER models. These data support rather than substitute for the perceptual data that can be provided by aircraft crews, maintenance personnel, and airline executives. Most consumer and industrial products lend themselves to this extended graphic analysis.

CONJOINT ANALYSIS OF THE OFFER

When developing new products and services, marketers would like to be able to judge the consumers' response to their offer before it is introduced. They would also like to judge consumer reactions to possible competitive changes before

FIGURE 5-7   Boeing and Airbus major aircraft models.

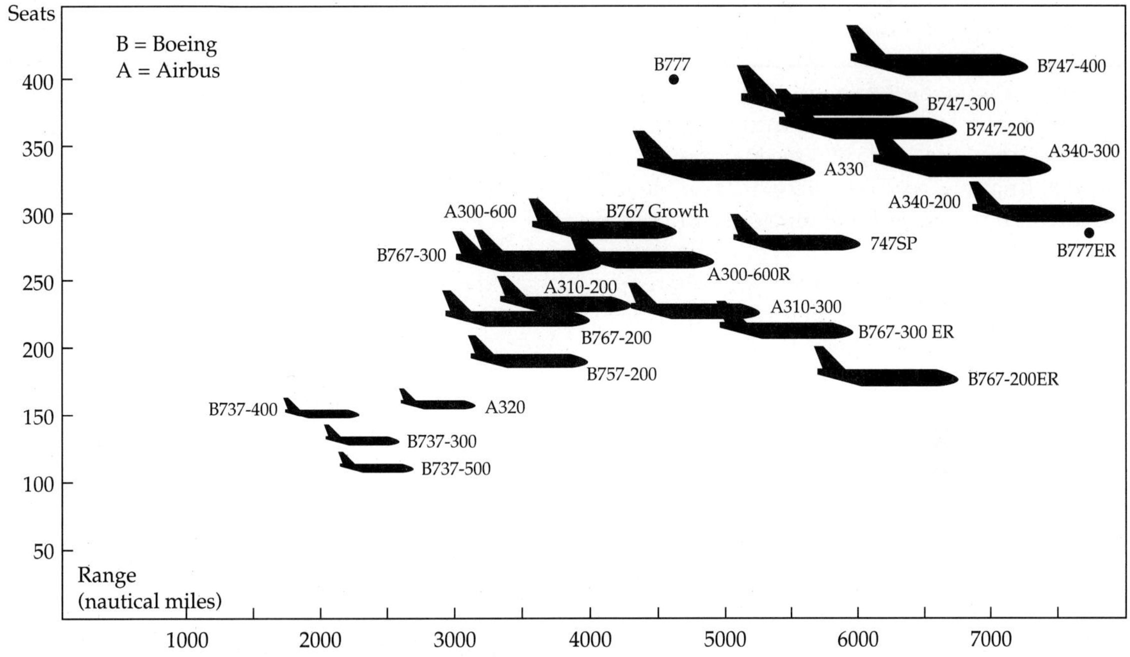

Source: *Adapted from March (1990, p. 36) and Business Week (October 29, 1990, p. 32).*

they are made. One way to deal with this problem is to perform traditional concept tests (Moore, 1982). Here the customer is presented with a description for a new product and is asked how likely that person would be to purchase it. This can be done either monadically (where the consumer is presented with only one concept to evaluate) or in some sort of a competitive environment test (in which a concept for the new product would be presented along with descriptions of several existing products and the consumer is asked which product he or she would be most likely to buy or how often he or she would buy each product).

Although concept tests have a good track record of predicting trial, they suffer from one major problem. If either the concept or the competitive set changes, the results may be invalid. In order to minimize this problem, researchers have tried to break preference, utility, or relative value of the overall concept down into its various attributes or components. Then if one of these attributes changes, they can estimate the impact of that change alone.

One of the first ways of evaluating the impact of a change was to ask people directly what they were looking for in a product (How would they describe a perfect or ideal car?) or what they thought of various possible features (How desirable is a blue car? How desirable is a red car?). Also, people were asked how important the various characteristics were (For example, how important is color when choosing a car? how important is price?). By knowing the desirability of different levels of an attribute (say, twenty-five versus thirty-five miles per gallon) it is possible to estimate the effect that changing gas mileage would have on the desirability of that car. This method of directly eliciting the desirability of various attribute levels and the importance of each attribute is called a "self-explicated" method.

There have been several problems with the self-explicated method. First, when asked to describe what they would like in a product, people tended to respond to these questions by saying that they want the best of everything at the lowest price. This answer may be truthful, but it is not very helpful. Second, while consumers seem to be able to judge how desirable different levels of an attribute are (e.g., I like blue cars much better than red cars), they are not as good at stating how important various attributes are. There is a general tendency to understate the importance of the more important attributes and overstate the importance of the less important attributes. The final problem is that statements about importance depend on the range of values that an attribute might take. For example, it may be very important for price not to be over a certain level, but if it is under that level, price may not have much influence. So an answer to a general question like how important is price may be misleading.

Therefore, some marketers use a technique called conjoint or trade-off analysis to analyze how consumers might respond to new product concepts. Here, consumers are asked either to evaluate complete descriptions of hypothetical new products or to compare partial descriptions of them. Conjoint analysis uses regression (or a similar technique) to decompose overall responses to hypothetical concepts, or offers, into the utilities of various attribute levels. Once the utilities of the attribute levels are known, it is possible to specify a new product or service that should have maximum desirability.

These related procedures are based on a number of assumptions (Clarke, 1987, p. 168):

It must make sense to view the product as a bundle of attribute levels—the product can be decomposed into separate features for which utilities can be computed.

The utility of the product is some simple function of the utilities of the product's attribute levels.

A respondent will buy the product for which he or she has the highest utility. It isn't necessary to assume that this happens at every purchase occasion. It may just be a purchase probability, but there is an assumption that utilities are translated into real purchase behavior.

The attributes in the questionnaire both are relevant and adequately describe the product.

There isn't any redundancy; that is, nothing gets counted twice.

We must assume that, in real product-buying decisions, people act the way they behave in the interview.

These assumptions may never be completely valid in any situation, but they are similar to the assumptions made in a large number of marketing research studies, and they are reasonable approximations in many situations. However, when only a small number of concepts is being tested or when a concept's positioning is based on an overall gestalt that cannot easily be broken down into a number of distinct attributes, traditional concept tests may be a more appropriate technique.

Method

The most popular method of conjoint analysis is called the full-profile method (Green and Wind, 1975; Louviere, 1988; Wittink and Cattin, 1989). In this method, the consumer responds to complete descriptions (full profiles) of hypothetical objects. The second most popular method is called the paired comparison method. In it consumers choose between two concepts or state their relative preference for each (Johnson, 1987). These pairs may or may not be complete profiles.

In either case, performing a conjoint analysis consists of several steps: selection of the attributes and the levels of each attribute to be included in the study, generation of the concepts

Collecting the data,

(product descriptions in terms of attributes) that will be presented to the consumers, parameter estimation, and use of the results for managerial decision-making. The primary differences between the full-profile and paired-comparison methods come in the steps of concept generation and estimation.

Attribute and level selection   Under either method, the first step is to decide which attributes and which levels of each attribute are to be analyzed. The analyst needs to determine which attributes are the most important factors in determining brand choice. For example, does a significant group of potential customers consider gas mileage to be an important attribute when choosing a new car? If so, what possible levels of gas mileage should be studied? This decision should be based on managerial judgment as well as on the opinions of both intermediate and final customers. Consumer judgments can be collected by using focus groups, individual open-ended interviews, or other, less structured techniques. Insight can also be obtained from studies of competitive offerings, consumer complaints and suggestions, and changes in what is technologically feasible. Usually more attributes are generated than are possible to analyze, so their number may need to be reduced. Typical conjoint analysis applications have employed between five and fifteen attributes.

Next, the specific attribute levels must be chosen. If an attribute is continuous, both the range of attribute levels and the number of levels need to be determined. The range should slightly exceed the range of what is currently being offered so that changes in offers will not render the study obsolete, but it should not be so far from current levels that credibility is lost. Enough intermediate levels should be used to cover the range adequately. Between two and five attribute levels are typically studied.

Special care must be taken to ensure that the attribute levels are meaningful to the consumer and that most respondents interpret them in a similar manner. Originally, this led most researchers to use only quantifiable (for example, price, miles per gallon, or dosage) or discrete attributes (for example, automatic transmission, aspirin-based, or domestically produced). However, through better descriptions, physical products, samples, drawings, examples, and so on, it is possible to express other types of attributes in such a way that people have a common understanding of each level. This may require that an advertising agency help with some of the statements or that R&D provide prototypes. It also means that the questionnaire should be carefully pretested.

Concept generation and parameter estimation
After the attributes and levels have been determined, the concepts that will be shown to the respondents need to be generated and the model's parameters must be estimated. At this point, there will be some differences between the full-profile and paired-comparison methods. First, the steps for the full-profile method will be discussed. This will be followed by a discussion of these steps for paired-comparison analysis.

Full profile   Once attributes and levels have been chosen, it may be possible to ask the respondents to evaluate every possible combination of attribute levels. This is called a full factorial design. In most cases this design results in too many concepts and respondent fatigue. For example, consider the situation in which five attributes are studied, two of which can take on one of two different levels, and three of which have three possible levels. This is not a very large problem, but all possible combinations of these attributes and levels result in 108 ($=2\times2\times3\times3\times3$) concepts; this is clearly too many for most respondents to judge. Therefore only a subset of these concepts, called a fractional factorial design (Addelman, 1962; Green, Carroll, and Carmone, 1978), is presented to the respondent. (It should be noted that several programs, such as Intelligent Marketing Systems' CONSERV and Bretton-Clark's Conjoint Designer, will automatically generate the appropriate design.)

The stimulus design problem can be illustrated with a simple example. Suppose that personal computers could be described in terms of three attributes: price, brand name, and storage capacity of the hard disk. Furthermore, the three brand names are IBM (I), Apple (A), and Epson (E); the three prices are $4,000, $3,000, and $2,000; and the two possible capacities of the hard disk are thirty megabytes and ninety megabytes. There are eighteen (=3×3×2) possible combinations of these attribute levels, yet we can devise a fractional factorial design with only nine combinations. It is displayed in Table 5-2. Here, each row represents a different profile or concept. These are called "full profiles" because each description contains all of the attributes in the study.

The design is "balanced" in that each brand name is paired once with each price level (e.g., three IBM computers are listed, one at each of the three possible prices) and twice with a ninety-megabyte disk and once with a thirty-megabyte disk. Similarly, each price is paired once with each brand name, twice with a ninety-

megabyte disk, and once with a thirty-megabyte disk. Therefore, that person's utility for a certain brand can be measured independently of his or her utility for a ninety-megabyte disk, because all brands are paired an equal number of times with a ninety-megabyte disk and an equal number of times with a thirty-megabyte disk. This is another way of saying that the attribute levels are uncorrelated; that is, a ninety-megabyte disk is just as likely to occur with an IBM PC as with an Epson. All nine concepts would be presented to each respondent. Typically, these concepts are in the form of verbal descriptions, but they can include drawings, prototypes, or actual products (see Page and Rosenbaum, 1987). If they were verbal descriptions, each concept would usually be presented on a different card.

After looking at the concepts, each respondent would be asked either to rank order these concepts from most preferred to least preferred or to rate each of these nine concepts on a liking, preference, or probability of purchase scale. In this example the concepts were rated on a likelihood of purchase scale, where ten is very likely to purchase and zero is very unlikely to purchase. Responses for one hypothetical respondent are given in the last column in the following table.

Fractional

TABLE 5-2   DESCRIPTION OF FULL-PROFILE CONCEPTS

	DESCRIPTION OF THE BRAND			
Observation Number	Brand Name	Price, $1,000	Hard-Disk Capacity, Megabytes	Customer Likelihood of Purchase
1	IBM	2	90	9
2	A	3	30	4
3	E	4	90	3
4	IBM	4	30	3
5	A	2	90	8
6	E	3	~~60~~ 90	5
7	IBM	3	~~60~~ 90	7
8	A	4	90	4
9	E	2	30	5
	3	3	2	

Full = 3·3·2 = 18

Once these responses have been collected, a regression is run to estimate the utility for each level of each attribute. Usually this is an ordinary least-squares regression. However, if the respondent has rank ordered the concepts, a monotonic regression can be used. If it is desired to constrain the predicted responses to a certain range, a logit regression might be run. See the Appendix.

Usually the independent variables are described in terms of dummy variables. First, each attribute has to be broken down into a number of discrete levels. In the case of some variables, such as brand name or presence of a feature like automatic transmission, these categories occur naturally. On the other hand, if the attribute is continuous, its possible values need to be categorized (for example, automobile gas mileage might be broken into the categories of twenty, twenty-eight, and thirty-five miles per gallon). Once each attribute has been converted into a series of levels, each level can be represented by a different dummy variable. (In the above example, a different dummy variable would be used to represent each of the three gas mileage categories.) A dummy variable is a variable that can take on one of only two values, either zero or one. A value of one is recorded if the object contains the level of the attribute in question and a zero if it does not. (For example, an observation describing a car getting twenty miles per gallon would be coded with a one for the dummy variable for twenty miles per gallon and zeros for the dummy variables representing twenty-eight and thirty-five miles per gallon).

In regression, an attribute can be modeled with one less dummy variable than there are attribute levels. For example, suppose an attribute could take on only one of three possible levels (e.g., Ford, Chevrolet, or Plymouth). If the observation does not contain either of the first two levels, then it must contain the third level. So the information contained in a third dummy variable is redundant. Therefore, one level is left out; it is called the reference level. Any one of the levels can be left out. In the

above example, if Epson, $4,000, and thirty megabytes are chosen as the reference levels, dummy variable coding for the previous example is given as in Table 5-3.

Here, the observations with a 1 in the column under D_I—observations 1, 4, and 7—are IBMs. The observations with a 1 in the column under D_A—2, 5, and 8—are Apples. The observations with 0's in both of the first two columns are Epsons.

Continuous variables are represented as dummy variables by breaking the continuum into a number of categories and assigning a dummy variable to each category. In our example, we could have used one dummy variable for prices under $2,000, a second for prices that are $2,000 and over but less than $3,000, and a third category for prices that are $3,000 and over.

The overall utility for each of the computers can be broken down into utilities for various levels of attributes by running a regression. Here the likelihood of purchase ratings in Table 5-2 forms the dependent variable and the dummy variables of Table 5-3 represent the independent variables. The regression would be of the following form:

$$P_i = \hat{a} + \hat{b}_1 D_{i1} + \hat{b}_2 D_{iA} + \hat{b}_3 D_{i2} \\ + \hat{b}_4 D_{i3} + \hat{b}_5 D_{i9} + e_i \quad (5\text{-}14)$$

TABLE 5-3   DUMMY VARIABLE CODING FOR FULL-PROFILE CONCEPTS

Observation Number	D_I	D_A	D_2	D_3	D_9
1	1	0	1	0	1
2	0	1	0	1	0
3	0	0	0	0	1
4	1	0	0	0	0
5	0	1	1	0	1
6	0	0	0	1	1
7	1	0	0	1	1
8	0	1	0	0	1
9	0	0	1	0	0

where $\hat{a}$ is the intercept, the $\hat{b}_i$s are the regression weights, and e_i is an error term.

The results of a dummy variable regression are interpreted in a manner similar to that of "regular" regressions. The only difference is that the regression weights represent the expected change in the dependent variable that is associated with a change *from* the reference level on that variable to the level associated with that weight.

If the likelihood of purchase responses from Table 5-2 were analyzed by a dummy variable regression using the independent variables shown in Table 5-3 the following equation would result:

$$P_i = 1.0 + 2.0\,D_{iI} + 1.0\,D_{iA} + 4.0\,D_{i2}$$
$$+ 2.0\,D_{i3} + 2.0\,D_{i9} + e_i \quad (5\text{-}15)$$

The implicit utility value for each of the reference levels is 0.0. This would put the utility for an IBM two units higher than it is for an Epson. The utilities for the various attribute levels are as follows:

U(IBM) = 2.0
U(APPLE) = 1.0
U(Epson) = 0.0

U($2,000) = 4.0
U($3,000) = 2.0
U($4,000) = 0.0

U(90 megabytes) = 2.0
U(30 megabytes) = 0.0

The importance of each attribute is defined as the difference between the highest and lowest utilities for that attribute:

Importance of brand name = U(IBM) − U(Epson) = 2.0

Importance of price = U($2,000) − U($4,000) = 4.0

Importance of disk capacity = U(90 megabytes) − U(30 megabytes) = 2.0.

This person places the greatest importance on price and the other two are tied for second (or least) in importance. It should be noted that the range of each attribute chosen by the researcher has a large influence over the importance of each attribute (for example, price would have probably been even more important if it had varied between $1,000 and $10,000), so attribute importances need to be interpreted in this light. The utility weights for price indicate that $1,000 difference in price is equal to two utility units. Therefore, this person is willing to pay $1,000 more for an IBM than a comparably equipped Epson, and an additional sixty megabytes of hard disk capacity is worth $1,000.

These results can be used to predict this person's preference for products other than the ones that were evaluated. For example, one would predict that this person would rate his or her likelihood of purchasing an IBM selling for $3,000 with a thirty-megabyte disk as five. The dummy variable coding for this concept is (1,0,0,1,0); that is, there are ones for the dummy variables representing IBM and $3,000 and zeros for the other dummy variables. The preference for this combination is estimated by inserting these values into Equation (5-15):

$$P = 1 + 2.0\,(1) + 1.0\,(0) + 4.0\,(0)$$
$$+2.0\,(1) + 2.0\,(0) = 5.0 \quad (5\text{-}16)$$

Preferences for any other attribute combinations can be predicted in this same manner.

Paired-comparison analysis   Here, pairs of concepts are directly compared and the respondent is asked how much better she or he likes one than the other or is likely to purchase one rather than the other. Instead of asking the respondent to compare each possible pair, the respondent is only asked to compare a subset of all possible pairs. As with the fractional factorial, the pairs have to be balanced, so each of the attributes would be independent of the others. Rather than a complete listing of pairs, a few pairs will be given to illustrate the way these dummy variables would be coded. As an example, the questionnaire might be shown in the following manner.

Circle the number that best reflects your relative preference for these two personal computers.

IBM		APPLE
$2,000		$3,000
90 MEGABYTES		90 MEGABYTES

PREFER   PREFER
10 8 6 4 2 0 2 4 6 8 10
LEFT   RIGHT

When these responses are recorded, preferences for the concept on the left are recorded as positive numbers and preferences for the concept on the right are recorded as negative numbers. The dummy variables for the concept on the left would be the very same as for the full-profile method (that is, a one if that concept contained that level and a zero if it did not). The dummy variables for the concept on the right would be the negative of the full-profile method (that is, a one if that concept contained that level and a zero if it did not). The dependent variable

is obtained by subtracting the preference for the right concept from that of the left concept and the independent variable is obtained by subtracting the dummy variable representation of the concept on the right from the description of the concept on the left. In this example the independent variable coding would be (1, −1, 1, −1, 0) with ones for the dummy variables representing IBM and $2,000, negative ones for Apple and $3,000, and a zero for ninety megabytes (because both computers had ninety-megabyte hard drives). Table 5-4 shows this method of coding for a few full-profile concepts from the very first example.

In the first example (shown in Table 5-2), concept one was an IBM selling for $2,000 with a ninety-megabyte hard drive (1, 0, 1, 0, 1) and had a nine likelihood of purchase. Concept two was an Apple selling for $3,000 with a thirty-megabyte hard drive (0, 1, 0, 1, 0) and had a likelihood of purchase of four. Therefore, in the first paired comparison the concept on the left is preferred (difference in preference of five) and the dummy variable representation of the concept on the right is subtracted from that of the concept on the left, giving independent variables of (1, −1, 1, −1, 1).

Sawtooth Software's Adaptive Conjoint Analysis (Johnson, 1987) allows one to generate the

TABLE 5-4   CODING FOR PAIRED-COMPARISON ANALYSIS

Circled Items Are Preferred

Left Concept	Right Concept	Difference Preference	D_I	D_A	D_3	D_4	D_9
①	2	5 = 9 − 4*	1	−1	1	−1	1[†]
③	④	0 = 3 − 3	−1	0	0	0	1
⑤	6	3 = 8 − 5	0	1	1	−1	0
⑦	8	3 = 7 − 4	1	−1	0	1	0
9	①	−4 = 5 − 9	−1	0	0	0	−1

*From the right-hand column of Table 5-3.

[†]From Table 5-3:
	Left	1	0	1	0	1
	Right	0	1	0	1	0
		1	−1	1	−1	1

paired-comparison profiles, conduct a computer-based interview, and analyze the responses.

Market Simulators

There are a number of ways conjoint results can be used. Typically, a choice simulator is developed. It is possible to predict the likelihood of purchasing any full-profile concept using Equation (5-16). As a first step, the model can be validated by comparing estimated and known market shares for the leading brands. This requires dummy variable descriptions to be constructed for the major brands in the market.

For example, assume there are only two products on the market. The first is an IBM for $4,000 with a ninety-megabyte hard disk and the second is an Apple for $2,000 with a thirty-megabyte hard disk. The choice simulator based on Equation (5-16) would predict this hypothetical person's likelihood of purchasing each as:

$$P_1 = 1 + 2.0\,(1) + 1.0\,(0) + 4.0\,(0)$$
$$+\,2.0\,(0) + 2.0\,(1) = 5$$

$$P_2 = 1 + 2.0\,(0) + 1.0\,(1) + 4.0\,(1)$$
$$+\,2.0\,(0) + 2.0\,(0) = 6$$

Usually, the concept with the highest utility for an individual (or homogeneous segment) is assumed to be the one chosen. In this case it would be the Apple. Notice that the Apple would have a higher utility regardless of whether or not the intercept was used in the calculations, so the full-profile and trade-off analysis would make the same prediction.

Some emphasis should be given to the fact that a conjoint market simulator can provide estimates of each brand's market share by employing an *ultimate form of market segmentation,* in which each customer is a segment. Here, individual behavior is modeled and the results are aggregated to obtain the predicted market shares. In most perceptual mapping and joint-space studies some type of prior aggregation is used, so the estimates about behavior apply to

the average behavior of group members, not necessarily to any individual in the group or market segment.

Since the numbers of people "choosing" each product are added up to calculate market shares, the sample of customers used in the analysis must be representative or steps must be taken to reweight these purchases. For example, one would reweight the observations if some segments of the population were underrepresented in the sample or if the sample failed to represent the heavier purchasers in the population adequately. In the planning methods that are used in the balance of this text, the market share of most direct interest is the share of the target market who will choose each product when people are aware of the products and have them readily available. Happily, this is the kind of data provided by the two main types of methods discussed in this chapter.

Since a simulation assumes that the properties of all brands are equally well known and that all brands are available, adjustments may be required to predict market share. Corrections will be needed for the appropriate levels of awareness and distribution, and possibly for the length of time that a brand has been on the market. When it is desirable to do so, the conjoint results can be modified to reflect the product's order of entry into the market.

The assumption that the product with the highest likelihood is always purchased has been criticized because a small difference in likelihood ratings could result in large changes in predicted market share. Also, in many situations, people do not always choose their favorite brand. Therefore, it may be more reasonable to assume that a person chooses products stochastically. This is typically done using a logit model, but it is possible to illustrate this idea with our example. Here, one must assume that the probability of choosing a product is proportional to its utility.[2] For example, the probability of choosing the IBM is .45 = 5/11 and the proba-

---

[2]Since ordinary conjoint utilities are interval rather than ratio measures, proportionality need not hold.

bility of choosing the Apple is .55 = 6/11. These choice probabilities would be added across all the respondents to estimate market shares.

A logit model's ratio-scaled estimates can be made with the full-profile method if the respondents have rated the concepts on a likelihood of purchase rating scale. If a trade-off approach is used to estimate the parameters for the attribute levels, some additional full profiles need to be evaluated on a probability of purchase scale. The latter data are used with a logit regression to calibrate the probability of choice function. The use of a logit analysis for these situations is described in Appendix 5-1.

Once the analyst is confident that the choice simulator can predict market shares for the existing products, concepts for several new or modified products can be generated and run through the choice simulator to see how many people choose one of the new concepts rather than an existing brand. The company can continue development with the one or two concepts that are most promising.

Another use of the results is to study the market by clustering respondents into segments that are homogeneous with respect to their regression weights. These clusters indicate how many people think brand name is most important, how many people like Apple best, and so on. It is possible that the company can design an alternative to appeal specifically to one of these groups. In addition, after clustering respondents into segments, it is possible to compare these different groups in terms of other variables, such as demographic or current usage characteristics. See Moore (1980) for an example.

Summary

Since its introduction in 1971, conjoint analysis has been one of the fastest-growing marketing research techniques. Cattin and Wittink (1982) did a study of commercial usage of conjoint analysis during its first decade and found approximately 600 commercial applications, of which more than 20 percent occurred in the last year of the study. During the 1981 to 1985 peri-

od, they estimate that about 400 applications have been performed annually (Wittink and Cattin, 1989). In large part this appears to be due to the actionability of its results and the relatively good predictive power it has displayed.

Montgomery (1985) presents some evidence of the ability of conjoint analysis to predict market shares. The results of Davidson's (1973) study of traffic between Montreal and downtown Ottawa and Robinson's (1980) study of the North Atlantic air travel market are given in Table 5-5. Their market share predictions are quite good. Wittink and Montgomery (1979) studied individual job choices and were able to predict each person's choice with more than 60 percent accuracy. This is compared with an approximate 30 percent chance figure.

One of the most important current developments in the field deals with trying to find ways to get consumer reactions to ever more complex concepts. As mentioned previously, one problem has been the inability to include all the attributes and levels that a manager might want. Two approaches have been introduced to deal with this problem. In both cases the solution is reasonably similar. Green (1984) developed hybrid conjoint analysis which combines some self-explicated information (i.e., desirabilities of different attribute levels and attribute importances) with responses to a smaller number of full profiles. Sawtooth Software has developed Adaptive Conjoint Analysis in a similar manner (Johnson, 1987). The self-explicated portion provides initial estimates and eliminates attributes that are unimportant and attribute levels that are totally unsatisfactory. Then a series of paired-comparison judgments are elicited from the reduced set of the most important attributes and desirable levels.

Model Structure

All of the models discussed here have a simple additive structure. They assume that attributes independently affect the desirability of the product. In a majority of well-designed studies, this simple structure is sufficiently realistic to yield

TABLE 5-5   EVIDENCE OF PREDICTIVE VALIDITY OF CONJOINT ANALYSIS

Forecast of Traffic Montreal to Downtown Ottawa

Transportation Mode	Actual Share, %	Conjoint Prediction, %
Air	3.2	3.2
Train	10.9	10.4
Bus	15.1	15.5
Car	70.7	70.9

North Atlantic Air Travel

Fare Type	Actual Share,%	Conjoint Prediction, %
Economy	25	23
Excursion	14	12
(14–21 day) Excursion	43	49
(22–45 day) GP Fares	18	16

useful results. It is not difficult, however, to find product classes where the effect that the level of an attribute has on preference depends on the level of one or more other attributes. For example, a large random access memory in a personal computer may be more valuable in a machine with a high-capacity central processor than in a less powerful machine.

When necessary, there are two main ways to handle attribute dependence. The most common procedure is to include one or more interaction terms that account for the effect of attribute combinations. A less common approach is to use a multiplicative rather than an additive model. Although a detailed discussion of these matters is beyond the scope of this text, if a simple additive model seems inappropriate because of attribute dependencies, a prospective user of conjoint analysis should seek technical advice.

Operational Aspects

As pointed out several times, conjoint analysis can be run with any regression program. Any multivariate package such as BMDP, SAS, or SPSSX that has a regression subroutine can be used. It is also possible to perform these regressions using the forecasting option in Lotus 123®.

Additionally, there are several software packages that allow one to perform conjoint analysis. Smith (1988) has a number of MDS, clustering, and conjoint analysis programs in a single package for use on PCs. Of specific interest to this discussion are the regression, MONANOVA, TRADEOFF, and CONJOINT routines. MONANOVA allows one to perform a full-profile conjoint analysis when the input data are rank ordered. TRADEOFF allows one to perform two attributes at a time trade-off analysis. CONJOINT allows one to perform an ordinary least-squares regression and a market-share simulation. The input data need to be collected in a paper-and-pencil manner or via another computer program for use in the conjoint program. Smith's package also contains the Howard-Harris clustering algorithm, making it possible to cluster respondents on the basis of their regression weights.

The Adaptive Conjoint Analysis package (Johnson, 1987) from Sawtooth Software is a combined interviewing, analysis, and simulation program. The program first questions the respondents about which attributes are most important and whether any levels are totally unacceptable to the respondent. Then it has the option of limiting the analysis to acceptable levels of the most important attributes. This program uses a paired-comparison methodology (usually on a reduced set of attributes) rather than a full-profile method. However, a number of full profiles are evaluated on a likelihood of purchase scale to estimate the logit regression. It also has a number of simulation capabilities.

Intelligent Marketing Systems' CONSERV and Bretton-Clark's Conjoint Designer (1985) are flexible packages that generate the conjoint design on the basis of user-specified attributes and levels of each attribute. Additionally, they will generate the stimulus cards. CONSERV can also analyze the data and run simulations. Bretton-Clark does not analyze the data, but it is possible to read the design file into Smith's CONJOINT program.

A COMPARISON OF PERCEPTUAL MAPS, JOINT SPACES, AND CONJOINT ANALYSES

At first glance, joint-space and conjoint techniques seem quite similar. Both techniques ask a number of respondents about what they would do or what they think about certain brands. Both techniques use relatively sophisticated statistical techniques to analyze these answers. One of the main outputs from each technique is information about which attributes are most important in determining preference or likelihood of purchase. This can lead one to ask which technique should be used, or when each technique should be used.

A number of similarities and differences between these procedures are of special interest. The primary objective of perceptual mapping and joint-space analyses is to provide a picture of the competitive structure of a market. How are the various brands perceived? What characteristics differentiate the brands? How well satisfied are the consumers? Where are the "holes" in the space that contain ideal points but no brands? Joint spaces do a very good job of summarizing a lot of information about product competition.

The joint space is probably not as good as conjoint analysis at determining which attributes are most important or at predicting the response to new brands. If two attributes are correlated within most brands, it is difficult to tell how much each one is related to preference. For example, if size, price, and poorer gas mileage are correlated across automobiles, it is almost impossible to determine if a person prefers a car because it is small, is inexpensive, or gets good gas mileage. Similarly, if none of the current brands possesses a certain attribute, such as four-wheel steering, it is not possible to determine how important this attribute is from a joint space.

Conjoint analysis can be based on the reaction to existing products and/or products with novel attributes. Therefore, it is possible to ask people whether they would be more likely to purchase a small inexpensive car, a large inexpensive car, a small expensive car, or a large expensive car. In this way it is possible to separate the effect of two attributes on preference even if they are environmentally correlated. Similarly, one can ask people whether they would be more likely to purchase a car with front-wheel steering or four-wheel steering. On the other hand, conjoint analysis does not provide any information about people's perceptions of current offerings.

These two techniques are similar in that they deal with the importance of various attributes, but they provide a complementary rather than a common point of view. So, to decide which of these to use, one must decide what information is desired from the study. Additionally, there are times when one technique may be more appropriate than the other. In some product categories, consumers may know enough to make rational decisions, but not enough about individual brands to rate them on a number of attributes. For example, lots of consumers can make intelligent trade-offs between size, price, energy efficiency, and freezer space when choosing a refrigerator, but they would not be able to rate current models on these same attributes. In this case, conjoint analysis would be a more appropriate technique. Conjoint analysis is more appropriate when the attributes are easily describable and the respondents agree upon what a specific level means. It is believed to be more difficult to ask respondents about automobile safety, handling, reliability, or styling (without drawings or mock-ups) than it is to ask about gas mileage, size, price, or front-wheel drive.

In both cases, it is assumed that people view the brands as bundles of attributes or benefits and not as unitary objects. It would be difficult to analyze preferences for paintings using either of these techniques. Similarly, both of these tech-

niques assume that people make consistent decisions. For example, if a person was most likely to purchase a certain brand, we would guess that the person's second choice would be similar. Neither of these models would work well if a person's most preferred television shows were "College Football," "60 Minutes," and "Murphy Brown," and least preferred shows were "Pro Football," "20/20," and "Cosby."

This latter case may be the result of some sort of variety seeking. See Figure 5-8 for a way to classify the various sources of variety seeking. It is possible that it would be derived variety-seeking behavior in which variation in preference is due to external influences such as different situations or use occasions. For example, a person may want a small car for commuting and a station wagon for family vacations, or different brands of catsup depending upon whether it will be used for cooking or put on hamburgers.

Varied behavior could also be due to direct

FIGURE 5-8   Causes of varied behavior.

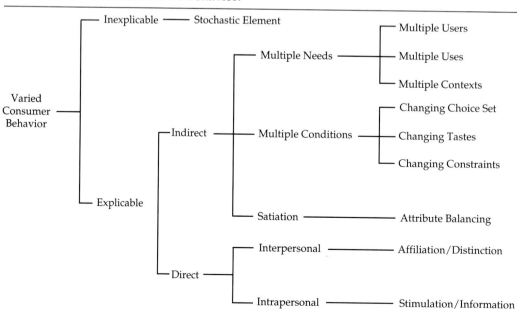

Source: *Pessemier (1985, p. 79).*

variation. Here, someone might seek variety because of satiation or because novelty is inherently desirable. There is a limit to the number of news or sports programs that a person wants to watch in a given period, so a product's value also depends on past consumption behavior. See McAlister and Pessemier (1982) and Pessemier (1985) for further discussion of variety seeking. If variety seeking is of the derived type, the situation or use of a product should be specified and analyzed separately. Direct varied behavior is hard to model with either of these techniques because part of a product's value is derived from its relationship to other products or to the behavior of other individuals.

CONCLUDING REMARKS

This chapter has covered joint-space analysis and conjoint analysis, two techniques that can help one to design both a product or service and the associated communications message.

When designing new or improved products and services that offer superior value, consumer input is a must. The manager must know how the competing products are perceived, as well as which features or attributes are most valued. These techniques present systematic ways for gathering these data.

In spite of their usefulness, they should not replace the less formal face-to-face interaction with customers that companies have successfully employed. However, that approach should not be used at the expense of these two more formalized approaches.

Pricing is covered in Chapter 6. Then Chapter 7 contains three extended examples of how these techniques either might have been or were actually used to solve important marketing problems.

REFERENCES

Addelman, Sidney: "Orthogonal Main-Effect Plans for Asymmetrical Factorial Experiments," *Technometrics*, 4, February 1962, 21–46.

Boyd, Harper W., Jr., Michael L. Ray, and Edward S. Strong: "An Attitudinal Framework for Advertising Strategy," *Journal of Marketing*, April 1972, 27–33.

Carroll, J. Douglas: "Individual Differences and Multi-dimensional Scaling," in *Multidimensional Scaling: Theory and Applications in Behavioral Sciences*, Vol. 1, Roger Shepard, A. Kimball Romney, and Sara B. Nerelove (eds.), New York: Seminar Press, 1972, 105–155.

Cattin, Phillipe, and Dick R. Wittink: "Commercial Use of Conjoint Analysis: A Survey," *Journal of Marketing*, 46, Summer 1982, 44–53.

Clarke, Darral G.: *Marketing Analysis and Decision Making: Text and Cases with Lotus 123*. Redwood City, Calif.: Scientific Press, 1987.

Conjoint Designer, New York: Bretton-Clark, 1985.

Davidson, J. D.: "Forecasting Traffic on STOL," *Operational Research Quarterly*, 1973, 561–569.

Day, George S., Allan D. Shocker, and Rajendra K. Srivastava: "Customer-Oriented Approaches to Identifying Product Markets," *Journal of Marketing*, 43, Fall 1979, 8–19.

Ginter, James, and Edgar A. Pessemier: "Analysis of Brand Preference Segments," *Journal of Business Research*, May 1978, 111–131.

Green, Paul E.: "Hybrid Models for Conjoint Analysis: An Expository Review," *Journal of Marketing Research*, 21, May 1984, 155–169.

_____, Frank J. Carmone, and Scott M. Smith: *Multidimensional Scaling*, Needham Heights, Mass.: Allyn and Bacon, 1989.

_____, J. Douglas Carroll, and Frank J. Carmone: "Some New Types of Fractional Factorial Designs for Marketing Experiments," in *Research in Marketing*, Vol. 1, Jagdish N. Sheth (ed.), Greenwich, Conn.: JAI Press Inc., 1978, 99–122.

_____ and Vithala R. Rao: *Applied Multidimensional Scaling*, New York: Holt, Rinehart and Winston, 1972.

_____ and Yoram Wind: "New Way to Measure Consumers' Judgements, "*Harvard Business Review*, July–August 1975, 107–117.

Johnson, Richard M.: "Market Segmentation: A Strategic Management Tool," *Journal of Marketing Research*, February 1971, 13–18.

_____: "Trade-Off Analysis of Consumer Values," *Journal of Marketing Research*, May 1974, 121–127.

_____: "Adaptive Conjoint Analysis," in *Proceedings of the Sawtooth Software Conference on Perceptual Mapping, Conjoint Analysis and Computer Interviewing*, Richard M. Johnson (ed.), Ketchum, Idaho: Sawtooth Software, Inc., 1987, 253–266.

_____: "Adaptive Perceptual Mapping," in *Proceedings of the Sawtooth Software Conference on Perceptual Mapping, Conjoint Analysis and Computer Interviewing*, Richard M. Johnson (ed.), Ketchum, Idaho: Sawtooth Software, Inc., 1987, 143–157.

Hoffman, Donna L., and George R. Franke: "Correspondence Analysis: Graphical Representation of Categorical Data in Marketing Research," *Journal of Marketing Research*, August 1986, 213–228.

Kotler, Philip: *Marketing Management: Analysis, Planning, Implementation, and Control*, Englewood Cliffs, N.J.: Prentice-Hall, 1987.

Louviere, Jordan J.: *Analyzing Decision Making: Metric Conjoint Analysis*, Newbury Park, Calif.: SAGE Publications, 1988.

McAlister, Leigh, and Edgar A. Pessemier: "Variety Seeking Behavior: An Interdisciplinary Review," *Journal of Consumer Research*, December 1982, 311–322.

McLauchlan, Bill: "How to Design a Perceptual Mapping Study," in *Proceedings of the Sawtooth Software Conference on Perceptual Mapping, Conjoint Analysis and Computer Interviewing*, Richard M. Johnson (ed.), Ketchum, Idaho: Sawtooth Software, Inc., 1987, 179–187.

March, Artemis: "The Future of the U.S. Aircraft Industry," *Technology Review*, January 1990, 27–35.

Montgomery, David B.: "Conjoint Calibration of the Customer/Competitor Interface in Industrial Markets," Marketing Science Institute Report No. 85–112, 1985.

_____ and Dick R. Wittink: "The Predictive Validity of Conjoint Analysis for Alternative Aggregation Schemes," in *Market Measurement and Analysis: Proceedings of the 1979 ORSA/TIMS Conference on Marketing*, D. B. Montgomery

and D. R. Wittink (eds.), Cambridge, Mass.: Marketing Science Institute, 1979, 298–309.

Moore, William L.: "Levels of Aggregation in Conjoint Analysis, An Empirical Comparison," *Journal of Marketing Research*, 17, 1980, 516–523.

_____: "Concept Testing," *Journal of Business Research*, October 1982, 279–294.

_____ and Russell S. Winer: "A Panel Data-Based Method for Merging Joint Space and Market Response Function Estimation," *Marketing Science*, Winter 1987, 25–42.

Pessemier, Edgar A.: "Varied Individual Behavior: Some Theories, Measurement Methods and Models," *Multivariate Behavioral Research*, 20, 1985, 69–94.

_____: *Product Management: Strategy and Organization*, 2d ed. New York: John Wiley & Sons, 1982.

Pilon, Thomas: "Discriminant vs Factor-based Perceptual Maps: Practical Considerations," in *1989 Sawtooth Software Conference Proceedings—Gaining A Competitive Advantage Through PC-Based Interviewing and Analysis*, Vol. 1, Margo Metegrano (ed.), Ketchum, Idaho: Sawtooth Software, Inc., 1989, 166–182.

Robinson, Patrick J.: "Applications of Conjoint Analysis to Pricing Problems," in *Market Measurement and Analysis: Proceedings of the 1979 ORSA/TIMS Conference on Marketing*, D. B. Montgomery and D. R. Wittink (eds.), Cambridge, Mass.: Marketing Science Institute, 1980, 183–205.

Smith, Scott M.: *PC-MDS: Multidimensional Scaling and Conjoint Analysis*, Provo, Utah: Brigham Young University, 1988.

Williams, Jeffery R., and George S. Yip: *Vicks Health Care Division: Project Scorpio*, case, Boston: Harvard Business School, 1981.

Wittink, Dick R., and Phillipe Cattin: "Commercial Use of Conjoint Analysis: An Update," *Journal of Marketing*, 53, July 1989, 91–96.

APPENDIX 5-1 LOGIT REGRESSIONS

The purpose of this appendix is to discuss the use of logit regressions to estimate purchase probabilities. The primary advantage of the logit is that the estimated purchase likelihood for any concept is within a given range—say, zero to one (or zero to ten). With a regression, even though the respondent rated all of the full profiles between zero and ten, it is possible that forecast P_is for some concepts would fall outside that range; that is, the forecasts could be either negative numbers or numbers greater than ten. This range restriction allows one to convert purchase likelihoods estimated by using a logit into purchase probabilities for any group of concepts such that the sum of the probabilities is 1.0. Logit analysis can be performed with any standard regression program.

Earlier, the likelihood of purchase in a full-profile conjoint analysis was a linear function of the attribute levels, as shown in Equation (5-14), which is reproduced as Equation (A-1) in summation notation:

$$P_i = \hat{a} + \sum_{k=1}^{5} \hat{b}_k D_{ik} + e_{ik} \qquad \text{(A-1)}$$

Here $\hat{b}_k$ represents the kth regression weight and D_{ik} is the kth dummy variable for the ith concept. They represent the same five dummy variables as in Table 5-3 and Equation (5-14).

When a logit regression is used with a zero to ten likelihood of purchase scale, the likelihood of purchase is written as the following function of the attribute levels:

$$P_i = 10.0 \Big/ \left(1.0 + \exp - \left(\hat{a} + \sum_{k=1}^{5} \hat{b}_k D_{ik} + e_{ik} \right) \right) \qquad \text{(A-2)}$$

With a little algebraic manipulation we can rearrange Equation (A-2) to the following:

$$P_i / (10.0 - P_i) = \exp \left(\hat{a} + \sum_{k=1}^{5} \hat{b}_k D_{ik} + e_{ik} \right) \qquad \text{(A-3)}$$

Taking the natural logarithm of each side results in the following equation:

$$\ln \left(P_i / (10.0 - P_i) \right) = \hat{a} + \sum_{k=1}^{5} \hat{b}_k D_{ik} + e_{ik} \qquad \text{(A-4)}$$

The parameters of this expression can be estimated with a regression program. Note that the only difference between (A-1) and (A-4) is the form of the dependent variable. In Equation (A-1) it is the likelihood rating from the consumer. In Equation (A-4) it is the log odds of the likelihood rating, which is called the logit of the likelihood rating. No matter how big or small $\hat{a} + \sum \hat{b}_k D_{ik}$ gets to be, P_i will always lie in the interval between 0.0 and 10.0. (If the consumer rated these products on a 0.0 to 1.0 probability of purchasing scale, the dependent variable would be $\ln (P_i/(1.0 - P_i))$.)

Once the parameters of Equation (A-4) have been estimated, it is possible to estimate a consumer's likelihood of purchasing or utility for any concept using Equation (A-2). These P_is can then be used to estimate the probability of choosing the ith object out of any set. Suppose there are three brands in a consideration set (X_1, X_2, X_3) and they have the following purchase likelihoods: P_1, P_2, and P_3. The probability of choosing the ith brand out of that set of three is

$$\Pr(X_i; \{X_1, X_2, X_3\}) = P_i/(P_1 + P_2 + P_3) \qquad \text{(A-5)}$$

Market shares can be estimated by averaging these probabilities over all people.

REVIEW QUESTIONS

Q5-1 What is the purpose of a joint space and what are its essential parts?

Q5-2 What measurements and other data are needed to build a joint space?

Q5-3 In principal and perhaps in fact, what strategic marketing questions can be answered with the aid of a joint space?

Q5-4 How does one select the attributes used to construct a joint space? How does one measure the product preference values that are used in constructing a joint space?

Q5-5 Describe the nature of a perceptual space developed by discriminant analysis using product attribute ratings. How does it differ from a principal component analysis of the same attribute ratings?

Q5-6 How does a perceptual space developed by multidimensional scaling (MDS) methods differ from a space developed by discriminant or principal component methods?

Q5-7 Using only the raw data in Table 5-1, explain which attributes discriminate between which brands, and which brands have the most unique brand positions.

Q5-8 What are the pros and cons of using correspondence analysis to produce a perceptual map?

Q5-9 What is conjoint analysis and how does it differ from joint-space analysis?

Q5-10 What are the major pros and cons of conjoint analysis?

Q5-11 What are the principal advantages of adaptive joint-space and conjoint analyses?

Q5-12 Discuss how a market simulator works for conjoint analysis, and how it can be used for marketing planning.

Q5-13 What are the advantages and limitations of using a logit regression?

Q5-14 How does variety seeking behavior limit the use of joint-space and conjoint analysis models?

COMPUTER EXERCISE

CONJOINT ANALYSIS EXERCISE

Questionnaire—Automobile Choices

Assume you are graduating and need a new automobile. The following cars are described in terms of five attributes: gas mileage, base sticker price, country of manufacture, top speed, and seating capacity. Assume that the same options (e.g., air conditioning and choice of two or four doors) are available on all cars, but that they will cost more on cars with higher base sticker prices. Assume that all unmentioned features (e.g., distance to the nearest dealer and safety) are the same on all cars unless you feel that they are related to the mentioned features (e.g., some people might feel that Japanese cars are more reliable than U.S. cars).

First, read the descriptions for all eighteen-calibration automobiles in Table 5-6 to get a feel for the range of your choices. Then rate how likely you would be to purchase each one on a 0.0 to 10.0 scale, where 0.0 means that you would be *very unlikely* to purchase the car and 10.0 means that you would be *very likely* to purchase it.

Please perform the same rating exercise on the following test automobiles in Table 5-7. First read all six descriptions to see your range of choices, then rate the likelihood of purchasing each one on a 0.0 to 10.0 scale.

TABLE 5-6 CALIBRATION AUTOMOBILES

RATING	GAS MILEAGE	PRICE, $	MANUFACTURE	TOP SPEED	SEATING
1 _____	20	7,000	AMERICA	90	4
2 _____	20	10,000	JAPAN	90	6
3 _____	20	13,000	EUROPE	120	4
4 _____	25	7,000	JAPAN	120	6
5 _____	25	10,000	EUROPE	90	4
6 _____	25	13,000	AMERICA	90	4
7 _____	30	7,000	EUROPE	90	6
8 _____	30	10,000	AMERICA	120	4
9 _____	30	13,000	JAPAN	90	4
10 _____	20	7,000	EUROPE	120	4
11 _____	20	10,000	AMERICA	90	6
12 _____	20	13,000	JAPAN	120	4
13 _____	25	7,000	AMERICA	90	4
14 _____	25	10,000	JAPAN	120	4
15 _____	25	13,000	EUROPE	90	6
16 _____	30	7,000	JAPAN	90	4
17 _____	30	10,000	EUROPE	90	4
18 _____	30	13,000	AMERICA	120	6

TABLE 5-7 TEST AUTOMOBILES

RATING	GAS MILEAGE	PRICE, $	MANUFACTURE	TOP SPEED	SEATING
1 _____	20	7,000	JAPAN	90	4
2 _____	20	10,000	EUROPE	120	4
3 _____	25	13,000	AMERICA	120	4
4 _____	25	7,000	JAPAN	90	6
5 _____	30	10,000	EUROPE	120	6
6 _____	30	13,000	AMERICA	90	6

After filling out the questionnaire, analyze your responses to the calibration automobiles using conjoint analysis and predict your likelihood of purchasing each of the test automobiles.

First, define a set of eight dummy variables (two for each of the first three attributes and one for each of the last two) by choosing one level of each attribute as the reference and defining a dummy variable representation for each calibration automobile. For example, if the following levels are chosen as the reference levels—twenty miles per gallon, $7,000, American, ninety miles per hour, and four seats—the dummy variable representation for the first three calibration automobiles would be (0 0 0 0 0 0 0 0), (0 0 1 0 1 0 0 1), and (0 0 0 1 0 1 1 0). These will be the independent variables in a regression with your likelihood of purchase ratings as the dependent variable.

After running the regression, answer the following questions:

1. What is the R^2?

2. Which level of each variable was most preferred?

3. Which variable was most important?

4. How do the answers to 2 and 3 agree with your feelings?

Next, forecast your likelihood of purchasing each of the test automobiles. First, develop a dummy variable description of each of them using the same dummy variables that you used for the calibration automobiles. Then apply these descriptions to the estimated regression weights to get the predicted purchase likelihoods. Finally, answer the following two questions.

1. Was the model able to predict the order of your choice correctly? If not, which ones were predicted incorrectly?

2. What is the correlation between your stated likelihoods and the likelihoods predicted by the model?

6

PRICING THE OFFER

The last chapter discussed two principal techniques for assessing what customers desired and how they perceived the competitive offerings. This information can be used to help determine an offer, i.e., that combination of product, service, communications message, and price—the value that can be delivered to various customers. As that discussion pointed out, the offer should consist of an integrated mix of elements built around a common theme—a core strategy. In turn, a major objective of the core strategy is to create the desired image for customers of the offer's worth relative to the competition.

This chapter continues with that general theme and deals with pricing both new and improved offers. It is a continuation of the previous chapter, because the price needs to be consistent with the positioning, the product or service's design, and its communications message. In this context, the offer price is defined as the average return to the seller per unit excluding purely promotional price reductions. The offer price, or planning price, is the list price less established quantity and seasonal discounts. Occasional price promotions, including coupons, label allowances, and the like, are part of the marketing support that the offer receives. These latter items are seldom considered to be a persistent change in price; rather, they are an effort to induce some favorable short-run change in behavior by the customer or reseller. The offer price should be based on the seller's estimate of the value (relative to the competition) of the offer to a defined target market. Extended discussions of pricing strategy and tactics appear in Monroe (1979) and Nagel (1987).

The current chapter focuses on setting the offer price for new and improved products as part of the marketing plan, but most of the analysis can be used when deciding whether the offer price should be changed. Oxenfeldt (1973) lists a number of symptoms of pricing problems. They include a decline in sales, prices that are too high (low) in some markets, the perception that the company is exploiting consumers, prices that are destabilizing the market, prices that place an unreasonable burden on resellers, and pricing actions that have made customers price sensitive and unappreciative of quality differences.

Another set of concepts that deserves attention applies to both product design and price. These concepts are the behavioral "laws" that govern just noticeable differences and their relationship to the amount of a product attribute or its price. If the change in the amount of an attribute is very small, no one may notice it, but if it is very large, everyone may take notice. Since changes in many product attributes provide some customer benefits, it is tempting to make these improvements. However, when the cost of doing so is high and few individuals notice the change, the "product improvement" can be ill-advised, creating needless cost pressure. Similar problems occur with respect to price. If a price reduction is too small to be noticed or to be meaningful to many customers, the erosion of unit margin is seldom justified. On the other hand, small price increases may be noticed by few customers but significantly enhance firm profits.

An associated behavioral phenomenon is that the size of a just noticeable difference is usually a constant percentage of the base from which the change is made. If a $10 increase in the price of a $100 product is noticed and influences 20 percent of a target market, it may take a $100 price increase to produce the same result for a $1,000 product. To obtain the same psychological impact, the size of the required increase typically goes up with each successive increase. For a price reduction, the size of an equally noticed reduction decreases with each successive reduction. In the case of product attributes other than price, the base from which a change is made also determines the size of the change needed to produce a given result.

PRICING CONCEPTS

Some managers with an internal orientation base prices primarily on costs. This is usually done by adding some industry standard markup to average costs. Although costs need to be considered when setting prices, this method ignores the market and results in lower profits than might otherwise be gained. Other managers set prices primarily on the basis of competition. Usually this means matching competitive prices, but it can also mean pricing at a slight premium or discount relative to the competition. Competition needs to be considered; however, this mechanistic approach does not allow the manager to take advantage of the product's unique strengths or compensate for its weaknesses (Shapiro and Jackson, 1978).

The fact that consumers generally determine the value of a product or service by comparing its benefits to its price leads to the fundamental principle of pricing. Price should be based on the perceived value of the offer rather than on the cost of production. Price setting should be thought of as a three-step process of:

1. Creating value in the mind of the consumer

2. Measuring the amount of perceived value

3. Capturing an appropriate portion of this value through price (Hulbert, 1983)

Taking these steps is not easy, even in the simplest of situations where:

the product is sold directly to the final consumer,

the competitive offerings are based on easily compared attributes,

consumers agree on the value of various attributes,

the company has an objective of maximizing relatively short-term profits, and

competition is understood.

Complications are the norm. When the product is not sold directly to the final customer, the manufacturer usually cannot set prices to the final customer; it can only set a price to the reseller. The reseller then adds a markup to arrive at a price to the final customer. Since value is always judged relative to the competition, competitive offers, prices, and reactions must be considered. Rarely can one ignore differences across various groups of customers in the value they place on different attributes and in their price sensitivity. Furthermore, ways to measure relative value and models for setting prices are not well developed.

Nevertheless, one should remember this three-step process when setting price; it should lead to more profitable prices.

MEASURING VALUE AND DEMAND

The relative value of an offer sets the maximum that can be charged; people won't pay more for a product than they feel it is worth. Furthermore, different people—and even the same person at different times—will place different values on the offer. Over time, costs set the minimum that can be charged and remain in business. Therefore, the company needs to determine both the relative value of an offer and its costs.

However, the role of costs is only an arithmetic one; that is, costs are needed to calculate profits at different price and volume levels. The price chosen should be the one that best meets profitability and other goals. If an adequate level of profits cannot be obtained with any likely price and volume combination, the product either should be dropped or never introduced. Still, many companies spend much more time calculating costs and figuring out the minimum price they can charge than in estimating the relative value of the offer, which sets the maximum. Even though value assessment methods are far from perfect, more effort should be expended in trying to determine the maximum prices.

The steps of value creation and measurement are related. The starting point is to determine what the customer wants and how well he or she is satisfied with the current offerings. Joint

spaces can be used to find desirable locations for both new and improved products. Similarly, conjoint analysis can forecast the likelihood of purchasing new concepts under different competitive scenarios and prices. By determining what various groups of customers want and how they trade off features and prices among the competitive offerings, one can explore a number of value-creating changes in the physical product or service, the associated communication message, and its price.

Once a potential offer has been created, there are several ways of assessing its value, or, equivalently, of estimating how much will be purchased at various prices.

Managerial Judgment

A manager's judgment should form the starting point when attempting to determine the value of an offer. Many managers have a good sense of the relative value of their products. The sales force and/or resellers may have important insights regarding the value of the firm's products compared with those of the competition. Other knowledgeable executives in the firm may also have valuable insights. Even if surveys, experiments, or statistical analyses are employed, the final pricing decision must rest on the judgment of the manager who accepts profit responsibility. When you consider the complexity of a typical situation (one must forecast how much of a price change given to a reseller will be passed along, what the competitive reaction will be, and how the final consumer will react), you can see that informed managerial judgments are crucial. Usually, a manager's judgment and responsibilities extend to related policies and procedures, such as discount schedules and how competitive moves will be met when time is of the essence.

There are several pricing factors about which managerial judgments can profitably be elicited. Managers should be asked to provide information about competitive offers and reactions, the value of different attributes, and consumer responses to different price levels. Also, if information is collected from managers formally, there are different ways of gathering this information. For example, managers can fill out questionnaires similar to the ones developed for consumers in the next section. If this is done, managers should complete a separate questionnaire for each major market segment. In any case, a manager can gain further insight by comparing personal expectations with consumer responses.

Graphic displays of price and value   If the company has not built any joint spaces from consumer judgment, a manager might try to build a two-dimensional product space by plotting each of the competing offerings on the two most important attributes or benefits provided (Shapiro and Jackson, 1978). This forces the manager to think about the relative strengths and weaknesses of various offers. When this information is combined with estimates of the value that different segments place on these benefits, one can evaluate the appropriateness of various prices.

Graphing the price per unit against one or more performance measures for each product in a category is another valuable form of analysis. When the data include trends, the graphs become even more valuable. Figure 6-1 illustrates changes in a class of computer equipment, where the performance measure refers to the speed of the machine's central processor. The usefulness of Figure 6-1 can be enhanced by representing the firm's product offerings by unique symbols and giving a similar treatment to the offerings of leading competitors. The average unit price, performance, and performance per dollar during each time period could be noted. Projecting these figures provides rough targets for product development and pricing. A companion graph, overlay, or third dimension could show the estimated volume of each product that has been sold or is on order. Finally, a variety of other physical properties, such as the size of the machine's random access

memory, can appear in a companion graph, or in two-at-a-time graphs with price as the third dimension. For example, showing the price of various combinations of central processor speeds and memory size over time might be highly instructive. These layouts do not exhaust the useful possibilities. Furthermore, this technique can be applied to most categories of products and services.

Economic value analysis   With many industrial products, it is possible to calculate the economic value of various products that might meet the same need (Forbis and Mehta, 1981). Forbis and Mehta suggest first calculating the consumer's life cycle cost of a "reference product," usually that consumer's current product. Then the differences in life cycle costs and relative benefits between a competitive product and the reference product are calculated. The consumer should be indifferent between the reference product at its current price and the competitive product with a price difference equal to the difference in relative value.

For example, assume that a company has developed a washer out of a new material that is used to seal joints in chemical plants making corrosive materials. The old washers cost $5 and had to be replaced every 200 hours. The cost of downtime for each replacement was $100. If the new washer will last for 600 hours, its relative economic value is $215.

In general, raw materials can be compared on such factors as cost per weight or volume, processing or assembly cost, and the ease of cleanup, as well as on differences they make in the final product that can be reflected in different prices. Equipment can be compared on the basis of output and price of the resulting products.

Invariably these value comparisons differ across customers and situations because of differences in the way the product is used. Additionally, customers will differ in their inertia or the size of the premium required to

FIGURE 6-1   Evolving value of computer equipment.

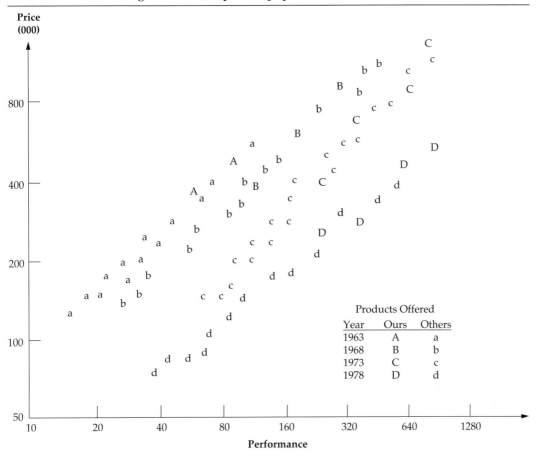

switch. A useful segmentation of the market can be developed from these facts and used to forecast how much will be sold at different prices. This approach is harder to take with many consumer products because the purchaser is usually less aware of performance and price differences. However, it is potentially appropriate when consumers make price and performance trade-offs between competing brands.

Managerial estimates of price sensitivity Managers can also make judgments about how price sensitive the customer is. Price sensitivity is due to several factors. The first is the per-

ceived difference in the offers. Consumers will be less price sensitive when they perceive a great difference in offers or when there are few known substitutes. Product differentiation is ordinarily achieved by carefully developing the product's physical characteristics and the ancillary benefits provided during purchase and use. Furthermore, the type and quality of the product's distributors are important. This is true of high fashion apparel and automobiles as well as for industrial goods where quick delivery and reliable technical service are important. Also, products can be favorably differentiated in terms of the image that has been created in the customer's mind. Also price can be a powerful way to differentiate a product, especially when a low price is sustainable, but many other opportunities exist for favorably influencing selective demand.

If the consumers feel they are able to judge product quality and perceive little difference in the offers, they will be quite price sensitive, and small unmatched changes in price will result in much larger changes in volume. This phenomenon suggests that consumers generally become more price sensitive as products move through the life cycle. First, consumers are better judges of product quality as they become more familiar with the various brands. Second, differences in the quality of competing products sold to a segment tend to narrow as good ideas get copied and unpopular products are taken off the market.

Conversely, if it is hard to judge quality independent of price or if a higher price contributes to a better image, price may be used as a cue for quality and people will not be as price sensitive. Also, customers tend to become less price sensitive when their risk of making a wrong decision increases. Risk decreases as one's ability to judge product quality increases and as the reactions of peers become less important. If there is a large nonprice risk in purchasing a new product, lowering the price may not increase sales much. On the other hand, consumers become more price sensitive when the product in question represents a large purchase or a large portion of their budget.

Forecasting sales   Even without questioning customers, managers can use the above factors to make a judgment about how price sensitive consumers will be for their product. The information from these analyses can be combined into an estimate of how much will be sold at various prices. When making this assessment, each responding manager should explicitly state his or her assumptions about competitive reactions. Figure 6-2 provides one possible format for collecting this information.

FIGURE 6–2   Framework for assessing responses to price changes.

Instructions: In the row labeled *Base* is our best estimate of next year's price and sales volume at that price as well as the forecast price of four of our major competitors. For each change in price, first fill in your assessment of competitive reaction, then fill in your forecast for our sales volume.

Percent Price Change	Price in Dollars	Competitive Prices				Our Unit Sales
		A	B	C	D	
+15%	*					
+10%	*					
+5%	*					
Base	*	*	*	*	*	*
−5%	*					
−10%	*					
−15%	*					

Please provide any comments on your forecasts that you think are helpful in evaluating them.

_____

_____

_____

* - Cells to be completed before the form is given to a respondent.

Consumer Judgments

There are two related ways to assess consumers' perceptions of prices. In the first case, consumers are questioned directly about how much more valuable one product is than another, or, equivalently, how much the price of the more preferred product would have to rise to induce a switch to the less preferred product. In the second, consumers are presented with two or more products whose prices are included and are asked which, or how much, of each product they would purchase. (Alternatively, they may be allowed to make an actual purchase.) This exercise can be repeated, using different prices to infer the relative value of the various products. Furthermore, both general types of questions can be asked about either the overall product or about various attributes.

The next two examples deal with using direct questions to estimate the relative value of different products or attributes. In each case, the methodology is based on Pessemier's dollar metric procedure (1963). First, the customer is presented with two alternatives and is asked to make a choice. Then the customer is asked how much the price of the more preferred would have to rise before the other would be chosen.

Value of the brand   The first case deals with preferences for different brands. It assumes that the product can be fully identified by its brand name. Examples of this kind of product include soft drinks, cereals, toothpastes, records, books, and wine. On the other hand, the value of a personal computer can vary on the basis of such options as memory, peripheral devices, type of monitor, and inclusion of a math co-processor. It may make sense to talk about comparably equipped models with some products such as automobiles. Alternatively, it is possible to state which options are included with each of the various brands.

The first step in this type of study is to choose the relevant brands. This choice should reflect concerns similar to those discussed in conjunction with perceptual maps and joint spaces. Once the list is complete, each respondent would be presented with all possible pairs of brands (or at least a balanced subset of them) with which they are familiar. For each pair the respondent would be asked which one was more preferred and how much its price would have to rise before he or she would choose the other. If prices for the various brands differ, it is possible to include the price for each brand in the questionnaire.

Figure 6-3 provides an example of a questionnaire dealing with the value of four different soft drinks. The output of this questionnaire can be analyzed with either of two equivalent methods. First, if every brand has been compared to every other brand, one can calculate the average value for each brand by averaging the responses across all the pairs of which that brand is a part. The number to be averaged is the *difference* in price needed to switch. It is equal to the sum of the increase in price needed to switch and the

FIGURE 6–3   Example of a questionnaire to determine the value of four soft drink brands.

Please complete the following task for each of the pairs of soft drinks. First, consider just the two available brands and their price per six-pack, and circle the soft drink you would purchase at these prices. Then in the space provided at the right state how much the six-pack price of the more preferred soft drink would have to rise before you would choose the other brand.

Pair	Brand 1	Brand 2	Price Increase to Switch
1	Pepsi ($2.25)	(Coke) ($2.30)	.25
2	(7 Up) ($2.20)	Sprite ($2.25)	.35
3	(Coke) ($2.30)	7 Up ($2.20)	.85
4	Sprite ($2.25)	(Pepsi) ($2.25)	1.00
5	(Coke) ($2.30)	Sprite ($2.25)	1.25
6	7 Up ($2.20)	(Pepsi) ($2.25)	.70

current price difference. If that brand is more preferred, the number is positive; if it is not preferred, the number is negative. For example, using the hypothetical responses in Figure 6-3, Coke is preferred over Pepsi by $.30 (which is the current $.05 difference plus the additional $.25 that Coke would have to increase for a switch to take place); Pepsi is preferred over 7Up by $.75 and Sprite by $1.00. The relative value for Pepsi is $.483 = ($1.00 + $.75 − $.30)/3. The corresponding values for the other brands are: Coke $.85, 7Up −$.477, and Sprite −$.877.

It is also possible to calculate these values with a dummy variable regression. In this application, each brand is represented by a dummy variable. There will be a different row, or observation, in the regression for every decision the consumer makes.[1] The dummy variable associated with the brand that is listed as brand 1 in any observation will be coded as 1. The dummy

---

[1]This example assumes that the regression program will allow the suppression of the intercept. If that is not true, every observation will be repeated, with the signs on the dependent and all of the independent variables reversed.

variable associated with brand 2 will be coded −1. All of the other dummy variables will be coded with a 0. The dependent variable is the difference in price that will cause the person to switch from the more preferred to the less preferred item. This difference is coded as a positive number if brand 1 is the more preferred and is coded as a negative number if brand 2 is more preferred. When prices are not included, the dependent variable is the number the respondent filled in. If prices are included, the number is equal to the price needed to switch plus the price of brand 1 minus the price of brand 2.

This exercise deals only with price differences that are associated with switches, and not absolute price levels. Therefore, an additional row needs to be added to the regression problem. Here the independent variables are all ones and the dependent variable is zero. This forces the sum of the price differences to be zero. The coding is illustrated in Table 6-1.

The first observation involves Pepsi as brand 1 (it is coded with a positive one) and Coke as brand 2 (coded as negative one). Brand 2 was preferred. Its price would have to rise by $.25 per six-pack before this person would switch to brand 1 so the price to switch is coded as a nega-

tive. Brand 1 is already $.05 less than brand 2, so the price difference is negative and the total difference in price needed to switch is $.30. The other observations can be interpreted in a similar manner.

If this regression were run, the following coefficients would be generated: Coke $.85, Pepsi $.483, 7Up −$.477, and Sprite −$.877. These are the same numbers as the averages calculated earlier. Because the difference in value of Coke and Pepsi is $.37 ($.85 - $.48), the indication is that this person will continue to choose Coke over Pepsi until the difference in their prices gets to be greater than $.37 per six-pack. Similarly, this person will continue to choose Coke over Sprite until the difference in price is $1.72 per six-pack. Given typical grocery store specials of $.70 to $.80 per six-pack, this person might switch to Pepsi when it was on special, but would not switch to Sprite unless it were part of a very unusual deal.

If this information is collected from a number of people, it is possible to build a demand curve for one of the brands; say, Pepsi. First, to calculate how much volume would be lost if Pepsi's price were raised above $2.25 per six-pack, one needs to look at those people who preferred

TABLE 6-1   DUMMY VARIABLE CODING FOR HYPOTHETICAL ANSWERS TO THE QUESTIONNAIRE IN FIGURE 6-3

PAIR	PRICE TO SWITCH[1]	PRICE DIFFERENCE[2]	DEPENDENT VARIABLE[3]	PEPSI	COKE	7UP	SPRITE
1	−.25	−.05	−.30	1	−1	0	0
2	.35	−.05	.30	0	0	1	−1
3	.85	.10	.95	0	1	−1	0
4	−1.00	.00	−1.00	−1	0	0	1
5	1.25	.05	1.30	0	1	0	−1
6	−.70	−.05	−.75	−1	0	1	0
			0.00	1	1	1	1

[1]This is the questionnaire response. It is negative if brand 2 was preferred and positive if brand 1 was preferred.

[2]This is the price of brand 2 subtracted from the price of brand 1.

[3]The sum of the two previous columns.

Pepsi over all other brands and determine how many would switch away as Pepsi's price rose relative to their second choice. Then, to determine how much volume would be gained as Pepsi lowered its price, one needs to look at the number of people who would switch from their favorite brand to Pepsi as Pepsi's price dropped relative to that brand.[2]

By recording the source of the purchases gained when Pepsi lowered its price and the destination of brand switchers lost when Pepsi raised its price, further insight could be gained into Pepsi's strengths and weaknesses. We realize that permanent price changes would probably be matched, so this information might be more useful in terms of short-term deals than in planning prices.

The issues surrounding brand loyalty (DuWors and Haines, 1990) and resistance to compromise (Olver and Farris, 1989) are closely linked to the value of a brand. It is one thing for someone to prefer a brand to its competitors but readily accept a compromise choice; it is quite another matter to be so loyal as to reject all substitutes. Like the measures of preference presented in the foregoing chapter, the measure of brand value presented here accounts for the individual's strength of preference and willingness to compromise. It measures one's resistance to price cutting by less preferred brands and the willingness to postpone a purchase when the preferred brand is unavailable. Like most of the other measures of preference used in this text, it leads to estimates of a brand's market share in a full awareness and availability environment.

Value of individual attributes   It is possible to use the same basic technique to estimate the value of enhanced levels of individual product attributes. This is illustrated in the next example. The process is similar to both the previous

method and to the form of conjoint analysis in which two concepts are placed side by side and directly compared. Here, the person is presented with two hypothetical concepts which include prices and is asked first to circle the one that is more likely to be chosen, then to state the increase in price that is required to get that person to switch. Figure 6-4 illustrates part of a questionnaire for this technique.

These responses can be analyzed with regression. The dummy variables for the different price levels are not included because they are absorbed in the dependent variable. Otherwise, the procedure is the same as discussed in the last chapter. One level of each attribute is chosen as the reference level and a separate dummy variable is created for every other level of that attribute. Each decision is recorded as a separate observation. The independent variables are

FIGURE 6–4   Example of a questionnaire to determine the value of various computer concepts.

Please complete the following task for each of the pairs of the personal computer concepts. First, consider the two concepts and their price and circle the computer you would purchase at these prices. Then in the space provided at the right state how much the price of the more preferred computer would have to rise before you would choose the other.

Pair	Brand 1	Brand 2	Price Increase to Switch
1	IBM $4K 90 MB	Apple $3K 30 MB	$500
2	Epson $4K 90 MB	IBM $5K 30 MB	$1000
3	Epson $4K 30 MB	Apple $3K 30 MB	$1500
4	Apple $5K 90 MB	IBM $4K 90 MB	$3000

[2]Ideally, these estimates would be made from data gathered by a separate set of questions, with subjects being asked how much of a price reduction in the nonpreferred brand would be required to induce a switch to it.

dummy variable descriptions of the differences in the concepts. If the concept on the left possesses a certain level of an attribute, the dummy variable associated with that attribute level is coded with a 1. If the concept on the right possesses a certain level of an attribute, the dummy variable associated with that attribute level is coded with a −1. If both concepts have the same level of a given attribute or if neither concept has a given level of a certain attribute, it is coded as a 0.

The dependent variable is the difference in price that would cause the person to switch from the more preferred to the less preferred alternative. This number is equal to the price needed to switch plus the price of the first alternative minus the price of the second alternative. The dependent variable is positive if the concept on the left is more preferred and negative if the concept on the right is more preferred. The same attributes and reference levels that were used in the last chapter are used in this example. Table 6-2 shows some hypothetical responses to the questionnaire in Figure 6-4 as well as the associated dependent and independent variables.

The regression weights indicate the difference in dollar value between the level associated with that dummy variable and the reference level for that attribute. The reference level can be thought of as having a zero value. The reference level

will not necessarily be the least desired level; it is quite possible that some of the attributes will have negative regression weights associated with them.

The attribute levels can be ordered from least to most valued. The least valued level is designated $j = 1$, the next higher valued level is designated $j = 2$, and so on. If the reference level is not the least valued, the least valued level will have the largest negative number associated with it. In that case, the absolute value of that largest negative number should be added to each regression weight for every level of that attribute (including the reference level, which has an implicit value of zero). After this is done, the value of the least valued level will be zero and every other level will be positive, with the most valued level having the largest number.

As in the soft drink example, when a respondent is choosing between a pair of alternatives which differ in terms of the levels of various attributes they possess, that person is expected to choose the alternative whose attributes have the highest value, unless the difference in value is less than the price difference. In this example, as long as an IBM is priced within $2,000 of a comparably equipped Epson, this person would choose the IBM. One could use this information to calculate the relative value of the offerings currently on the market. These relative values could be used to estimate the market share of

TABLE 6-2   CODING FOR FULL PROFILE TRADE-OFFS

PAIR	PRICE TO SWITCH[1]	PRICE DIFFERENCE[2]	DEPENDENT VARIABLE[3]	IBM	APPLE	90MB
1	$500	$1,000	$1,500	1	−1	1
2	$1,000	−$1,000	0	−1	0	1
3	−$1,500	$1,000	−$500	0	−1	0
4	−$3,000	$1,000	−$2,000	−1	1	0

[1]This is the response on the questionnaire. It is coded as a positive number if the first concept was chosen and as a negative number if the second was chosen.

[2]This is the price of the concept on the left minus the price of the concept on the right.

[3]This is the sum of the first two columns.

any offering in a manner similar to a conjoint simulator. Each person's regression weights are used to estimate the value of the alternatives under consideration. Then these values are compared to current prices to predict brand choice.

The value of the *base* product design (i.e., the one of minimum value) to a subject is estimated from purchase behavior by noting the attribute features and price paid for the last product purchased. When the price is adjusted downward for the increments in value provided by the purchased product's enhancements, one obtains the dollar value of the basic product. The latter least-cost product design is assigned $j = 1$ for all nonprice attributes. Once the estimated acceptable price of the base product has been determined, the estimated acceptable price can be computed for all other design possibilities. When these are averaged over all subjects, the imputed price should be close to the market price. If it is not, price and value increments can be rescaled to achieve an acceptable fit.

Comparing the cost and value of attribute levels   The above method allows one to estimate the monetary value of each attribute to each individual. If the cost of providing each level can be estimated by design and manufacturing

personnel, the value per dollar of cost can be determined to identify efficient designs. The value delivered by a design when compared to the value delivered by competing products is a predictor of purchase behavior on the part of individual subjects. When these results are aggregated across individuals, you can predict sales, costs, and profits.

Individuals can be clustered into segments that are homogeneous with respect to the value that they place on the various attribute levels. The following summary tables display information on the value of various attribute levels. Table 6-3 could be for an individual respondent or for an average respondent of a preference segment. If the market is heterogeneous, averaging over the entire market can produce meaningless results. When predicting choice and market potential, the best approach is the *ultimate segmentation* scheme found in most conjoint simulator studies, in which each respondent is analyzed separately to compute market predictions.

Table 6-3 lists the levels of all the attributes in order of increasing value (level 1 always has the lowest value). Then the value of each level (determined by consumer input) is divided by the incremental cost estimated by operations.

TABLE 6-3   VALUE OF VARIOUS ATTRIBUTE LEVELS FOR AN INDIVIDUAL

ATTRIBUTE LEVEL		Incremental $ Value	Incremental $ Cost	Incremental $ Value Per Incremental $ of Cost
i Description	*j* Description			
1	1	____[1]	____[2]	____
	2			
2	1	____[1]	____[2]	____
	2			
	3			
3	1	____[1]	____[2]	____
	. . .		. . .	

[1] $ value of the basic design $_____. This amount cannot be allocated to individual attributes.

[2] $ cost of the basic design $_____. This cost cannot be allocated to individual attributes.

For each design of interest to a marketing manager, the value and cost can be computed, *provided* customer behavior is guided by the relative value of the firm's and its competitors' product designs. Since the price attribute must be subtracted from the imputed dollar value of the other attributes, an increase in price directly reduces the net dollar value or buyer surplus. A price decrease has the opposite effect. *The task of the manager is to increase the revenue obtained from his or her product net of the product's cost.* Since the baseline design is assumed to be a minimum cost design, attributes should be upgraded in a manner that delivers the largest increase in revenue for the cost that is incurred. This value–enhancing strategy opens the door to possible price changes. The extent to which minimum

(low cost and low price) designs are attractive compared to enhanced (higher cost and higher price) designs depends on how responsive customers will be to various levels of price for a given design.

An indication of the dispersion of customer desires for all of the attributes can be gained by clustering people on the basis of how much they value the basic design and the possible incremental improvements. If there are sizable groups that want quite different product characteristics, multiple product offerings may be called for. On the other hand, all of the more desirable design options may already be offered by competitors. In this case, opportunities to be price competitive, to develop a more attractive image, or to use a superior pattern of support

TABLE 6-4   ATTRIBUTE VALUES BY VARIOUS SEGMENTS

DESCRIPTION	SEGMENT 1	SEGMENT 2
Number of Individuals		
Average Value of Basic Design		
Mean Deviation from Average		
Incremental Attribute Values		
Attribute 1, Level 2		
Average $ Value		
Mean Deviation		
Level 3		
Average $ Value		
Mean Deviation		
Attribute 2, Level 2		
. . .	. . .	. . .
Trial Design I (, ,...,)[1]		
Est. Share of Purchases		
Est. Before Mktg. Contribution		
Trial Design II (, ,...,)[1]		
Est. Share of Purchases		
Est. Before Mktg. Contribution		
Trial Design III (, ,...,)[1]		
. . .	. . .	. . .

[1]A vector of attribute levels defining the design.

spending must be explored. A table like Table 6-4 is a useful way to display group differences and the degree of within-group consensus. The bottom section of the table is compiled by using the attribute value data to determine how many of the people in a segment find that a particular trial design offers the greatest net value at the proposed price.

Analyzing demand at various price levels
The above methods allow you to calculate a demand curve indirectly by estimating how many people would switch on the basis of how much they value each product's attributes. This section discusses a more direct way to estimate demand at different price levels. Additionally, this method can be used to estimate the effect of different offers on primary demand. As noted earlier, there are many ways to shed light on this subject. Here, the discussion is directed solely to the effect of the offer, design, communications message, and price, before it is affected by future marketing spending. Like analyzing the value of design elements, a simple survey method is presented.

Subjects should be asked to specify which products are familiar and which attributes materially influence choice and use. This approach allows subjects to respond to tailor-made stimuli that are relevant to their purchase decisions. The stimulus format shown in Table 6-5 can be used. In this layout, the assortment includes the firm's proposed product and price as well as the other products that are known to the subject (and their expected prices). If acceptance is materially modified by product images and/or distribution, steps must be taken to convey the images verbally, in print, or on a video screen as well as to provide descriptions of the product's distribution. When several proposed products and prices are being tested, multiple stimuli and possibly multiple samples are needed. By presenting a suitable sample of subjects with this type of stimuli, the attractiveness of the proposed design and price can be measured.

Once the data are in hand, it is easy to estimate the share of demand that a proposed product and price will attract and the extent to which the price level does or does not change primary demand. Since this approach provides market-

TABLE 6-5 EXAMPLE OF A QUESTIONNAIRE TO ELICIT DEMAND FORECASTS

Attributes	Brand A	Brand B	Brand C	
Attribute 1	XXXXXX	XXXXXX	XXXXXX	. . . .
Attribute 2	XXXXXX	XXXXXX	XXXXXX	. . . .
Attribute 3	XXXXXX	XXXXXX	XXXXXX	. . . .
. . .	. . .	. . .		
Price	XXXXXX	XXXXXX	XXXXXX	. . . .
Planned Purchases	[ ]	[ ]	[ ]	. . . .

Instructions: If this is the available assortment, how many total units will you buy during the next YYYYY months?_____
Indicate the most likely pattern of purchases by distributing this amount across the products shown above. Do this by entering an appropriate number (greater than or equal to zero) in each box.

ing management with both sales forecasts and estimates of the total contribution to profit, the selection of the best design is straightforward. Although testing multiple positioning strategies may require different groups of subjects and possibly a larger number of product sets, no additional methodological issues are encountered.

Two things about this procedure should be noted. First, the products do not always need to be described in terms of attributes. Sometimes the brand names convey all the required information, as in the earlier example dealing with soft drinks. Second, one does not have to stop with asking how many units a person would purchase at one set of prices. A person could be asked a number of questions that involve a group of systematically varying prices.

If one is not concerned with competitive reaction at this time, a manager could vary only the price of the company's product and leave all the competitive prices constant. This would give an indication of how much could be sold at various price levels. On the other hand, it is possible to vary the prices of all of the competing products. In this case, you can look at sales not only under different prices, but also under different competitive reactions.

This procedure is illustrated with an example. Assume that brand A is a mid-priced brand competing with brands B and C. The current market prices for the three are $60, $80, and $50, respectively. Furthermore, assume that you want to study three possible prices for each of the brands: A—$50, $60, and $70; B—$60, $80, and $90; and C—$40, $50, and $60. Each respondent would be asked to fill out nine cards like that in Table 6-5. Each would be identical except for the prices. The prices for each of the nine cards as well as hypothetical responses for the quantity of brand A demanded are given in Table 6-6.

The impact of any brand's sales can be studied by using a dummy variable regression analogous to conjoint analysis. There are three prices

TABLE 6-6 EXAMPLE OF PRICE COMBINATIONS GIVEN TO EACH RESPONDENT

Quantity of Brand A Demanded	Price of Brand A	Price of Brand B	Price of Brand C
46	$70	$90	$50
47	$70	$80	$60
36	$70	$70	$40
54	$60	$90	$40
53	$60	$80	$50
52	$60	$70	$60
70	$50	$90	$60
61	$50	$80	$40
58	$50	$70	$50

for each brand. One price for each brand needs to be designated as the reference level and dummy variables must be constructed for each of the other two levels. In this example, the highest price for each brand will be the reference level. Table 6-7 gives the dummy variable coding for these nine cards as well as a set of hypothetical responses for the quantity of brand A, Q_A, that would be purchased under each of the price conditions. For example, the first row shows that when the prices of brands A, B, and C are set at $70, $90, and $50, respectively, this person wanted forty-six units of brand A.

Running this regression would result in the following set of regression weights:

$$Q_A = 50 + 10\,D_{AM} + 20\,D_{AL} - 3\,D_{BM} - 8\,D_{BL} - 4\,D_{CM} - 6\,D_{CL}$$

where Q_A is the quantity of brand A that would be purchased and D_{ij} is the dummy variable associated with the jth price (medium or low) of the ith brand (A, B, or C).

This regression shows that when all brands are at the highest price, fifty units (i.e., the intercept) of brand A will be purchased. Lowering

TABLE 6-7   CODING FOR PRICING QUESTIONS

Quantity of Brand A Demanded	DUMMY VARIABLES FOR BRAND PRICES					
	BRAND A		BRAND B		BRAND C	
	$60	$50	$80	$70	$50	$40
	D_{AM}[1]	D_{AL}	D_{BM}	D_{BL}	D_{CM}	D_{CL}
46	0	0	0	0	1	0
47	0	0	1	0	0	0
36	0	0	0	1	0	1
54	1	0	0	0	0	1
53	1	0	1	0	1	0
52	1	0	0	1	0	0
70	0	1	0	0	0	0
61	0	1	1	0	0	1
58	0	1	0	1	1	0

[1]The first subscript of the dummy variable indicates the brand and the second subscript indicates whether it is the medium or the low price for the brand.

the price of brand A will increase its sales, but lower prices for brands B or C will decrease the amount of brand A sold. Comparing the regression weights associated with B and C, it is seen that a decrease from $90 to $80 for brand B has a smaller effect (−3) on brand A than does a decrease from $60 to $50 for brand C (−4). However, the decrease from $90 to $70 for brand B has a bigger impact on brand A (−8) than does the decrease from $60 to $40 for brand C (−6). Finally, the regression shows that price changes for brand A have a bigger impact on its sales than do price changes do for either B or C. A similar analysis could be carried out for any of the other brands or for the total quantity of all three brands purchased.

It is possible to use this same basic procedure to ask people what portion of their purchases would be allocated to each brand rather than ask them to specify purchase quantities. Usually, a logit model is used to analyze this type of data. However, it is possible to approximate the logit by running an ordinary least-squares regression on these data and setting any predicted proportions that are greater than one equal to one and

any predicted proportions that are less than zero equal to zero. Use of a logit is illustrated in Appendix 6-1.

Limitations of this type of pricing research There are several problems with the foregoing type of pricing research. With all questionnaire-based research, there must be a concern about the consistency between what people say they will do and what they actually do. First, this problem is greater when respondents are asked questions that they have not considered before. Second, if consumers are not aware of competing prices, a heightened awareness of prices in an experimental situation may make them more price sensitive than normal. Third, none of these methods can model the long-term impact of price changes. It is possible that a person will buy a product once or twice because of a lower price, but will switch to another brand if quality is not perceived to be as good.

Furthermore, many industrial buyers may not want to discuss their buying intentions or may resort to game-playing in order to get lower prices than they otherwise would. Also, people seldom know how much they are going to purchase in the future. Finally, all pricing research is costly and time consuming, often making intolerable demands on a manager. Still, these methods offer some potentially useful information and deserve serious consideration.

Field Experiments and Historical Analyses

Rather than asking consumers what they would do in various circumstances, it is possible to observe their actions in the marketplace. For example, the value of enhancements to a basic design may be estimated from price-performance curves. Here an important measure of performance, such as horsepower, top speed, or hauling capacity, can be plotted on the horizontal axis, with the associated price on the vertical axis. Furthermore, several price-performance curves from different time periods can be plotted to aid in forecasting trends in price, performance, and value. See Figure 6-1 and the associated text.

One can also analyze the historical pattern between price and sales volume. However, several factors make this option less attractive than it might appear. First, there is usually a clear long-term trend in price levels, but other than promotional prices, relatively little variation can be observed around this trend. Second, historical information is needed on competitive prices during this period. Third, volume changes are due to a number of marketing activities the firm and its competitors undertake; so these effects must also be considered.

A more precise measure of the relationship between price and sales volume can be obtained through field experiments. If the entire selling area can be split into a number of regional markets, it is possible to perform pricing experiments by raising the price in some areas, lowering it in others, and maintaining the original price in the rest. This process should have a lot of basic appeal and is encouraged.

However, several problems are associated with the process. First, the changes need to be communicated as permanent changes and not temporary changes. Second, the territories must be comparable, so the effects of price changes in one area can be extrapolated to the entire selling area. Third, competitors may discover the experiment and will either learn as much as the company running the experiment or try to interfere with it. Finally, it may be difficult to conduct pricing experiments in industrial markets. Some customers detect the regional price differences because they are purchasing in multiple areas and are negotiating price along with other terms of the sale.

Numerous difficulties can be encountered when using field experiments or historical analysis to study the effect of price on sales. Coupons given to customers and display allowances given to retailers are logically classified as marketing support spending rather than as an adjustment in the product's basic price; that is, the offer price. Furthermore, the effect on sales of support items is frequently confounded with the effect of price. Suppose a manufacturer uses a label allowance promotion and requires participating retailers to provide special displays. Temporarily, customers buy more and pay less per unit. These sales can be recorded in a way that prevents management from separating the short-term promotional results from the effects that might be produced by changes in the product's basic price level. In addition, it may be difficult or impossible to adequately account for the degree to which the added sales were due to the label allowance and the special display.

The above conditions indicate that managers need to examine price and sales data thoughtfully. The time intervals for the analysis must be chosen with care and the related influences on sales must be monitored. These matters have been discussed by Clarke (1987, pp. 384–389). Clarke also displays a graph that illustrates the presence of interactions among promotional prices, supporting displays, and feature advertising. As expected, volume increases as price is reduced, but the extent of the effect is substantially intensified when supported by nonprice elements. Support spending on nonprice elements appears to be considerably more effective at larger price reductions than it is at smaller price reductions. The final choice of an action or set of actions must be justified in terms of both the sales effects and the costs of obtaining the results.

Summary

Each of the above-mentioned techniques has certain strengths and weaknesses. Furthermore, there is no one best way of estimating demand curves or the relative value of different offers in all situations. Still, in the end, managers must base these estimates on their own judgment. However, because their unaided judgments may be biased, they need to consider what the consumers say they will do and/or what they have done in the past.

CAPTURING VALUE

Once the relative value of the offer has been estimated and one has some idea about how much might be sold at different prices, the manager must decide how much of the value created by the offer should be captured through price. As more of the value is captured through higher prices, the customer has less incentive to purchase the product and fewer units will be sold. Some of the factors that should enter into this decision include the strategic objectives of the firm, the need for support spending, consumer price sensitivity, the firm's cost structure, competitor and reseller reaction, and production capacity.

Strategic Considerations

Strategic factors include all of the longer run and product line objectives which can modify the pricing actions that might otherwise be adopted.

The most common example of the interaction between objectives and pricing is in the choice between a penetration and a skimming strategy for a new product. A penetration strategy may be employed to gain a large market share quickly at the expense of early profits. By way of contrast, with a skimming strategy, a product is introduced at a relatively high price, which is gradually lowered. This skimming action might allow the successful liquidation of a large inventory of an existing product by taking advantage of the new product's special appeal to some customers. Another common interaction between objectives and pricing strategies occurs later in a brand's life cycle, when a harvesting strategy is an option. In this case, a comfortable margin is maintained at the expense of a continuing erosion of sales.

However, these interactions between strategic objectives and pricing strategies are present at all points in a brand's life cycle. At any time, there are conflicting objectives in terms of enhancing the brand's image, balancing current profits against growth, stabilizing the market, discouraging others from cutting prices, discouraging entrants, speeding the exit of marginal firms, and maintaining reseller loyalty and support. One must look at all these objectives when determining price. A price increase to improve a brand image could also result in lowered volume.

This interaction between objectives and pricing strategies points to the need for an integrated marketing mix and reinforces the idea that the entire mix should be focused on a specific objective. Therefore, one must first determine objectives and a general strategy, then decide how price can best be used in conjunction with other parts of the offer and marketing support spending to achieve the desired results.

When choosing a price to achieve a certain objective, a frequent trade-off occurs between current profits and growth. There is a strong relationship between relative market share and contemporaneous profitability (Buzzell, Gale, and Sultan, 1976), possibly because they are two different measures of how well the business is doing. However, there is a continuing debate on the relationship between current market share and future profitability (Anterasian and Phillips, 1988; Jacobson and Aaker, 1985).

At present, the relationship appears to be much weaker than was previously thought. To the extent that share increases are due to satisfied customers, market share is a good indication of the health of the business. But, trying to gain share for its own sake through low prices is frequently unwise. Share is not intrinsically valuable if higher shares do not translate into higher future profits or if share that is gained through lower prices is easily lost when prices are raised or when a competitor offers lower prices. Furthermore, one study (Buzzell and Wiersema, 1981) found that price changes did not appear to be related to increases in share. These comments do not suggest that a positioning of very good value (a good product at a low price) is incorrect. They caution that seeking a large increase in share through price cutting can be a risky strategy.

Price Sensitivity

The second factor that should be considered is consumer price sensitivity. Consumers' price sensitivity can be represented by a demand schedule or curve. This curve can represent the demand either for the product class as a whole (primary demand) or for an individual brand (selective demand). The greatest interest is usually on the selective demand curve. Several methods to estimate this curve were presented in the last section. Except for unusual circumstances, unit sales are expected to increase as price decreases, given no changes in the other variables that influence volume. This results in a downward-sloping demand curve.

Price elasticity is the relative change in the quantity sold divided by the relative change in price. Although this general relationship applies

to a fixed time interval, it helps managers think about the effects of a price change. If q is the original quantity demanded at price p and q' is the quantity demanded at a new price p', the price elasticity equals $((q' - q)/q)/((p - p')/p)$. If this ratio is greater than one, the percentage change in unit sales is greater than the percentage change in price. This means that total revenue will increase when prices are lowered but will decrease when prices are raised. When the ratio is less than one, the opposite is true. Usually consumers are more price sensitive within certain ranges than others. Therefore, price elasticity is not constant over the range of prices.

The Effects of Cost Structure on Unit Price

Although prices should not be set simply by adding a fixed percentage markup to the cost, costs do play an important role in determining the proper price to charge. This is an arithmetic role in which costs are used to calculate profitability under different price and volume combinations. Furthermore, if factors such as experience curves create dynamic cost effects, the analysis must be carried past the current period, as current decisions will have an impact on future profits at different price and volume combinations.

Cost structure refers to the fixed- and variable-cost mixture at different volumes. Variable costs are fixed per unit but increase in total as unit sales increase. Fixed costs do not change as volume increases (within reasonable limits) but their allocation per unit decreases as the number of units sold increases. The following discussion makes the simplifying assumption that all costs can be classified as either fixed or variable. When applying these concepts, one must realize the limits of this assumption. Most fixed costs become variable with enough changes in volume. Also, most fixed costs become variable when time horizons are extended (Johnson and Kaplan, 1987).

Variable costs Price changes have more leverage on the bottom line than any other variable. Holding everything else constant, a 10 percent increase in price adds more to profit than a 10 percent increase in volume or a 10 percent decrease in cost (either fixed or variable). However, the relative effect of these various changes differs, depending on the cost structure. Therefore, the relationship between costs and prices has an important impact on the firm's options.

For example, consider a small difference between price and variable costs. Then the contribution margin, CM (equal to price, *P*, minus unit variable cost, VC), and the percentage contribution margin, PCM (equal to CM/*P*), are quite low. Under these circumstances it is usually easier to try to increase profits by raising prices than by increasing volume. If PCM = 10 percent, a 10 percent price increase will add as much to profit as a 100 percent increase in volume, because the price increase doubles the contribution margin. Stated differently, if price is increased by 10 percent and volume does not drop by 50 percent, the firm will be more profitable. On the other hand, if the PCM = 70 percent, a 10 percent price increase will add about as much to profits as a 15 percent volume increase.

To demonstrate these results numerically, let unit volume be 1,000, unit price equal $100, and variable cost equal either $90 or $30. In the first case, CM = $10 and PCM = .1. In the second case, CM = $70 and PCM = .7. The following examples show the change in volume (at current price) required to equal the total contribution, TC, achieved by a 10 percent increase in price (with current volume).

Case 1: CM × *V*   = TC
$10 × 1,000 = $10,000   Original condition
$20 × 1,000 = $20,000 $10 price increase
$10 × 2,000 = $20,000   100 percent volume increase needed to match the results of the price increase

Case 2: CM × *V*   = TC
$70 × 1,000 = $70,000   Original condition
$80 × 1,000 = $80,000 $10 price increase
$70 × 1,143 = $80,000   14.3 percent volume increase needed to match the results of the price increase

This suggests that when variable costs are quite high relative to prices, one should focus on strategies to increase price, especially if it can be done without raising variable costs. On the other hand, when variable costs are quite low, increasing either price or volume can be a viable strategy to increase profits, depending upon their relative ease of accomplishment.

This general line of reasoning can be extended to any level of contribution margins (Dolan, 1984). As noted above, total contribution to fixed costs and profits, TC, is equal to CM times unit volume, *V*. Given these relationships, one can determine how large the new unit volume, *V'*, would have to be to preserve or increase current contribution to profit when the price is changed by *F* dollars or cents. (If price is decreased, then *F* is negative.)

The following formula sets the old total contribution, CM × *V*, equal to the new total contribution, CM' × *V'*, so it is possible to solve for the new volume required to maintain total contribution:

$$CM \times V = (F + CM) \times V' = CM' \times V'$$

Rearranging this equation yields:

$$\frac{CM}{F+CM} = \frac{V'}{V}$$

Knowing that the new volume as a fraction of the old volume must be at least as big as the ratio of the old contribution margin, CM, to the new contribution margin, CM' = *F* + CM provides a helpful decision criterion. Substituting various price changes into the expression yields an informative series of "break-even" unit sales hurdles. If CM = \$10 and F changes as shown in the left-hand column, the right-hand column shows the required minimum ratio of the new to the old volume.

$F = -\$2$ $V'/V = 1.25$

$F = -\$1$ $V'/V = 1.11$

$F = \$1$ $V'/V = .901$

$F = \$2$ $V'/V = .883$

Now the manager's job is one of deciding whether the firm can get at least the break-even volume associated with the price change. This is a function of price sensitivity, the subject of the previous subsection.

Fixed costs   It is equally important for management to recognize the effects of fixed costs on marketing decisions. When fixed costs are high and variable costs are low, profits are much more sensitive to swings in unit sales, whether these swings are caused by competitive actions or by broad economic movements like recessions and expansions. High fixed costs create tremendous pressure to cut prices to try to maintain or increase volume; however, these price cuts are usually matched by competition, with the result that no one gains any volume. This price-cutting pressure is cited as a primary reason for the observed negative relationship between investment intensity and profitability in the PIMS data base (Schoeffler, Buzzell, and Heany, 1974). Currently, this effect is seen most clearly in airline ticket prices. Several years ago, the same phenomenon could be seen in the gasoline price wars.

A second impact of fixed costs occurs when they are related to significant economies of scale. Economies of scale occur when the minimum plant size, national advertising, R&D budget, or fixed cost of servicing or distribution is quite high. In this case, increases in volume allow sig-

nificant reductions in unit costs, so attempting to gain share may be an appropriate objective. It is usually better to reach this goal through some avenue other than price cutting.

Design and policy effects   It is important to remember that design changes can change the levels of fixed and variable expenses. A simple design can save direct costs of assembly and perhaps eliminate the need for some increment of investment. Enhancing the product's features can have the opposite effect. Therefore, R&D, manufacturing, and marketing personnel should work closely with each other to develop appealing products that can be efficiently produced. The cost saved by a new design that does not affect the product's desirability adds directly to unit contribution margin, just as a price increase does, but unlike a price increase, it need not reduce volume.

A less common shift in the mix of variable and fixed expenses occurs when all or part of the production work is performed outside the business unit. In such cases, the entire cost of the unit becomes variable. The desirability of such an arrangement depends on numerous factors, but obtaining a dependable, low-cost source of supply is a central consideration.

Dynamic cost and performance effects   Although the fundamental cost structure may not change over time, it is possible that unit costs will go down for various reasons. In many cases, these reductions can be modeled with an experience curve, a curve that is based on the assumption that costs decline by a constant percentage every time cumulative volume doubles. This relationship can be expressed with the following formula:

$$c_n = c_1 \, n^{-b}$$

where c_n is the cost of the nth unit, c_1 is the cost of the first unit, and $-b$ is the slope of the experience curve. This function can be written in logarithmic form as:

$$\ln c_n = \ln c_1 - b \ln n$$

or

$$\ln (c_n / c_1) = - b \ln n$$

Here, the logarithm of the ratio of the costs is a function of the logarithm of the cumulative number of units. Therefore, the slope, $-b$, can be estimated with a regression. Furthermore, if pc is the percentage by which costs decline every time that cumulative volume doubles, then

$$\text{pc} = 1 - 2^{-b} \text{ and } b = \ln (1 - \text{pc}) / - .69315$$

If $b = .235$, then pc $= .15$ and every time volume doubles, costs will crop by 15 percent. This is usually referred to as an 85 percent experience curve.

This phenomenon of costs declining by a constant percentage as cumulative volume doubles has been commonly observed (Abell and Hammond, 1979; Day and Montgomery, 1983). The systematic decrease in costs is due to three factors.

1. Learning is the first factor. People learn to do their jobs better and faster over time. For example, they learn how to run the manufacturing equipment better, or they learn how to do a better selling job.

2. Technological changes also lower costs. Examples of this include the substitution of capital for labor in automation, the use of different raw materials or components, product redesign for ease of manufacturing, and substituting telemarketing for personal sales calls.

3. Economies of scale may enter into cost reduction if volume per period is growing.

Some of these cost reductions, such as economies of scale and some learning, occur almost automatically. Others, such as raw material substitution and product redesign, are the result of conscious managerial decisions. Therefore, a company can affect the slope of the experience curve by its decisions.

If an experience curve is used to forecast future costs, a different curve should be calculated for every major subcomponent as well as for the assembly process. The slope of each of these curves can be estimated with the logarithmic regression mentioned earlier, or on the basis of experience with similar products. Future costs and prices can be forecast with the aid of a small computer program, EXPER, that is in the set of programs developed for this text. Its principal features are described in Appendix 6-2.

In many cases, the costs required by a marketing plan must be based on engineering estimates or managerial judgment. The EXPER computer program can use simple cost and production estimates as input in lieu of the (equally acceptable) parameter estimates of the type described above. The program output includes projected average annual unit costs. These latter figures are more useful for planning purposes than the cost of the last unit produced at various levels of cumulative production is.

Not only does real cost tend to decline over time, but in most product categories, product performance continuously improves. Under these conditions performance per dollar can increase even if the price per unit increases or remains nearly constant. In a number of fields, it has been possible to observe regular advances in both performance and performance per dollar by plotting the rates by which these variables change on suitable graph paper. See Figure 6-1. Not only do these data help a manager predict price changes, they also help predict the design and performance characteristics that the products must have to remain competitive in the years ahead. This problem is especially troublesome in product categories subject to both rapidly changing technology and long development lead times.

A related subject concerns the rate at which superior substitute products affect sales and prices. Substitution cycles are usually long because users have to learn about the new product and adjust to using it. In the short run, the established inferior product can fight an intruder with product improvements and lower prices. In time, however, the substitute product will prove its superiority. Experience in production and distribution will accumulate and increased scale will permit price reductions. Furthermore, the passage of time will yield product improvements that will further enlarge its market. The recent history of the pocket calculator replacing the slide rule and the transistor replacing the vacuum tube illustrates the process. See Chapter 2 and Foster (1986) for an expanded discussion of this topic.

Other cost analyses   A more traditional form of break-even analysis deals with the number of units that must be sold at a given contribution margin to cover the costs of producing and marketing the product. If at least this level of volume is not predicted at the given unit price, the price is unattractive. Computing the break-even unit sales and the associated market share figures helps management assess the attractiveness of various prices and the risks implied by adopting any one of them. If none of the price and volume combinations produces enough profits (during an appropriate time interval), management should consider either dropping the product or not introducing it.

Pricing and Resellers[3]

In pricing a product that is not sold directly to the final customer, allowance must be made for the margins which the reseller needs to perform the tasks that management wants performed on behalf of the product. If the reseller must exert considerable sales effort or if the product is expensive to store, the reseller will want a large margin. If the product has a large market, is presold, and has small inventory requirements, resellers will handle the product for a lower margin. A useful procedure in setting the price to one or more types of resellers is to analyze the attractiveness of the product from the point of view of each reseller in the chain. Each successive buyer must believe that the purchase offers a better opportunity for profit or greater value than an alternative use of his or her time and money.

The effects of resellers and some of the relationships between price and profit can be observed in a four-quadrant graph like the one described by Alderson and Green (1964, pp. 255–265). Figure 6-5 displays an illustrative graph. Using the connected effects depicted in Figure 6-5 a manager can examine what market

FIGURE 6–5   The effects of resellers on a product's price and sales.

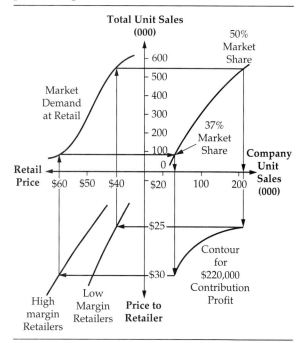

Source: *Alderson and Green, 1964.*

---

[3]See Monroe (1979), Chapter 12.

share is required if a low $25 price and low-margin, mass-retail distribution are used instead of the high $30 price and specialized high-margin retailers currently being employed. The figure shows the principal effects, particularly how the price paid by final customers will change, the effect this change will have on the number of units demanded, and the share of the market that is needed for the firm to obtain the same level of contribution to profit that it expects to obtain under the present price and distribution policy.

In this case management sees that primary demand is responsive to the lower price. Also, management might conclude that a 50 percent market share is unattainable given the small contribution per unit available from the low price to support marketing activities. A higher price calls for the use of retailers who will support the product with a good deal of sales and service. The margin requirements of these resellers typically increase the price to the final buyer. These are the types of trade-offs that confront marketing managers who must reach final customers through resellers.

In light of the above discussion, it is clear that resellers can make important additions to the value received by buyers and users. These contributions are most direct when resellers modify the product. For example, some industrial supply houses cut and otherwise fabricate materials for their customers, and many stores alter both men's and women's apparel. If an appropriate charge is made, these actions become self-supporting services. If a charge is not made to cover that cost, the price must be increased to provide the required operating margin. In analyzing the price charged to resellers and the price paid by final buyers and users, the value-enhancing contribution of resellers must be accounted for.

Predicting Competitive Response

All marketing actions should be preceded by a careful appraisal of the likely competitive re-

sponse. The magnitude of the response is likely to be proportional to both the degree of injury or the extent of the opportunity an action provides and competitors' capacity to respond. For this reason, the effect that a lower (or higher) than expected price would have on competitors should be examined carefully before the price change is implemented. A price reduction that takes substantial volume from a product that is the competitor's principal source of income is very likely to induce the strongest feasible retaliation.

Furthermore, if fixed costs are high relative to variable costs, competitors may have a strong incentive to match a price cut. On the other hand, if the threatened product is unimportant to a competitor, the pricing action may be ignored. Although pricing actions are most often met with pricing responses, many nonprice moves are available, such as increasing quality or offering new associated services to interested market segments.

One potentially important part of competitor analysis is cost analysis. Knowledge of the cost structures of the primary competitors is an important input to the strategizing process. Some products have the advantage of a relatively low unit cost compared to competitors. A product with a cost advantage has the freedom of adopting a low price in the hope of gaining market share and discouraging the entry of competitors, or making it difficult for competitors to mount aggressive marketing campaigns. Alternatively, a low-cost producer may simply meet the market price and bank the added margin, modernize production facilities and product designs, or adopt any of a wide range of aggressive marketing tactics. On the other hand, a high-cost producer is faced with reduced margins and fewer resources with which to manage the effectiveness of the offer and the supporting marketing program.

Determining competitor costs should be a key part of the competitive analysis discussed in Chapter 1. Also, competitive reactions to price changes should be predicted, monitored, and saved for future reference. One way to make sure this gets done in a systematic manner is to assign one or more people to play the role of each competitor when competitive responses are being forecast. Those same people should attempt to mimic all of that competitor's decisions, not just pricing decisions.

The fact that competitive responses are usually important and hard to predict increases management's uncertainty about the link between price and sales volume. In the end, price setting is a dynamic process in which price is set, the market results are tracked, and price is adjusted. A number of market changes that influence demand and price have already been noted; for example, accumulated customer and production experience or design improvements. Through all of these shifts, management must keep an eye on the overriding marketing objectives that pricing actions should serve. Some firms strive for price leadership, others try to minimize the importance of price by providing complex, highly differentiated offers. Unless the strategic context is well understood, it is impossible to set a product's price with confidence.

Integration of Factors Influencing Prices

New products   The following discussion shows how a number of the factors described above might be combined into an overall pricing strategy for new products. Under certain conditions, a company can attempt to capture less value (a penetration pricing strategy) in order to gain market share, possibly at the expense of short-term profits.

1. The customers must be price sensitive; that is, they must be willing to buy more of the firm's product at lower prices.

2. Penetration pricing may be appropriate if there are significant economies of scale or experience curve effects. In this case, selling more enables a company to lower the cost of the product and receive higher margins in the future. If either of these effects is pro-

nounced, it may be possible to drop prices quickly enough to keep other companies out and still maintain acceptable margins.

3. Penetration pricing is appropriate if competitors are likely to enter the market if a higher price is charged, but will stay out if they must meet a lower price. Pricing below the competition when entering an existing market may be appropriate if the competition will not match the price or if a lower price will increase primary demand substantially.

4. The product should be as free from defects as possible to avoid a large volume of unsatisfactory sales.

On the other hand, trying to capture a large part of the value (a skimming strategy) is appropriate under a different set of circumstances:

1. A skimming strategy should be used when the customers are not price sensitive or if there are few, if any, economies of scale or experience curve effects.

2. Premium pricing should be used when capacity is insufficient to meet the demand that would be generated at a lower price.

3. When there is little danger that competition will enter or when a lower price will not keep it out, prices should be higher.

Existing products   With existing products, one might think of a premium pricing strategy, a parity strategy, and a discount strategy to deal with the competition. Although competitive pressure and established customer expectations generally restrict the opportunity to change the prices of existing products, the same principles should apply.

Particular attention needs to be paid to competitive reactions. It may be appropriate to attempt to price below the competition if one is currently losing market share. However, a discount strategy designed to increase market share is appropriate only if consumers are price sensitive and if one of two additional conditions holds. First, a discount pricing strategy may yield increased sales or profits when competitors do not match the price cut. Typically, this will occur only when the competitors' contribution margins are already quite low. In this case, the price-cutting firm's contribution margin must be higher than that of the competition. Otherwise, even a substantial increase in volume may not generate enough profits to make up for the lost contribution per unit. Second, a price cut may be profitable even when competition matches the reduction (which means the strategy is not a discount strategy) if the demand for the product class increases enough so that all of the firms are better off. These situations will occur relatively infrequently. A different way of achieving a discount strategy is by failing to raise prices when competitors do. Ross (1984) feels that even a delay in following competitive price increases may leave the image of a low-price competitor.

On the other hand, a premium price strategy is most appropriate when consumers, or at least one segment, are not price sensitive. Usually, a premium price strategy is associated with a superior product, service, or image. Here, an increase in price is usually associated with a product improvement or repositioning.

In any case, prices should be set with an eye to the relative value of the offer and competitive reactions. Costs should be used only to decide whether it is worthwhile to enter the market, assess possible competitive reactions, and calculate profits at different price and volume combinations.

CONCLUDING REMARKS

This chapter and part of the section on conjoint analysis in Chapter 5 have developed methods which can help a manager price the company's product. The key aspects of the pricing problem which have been treated are (1) measuring

value, (2) estimating how demand will change, (3) estimating unit cost and how it may change as volume changes, and (4) understanding the variety of market forces that can influence a firm's pricing decisions.

Measuring Value and Forecasting Sales

Customer analysis   The worth of a product can be directly assessed by using several price levels for the firm's product in a conjoint analysis. Plotting market share for a set of three to five suitably spaced prices can yield a rough demand schedule for a specific product and set of competitors. Furthermore, dollar differences in the value of all competing products can be measured by the methods illustrated in Figures 6-3 and 6-4. The value and sales effects of design changes can be studied by the approach illustrated in Tables 6-3 and 6-4. Design and price effects on primary as well as selective demand can be investigated by surveys using inputs like those shown in Table 6-5.

One way or another, a manager must judge P, the percentage of potential buyers who prefer his or her product over competing offers *when buyers know the products and have them available.* This percentage is a critical measure of the offer's market power, since it sets an upper limit on the number of people that support spending can attract to try the product. As Figure 6-6 points out, the offer's lost purchasers are $(1-P)$ times the number of product class buyers, #PCB.

Many of the ways in which P can be increased have been reviewed in the foregoing text. Since all competitors will be trying to use these same methods to their advantage, a product manager usually must settle for a P value less than .5. If all n products are equally appealing, each product will attract $1/n$ share of the product class buyers. In this case, each offer's (expected) loss of potential purchasers is #OLP $= ((n-1)/n) \times$ #PCB, and the expected maximum number of potential first-time buyers for each product is #PT $= (1/n) \times$ #PCB. A successful product

FIGURE 6-6   Offer's division of the target market.

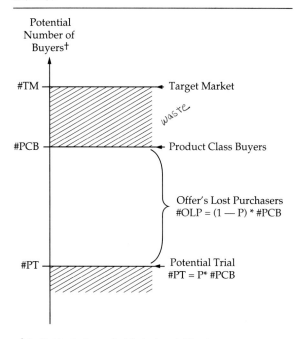

† Individuals, households, industrial buying centers, etc.
P = Share of buyers who prefer the product over competing products, given knowledge and availability.
    Here, P is based on # PCB.

should attract more than the latter number of first-time buyers unless it is targeted at a sub-market.

Managerial inputs   Most managers will have a substantial body of historical data that bear on pricing, design, and positioning decisions. In addition to the formal and informal analysis of such data, managers often profit from close contact with customers, the trade press, and other sources of information about present market conditions and the prospects for the coming year. In a study of managerial intuition (judgment), Blattberg and Hoch (1990) concluded that "both statistical and human inputs should guide final decision." They found that a fifty-fifty contribution from each domain leads to substantial-

ly more accurate forecasts of demand. As the form in Figure 6-2 implies, the managerial judgments formed from all sources should be assembled in usable form and given due weight. At the final point of decision, however, the responsible decision-maker's judgment should define the offer. The design, positioning, and price that this person chooses is the one for which market acceptance must be estimated and whose success or failure will determine the decision-maker's success or failure.

Estimating Unit Cost and Volume-induced Changes in Unit Cost

Marketing managers usually rely on others to estimate the variable unit cost and to indicate how accumulating experience will reduce this cost. They also rely on others to assess the cost of alternative product designs. Nevertheless, product managers must keep in mind the linkages between price, demand, and unit cost, adopting a set of strategies and budgets that will stand the test of evolving market conditions. Preliminary explorations of the effect of alternative offers, especially alternative relationships among price, volume, and profit, can be completed with the aid of the EXPER program (see Appendix 6-2).

Accounting for Market Conditions

Many market conditions can have an important effect on the success of an offer. For example, new competitive products may enter the product class, or currently marketed products may be redesigned, repositioned, repriced, or dropped. The effect of these possible actions can be examined before the fact with the aid of joint spaces and conjoint studies. Also, conjoint studies conducted at regular intervals should indicate the extent to which buyers are changing their preferences for design features and are becoming more or less price sensitive. Similarly, the margins taken by resellers and the contributions they are making to a product's sales can be monitored by relatively simple methods. General price levels and price levels within the product class can be recorded at regular intervals and forecasts made for the planning period(s).[4]

---

[4]For a discussion of such issues as product line pricing and competitive bid pricing, see Monroe (1979).

REFERENCES

Abell, Derek F., and John S. Hammond: *Strategic Market Planning: Problems and Analytical Approaches,* Englewood Cliffs, N.J.: Prentice-Hall, 1979.

Alderson, Wroe, and Paul E. Green: *Planning and Problem Solving in Marketing,* Homewood, Ill.: Richard D. Irwin, 1964.

Anterasian, Cathy, and Lynn W. Phillips: "Discontinuities, Value Delivery, and the Share-Returns Association: A Reexamination of the 'Share-Causes-Profits' Controversy," Marketing Science Institute working paper, April 1988. Cambridge, MA.

Blattberg, Robert C., and Stephen J. Hoch: "Database Models and Managerial Intuition: 50% Model + 50% Manager," *Management Science,* 36 (8), 1990, 887–899.

Buzzell, Robert D., Bradley Gale, and Robert Sultan: "Market Share: A Key to Profitability," *Harvard Business Review,* 53, January–February 1975, 97–106.

_____ and Frederik D. Wiersema: "Successful Share Building Strategies," *Harvard Business Review,* 59, January–February 1981, 135–144.

Clarke, Darral G.: *Marketing Analysis and Decision Making: Text and Cases with Lotus 123,* Redwood City, Calif.: The Scientific Press, 1987.

Day, George, and David B. Montgomery: "Diagnosing the Experience Curve," *Journal of Marketing,* 47, Spring 1983, 44–58.

Dolan, Robert J.: "Pricing Policy," in *Marketing Management: Principles, Analysis, and Applications,* Vol. I, Benson P. Shapiro, Robert J. Dolan, and John A. Quelch (eds.), Homewood, Ill.: Richard D. Irwin, 1985.

DuWors, Richard, and George Haines: "Event History Analysis Measures of Brand Loyalty," *Journal of Marketing Research,* 27, November 1990, 485–493.

Forbis, John L., and Nitin T. Mehta: "Value-Based Strategies for Industrial Products," *Business Horizons,* 24, May–June 1981, 32–42.

Foster, Richard: *Innovation: The Attacker's Advantage,* New York: Summit Books, 1986.

Hulbert, James M.: *Marketing: A Strategic Perspective,* Chapter 10, draft book, New York: Columbia University, 1983.

Jacobson, Robert, and David A. Aaker: "Is Market Share All That It's Cracked Up To Be?" *Journal of Marketing,* 49, Fall 1985, 11–22.

Johnson, Thomas H., and Robert S. Kaplan: "The Importance of Long-Term Product Costs," *The McKinsey Quarterly,* Autumn 1987, 36–47.

Mahajan, Vijay, Paul E. Green, and Stephen M. Goldberg: "A Conjoint Model for Measuring Self- and Cross-

Price/Demand Relationships," _Journal of Marketing Research_, 19, August 1982, 334–342.

Monroe, Kent B.: _Pricing: Making Profitable Decisions_, New York: McGraw-Hill, 1979.

Nagel, Thomas T.: _The Strategy and Tactics of Pricing_, Englewood Cliffs, N.J.: Prentice-Hall, 1987.

Olver, James, and Paul Farris: "Push and Pull: A One-Two Punch for Package Product," _Sloan Management Review_, Fall 1989, 53–61.

Oxenfeldt, Alfred R.: "A Decision-Making Structure for Price Decisions," _Journal of Marketing_, 37, January 1973, 48–53.

_____: _Pricing Strategies_, New York: AMACON, 1975.

Pessemier, Edgar A.: _Experimental Methods of Analyzing Demand for Branded Consumer Goods with Applications to Problems in Marketing Strategy_, Bureau of Economic and Business Research, Pullman: Washington State University, 1963.

_____: _Product Management: Strategy and Organization_, 2d ed., New York, John Wiley & Sons, 1982.

Schoeffler, Sidney, Robert D. Buzzell, and Donald F. Heany: "Impact of Strategic Planning on Profit Performance," _Harvard Business Review_, March–April 1974, 137–145.

Shapiro, Benson P., and Barbara B. Jackson: "Industrial Pricing to Meet Customer Needs," _Harvard Business Review_, November–December 1978, 119–127.

APPENDIX 6-1 USE OF A LOGIT TO ESTIMATE PURCHASE PROPORTIONS

In many cases a logit is used to obtain logically consistent estimates of purchase proportions. That is, a logit is used when one wants to ensure that all of the predicted proportions fall between zero and one and that the sum of the proportions equals one. This is the same as the reasoning behind the use of the logit in Appendix 5-1.

In the present case, a conditional logit is used. In addition to the reference levels chosen for the dummy variables, a _reference brand_ must be chosen. As with reference levels of dummy variables, any brand can be chosen as the reference brand. In Chapter 5, the dependent variable was $\ln (p_i/(1 - p_i))$, where p_i was the probability of choosing the ith alternative (or the proportion of the next group of choices that would be allocated to the ith alternative). In a conditional logit, the dependent variable is

$$L_{irj} = \ln (p_{ij}/p_{rj}) \qquad \text{(A-1)}$$

where p_{ij} is the probability of choosing the ith brand $(i \neq r)$ in the jth pricing condition and p_{rj} is the probability of choosing the reference brand in the jth pricing condition.

In the pricing example of Tables 6-6 and 6-7, the independent variables of Table 6-7 would not change. However, the dependent variable (the quantity of brand A purchased) would be replaced by L_{Arj}. A separate regression could be run for each of the nonreference brands (denoted by i) After these regression weights have been estimated, the predicted logits, $\hat{L}_{irj}$, can be converted into probabilities or proportions using the following formulas:

$$\hat{p}_{ij} = e^{\hat{L}_{irj}} \Big/ \left(1 + \sum_{i}^{i \neq r} e^{\hat{L}_{irj}}\right) \qquad \text{(A-2)}$$

An expanded discussion and technical details appear in Mahajan, Green, and Goldberg (1982).

APPENDIX 6-2 EXPERIENCE CURVE COST PREDICTIONS

Frequently, the cost of manufacturing a product or delivering a service will decline as experience accumulates. This process can affect the price that is set by a manager as well as the prices charged by competitors. To ease predicting unit cost at any level of experience and the average unit cost in the experience interval before each level, it is usually preferable to make a simplifying assumption and use a computer program. The assumption is that unit cost declines at a constant rate as experience accumulates. In this case, each doubling of experience is expected to reduce the cost of the last unit produced by a constant percentage of the cost of the last unit produced before production was doubled.

The program which is illustrated below provides five types of output:

1. The slope coefficient b and the imputed cost of the first unit, c_1, in the model that predicts the cost of the nth unit, $c_n = c_1 * n^{-b}$

2. The unit cost of a product at any level of production

3. The total cost of the output to the end of a period and the average unit cost to date

4. The total cost of the output during a period and the average unit cost of the products produced during the period

5. The unit and total manufacturing margin in each period and the present worth of these margins

To obtain these useful figures, a user of the EXPER computer program must supply the following inputs:

1. The expected level of cumulative production to the end of each period of analysis.

2. The expected cost of the last unit produced in period 1, and the number of additional units that must be produced to reduce the unit cost by 10 percent. (Alternatively, a manager can provide the values of the model's slope parameter *b* directly.)

3. If the analysis of manufacturing margins is desired, a user must also provide the expected average unit price during each period and the discount rate for the present-value computations.

Appendix 15-1 includes information on how to install and use the EXPER program. The following illustrative output covers just five years. Longer periods of analysis are common.

Period	Total Cost to Date	Aver. Unit Cost to Date
1	3,390.	33.90
2	7,627.	30.51
3	12,831.	28.51
4	18,971.	27.10
5	26,013.	26.01

Period	Total Cost in Period	Aver. Unit Cost in Period
1	3,390.	33.90
2	4,237.	28.25
3	5,204.	26.02
4	6,140.	24.56
5	7,041.	23.47

EXPERIENCE CURVE COST ANALYSIS

Problem: TEST PROBLEM 1

The period of analysis is Year

The number of periods in this analysis are: 5

Cum. Production to the End of Period	1	100
Cum. Production to the End of Period	2	250
Cum. Production to the End of Period	3	450
Cum. Production to the End of Period	4	700
Cum. Production to the End of Period	5	1000

Expected unit cost of last unit produced in period 1   30

Added units to reduce cost of the last unit by 10%   150
The model parameters are:

  The slope coefficient, negative lambda -0.115
  The imputed cost of the first unit produced 50.94

The unit cost of UNIT 250 is   27.00

The unit cost of UNIT 500 is   24.93

The unit cost of UNIT 1000 is   23.02

The discount rate is .1

The average unit price in Year 1 is 50
The average unit price in Year 2 is 49
The average unit price in Year 3 is 48
The average unit price in Year 4 is 47
The average unit price in Year 5 is 46

Year	Unit Mfg. Margin	Total mfg. Margin
1	16.10	1,610.22
2	20.75	3112.78
3	21.98	4,395.62
4	22.44	5,610.18
5	22.53	6,758.51

Present Worth of Mfg. Margin
15,367.21

REVIEW QUESTIONS

Q6-1 What is the fundamental principle of pricing?

Q6-2 What applications to product design and price can be made of the behavioral concept of a just noticeable difference?

Q6-3 What can be said about the role of managerial judgment in setting price?

Q6-4 Discuss the aspects of consumer judgments that concern price setting.

Q6-5 How can consumer value and producer costs be integrated to influence product design and product cost?

Q6-6 What are the advantages and limitations of using market experiments and historical records as aids to price setting?

Q6-7 Discuss the main issues concerned with capturing value.

Q6-8 Does price elasticity tend to change from one price level to the next? Why or why not?

Q6-9 Discuss the effects of cost structure on pricing decisions.

Q6-10 When and how do experience effects influence price setting?

Q6-11 Discuss competitors' influence on price setting.

Q6-12 Discuss the offer's lost purchasers, how they are measured, and the kinds of par value or target values against which they might be judged.

COMPUTER EXERCISES

EXPERIENCE CURVE EXERCISES

1. Using the air conditioner data, fit an experience curve (on three-cycle log-log paper; the x-axis for the units produced and the y-axis for unit cost) that runs through $220 cost at 420,000 units and $160 cost at 6 million units. Estimate the unit cost at 28,000 units and the number of units at a unit cost of 10 percent less than that estimated at the 28,000 unit level. Using these data, run the EXPER program to estimate the unit cost at 420,000 units and at 6.4 million units. Comment on the results.

ROOM AIR CONDITIONER DATA

Date	Cost of Last Unit Produced	UNITS (000)		
		Added	Cum. Added	Scrapped
1947			28	0
1948		48	76	0
1949		58	134	0
1950		130	264	0
1951	$220	155	419	0
1952		235	654	0
1953		708	1,362	1
1954		1,004	2,366	5
1955		844	3,210	17
1956		1,160	4,370	37
1957		1,000	5,370	61
1958	160	1,037	6,407	98
1959		1,187	7,594	154
1960		908	8,502	270
1961		709	9,211	520
1962		800	10,011	761

Source: *Adopted from Carrier Corporation (A): Harvard Business School Case, 9M84, M99, 1964, p. 16.*

2. Using the illustrative data analyzed in Appendix 6-2, run the program with the slope coefficient set at −.05. Repeat the analysis using a slope coefficient of −.2. Discuss the changes in the present worth of the manufacturing margin.

3. Rerun the original illustrative data (slope coefficient = −.115) after changing the discount rate to .2. Discuss the result.

4. Rerun the data in 3 after changing the unit price to a constant $49. Discuss the result.

5. Repeat the analysis in 4 but change the slope coefficient to −.2 and the unit price to a constant $47. Discuss the result.

6. Repeat the analysis in 5 but change the units produced to reflect a 10 percent increase in demand that the new price might produce. Discuss the result.

7. Repeat 6 but this time use the following unit prices; $48, $46, $45, and $44. Discuss the result.

7

ILLUSTRATIVE OFFER DEVELOPMENT

The diverse illustrative applications that appear in this chapter relate to the methods that were developed in Chapters 5 and 6. The first illustration deals with a new piece of industrial machinery. The second illustration describes the perceptual mapping of a class of automobiles both before and after the introduction of a new model. The third illustration describes the design of a new hotel chain. The fourth illustration deals with the services offered by a university library. Although these cases cover very different domains, the range of possible applications is much larger, including any choice objects that can be decomposed into determinant attributes. The reader might consider how the value of a vacation destination, restaurant, job, political candidate, or other entity can be determined and enhanced by these methods. Also, a brief discussion is included on an important psychological property of choice objects. The chapter concludes with a discussion of the temporal sequences by which the three aspects of an offer—design, communications message, and price—can be developed and integrated.

ILLUSTRATIVE DEVELOPMENT OF THE OFFER FOR AN INDUSTRIAL PRODUCT

The following product offer problem is fabricated to illustrate the use of several research approaches. Apparently these approaches were not used in the case on which this illustration is based. See Kearney & Trecker (A) and (B), HBS Case Series 9-580-143, Rev. 6/81 and 9-580-144 (1981). An interesting discussion of some related matters can be found in *When the Machine Stopped* (Holland, 1989).

Illustrative Company's Profile

The company discussed in this illustration can be thought of as a major manufacturer of high-quality, high-priced machine tools. The industry

211

to which it belongs is composed of three large machine tool builders, three large providers of the associated numerical controls, and a modest number of smaller firms. The largest firms account for about 80 percent of the industry's sales. Machining centers are the product type considered in this illustration. The machine mills, drills, bores, taps, and reams. These actions remove metal to produce precision parts. The tool-holding and the workpiece-holding elements of the machine are movable and are usually directed by numerical (computer) controls. Although customers can specify the machine and the numerical controls to which it is connected separately, most machine tool builders also sell fully integrated packages.

Machining centers are primarily used by firms that do not have production runs that are long enough to take advantage of automated transfer lines and other hard automation systems, but need to avoid the high labor costs imposed by manually operated machines. A need for flexible but efficient equipment often motivates the choice of a machining center. Makers of aircraft, office and computing equipment, and construction equipment often fall into this category. Quality and efficiency considerations, however, vary a good deal by industry and firm size. When choosing among machines that fall within acceptable precision ranges, savings in direct labor and tooling become major considerations.

Orders for machining centers were expected to grow by about $300 million in the decade for which product planning was being conducted. The company wanted to exert the kind of technical and quality leadership in this growing area that it had historically enjoyed in many segments of the machine tool industry. Tracking machine performance and customer needs over time in the manner described in Chapter 5 convinced management that increased precision, speed, and reliability would have to be delivered at stable or reduced prices.

Currently, the firm competed aggressively with one large machine tool builder that had a very wide line and an excellent reputation for high-quality products. The firm also competed with a number of smaller firms and expected to encounter aggressive foreign competition in the years ahead. The machining centers in the firm's present product line were high-quality models based on earlier technology. An additional machine was produced for the value-conscious market but it had proven to be a weak contender. To grow in this market environment, management concluded that it must become more volume oriented to benefit from cost-reducing experience and to cover development cost. Unless costs could be materially reduced, the company was likely to remain a medium-size supplier of premium-priced equipment.

Formulating the Offer

Some members of management believed that attempting to produce a low-cost, high-volume machine might not be feasible, and even if it were, it might damage the company's current quality image. Other executives saw the introduction of such a machine as a way to grow the firm and make needed adjustments in the firm's line. After extended deliberations, top management approved the necessary market assessment and the development work. It also appointed a project leader with the necessary authority to move the work forward rapidly.

Seeing the problem largely in technical manufacturing terms, the project leader traveled overseas to assess the extent of foreign competition and to find out if it was feasible to source the new machine overseas. In the short run, serious foreign competition or sourcing was ruled out. Nevertheless, the trip began to clarify some of the technical options and how the new machine design might be positioned. He believed that a full-featured machining center in a smaller size and at a lower price would attract a large number of customers not well served by the company's current product line.

On returning to the United States, the project

leader initiated two parallel activities. First, he established a design team charged with exploring how the company could make a low-cost, high-quality machine. Second, he began to explore the size and characteristics of the potential market. The latter work involved attempts to segment the market by customer size and industry to see if perception of currently available machines and the needs for product attributes varied across these segments. Focus group interviews were held with groups representing the more important classes of potential customers and with members of the company's sales force. These discussions led the company to believe that a lower-priced but high-quality machining center would be well received. However, there was some confusion about the specific characteristics the machining center should have. The debate centered around the following characteristics:

Price

Horsepower of the drive motor

Maximum size of the workpiece

Distance the workpiece can travel

Number of tools the machine can store

Type of work coolant

Largest tool size

Precision with which the workpiece could be rotated

Fast work loader

Rapid speed changes

Air conditioning

Managerial judgment was used to cut this list to five characteristics: price, horsepower of the drive motor, maximum size of the workpiece, number of tools the machine can store, and type of work coolant. In order to study competitive reaction, the name of the company producing the machine tool was added as a sixth character-

istic. It was decided that the largest tool size had to conform with the rest of the line to allow a user to interchange tools if desired. In order to maintain the company's image of quality, the precision with which the workpiece could be rotated was to be the same as the rest of the line. The last three elements were provided as options, as the preliminary interviews had indicated these were not equally appealing to all groups. The maximum size of the workpiece and the distance the workpiece could travel were highly correlated, so they were combined into one characteristic to simplify the study. These six attributes formed the basis of a conjoint analysis study. All combinations of these attribute levels yield $3 \times 3 \times 3 \times 2 \times 2 \times 3 = 324$ possible machining centers.

This study investigated three price levels: $120,000, $130,000, and $140,000; three levels of horsepower: 7.5, 10, or 15; three maximum workpiece sizes: 16″ cube, 24″ × 20″ × 20″, and 30″ × 20″ × 20″; two levels of the number of tools that could be stored: fifteen or thirty; two types of workpiece coolant: flood only or flood and mist; and three companies, competitor A (which was this company), competitor B (its main domestic competitor), and competitor C (a foreign competitor).

A survey was conducted among 195 companies. The respondents were all decision-makers in the selected target markets. This study as well as the focus group and questionnaire studies previously mentioned, was conducted by an independent research contractor who did not disclose the name of the study's sponsor. The respondents answered a number of questions about the industry they were in, the types of products they made with machining centers, and the intensity with which they used their machining centers. Then they rated their likelihood of purchasing each of twenty-seven profiles. These ratings were used to estimate the weights of a conjoint analysis model for each respondent. The average utility levels for the various levels are given below (the utility for the reference level is always 0):

	BASE PRICE	
U($120,000)	U($130,000)	U($140,000)
0.0	−2.0	−8.0

	HORSEPOWER	
U(7.5 hp)	U(10 hp)	U(15 hp)
0.0	4.0	5.0

	MAXIMUM SIZE OF PIECE	
U(16″)	U(24″)	U(30″)
0.0	1.0	2.0

	NUMBER OF TOOLS
U(15)	U(30)
0.0	1.5

	WORK COOLANT
U(FLOOD)	U(FLOOD/MIST)
0.0	0.5

	MANUFACTURER	
U(COM. A)	U(COM. B)	U(COM. C)
0.0	−1.0	−2.0

As expected, the most popular levels were $120,000 price, 15 horsepower, 30″ × 20″ × 20″ size of workpiece, thirty tools, and a combination flood and mist cooling system. Furthermore, these people were very much opposed to paying $140,000 for a machining center. Also, the difference in utility between 10 and 15 horsepower as well as between all levels of the other attributes was quite small. Finally, there was a higher utility for a machining center made by this company than by either of the competitors included in the study.

The results of the conjoint study and the preliminary design work were used to establish the product specifications. First it was assumed that neither competitor B nor C would introduce a new machining center. A choice simulator was run for each of the 195 respondents to forecast the respondent's choice among a current model of competitor B, a current model of competitor C, or the model that was being analyzed for this firm. First, that respondent's utility for each of the three choices was computed using his or her estimated utility weights along with a dummy variable description for each of the three machining centers. Then the respondent was assumed to choose the machining center that had the highest utility.

Analyzing a number of different possible product configurations allowed the management to estimate the sales volume that would be expected at various prices, and the value of

adding any design feature could be compared to the added cost of production. This simulation suggested that the most profitable design would consist of $130,000, 10 horsepower, 16″ cube, thirty tools, and a combined flood and mist cooling system. This had a forecast market share of 40 percent. In the first three decisions, the most popular level of an attribute was not chosen because cost or foregone revenue of providing that level was greater than the difference in utility between the most popular and the chosen level. In the case of the last two attributes, the most popular level cost little more and was chosen even if the difference in utility was small.

As would be expected, models that were quite similar to the chosen one had similar forecast market shares. One very different model that was also relatively popular was one that had a 7.5-horsepower motor and cost $120,000. It had a forecast market share of 25 percent. This prompted management to segment the sample into two groups, one of which used machining centers very intensively (two-thirds of the sample) and one of which used them much less intensively (approximately one-third of the sample). The average utilities for these two groups differed significantly on both price and horsepower; the less intensive users were much more price sensitive and did not gain as much utility for a larger drive motor. The utilities for each segment as well as the total are shown below:

	BASE PRICE			HORSEPOWER		
	U($120,000)	U($130,000)	U($140,000)	U(7.5 hp)	U(10 hp)	U(15 hp)
Total	0.0	−2.0	−8.0	0.0	4.0	5.0
Intensive	0.0	−1.5	−7.0	0.0	5.0	6.0
Less Intensive	0.0	−3.0	−10.0	0.0	2.0	3.0

The existence of two segments prompted the question of whether the company should offer two models instead of one. This led to a second round of choice simulations. In this case, the simulator was used to forecast whether each respondent would choose one of the products offered by the competition or one of two models offered by this company. In the first simulation, this company offered a large model ($140,000 and 15 horsepower) and a small model ($120,000 and 7.5 horsepower). The simulator forecast the company would achieve a market share of 42 percent with this combination. In the second simulation, the previously chosen option was paired with the small model. This resulted in a forecast market share of 46 percent. Although this was significantly higher than the share achieved only with the previously chosen alternative, the additional tooling costs made this option slightly less attractive economically.

One final simulation was run in which it was assumed that competitor B would introduce a smaller model in addition to its current machining center. In this case the previously chosen alternative was forecast to achieve a 36 percent share, the combination of the large model and the small model would receive a market share of 40 percent, and the combination of the previously chosen alternative and the small model would receive a 45 percent share. This time, the difference in share between the previously chosen alternative alone and the previously chosen alternative along with the small model was large enough to make it economical to introduce both in spite of the additional tooling cost.

Management assumed it was unlikely that competitor B would introduce a small model in the next two years. Therefore development was

undertaken only on the previously chosen alternative. However, some additional feasibility studies were carried out on the small model so that it could be introduced more rapidly in the event of a competitive introduction.

Later a pricing study was conducted. A description of the chosen model was presented along with descriptions of four other smaller machining centers. Brand names were included in these descriptions as focus groups indicated that brand name had an important impact on choice. Competitive prices were not varied, but the price of the model was varied between $120,000 and $140,000 in $4,000 increments. This study indicated that little volume was gained as price dropped below $128,000, but that demand dropped off substantially when price rose above $132,000. Therefore, a decision was made to keep the price at $130,000.

Bringing the Product to Market

The first lot of machines was completed by the proposed tooling and production methods before the product was announced. This procedure was in opposition to the industry's usual practice of building to order. However, it let management verify costs before the price was announced. It also allowed salespeople to book orders for immediate delivery. While the product-oriented work moved ahead, a good deal of time was devoted to developing an exciting market introduction that presented both the company and the product in a favorable light. First, it was important to preserve the company's quality image and current customer base. Second, it was important for the company to establish itself as a credible supplier of lower-price, high-value equipment to the price-sensitive elements in the market. The target price for the new machine and its expected high-performance characteristics allowed the company to pursue these twin objectives.

Before the aggressive, newsworthy product introduction was initiated, a benchline company image study was completed among the company's current customers as well as among the target market for the new machining center. After the product was introduced, corporate image and associated product positioning studies were scheduled for six-month intervals over a period of eighteen months. Interest centered on any favorable or unfavorable changes in the company image following the product's introduction and the perceptions of the product and competing products in the target market.

The introductory advertising and publicity were powerful enough to establish the product's favorable features quickly and to greatly improve the firm's value rating in the industry. The product was so successful that it sold more units than any of the firm's previous products. In addition, it greatly expanded the firm's customer base among smaller buyers who had not previously purchased the company's machines.

ILLUSTRATIVE PROCEDURE FOR MEASURING AUTOMOBILE IMAGES

The following illustration has been fabricated to illustrate the use of perceptual mapping to monitor the changes in mid-size car images. It is loosely based on Douglas Scott and Flaurel English, "How Competitive Activity Can Change Attitudes Toward Your Brand," paper presented at the AMA Attitude Research Conference in Orlando, Fla. (1989a), and Douglas Scott and Flaurel English, "Tracking Automobile Intentions and Imagery: A Case Study," *Journal of Advertising Research*, 29, February–March 1989b, RC13-20. However, because of important differ-

ences in the techniques of that article and this illustration, specific statements in this illustration should not be regarded as factual.

It typically takes a U.S. automobile manufacturer five years to complete the steps from development of a new car concept to market introduction. Although perceptual maps may have been used in the initial specification and positioning of the Taurus,[1] these decisions are not the focus of this illustration. The purpose of this research is to monitor the position of the Taurus over time so that changes in the offer could be made in a timely fashion.

Purchasing a new car is a complex task that differs for each person. However, in many cases, it can be described by the following general sequence. First, someone decides on a general size or type of vehicle desired. Then an evoked or consideration set is formed of vehicles in this general category and information search via dealer visits, conversations with acquaintances, and reading is conducted primarily within this group. Eventually a brand from this group is chosen or the process is terminated. The consideration set may be expanded or contracted with additional information, but the general image that a person has of a particular brand will have a major influence on whether it is part of the consideration set. Therefore, it is very important to track these images over time and to make appropriate changes when warranted.

One of the most important product segments to domestic manufacturers is called the upper middle segment. Depending on the definition of mid-size cars, this segment can equal approximately 25 percent of the U.S. automobile market. It consists of five- and six-passenger cars that have base sticker prices between $10,000 and $20,000. Some of the cars that were in this segment as of 1985 included: Chevrolet Celebrity, Oldsmobile Ciera, Pontiac 6000, Chrysler

---

[1]All names are registered trademarks of the respective manufacturers.

Lebaron, Audi 4000, Nissan Maxima, Toyota Cressida, and Ford LTD. This is the segment into which the Ford Taurus was introduced in December 1985. It is a segment defined by manufacturers, but many consumers feel that these cars are similar and are substitutes for each other.

Not only do car images determine which brands get into the consideration set, but also purchase intentions are related to future purchases. This latter fact is seen in Figures 7-1 and 7-2, which show the relationship between aggregate intentions to purchase in the next six months and actual sales for both General Motors as a whole and Buick Century[2] by itself. Although these figures illustrate the strength of the

---

[2]These data come from the Allison-Fisher Automotive Intentions Study. Every quarter they survey 200,000 representative households about new-car purchasing intentions.

FIGURE 7-1 Market share versus intention share for GM.

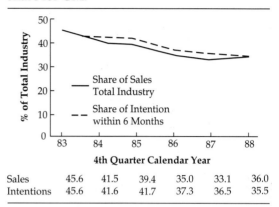

	83	84	85	86	87	88
Sales	45.6	41.5	39.4	35.0	33.1	36.0
Intentions	45.6	41.6	41.7	37.3	36.5	35.5

Source: *Scott and English (1989a).*

Purchase intentions are related to future purchases. But // lots of individual variation.

FIGURE 7-2 Market share versus intention share for Buick Century.

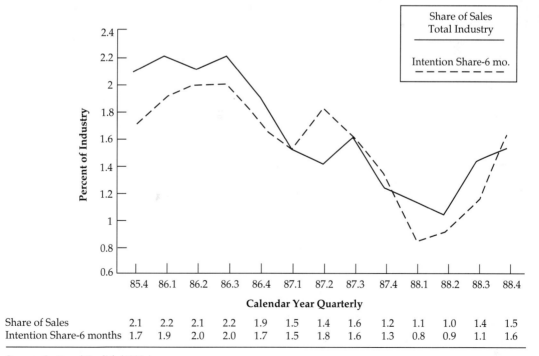

	85.4	86.1	86.2	86.3	86.4	87.1	87.2	87.3	87.4	88.1	88.2	88.3	88.4
Share of Sales	2.1	2.2	2.1	2.2	1.9	1.5	1.4	1.6	1.2	1.1	1.0	1.4	1.5
Intention Share-6 months	1.7	1.9	2.0	2.0	1.7	1.5	1.8	1.6	1.3	0.8	0.9	1.1	1.6

Source: *Scott and English (1989a).*

aggregate relationship between these two variables, they mask a lot of individual variation. (In
an extreme example, it is possible that one
group of consumers would state that they will
buy a certain brand, but none of them does,
while the people in an equivalent-sized but
totally different group say they will not purchase that brand, but actually do. In this case,
the aggregate prediction was perfect even
though each of these individuals was predicted
incorrectly.)

In any case, the inconsistencies at the aggregate level indicate that a number of factors can
influence the actual purchase decision after purchase intentions have been assessed. For example, a test drive may not be satisfying, some
desired options may not be available, or an
acceptable price or financing terms may not be
negotiated. As a general rule, when sales are
much higher than intentions, it means that the
company has paid too much for the sales
through rebates, financing, or special promotions. Sales that are too far below intentions
could indicate strength of competitive activity or
ineffective dealer support. Still, this evidence
argues strongly for the collection of this type of
information and the development of marketing
programs that will increase the purchase intention level.

June 1985

In order to determine what attributes best differentiate these automobiles several focus group
interviews were held in early 1985 with people
who were considering the purchase of an automobile within this general size and price category. When these consumers were asked what
they wanted in an automobile, the general
answer was a "good value." They needed more
room than that offered by compacts, but did not
want the exterior size present in full-size cars.
They wanted a good-quality car, but were not
willing to pay prices in excess of $15,000 to
$20,000. They wanted a car they could be proud

of without paying too much. However, these
qualities were possessed by most of the cars in
this product segment so they did not differentiate among these cars very well.

Therefore, the next step in the focus groups
was to show the consumers pairs of cars in this
segment and ask how they differed. These focus groups used approximately fifty words or
phrases to describe automobiles in this segment.
In order to reduce the number of attributes to a
more manageable number without losing any
more information than necessary, a factor analysis was conducted. A new group of 150 respondents was recruited and each respondent rated
one of three upper middle automobiles on those
fifty attributes. The ratings of each automobile
were factor analyzed separately to see which
attributes were most highly correlated with each
other. (Attributes that are highly correlated generally mean that they are measuring similar
characteristics.) This analysis suggested that
these cars were measured or evaluated on six
dimensions: economy, dependability, luxurious-
ness, suitable for families, suitable for young
people, and innovative.

Two attributes were chosen to represent each
of these factors. The specific attributes were:

Excellent gas mileage

Economical to operate

A really dependable car

Excellent workmanship

Luxurious car

Prestigious car

Family car

Interior roominess

For young people

Sporty car

Innovative styling

Technologically advanced

In June 1985, a sample of 1,000 customers interested in this product segment was asked to rate the degree to which each of eight representative cars possessed each of these twelve attributes, specify which one they would choose, state the likelihood of choosing each of the eight, and rate themselves on a number of demographic and life-style dimensions. Because they were interested in "top of the mind" perceptions that would be similar to those held when starting the search for a new car, no information on any of the cars was given to the respondents before they filled out the questionnaire.

When a discriminant analysis was performed on these ratings, the discriminant functions shown in Table 7-1 were obtained. The first dimension contained 46 percent of the discriminating power. Positive positions on this dimension were associated with cars that had interior roominess (.79) and were viewed as family cars (.76). Negative positions on this axis were associated with cars that had excellent gas mileage (−.77), were economical to operate (−.57), and had excellent workmanship (−.40).

This set of weights caused all of the imports to fall on one side of the origin and all of the domestic cars to fall on the other. Therefore, this

axis could have been labeled Import–Domestic. However, that does not result in a very actionable dimension. That is, there is little that management can do to change a car's perception on that dimension short of moving the company to another country (most people view "Japanese" cars that are made in the United States as "imports" and "American" cars that are produced elsewhere as "domestic"). Looking at the discriminant function weights, this dimension could also be labeled Larger–Smaller or Family–Single. In Figure 7-3 the first axis is labeled Large–Good Gas Mileage. This label suggests definite steps that one can take to reposition a car.

The second dimension contained 31 percent of the discriminating power of the attributes. Positive positions on this axis are associated

FIGURE 7-3   Perceptual map—June 1985.

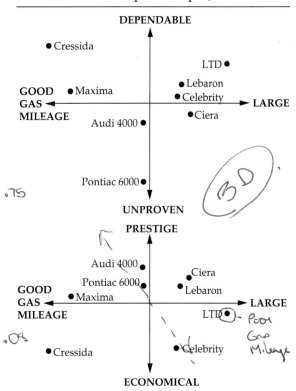

TABLE 7-1   DISCRIMINANT ANALYSIS FUNCTIONS—JUNE 1985

ATTRIBUTE	DF1	DF2	DF3
Excellent gas mileage	−.77	.11	−.39
Economical to operate	−.57	−.12	−.34
A really dependable car	−.11	.67	.09
Excellent workmanship	−.40	.72	.14
Luxurious car	.26	−.12	.71
Prestigious car	−.22	.11	.79
Family car	.76	.15	−.16
Interior roominess	.79	−.14	.06
For young people	.14	−.75	−.11
Sporty car	−.23	−.70	.11
Innovative styling	.08	.25	−.09
Technologically advanced	.38	.17	.14
Discrimination, %	46	31	10

with cars that were dependable (.67) and of excellent workmanship (.72). Negative positions on this axis were associated with cars that were for young people (−.75) and sporty cars (−.72). This axis has been labeled Dependable–Unproven. It could also have been labeled Dependable–Sporty, or Conservative–Sporty.

The third dimension explained 10 percent of the discrimination. Positive positions on this axis were associated with cars that were prestigious (.79) or luxurious (.71). Negative positions on this axis were associated with cars having excellent gas mileage (−.39) and being economical to operate (−.34). This axis was labeled Prestige–Economical.

Looking at the variables that load positively and negatively on the various axes, sometimes there is a reason for this association. For example, on the first dimension, cars that have a roomy interior will generally get poorer gas mileage. On the other hand, there is no reason cars that have roomier interiors should have poorer workmanship. It was just that in this sample of cars and people, the less roomy cars were perceived to have better workmanship. Similarly, looking at the second dimension, there is no reason sporty cars should be less dependable than less sporty cars. In some cases, it is possible

to get rid of these "messy" results by rotating the axes to simple structure. When this was attempted, the attribute weights on the dimensions became more "polarized"; that is, closer to zero or one, but the same attributes weighted heavily on the same axes under either orientation, so the original solution is presented here.

Table 7-2 contains the average ratings for each of the cars on each attribute. Because the means have been subtracted, a car that has a rating close to zero on a certain attribute is perceived to be about average on that attribute. The location of a car on any dimension is determined by taking a linear combination of that car's average ratings weighted by the discriminant weights for that dimension. For example, the location of the Ford LTD on the first dimension is given by the following formula:

$$
\begin{aligned}
D_{1F} = & -.77\,(-.76) - .57\,(-.81) - .11\,(-.35) \\
& -.40\,(-.85) + .26\,(-.49) - .22\,(-.47) \\
& +.76\,(1.08) + .79\,(1.06) + .14\,(-1.20) \\
& -.23\,(-1.75) + .08\,(-.50) + .38\,(.06) \\
= & \;3.28
\end{aligned}
$$

(7-1)

Plots of dimensions one and two as well as one and three are shown in Figure 7-3. The first dimension shows Ford LTD and Chevrolet

0 = average on that attribute

TABLE 7-2   AVERAGE AUTOMOBILE RATINGS—JUNE 1985[1]

Attribute	Ford LTD	Chevrolet Celebrity	Oldsmobile Ciera	Chrysler Lebaron	Pontiac 6000	Audi 4000	Nissan Maxima	Toyota Cressida
Gas mileage	−.76	−.76	−.86	−.66	−.66	−.26	1.94	**2.04**
Economical	−.81	−.71	−.61	−.81	−.71	−.11	1.49	**2.29**
Dependable	−.35	−.45	−.35	−.25	−.35	−.55	.55	**1.75**
Workmanship	−.85	−.65	−.15	.45	−.65	.45	.15	**1.25**
Luxurious	−.49	−1.49	.41	.21	.31	**.81**	**.81**	−.59
Prestigious	−.47	−1.27	.33	.23	.43	**.83**	.63	−.67
Family car	**1.08**	.38	.38	.58	−.92	.28	−.92	−.82
Roominess	**1.06**	.36	.46	.16	−.54	−.24	−.74	−.54
Young person's	−1.20	−.30	−.20	−.10	**2.00**	0.00	−.20	0.00
Sporty car	−1.75	−.95	.25	.35	**2.05**	1.25	−.65	−.55
Innovative style	−.50	.10	−.20	.10	−.30	**.80**	−.30	.30
Technologically advanced	.06	−.64	−.24	.36	−.24	−.14	**.66**	.16

[1]Underlined numbers are the lowest in their respective rows. **Bold** numbers are the highest in their respective rows.

(1) locate the brands
(2) embed the ideal points

Celebrity farthest out on the Large axis and Toyota Cressida and Nissan Maxima anchor the Good Gas Mileage axis. There is less general variation on the second axis, as most of the cars are viewed to be more similar. The two exceptions are Toyota, which is viewed as having good workmanship, and Pontiac 6000, which is viewed as a younger person's sporty car.

Several things should be noticed about the third dimension. First, the three GM cars appear to be in the appropriate order, as the Oldsmobile and the Pontiac are viewed as being more luxurious than the Chevrolet. Although the Ford LTD may not be perceived as being particularly luxurious, it is high on this scale partly because of its relatively poor gas mileage. Similarly, the Toyota Cressida is lower on this axis than might otherwise be thought because it is perceived to have good gas mileage and to be economical to operate. The Audi and the Nissan are higher on this dimension in part because they are not perceived to be as economical to operate.

Next, ideal points were embedded in the space. This was done by using Equation (5-11), in which each person's likelihood of purchase rating for each of the cars was used as the dependent variable and the locations of the cars in the perceptual space were the independent variables. With 1,000 respondents, segment ideal points were deemed to be more informative than individual ideal points. The individuals were clustered into segments on the basis of the similarity of their ideal points. The joint space for June 1985 is shown in Figure 7-4.

Segment one was the largest, segment two the second largest, and so on. There were few demographic differences across the segments. Segments one and two were slightly older and had more children. Segment three was slightly younger and segment four had a higher level of education.

ideal pts based on likelihood of purchasing

December 1985

In December 1985, Ford introduced its aerodynamically styled Taurus with a very large campaign. At this point, more data were collected

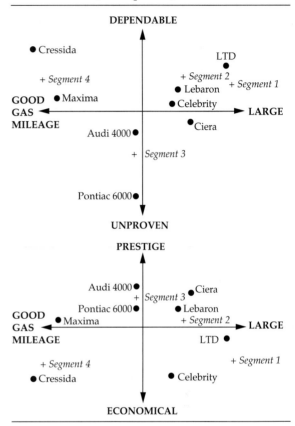

FIGURE 7-4 Joint space—June 1985.

and a second space was generated. Except that Taurus was substituted for the LTD, the same questionnaire was used.

The addition of the Taurus and the passage of time changed both the perceptions of the existing cars on various attributes and the relationship among the attributes in terms of their power to discriminate among the brands. The discriminant function weights and average ratings for each of the automobiles are given in Tables 7-3 and 7-4.

As shown in these tables and Figure 7-5, the dimensions of this space were generally similar to those of the previous study; however, some of the cars had moved substantially. The first dimension was still labeled Large–Good Gas Mileage; however, gas mileage was less impor-

Time + Taurus ∆.

Gas Mileage less important

TABLE 7-3   DISCRIMINANT ANALYSIS FUNCTIONS—DECEMBER 1985[1]

Attribute	DF1	DF2	DF3
Excellent gas mileage	−.56	.10	−.20
Economical to operate	−.55	−.08	−.38
A really dependable car	−.15	.68	.05
Excellent workmanship	−.20	.75	.12
Luxurious car	.27	−.14	.69
Prestigious car	−.21	.12	.80
Family car	.81	.17	−.14
Interior roominess	.74	−.18	.09
For young people	−.60	−.35	−.21
Sporty car	−.33	−.65	.19
Innovative styling	.10	−.62	−.12
Technologically advanced	.10	−.73	.15
Discrimination %	45	43	12

[1]**Bold** numbers are the highest in their respective rows.

tant (−.56 versus −.77) and a young person's car was now more heavily associated with this axis (−.60) than the second dimension (−.35), which was opposite to the first study, where the respective weights were .14 and −.75. As a result, this dimension could also be viewed as one of Large versus Young and Sporty.

The second dimension is now labeled Dependable–Innovative; dependable (.68) and excellent workmanship (.75) are weighted positively and sporty (−.65), innovatively styled (−.62), and technically advanced (−.73) have large negative weights. The latter two attributes did not differentiate the cars very well in the June study. (Table 7-1 shows that their weights were close to zero on all three dimensions.) All of the existing cars moved up on the second dimension and the Taurus is the only car in the lowest part of the space. It is seen as clearly differentiated. The Pontiac 6000 has lost some of its distinctiveness.

The third dimension is quite similar to the earlier plot. It is still labeled as Prestige–Economical. The primary change is that gas mileage is less important (−.20). At this point (and without the LTD) the cars are all seen to have relatively similar gas mileage ratings. So it ceases to be a differentiating factor.

The introduction of the Taurus (as well as the passage of time) has altered the perceptions of the existing brands. For example, the three imported cars have moved closer together. However, the biggest change is that Pontiac has moved closer to the other two GM cars. Taurus has preempted the high-tech, innovatively styled position.

TABLE 7-4   AVERAGE AUTOMOBILE RATINGS—DECEMBER 1985[1]

Attribute	Ford Tauras	Chevrolet Celebrity	Oldsmobile Ciera	Chrysler Lebaron	Pontiac 6000	Audi 4000	Nissan Maxima	Toyota Cressida
Gas mileage	.46	−.64	−.74	−.84	−.64	.16	1.06	**1.16**
Economical	−.22	−.52	−.72	−.62	−.62	.28	1.08	**1.38**
Dependable	−.40	−.40	−.30	−.20	−.30	.00	.60	**1.00**
Workmanship	−.71	−.61	−.11	.49	−.21	.19	.19	**.79**
Luxurious	.28	−.52	−.02	−.22	−.42	**.38**	.38	.18
Prestigious	.13	−.37	−.17	−.07	−.17	**.33**	.13	.23
Family car	−.44	.46	.66	**.76**	−.14	−.44	−.54	−.34
Roominess	−.25	.35	.55	**.75**	.25	−.75	−.55	−.35
Young person's	.14	−.16	−.16	−.16	**.44**	.04	−.16	.04
Sporty car	.16	−1.14	.06	−.04	**.96**	.46	−.24	−.24
Innovative style	**.44**	.04	−.36	−.06	−.16	−.06	.04	.14
Technologically advanced	**.99**	−.51	−.31	−.21	−.31	−.31	.59	.09

[1]Underlined numbers are the lowest in their respective rows. **Bold** numbers are the largest in their respective rows.

FIGURE 7-5 Perceptual map—December 1985.

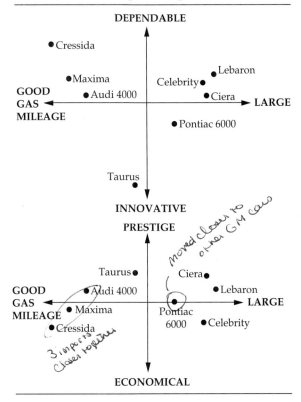

As before, the location of individual ideal points is based on the likelihood of purchasing the various cars. These were clustered into segments with similar automobile preferences. This joint space is shown in Figure 7-6. Again, segment one is the largest, segment two the second largest, and so on.

Consistent with the movement of the GM cars into a tighter cluster, segments one and two have moved closer together. Segment three is midway between the Audi and the Pontiac and is not as young as it was previously. Segment four is still between the two Japanese cars but has moved closer to Audi. It continues to be better educated than average. The major difference between the two studies was the emergence of a fifth segment relatively close to Taurus. Although all of the original four segments are slightly smaller than before, segment five has

drawn a greater proportion of people from segments two and three.

December 1987

The December 1985 study was repeated two years later with the same brands and attributes. The perceptual map shown in Figure 7-7 shows the changes over this period. Again, the biggest movement within the cars that were on the market prior to the introduction of the Taurus is that of the Pontiac 6000, which is seen as being even more of a family car than in the December 1985 study. It has lost almost all of its distinctiveness versus the other GM cars. The other major movement is that of Taurus. It has made a significant movement on the first two axes. It moved to the right on the first axis because it

FIGURE 7-6 Joint space—December 1985.

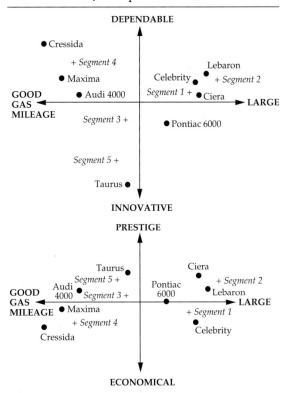

is viewed as more of a family car. People are beginning to realize that it has the interior room and trunk space of a family car. It has moved up on the second axis partly because its style is viewed as being less radical than previously, so it is not perceived to be as high tech as before, but it is also being viewed as more dependable.

Corresponding to these perceptual movements, there have been a number of shifts in the market segments. These are shown in Figure 7-8. Segments one and four remain relatively unchanged. Segment three has disappeared and people in that segment have migrated to segments two, four, and five. The other big change is that segment five has more than doubled in size and it has taken people almost proportionately from each of the other segments.

FIGURE 7-7   Perceptual map, December 1987.

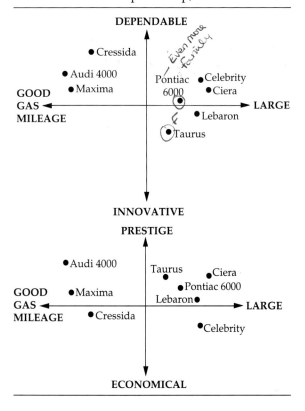

FIGURE 7-8   Joint space, December 1987.

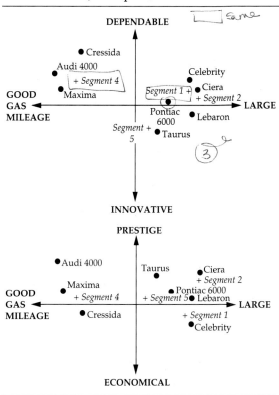

The sum of these movements indicates that Taurus has developed an image with which many of the customers for this segment are comfortable. This is reflected in the changes in intentions and sales shown in Figure 7-9.

Summary

Although this example has been partly fabricated, it illustrates a number of important points about perceptual mapping. *First*, these maps change over time and it is dangerous to conduct one study and assume that perceptions remain constant for long. In this study, the introduction of Taurus was associated with movements of a number of existing brands. The most obvious of these was that of the Pontiac 6000. Also, the introduction of the Taurus led to changes in the

FIGURE 7-9   Market share versus intention share for Ford Taurus.

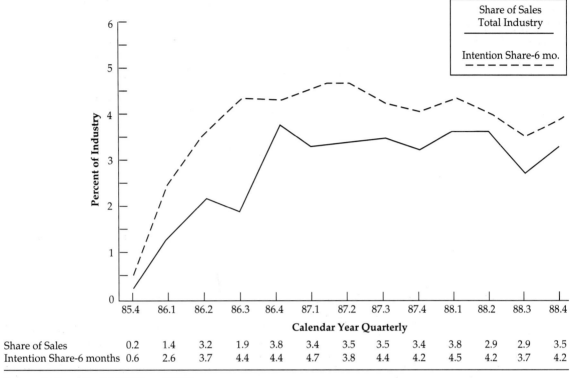

	85.4	86.1	86.2	86.3	86.4	87.1	87.2	87.3	87.4	88.1	88.2	88.3	88.4
Share of Sales	0.2	1.4	3.2	1.9	3.8	3.4	3.5	3.5	3.4	3.8	2.9	2.9	3.5
Intention Share-6 months	0.6	2.6	3.7	4.4	4.4	4.7	3.8	4.4	4.2	4.5	4.2	3.7	4.2

Source: *Scott and English (1989b, p. RC-15).*

importance of some of the attributes used to define the dimensions. The attributes technologically advanced and well styled became more important as consumers saw greater differences across the cars in these two attributes after the introduction of Taurus. Similarly, gas mileage became less important as the cars were viewed as being more similar on this attribute with the exit of the Ford LTD. Finally, the relationship among the attributes changed between the first two studies as the attribute a car for younger people became more of an opposite to interior roominess and family car instead of being the opposite of a dependable car.

Looking at the last two perceptual maps, a major change was in the position of the Taurus. As people became more comfortable with its styling, they saw it as less technologically advanced and more of a family car. This move appeared to be good for sales. It is common for the perceptions of a new object like the Taurus to become less varied (confused) with increased experience.

Second, the only attributes that appear in a perceptual map formed with discriminant analysis are attributes on which the brands differ. For example, technologically advanced was not an important variable until the introduction of the Taurus. This implies that these maps cannot say anything about the value of improving upon an attribute on which the current brands do not differ unless one or more artificial products are introduced by the researcher. This latter approach may also be used to study the perceptions of and preferences for new designs prior to their possible introduction.

ILLUSTRATIVE DEVELOPMENT OF THE OFFER FOR A NEW SERVICE

The following example of the research to develop a new hotel concept is based on the paper by Jerry Wind, Paul E. Green, Douglas Shifflet, and Marsha Scarbrough, "Courtyard by Marriott: Designing a Hotel Facility with Consumer-Based Marketing Models," *Interfaces,* 19, January–February 1989, 25–47. In an effort to increase the understanding by nontechnical readers and avoid introducing too much new terminology, the description in this example differs from what was actually done. It is hoped that the essential features of the analysis have been captured.

In the early 1980s the Marriott Corporation was becoming increasingly concerned over meeting expansion and profitability goals through traditionally designed Marriott Hotels. This led to the decision to examine the possibility of developing a new hotel chain for travelers dissatisfied with current offerings. The target was to be business travelers who stay in mid-level hotels and motels and pleasure travelers. A successful new concept had to offer consumers a good value, minimize cannibalization of other Marriott facilities, and establish a positioning that offered a competitive advantage. Previous corporate experience suggested that this would result in a smaller version of a typical Marriott hotel.

This study was conducted with 346 business and 255 nonbusiness travelers. Because the study was used to gain insights about the entire hotel, a total of fifty attributes, or factors, containing between two and eight levels were studied. This resulted in a total of over 160 attribute levels. This was clearly too many attributes and levels to be evaluated in a typical conjoint analysis task as described in Chapter 5. Therefore, Marriott employed a hybrid conjoint analysis (Green, 1984), in which the results of a consumer self-explicated task (Wilkie and Pessemier, 1973) were combined with a conjoint analysis.

First, the fifty factors were divided into seven sets called "facets" of the design. These facets included (1) external factors (such as building size and shape), (2) room factors (such as size and decor), (3) food-related services (for example, type of restaurant), (4) lounge facilities (such as atmosphere and clientele), (5) services (for example, reservations, registration, and checkout), (6) leisure-time activities (for example, sauna), and (7) security factors (such as smoke detectors). The complete list of attributes and levels is given in Figure 7-10.

Hybrid Conjoint Analysis

Self-explicated portion   In this phase, each respondent rated the desirability of each of the 160-plus attribute levels. Each respondent was given a card for each of the seven facets, one facet at a time. Each card listed all of the attributes associated with that facet.

For each attribute, the most basic (or least valuable) level was presented first, followed by all the other levels as well as their associated incremental price per day. For example, the following levels would be associated with the attribute "television": (1) color TV, (2) color TV with thirty cable channels (.25), (3) color TV with HBO and ESPN (.40), and (4) color TV with free in-room movies—a choice of three (2.50). In this case, a room containing a color TV with thirty cable channels would cost $.25 a day more than a room with just a color TV.

First, the respondent indicated which level best described the service offered in his or her most frequently used hotel chain. Then the respondent rated the desirability of each level (at its associated price) on a 0 to 10 scale, where 0 was completely unacceptable and 10 was extremely desirable.[3]

---

[3]In actuality, the respondents just chose their most preferred level as well as any levels that were unacceptable for each factor. These responses were analyzed with a technique called categorical conjoint analysis.

FIGURE 7-10 The fifty hotel features and services factors and the associated (167) levels. (The boxed items were included in the final design of the hotel.)

ATMOSPHERE

Building shape
  L-shaped w/landscape
  Outdoor courtyard

Landscaping
  Minimal
  Moderate
  Elaborate

Pool type
  No pool
  Rectangular shape
  Free form shape
  Indoor/outdoor

Pool location
  In courtyard
  Not in courtyard

Corridor/view
  Outside access/restricted
    view
  Enclosed access/
    unrestricted view/balcony
    or window

Hotel size
  Small (125 rooms, 2 stories)
  Large (500 rooms, 12 stories)

ROOMS

Entertainment
  Color TV
  Color TV w/movies at $5
  Color TV w/30 channel cable
  Color TV w/HBO, Movies, etc.
  Color TV w/free movies

Entertainment/rental
  None
  Rental cassettes/in-room
    Atari
  Rental cassettes/stereo
    cassette playing in room
  Rental movies/in-room BetaMax

Size
  Small (standard)
  Slightly larger (1 foot)

  Much larger (2 1/2 feet)
  Small suite (2 rooms)
  Large suite (2 rooms)

Quality of decor (in standard
    room)
  Budget motel decor
  Old Holiday Inn decor
  New Holiday Inn decor
  New Hilton decor
  New Hyatt decor

Heating and cooling
  Wall unit/full control
  Wall unit/soundproof/full
    control
  Central H or C (seasonal)
  Central H or C/full control

Size of bath
  Standard bath
  Slightly larger/sink
    separate
  Much larger bath w/larger
    tub
  Very large/tub for 2

Sink location
  In bath only
  In separate area
  In bath *and* separate

Bathroom features
  None
  Shower massage
  Whirlpool (Jacuzzi)
  Steam bath

Amenities
  Small bar soap
  Large soap/shampoo/
    shoeshine
  Large soap/bath gel/shower
    cap/sewing kit
  Above items and toothpaste,
    deodorant, mouthwash

FOOD

Restaurant in hotel
  None (coffee shop next
    door)

FIGURE 7-10   The fifty hotel features and services factors and the associated (167) levels. (The boxed items were included in the final design of the hotel.) *(Continued)*

FOOD *(Continued)*

Restaurant/lounge combo, limited menu
Coffee shop, full menu
Full-service restaurant, full menu
Coffee shop/full menu and good restaurant

Restaurant nearby
None
Coffee shop
Fast food
Fast food or coffee shop and moderate restaurant
Fast food or coffee shop and good restaurant

Free continental
None
Continental included in room rate

Room service
None
Phone-in order/guest to pick up
Room service, limited menu
Room service, full menu

Store
No food in store
Snack items
Snacks, refrigerated items, wine, beer, liquor
Above items and gourmet food items

Vending service
None
Soft drink machine only
Soft drink and snack machines
Soft drink, snack, and sandwich machines
Above and microwave available

In-room kitchen facilities
None
Coffee maker only
Coffee maker and refrigerator
Cooking facilities in room

LOUNGE

Atmosphere
Quiet bar/lounge
Lively, popular bar/lounge

Type of people
Hotel guests and friends only
Open to public—general appeal
Open to public—many singles

Lounge nearby
None
Lounge/bar nearby
Lounge/bar w/entertainment nearby

SERVICES

Reservations
Call hotel directly
800 reservation number

Check in
Standard
Pre-credit clearance
Machine in lobby

Check out
At front desk
Bill under door/leave key
Key to front desk/bill by mail
Machine in lobby

Limo to airport
None
Yes

Bellman
None
Yes

Message service
Note at front desk
Light on phone
Light on phone and message under door
Recorded message

Cleanliness/upkeep/management skill
Budget motel level
Holiday Inn level

FIGURE 7-10 The fifty hotel features and services factors and the associated (167) levels. (The boxed items were included in the final design of the hotel.) *(Continued)*

Nonconvention Hyatt level

Convention Hyatt level
Fine hotel level

Laundry/valet
None
Client drop off and pick up

Self-service
Valet pick up and drop off

Special services (concierge)
None

Information on restaurants,
   theaters, etc.
Arrangements and
   reservations
Travel problem resolution

Secretarial services
None

Xerox machine
Xerox machine and typist

Car maintenance
None

Take car to service
Gas on premises/bill to
   room

Car rental/airline
   reservations
None

Car rental facility
Airline reservations
Car rental and airline
   reservations

PLEASURE

Sauna
None

Yes

Whirlpool/jacuzzi
None
Outdoor
Indoor

Exercise room
None
Basic facility w/weights

Facility w/Nautilus
   equipment

Racquet ball courts
None

Yes

Tennis courts
None

Yes

Game room/entertainment
None

Electric games/pinball
Electric games/pinball/
   ping pong
Above and movie theater,
   bowling

Children's playroom/playground
None

Playground only
Playroom only
Playground and playroom

Pool extras
None

Pool w/slides
Pool w/slides and equipment
Pool w/slides, waterfall,
   equipment

SECURITY

Security guard
None
11 a.m. to 7 p.m.
7 p.m. to 7 a.m.

24 hours

Smoke detector
None
In rooms and throughout hotel

Sprinkler system
None
Lobby and hallways only
Lobby/hallways/rooms

24-hour video camera
None

Parking/hallway/public areas

Alarm button
None

Button in room, rings desk

Source: *Wind et al. (1989, p. 26).*

Add Cost

After this task was completed for all seven facets, the total incremental cost associated with the most desired level for each attribute was added to the base price of the room (the price of the room with the most basic level of each attribute). If the total cost associated with this room was too high, the respondent could revise his or her judgments about the most desired levels.

Revise

Conjoint analysis portion   In the conjoint analysis portion, each of the seven facets was treated as a separate factor (or "super" attribute) and five levels were constructed for each factor. For example, the facet "room" was described in terms of size, decor, TV (as shown in the self-explicated example), heating and cooling controls, size of bath, sink location(s), bathroom features, and amenities. Five different rooms, or "levels," were made up. Each "level" was internally consistent; larger rooms were furnished more luxuriously, had a better-equipped TV, and so on. However, each facet was independent of the other six. A large and luxurious room was just as likely to be paired with minimal food service as it was to be paired with a nicer restaurant. A main-effects fractional factorial design of the five levels of each of these seven factors contained a total of fifty concepts. However, each respondent rated only five of these fifty concepts, using a scale that expressed the likelihood of that person staying at that hotel.

indiv. factors

Hybrid conjoint analysis   The combination of the self-explicated desirabilities for each of the levels of each attribute (such as the TV example given above) and the reactions to the full-profile concepts allowed the estimation of the utilities for each of the levels. First, the desirability for the *i*th hotel description, $\hat{Y}_i$, is equal to the sum of the self-explicated desirabilities of the attribute levels contained in that description

$$\hat{Y}_i = \sum_{k=1}^{50} D_{ik} \qquad (7\text{-}2)$$

desirability *I'th desc.*   *desirability of indiv. attribute*

where D_{ik} is the desirability of the *k*th attribute in description *i*. A different desirability is calculated for each of the five concepts that a person rated on a likelihood of staying.

This overall desirability forms one of the independent variables in a hybrid conjoint regression. The other independent variables are dummy variables used to describe the levels of each of the seven facets. One level in each facet is chosen as the reference level and a dummy variable is used to describe each of the other levels. The dependent variable is the rated likelihood of staying at that hotel. Because each person rated only five of the fifty hotel concepts, the conjoint regression is run across all people or all of the people in a certain segment (for example, all pleasure travelers). The regression takes the following form:

$$Y_{im} = \hat{a} + \hat{b}_0 \hat{Y}_{im} + \sum_{j=1}^{20} \hat{b}_j X_{ij} + e_{im} \qquad (7\text{-}3)$$

where Y_{im} is the *m*th person's likelihood rating of the *i*th hotel description, $\hat{Y}_{im}$ is the *m*th person's self-explicated desirability of the *i*th hotel description, X_{ij} is the *j*th dummy variable description of the *i*th hotel concept (*j* runs from one to twenty, with the first four dummy variables representing levels of the first facet, the second four dummy variables representing the second facet, and so on), $\hat{a}$ and the $\hat{b}_i$s are parameters to be estimated, and e_{im} is an error term.

The output from this hybrid conjoint analysis included a model that could be used to estimate the utility associated with any combination of attribute levels desired. It also showed which level of each attribute was the most desired. Comparing the most desired level with the level that the respondent normally enjoyed with his or her most frequently visited hotel suggested which attributes were most important from the standpoint of differentiating this hotel.

After describing each of the competing hotels in terms of the same features, the likelihood of staying in each was estimated. These likelihoods were used to simulate hotel choices under a variety of conditions. The description of the new hotel was manipulated to see what configuration would generate the maximum market share and/or the smallest cannibalization of existing Marriott Hotels.

Pricing Analysis

Next, five hotel concepts that Marriott had been considering were used in a pricing study. First, the respondent read a description of a hotel in terms of the seven facets shown earlier. Then he or she was given the price of both a room and a suite in that hotel as well as the price of a room in each of four competing hotels and was asked to allocate 100 points across those six hotels (counting the room and the suite as different hotels) based on the likelihood of staying at each of the hotels. This point allocation task was repeated three more times with different prices.

Four different prices were tested for each of the six hotels. A main-effects fractional factorial design of the four levels of these six hotels contained thirty-six combinations. However, each person saw only four of these. An example of a description for one of these hotels is given in Figure 7-11, and an example of the card used to allocate points is shown in Figure 7-12. These data were analyzed by using a conditional logit regression as discussed in Appendix 6-1. One of the hotels, say the "older Holiday Inn," was chosen as the reference hotel, and one of the price levels for each of the hotels was chosen as a reference price level for that hotel. A different regression was run for every hotel except the reference hotel. Then the dependent variable in each regression was the logarithm of the ratio of the points allocated to the hotel in the regression to the points allocated to the reference hotel. The independent variables included an intercept and a dummy variable for every nonreference level price of each of the five hotels (including the reference hotel).

Other Tasks

The respondents also had to perform several other tasks. They were asked to allocate 100 points among a set of locations that were defined in terms of closeness to business, shopping, sightseeing, night life, and so on. The respondents also described themselves in terms of a number of demographic and travel characteristics. They also rated how much they liked each of eleven possible names for the hotel. Finally, they were asked to react to a number of hotel descriptions, such as "a busy, efficient, modern hotel" or "a good, no-frills, basic hotel."

Results

1. The study indicated that the respondents were dissatisfied with current offerings. Some hotels cost too much and others did not offer a number of highly desired features. This finding plus the finding that the description of the most preferred hotel was "an informal, quiet, relaxing hotel or motel with charm and personality" suggested a positioning of "A special little hotel at a very comfortable price."

2. The study provided guidelines for the selection of close to 200 features and services. For example, they found that about two-thirds of the people were currently getting only color TV in their rooms and about 70 percent wanted more than just color TV. Of these people, about 40 percent wanted HBO and ESPN. This was the television option selected.

3. The simulations estimated the likely share of any combination of attribute levels, the source of the business (which hotels would lose business to the new hotel), and the characteristics of the consumers who would be attracted to various hotel concepts.

4. The pricing studies based on the five concepts indicated which hotels would be the

FIGURE 7-11   Illustrative concept description used in Elasticon task.

HAMPTON SUITES

MOTELS PROVIDING QUALITY SMALLER 2-ROOM SUITES, SET AROUND A WELL-LANDSCAPED COURTYARD WHICH PROVIDES A SENSE OF CHARM AND RELAXATION

| Price In Suburban Areas |

About *$45 per night* on weekends (Friday–Sunday)

| Atmosphere |

Two-story, 125-room building surrounding a *central courtyard* creating a *"garden"* or *"park" atmosphere*. Courtyard can be enjoyed as a *"view"* and by using it for *relaxation and recreation*.

| Rooms |

- *Quality similar to better Hiltons and Marriotts*
  - Color TV with free movies.
- *Two-room suite:*
  - Separate *living room:* sofa bed, 4 chairs, coffee table, and work/dining table.
- *Bedroom:* Two double beds or king and large desk.
  - Dressing area between rooms includes dresser, coffee maker, and small refrigerator.
- *Balcony or patio* off living room with view of courtyard.

| Food & Beverage Services |

- *Small, moderately priced lounge-restaurant combined* in a club or living room like setting. Not open to public; for guests and their friends only. No entertainment.

  - Serving breakfast, lunch, and evening meal from a *limited menu* including sandwiches and hot entrees in the evening.
  - *Free continental breakfast* with juice, fruit, cereal, and pastry.
  - *Carryout* food available. No room service.

| Services & Other Facilities |

- *Upkeep and management skills as in nonconvention Hyatt and Marriott Hotels*
  - Fast check in and out. Wake up call. Reliable message service.
- Two *meeting rooms*.
- *Swimming pool* in terraced, well-landscaped *courtyard*. Areas to sit, sun, & eat.
- Indoor *whirlpool*. Well-insulated *game room*.

| Security |

Good security and fire safety systems.

Source: *Wind et al. (1988).*

FIGURE 7-12   The Elasticon task.

Below are 4 boxes containing hotel/motel names. For each of the boxes you have 100 points which we would like you to divide among hotels. Please divide the 100 points based on how likely you would be to stay at each hotel. Please start with Box 1.

You can give as many of the 100 points to any of the hotels. The more points you give to any hotel, the more likely you would be to stay there. You may give zero points to one or more of the hotels/motels listed if you think the chances of your staying there are zero.

Remember to distribute all the 100 points among your choices. Your points must add up to 100. After you have finished Box 1, go to Box 2, then 3, etc.

LaQuinta	La Quinta	La Quinta	La Quinta
$30.00 : _____	$30.00 : _____	$26.00 : _____	$26.00 : _____
Marriott	Marriott	Marriott	Marriott
$60.00 : _____	$60.00 : _____	$66.00 : _____	$66.00 : _____
Newer Holiday Inn	Newer Holiday Inn	Newer Holiday Inn	Newer Holiday Inn
$48.00 : _____	$42.00 : _____	$42.00 : _____	$48.00 : _____
Older Holiday Inn	Older Holiday Inn	Older Holiday Inn	Older Holiday Inn
$31.00 : _____	$35.00 : _____	$31.00 : _____	$35.00 : _____
Hampton	Hampton	Hampton	Hampton
$46.00 : _____	$50.00 : _____	$38.00 : _____	$42.00 : _____
Hampton Suites	Hampton Suites	Hampton Suites	Hampton Suites
$60.00 : _____	$55.00 : _____	$70.00 : _____	$65.00 : _____
_____ 100	_____ 100	_____ 100	_____ 100

Source: *Wind et al. (1988).*

primary source of new business. Also, they forecast the effect on share if the price of either the new or one of the existing hotels changed from the predicted level.

5. The location analysis provided valuable guidance about the proximity to business, shopping, theaters, and so forth.

Implementation

Courtyard, the resulting hotel, closely follows the recommendations of the study. In every case the chosen level had a high utility to the consumers surveyed. The predicted share of the concept was within four percentage points of the actual share achieved. Guest tracking studies have indicated that the features and services offered by Courtyard are very important to them. Of special interest is the finding that one of the hotel amenities that was found to be highly valued in the study, but not offered, has been missed by consumers who complained of its omission. The Courtyard has been a major success for the Marriott Corporation. Currently, it has more than 200 hotels either open, under construction, or under contract. It is the fastest-growing moderately priced hotel chain in the country.

Summary

This example has demonstrated that these techniques can be used to help design a new service. Furthermore, the ability to predict market share was quite good. The good predictive ability is in part due to the familiarity that the respondents had with the concepts being discussed. All of the attribute levels were within the range of their experience.

This example has also shown that it is possible to study very big problems with conjoint analysis. However, the complexity of this problem required that some of the details remain fairly sketchy.

AN ILLUSTRATIVE APPROACH TO OFFER DEVELOPMENT IN A NOT-FOR-PROFIT ENVIRONMENT

The following illustration is based on the research described in Library Services (A), (A1), (B), (B1), (C), and (D), Darden Graduate School of Business case numbers UVA-M-296, UVA-M-314, UVA-M-297, UVA-M-315, UVA-M-298, and UVA-M-300, respectively, Pessemier, et al. (1986).

In the absence of a simple, readily measurable index of organizational effectiveness, it is difficult to specify the types and amounts of services that should be offered by not-for-profit organizations. Determining the services that should be offered by a hospital, county office, and United Way agency are illustrative.

Here, the service offerings of a graduate business school library will be examined. A library can serve widely varied purposes. It can be a study hall, a meeting place, a repository for seldom used but highly prized reference materials, a source of assigned readings and recreational materials in print and on film, a place to check out and possibly use microfilm and computer-readable media, and a place where printed material can be copied. A business school library can have an equally varied clientele. The Darden Graduate School library at the University of Virginia serves significant numbers of MBA students, undergraduate business students, business school faculty, executive program participants, school and university staff, nonbusiness university students, nonbusiness university faculty, and people who are not directly affiliated with the university.

Librarians may have a count of the total number of people who enter their library, but they seldom know who these people are or how satisfied they were with the available materials and services. With the exception of materials that are checked out, librarians seldom know the rate at which available materials and services are being used or who is generating the usage.

Since libraries have controlled access, it is a relatively simple matter to determine the number of people who are in a library during each day and hour. By annually surveying the patrons of the library during representative periods, one can estimate who is using the library during any interval, how long they stay, what they use, and how well the library has satisfied their needs. Simple tabulations of these data can go a long way toward helping a librarian understand demands on the library, strengths and weaknesses of the services offered, and the absence of materials and services desired by patrons. Some of the results of an entry/exit survey conducted at the Darden Library appear in Table 7-5. Table 7-6 shows three of the many summary tables that were developed from the survey.

To expand the Darden librarian's understanding of individual complaints, several focus group interviews were completed. Each focus group represented a particular type of patron: MBA students, undergraduate business students, business school faculty, and nonbusiness users. In the focus group interview setting, the discussion leader encouraged in-depth coverage of broader problem areas and elicited suggestions for improving a library's offerings. Table 7-7 lists the ten most frequent complaints recorded during focus group discussions with MBA students.

In addition to the information provided by the methods outlined above, the Darden librarian wanted to know the degree of capacity utilization of each major library facility, such as reference materials, copying machines, and reading room seating. A work sampling study produced counts of the clients waiting, the empty seats, and so forth by time period. Checkout records and records of unsatisfied requests provide similar data for collections.

In the research described above, traditional marketing research methods were adapted to help a librarian understand his clientele and to improve the library's offering of services. Since a library's budget is usually provided by more senior administrators, attempts to improve services usually involve adjusting the allocation of funds to collections and the pattern of work performed by library staff. Nevertheless, such adjustments can involve major trade-offs, calling for a more formal examination of alternative expenditure patterns and/or alternative deployments of fixed resources such as space. The trade-off problem becomes particularly acute when library space is subject to either expansion or reduction. At the time of the Darden library cases, three levels of space were considered: no change, adding 2,000 square feet, and adding 7,500 square feet to the 12,000 square feet available at the time.

To start the process of producing a more effective mix of services, a librarian can formulate promising ways in which major library ser-

TABLE 7-5 MEANS AND PERCENTAGES FOR LIBRARY ENTRY/EXIT SURVEY DATA

(N = 999)

	Mean	Percent
Minutes per library visit	71.2	
Hours visited per week	15.6	
Type of visitor		
Darden: students		82.0
faculty		2.9
staff		.7
Other: undergraduates		5.8
graduate students		3.3
faculty		.3
other		1.5
Materials used during a visit[1]		
Assigned readings		48.6
Research		46.2
Biblio-catalog files		6.3
Electronic media		12.7
Equipment used[1]		
Copiers		26.4
Computers		26.1
Microfilm reader		2.6
Microfiche reader		2.1
Transparency machine		3.2
Activities[1]		
Checkout materials		13.1
Return materials		8.0
Individual work		64.8
Group work		10.7
Rest/socialize		16.9
Other		10.9
Use a reference librarian		18.3
Level of satisfaction		
Very satisfied 1		33.8
2		36.9
3		15.3
4		5.8
5		2.0
Very dissatisfied 6		1.0
No response		5.2

[1]Percentages may not add up to 100 because of multiple responses per person.

TABLE 7-6   TABULATION OF ENTRY/EXIT SURVEY DATA

Sample of Data Analysis

Table 1 Satisfaction by Time of Visit

Count Row Pct. Col. Pct.	Time of Day			Row Total
	8:00-12:00	12:00-6:00	6:00-12:00	
Satisfied	209	263	235	707
1–2	29.6	37.2	33.2	
	74.4	73.1	76.5	74.6
Dissatisfied	72	97	72	241
	29.9	40.2	29.9	
	25.6	26.9	23.5	25.4
Col. Total	281	360	307	948
	29.6	38.0	32.4	100.00

$X^2 = 1.07$; DF = 2; Sig. = .585; Cell w/EF<5, None

Table 2 Length of Visit in Minutes by Time of Day

Time of Day	Mean	Std. Dev.	No. Cases
8:00-12:00	74.6	93.6	289
12:00- 6:00	74.5	87.3	378
6:00-12:00	64.5	58.7	332
			999

Table 3 Time of Visits by User Segments

Count Row Pct. Col. Pct.	Time of Day			Row Total
	8:00-12:00	12:00-6:00	6:00-12:00	
Darden Students	246	312	261	819
	30.1	38.1	31.9	
	89.1	86.0	80.3	85.0
Darden Faculty	11	17	1	29
	37.9	58.6	3.4	
	4.0	4.7	.3	3.0
Darden Staff	6	19	18	43
	14.0	44.2	41.9	
	2.2	5.2	5.5	4.5
Undergraduate	6	11	41	58
	10.3	19.0	70.7	
	2.2	3.0	12.6	6.0
Other UVA	7	4	4	15
	46.7	26.7	26.7	
	2.5	1.1	1.2	1.6
Column Total	276	363	325	964
	28.6	37.7	33.7	100.0

$X^2 = 56.2$; DF = 8; Sig. = .0000; Cells w/EF <5, 1 of 15

TABLE 7-7 TEN MOST FREQUENT COMPLAINING COMMENTS DURING MBA FOCUS GROUP DISCUSSIONS

1. Library is too dark; need better lighting, especially in the open carrels.
2. Library is too noisy.
3. Need more and better copying machines.
4. Should allow eating and drinking in library, not computer room.
5. Should not permit smoking in the library.
6. Extend library hours at least until 1:00 A.M.
7. Need more phones in the computer room.
8. Need more computers in the computer room.
9. Need more comfortable chairs in the library.
10. Need separate room for conversation, group study.

vices can be increased or decreased, estimate the effect of doing so on such matters as waiting time and availability, *and* note what changes will occur in the required resources. These alternatives can be presented to patron subjects, who are asked to choose a preferred alternative of each type without exceeding the resource limits. Stated another way, a subject is asked to design an improved set of service offerings while observing the resource constraints.

In a fixed space, a subject might choose to increase the space allocated to study carrels at the expense of reduced seating in the general reading room. If added space were becoming available, the same subject might choose to make a large addition of space to study carrels and a small addition of space to reading room seating. Similar trade-offs can be made among the budget allocations to various collections and the assignment of library staff. Finally, a subject could elect to introduce previously unavailable services or drop existing services.

Note that the above approach has some of the properties of conjoint analysis but can more easily handle diverse alternatives and the resource constraints inherent in the case of providing library services. By placing subjects before an interactive computer that has been programmed to perform the resource accounting, subjects should be able to deal with a sizable number of

choice types and alternatives per type. When the data from a suitable sample of clients are tabulated, a librarian will know what proportion of the patrons are likely to favor each feasible set of changes that can be made given the change (if any) in the resource base. Such information is particularly helpful when it is tabulated separately for different classes of patrons (market segments). The size and character of each class will influence the final decision.

If patron subjects do not want to make significant changes in the distribution of the library's resources and the nature of its service offerings, the library's offerings are efficiently designed. On the other hand, if a large or rapidly growing class of patrons wants important changes, the offerings may require modification. If a generally satisfied clientele cannot be obtained within the current resource base, expansion may be in order. A librarian can use the results of this type of study and knowledge about expected changes in the size of patron groups to argue for increased library resources or changes in their deployment.

To close this short illustration, several additional aspects of libraries are worth noting. First, they very often are monopoly suppliers of their clientele. This fact makes it especially important that they monitor demand and that their service offerings be responsive to the changing circumstances. Second, information technology is evolving very rapidly, creating surprisingly dynamic demand and altering the very nature of libraries. Historically, libraries were almost exclusively repositories for books and periodicals. Budgets concerned little beyond funds for acquisitions and for personnel to handle the printed materials. Today, items like copy machines, expensive computer-readable media, computers, and on-line information services are absorbing large portions of library budgets. Library personnel are being forced to learn a wide range of new skills to properly manage this new high-tech environment. Furthermore, many clients' needs are being met at least in part by direct personal-computer access to remote data bases and huge data files on small optical disks.

In this climate, it is increasingly important for libraries to understand their clients' needs and to respond promptly with modern, efficient service offerings. Budget demands made by these changes can encourage the growth of user fees for services that have predominantly been a "free" good. It is not difficult to believe that other not-for-profit institutions will also need to be more responsive to their clients.

THE ANALYZABLE-UNITARY CONTINUUM

The foregoing illustrations are diverse enough to emphasize an important property of choice objects that an analyst or manager must pay particular attention to. A choice object is "analyzable" if its appeal can be described by the object's attributes, and it is "unitary" if its appeal cannot easily be described by its attributes. Here the term "attribute" is confined to the characteristics of an object that can be observed directly when the object is examined and used. A machine tool and a garden hose illustrate analyzable objects and a neon sign over a corporate headquarters and a bottle of vodka illustrate unitary objects. One kind of uni-

tary object forms a gestalt which must be taken in its entirety to be fully appreciated. The second kind of unitary object has few distinguishing characteristics and must be evaluated by its association with people, places, and things.

An oil painting must be seen to be appreciated even though it can be described in part by various characteristics. It may be a landscape, portrait, still life, or abstract; colorful or drab; cheerful or depressing; large, medium, or small in size; from a particular school or period; by a given artist; and so on. Much can be learned about one's preferences for a painting from such descriptors, but in the final analysis the whole painting must be examined. It is also noteworthy that a small visible defect may greatly devalue an otherwise "priceless" work of art. Therefore, great care must be taken when analyzing the desirability of such objects. It is unlikely that a superior painting will ever be produced with the aid of a joint-space or conjoint analysis.

A similar problem is encountered with products that have few, hard-to-measure, or indirect characteristics. Vodka and perfume are illustrative. Such objects often gain acceptance by their association with users, use contexts, and other persons, places, and things that have value to prospective buyers. In part, the perceptual map of the brands of beer in Figure 5-5 was fitted by using the variables popular with men, popular with women, blue collar, and good for special occasions. These descriptors concern indirect properties of the beers or are beliefs about how they are consumed. Knowledge about how the market judges beers on these variables offers little help in designing the product's physical features, but they can be very helpful in developing a favorable positioning for a beer.

Finally, it is worth observing that most products are located away from the extremes of the analyzable-unitary continuum. Beers tend toward the unitary pole and machine tools toward the analyzable pole, but neither one is a pure case. Few objects are.

THE ORDER OF OFFER DEVELOPMENT—ILLUSTRATIONS BASED ON THREE CONSUMER PRODUCTS

The foregoing discussions have covered decisions about product design, positioning, and price. Although it was emphasized that these three elements must ultimately make up an integrated whole, little was said about the order in which the elements are considered. Typically, this order is dictated by the specific circumstances. To illustrate various development paths, three well-known cold cereals will be discussed.

Shredded Wheat® has been on the market for a long time, although the bite size and other versions have more recent origins. The fundamental ingredients and form of the product have changed little, but the demands of the market and competition have been dynamic in recent years. In particular, health questions became more important, interest in natural products increased, and concern about the intake of sugar and salt grew rapidly. Since the product's physical properties were advantageous, management has been able to emphasize the product's health benefits that could not easily be matched by other cereals. The pricing strategy for the product recognizes the need to communicate these benefits to target market segments and to gain the support of wholesale and retail distribution. These facts precluded the adoption of a bargain price strategy.

Total® cereal is very likely to have had a different history. When it was introduced in the mid-1960s the product had to have very specific product characteristics to support the claim built around the name, supplying one's *total* daily minimum requirements of essential vitamins. In such a situation, a product's positioning strategy comes before the product's design. Furthermore, a product's price cannot be set until after the design is fixed and an assessment had been made of the amount of support spending that is required to make the product and its positioning a market success. Because the product and its principal claim were relatively novel, one suspects that vigorous marketing support was a necessity.

Private-brand Corn Flakes has been a chain store offering for many years. Some chains desired to offer a generic cold cereal at a price below that required by national-brand corn flakes. Each chain's reputation for value and its capacity to give the brand favorable display treatment are the essential features of these marketing programs, which put price first. Savings on the typical marketing support given to a private brand represent a large part of the cost savings which chains can recognize and share with their customers.

As the above cases illustrate, it is less important that the development of the offer follow a particular path than that the strategy for the offer make good market and economic sense. What customers should face is a marketing program that makes them aware of the product, that keeps the product readily available, and that provides an offer with enough benefits to be attractive in the face of competitive programs.

CONCLUDING REMARKS

This chapter has illustrated a number of research techniques associated with designing an offer and monitoring its effectiveness. In each case, the particular methods employed had both advantages and disadvantages. Carefully choosing an approach that exploits the advantages and minimizes the drawbacks lies at the heart of effectively developing the offer. In spite of the various cautions that have been pointed out, the methods reviewed in Chapters 5 and 6 are powerful aids in improving the desirability of one's offer.

Chapters 8 and 9 are devoted to testing one or more offers and to developing suitable marketing support programs. In the process of developing this support the offer may be revised. In the end, however, the support program will apply to one and only one well-defined offer. When viewed in its entirety, a successful offer and its marketing support must deliver more value to a significant proportion of the target market than the competition.

REFERENCES

Green, Paul E.: "Hybrid Models for Conjoint Analysis: An Expository Review," *Journal of Marketing Research*, 21, May 1984, 155–169.

Holland, Max: *When the Machine Stopped*, Boston: Harvard Business School Press, 1989.

Kearney & Trecker (A) and (B), HBS Case Series 9-580-143, and 9-580-144 , 1981.

Library Services (A), (A1), (B), (B1), (C), and (D), Darden Graduate School of Business case numbers UVA-M-296, UVA-M-314, UVA-M-297, UVA-M-315, UVA-M-298, and UVA-M-300, respectively, 1986.

Scott, Douglas, and Flaurel English: "How Competitive Activity Can Change Attitudes Toward Your Brand," paper presented at the AMA Attitude Research Conference, Orlando, Fla., January 31, 1989a.

_____ and _____: "Tracking Automobile Intentions and Imagery: A Case Study," *Journal of Advertising Research*, 29, February–March 1989b, RC13-20.

Wind, Jerry, Paul E. Green, Douglas Shifflet, and Marsha Scarbrough: "Courtyard by Marriott: Designing a Hotel Facility with Consumer-Based Marketing Models," Wharton working paper 88-008, March 1988.

_____, _____, _____, and _____: "Courtyard by Marriott: Designing a Hotel Facility with Consumer-Based Marketing Models," *Interfaces*, 19, January–February 1989, 25–47.

Wilkie, William L., and Edgar A. Pessemier: "Issues in Marketing's Use of Multiattribute Attitude Models," *Journal of Marketing Research*, 10, November 1973, 428–441.

REVIEW QUESTIONS

Q7-1 In the machining center illustration, what are the advantages of using conjoint analysis over perceptual mapping?

Q7-2 Brand name was known to be important. Should it have been one of the attributes in the conjoint analysis?

Q7-3 What could the company learn from a joint-space study? What wouldn't they have learned from a joint-space study?

Q7-4 In the automobile illustration, what other attributes should Ford have included? What other methods might have been used to generate attributes?

Q7-5 Ford could have given the consumers a description of the various automobiles, including sticker prices, or it could have let them see the cars before they were rated on the various attributes. What would Ford have learned from this type of a study that it did not learn from the study described in the text?

Q7-6 Ford could have produced a joint space for December 1985 that did not include the Taurus.

What additional information would it have learned from the joint space?

Q7-7 Ford could have used explicitly rated ideal points rather than ideal points based on the likelihoods of buying the cars currently on the market. How do you think these would have differed? What would Ford have learned by using this methodology?

Q7-8 How could Ford study the importance of attributes along which current offerings did not differ?

Q7-9 What would Marriott have learned from a joint-space study? How could it have used this information to design a new hotel chain?

Q7-10 Why did Marriott need both the self-explicated portion and the conjoint analysis portion in hybrid conjoint analysis?

Q7-11 Could Marriott have used location as one of the variables in the conjoint analysis? If yes, why didn't it include location in the conjoint analysis?

Q7-12 If you were studying the Darden library's operations, would you add to or delete any of the methods used to understand its clientele and the demands they make for services?

Q7-13 Evaluate the method that was used to adjust the facilities and services offered by the library.

Q7-14 How, if at all, can conjoint analysis be used to improve the services offered by the Darden library?

PART 3

TESTING THE OFFER'S VALUE

CONCEPT AND PRODUCT TESTING

PRETEST MARKET MODELS AND TEST MARKETS

8

CONCEPT AND PRODUCT TESTING

This chapter deals with various ways to test and evaluate new product concepts and products. The tests have two primary purposes. The first is to evaluate the idea or product to see whether there is enough promise to continue the new product development process. The second is to determine ways to improve the concept or product.

This chapter, as well as Chapter 5, may look like applied marketing research. Nevertheless, most of the decisions that must be made about product design and tests should be made by, or in consultation with, marketing management. When using the models discussed in these chapters, one needs to remember all the assumptions that went into the computations, not just the output, such as market share or first-year profits. This chapter will not make you a "model builder" but it should enable you to make better decisions.

One can evaluate new products by the number of respondents that reacts positively to it. However, the position taken here is that one should evaluate concepts and products by attempting to forecast the sales and profits associated with a given product and marketing program. To do so, one needs to make an initial forecast of sales and refine it as more is learned through additional tests. In this case, a model of new product sales is needed to provide a framework for integrating the test results.

The following section covers a general model for forecasting new product sales. The parameters of this model can be based on managerial judgments and experience with similar products prior to any testing. The parameter estimates should be updated and refined through concept, product, and market testing. Finally, the model can be used to track the progress of a product as it is launched. Experience with one product should be incorporated into the planning of the next. In spite of differences in the way the parameters are estimated at different points in the new product development process, the same general model is used to forecast sales. After the general model is discussed, subsequent sections cover concept and product testing.

MODELING NEW PRODUCT SALES AS A FUNCTION OF TRIAL AND REPEAT OR REPLACEMENT SALES[1]

Sales of a product are related to both the desirability of the offer and the amount of support that is provided. Most of this chapter deals with measuring the desirability of the offer and determining ways to increase its desirability. However, to make a sales forecast, an estimate of the level of marketing support must be made. At this point little will be said about determining an optimal level of support, but a given level will be assumed. In contrast, Chapters 10 through 15 hold the desirability of the offer relatively constant and vary the level and allocation of support.

The model discussed in this section breaks overall sales into trial or first purchases and repeat or replacement purchases. This decomposition results in more work, but the additional insights gained should be worth the effort. As discussed in Chapter 1, the primary reason for this division is that different factors influence trial and repeat sales. The first subsection deals with estimating trial purchases. It covers three related issues: the percentage of people who will ever try the product, how quickly they will try it, and the pattern of trial over time.

A Model of Trial and Repeat Sales

Total number of triers   Before describing the model, some definitions concerning the nature of trial purchasers are required. The following mar-

---
[1]Some of the variables in this section will not have temporal subscripts. If they are forecast to change over the period of the analysis, such subscripts should be included.

ket definitions will be used throughout this book. Their relationship is illustrated in Figure 8-1.

1. *Target Market,* #TM: the group of individuals or entities to whom the marketing plan is directed. This group may include many nonbuyers of the relevant product class if market segments are formed on the basis of general characteristics.

2. *Product Class Buyers,* #PCB: the group of buyers who are expected to buy the firm's product or other important substitute products.

3. *Potential Triers,* #PT: the group of buyers who like the firm's product well enough compared to competing products to make a trial purchase, given knowledge and availability. #PT = $P \times$ #PCB, where P is the percentage of #PCB who will try the product if they are aware of it and can find it.

4. *Cumulative Trial Rate,* CTR_t: the percentage of people in #PCB who have tried the firm's product by the end of period t. CTR_t is a function of the product's preference, awareness, and distribution. Letting A_t be the percentage who are aware and D_t be the percentage distribution coverage in period t, $CTR_t = P \times f(A_t, D_t)$.

5. *Triers,* $\#T_t$: at any point in time or cumulative level of marketing spending, the number of people or organizations that has tried the product and can make repeat purchases. $\#T_t = CTR_t \times$ #PCB.

6. *Maximum Number of Triers,* $\#T_{max}$: along the continuum for cumulative spending and/or the passage of time, the largest number of buyers who make a trial purchase of the product. Negative trial purchases can occur because of deaths, important changes in product preferences, forgetting the product, and so on.

The target market, #TM, contains the people to whom the marketing effort will be directed.

FIGURE 8-1 Division of the target market.

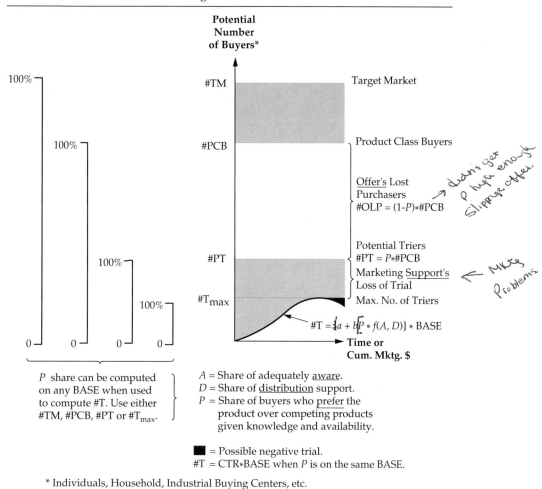

People who fit into a specific age or income bracket, people who live in a particular geographic region, and companies in a certain industry illustrate possible targets. In most cases, a target market will include a number of people who will not be customers of the product class. The possible reasons are legion: religious attitudes, insufficient income, health considerations, and so on. It is important to recognize these limitations whether or not they are matters over which a manager can exercise control.

The remaining potential customers, or the product class buyers, #PCB[2], become the group upon which analysis is most directly focused. They are the final customers who, if made aware

[2]In this chapter's notation,
# indicates the number of individuals,
$ indicates dollars,
U indicates units, and
t is a subscript that indicates the time period.
To simplify notation at various points, these sysmbols may be dropped or moved.

of the products and have them available, will be purchasers of the product class on at least one occasion.

The number of potential triers #PT of a product is defined to be #PCB $\times$ P; that is, #PT is based on the number of potential product class buyers. It could just as easily have been defined in terms of the target market, #TM. For example, one could use either the demographic target market, of men eighteen to thirty-five, or the product class buyers in that target market, male smokers between eighteen and thirty-five. If one-third of the males in the target market smoke, the P associated with the BASE = #PCB would be three times as large as the P associated with the BASE = #TM. Both cases give the same estimate of trial, so the specific BASE used does not matter, but the appropriate BASE definition must be made and kept in mind. In this book, if #PCB is the BASE, the preference measure will be designated as P. If #TM is the BASE, the preference measure can be designated as P'.

Trial will generally be discussed in terms of the *percentage* of people who have tried the product; that is, the cumulative trial rate at time t, CTR_t, rather than the *number* who have tried the product, $\#T_t$. However, either terminology can be used, as they are related by the following equation.

$$\#T_t = \#PCB \times CTR_t \qquad (8\text{-}1)$$

Whether one is interested in predicting trial in each period or just the total number of people who will ever try the product, a forecast of the cumulative trial rate, CTR_t, needs to be made. Conceptually, one can think of CTR_t as being equal to the product of P, the percentage of people who would prefer the product, as measured by a full-awareness preference task, times A_t, the percentage who can be made aware of it, times D_t, the percentage who can find it.

$$CTR_t = P \times A_t \times D_t \qquad (8\text{-}2)$$

For example, assume that a choice simulator in a conjoint analysis predicts 30 percent of the prod-

uct class buyers would try this product, the marketing support program is predicted to make 80 percent of them aware of the product, and 85 percent of those people who are aware of the product will be able to find it. The predicted trial level would be 20.4 percent (= .30 $\times$ .80 $\times$ .85) of the product category buyers.

In some cases, CTR_t may be a more complicated function of these three variables. First, the awareness rate, A_t, does not have a natural scale. Instead, its level can vary considerably from one type of measure to another. Furthermore, the percentage of distribution coverage, D_t, is usually defined as a volume-weighted distribution coverage. If consumers are willing to search for the product, this measure of distribution may understate the percentage of people who are able to find it. Therefore, this more general relationship is represented as:

$$CTR_t = P \times f(A_t, D_t) \qquad (8\text{-}3)$$

This book will generally use the simpler formula in Equation (8-2). If one were interested in the percentage of the product class buyers that would ever try the product, CTR_{max}, it could be forecast with the following equation:

$$CTR_{max} = P \times A_{max} \times D_{max} \qquad (8\text{-}4)$$

Awareness is created through advertising, sales force calls, word of mouth, and publicity. Distribution coverage is increased with trade promotions, sales force calls, and attractiveness of the offer to intermediaries. A primary job of the product manager is to design a support program that will effectively and efficiently generate trial for the product.

Trial and adoption curves[3]   Forecasting the level of trial in each period can be done by extrapolating along a curve that has CTR_{max} as an asymptote. The shape of this curve is usually

---

[3]Although the terms are used interchangeably here, adoption usually refers to a more innovative product and trial typically refers to significant line extensions and other less novel new products.

taken from similar products launched previous-ly. The speed with which the curve rises is usually forecast on the basis of estimates of the marketing program or through comparisons with other products.

Typically, trial curves are drawn as *cumulative* trial curves; that is, the vertical scale is the total percentage, CTR_t, or number, $\#T_t$, of people who have tried the product by the end of period t. The horizontal axis represents either time or the amount of money spent on the product since introduction. However, trial curves can also be drawn as *incremental* trial curves that represent the percentage of people who try the product in the tth period after introduction, ITR_t, where

$$ITR_t = CTR_t - CTR_{t-1} \quad (8\text{-}5)$$

Two primary patterns of first purchases have been observed. The first is like the pattern for the diffusion of innovations (which refers to an entire product class). However, many brands in that product class follow a similar pattern. In this pattern, a small number of people try the product soon after introduction; then the number of triers per period increases and finally decreases. This results in a bell-shaped incremental trial curve or an S-shaped cumulative pattern.

The above process has been likened to a contagion process in which the percentage of new triers, ITR_t, is proportional to the product of the percentage of previous purchasers, CTR_{t-1}, times the percentage left to try it, $CTR_{max} - CTR_{t-1}$. Early in the process few people have tried it, so the product of the previous users times the percentage left is small. The incremental trial rate increases as the group of previous triers and potential triers becomes more equal, but the rate starts to decrease when the number of previous triers becomes larger than the number of potential triers.

This pattern occurs when new triers are influenced by previous purchasers and/or when the product's price performance ratio improves with increased cumulative sales. Under either of these conditions, the incremental trial rate, ITR_t, is:

$$ITR_t = b \times [CTR_{t-1} \times (CTR_{max} - CTR_{t-1})] \quad (8\text{-}6)$$

where b, the proportionality constant that determines how quickly the product is tried, is a function of the offer's relative advantage, communicability, ease of trial, complexity, risk, and marketing support.

As an example, assume that 80 percent of the market will eventually try the product, b is equal to .7, and trial in the first two periods is 2.4 percent and 2.6 percent, respectively. Then Equation (8-6) predicts the following percentages trying the product in each period between period 3 and period 13.

t	ITR_t	CTR_{t-1}	$(CTR_{max} - CTR_{t-1})$
1	2.4%	0%	80%
2	2.6	2.4	77.6
3	2.6*	5	75
4	3.9	7.6	72.4
5	5.5	11.5	68.5
6	7.5	17.0	63.0
7	9.5	24.5	55.5
8	11.0	34.0	46.0
9	11.0	45.0	35.0
10	9.7	56.0	24.0
11	6.7	65.4	14.6
12	5.7	72.1	7.9
13	1.2	77.8	2.2

* $.026 = .7 \times .05 \times .75$.

Even though the incremental trial starts slow and increases, it eventually peaks and goes down, and extra dollars spent on marketing support will bring in fewer and fewer triers. The graphs of both the incremental trial curve and the cumulative trial curve for these data are given in Figure 8-2.

The second typical pattern occurs when the largest number of people try the product in the first few periods after introduction and then the number of new triers per period continually decreases. This pattern results in a cumulative trial curve that is concave downward and an incremental trial curve that is concave upward. This pattern is usually observed in connection

FIGURE 8-2   Incremental and cumulative trial; S-shaped cumulative curve.

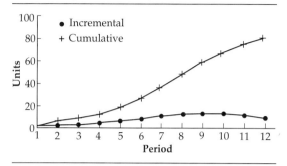

with frequently purchased products (e.g., Fourt and Woodlock, 1960; Eskin, 1973; Pringle, Wilson, and Brody, 1982).

This process can be viewed as a pool of potential triers with a constant percentage of them, a, trying the product in each period. Formally stated:

$$\begin{aligned} \text{ITR}_t &= a \times (\text{CTR}_{max} - \text{CTR}_{t-1}) \\ &= a \times (1 - a)^{t-1} \times \text{CTR}_{max} \end{aligned} \quad (8\text{-}7)$$

where a is the fraction pulled out of the pool each period and $(\text{CTR}_{max} - \text{CTR}_{t-1})$ is the fraction remaining in the pool. An example of the sales pattern generated by this model is given in the following table. The assumptions that CTR_{max} is equal to 20 percent and a is equal to .3 result in the following percentages trying the product in each of the first ten periods.

t	ITR_t	$(\text{CTR}_{max} - \text{CTR}_{t-1})$	CTR_{t-1}
1	6.0%	20.0%	0.0%
2	4.2	14.0	6.0
3	2.9	9.8	10.2
4	2.1	6.9	13.1
5	1.4	4.8	15.2
6	1.0	3.4	16.6
7	.7	2.4	17.6
8	.5	1.7	18.3
9	.4	1.2	18.8
10	.2	.8	19.2

The incremental and cumulative trial graphs for these data are given in Figure 8-3.

In order to forecast trial for a new product, one needs to choose one of the two curves and estimate values for CTR_{max} and either a or b. Prior to any testing, these judgments would be based on similar products. The estimate for CTR_{max} can be refined through concept testing, laboratory test markets, and test markets. The values for a and b can be refined through test markets and judgments about the level of marketing support. Once the product is on the market, these estimates can be further refined through experience in the marketplace.

Alternatively, when using the concave trial curve it is possible to make ITR_t a direct function of $P \times f(A_t, D_t)$. Doing so still results in a concave downward-shaped cumulative trial curve because the levels of awareness and distribution usually increase at a decreasing rate for additional spending on marketing support. However, when awareness and/or distribution build up slowly, S-shaped cumulative trial curves can be observed. The above representations of trial are the ones most often found in the marketing literature and used in practice. In some cases, a modest modification may be desirable. If one thinks about the pool of individuals who are potential repeat purchasers, trial purchase provides membership in this group. Nevertheless, other events provide an exit from the group. For example, people who have tried the product can

FIGURE 8-3   Incremental and cumulative trial; concave downward cumulative curve.

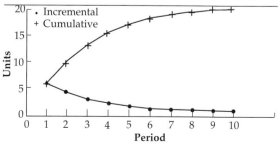

cease to be purchasers. Death, permanent changes in taste, and so on, can produce what is in effect negative trial or withdrawal from the pool of potential repeat buyers.

Repeat purchases and the retention rate Having made an initial purchase, a customer may make one or more repeat, replacement, or additional purchases. If the interpurchase times are more than ten years, as in the case of some major household appliances, or if planning is done for models that have shorter life cycles than interpurchase times, repeat purchases will seldom influence the strategy and budget covering a normal new product planning horizon. In these cases sales are a function only of "trial" purchases.

If the interpurchase times are shorter, repeat or replacement purchases play a more important role. When the times are short enough, they play the dominant role in determining the success of a product. Repeat purchases are especially important for most packaged goods and many industrial supplies. When repeat purchases are important, the *Long-run Retention Rate*, LRR, needs to be considered. This is the long-run market share of the brand *among those people who have tried the product.*

Assuming that purchasers of the brand under study have average consumption rates, one could forecast steady-state market share of a frequently purchased product as:

$$MS = CTR_{max} \times LRR \qquad (8\text{-}8)$$

If each person who tried the product repurchased only that brand, its market share would be equal to the percentage of people ever trying the product, CTR_{max}. However, some of these triers will never repurchase this brand and others will spread subsequent purchases across several brands in the category. Therefore, ongoing market share will be a fraction of the percentage of people that try it.

One way of estimating LRR is with repeat ratios. In most frequently purchased goods, a decay across depth of repeat classes is observed. That is, many people who try a new brand never repurchase it and many people who make one repeat purchase never make a second. In general, only a fraction of the people who make i repeat purchases make another. $R(i)$, the ith repeat ratio, is the proportion of people who made $i - 1$ repeat purchases and will also make i repeat purchases. $R(1)$, the first repeat ratio, is the percentage of people who have tried the product and will repurchase it.

This decay means that the pool (as a percentage of those who tried the product) gets smaller at each depth of repeat class. Typically $R(i) < R(i + 1) < R(\infty) \leq 1.0$; that is, the more repeat purchases a person has made, the more likely that person is to make one more. The following table is representative of repeat ratios and the percentage of loyal triers for a very successful, new, frequently purchased product.

Depth of Repeat Class	$R(i)$—the ith repeat ratio	Percent of triers making i repurchases
1	60%	60%
2	84	50*
3	94	47
4	97	46
5	99	46
6	100	46

*Where 50% = 60% × 84% and 47% = 50% × 94%.

In this case, 46 percent of the people who tried the product made four or more repurchases. This pattern indicates that a brand's market share among people who have tried it tends to start off relatively high, is gradually reduced, then stabilizes at a lower level.

These regular patterns have not been observed with durable goods, as there may be considerable change in the relative attractiveness of the competitive offerings over time.

Rather than estimating LRR directly, it may be better to estimate it with the following formula

(Maffei, 1960; Hartung and Fisher, 1965; Silk and Urban, 1978; and Clarke, 1987):

$$LRR = SBR/(1 + SBR - RR) \qquad (8\text{-}9)$$

where SBR is the switch back rate, the percentage of triers who bought another brand last time but will switch back to the manager's brand on the next purchase occasion. RR is the repeat purchase rate, the percentage of customers who bought the manager's brand last time and will repurchase it next time.

This formula is important for two reasons. First, it provides a method to estimate LRR from a small number of purchase cycles. Second, it focuses attention on two different actions: retention of current customers and attraction of customers of competitive products.

Steady-state market share can be estimated by using Equation (8-8), where it was equal to trial times long-run retention. However, that equation does not tell how soon this equilibrium market share will be reached. The path to this level can be modeled through dynamic repeat-purchase analysis.

Dynamic repeat-purchase analysis   In many cases repeat purchases follow curves that are similar in form to trial curves, as both curves either are S-shaped or concave downward (e.g., Eskin, 1973). Under this assumption, it is possible to model repeat purchases over time by creating separate repeat curves for each cohort of trial purchasers. A brief example of this method is given in Appendix 8-1. Although the method is relatively straightforward, it requires a lot of "bookkeeping" to keep track of all the depth of repeat classes. It is very useful if one wants to track the shorter term (e.g., quarterly) progress of a new product versus forecasts.

However, when one is interested only in annual forecasts, a much simpler method can be used. In addition to the trial rates introduced earlier, CTR_t and ITR_t, several other definitions are needed.

1. RFP_t is the *R*epeat purchase in period t by people who also made their *F*irst *P*urchase in period t. In many cases, people will make a repeat purchase during the same period that they made their trial purchase.

2. RBP_t are the *R*epeat purchases in period t made by people who made their initial purchase *B*efore period t.

3. RP_t is the total number of *R*epeat *P*urchases made in period t and is equal to the sum of RFP_t and RBP_t.

4. TUP_t is the *T*otal number of *U*nits of all brands in the product class *P*urchased in period t by the PCB.

Frequently purchased products   The number of repeat purchases of the firm's brand in period t made by people who also made their first purchase in period t is given by:

$$RFP_t = 1/2 \times ITR_t \times LRR \times TUP_t \quad (8\text{-}10)$$

The product of ITR_t and LRR gives the market share of purchases accounted for by those people who purchased the brand for the first time in period t. This is divided by two because the average trier in this period will be able to make only half as many repeat purchases of this brand during this period as an average purchaser of the product class. Total repurchases are found by multiplying market share by the number of Total Units Purchased, TUP_t.

The number of repeat purchases in period t made by people who made their first purchase prior to period t is

$$RBP_t = CTR_{t-1} \times LRR \times TUP_t \quad (8\text{-}11)$$

Finally, the total number of repeat purchases is the sum of these two numbers.

$$RP_t = \boxed{RFT_t} + RBP_t \qquad (8\text{-}12)$$

RFP_t

Infrequently purchased products   When products have longer purchase cycles, a slightly different model can be used. Assuming an average replacement cycle of T years, some people will replace sooner than this and others later, so replacement purchase will be distributed in a bell-shaped pattern around this mean. As a simplifying assumption, this section models all replacement purchases as occurring exactly T years after the initial purchase. It also assumes that the product is purchased in single quantities. Replacement purchases are modeled with the following formula:

$$RFP_t = ITR_{t-T} \times LRR \times \#PCB \quad (8\text{-}13)$$

In this case a certain fraction of people who made an initial purchase T years ago will repurchase in the present year. If the purchase cycle is short enough relative to the analysis period, the total repurchases, one and two purchase cycles after the initial purchase, could be modeled with the following formula:

$$RFP_t = (ITR_{t-T} + ITR_{t-2T}) \times LRR \times \#PCB$$
$$= ITR_{t-T} \times LRR \times \#PCB + RFP_{t-T} \quad (8\text{-}14)$$

This formula does not require all people who made an initial purchase in period $t - 2T$ to make a third purchase of this brand in this period. Some people could have purchased this brand in period $t - 2T$, switched to another brand in period $t - T$, and switched back to this brand in period t. LRR is just the market share among people who tried the product $t - 2T$ periods ago.

After this introduction, as a way to model sales the next two sections discuss ways of testing concepts and new products in order to estimate parameters for these models.

CONCEPT TESTING

Customer acceptance should be established before committing time and resources to product development, pilot plant construction, or the larger investments that follow. Concept tests are a rapid, inexpensive way to determine:

1. Whether there is sufficient consumer appeal to warrant further development. Here, one is interested in the percentage who would be interested in purchasing the product, whether they appreciate its major benefit, and whether there are any overwhelming negatives.

2. What the most appropriate target market is. Usually a new product will not appeal equally to all customers or will not be equally appropriate in all situations. If some people or organizations are more interested in the concept or its major benefit, they may be better targets.

3. Ways to improve the concept. This can either mean improving the concept statement—stating the benefits more clearly—or it can mean changing the idea behind the new product. One can ask consumers what they think the major benefit of the concept is and compare it to what the company thought. Frequently, consumers are able to suggest improvements in the concept.

4. Forecast trial. Concept tests can provide an estimate of P, the percentage of people who will try the new product if they are made aware of it and can find it. It is much more difficult to predict sales volume, because it depends on repeat purchases, which, in turn, depend on buyer satisfaction with the product.

Additionally, if the concept is a complement, substitute, or line extension, such as Tartar Control Crest, Ivory Flakes, Bud Light, Cherry Coke, or IBM PS/1, it is also possible to estimate:

1. How much new business the extension will bring to the total brand,

2. How many sales will be lost to cannibalization, and

3. What will happen if a competitor brings out a similar product.

Concept testing can also be used to help determine advertising or positioning approaches for a product by assessing which benefits should be offered, whether they should be rational or emotional, and what arguments best support the main benefit.

Concept Statements

Holbert (1977) makes the point that we never test "concepts." They are ideas that are in someone's head. Instead, we test *concept statements;* that is, descriptions of the concept. This distinction is important because it emphasizes the fact that the consumer is responding to the concept, the positioning, and the execution. Furthermore, a poor reaction may be due to poor positioning or poor execution of a good idea.

Schwartz (1987) defines a concept (statement) as "a printed or filmed representation of a product or service. It is simply a device to communicate the subject's benefits, strengths, and reasons for being." Holbert (1977) says it is a "selling proposition" or an "expression of an offer." The concept statement is a description of the product that includes its essence and the benefits it offers. In many industrial situations, the description of the product may include blueprints, videos, scale models, or prototypes.

There are two major types of concept statement: *core ideas* and *positioning concept statements.* Core ideas are short, bland descriptions of what the product can do for the customer. They usually make little attempt to persuade the consumer to buy the product. Typically, a statement of the core idea is a brief paragraph that is accompanied by simple or no artwork. Schwartz (1987) gives an example of a core concept for Secret Solid Antiperspirant in Figure 8-4.

FIGURE 8-4   Secret Solid Antiperspirant core idea concept.

Secret Solid Antiperspirant is comfortable to apply to the body because it goes on dry.

It contains a pleasant feminine scent and provides the wearer with effective, all-day protection.

Source: *Schwartz (1987, p. 8).*

A positioning concept statement is longer, usually several paragraphs. In addition to the main benefits, it also lists secondary benefits and contains a positioning statement or comparison with other products. It is usually more promotional, as it makes statements about the product's relative advantages. It may contain high-quality artwork. Alternatively, it may be in the form of story boards, animatics, or a rough or finished commercial. Figure 8-5 gives an example of a positioning concept statement for Secret Solid.

Concept statements for industrial products and services tend to be more factual. They should provide an unbiased comparison of the new product's likely performance characteristics with those of competitive products. They list

FIGURE 8-5   Secret Solid Antiperspirant positioning concept.

Secret Solid Antiperspirant

**Goes on Drier than roll-ons,
so it feels good on a
woman's underarm.**

Secret Solid Antiperspirant is different. It goes on drier than wet, sticky roll-ons, so it feels more comfortable when a woman puts it on.

And Secret Solid gives you effective, all-day protection that's strong enough for a man, yet its pleasant feminine scent tells you it's made for a woman. Secret Solid Antiperspirant.

Source: *Schwartz (1987, p. 9).*

specific advantages and disadvantages. A price, or price range, is usually indicated. As with consumer products, the objective is to elicit realistic judgments. If the respondent will check prices and specifications of competing products when making a decision, they should be provided as part of the concept test.

Sometimes consumers have ill-formed ideas of an innovative product's advantages and disadvantages. These pose a special problem. Wilton and Pessemier (1982) used a video presentation of an innovative product in use and a discussion of the product's operating characteristics. Subjects exposed to this stimuli were able to judge the desirability of an electric vehicle as a means of personal transportation. Other products that must be visualized or that need explanation may lend themselves to similar treatment.

In a sophisticated forecasting model for a mainframe computer laser printer, Xerox collected data on the characteristics of the computer operation of each respondent. [See Oren, Rothkopf, and Smallwood (1980) for a complete description.] This information included the site's workload profile, existing printers, and modes of operation. These data were used to calculate the operating cost of additional printers. After the data processing manager adjusted the assumptions to be compatible with company practices, the manager was given the throughput costs for several hypothetical printers. Because she or he would have made these same calculations in a real purchase situation, it was believed that providing this information led to better judgments about the value of various printer features.

Choice of a core idea or positioning concept statement   There is considerable debate on whether one should test core idea concept statements or positioning statements as well as on how much "sell" or "ad talk" should be included. Looking at the first issue, Tauber (1972) tested three products using both finished advertise-ments and a paragraph description. He found that although the print ads scored higher, the relative scores were unchanged, so the central finding remained the same. On the other hand, Haley and Gatty (1971) performed an experiment in which three copywriters provided concept statements for each of eight positionings of a concept. They found that consumer reaction was based on the concept, the positioning, the copywriter, and the interaction between the positioning and the copywriter. So the best positioning varied by copywriter.

Armstrong and Overton (1971) compared brief and comprehensive descriptions of minicar leasing systems and found no significant differences in consumer judgments. On the other hand, Wilton and Pessemier (1982) found that the amount and type of information provided about electric cars had a significant impact on consumer judgments. Proprietary studies comparing rough and finished ads for the same product found that the reactions to rough ads were positively correlated with reactions to finished ads, but the latter were generally higher (Moore, 1982; 1985). However, the high correlation appeared to be due to a small number of ads that scored very well or very poorly in both cases. There was a much lower correlation between average scoring ads.

In light of a number of these studies, it is often argued that concepts should be "dressed up" to a level comparable to the advertisements of the products with which it will be competing. However, it appears that the amount of positioning, selling, and ad talk required is negatively related to the size of the benefit, the social acceptability of the benefit, and how widely recognized the benefit is.

Although a number of companies use rough print advertisements as concept statements, Schwartz (1987) points out that concept statements are not advertisements. Advertisements are designed to break through competitive clutter, be remembered, and persuade one to buy the product. Concept statements are presented in a forced exposure situation and he feels that they should focus on forthright communication rather than persuasion. Still, concept statements should be as realistic as possible. For example, one should not list more benefits than could be presented in a real selling situation—either advertisement, commercial, or sales message.

Most people in Moore's (1982) survey were in favor of concept statements that were not too promotional. However, they also felt that short statements which did not adequately convey the benefits and uses were inappropriate. Across a number of studies, Schwartz (1987) has found that neither headlines nor illustrations (unless one was needed to demonstrate the product) have an impact on concept test scores. Perhaps this finding also argues for fewer promotional concept statements.

Writing concept statements   Regardless of the type of concept statement being prepared, it is important to write a good concept statement. Poorly written concept statements are one of the primary reasons for the rejection of potentially good ideas.

Holbert (1977) says concept generation tests should be used to develop a clear and meaningful concept statement. These tests can be carried out with one or more focus groups or with a series of individual personal interviews. During the process, the respondents are shown a preliminary concept statement and are asked to respond to it. Here, the researcher is trying to find the answer to questions such as: What are the major benefits? Are they important and believable? Is the concept statement clear? Is there a better way of stating it? How relevant is the benefit? What are the concept's advantages and disadvantages? How likely is the consumer to buy it? It is possible to ask the consumer to underline words or phrases that are interesting or important.

This iterative process can be thought of as *concept optimizing*, with consumer reactions on one iteration used to improve the concept state-

ment on a subsequent iteration. When practical, the concept statement writer should do this work himself or herself.

Test Design

There are three basic designs, or ways to present concepts to respondents: screening tests, monadic tests, and competitive tests.

Concept screening tests   In a concept screening test, each respondent receives concept statements for a number of new products within the same class. Concept screening is employed when a large (more than six) number of competing ideas must be reduced to a more manageable number. In this type of test, core idea concept statements are presented to each respondent in sentence or short paragraph form. These concepts are rated on one *primary affective scale* such as intention to purchase, interest, probability of shopping for, or liking—and possibly a *few secondary scales* such as importance, uniqueness, or believability of the main benefit. Each concept is judged by the number of people who rate it in the "top box" (most favorable category). The concepts are compared on secondary criteria to choose between concepts that score similarly on the primary criterion or to locate potential trouble spots.

Because the task is complex, data are usually collected through personal interviews conducted in a central location or in the respondent's home or place of business. Sample sizes for this stage can vary from a low of forty to fifty, when a small number of concepts is involved and the analysis is univariate, to a high of 300 to 500. Larger samples tend to be used when each respondent rates only a subset of the concepts and/or multivariate analysis is used to cluster the concepts into groups to identify superior concepts.

Many practitioners observe that comparing

ten to fifty concepts from one category is a difficult, left-brain task that may be biased against emotional concepts. They believe that strategic research should permit managers to select the four or five ideas that are worthy of further study. Nevertheless, one firm that has done some validation research on concept screening tests states that concepts scoring well at this stage also score well in subsequent concept tests and concepts scoring poorly here also tend to score poorly in a later phase.

Monadic tests   In a monadic test each respondent is presented with one concept to evaluate and is asked to respond to several questions about it. If more than one concept is evaluated, matched samples are used and comparisons are made across different samples.

Competitive tests   The CET® is a trademarked name of AHS Research and is representative of a number of tests. Typically, the CET® is a pre–post design. First, concept statements for the leading brands, which may include price and brand name, are presented to the respondent, who distributes ten chips across the brands in proportion to past purchases, expected purchases, or preferences. Then the new concept is presented and the respondent is asked to redistribute the chips according to expected purchases or preferences. All concept statements must be in a similar form, usually a print ad. A monadic test can be embedded in the pre–post test by questioning the respondent about the new brand. Two variations on this basic design are: (1) presenting the old and the new concept at the same time (i.e., the "post" only design) and (2) presenting more than one new concept along with several old concepts.

Choosing between monadic and competitive tests   There are several arguments for using monadic tests. The primary reason is that many firms report successful applications. Many users

of monadic tests argue that the consumer responds to a new concept in a comparative way anyway, so a direct comparison is not needed. Most of these users also favor relatively bland concept statements and believe that it is unrealistic to ask consumers to judge bland, disguised statements for existing brands. Furthermore, proponents of monadic testing feel that the reaction to the concept being tested is influenced by the competitive concepts. In some categories such as wine, it is hard to determine the proper competitive products. Finally, some of these people also thought making all competing concepts equally prominent decreased realism.

People who favor comparative tests generally do so because they feel they are more realistic. These people tend to use print ads for their concepts and use their competitors' ads for comparison concepts. Arguments about the proper test design are confounded with ones about the amount of "sell" in the concept statement.

In sum, people have reported considerable success in predicting trial with both concept testing methods. Comparative tests may be preferable in the case of durables, where multiple concepts can simulate the search process and provide information about alternatives. This additional "education" may not be needed for many frequently purchased goods. In this case, the simpler, and less expensive monadic test may be preferred. A monadic test is preferred when a concept does not have a clear set of competitors. However, companies should try to stick with one method as much as possible to build up expertise and useful norms.

Respondents

Typically respondents are either purchasers or users who influence the purchase decision of a particular product. Although sample sizes vary widely, most companies use between 100 and 300 respondents per concept for consumer goods.

Sample sizes for industrial products may be much smaller, depending on the number of customers in an industry. Furthermore, concept tests may be performed at more than one point in the new-product development process. As the product proceeds through the process, the sample size involved tends to increase.

Focus groups   In addition to using focus groups to generate product ideas, some companies use them to test concepts. The general feeling of the people interviewed by Moore (1982) as well as Schwartz (1987) is that focus groups are appropriate for generating and refining concept statements; but they should not replace the quantitative testing methods discussed in this chapter.

Personal interviews at the place of the customer
In most industrial as well as some consumer situations, concept testing is done through personal interviews conducted either at the respondent's home or place of business. The biggest disadvantage of this approach is its cost, which may be exacerbated by the geographic spread of respondents. On the other hand, it may be the easiest way to get cooperation for a longer interview and is the only way to reach certain groups.

Central locations   Many consumer concept tests are conducted at central locations like shopping malls. This is much less costly than in-home personal interviews and allows fairly complicated interviewing instruments that can be administered by computer, but it can yield nonrepresentative samples. This problem can be overcome to an extent by conducting interviews at differing times of the day and week as well as through the use of quota sampling—for example, requiring that half of the sample be men and half be women, half between the ages of twenty-four and thirty-four and half between thirty-five and forty-five. However, the respondents still

may not be representative of people in these categories.

Industrial companies may conduct concept tests at trade shows, but they will encounter some of the same drawbacks of mall testing with consumer products. Additionally, it is quite likely that competitors will find out about the new product.

Telephone interviews   Although telephone interviews are infrequently used for concept tests or to predict market success, a study by Jamieson and Bass (1989) produced positive results. Three phone interview waves were conducted at three-month intervals. The starting sample size was 800. It shrank to 412 on the second wave and 200 on the third, but the demographic profile of the respondents remained constant. The surviving subjects produced a total of 912 exposures to product concepts. The satisfying level of market share prediction for both frequently and infrequently purchased products will be displayed later in this chapter. The efficiency and demonstrated predictive power of telephone interviews may encourage wider use of this approach.

Mail interviews   Finally, it is possible to conduct concept tests through the mail. This can be done through either a random sampling procedure or a mail panel. A number of marketing research firms have constructed mail panels which contain representative groups of consumers who have agreed to participate in a certain number of marketing research studies in order to receive a small gift or to be included in a drawing for something more substantial.

Many industrial companies also use mail panels to conduct concept tests. In some cases research companies maintain the mail panels and in other cases the producer maintains a private panel. For example, McGuire (1973) cites an example of a steel company that regularly sends out surveys and new products (alloys) to machine designers. In either case, the respondents are typically compensated by receiving a copy of the survey results or early access to the new product.

Recently companies have begun doing industrial marketing research by mailing computer disks, called Disk-By-Mail (DBM) surveys. The novelty of DBM has probably helped obtain a higher response rate than paper-and-pencil surveys; however, this advantage may disappear over time. Through automated branching instructions it is possible to ask complex questions. Although DBM currently costs somewhat more than paper-and-pencil surveys (the higher cost of questionnaire development and mailing may more than offset the lower costs of coding and data entry), most respondents like it better than traditional surveys (Wilson, 1989). Problems of DBM include: access to a computer and disk drive that is compatible with the disk in the mail, computer phobia, and quality of the disk. See Zandan and Frost (1989) for a more complete discussion.

Mail interviews can be the least expensive way of conducting concept tests, but they may offer a number of other drawbacks. First, the response rate is typically quite low and respondents are not necessarily the people to whom the mailing was directed. Therefore, respondents may be atypical even if the sample was drawn randomly. Second, it is not possible for the respondents to ask any questions unless an 800 number is provided. Third, the time to complete the study is much longer than with other methods. Fourth, it is harder to get answers to open-ended questions with this method than with others. Finally, it is not possible to keep these respondents from looking ahead or back in the questionnaire.

There are a number of ways of choosing respondents for concept tests. All of them have strengths and weaknesses. The best trade-off among these factors depends on the specific situation.

Questions

After the concept statements are presented to the respondents in one of the above-mentioned designs, a number of questions are asked. These may be divided into three categories: *primary criterion, diagnostic,* and *classification.*

Primary criterion *Purchase intention* The purchase intention question is probably the most frequently used question to evaluate the overall appeal of a new product concept.

How likely would you be to purchase the product described above if it were available in your local store?

Definitely would buy it ☐

Probably would buy it ☐

Might or might not buy it ☐

Probably would not buy it ☐

Definitely would not buy it ☐

Probability of purchase A second popular response scale is the probability of purchase scale. One example of how this question might be worded has been modified from Infosino (1986, p. 374):

Please circle the number from zero to ten on the scale below that best indicates how likely you might be to buy the product. If you definitely would buy it, circle 10; if you definitely would not buy it, circle 0. Of course, you may indicate a number somewhere in between.

Definitely would not buy										Definitely would buy
0	1	2	3	4	5	6	7	8	9	10

Point allocation The primary criterion with a competitive concept test is usually an allocation of preferences or future purchases across all brands.

Based on the advertisements you have just seen, allocate these ten chips across these brands in proportion to the number of times you will purchase each brand during your next ten purchase occasions.

_____	_____	_____	_____	____
Brand A	Brand B	Brand C	Brand D	Other

Diagnostic questions   In addition to the primary criterion question, a number of diagnostic questions should be asked to determine ways to improve the concept, understand reasons for the rating on the primary criterion question, and identify the best targets for the product.

Uniqueness   One of the primary differentiators between successful and unsuccessful products is their uniqueness. Therefore, one should ask whether a concept was unique or not. For example:

Check the box that best describes how different this product is from other products in the product category.

Very different   ☐

Somewhat different   ☐

Slightly different   ☐

Not different at all   ☐

Alternatively, one could ask:

Check the box that most closely fits the description you just read.

An ordinary ☐ ☐ ☐ ☐ ☐ A unique product   product

Relevance   The relevance or appropriateness of the product to the respondent can differentiate successful from unsuccessful products. A relevance question might be worded as follows:

Check the box that best describes the relevance of this product to your needs

Relevant ☐ ☐ ☐ ☐ ☐ Not Relevant

Main idea   This open-ended question allows one to determine whether the concept was able to communicate its primary benefits to the respondent. Furthermore, it can be analyzed in conjunction with other responses, such as purchase intention, to see if they are related. One can ask about the main idea in the following manner.

Other than trying to sell the product, what was the *main idea* of the description you just read? What was the *main thing* it was trying to communicate to you?

_____
_____
_____

Usually, this should be followed up with a question on the importance of this idea.

How important is the main idea you indicated in the previous question?

Very Important   ☐

Somewhat Important   ☐

Somewhat Unimportant   ☐

Very Unimportant   ☐

Believability   Another open-ended question covers how believable the concept is.

Is there anything about this product that is hard to believe? If so, what? _____
_____

Comprehension   Comprehension can be tested either by directly asking whether there were things about the concept that were not clear or by asking specific questions about the concept whose answers would indicate comprehension.

Likes and dislikes Another open-ended question deals with specific things that were liked or disliked about the concept. This can also be asked in terms of significant negatives.

Is there anything about this concept that you especially disliked? If so, what?_____
_____

Attribute ratings Finally, the concept should be rated on a number of attributes. Additionally, the importance of each attribute should be assessed. An example of these questions is given in the table below.

Classification questions In addition to determining the respondent's reaction to the concept statement, the questionnaire should include a number of questions about the respondent in order to learn to which groups the concept appeals most and least. At a minimum, respondents should be asked a battery of demographic and socioeconomic questions. Additionally, they should be asked what brands they are currently using and how they compare to the concept.

Analysis

There are three main purposes of concept tests: to determine whether there is enough appeal to warrant further work, to determine the most appropriate targets, and to learn how the concept might be improved. In many cases, there is an overemphasis on the first objective and an underemphasis on the latter two, especially the third.

The analysis of concept test data often consists of frequencies; that is, counting how many people answered a question in a certain way—for example, what percentage of the people gave a top box rating to the purchase intention question. A second typical form of analysis is crosstabulation. Here one looks at how many people rated each of two questions in a certain way; for example, how many people said they were likely to purchase the product and said it was unique. Correlations and regressions can also be run. Finally, if attribute ratings have been collected, it is possible to produce perceptual maps.

Norms Typically questions arise about what is a good top box score on the purchase inten-

Circle the number that best describes this concept on each of the following scales:

Nutritious	1	2	3	4	5	Not Nutritious
Delicious	1	2	3	4	5	Not Delicious
Easy to Prepare	1	2	3	4	5	Hard to Prepare
Appropriate for Dinner	1	2	3	4	5	Not Appropriate

How important is it that a product like this be:

	Very Important				Very Unimportant
Nutritious	1	2	3	4	5
Delicious	1	2	3	4	5
Easy to Prepare	1	2	3	4	5
Appropriate for Dinner	1	2	3	4	5

tion question or what percentage typically rates a product as being very different from existing products. To answer these questions one can use scores from previous concept tests, called "norms." They act as a benchmark or point of reference. Many researchers and companies have an assembled data base of norms and it is in managers' best interest to collect their own.

Norms are based on a series of concept test results and market success indicators. These can be collected from all products introduced by a company as well as from competing products. If a competing product is introduced regionally or is in test market, it is possible to test the concept and compare its scores to its market success. Even if it is introduced nationally, it is quite possible to conduct a concept test before many consumers are aware of the product.

At a minimum, Schwartz (1987) suggests collecting the following measures: top box; total positive, neutral, and negative percentages of responses to the purchase intention question; the percentage that lists advantages and disadvantages both in total and for major items; some information on uniqueness, believability, ease of understanding, and persuasiveness; and the percentage of respondents who suggest improvements in the concept.

Average norms both for a product category and for successful products in a category should be calculated. Schwartz (1987) lists averages for top box purchase intention scores; for example, detergents, 12 percent; fragrances with prices, 18 percent; food, 20 percent; and cleaning products, 28 percent.

Norms are useful, but they can be misleading; some brands are successful because of a small number of very loyal customers rather than a larger base of customers with average loyalty.

Primary criterion   The first question to be analyzed is the primary criterion. A tabulation of the percentage of people who marked each of the intention to purchase categories can be compared with norms or used to predict the percentage of people who will try the product.

In the simplest prediction system, the percentage of people marking the top box (most favorable category) would be an estimate of the number of people who would try the product if they were aware of it and could find it easily. However, because advertising will not make everyone aware of the product and because the product will not achieve 100 percent distribution, this concept test score must be adjusted downward to predict trial. The following formula can be used to predict trial at the end of the first year.

$$CTR_1 = TBS \times A_1 \times D_1 \qquad (8\text{-}15)$$

where CTR_1 is the proportion of people who will have tried the product by the end of the first year, TBS is the top box score (percentage) for the concept, A_1 is the proportion of people who are expected to be made aware of the product during the first year, and D_1 is the fraction distribution coverage that can be expected at the end of the first year. The number of trial purchases can be estimated by multiplying CTR_1 by the number of product class buyers, #PCB. Estimates of A_1 and D_1 need to come from expected expenditures and experience with past new product introductions.

The relationship between trial and the response to a concept test is a function of a number of variables, such as the product category, its purchase cycle, the type of concept statement, and questionnaire wording. Therefore, as a company observes several launches, this formula can be modified to fit its experience. NPD Research uses the total percentage of positive responses (the top two boxes on a five-point scale) instead of the top box score in their Concept ESP® system. This system is based on a factual concept statement that is administered through a mail panel (Tarshis and Robinson, 1982). When combined with estimates of marketing spending and distribution, they have been able to estimate the actual trial level, with a standard deviation of 14 percent across sixty-five validation cases. Others have used other measures of TBS, such as the percentage who marked the top box plus half of the percentage who marked the next to the top box. Frank (1972) has found that taking one-half of the top box percentage and not correcting for awareness and distribution gives a good estimate in many instances.

Johnson (1979) surveyed several firms and found that several other weighting schemes were used in addition to taking all the top box or the total positive responses. Two of these were 80 percent of the top box and 20 percent of the next to the top box and 75, 25, 10, 5, and 2 for each of the possible responses on a five-point scale.

A weighted average can be calculated with the probability-of-purchase scale where the people marking 10 are weighted by 1, those marking 9 are weighted by .9, etc. This produces an average likelihood of purchasing. However, not all of the people circling a 10 will buy the product, and some of the people circling a 0 will buy it. Therefore, these ratings may need to be transformed to give an accurate prediction. One example of the relationship between stated likelihood and actual purchase proportions appears in Figure 8-6 (Infosino, 1986, p. 375). The horizontal axis gives the stated likelihood of purchasing and the verticle axis gives the actual percentage of each group that made a purchase.

In their telephone interview study, Jamieson and Bass (1989) questioned people about the affordability and availability of a new product as well as their purchase intention. For each of the products, they calculated the percentage by which intentions overstated actual purchases. Then they modeled the amount of overstatement as a function of availability and affordability.[4] Next, they adjusted purchase intentions on the basis of the respondents' assessment of the products' availability and affordability. They were able to produce good forecasts of trial probabilities; the average error in predicting

FIGURE 8-6 Likelihood of purchase ratings versus observed purchase proportions.

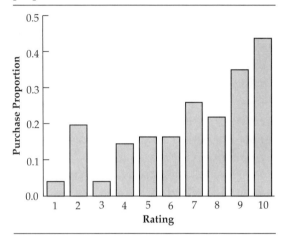

trial share across ten products was .023. These results are shown in Table 8-1.

In competitive concept tests, the number of chips allocated to each brand is used to measure the probability of purchasing each of the various brands. Additionally, intention-to-purchase responses can be analyzed with responses to other questions to determine the target market or ways to improve the concept.

Diagnostic questions   As with the intention-to-purchase question, the first step is usually a simple tabulation of the responses to the various diagnostic questions. The results provide some information about product uniqueness, relevance, the importance of main ideas, and the perception of the product on various attributes.

Second, one can perform cross-tabulations to see the relationship between responses to different questions. For example, consider the responses in Table 8-2. Looking at the top left number, it is seen that 22 percent had a positive intention to purchase the concept (marked one of the two top boxes). This number could either be compared with a category norm or used in a formula like Equation (8-12) to predict first-year trial.

---

[4]This analysis was repeated ten times, so the information on the product to be forecast was not used in this modeling stage.

TABLE 8-1   PREDICTING TRIAL FROM PROBABILITY OF
PURCHASE JUDGMENTS

| | TRIAL | | | |
	Predicted	Actual	Predicted less Actual	Predicted to Actual
Pump Toothpaste	.412	.422	−.010	.971
Diet Drink Mix	.254	.283	−.029	.898
Fruit Sticks	.196	.227	−.031	.898
Stay Fresh Milk	.058	.030	.028	1.933
Salad Dressing	.291	.230	.061	1.265
Home Computer	.039	.060	−.021	.650
Cordless Phone	.129	.110	.019	1.173
Touch Lamp	.047	.029	.018	1.621
Cordless Iron	.003	.010	−.007	.300
Shower Radio	.012	.022	−.010	.545

Source: *Based on Table 8 in Jamieson and Bass (1989).*

Table 8-2 examines the relationship between relevance and purchase intention. The bottom of the second column shows that 40 percent of the respondents rated this concept as being relevant to them. Looking within this column (that is, at only those people who thought the concept was relevant), 38 percent of them had positive intention to purchase. However, only 11 percent of the people who felt the concept was not relevant to them had a positive purchase intention.

TABLE 8-2   RESPONSES TO PURCHASE INTENTION
AND PRODUCT RELEVANCE

Purchase Intention Response	Total	Relevant	Not Relevant
Positive	22%[1] (33)[2]	38% (23)	11% (10)
Neutral or Negative	78% (117)	62% (37)	89% (80)
Total	100% (150)	40%[3] (60)	60% (90)

[1]The percentages in the first two rows are taken within column. In this case 22% of the total sample (33/150) had a positive intention to purchase this product.

[2]The numbers in parentheses represent the actual number of people. In this case thirty-three out of a total of 150 people had a positive intention to purchase this product.

[3]The percentage numbers in the last row are taken across the columns. In this case, 40% of the people (60/150) rated this concept as relevant to them.

In turn, this could lead one to investigate which people found the concept to be relevant; they may be good targets. Possibly people with certain needs, problems, or life styles find the product more relevant than others. On the other hand, one can look at what made the product relevant. Maybe the people who understood the main benefit saw the product as being more relevant. These findings would suggest that if the main benefit were communicated more successfully, more people would find the product relevant and overall purchase intention might go up.

Finally, rather than looking at the relationship between purchase intentions and other variables one at a time, it is possible to run a regression where the dependent variable is the purchase intention and the independent variables are the ones that are hypothesized to be related to it.

Classification questions One can perform cross-tabulations of the classification variables with purchase intention, just as was done for relevance and purchase intention in the previous section. For example, an analysis relating age to purchase intention would reveal whether some age groups would be better targets than others.

Summary

Concept testing is used to assess whether there is enough interest in a new product idea to warrant further development effort. It is also used to help ascertain the best targets and suggest improvements that could be made in the concept.

A number of research companies have produced evidence showing a good ability to predict first-year trial from concept tests and estimates of awareness and distribution.

However, in a number of situations concept tests cannot predict marketplace success as well as in others. First, concept tests can only estimate the number of people who will try the product. In many instances, product satisfaction is important to generate either repurchases or positive word of mouth. The success of a product may be tied more closely to satisfaction than to the quality of the idea. Second, a single exposure may not be a good predictor of eventual reaction to a product. In some categories, reactions may be due more to word of mouth than they are to advertising messages. Similarly, when a product is radically different, multiple exposures may be required to form a stable opinion. When a new product is not part of a well-defined product category, it may be much more difficult to forecast trial.

Several other factors can influence the predictive quality of concept tests. First, other new products may be introduced between the time of the concept test and market introduction. Second, attitudes can change, such as when long gas lines in the late 1970s radically altered people's preferences for high-mileage cars. Third, the concept may change between the original concept test and market introduction. Finally, alterations to the marketing plan may change awareness and distribution levels. These "problems" are not caused by concept tests, but they all affect their predictive power. Still, when used intelligently, even if they cannot perfectly separate "winners" from "losers," concept tests do provide a good value for the money.

PRODUCT TESTING

Product testing refers to the evaluation of a product or service after usage. This can be as simple as a taste test or a sniff test done in a central location or it can be a complex usage test lasting several months. In some cases, product tests are used in conjunction with concept tests to determine if the product lives up to the promises made in the concept test. Sales waves product tests (Data Development Corp., undated) allow the subject to make repeated choices among a number of competing brands.

Product tests can be used in the new product process to determine:

1. Whether the product lives up to the promises made in the concept statement.

2. How the product compares with other brands currently on the market. The percentage that plan to repurchase.

3. How the product can be improved. What is liked and disliked about the product.

4. How preference changes after extended usage. In some cases, preference may increase as a product gets easier to use over time. In others, consumers may tire of the product after repeated contact.

Similarly, product tests can be used when a product is being improved or reformulated. In a number of cases a reformulation may result in a product that does not perform as well as the one it is replacing. Some ingredients may have to be replaced in order to control costs, or government regulations may limit or ban certain substances. One example of a reformulation decision is Campbell Soup Company's decision to reduce the cost of its vegetable soup by taking out some of the more exotic vegetables like okra. In the early 1970s Schlitz lost a major share of the domestic beer market when it reduced the cost of its beer.

When used in reformulation decisions, product tests can help determine:

1. How the new product compares with the one it is potentially replacing. How it compares with other brands on the market.

2. If the consumers can tell a difference. If a product is being cost reduced, the company should test whether the consumer can tell the difference and cares.

Product testing can also be used to monitor brands currently on the market. If one is trying to determine why a brand has experienced a change on its market share, product testing can be used as part of this search, to determine if consumers' evaluations of the product after use have changed.

When product tests are conducted, the following decisions need to be made.

Blind Versus Identified Tests

In a "blind" test the consumer does not know the name of the brand or the company that made the product being tested. In blind tests, the consumer is reacting only to the physical product. In identified tests, the consumer is given the product as it appears in the marketplace. In this case, the evaluation is based not only on the physical product but also on any positive or negative bias due to the brand name, packaging, or manufacturer reputation.

Blind tests are used to compare physical products. For example, if a product has been cost reduced and the company wants to know if the consumer sees a difference, a blind test may be more appropriate. Similarly, if a brand has been losing share and the company is interested in whether it has an image problem or the actual product has lost its appeal, a blind product test could determine if the latter is the problem.

Identified tests are likely to do a better job of determining how the product would do in the marketplace. One brand may outperform another in a blind test, but not when the brand names are known. It is possible that people preferred New Coke to Classic Coke in a blind taste test, just as Pepsi was preferred to Coke in blind taste tests. However, many Coke drinkers preferred Classic Coke in an identified situation. Traditionally, P&G has used blind product tests to establish superiority, possibly on the view that if the product is perceived to be better, their marketing skill can make it a success in an identified setting.

Because blind and identified procedures test different aspects of the product, this decision is based on the objectives of the test. If it is more important to test physical characteristics, blind tests should be used. If determining the reaction to the entire offer is more important, an identified test is called for.

Test Design

There are three major types of product test designs: monadic, simultaneous, and sequential. A decision on the proper test design should be based on realism (approximation to normal consumption situations), sensitivity (how readily subjects will report differences), and cost.

Monadic product tests In a monadic product test each consumer tests one product. This can be a single consumption occasion test or it can be an extended usage test. After the consumer uses the product he or she evaluates it.

Simultaneous product tests In simultaneous product tests, the subject is usually given two products and is asked to use them at the same time. Sometimes they need to alternate their trials of each in one sitting. The "Pepsi Challenge" commercials showed a depiction of a simultaneous taste test, where the subjects could try both Pepsi and Coke at the same sitting. Listening to different stereo speakers in a listening room is another situation that resembles simultaneous product tests. Similarly, sampling two different brands of canned peas at the same meal would be a simultaneous product test.

Sequential product tests Sequential product tests also usually involve two products. In this case, the subject is asked to use one product first, then use the second some time in the future. Typically, the research company will give only the first brand to the subject, then return with the second brand after the first has been consumed. An example of a sequential test would be consuming one brand of soft drink on one day and another brand two days later. Similarly, a subject could drive one type of automobile for a month, then drive a different brand the next.

There are several subcategories of sequential product tests (Golden, 1972). A sequential monadic test occurs when the consumer tries and rates the first product, then tries and rates the second product without any direct comparison. In a sequential monadic with paired comparison, the sequential monadic test is followed by an explicit comparison. In a sequential paired comparison test, the subject tries both products before rating either. After both have been tried, they are compared. In a proto-monadic with paired comparison, the first product is tried and rated, then the second product is tried, and the two are compared. The second product is not explicitly rated. This test might be performed when the second product is a standard that is used in many tests.

The main difference between these designs is whether the first product is rated before the second is tried. This is undesirable if rating the first product will influence the evaluation of the second. For example, if one is asked to rate the first product on an unexpected attribute, the subject will probably pay closer attention to it when using the second. On the other hand, if the consumer is likely to forget some aspects of the first product if it is rated only after the second is used, the first product should be rated after its usage. Under any circumstances, the order of product usage should be randomized across subjects.

Comparison of methods Greenberg (1963) ran a taste test of two visibly different brands of matzo (an unleavened bread used primarily by Jewish people during Passover), labeled A and B. It was conducted with two groups of subjects (I and II). A sequential monadic test was performed on the first day, with one brand consumed in the morning and the other in the afternoon. Group I (II) tasted brand A (B) in the morning and brand B (A) in the afternoon. One or two days later, the subjects underwent a simultaneous paired comparison test of the same two brands. This time group I (II) was instructed to eat brand B (A) first and brand A (B) second, with a cup of water between tastings. The results for this test are given in Table 8-3.

Several findings are noteworthy. First, the

TABLE 8-3   *MATZO BREAD PRODUCT TEST*

| | PERCENT PREFERRING BRAND | | |
	A	B	No Preference
Monadic	4.0	4.0	NA
Sequential Monadic	30%	26%	44%
Group I (A first)	45%	16%	39%
Group II (B first)	15%	36%	49%
Simultaneous P.C.	47%	48%	5%
Group II (A first)	57%	36%	7%
Group I (B first)	36%	60%	4%

combined (over both groups) results of all tests indicates little overall difference in preference in spite of the fact that the two breads are visibly different. Second, there are relatively large order effects. The brand tried first tended to be more preferred. Finally, the simultaneous test was much more sensitive than the sequential monadic test.

This leads to a comparison of the strengths and weaknesses of the various designs. The *monadic* best approximates the way most products are tried—one at a time. It is also the least sensitive partly because many people tend to evaluate brands in a test favorably and partly because no direct comparison is made. The monadic test is the only test possible if use of one product makes another unnecessary, such as a cold remedy, a book that teaches someone how to use a word processor, or a diet product. It is also the most appropriate test when there is no good benchmark. However, it is usually the most expensive way to compare two brands, because one needs two comparable groups and each respondent usually needs to be visited twice (once at the start to give out the product and once at the end after usage). Furthermore, because of a larger sampling variance (due to different people evaluating each product), larger sample sizes may be needed.

The strengths and weaknesses of *simultaneous tests* are the mirror image of the monadic. They are the most sensitive, because the products are

used at the same time and are directly compared. They are the least realistic, because few products are typically compared in this fashion. Finally, they are usually the least expensive way to compare two brands, because only one sample of respondents is needed and each respondent needs to be visited twice (as with the monadic).

Sequential tests occupy a position between the simultaneous and the monadic tests. They are relatively realistic; trying different brands on different occasions and deciding which is preferred is typical. They are more sensitive than a monadic test, especially if direct comparisons are made. They are also in the middle as far as the cost of comparing two brands. Like the simultaneous test, they require only one group to test two brands, but in many cases, three contacts with each subject are required (once to deliver each of the products and once to collect the evaluations). The order effects tend to be more pronounced in these tests. Finally, the subjects may get conditioned after using the first product.

As can be seen from this comparison, no design is best in every situation. An important factor to consider is how sensitive the test should be. When comparing new and old formulations of the same brand, sensitivity may be required. On the other hand, if there is so little difference between a new product and its competition that the new brand can be seen as superior only in a simultaneous (if unrealistic) usage situation, its superiority may not translate into marketplace success. In many cases, sensitivity is directly opposed to realism. Therefore, in many new product situations, the monadic and sequential product tests are favored in predicting marketplace success.

Subjects

The source of subjects for product tests is quite similar to that of respondents for concept tests. The primary difference is that users or consumers are required for product tests and purchasers or influencers are required for concept tests. However, in many instances, these are the same people.

Employees   In numerous situations employees can profitably be used in product tests. Many times industrial companies use the products or services they make in their own business. Therefore, their employees can be quite useful in terms of determining what features a new product should have. Similarly, many food companies have test kitchens where employees try out new foods. Apple has given its employees a discount on its computers. Many of its employees are novices. Several years ago, they told the company that there were too many manuals and that the computer was too hard to hook up. This feedback was one of the factors that made Apple design the Macintosh to be easy for the user to assemble and start up.

Employees may create certain problems for product testing. The most obvious is that they may not want to go on record as saying anything bad about their company's product. In some cases, employees may be much more familiar with the product than its typical consumers and they may evaluate products or features differently than the rest of the market. In the 1950s, when Dow developed HandiWrap, its engineers took it home and tested it. Many of the engineers' comments centered on the fact that it was made of plastic. This led to the first slogan, "It's Plastic, not Wax." Although this impressed Dow's engineers, it did little for the average consumer. However, the employee tests did reveal a number of packaging and quality problems.

There are at least two ways to minimize problems with employee testing. First, one should perform blind rather than identified tests and test competitors' products as well as the company's. Second, other family members may make more representative subjects.

Central locations   It is possible to test both consumer and industrial products in central locations. Consumer products can be tested in shopping malls. Industrial products can be tested at trade shows or on the premises of the company developing the product. Central location tests work best when the product does not require extended usage to evaluate. If the piece of equipment is expensive or difficult to install, a central location may be best. For example, GE has test kitchens. By watching people cook in them, it has learned about the placement of large burners, the location of oven windows, and so on.

Central location tests also work well when a food product requires little preparation or when controlled serving conditions are required. For example, it is possible to run taste tests for soft drinks in a mall. On the other hand, Green Giant tested Oven Crock Baked Beans in a central location taste test. They were highly preferred to the leading brand in this test. However, when people bought them and fixed them at home, they added their own seasonings and the product failed.

Home or workplace placement   Home or workplace placement is often required where central location testing does not work. The home or workplace is usually the only possible location for extended usage tests. It is also the preferred place when the consumer is likely to "customize" the product. Like baked beans, the product needs to be tested in the way in which it will be used after purchase.

Circle the number that best describes the taste of the following cereals:

	Delicious									Not Delicious
Product A	1	2	3	4	5	6	7	8	9	10
Product B	1	2	3	4	5	6	7	8	9	10
Cheerios	1	2	3	4	5	6	7	8	9	10
Grape Nuts	1	2	3	4	5	6	7	8	9	10

Questions

The questions asked during a product test and the methods of analysis are quite similar to those used for concept tests. Therefore, they will not be discussed in the same detail as before. The questions may be divided into the same three categories: *primary criterion, diagnostic,* and *classification.*

Primary criterion   Monadic tests usually ask subjects to state their intention to purchase a product by using a five-point scale, ask a probability-of-purchase question, or ask for a chip allocation across several brands on the basis of either purchase probabilities or frequencies.

In paired comparison tests the subjects are asked to choose which product they liked better. Sometimes they are asked a graded paired comparison question in which they are to state their relative preference for each product. The preference could be requested in the following manner:

Circle the number between 0 and 10 that best represents your relative preference for the two products you have just tried. Circle 5 if you are indifferent between them. Circle a number closer to 0 if you preferred product A and a number closer to 10 if you preferred product B. Circle numbers closer to one of the ends to indicate a stronger preference.

Very Strong Preference For Brand A										Very Strong Preference For Brand B
0	1	2	3	4	5	6	7	8	9	10

Diagnostic questions   Many of the diagnostic questions for concept statements are communications questions and are not asked in product tests. For example, there is no need to ask about the main idea in the concept statement. Similarly, believability is less of an issue in product tests. The primary diagnostic questions deal with attribute ratings and likes and dislikes of the products tested.

Attribute ratings.   Attribute ratings of both the test product and brands typically consumed, as well as the importance of those attributes, should be collected. These questions can be asked in the following manner, illustrated in the two tables on this page.

How important is it that a cereal be:

	Very Important			Very Unimportant	
Delicious	1	2	3	4	5

If the most preferred level of an attribute is not obvious, that information should be collected as well. See the example on the next page.

Likes and dislikes   Also, it is important to ask about specific likes and dislikes, as was done in the concept test. Similarly, one should ask why a brand would or would not be repurchased.

Classification questions   The same types of classification questions should be asked in a

Circle the number that best describes the sweetness of the following cereals. On the "desired level" line, circle the number that best describes your preferred level of sweetness relative to the cereals you just rated.

	Sweet									Not Sweet
Product A	1	2	3	4	5	6	7	8	9	10
Product B	1	2	3	4	5	6	7	8	9	10
Cheerios	1	2	3	4	5	6	7	8	9	10
Grape Nuts	1	2	3	4	5	6	7	8	9	10
Desired Level	1	2	3	4	5	6	7	8	9	10

product test that were asked in a concept test. They include demographic, socioeconomic, and psychographic questions. Additionally, brands used most frequently, last brand used, and purchase quantities can provide useful information.

Analysis

Most product test analysis consists of frequencies and cross-tabulations. Frequencies give a count of the number of people who answered each question in a certain way. Cross-tabulations count the number of people who answered two questions in a certain way. Correlations and regressions should also be run.

With most new products, one wants to know whether the product lived up to what was promised in the concept statement. One can do this with a monadic test by comparing the percentage who marked a top box on a purchase intention question on the concept test with the corresponding response on the product test. It is also possible to cross-tabulate the answers to the two purchase intention questions to see who changed their minds after contact with the product. This comparison may indicate whether the concept or the product should be changed.

Depending on the question associated with the primary criterion, one needs to calculate the percentage marking the top box, the number of points allocated to a brand in a point allocation task, or the percentage of people who preferred the new product to the leading brand in the cat-

egory. These results can be compared with norms, but their primary use should be to help forecast the financial consequences of introducing the product.

The percentage marking the top box (or the percentage who had a positive intention to repeat and had no negatives about the product) can be used to estimate the percentage of people who will make a first repurchase, given that they made an initial purchase, $R(1)$. This estimate can be used in a depth of repeat model like the one described in Appendix 8-1. Alternatively, this top box number can be used as an approximation of RR, the repeat rate in a repeat and switchback model.

If the subjects are asked to allocate chips among the new brand and members of their consideration set (i.e., the brands they would consider buying), the percentage of chips allocated to the new brand is an estimate of LRR for that person. LRR needs to be calculated across only those people who tried the product.

If a new formulation is compared with a product that is currently on the market, current users of the product should be analyzed separately from nonusers. Villani and Morrison (1976) suggest that both groups should be analyzed in terms of their size, the probability they would try the product, and the percentage of each group who likes the new formulation better than the old. The reason for their approach can be seen in the following example.

A brand with a 15 percent market share is contemplating a reformulation. Twenty percent of the current users of the brand like the refor-

mulation better and 80 percent like the old formulation better. Nonusers prefer the new formulation over the old 60 percent to 40 percent.
The current users of the brand are considered
certain to try the new formulation, but only 10
percent of the rest of the market will try it. The
results shown in Table 8-4 contain a sample of
1,000 people. If users are not separated from
nonusers, it appears that consumers like the
reformulation better than the original product
(540 to 460). However, if one looks at those
people who will try the new formulation, the
old formulation is preferred to the new (154
to 81).

In addition to determining what percentage
of the people say they will purchase the product, one should analyze who will purchase the
product. First, one can cross-tabulate each subject's response to the intention to purchase question with some of the classification questions.
Doing so indicates whether any demographic or
socioeconomic groups are more likely to purchase the product than others. Also, purchase
intention can be cross-tabulated with the last
brand used (or most frequently used brand) to
determine which brands will be most affected
by the product. Finally, one can cross-tabulate
answers to the intention to purchase question
with the answers to attribute ratings to see
which product qualities are associated with purchasing.

In addition, attribute ratings can be related to
purchase intention by running a regression with
purchase intention as the dependent variable
and various attribute ratings as the independent
variables.

Sales Waves Experiments

A different type of product test is a sales waves
experiment (Data Development Corporation,
undated). Typically, the first stage is a concept
or product test. After the initial placement, a
researcher visits the subjects periodically and
allows them to repurchase the test brand. As an
alternative, the researcher may offer a full selection of brands from the category. If it is just the
brand being tested, the price needs to be comparable to marketplace prices.

The length of time between visits is based on
the purchase cycle. For example, a new soft
drink may require weekly visits, whereas a new
toothpaste would entail only monthly visits.
During each visit, the brand(s) purchased need
to be recorded.

A sales waves experiment can be used to estimate market share in the following manner.
Suppose a representative sample of 300 families
was given a concept or product test and sixty of
the families rated the tested concept in the top
box or said they would like to purchase the associated product. This would represent a trial
probability (assuming 100 percent awareness
and distribution) of 20 percent (60/300).

Of these sixty families, suppose that during
each repurchase period the following percentages of total purchases were directed toward

TABLE 8-4   ANALYSIS OF USERS AND NONUSERS

	Nonusers	Users	Total
Number	850	150	1,000
Like new formulation better	510	30	540
Like old formulation better	340	120	460
Will try new formulation	85	150	235
Try and like new formulation better	51	30	81
Try new formulation and like old better	34	120	154

this brand: 55 percent, 40 percent, 37 percent, 38 percent, and 36 percent. Under the typically made assumption that repeat purchases tend to stabilize after five or six repurchases, one would guess that the new brand will have a 35 percent share among the people who have tried it. This information can be used with the expected cumulative trial rate, CTR_{max}, of 20 percent in Equation (8-5) to forecast market share

$$MS = CTR_{max} \times LRR = 20\% \times .35 = 7\% \quad (8\text{-}16)$$

Alternatively, one can run a regression of the following form to estimate LRR:

$$\hat{LRR}_t = \hat{a} + \hat{b}/t + e \quad (8\text{-}17)$$

Where $\hat{LRR}_t$ is the market share in period t among those people who have tried the brand of interest, $\hat{a}$ and $\hat{b}$ are regression weights and e is an error term. This equation fits a downward sloping curve that has a lower limit of $\hat{a}$, as the second term in the equation approaches zero when t gets large. When this regression is run the following curve is estimated:

$$\hat{LRR} = .304 + .236/t \quad (8\text{-}18)$$

These data and the resulting curve are shown in Figure 8-7. This regression implies that the equilibrium market share among those who tried the product will be 30.4 percent. Combined with the

^ means estimate

FIGURE 8-7   Long-run retention.

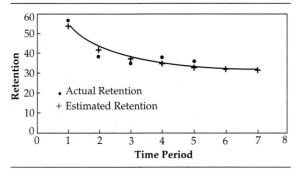

estimated trial rate of 20 percent, this results in a forecast market share of 6 percent.

Summary

Product testing is an important part of new product research. One of the primary differences between successful and failing new products is a high relative value to the customer. Some form of product testing is the only way to determine if the product is perceived to be superior to what is currently on the market.

Product testing is able to identify many unsuccessful products. However, a success at this stage does not ensure a winner. Many product tests that are performed over a small number of trials may not be able to predict marketplace success. In many frequently purchased categories, a large number of repeat purchases are typically needed to ensure success. In addition to indicating possible market success, product tests can suggest important opportunities to improve the product.

CONCLUDING REMARKS

A successful new product needs to be based on a concept that promises something to the consumer that is not available in current offerings. Next, the product must live up to the promises made in the concept statement. Finally, the introductory marketing program must be well directed and appropriately funded. The techniques discussed in this chapter can help ensure that the first two of these goals are reached.

Concept tests allow the company to determine the level of consumer interest in the benefits promised by the new product. This information can be used to forecast the number of people who might try the product, which market segments would be most likely to try it, and ways the concept could be improved.

Product tests are used to compare the actual performance of the product with what was promised in the concept statement. Product tests also determine how the product compares with the ones currently on the market and how this evaluation changes with extended usage. This information can be used to forecast the long-run retention rate. Finally, one can learn ways to improve the product.

REFERENCES

Armstrong, J. Scott, and Terry Overton: "Brief vs. Comprehensive Descriptions in Measuring Intention to Purchase," *Journal of Marketing Research,* 8, February 1971, 216–220.

Bass, Frank M.: "A New Product Growth Model for Consumer Durables," *Management Science,* 15, January 1969, 215–227.

Clarke, Darral G.: *Marketing Analysis and Decision Making,* Redwood City, CA: The Scientific Press, 1987, pp. 111–133.

Data Development Corporation: *Sales Waves Experiments,* New York: Data Development Corporation, undated.

Eskin, Gerald J.: "Dynamic Forecasts of New Product Demand Using a Depth of Repeat Model," *Journal of Marketing Research,* 10, May 1973, 115–129.

Fourt, L. A., and J. W. Woodlock: "Early Prediction of Market Success for New Grocery Products," *Journal of Marketing,* 25, October 1960, 31–38.

Frank, Newton: "Can We Predict New Product Success From Concept Testing?" talk given at the AMA New York Chapter New Products Conference, November 30, 1972.

Golden, Robert: "Monadic vs. Paired Comparison Product Testing—Is the Battle Still Raging," presented at the AMA New York Chapter Conference, "Product Testing—Today and Tomorrow," January 1972.

Greenberg, Allan: "Paired Comparison vs. Monadic Tests," *Journal of Advertising Research,* 3 (4), 1963, 44–47.

Haley, Russel I., and Ronald Gatty: "The Trouble with Concept Testing," *Journal of Marketing Research,* 8, May 1971, 230–232.

Hartung, P. H., and J. L. Fisher: "Brand Switching and Mathematical Programming in Market Expansion," *Management Science,* 11, August, pp. 231–243, 1965.

Holbert, Neil: *Research in the Twilight Zone,* AMA Monograph Series no. 7, Chicago: American Marketing Association, 1977.

Jamieson, Linda F., and Frank M. Bass: "Adjusting Stated Intentions Measures to Predict the Trial Purchase of New Products: A Comparison of Models and Methods," *Journal of Marketing Research,* 26, August 1989, 336–346.

Johnson, Jeffery S.: "A Study of the Accuracy and Validity of Purchase Intention Scores," privately circulated working paper, Phoenix, Ariz.: Armour-Dial Co., 1979.

Maffei, R. B.: "Brand Preference and Simple Markov Processes," *Operations Research,* 8, 1960, 210–218.

McGuire, E. Patrick: *Evaluating New-Product Proposals,* New York: The Conference Board, 1973.

Moore, William L.: "Concept Testing," *Journal of Business Research*, 10, 1982, 279–294.

_____: "Testing Advertising Concepts: Current Practices and Opinions," *Journal of Advertising Research*, 14 (3), 1985, 45–51.

Oren, Shmuel S., Michael H. Rothkopf, and Richard D. Smallwood: "A Market Forecasting System for Non-impact Computer Printers," *Interfaces*, 1980.

Parfitt, J. H., and B. J. K. Collins: "Use of Consumer Panels for Brand Share Predictions, *Journal of Marketing Research*, 5, May 1968, 131–145.

Pringle, Lewis G., R. Dale Wilson, and Edward I. Brody: "NEWS: A Decision-Oriented Model for New Product Analysis and Forecasting," *Marketing Science*, 1, Winter 1982, 1–29.

Pessemier, Edgar A.: Experimental Methods of Estimating Demand," *Journal of Business*, October 1960, 373–383.

_____: *Experimental Methods for Analyzing the Demand for Branded Consumer Goods With Applications to Problems in Marketing Strategy*, Pullman, Wash.: Washington State University Press, 1963.

_____: *Product Management: Strategy and Organization*, 2d ed., New York: John Wiley and Sons, 1982, pp. 170–174.

_____: "Varied Individual Behavior: Some Theories, Measurement Methods and Models," *Multivariate Behavioral Research*, 20, January 1985, 69–94.

Rogers, Everett M.: *Diffusion of Innovations*, 3rd ed., New York: Free Press, 1982.

Sales and Marketing Management: "The True Test of Test Marketing Is Time," *Sales and Marketing Management*, March 14, 1983, 74, 78.

Schwartz, David: *Concept Testing: How to Test New Product Ideas Before You Go to Market*, New York: American Management Association, 1987.

Silk, Alvin J., and Glen L. Urban: "Pretest Market Evaluation of New Package Goods: A Model and Measurement Method," *Journal of Marketing Research*, 15, No. 2, May 1978, 171–191.

Shocker, Allan D., and William G. Hall: "Pretest Market Models: A Critical Evaluation," *Journal of Product Innovation Management*, 3, 1986, 86–107.

Tarshis, Andrew, and Joel Robinson: "Concept ESP: Estimating Sales Potential From Written Concept Statements," in *Concept Testing, Screening, and Analysis*, PDMA Proceedings, Friedhelm W. A. Bliemel and George Tesar (eds.), 1982, 11–25.

Tauber, Edward M.: "What Is Measured by Concept Testing," *Journal of Advertising Research*, 12, December 1972, 35–37.

Urban, Glen L., and Gerald M. Katz: "Pre-Test-Market Models: Validation and Managerial Implications," *Journal of Marketing Research*, 20, August 1983, 221–234.

Villani, Kathryn E. A., and Donald G. Morrison: "A Method for Analyzing New Formulation Decisions," *Journal of Marketing Research*, 13, August 1976, 284–288.

Wilson, Brant: "Disk-By-Mail Surveys: Three Years' Experience," in *Gaining a Competitive Advantage Through PC-Based Interviewing and Analysis*, Vol. 1, 1989 Sawtooth Software Conference Proceedings, Margo Metegrano (ed.), 1989, 1–4.

Wilton, Peter C., and Edgar A. Pessemier: "Forecasting the Ultimate Acceptance of an Innovation: The Effects of Information," *Journal of Consumer Research*, 8, September 1981, 162–171.

Zandan, Peter, and Lucy Frost: "Customer Satisfaction Research Using Disks-By-Mail," in *Gaining a Competitive Advantage Through PC-Based Interviewing and Analysis*, Vol. 1, 1989 Sawtooth Software Conference Proceedings, Margo Metegrano (ed.), 1989, 5–18.

APPENDIX 8-1 USING DEPTH OF PURCHASE CLASSES TO FORECAST SALES OF A FREQUENTLY PURCHASED GOOD

The depth of purchase method is straightforward, but requires lots of "bookkeeping" to keep track of the various sources of sales. First, trial sales in each period are modeled using Equation (8-7):

$$
\begin{aligned}
ITR_t &= a \times (CTR_{max} - CTR_{t-1}) \\
&= a \times (1 - a)^{t-1} \times CTR_{max}
\end{aligned}
\qquad (8\text{-}1A)
$$

ITR_t is the proportion of trial sales in period t, a is a constant that determines the proportion of those left to try the product who will do so each period, and CTR_{max} is the maximum proportion who will ever try the product. In this example, it is assumed that 30 percent will ever try the product and 40 percent of those left in the pool to try the product will try it during that period. Inserting these values into Equation (8-1A) results in the following equation:

$$
ITR_t = .4 \times (.6)^{t-1} \times .30 \qquad (8\text{-}2A)
$$

It yields the following trial percentages for the first five periods: 12 percent, 7.2 percent, 4.3 percent, 2.6 percent, and 1.6 percent. These fractional numbers are multiplied by the number of product category buyers,

#PCB, to determine the number of trial sales in each period. In this case, #PCB is assumed to be 1,000, so trial sales in the first five periods are 120, 72, 43, 26, and 16, respectively.

Repeat sales are modeled with a depth of repeat model. $R(i)$ is the repeat probability for the ith depth of repeat class; that is, it is the probability that a person who makes an $i - 1$th repeat purchase will make an ith repeat purchase. In general, $R(i) \leq R(i + 1)$ and $R(\infty) \approx 1$. Successive depth of repeat probabilities are typically modeled with the following equation:

$$
R(i) = R(\infty) \times (1 - I^{ti}) \qquad (8\text{-}3A)
$$

If $R(\infty) = 1$ and $\Gamma = .6$, then $R(1)$, $R(2)$, and $R(3)$ equal .4, .64, and .78, respectively.

Just as all the people who try a product will not try it during the same period, all the people making a first repeat purchase will not make it during the same period after they tried it. However, just like trial, most people who are going to make a repeat purchase will make it soon after making their previous purchase. This means that the pattern of repeat purchases after a previous purchase should be similar to the pattern of trial purchases. Therefore, the following equation is used to model the proportion of people who will make their ith repeat purchase t periods after their $i - 1$th repeat purchase:

$$
R(i)_t = b \times (1 - b)^{t-1} \times R(i) \qquad (8\text{-}4A)
$$

where $R(i)_t$ is the proportion who will make an ith repeat purchase t periods after the $i - 1$th repeat purchase and b is the fraction of those who will make an ith repeat purchase during each period. In this example, it is assumed that b is equal to .5. Using the values from the repeat probabilities, Equation (8-4A) can be rewritten as follows:

$$
R(i)_t = .5 \times (.5)^{t-1} \times R(i) \qquad (8\text{-}5A)
$$

The first repeat probability, $R(1)$, is .4 and Equation (8-5A) is used to calculate the first repurchase probabilities in the first three periods after trial as $R(1)_1 = .2$, $R(1)_2 = .1$, and $R(1)_3 = .05$. Similarly, with $R(2)$ equal to .64, the second repeat purchase probabilities for the first three periods after a first repeat purchase are $R(2)_1 = .32$, $R(2)_2 = .16$, and $R(2)_3 = .08$.

These ideas are combined in the following chart. Each row represents the number of purchases in a given period. The columns contain trial and depth of repeat classes. To simplify the ~~chart~~ table, only first and second repeat purchases are shown. Furthermore, only those repeat purchases that are made within two periods of a previous purchase are shown.

Period	ITR$_t$	R(1)$_1$	R(1)$_2$	R(2)$_1$	R(2)$_2$	Total
1	120[1]					120
2	72	24[2]				96
3	43	14	12[3]	7[4]		76
4	26	9	7	8[5]	3[6]	53

[1] Of the 1,000 people, 12%, or 120, tried the product in period 1; 7.2%, or 72, tried it in period 2, and so on.

[2] Of the 120 people who tried the product in period 1; 20% of them, or twenty-four, made a first repeat purchase in period 2. All other entries in this column follow similar logic.

[3] Of the 120 people who tried the product in period 1; 10% of them, or twelve, made a first repeat purchase two periods later, in period 3.

[4] Of the twenty-four people who made a first repeat purchase in period 2, 30%, or seven, made a second repeat purchase one period later, in period 3.

[5] Of the twenty-six (14 + 12), people who made a first repeat purchase in period 3, 30% of them, or eight, made a second repeat purchase one period later.

[6] Of the twenty-four people who made a first repeat purchase in period 2, 15% of them, or three, made a second repeat purchase two periods later, in period 4.

REVIEW QUESTIONS

Q8-1 What is a target market? How can it be divided up?

Q8-2 How does one account for the fact that only a fraction of all potential triers ever make a first purchase?

Q8-3 What are some of the distinct meanings one can assign to the term "market share"?

Q8-4 Discuss the meaning of the cumulative trial rate and the incremental trial rate.

Q8-5 Discuss the rationale for the formula CTR$_t$ = $P \times f(A_t, D_t)$.

Q8-6 What is the meaning of LRR? What is it a function of?

Q8-7 What are the main types of concept tests and when is each one most suitable?

Q8-8 Discuss some of the principal problems that must be dealt with to successfully execute a concept test.

Q8-9 How many and what kinds of respondents are used in concept tests?

Q8-10 What questions are asked in a concept test? Why?

Q8-11 Contrast the purposes of concept and product tests.

Q8-12 What are the pros and cons of blind product tests?

Q8-13 What questions are typically asked after a product test?

Q8-14 How are sales waves product tests used to estimate market share? How can response bias and sample composition affect the estimate?

9

PRETEST MARKET MODELS AND TEST MARKETS

The last chapter focused on the use of concept and product testing to evaluate the offer. This chapter extends the scope of evaluation to simulated test markets and test markets. Both of these new tools are more realistic than previous types of tests. Respondents usually see finished commercials, are given the chance to purchase the product, and may receive free samples. Thus both methods are able to test more of the marketing mix. Pretest market models are calibrated in a laboratory (or simulated test market), so they are somewhat artificial from the consumer's standpoint. However, they are much faster and less expensive than test markets. Test markets are able to test the entire marketing mix, are most realistic, and may test trade acceptance, but are the most expensive, most time consuming, and easiest for competition to observe.

PRETEST MARKET MODELS

Pretest market models were developed in the late 1960s as a lower-cost way to predict new product success for packaged goods. This general approach follows Pessemier's work (1960, 1963), which demonstrated the usefulness of laboratory data in predicting price elasticities and demand. Since this time, there have been a few attempts to apply this general method to durable goods, industrial goods, and services. Although there are a relatively large number of suppliers of these methods, they share a number of characteristics. This discussion will tend to focus on the commonalities rather than the differences. However, only a portion of the research suppliers have described their methodology in detail [for example, ASSESSOR (Silk and Urban, 1978), LITMUS (Blackburn and Clancy, 1982), and NEWS/Planner, which will be referred to as NEWS (Pringle, Wilson, and Brody, 1982)[1]]. They will be the primary focus of this discussion.

---

[1]Because these models can be reasonably complicated, this discussion will make a number of simplifying assumptions, which are not always mentioned. Hopefully, this discussion presents the essence of the models. To learn about the specific models, one should consult the original sources, or insightful review articles by Shocker and Hall (1986) and Dolan (1988).

General Description

A pretest market model, which may also be called a Simulated Test Market (STM), consists of showing an advertisement for a new brand to a number of people, giving them the opportunity to purchase the brand in a convenient store, and recontacting them after they have used it. An STM is usually run in several geographically separated shopping malls.

Before the test is run the company needs a complete new product marketing plan, because the results of the test are combined with a number of managerial assumptions to forecast sales. This plan needs to specify the amount that will be spent on advertising, the gross ratings points (GRPs)[2] generated, target awareness levels, distribution levels, a specific promotion plan (including the number of samples and coupons to be distributed), price, a volume target that is a minimum for continuing, and a competitive frame. Furthermore, the packaging and advertising should be reasonably finished.

There are several common steps to the data-gathering process.

1. Between 300 and 600 respondents are recruited. The respondents are chosen to fit certain demographic categories and may be screened to be users of the product category if the new brand fits into an existing category. BASES II does not screen on category usage, because it estimates volume directly rather than going through market share.[3]

2. The respondents are shown a print ad, story boards, or a commercial for the new brand. They may also be shown commercials for a number of other brands in that category.

3. They may be questioned about attitudes and brand usage either before or after the commercials are shown.

4. ASSESSOR and LITMUS request the respondents to go on a shopping trip in either a simulated or a real store nearby. In these cases, they are usually given either coupons or seed money to purchase a brand in the relevant product category. If they do not buy the new brand, they may be given a free sample at the checkout counter. Rather than put them through a simulated shopping trip, BASES II and NEWS ask the respondent several questions about the new brand. These include likes and dislikes, value for the money, and purchase intention.

5. The respondents are recontacted at home by phone after they have had a chance to use the product and are asked a number of attitudinal, preference, and intention-to-purchase questions. They are also given the opportunity to make a mail-order purchase of the test product. Sometimes a sales waves test is added in order to track repurchases over several cycles.

The measurements from the STM are combined with managerial judgments about the level of support that will be given to the product to produce a forecast steady-state market share using either a trial-and-repeat model (ASSESSOR) as in Equation (8-8) or a trial-and-depth-of-purchase model (LITMUS and NEWS) similar to that in Appendix 8-1.

In the case of BASE II and NEWS, an STM is similar to a concept-product test except that the packaging and advertising are comparable to what is done for brands already on the market, a firm price is established, and a more detailed marketing plan is needed for better sales forecasts. ASSESSOR and LITMUS have an additional point of differentiation in that the respondent actually purchases the product in a store rather than responding to a questionnaire.

Simulated test markets have a number of advantages over traditional test markets. They

---

[2] Gross ratings points are the product of reach (the percentage of people who will see a commercial) times frequency (the average number of times that a person who sees a commercial at least once will see it) times 100.

[3] See the discussion on the use of #TM and #PCB as the appropriate BASE on page 248 of Chapter 8.

are much less expensive, $35,000 to $100,000 versus $1 millon. They are much quicker, eight to twelve weeks versus a year. They are not as visible to competition. They are also able to screen out a large proportion of potential test market failures. Approximately 80 percent of the time that a new product meets its objectives in a well-run STM, it will also meet them in a test market. This compares with a 40 percent success rate in traditional test markets for products that have not gone through an STM (Shocker and Hall, 1986).

However, in many cases STMs should not be a substitute for test markets. STMs are somewhat artificial; the sample sizes are relatively small and the people usually know what the new brand is. STMs are not able to test trade acceptance or the ability of the manufacturing and distribution system to deliver the product. A number of important marketing support variables, such as the level of advertising, cannot be tested directly. Finally, competitive reactions are not fully tested.

Trial Models

One can either model steady-state trial—that is, how many people will try the product within one or two years—or one can model the number of people who will try the product in every period (usually monthly or quarterly periods, but the length of the period may be based on the length of the purchase cycle). The advantage of modeling trial by period is that one can compare each period's forecasts to actual trial to see whether the product is on track or not. However, this leads to a much more complex model.

Steady-state trial   Steady-state trial is incorporated into one of the two principal models in ASSESSOR (Silk and Urban, 1978). The following formula is used to predict steady-state trial due to advertising:

$$CTR_A = P \times A \times D \qquad (9\text{-}1)$$

where CTR_A is the cumulative trial due to advertising, P is the proportion who tried this brand in the simulated shopping trip or marked the top box in response to an intention to purchase question, A is the proportion of the target market expected to become aware of this product through the company's advertising, and D is the proportion of all category distribution that is expected to be achieved. Both A and D are based on managerial judgment as reflected in the preliminary marketing plan.

In addition to advertising, it is assumed that some people will try this product by using a free sample they receive. The fraction who will try the product through a sample is

$$CTR_S = C \times U \qquad (9\text{-}2)$$

where CTR_S is the trial due to sampling, C is the probability the person will receive a sample, and U is the probability that the person will use the sample received. U can be estimated from the percentage of people who tried the free sample given to them in the simulated store or may be based on managerial judgment of past responses. C is based on managerial judgment of the amount that will be spent on samples as reflected in the marketing plan.

With this formulation, some of the people would try the product twice, once because of advertising and once because they received a free sample. This double counting is eliminated with the following steady-state trial function:

$$CTR = CTR_A \ast CTR_S - (CTR_A \times CTR_S) \qquad (9\text{-}3)$$

Trial by period   This type of model is a part of both the NEWS (Pringle, Wilson, and Brody, 1982) and LITMUS (Blackburn and Clancy, 1982) models. These models assume that each consumer moves through a series of stages. These are shown in Figure 9-1.

The first stage is being unaware of the product. Initially, all customers start out in this stage. The people in the next stage are aware of the

FIGURE 9-1   Consumer stages in the trial and repeat model.

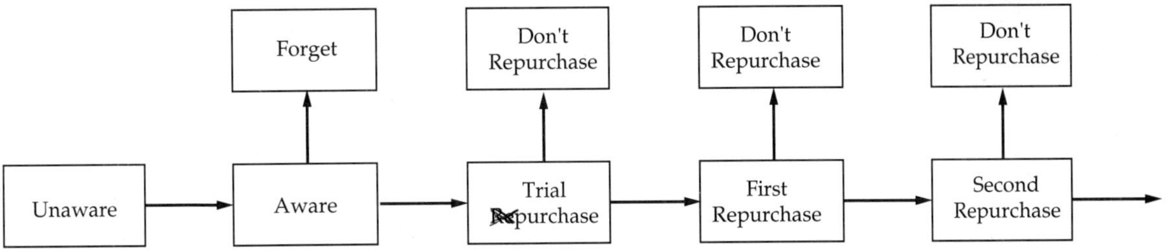

product, but have never purchased it. People enter this stage by becoming aware of the product through advertising, free samples, coupons, word-of-mouth, or by seeing it in the store. This discussion will make the simplifying assumption that awareness can be generated only through advertising, which greatly simplifies the mathematics but does not change the logic.

People can leave this stage either by trying the product or by forgetting about it. The people in the next stage have made one and only one purchase of this brand. People enter this stage by making their first purchase. Typically, people who are going to try the product do so relatively soon after becoming aware of it. The longer they have been aware but have not purchased, the lower their probability of trying it becomes. They leave the trial group by making a second purchase of the brand (in which case they go to the first repeat stage) or they exit from the system if they do not repurchase the brand within two purchase cycles. Again, it has been found that if someone does not repurchase relatively quickly, the probability of ever repurchasing goes down. The various depth of purchase groups will be discussed in a subsequent section.

Awareness.   When the relationship between advertising expenditures and brand awareness has been studied, three things are generally found. There is usually some level of awareness of a brand without any advertising. As more is

spent on advertising, awareness increases, but at a decreasing rate. Finally, there appears to be an upper limit on awareness. Equation (9-4) represents one way of modeling this relationship.

A_0 is the minimum awareness level without any advertising. This could be thought of as the awareness that is generated by having the product on the shelves or the tendency of some people to say they have heard of a brand even if it does not exist. A_* is the maximum awareness that is attainable. Usually it is close to one. The fraction who are made aware from current advertising (and yea saying) in period t, AA_t, is:

$$AA_t = A_0 + (A_* - A_0)(1 - e^{-\alpha G_t}) \qquad (9\text{-}4)$$

where α is a term that reflects the quality of the advertising and interest in the product category and G_t is the advertising's gross ratings points (in hundreds) during period t. In an STM, α, A_0, and A_* are based on management's experience with other products and may be aided by copy tests. G_t is based on spending plans as reflected in the new product marketing plan.

The function in Equation (9-4) has a minimum value of A_0 when G_t is zero. $(1 - e^{-\alpha G_t})$ is a concave downward function that takes on values between zero and one. It is zero when G_t is zero and approaches one as G_t approaches infinity. As G_t increases, a bigger portion of the difference $(A_* - A_0)$ is added to A_0. AA_t has a maximum of A_* when an infinite number of GRPs are achieved.

In Figure 9-2, as well as in the example to fol-

FIGURE 9-2   Awareness due to advertising.

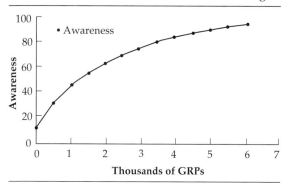

low, it is assumed that $\alpha = .040$, $A_0 = 8$ percent, and $A_* = 92$ percent[4]. These assumptions result in the following relationship between G_t and AA_t.

Some fraction of those aware in the previous period, A_{t-1}, will forget if they do not see an advertisement in period t. The fraction of those who were aware in a previous period and who will see an advertisement in this period is $(1 - e^{-\alpha Gt})$, therefore, one minus that fraction, or $e^{-\alpha Gt}$, will not see an advertisement. Making the simplifying assumption that those who became aware through distribution, A_0, are not affected, the fraction previously aware who will not see an advertisement is $(A_{t-1} - A_0) e^{-\alpha Gt}$. Of this group not seeing an advertisement, some fraction, δ, will retain their awareness. (This retention parameter is estimated from past experience.) Therefore, the fraction who will not see an advertisement but will retain awareness, AR_t, is

$$AR_t = \delta (A_{t-1} - A_0) e^{-\alpha Gt} \qquad (9\text{-}5)$$

Putting Equations (9-4) and (9-5) together, the total fraction aware in period t is

$$
\begin{aligned}
A_t &= AA_t + AR_t \\
&= A_0 + (A_* - A_0)(1 - e^{-\alpha Gt}) \qquad (9\text{-}6) \\
&\quad + \delta (A_{t-1} - A_0) e^{-\alpha Gt}
\end{aligned}
$$

[4]This example is adapted from Pringle, Wilson, and Brody (1982).

The percentage of people who become aware for the first time in period t, AN_t, is the difference in the number aware between the last period and the present one.

$$AN_t = A_t - A_{t-1} \qquad (9\text{-}7)$$

Continuing with the example in Figure 9-2, assume that the company achieves 2,000 GRPs in the first period and 1,500 GRPs in each of the next two periods, that initial awareness (above A_0) is zero, and that $\delta = .75$. Then the following levels of awareness would be predicted by Equations (9-4) to (9-7):

Period	AN_t	A_t	AA_t	AR_t	$e^{-\alpha Gt}$
1	54.3	54.3	54.3	0.0	.44
2	7.2	61.5	45.9	15.6	.55
3	2.5	64.0	45.9	18.1	.55

Trial   In keeping with the empirical observation that if a person tries a brand, that person will do so relatively quickly after becoming aware, these models assume that people try in either the first or the second period in which they become aware. The fraction of people who become aware of the product and try it in the same period t, $ITR1_t$, is

$$ITR1_t = AN_t \times D_t \times \tau \qquad 0 \le \tau \le 1 \quad (9\text{-}8)$$

where τ is the proportion of the people who are newly aware and can find the product who will try it within one period. D_t is the level of distribution in period t. The percentage of the people who purchased the new product in the simulated shopping experiment or marked the top box on purchase intention is used as the estimate of τ.

If people do not try the product in the period in which they become aware, their probability of trial decreases considerably. This decrease in the probability of trial is modeled by setting the probability of trying the product one period after becoming aware equal to τ^2. The fraction who became aware in period $t - 1$ but did not try the product is $(AN_{t-1} - ITR1_{t-1})$. Therefore, the fraction who became aware of the product in period $t - 1$ and try it in period t is

$$ITR2_t = (AN_{t-1} - ITR1_{t-1}) \times D_t \times \tau^2 \quad (9\text{-}9)$$

The total trial in period t, ITR_t, is

$$ITR_t = ITR1_t + ITR2_t \quad (9\text{-}10)$$

People who do not try the product within two periods of becoming aware exit the system.

To continue the example, assume that D_t is .67, .77, and .89 in the first three periods, respectively, and that $\tau = .23$. The model predicts the following percentages of trial in the first three periods.

Period	ITR_t	$ITR1_t$	$ITR2_t$	AN_t
1	8.4	8.4	0.0	54.3
2	3.2	1.3	1.9	7.2
3	0.8	0.5	0.3	2.5

Summary. The mathematics looks complicated (and it does take a computer to keep track of the people in the various groups), but the logic is reasonably simple. The percentage of people who become aware of the product is a function of the amount and quality of the advertising. Most people who will try the product do so within the same period in which they became aware of it. If they do not try it then, their probability of trying it goes down considerably. This model is more complicated than the steady-state model, but it allows one to forecast awareness and trial in each period. When the product is launched either in test market or nationally, the actual levels of awareness and trial can be compared with the forecast levels.

Repeat Models

Again there is a dichotomy between a steady-state repeat model and a repeat by depth-of-purchase-class model. The first is simpler but does not offer market share predictions for periods leading up to the steady state.

Steady-state models These models predict the long-run retention (LRR) rate, or the market share of that brand among the people who have ever tried it. ASSESSOR uses the repeat and switchback method of Equation (8–9) and repeated here.

$$LRR = SBR / (1 + SBR - RR) \quad (9\text{-}11)$$

The estimates of RR and SBR are obtained from the call-back interviews after product usage. RR is that proportion of the people who purchased the product in the simulated store who will make a mail-order repurchase of the brand. SBR could be measured as the proportion of the people who did not purchase the brand in the simulated store but want to make a mail-order purchase in the call-back interview. However, it is estimated from a preference model that is discussed in a later section.

Another way to estimate LRR is with a sales waves experiment in which the respondents are given multiple chances to purchase the brand of interest. LRR is an estimate of the steady-state market share among the people who purchased in the simulated store. LRR can be estimated with a regression-based Equation (8-17), which is repeated here:

$$LRR_t = \hat{a} + \hat{b}/t + e \quad (9\text{-}12)$$

where LRR_t is the market share of the brand among those who have tried it—the dependent variable—and $1/t$, where t is the time period, is the independent variable. Once this regression has been run, $\hat{a}$ is the estimate of LRR.

This estimate of LRR can be combined with the estimate of CTR from Equation (9-3) to estimate steady-state market share MS as follows:

$$MS = CTR \times LRR \quad (9\text{-}13)$$

Repeat ratios   There is a separate group for each depth-of-repeat-purchase class. The groups are composed of those people who have made one, two, three, or more repeat purchases. People enter the first repeat purchase group by making a purchase after initial trial. They leave this group when they make a second purchase or when they fail to make a purchase for two-periods. This two period cutoff is applied because it has been observed that most people make a repurchase shortly after the previous purchase or they do not make it at all.

The fraction of people who made a trial purchase in period $t - 1$ and a first repeat purchase in period t is denoted as $R11_t$. The fraction who made a trial purchase in period $t - 2$ and a first repeat purchase in period t is denoted as $R12_t$. The probability that a person will make a first repeat purchase one period after trial is $0 \leq \tau_1 \leq 1$. This is estimated from the fraction of people who wanted to make a mail order repurchase. If they do not make a first repeat purchase in the period immediately following trial, the probability of making a first repeat purchase two periods after trial drops to τ_1^2. The fraction who make a first repeat in period t after a trial purchase in period $t - 1$ is:

$$R11_t = \tau_1 \times ITR_{t-1} \qquad (9\text{-}14)$$

The fraction of the people who did not make a first repeat purchase in period $t - 1$ after a trial purchase in period $t - 2$ is $(1 - \tau_1)$. The probability that one of these people will make a first repeat purchase in period t is τ_1^2. Therefore, the fraction of the population who will make a first repeat purchase in period t after making a trial purchase in period $t - 2$ is:

$$R12_t = \tau_1^2 \times (1 - \tau_1) \times ITR_{t-2} \qquad (9\text{-}15)$$

Total first repeat purchases in period t, $R1_t$, is

$$R1_t = R11_t \ast R12_t \qquad (9\text{-}16)$$

Similarly, it is assumed that a person will either make a second repeat within two periods

of making a first repeat or drop out of the system. The probability of making a second repeat is $\tau_2 > \tau_1$. The fraction of people who make a second repeat in period t following a first repeat in periods $t - 1$ and $t - 2$, respectively, is given in the next two equations:

$$R21_t = \tau_2 \times R1_{t-1} \qquad (9\text{-}17)$$

and

$$R22_t = \tau_2^2 \times (1 - \tau_2) \times R1_{t-2} \qquad (9\text{-}18)$$

The total fraction of second repeat purchases in period t, $R2_t$, is given by:

$$R2_t = R21_t + R22_t \qquad (9\text{-}19)$$

Higher depth of repeat classes can be handled in the same manner. Under the assumptions that the purchase cycle is equal to one period and the average purchase quantity is one, total unit sales in period t, TUS_t, can be calculated by multiplying these fractions by the number of product class buyers, #PCB:

$$TUS_t = \#PCB \left(ITR_t + \Sigma_i \, R(i)_t \right) \qquad (9\text{-}20)$$

Actual total sales during each period can be compared with forecast sales to see if they are on target.

Preference Models

ASSESSOR also uses an alternative forecasting procedure based on a preference model (Silk and Urban, 1978). Before seeing any commercials, the respondents are asked to name the brands in this product class they would consider buying. Next, they are presented with each pair of brands in their consideration set and are asked to allocate eleven chips between each pair based on their relative preference for each. A logit regression is used to convert the point allocations for each pair of brands into a set of scale values, S_i, one for each of the brands. (See Appendix 9-1 for an example.) Each brand's scale value is proportional to the probability of choosing that brand out of the consideration set. This is illustrated with the following formula:

$$P_i = S_i / \Sigma_j S_j \qquad (9\text{-}21)$$

where P_i is the probability of choosing brand i out of the consideration set. For example, if three brands were in a respondent's consideration set and a logit regression resulted in the following scale values, 5, 3, and 1, the probability of choosing each brand would be approximately 56 percent = 5/9, 33 percent = 3/9, and 11 percent = 1/9. These choice probabilities are averaged over the entire group of respondents to predict the market shares for each of the existing products. These predicted market shares can be compared with the actual market shares to give a check on this procedure.

In the call-back phase of the simulated test market, the respondents are asked once again which brands they would consider purchasing. At this point, the new brand will be in the consideration set of some of the people. Next, they are presented with all pairs of brands in their consideration set and are asked to allocate eleven points between each pair based on their relative preference. These point allocations are converted into a new set of scale values for each respondent, using the logit regression mentioned earlier. In turn these scale values are converted to forecast brand purchase probabilities. These probabilities are averaged[5] over the population to forecast market shares.

The latter estimate of market share is compared with the predicted steady-state market share. If these two methods give similar answers, one should have increased confidence in the estimate. If there is some disagreement, the two estimates should be examined further in order to reconcile them.

Pretest Market Models for Other Types of Products

Although this methodology has been applied primarily to packaged goods, it is possible to apply it to other areas. For example, Urban, Hauser, and Roberts (1990) have used this general technology to forecast new automobile sales. Rather than following the consumer through the stages of unaware => aware => trial => repeat purchases, the movement for durable goods may be more similar to unaware => aware => visit showroom => purchase. Parameters for a model like this can be estimated from data collected from a car clinic. A pretest market model for a product like this could contain the following steps.

1. Respondents are screened on being in the market and being possible buyers of a car like the one to be tested.

2. Respondents are shown a commercial for the new car (along with commercials for competing cars) and some are exposed to videotaped conversations that would simulate word-of-mouth (WOM) discussions of the new car.

3. Respondents provide information on perceptions and preferences for automobiles in their consideration set. Included in this information would be their likelihood of visiting a showroom to learn more about cars in their consideration set.

4. Respondents with a positive intention to visit a showroom are sent to a showroom to receive a videotaped sales presentation and take a test drive.

5. Respondents who see the sales presentation are asked to provide perceptual and preference information on cars in their consideration set. Included in this would be an intention to purchase the test car.

Awareness of the new brand is modeled as a function of both the amount of advertising [as in

---

[5]The purchase probabilities may be weighted for differences in purchase quantities if need be.

Equation (9-6) for packaged goods] and WOM communication. WOM would depend on the number of previous purchasers.[6] In a simplified form, awareness in period t, A_t is a function of net awareness due to advertising, NAA_t, and net awareness due to WOM, NAW_t

$$A_t = NAA_t + NAW_t - (NAA_t \times NAW_t) \quad (9\text{-}22)$$

where net awareness is due both to activity during period t and to retention from previous periods.

The fraction who would visit a dealer, VD_t, is

$$VD_t = A_t \times IM_t \times \tau \quad 0 \le \tau \le 1 \quad (9\text{-}23)$$

where IM_t is the fraction of the people who are in the market for a new car and τ is the fraction who marked the top box on intention to visit a dealer. IM_t is a function of general economic conditions and the average age of the present car fleet.

The fraction who would purchase this car, IP_t, is

$$IP_t = VD_t \times \tau_1 \quad 0 \le \tau_1 \le 1 \quad (9\text{-}24)$$

where τ_1 is the fraction who marked the top box on an intention to purchase after taking a test drive. Because a specific model is likely to become less popular as it ages and newer competitive models are introduced, τ_1 would generally decrease over time.

Many pretest market models (such as the one by Urban, Hauser, and Roberts, 1990) are very complicated. The purpose of this section has been to present a simple illustration of how the technology can be applied to other types of products.

---

[6]Urban, Hauser, and Roberts (1990) modeled the effects of both positive and negative word-of-mouth communications. This model allows one to forecast sales accurately after a car is introduced and actual WOM is received.

Summary

In many cases, STMs do a very good job of predicting steady-state market share. All of the mentioned models have reported very good validation results, with unadjusted prediction errors that averaged about 20 percent, If a model predicted a market share of twenty, chances were good that the actual share would fall between sixteen and twenty-four. When ASSESSOR corrected its forecasts for management errors in terms of levels of awareness and distribution achieved, the average error dropped to the 11 to 12 percent range (Dolan, 1988). For products that were introduced into test markets, the market share predicted by ASSESSOR had a .95 correlation with the actual market share (Urban and Katz, 1983).

These models work best when testing products that are introduced into well-defined categories. In many cases, sales predictions must make allowance for capacity constraints. In some of these instances the STM forecast can be made early enough to influence capacity. Additionally, they work best when a consumer will make a purchase after a single advertising exposure. This occurs when the product is not very different from the products currently on the market. In most cases, these approaches do not observe a large number of repeat purchases. Therefore, they will work better with products for which opinions are formed reasonably quickly and preference is not subject to wear out. Pretest market models usually represent a very good value for the money.

TEST MARKETS

Like simulated test markets, test markets are used primarily for frequently purchased goods, but many of the general principals apply equally to regional rollouts in industrial goods and introductory marketing campaigns for all kinds of durable goods.

The main purposes of test markets are threefold. First, test markets represent the best estimate of volume and share that will be obtained. Second, they are the only way to test some elements of the marketing mix, such as distributor support, advertising expenditure levels, and some sales promotions. They also represent the only time that the entire marketing mix is tested. The final purpose is that of a dress rehearsal. This is a time to practice making, selling, and delivering the product.

Deciding whether or not to test market depends on the size of the risk and required investment with and without the test market. The risk is associated with the size of an error that would be made without a test market in terms of predicting sales and the response to some of the marketing variables (including the reaction of the trade), or overestimating the firm's ability to make, sell, or distribute the product. A second risk factor is the company reputation and employee enthusiasm. If a major part of the investment—like the tooling and plant for a new car model—must be made whether the firm enters a test market or a national introduction, the value of a test market is much less. On the other hand, if test market volumes can be produced in existing plants or a lower-cost pilot plant and if a large part of the marketing support can be saved by doing only a test market, it has much greater value. Finally, if, as in the case with many line extensions, the product can be made on existing equipment and little advertising or sales force time is required, the risk may be low enough to skip the test market.

A second factor is the opportunity cost. Every month that a product sits in a test market is a month that it could be earning revenue on a national introduction. A second opportunity cost of test marketing is that of sales force time and enthusiasm. If the company has done a simulated test market and is confident that it can get distribution, execute the marketing plan, and meet its objectives nationally, a test market may be bypassed.

A third factor is competitive reaction. First, the competition may engage in such activities as price reductions or trade or consumer promotions to cloud the test market results. In this case, the sales forecasts could be very inaccurate. The second and more important factor is that competition may learn as much from the test market as the company performing it. It may beat or closely follow the firm into national introduction. For example, Hunt-Wesson's Prima Salsa spaghetti sauce was first into the test market, but Ragu's Extra Thick and Zesty spaghetti sauce beat it into national distribution. Similarly, Hill's Brothers High Yield coffee was first into the test market, but it was preempted nationally by Folger's Flakes.

The question discussed so far is whether the product should be put into test market or rolled out nationally. Another question is whether the product should be dropped instead of going into test market. Nielsen (1979) found that only 35 percent of the 228 grocery products that entered a test market made it to full national distribution. With proper concept and product testing (including extended use testing) and possibly a simulated test market, the success percentage should be more than 65 percent. Therefore, the purpose of a test market should not be to learn whether people will try the product or whether they will lose interest after a couple of purchases. These questions should have been answered well before the test marketing stage.

Test Market Design

As with concept tests, product tests, and simulated test markets, several decisions have to be made. Before these decisions are made, a national marketing plan must be constructed. It should contain all the elements specified in the plan prior to simulated test markets. Additionally, advertising and packaging must be finished. Planned national media expenditures need to be converted into GRPs. Then test market expenditures should be planned that will yield the same number of GRPs in the test market. Finally, a sales target that is a minimum for national introduction needs to be specified.

Sell-in or forced distribution test market
Possibly the first decision is whether or not the
test market should be forced distribution. In a
forced distribution test market, sometimes called
a controlled store test or a minimarket test, a
research company warehouses, stocks, prices,
and displays the product, presents the new
product to the trade, maintains adequate stock
at retail, and audits sales of the new product and
its competition. The manufacturer can specify
store location, number of facings, price, and special displays. This is possible because of the
research company's relationship with the retailers in certain areas as well as the fees that are
paid (typically about $100 for each weekly store
visit).

In a sell-in test market, which is also called a
traditional test market, the manufacturer's sales
force must convince the local retailers to carry
the test product. The manufacturer ships the
product to the retailer (or wholesaler) and the
retailer stocks, prices, and displays the product.

Usually forced distribution test markets take
place in smaller cities than sell-in test markets.
For example, Nielsen's Controlled Market Testing Cities include Boise, Eugene, Evansville
(Indiana), Green Bay, Peoria, Portland (Maine),
and Tucson. When they were chosen, they had
under 500,000 in population, but had at least
two television stations, a daily and Sunday
newspaper, and several radio stations. This size
contrasts with Nielsen's Marketplace Cities, the
first four (alphabetically) of which are Atlanta,
Boston, Buffalo, and Chicago. In most cases, the
area includes the central city, suburbs, and the
remaining television area. Additionally, most of
these cities contain at least 1.5 percent of total
U.S. households.

Forced distribution test markets offer several
advantages over traditional test markets. First,
they are quicker to set up (three weeks verse
two months) because of the relationship between
the research company and the retail organizations. Second, the controlled conditions (for
example, same number of facings in comparably
sized stores and same price everywhere) reduce

the random variation and make it easier to
"read" such variables in the test market as the
effect of different levels of advertising. There is
very good surveillance of competitive activity,
as the researchers are in each store at least
weekly and do a complete audit of the category.
Because distribution is gained quickly and uni-
formly and fewer out-of-stock problems or
changes in the number of facings are encountered, measurements stabilize rapidly. There
may be a small gain in security from competitive surveillance, because forced distribution
test markets do not go through regular trade
channels. However, these markets are well
known and are closely watched. Finally, forced
distribution tests cost about 35 percent as
much as a traditional test market, primarily
because advertising costs are lower in smaller
population areas.

On the other hand, forced distribution tests
are not as realistic, partly because the cities used
are not as representative of major population
centers and partly because they are researcher
stocked. Also, they do not provide any practice
in dealing with the trade.

It is possible to use forced distribution test
markets for many of the same purposes as simulated test markets. Large companies may use
them when they do not foresee any trade problems and when there is little uncertainty or risk
(such as with line extensions). Smaller companies may use them to gain credibility before
going into a traditional test market.

Choice of test market cities   To achieve good
projectability (ability to predict national results)
with traditional test markets, two or more markets totaling 3 percent of U.S. households
should be used. In choosing test markets one
should look for representative and reasonable
cost locations. Usually, one looks at demographic representativeness on key variables, such as
age, income, ethnic composition, and household
income distributions. In order to predict results
in major population centers, the testing should
be done in relatively large cities. However, city

size must be balanced off against greater media costs in larger cities. For some products climatic conditions are important.

Another way of assessing markets is to use the Category Development Index (CDI), which is that city's average per-capita consumption of the product category divided by the national average per-capita consumption. Sometimes a Brand Development Index (BDI) is also calculated if one is testing a brand extension or is particularly interested in one major competitor.

A second factor is media isolation. "Spill in" occurs when the city gets some of its media from other cities. For example, Newark gets much of its media from New York City. This makes it difficult to simulate a national media campaign in that location. Typically, one would want no more spill in than 20 percent for television and 50 percent for radio. Spillage out occurs when advertising in the test market reaches areas that are outside of the test market. With spillage out, media costs are distorted, because one is paying to advertise to many people who cannot buy the product. It also increases the costs of the test market.

Other considerations include whether the firm is trying to run a number of sales promotions for other brands in the area. They will take away from the time the sales force has to spend on the new product. Similarly, many firms want to avoid cities that are used too often for test markets because they are afraid that the consumers may become sensitized to new products. Also, one must have research services that audit sales, have customer or scanner panels, or data collection capabilities. These services are now available in virtually all potential test market cities. One should look for an area where retail cooperation is reasonably high. Finally, when testing in several locations there should be some dispersion geographically as well as on other key variables.

Because there is no "magic town" and multiple cities are needed in most instances, there is a wide range of popular test marketing cities. One list is presented in Table 9-1.

Length of the test market Typically, test markets run for ten to twelve months; however, their length is a function of the length of the purchase cycle and the way the test market is read. Products with longer purchase cycles require more lengthy test markets than products with shorter cycles. Similarly, test markets that are read just in terms of market share must be carried on longer than test markets where share is estimated from trial and repeat measurements.

A test market should be run for at least two to three repurchase cycles; five to six is much better. Nielsen (*Sales and Marketing Management*, 1983) examined the ability of various time periods to forecast eighteen-month market share. It found the following percentages of correct predictions: after four months, 37 percent; after six months, 55 percent; after ten months, 85 percent; and after twelve months, 95 percent. It concluded (if one were monitoring market share and not trial and repeat percentages) that ten months is the minimum time to be confident about market share. On the other hand, if trial and repeat percentages are measured separately one can make reasonable predictions of market shares after about three months (Blattberg and Golanty, 1978; Pringle, Wilson, and Brody, 1982). The only time that test markets are stopped early is when it is clear that the new product will not come close to meeting its objectives. However, it is possible to start making plans for national introduction before the test market is completed.

Other considerations include seasonality. Some products should be tested through an entire season. For example, cold medicines should be tested at least from October through April. When there are problems gaining distribution or with out-of-stock conditions, a test market may have to be extended. However, these issues must be balanced against a desire to preempt competition on national introduction.

Marketing mix variables to be tested Only variables that cannot be tested elsewhere should be tested in a test market. Consumer and trade

TABLE 9-1   SAATCHI & SAATCHI; DFS COMPTON RECOMMENDED TEST MARKETS, 1987

1. Albany-Schenectady-Troy, N.Y.	23. Louisville, Ky.
2. Atlanta, Ga.	24. Milwaukee, Wis.
3. Boise, Idaho	25. Minneapolis-St. Paul, Minn.
4. Buffalo, N.Y.	26. Nashville, Tenn.
5. Cedar Rapids-Waterloo-Dubuque, Iowa	27. Oklahoma City, Okla.
6. Charlotte, N.C.	28. Omaha, Nebr.
7. Cincinnati, Ohio	29. Orlando-Daytona Beach, Fla.
8. Cleveland, Ohio	30. Peoria, Ill.
9. Colorado Springs-Pueblo, Colo.	31. Pittsburgh, Pa.
10. Columbus, Ohio	32. Portland-Poland Spring, Maine
11. Dayton, Ohio	33. Portland, Oreg.
12. Denver, Colo.	34. Rochester, N.Y.
13. Des Moines, Iowa	35. Sacramento-Stockton, Calif.
14. Erie, Pa.	36. St. Louis, Mo.
15. Evansville, Ind.	37. Salt Lake City, Utah
16. Fargo, N. Dak.	38. Seattle-Tacoma, Wash.
17. Fort Wayne, Ind.	39. South Bend-Elkhart, Ind.
18. Grand Rapids-Kalamazoo-Battle Creek, Mich.	40. Spokane, Wash.
19. Green Bay-Appleton, Wis.	41. Springfield-Decatur-Champaign, Ill.
20. Greensboro-High Point-Winston Salem, N.C.	42. Syracuse, N.Y.
21. Indianapolis, Ind.	43. Toledo, Ohio
22. Kansas City, Kans.-Mo.	44. Tulsa, Okla.
	45. Wichita-Hutchinson, Kans.

promotions, price, and advertising expenditure levels can be tested in a test market, but such variables as packaging, advertising message, and product formulation should be tested elsewhere.

Most of the time a variable is tested at two levels; high and low in the case of advertising expenditures and price, and present and absent in the case of various promotions. One would like to have two cities test each combination of variables. This means that if a firm is testing two different advertising expenditure levels and the presence or absence of a sales promotion, it would take eight test market cities. In most cases, with two variables only four cities are used, in the following manner.

In this case city A receives a high level of both advertising expenditures and sales promotions, B gets the combination of low advertising and sales promotion, C gets high advertising but no sales promotion, and D gets low advertising and no sales promotion. This allows one to compare high to low advertising by looking at the difference between the pair A–C versus B–D. Similarly, the effect of sales promotions can be determined from a comparison of A–B versus C–D. A second city in each of these four cells would guard against the possibility of something going wrong in a measurement cell, but it would also double the cost of the test market.

The test market should be based on a marketing plan, with the level of support comparable to that in the plan. For example, in media advertising GRPs are usually equalized. That is, a national advertising budget is translated into GRPs, then that same number of GRPs is purchased in the test market. The cost of an equivalent number of GRPs is usually higher on a per-capita basis in a test market. A problem that many firms face is that they spend at a higher level in a test market than they can afford in the national introduction. Once a planned level of support is determined, it is possible to test different levels in a test market to estimate a portion of an advertising response curve.

Monitoring the Results

Next, one must decide what information will be collected and the best way to collect it.

Store audits   Traditionally, the success of a new product in a test market has been measured with retail store audit data which are used to measure retail sales. The manufacturer has information on shipments to wholesalers, but retail store audits are needed because much of the firm's early sales go to fill the pipeline and because there is a delay in seeing consumer response to marketing actions. Furthermore, the other information collected during retail audits,

such as competitive prices and dealing activity, may be valuable.

In the past, researchers visited all cooperating stores periodically (biweekly, monthly, or bimonthly) to ascertain the quantity of each size and flavor of all major brands in the category ordered during the last period and in inventory. By comparing orders and inventory with the previous period's measurements, they calculated retail sales during the period. Additionally, they collected information on the prices charged and whether any promotions were run during the period.

Now, both Information Resources Inc. (IRI) and A.C. Nielsen purchase raw scanner data from retailers to collect retail sales information without going into stores. In addition to sales volume, the scanner data include price, whether a purchase was at regular or a special price, and whether the product was purchased with a coupon. In late 1990, IRI was purchasing raw scanner data from 2,700 stores in sixty-six markets and Nielsen was purchasing data from 3,000 stores in about fifty markets (Caminiti, 1990). Traditional store audits are conducted only in outlets that do not have checkout scanners, such as drugstores and convenience stores.

Auditing marketing support   The firm running a test market also needs information on the advertisements and sales promotions that are run, both for the test brand and for competitive brands. Both Nielsen and IRI provide these data as well. The combination of retail sales information, advertising levels, and promotional support is called single-source data. The benefit of single-source data is that they are all consistent. That is, some research suppliers might define the Chicago area as the six surrounding counties; others include eight counties. Some firms measure time periods in terms of four-week months, others use five-week months, and still others use calendar months. Single-source data allow all of these measures to be consistent.

Both Nielsen's service, called SCANTRACK, and IRI's InfoScan provide the retailer advertising support in terms of A, B, and C ads, retailer display activity (stocking of a brand in a location separate from its normal location), and retailer coupon distribution level all measured in terms of ACV[7] volume. Nielsen estimates the number of GRPs delivered to a geographic area. IRI has a household panel whose members' television sets are equipped with meters to record what channel is being played.

Consumer surveys   Although store audit data provide valuable information on sales, they do not provide any breakdown between trial and repeat sales. The only way to estimate a steady-state market share with store audit data is by letting the test run until market share has stabilized. Also, store audits do not provide any information on why sales are different from what was predicted.

Therefore, many firms perform periodic surveys to collect information on brand awareness, advertising recall, receipt of coupons or samples, trial, repeat, other brands purchased, primary brand used, and satisfaction with the product. Various classification variables can also be collected to aid in the identification of target markets. Early in the test market, these data can be collected monthly, but later, they may be collected only quarterly.

Survey data have two very different functions. First, they can be used in models such as TRACKER (Blattberg and Golanty, 1978) or NEWS/Market (Pringle, Wilson, and Brody, 1982) to make an early prediction of steady-state market share. Second, they offer valuable diagnostic information.

As examples of diagnostic information, if brand awareness and advertising recall are lower than forecast, it may indicate that the advertising is not memorable or that too little is

being spent. If awareness (and level of distribution) is close to forecast and trial is low, it would indicate that the advertising is not doing a good job of convincing people to try the product. If trial is on target but the repeat rate is low, it suggests some problem with the product (or the price). Similarly, if the brand is not used regularly by a portion of the sample, there may be a problem of wearout.

Diary or scanner panels   In a diary panel, a group of consumers records everything purchased in certain product categories. The record lists the quantity, price, size, flavor, brand, whether the product was purchased with a coupon, store, and date of purchase. In IRI's scanner panel and Nielsen's local scanner panels, the panel members have an identification card (much like a credit card), which is given to the grocery store every time they check out. This records all of their purchases and creates a record like the diary panel. Nielsen's national panel members use a hand-held computer that is used to scan the bar codes of purchases once they get home. The benefits of the "credit card" panel are the record of all purchases in participating stores and the convenience of recording purchases in this manner. The primary benefit of the hand-held computer panel is that its members are able to record purchases made in locations that do not have scanner checkouts. This may be important if a significant part of a category's purchases are made in drugstores and discount stores that do not have scanners.

The benefits of a scanner panel over a diary panel are accuracy, the willingness of people to agree to participate (so the group is more representative), and speed of response. Additionally, the television shows watched by IRI's InfoScan panel members are also recorded, so it is possible to monitor television viewing and product purchases by the same household. IRI has a second product called BehaviorScan in Pittsfield, Mass.; Marion, Ind.; Eau Claire, Wis.; Midland, Tex.; Grand Junction, Colo.; and Cedar Rapids,

---

[7]ACV is All-Category Volume. A 40-percent ad level means that stores accounting for 40 percent of total sales in a market ran a certain ad.

Iowa. There is a panel of 3,000 in each city. Each is equipped with an identification card to use in grocery store and drugstore scanners. Additionally, each of these markets is located far enough from major media centers that cable television is required for good reception. Therefore, not only are the panel members' television sets monitored, but IRI has the capability to show different commercials to different panel members. These effects can be measured in terms of purchases by the same households.

In either case, one is able to get an accurate record of trial, repeat, and depth-of-purchase classes. Furthermore, one gains information on which brands are most affected by the new brand.

Analyzing Test Market Results

There are two basic ways of "reading" test markets. One is to measure market share directly from retail audit or retail scanner data. The other way is to estimate market share on the basis of trial and repeat measures based on individual households. Direct market share measurements usually take longer to reach a steady-state. Once trial and repeat measures have been estimated, they can be used to forecast steady-state market share at some time in the future. On the other hand, if the percentage of triers and repeat users is relatively small, the number of households on which estimates are based may be quite small and therefore contain considerable sampling variance. With everything else equal, it is recommended that market share be estimated both ways. The direct measurements provide a good check on the trial and repeat measurements and the trial and repeat measures provide valuable diagnostic information whether or not they are used to forecast market share.

There are two popular survey methods of using the trial and repeat proportions to predict market share, NEWS/Market and TRACKER. NEWS/Planner was discussed in the section on pretest market models. A model with the same

basic structure, called NEWS/Market, can be used to estimate market share in a test market. Additionally, if household purchase data are available, they can be used to estimate market share from trial and repeat data.

To estimate market share from trial and repeat measures using survey data, one needs a marketing plan with estimates of GRPs, G_t, and distribution, D_t, in each period. Typically, NEWS/Market is based on 200 to 1,000 customer interviews in each of the first three months of the test market. These surveys collect information on awareness, trial, and number of repeat purchases. The combination of survey results and estimates from the marketing plan are used to estimate the following parameters: advertising quality, α, probability of trial given awareness and distribution, τ, and probability of making an ith repeat given an $i - 1$th repeat, τ_i.

As a first step, Equation (9-6) is used to estimate advertising quality, α. This is restated as Equation (9-25). Actual awareness, A_t, in each time period is estimated through consumer surveys. Manufacturer or researcher judgment is used to set the values for minimum awareness, A_0, maximum awareness, A_*, and retention, δ. GRPs in each period, G_t, come from the marketing plan. Then the only unknown is the parameter for advertising effectiveness, α, which is estimated through a nonlinear least-squares estimation procedure.

$$A_t = A_0 + (A_* - A_0)(1 - e^{-\alpha G t}) + \delta (A_{t-1} - A_0) e^{-\alpha G t} \quad (9\text{-}25)$$

In order to estimate the probability of trial, τ, cumulative trial in each period, CTR_t, is estimated from consumer surveys or from panel data. The difference from the previous period's cumulative trial gives incremental trial in that period, ITR_t. This estimate is used along with fraction newly aware, AN_t, (calculated from changes in awareness) and manufacturer estimates of distribution, D_t, to estimate the probability of trial, τ, using Equation (9-10), which is restated as Equation (9-26)

$$ITR_t = ITR1_t + ITR2_t$$
$$= AN_t \times D_t \times \tau$$
$$+ (AN_{t-1} - ITR1_{t-1}) \times D_t \times \tau^2 \qquad (9\text{-}26)$$

Similarly, total first repeat purchases in each period, $R1_t$, is estimated from survey data. This is combined with estimates of the previous period's trial fractions, ITR_{t-1} and ITR_{t-2}, to estimate the first repeat ratio, τ_1, using Equation (9-16) which is restated here as Equation (9-27):

$$R1_t = R11_t + R12_t$$
$$= \tau_1 \times ITR_{t-1} + \tau_1^2 \times (1 - \tau_1) \times ITR_{t-2} \qquad (9\text{-}27)$$

Higher depth of repeat classes can be handled in a similar fashion.

In twenty-eight cases in which they were able to compare predictions on the basis of three months of data with sales or market share at the end of a test market, they found that the average error as a percentage of actual market share was 17.5 percent. When one of these cases was dropped, the level of error decreased to 12.3 percent. They came within 1.5 share points 90 percent of the time (Pringle, Wilson, and Brody, 1982).

Summary

On one hand, the data indicate that both pretest market models and test market models are able to do a good job of forecasting test market results at some point in the future. On the other hand, only half of the products that go into test market are successful nationally. This statistic raises some legitimate questions.

One primary cause of this discrepancy is lack of objectivity in analyzing test market results (Hardin, 1976). There appears to be a tendency to pick above-average cities for test markets, where CDIs or BDIs of 110 or 120 (where 100 is average) are much more common than ones of eighty or ninety. There is also a tendency to make more positive adjustments than negative ones. For example, if a distribution channel is

uncovered in a test market, researchers tend to predict above-average sales through that channel. On the other hand, sales force enthusiasm (because the salespeople know they are being watched) is usually assumed to carry over to national introductions. (Some feel that market share and sales estimates should be multiplied by .85 to correct for this problem.)

Second, changes are usually made to the marketing plan on the basis of test market experience. In most cases, these changes are not tested, but it is assumed that they will improve things. One investigation (Hardin, 1976) found that about half of the marketing plans for national introductions had been so drastically altered from the test market plans that projections were not possible. Sometimes spending levels are achieved in test markets that are not possible nationally. Also, competitive reaction may be much different in test market and national rollout.

Balancing the need for enthusiastic championing of the new product with objectivity in its measurement is always difficult but necessary.

TESTS FOR INDUSTRIAL GOODS

Industrial goods may have one or more special features that limit a firm's capacity to use some of the methods that were discussed for consumer goods. First, some industrial goods have a small number of customers or a small proportion of all potential customers who account for a very large share of all purchases. Typically, a seller will have a well-developed understanding of these customers' needs and will be in personal contact through a direct sales force or technical assistance staff. It is not uncommon for the working relationships to be close and durable. When a customer contemplates or requests a new product, a good deal of joint effort can develop. In such instances, the buyer may formally or informally extend commitments to purchase and the seller may offer performance guarantees. When it is feasible, buyers may be involved in various beta tests of prototypes or samples of new materials. The close personal contact during development tends to make it undesirable or unnecessary to conduct the kinds of market tests or test markets commonly used for consumer goods.

Second, some industrial goods can be tried at low risk on a small scale or must prove themselves during a long period of use. The seller may try to accelerate the latter process by providing test results and guarantees of satisfaction, but these will have little effect if the buyers need to acquire extended experience in their own environments.

Third, industrial goods often replace items that have long economic lives. In such cases, only a small proportion of the long-run potential market is ready to make an early purchase. Initially, special inducements to make a purchase may be called for, but later favorable application experience by others provides the assurance and incentives needed by most potential buyers.

Fourth, a great many industrial goods are designed for a single buyer and used over a relatively short period—say a year or two. Components supplied by outside vendors usually fall into this category. The buyer prepares the specifications and normally maintains close surveillance of the suppliers performance. In such instances, market tests and test markets have little or no role to play.

Fifth, trade shows and industry meetings provide a natural forum in which industrial goods producers can gauge buyers' interests in new or modified products. Often, prospective buyers can see products in use and compare them with new competing products displayed at the same site. An analysis of buyer interest and orders received may provide a sufficiently accurate forecast to let a manager approve full-scale marketing or to kill the project.

The above characteristics do not exhaust the possible reasons for the infrequent use of market tests and test markets on behalf of industrial products. Most of these characteristics do not apply to consumer goods, but in the case of consumer durables, a number of related conditions can be observed. The main point is that all tests must be justified by comparing the expected value of the new information with the time and expense required to obtain it.

CONCLUDING REMARKS

A successful new product needs to be based on a concept that promises more value to the consumer than current offerings. Next, the product must live up to the promises made in the concept statement. Finally, the introductory marketing program must be well directed and appropriately funded. The techniques discussed in the last two chapters can be used to ensure that these goals are reached.

Simulated test markets are a more realistic way to test the ability of the product's advertising to get people to try the new product. In most cases, consumers have to purchase the product rather than fill out a questionnaire. Simulated test markets can also test the ability of free samples to stimulate trial. Simulated test markets can be combined with an extended usage test to determine whether preferences hold up over time.

Test markets are the most realistic way to test new products as well as the most expensive and visible to competition. Furthermore, a test market is the only way to test some variables such as advertising levels and certain promotions. Because of the cost and visibility, test markets should be entered only after concept and product testing.

REFERENCES

Blackburn, Joseph D., and Kevin Clancy: "LITMUS: A New Product Planning Model," in *Studies in Management Sciences—Marketing Planning Models,* Andris Zoltners (ed.), North-Holland, 1982, pp. 43–61.

Blattberg, Robert, and John Golanty: "TRACKER: An Early Test Market Forecasting and Diagnostic Model for New Product Planning," *Journal of Marketing Research,* 15, May 1978, 192–202.

Caminiti, Susan: "What the Scanner Knows About You," *Fortune,* December 3, 1990, 51–52.

Clarke, Darral G.: *Marketing Analysis and Decision Making,* The Scientific Press, Redwood City: CA, 1987, pp. 111–133.

Claycamp, Henry J., and L. E. Liddy: "Prediction of New Product Performance: An Analytical Approach," *Journal of Marketing Research,* 6, November 1969, 414–420.

Dolan, Robert J.: *Note On Pretest Market Models* 9-588-052, Harvard Business School case note, 1988.

Eskin, Gerald J.: "Dynamic Forecasts of New Product Demand Using a Depth of Repeat Model," *Journal of Marketing Research,* 10, May 1973, 115–129.

Fourt, L. A., and J. W. Woodlock: "Early Prediction of Market Success for New Grocery Products," *Journal of Marketing,* 25, October 1960, 31–38.

Hartung, P. H., and J. L. Fisher: "Brand Switching and Mathematical Programming in Market Expansion," *Management Science,* 11, August 1965, 231–243.

Hardin, David K.: "The Final Decision: Are You Really Ready to Roll Out?," in *How to Develop and Market New Products. . .Better and Faster,* David Hoo (ed.), New York: Association of National Advertisers, 1985, pp. 254–258.

Maffei, R. B.: "Brand Preference and Simple Markov Processes," *Operations Research,* 8, 1960, 210–218.

Parfitt, J. H., and B. J. K. Collins: "Use of Consumer Panels for Brand Share Predictions," *Journal of Marketing Research,* 5, May 1968, 131–145.

Pringle, Lewis G., R. Dale Wilson, and Edward I. Brody: "NEWS: A Decision-Oriented Model for New Product Analysis and Forecasting," *Marketing Science,* 1, Winter, 1982, 1–29.

Pessemier, Edgar A.: Experimental Methods of Estimating Demand," *Journal of Business,* October 1960, 373–383.

_____: *Experimental Methods for Analyzing the Demand for Branded Consumer Goods with Applications to Problems in Marketing Strategy,* Pullman, Wash.:s Washington State University Press, 1963.

_____: *Product Management: Strategy and Organization,* 2d ed., New York: John Wiley and Sons, 1982; reprinted by Krieger, Malabar, FL, 1988, pp. 170–174.

_____: "Varied Individual Behavior: Some Theories, Measurement Methods and Models," *Multivariate Behavioral Research,* 20, January 1985, 69–94.

Sales and Marketing Management: "The True Test of Test Marketing Is Time," *Sales and Marketing Management,* March 14, 1983, 74, 78.

Silk, Alvin J. ,and Glen L. Urban: "Pretest Market Evaluation of New Package Goods: A Model and Measurement Method," *Journal of Marketing Research,* 15 (2), May 1978, 171–191.

Shocker, Allan D., and William G. Hall: "Pretest Market Models: A Critical Evaluation," *Journal of Product Innovation Management,* 3, 1986, 86–107.

Urban, Glen L., John R. Hauser, and John Roberts: "Prelaunch Forecasting of New Automobiles," *Management Science,* 36 (4), 1990, 401–421.

_____ and Gerald M. Katz: "Pre-Test-Market Models: Validation and Managerial Implications," *Journal of Marketing Research,* 20, August 1983, 221–234.

APPENDIX 9-1 USING LUCE'S CHOICE MODEL TO MODEL PREFERENCES

The section on preference models described a method for using a constant sum scale to determine choice probabilities. The purpose of Appendix 9-1 is to explain how to estimate the scale values and choice probabilities.

Equation (9-21) is sometimes referred to as a statement of Luce's choice model. It states that the probability of choosing one object out of a group is equal to its scale value, S_i, divided by the sum of the scale values of all of the items in the group, $\Sigma_j S_j$. (The scale values are ratio scaled; that is, they have a natural origin at zero.) Formally, the probability that object x_i is chosen is given by:

$$\text{Prob } x_i = S_i / \Sigma_j S_j \quad (9\text{-}1A)$$

In the case of two brands, x_i and x_j, the probability of choosing x_i in a paired comparison is:

$$\text{Prob } (x_i) = S_i / (S_i + S_j) \quad (9\text{-}2A)$$

Similarly, the ratio of the probability of choosing x_i to the probability of choosing x_j in a paired comparison involving these two brands is:

$$\frac{\text{Prob}(x_i)}{\text{Prob}(x_j)} = \frac{S_i}{S_j} = \frac{e^{v_i}}{e^{v_j}} \quad (9\text{-}3A)$$

where

$$S_i = e^{v_i} \quad \text{or} \quad v_i = \ln(S_i) \quad (9\text{-}4A)$$

Taking the logarithms of both sides of Equation (9-3A) and realizing that Prob (x_j) equals $(1 - \text{Prob}(x_i))$, the following result is achieved:

$$\ln\{\text{Prob}(x_i)/(1 - \text{Prob}(x_i))\} = \ln e^{v_i - v_j} = v_i - v_j \quad (9\text{-}5A)$$

Here, the log odds of the probabilities are equal to the difference in the v_is. Because this is a linear function, it can be estimated with a regression. These v_is are converted back to the S_is with Equation (9-4A). The resulting S_is are the ratio scaled affective values of the choice objects.

With this as background, consider the following example. A consumer says that he or she would consider purchasing three brands in a category: a, b, and c. In three paired comparison tasks, the consumer allocates the following points to each: 9–a, 2–c; 8–a, 3–b; and 6–b, 5–c. First the point allocations must be converted into ratios. For example, the point allocations of 9–a and 2–c are converted into the ratio 4.5 = 9/2. Then the natural logarithm of the ratio is taken: ln (4.5) = 1.504. These logarithms form the dependent variable in a regression. The independent variables are three dummy variables. There is one dummy variable for each of the three brands a, b, and c. In any equation, the dummy variable for a brand is 1 if the brand's points are in the numerator of the ratio, -1 if they are in the denominator, and 0 if the brand is not involved in the comparison. Finally, one more observation must be added. It has zero for the dependent variable and a one for each of the dummy variables. This is shown in the table below.

Pair	Point ratio	ln of point ratio	DV for brand a	DV for brand b	DV for brand c
a/c	4.5	1.504	1	0	−1
a/b	2.66	.98	1	−1	0
b/c	1.20	.18	0	1	−1
n/a	n/a	0.00	1	1	1

Next, one needs to run the following regression with the natural logarithm of the point ratio as the dependent variable and the three dummy variables as the independent variables to estimate the v_is.

$$\ln(\text{point ratio}) = \hat{v}_a \, DV_a + \hat{v}_b \, DV_b + \hat{v}_c \, DV_c + e \quad (9\text{-}6A)$$

Once this is done, the following parameters would be estimated: $\hat{v}_a = .828$, $\hat{v}_b = -.267$, and $\hat{v}_c = -.561$. By exponentiating each of the v_is, one can determine the S_is. In this case $S_a = e^{v_a} = 2.289$, $S_b = .766$, and $S_c = .570$. Using the formula in Equation (9-1A), this set of point allocations would predict the following market shares: a–63 percent, b–21 percent, and c–16 percent.

REVIEW QUESTIONS

Q9-1 Describe the steps in a simulated test market and the information that would be collected at each step.

Q9-2 Show how you would use the information from Q9-1 to forecast market share. Make up a set of numbers to illustrate your procedure.

Q9-3 Why have simulated test markets become widely used for frequently purchased consumer products? Why aren't they used for some other products?

Q9-4 What is usually the weakest link in a simulated test market? Why?

Q9-5 What is the purpose of a test market? Can a national rollout be a test market? Explain.

Q9-6 Discuss the pros and cons of test markets.

Q9-7 Why are test markets used for some types of products and not for others?

Q9-8 How are test market results measured? Why?

Q9-9 What factors would you consider when choosing a test market city?

PART 4

MARKETING DELIVERS VALUE: PLANNING A PRODUCT INTRODUCTION

MULTIPERIOD MARKETING PLANS AND BUDGETS:
NEW OR MODIFIED PRODUCTS

AN ILLUSTRATIVE PLAN FOR A NEW PRODUCT:
A SPREADSHEET MODEL

DIRECT FORMULATION OF MULTIPERIOD PLANS AND BUDGETS:
NEW OR MODIIFIED PRODUCTS

10

MULTIPERIOD MARKETING PLANS AND BUDGETS:

New or Modified Products

The purpose of this chapter is to build on the material in previous chapters. It is time to examine the unique problems of developing marketing plans and budgets that will increase the value of new and substantially modified products. As before, *the term "product" includes both single products and coherent groups of products. Also, a product is broadly defined to include products, services, or a mix of products and associated services. These are the revenue-producing units being analyzed.* A marketing plan serves at least two important purposes: It is a way to formulate and choose the most effective way to support the offer, and it lets senior management evaluate a forecast of the resource needs and economic results implied by these actions. Since more than one strategic approach might be considered when developing a new product marketing plan, the term "strategy/budget" will be used for each alternative.

The plan and its associated series of annual budgets are assumed to come after the business unit's overarching strategic plan has been formulated. The business unit strategic plan provides a frame of reference for the new product strategy/budget and indicates the kinds of opportunities that a product manager can consider and how aggressively they can be pursued.

PROBLEM DIMENSIONS

This section discusses the essential elements that a manager must consider when developing a marketing plan for a new product or when analyzing the prospects for repositioning an existing product. First, the opportunity must be assessed and the firm's prospects for success should be evaluated. In turn, objectives for the new product must be established. Then one needs to look at specific strategy/budget combinations that would lead to reaching the objectives. This final step includes the design of an integrated marketing mix. However, rather than attempting to develop the entire mix simultaneously, it is easier to break the mix into two principal parts: the *offer* and the *marketing support* for the offer. These two elements produce *market response,* a third key consideration.

Situation Analysis and Objective Generation

The starting point of a new product plan is a situation analysis. Its purpose is to uncover the problems and opportunities facing the new product. The industry should be analyzed to determine if it has the potential to be profitable. This analysis should include an assessment of current and future entry barriers, existing rivalry, and power of buyers and suppliers. Historical trends in sales, replacement purchases, and pricing strength should be analyzed and projected to the future. Companies that the firm may be competing more closely with should be analyzed to gauge current offerings and likely moves. Finally, the relevant buyers should also be analyzed. The analysis should include their satisfaction with current products, desires not currently being filled, and shopping patterns.

Only when one has a grasp of these factors is it possible to make sensible judgments about the likely success of the new product. In general, more attractive opportunities should lead to more aggressive objectives and greater potential resource commitments.

After objectives have been determined, it is time to formulate a strategy/budget that will reach them. That is the role of the offer, support, and responses.

The Offer

The offer is composed of three principal components; the physical product and/or service as described in terms of its design or *features,* the *communications message* that is sent to various customers, and *price.*

Chapters 5 to 9 focused on a number of methods to aid in the development of an offer and in forecasting its desirability to each of the differ-

ent actors in the market. These methods include conjoint analysis, joint space analysis, concept testing, and product testing.

In this chapter, it is assumed that an attempt has been made to find an offer that provides the greatest value to one or more market segments and therefore maximizes P— the offer's preference or probability of trial. The purpose of obtaining a percentage-of-choice index under controlled conditions is to see how attractive the offer is on its own merits, uninfluenced by differing levels of knowledge and availability. These last two influences are delivered by the marketing support programs of the various competing brands.

The marketing plan should be written after an offer has been formulated, but this does not mean that either the firm's or competitive offers will remain constant over time. Therefore, the temporal change in preference, P, should be reflected in the marketing plan. Part of a new product marketing plan should involve planned evolutionary changes in the offer that continually add value.

Support Spending

One of the primary purposes of marketing planning is to decide on the proper amount and distribution of marketing support to reach desired objectives. The immediate role of marketing support is to enhance value by creating favorable awareness, A_t, and distribution, D_t, for the offer. Typical support elements include advertising, personal selling, trade and consumer promotions, and the cost of maintaining company-owned distributors. Most of the marketing budget goes to marketing support.

When choosing spending categories for marketing support elements, one must usually go beyond typical accounting expense categories such as advertising or sales force. A broad category like advertising may be related to a large number of targets and objectives. Therefore, these categories should be broken down into subcategories, like advertising to intermediaries, seasonal discounts, and sample components sent to systems designers.

These kinds of expense categories typically have well-defined strategic objectives that are easily linked to useful measures of effectiveness. For example, a category like advertising in trade magazines can usually be associated with an objective like increasing dealer awareness and cooperation in some specific aspect of a marketing effort. It is possible to make post-expenditure reviews of these categories to determine their effectiveness. In that way, they force continuing attention to the "money-in/results-out" questions in strategy/budget formulation. Only categories that will have a significant response in terms of awareness, distribution, or trial or repeat purchases should be included. Also, a manager should use only expenditure categories over which she or he can exercise control. And to keep the analysis as simple as possible, include only significant expenditures.

Response

In order to determine the appropriate level of marketing support, one needs to be able to forecast the impact that different levels and allocations of marketing support will have on various responses. That makes it possible to see how much it will cost to reach an objective.

Response to marketing spending can be considered at two levels: *direct results*, like changes in the percentage of the target market that is aware of the offer, A_t, and the percentage of distribution coverage, D_t, and *indirect results*, such as purchase and use. Each level has a distinct role to play. Direct results measure how well individual mix elements in a budget are performing. For example, a measure like dealer support or the level of brand awareness may be predominantly influenced by a single category of marketing support—personal selling expenditures in the first case and advertising media expenditures in the second.

Indirect results, which focus on purchase and use, measure the overall economic effectiveness of a strategy and its supporting budget. The offer and supporting marketing expenditures *jointly* influence perceived value, purchase, and use.

Direct results   The majority of people who are aware of a brand reach that state by virtue of the pull marketing effort on behalf of the brand. Nevertheless, awareness can be produced in a variety of ways and may persist over an extended period of time. For example, Packard automobiles have not been manufactured for many decades but they are fondly remembered by many older drivers. In the distant past, these people may have owned one, ridden in one owned by a friend, observed them on the road when driven by others, heard word-of-mouth reports about them, seen print advertisements, visited a showroom, or, more recently, observed one at an antique automobile show.

The percentage aware of a product in period t is a function of current and past actions by both the company and other actors in the social system. Therefore, it is important to recognize the cumulative effects of a brand's communications and product exposures; predominantly advertising, purchase, and use. These dynamics are represented by the following schematic:

$$\begin{array}{c} \text{Current} \\ \text{Fraction} \\ \text{Aware, } A \end{array} = \left(\begin{array}{c} \text{Communications} \\ \text{Current} \\ \text{Past} \end{array} \right) + \left(\begin{array}{c} \text{Personal Exposure} \\ \text{Current} \\ \text{Past} \end{array} \right)$$

Advertising	Purchase and Use
Word-of-Mouth	Sample and Use
Personal Selling	Retail Exposure
. . .	Observation of Use
	. . .

In terms of marketing expenditures, awareness is primarily a function of the amount of money spent on advertising and personal selling.

Distribution typically refers to the proportion of outlets that carry a given product, but the quality of distribution also needs to be considered. In many cases, the most important issue deals with the support that retailers give the brand. In large part, distribution is a function of the push activities of the sales force and trade promotion.

Indirect results   The primary indirect response is unit, TUS_t, or dollar sales, $\$S_t$. In turn, unit sales can be decomposed into initial or trial purchases, T_t, and repeat or replacement sales, RP_t. As discussed in Chapters 1 and 9, this decomposition results in additional work, but it is important because different factors influence the two purchase categories. This classification also increases the ability to tie expenditures to specific responses and should aid in the planning of future expenditures.

A useful way to look at repeat sales is through the long-run retention rate, LRR, which is the brand's market share among people or organizations that have tried it. The following formula was used in Chapters 8 and 9 to estimate LRR:

$$LRR = SBR/(1 + SBR - RR)$$

where SBR is the switchback rate, the percentage of triers who bought another product last time but will switch back to the manager's product on the next purchase occasion. RR is the repeat purchase rate, the percentage of customers who bought the manager's product last time and will repurchase the product next time.

In those chapters, the formula was used as a way to estimate LRR. Here the emphasis is on the managerial significance of the repeat and switchback rates. RR is a function of the *availability* of the firm's product, user *satisfaction* with the firm's product, *special inducements* to repeat purchase the product, and other firms' *special inducements* to switch to their product. SBR is a function of the *availability* of the product bought last time and of the firm's product, *satisfaction* with the product bought last time and with the

firm's product, *special inducements* to switch to the firm's product, and other firms' special inducements to repurchase. The relationship between the offer and support and the market response is shown in Figure 10-1.

In considering the relationship shown in Figure 10-1, it may be helpful to examine the relative effort given to "push" and to "pull" elements in an overall strategy. The role of each element is:

PUSH— Cost-effective creation of convenient availability to final buyers.

— Cost-effective creation of appropriate sales effort at the point of sale.

Predominantly personal selling, price, and promotion directed toward resellers, but supported by pull activities.

PULL— Cost-effective creation of awareness, knowledge, and preference for the offer among final buyers.

Predominantly advertising, publicity, and promotions that emphasize the comparative value of the offer but are supported by push activities.

The relative emphasis given to each element should be influenced by competition, distribution, knowledge among final buyers, the life-cycle stage of the product, and an appraisal of the efficiency with which various support elements can contribute directly to push and pull and indirectly to total sales. A more detailed discussion of the effects of push and pull can be found in Farris, Olver, and de Kluyver (1989).

Intense special inducements, low product salience, and variety-seeking motives (Pessemier, 1985) are among the major forces behind high levels of brand switching. Whatever these forces may be, they decrease RR. In most instances, they cannot be easily influenced by a manager's offer or the offer's supporting marketing program.

FIGURE 10-1 Marketing causation.

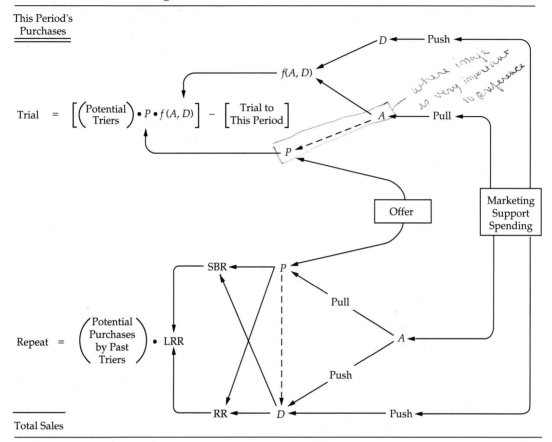

FORECASTING NEW PRODUCT
SALES IN TERMS OF TRIAL
AND REPEAT OR
REPLACEMENT SALES[1]

This section reviews and uses the concepts in Chapter 8 to build a series of annual sales forecasts for a product or service with a reasonably short repurchase cycle, that is, one in which repeat purchases need to be considered.

The data requirements for new product planning may appear to be very detailed at first, but they do help one to understand why a product is a success or a failure. Rarely will all of these data be available the first time a company launches a new product, but if good records are kept, an appropriate data base can be built up over time. Without such a data base containing standardized measures, the company's new product experience is much more likely to be fragmented and subjective.

Review of Trial and Repeat Sales

Trial sales   The same breakdown of the market outlined in Figure 8-1 will be used in the rest of the book. It is reviewed below.

---

[1]Some of the variables in this section will not have temporal subscripts. If they are forecast to change over the period of the analysis, such subscripts should be included.

The size of the target market, #TM: the number of people or entities in the group to whom the marketing effort is directed. This group may include many nonbuyers of the relevant product class if market segments are formed on the basis of general consumer characteristics such as age or income for consumer products or industry for industrial products.

The number of product class buyers, #PCB: the number of people or entities who are expected to buy the firm's product and/or other important substitute products if they are made aware of the products and have them available. In the remainder of the book #PCB is used as the BASE for analysis.

The number of potential triers, #PT: the size of the group of buyers who like the firm's product well enough compared with competing products to make a trial purchase, given knowledge and availability. $\#PT = P \times \#PCB$.

The cumulative trial rate, CTR_t: the percentage of people in #PCB who have tried the firm's product by the end of period t. CTR_t is a function of the product's preference, P, awareness, A_t, and distribution, D_t. Conceptually, one can think of CTR as being equal to the product $P \times A \times D$, the percentage of people who prefer the product times the percentage who are aware of it times the percentage who can find it.

The number of triers, $\#T_t$, at any point in time or cumulative level of marketing spending: the number of people or organizations that has tried the product

$$\#T_t = \#PCB \times CTR_t = \#PCB \times P \times A_t \times D_t \quad (10\text{-}1)$$

When making yearly forecasts, cumulative trial rate, CTR_t, needs to be converted into incremental trial rate, ITR_t, or trial in each period. The following formula can be used:

$$ITR_t = CTR_t - CTR_{t-1} \quad (10\text{-}2)$$

Repeat and replacement purchases When repeat or replacement purchases play an impor-

tant role in determining product success, the long-run retention rate, LRR, provides a useful way of analyzing them.

If one needs only a rough estimate of steady-state sales or long-run market share, LRMS, say for a preliminary decision, it can be obtained with the following formula:

$$LRMS = CTR_{max} \times LRR \quad (10\text{-}3)$$

LRMS can be multiplied by the size of the market to derive a long-run, or steady-state, sales forecast.

In most cases, one needs to derive annual sales forecasts to determine optimal levels and patterns of resource allocation. This requires that one estimate annual repeat purchases, RP_t, which can be done using the three equations that follow.

RFP_t is the number of repeat purchases made in period t by people who also made their first purchase in period t. It is modeled by:

$$RFP_t = ITR_t \times (TUP_t/2) \times LRR \quad (10\text{-}4)$$

The product of ITR_t and LRR is the market share of purchases accounted for by those people who purchased the product for the first time in period t. This share figure is multiplied by the size of the market, that is, total units purchased, TUP_t. Because on average the triers will be able to make only half as many repeat purchases during this period as an average purchaser of the product class, the total number of purchases must be divided by two.

RBP_t is the number of repeat purchases made in period t by people who made their initial purchase before period t. It is modeled by:

$$RBP_t = CTR_{t-1} \times TUP_t \times LRR \quad (10\text{-}5)$$

Finally, the total number of repeat purchases in period t, RP_t, is the sum of these two numbers.

$$RP_t = RFT_t + RBP_t \quad (10\text{-}6)$$

Over time RFT$_t$ gets progressively smaller and RBT$_t$ approaches the steady-state sales forecast.

Estimating the Parameters of Trial and Repeat Models Before Market Introduction

One can estimate the parameters of these models judgmentally, or by using survey, laboratory, or marketplace data. As one moves from managerial judgment to market-based estimates, the quality of the estimates should improve. However, the cost increases as one moves across these options and the value of the information decreases over time. For example, if you wait until a product has gone through its entire life cycle, you would get very good parameter estimates, but they would have no decision value for the product. On the other hand, estimates made prior to launch have much less certainty but can influence decisions about the future.

The following subsection covers premarket introduction estimates of trial rates and curves and the next subsection discusses premarket introduction estimates of repeat or replacement rates. The last section deals with updating these estimates on the basis of marketplace experience.

Trial forecasts   There are two different ways to estimate annual trial. The first is to estimate the maximum number of consumers who will try the product, then estimate how quickly they will try it. The speed of trial can be linked either to the firm's marketing support or to time (that is, based on managerial experience with other products). The second way is to estimate directly how many consumers will try the product each year. There are several common elements across these two approaches.

The total percentage of people who will try the product should initially be estimated as a function of *P*, *A*, and *D*. Without any other information, the simple multiplicative formula is a good starting place. Once some experience with

other new products has been gained and recorded, a more complex function can be used.

Equation (10-7) represents one way to estimate the maximum number of consumers who will try the product:

$$\#T_{max} = \#PCB \times CTR_{max} \\ = \#PCB \times P \times A_{max} \times D_{max} \quad (10\text{-}7)$$

Alternatively, Equation (10-1), repeated here, can be used to estimate the cumulative triers during any period.

$$\#T_t = \#PCB \times CTR_t = \#PCB \times P \times A_t \times D_t \quad (10\text{-}1)$$

Then an equation similar to Equation (10-2) can be used to forecast incremental trial, $\#IT_t$:

$$\#IT_t = \#T_t - \#T_{t-1} \quad (10\text{-}8)$$

A judgment has to be made about how important it is to forecast changes in awareness and distribution accurately over time. In either case, one needs estimates of *P*, A_{max}, and D_{max}, or estimates of *P*, A_t, and D_t for all time periods in the planning horizon.

P, Probability of trial   Although the percentage of the customers who will try the product, given awareness and distribution, can be estimated judgmentally, it is strongly advised that this estimate be based on consumer input. Many companies use the top box criterion in concept tests to estimate *P*. However, others have experimented with the top box criterion and have found that some other estimate, such as the "top box and a half" (that is, the sum of the percentage who say they will definitely purchase the product and half of the percentage who say they will probably purchase it), is a better predictor than the "top box" score in traditional concept tests.

Similarly, when using conjoint choice simulators, many companies assume that the profile with the highest utility will be the consumer's first choice. Others have argued that because P is typically measured on a single occasion, it does not directly make allowance for the level of brand switching that buyers may exhibit. Therefore, it is a less than perfect predictor of the share of potential buyers who will ultimately try a new product. The possible understatement has been reduced by estimating P with the aid of the Bradely-Terry-Luce choice model (see Appendix 9-1).

Regardless of the way in which P is estimated, the company should keep records of these estimates and the actual trial or Ps achieved in the marketplace. These methods have generally proven to be reliable, although it is possible that any of them will overestimate or underestimate the actual trial levels in certain situations. So the general guidelines should be modified on the basis of a particular company's experience.

A, Percentage aware   The relationship between dollars spent and awareness levels achieved varies considerably across industries. Therefore, one should look at the relationship between expenditures and awareness for similar products.

Clarke (1987, p. 165) shows a curve fitted to observations of aided awareness (based on data from Leo Burnett Co.) for a range of cumulative gross rating points, CGRP. The curve is concave downward and rises from a minimum of 23 percent to a maximum of 81 percent. The formula relating CGRPs to aided awareness is:

$$\text{Awareness} = .23 + (.81 - .23) \times (1 - e^{\,(-0.00089 \,\times\, \text{CGRP})}) \quad (10\text{-}9)$$

Once the cost of gross rating points is known, it is possible to estimate a relationship between dollars spent and awareness.

Clarke's chart points out two additional issues of importance. First, the observations are widely scattered around the fitted line, indicating a good deal of variability from case to case.

Possible explanations include differing quality of advertising copy and differing product saliences. Second, the fitted curve predicts a 23 percent level of awareness at zero CGRP and zero spending on the related media. Marketing managers need to understand this peculiar "free ride." The most appealing explanation is found in the use of aided awareness. When provided with a set of prompts, respondents will often indicate awareness when in fact they have never seen or heard of the brand. Some contol over this artifact can be obtained by including one or more fictitious brands in the prompts and adjusting the results. Alternatively, a unaided measure of awareness may be used.

Although Clarke's curve is a good approximation of the relationship between cumulative GRPs and awareness early in the product's life cycle, it does not model forgetting. Therefore, in later years, it may understate the need for continued advertising to maintain awareness.

Awareness is produced by more than the kind of media spending producing CGRPs. Carryover effects, sampling, coupons, and the availability of self-service displays can contribute significantly to buyer awareness. Similar curves can be constructed for the relationship between these other marketing variables and awareness. In particular, you would want to do this for sales force effort in situations in which salespeople are the primary communications vehicle.

When there is more than one important source of awareness, say awareness due to advertising, $A(\text{adv})_t$, and awareness due to free samples, $A(\text{fs})_t$, a formula like the following should be used to estimate overall awareness at time t:

$$A_t = A(\text{adv})_t + A(\text{fs})_t - A(\text{adv})_t \times A(\text{fs})_t \quad (10\text{-}10)$$

In this case, the last term subtracts the double counting of people who were made aware of the product by both advertising and free samples. Awareness carried forward from period $t - 1$ is ignored in Equation (10-10), but carryforward effects are modeled in Chapter 12.

D, Distribution level   Usually, distribution is defined in terms of weighted distribution coverage. That is, one calculates the share of total product category sales that is accounted for by outlets that stock the brand in question. With frequently purchased goods, this information is available through store audit data. In other categories, these data must be collected through surveys (sometimes carried out on a syndicated basis by a third party) or through sales force estimates.

Prior to introduction, an estimate of the level of distribution is usually based on the distribution level the company has achieved with similar products or, possibly, based on the experience that similar companies have achieved in the past.

Speed of trial   An initial estimate of how quickly people will try the product is usually based on experience with other products. Therefore, one needs to look at how quickly they gained sales.

The speed with which a curve rises is a function of time and money spent promoting the product. When one does not know the amount spent on marketing expenditures by other firms in a product class, the speed of diffusion can be viewed strictly as a function of time using the trial curves of similar products. For example, Bass (1969) studied ten innovative consumer durables and found the average time of the peak in the incremental adoption rate was nine years after introduction. Trial curves for individual brands typically have a similar shape, but may complete their rise more quickly.

Once one has estimated the rate with which one or more analogous products have been tried, those rates can be adjusted for the new product. Rogers (1962, 1982) found that the speed with which a new product is tried is posi-

tively related to its relative advantage over existing products, the ease of trying it on a limited basis, the compatibility of this product with the rest of the person's life, and the product's visibility. The speed of adoption has been found to be negatively related to the risk involved in trying the product and the product's relative complexity.

For example, one could model the speed of diffusion for an analogous new durable good with Equation (8-6), repeated here:

$$ITR_t = b \times [CTR_{t-1} \times (CTR_{max} - CTR_{t-1})] \quad (10\text{-}11)$$

The estimated parameter b models how quickly the product was tried. By looking at Rogers' factors, one could adjust this parameter for a new product. Similarly, one could model the speed of diffusion for an analogous frequently purchased product, using Equation (8-7):

$$ITR_t = a \times (CTR_{max} - CTR_{t-1}) \quad (10\text{-}12)$$

Again, the parameter a models the speed of trial. Rogers' factors could be used as a guide to make adjustments in it.

In the second approach, if data are available on the introductory marketing spending on a new product, it is possible to make the trial curve a function of money rather than time. For example, one could use Equations (10-1) and (10-9) along with a series of advertising budgets and a cost per CGRP to estimate awareness over time. This estimate of awareness can be combined with estimates of P and D to estimate trial.

Curves based on these two methods can then be merged to arrive at a *better* estimate of rate of trial for an alternative strategy/budget. One way to turn these estimates into a rough trial forecast over time is through the TRIAL model that is discussed in Appendix 10-1. This model requires that the user specify the *launch time* (the time it takes to achieve 10 percent of the maximum penetration) and *takeover time* (the time it takes to achieve 90 percent of the maximum penetration). Then the user can experiment with different pairs of points and the associated curves connecting these two points. On the other hand, when enough estimated or observed trial purchases are available (say for five or more budget periods) the model can be fit from data, and future cumulative trial can be forecast directly.

Repeat rates   It is relatively easy to estimate the average length of purchase cycles from other brands or similar products. However, it is harder to estimate LRR, the long-run retention rate, than it is to estimate P, because LRR is based principally on satisfaction after usage.

Prior to introduction, LRR should be based on a product test in which the consumer uses the product in a natural manner for a sufficient length of time to be able to make an informed decision. ASSESSOR® makes these predictions in two ways. First, after using the brand of interest, the consumer is asked to allocate chips among pairs of brands in relation to each brand's likelihood of being repurchased, a task that is similar to the chip allocation exercise in a competitive environment concept test. (When only one product can be used, it is possible to rate the likelihood that it will be repurchased.) This after-usage preference rating is used as an estimate of LRR. Although this procedure can be used with durable goods, its use is based on the assumption that the competing products' relative preferences will remain unchanged over several years.

In ASSESSOR's second method, one that is more appropriate for frequently purchased goods, $LRR = SBR/(1 + SBR - RR)$ can be used to estimate LRR from a small number of purchases. Again, SBR is the switchback rate and RR is the repeat purchase rate. Chapter 12 contains an extended discussion of how these two variables can be linked directly to marketing expenditures.

LRR has been successfuly estimated from RR

and SBR in simulated test markets by questioning people after only a single purchase. Because preferences may change with additional usage, estimating these rates over a larger number of purchases should produce more accurate estimates. However, the increased accuracy is gained at the expense of additional time and money.

Updating Premarket Estimates of Trial and Repeat Models

After the product has been introduced, a series of measurements should be made to determine how well the product is doing and why. Furthermore, the ability of the product to gain trial and repeat purchases needs to be analyzed separately, because problems in these two areas point to different actions. Consumer surveys are needed to measure the level of awareness, trial, last brand used, brand used most often, next brand to be purchased (or other kinds of preference measures), and the measures needed to build perceptual spaces for the product and its competitive set.

Either unaided (what brands in this product class are you aware of?) or aided awareness (which of the following brands are you aware of?) can be collected (and both can be collected in the same survey if unaided awareness is collected first). Aided recall is usually used in forecasting models, but it is possible to use unaided recall. At a minimum, one can compare actual and predicted levels of awareness. With systematic data collection, as shown by Clarke (1987), one can develop a relationship between marketing expenditures and awareness levels.

Similarly, distribution should be systematically monitored after introduction, both to alert management to possible problems and to provide data for future new product introductions.

Trial levels estimated from these surveys can be compared to forecast values of CTR_t. Product preference, P, can be estimated with the same technique used in its premarket estimate, or P

can be estimated after the trial levels have been recorded using the formula $\hat{P} = CTR_t / (A_t \times D_t)$.

This allows one to look at the relationship between P and $\hat{P}$. After estimates have been collected across several products one can look at the relationship between the two variables. One can then determine whether the simple multiplicative formula is appropriate to predict CTR_t or a more complex formula such as Equation (10-13) would be better. It also allows one to see if the method of estimating P is appropriate.

$$CTR_t = a + b \times [P \times f(A_t, D_t)] \quad (10\text{-}13)$$

These analyses can be used to ascertain the reasons for the deviation of CTR_t from forecast. Specifically, they will point to whether the value of the offer, P, is as good as forecast, whether the pull elements of the supporting mix are generating awareness as effectively as predicted, and whether the push elements are generating distribution as effectively as predicted.

One also needs to look at repeat purchases. If a product is purchased many times a year, LRR can be directly estimated from the product's purchase histories within a year of introduction. This can be done either by using the formula relating LRR to SBR and RR or by directly calculating the brand's share among people who have purchased it at least once (see, for example, Parfitt and Collins, 1969; Eskin, 1973; Pringle, Wilson, and Brody, 1982).

When the interpurchase times are of intermediate length, say every two to four years, an actuarial approach can be used in which each annual cohort of triers is followed through time to estimate their repurchase behavior (See Pessemier, 1982, pp. 170–171). If the average interpurchase time is three years, the LRR should be defined as the percentage of people who purchased this brand three or more years ago and who will repurchase it this year. In this case, the market share in the tth period could be estimated as the sum of the percentage trying the product that year plus the percentage who tried it three years ago and repurchased it in the tth period:

$$MS_t = ITR_t + ITR_{t-3} \times LRR \quad (10\text{-}14)$$

Additionally, to understand why LRR is at the level it is, each cell of the table at the bottom of the page should be examined at regular intervals to discover important trends and to forecast future levels of LRR.

The Quality of Awareness and Distribution

In the treatment of both awareness and distribution, possible quality variations have been ignored. In the case of awareness, it can range from an individual's capacity just to recall a brand name to awareness of the product's many attributes and the benefits that they promise. In the case of distribution, it can involve resellers doing no more than stocking the product to resellers aggressively supporting the product's sales to final buyers. If a manager believes it is essential to allow for the differences in quality across products, market entities, and/or over time, measures of awareness and distribution can be quality weighted. Alternatively, these measures can be elaborated to indicate the degree to which various quality levels have been attained (for example, the share of people who are aware of the brand's name, the share who

	Availability	Satisfaction	SPECIAL INDUCEMENTS	
			Repurchase	Switch
Ours				
Theirs				

SPECIAL INDUCEMENTS

Different Mktg Actions are required

know its main features, and the share who
know about its relative advantages). An effort
to account for quality differences will complicate the data requirements (and change
some coefficients), but will not alter the basic
structure of the models that are outlined in
Chapters 10 to 12.

When the intercept and slope coefficients, *a*
and *b* of Equation (10-13) for the cumulative trial
function, have been estimated from historical
observations, allowance is made for the specific
manner in which awareness and distribution
were measured. Furthermore, the quality of each
measure is unlikely to vary greatly between
competitors. For these reasons the above extension of the model will seldom be worth the
effort. This does not mean that a manager
should not actively try to improve the quality
of the awareness and distribution of the company product(s). For example, it may be possible
to increase the quality of awareness by making
the brand name signal a principal product benefit, say using Locfast as a brand name for a line
of industrial fasteners. In a similar manner, the
quality of an industrial goods manufacturer's
distribution can be improved by training the
resellers' sales representatives. For a consumer
packaged good, a package can emphasize a
product feature (for example, Pringles®) and the
producer can offer direct delivery or display fix-
tures to gain greater point-of-sale exposure.

In some situations, a manager will be more
interested in improving the quality of awareness
or distribution than in increasing the quantity.
The results of actions that are designed to
improve the quality of awareness can be monitored by noting the degree to which they raise
the level of product preference, *P*. The results of
actions designed to raise the quality of distribution must be accounted for by more complex
measurements.

Understanding Trial and Repeat

An important strategic question for any product
introduction is where do the trial sales come
from? Innovative products do not fit into an
established product class or use pattern, so their
trial and repeat purchases may not come directly from other, similar products. The more common situation concerns product introductions in
which sales come principally from directly competing products. In this case, one should predict
where the triers will come from. A good measure of competitive vulnerability is the share of
trial purchases coming from each brand (source
brand) divided by the source brand's market
share in the prior period. If this ratio is less
than one, the brand is undercontributing triers
to the new brand, and if it is greater than one,
the brand is vulnerable and is overcontributing
triers to the new brand. Of equal importance is
the trend in these data after a product's intro-

Source Brand	Source Brand Share	SHARE OF TRIERS ÷ SOURCE BRAND SHARE		
		Qtr 1	Qtr 2	Qtr 3
Q	.27	.9	1.0	1.1
J	.10	1.4	1.2	1.2
C	.35	1.1	.9	.85
E	.12	1.6	1.4	1.1

duction. The table on page 312 illustrates three quarters of results for a grocery product monitored by scanner data.

Large-share brand Q has shown little vulnerability, but it is increasing slightly. Large-share brand C showed some early vulnerability, but it has become far less vulnerable over time. The smaller share brands (J and E) were initially relatively vulnerable, but have also become less so with the passage of time. Data of this sort suggest problems and opportunities for the manager of the new brand.

Additional useful information during the early months and years of a product's life can be obtained by examining the repurchase rate among the triers contributed by each source brand. The following table illustrates scanner data that could be obtained about a grocery product.

Source	TRIERS' REPURCHASE RATES		
Brand	Qtr 1	Qtr 2	Qtr 3
Q	.2	.25	.26
J	.4	.41	.38
C	.1	.09	.07
E	.3	.31	.33

This table shows marked differences in the post-trial repurchase rates for individuals who used each source brand prior to trying the new brand. Triers who originally bought brand C are not very satisfied and repurchase rates are low. The situation with respect to source brand Q is somewhat better and improving. The results concerning source brands J and E are encouraging, as they have high stable or improving repurchase rates.

Understanding Market Responses

Market response can be direct or indirect. Most of the foregoing discussion has been focused on direct responses, ones that can easily be linked to simple, discrete marketing actions. Unfortunately, a number of useful response measures are not easily linked to single mix elements or they are functions of several prior measures. Some characteristics of this class of indices require additional attention.

Long-run retention rate and market dynamics The *Long-run Retention Rate* is a function of the *Repeat purchase Rate* (among those who bought the brand last) and the *SwitchBack Rate* (among those who bought another brand last time), LRR = SBR /(1 + SBR − RR). Even when RR and SBR do not change over time (the base case explored in the following exposition), LRR will not accurately reflect a brand's share of purchases during the first three to five repurchase cycles by triers. The market dynamics of a new or improved brand are such that a brand's share of last-time buyers who can repeat and last-time nonbuyers who can switch back can change noticeably for a number of periods following a brand's introduction. How rapidly change occurs and the process stabilizes depends on the brand's relative appeal and the general propensity of customers to switch from brand to brand in the product class. This fact can best be illustrated by examining the following relationships.

$S(t − 1)_i$ = the number of non-first-time customers buying brand i in the period ending at time $t − 1$.

$S(t − 1)_i \times RR(t)_i$ = the number of customers loyal to brand i at time t.

$S(t − 1)_i \times (1 − RR(t))$ = the number of customers who switched from brand i in the period ending a time t.

$\#T(t)_i$ = $CTR(t)_i \times T\#P(t)$ = the number of triers of brand i who could switch brands.

Dropping the i subscript and the time on RR and SBR

$$S(t) = \underbrace{(S(t-1) \times RR)}_{\substack{\text{retained} \\ \text{buyers}}} + SBR \times \underbrace{\{\#T(t) - \overbrace{(S(t-1) \times (1 - RR))\}}^{\substack{\text{eligible to be gained} \\ \text{by brand } i}}}_{\text{gained brand switchers}}$$

(10-15)

Equation (10-15) provides a limited picture of market behavior that can be used to compute market shares for ten initial time periods using a variety of inputs. The required data include $S(0) = 0$, the brand's repeat rate RR(t), the brand's switchback rate SBR(t), and the total number of triers $\#T(t)$. Two values of $S(0)$ will be used but, the last three variables will remain constant. For a variety of inputs, the results appear below.

In typical cases like those shown, market share quickly converges to its long-run value. This is true when a brand starts with a zero share or a share that is larger than the long-run value. During the first few years of a marketing plan for a new or improved product, the spreadsheet results that employ the formula for LRR should be adjusted for the effects shown above and for temporal changes in RR and SBR.

When RR and SBR are constant over time, these two values determine the brand's equilibrium market share. But the values of these variables do not remain constant. They are subject to change by the firm's marketing actions, the actions of competitors, and market maturation. If all firms had equally strong values of RR and SBR, the equilibrium market shares would be $1/n$, where n is the total number of brands in the product class (Pessemier, 1982, pp. 115–118). Any departure from this par share is evidence of a strong or weak brand(s) and/or marketing support.

RR and SBR as components of LRR   To the extent that RR and SBR are subject to differential influences by the firm's marketing actions, it is useful to see how much each one influences the long-run retention rate and the degree to which the effect of one variable depends on the value of the other variable. The table on the next page contains the essential relationships. If RR $= .3$ and SBR is increased by .1 when the original SBR is .1, the increase in LRR is .097. But if the original SBR is .8, the increase in LRR is only .03. The lower the original value of SBR, the greater will be the effect on LRR for a given incremental increase. If SBR is .3 and RR is increased by .1 when the original RR is .1, the increase in LRR is .023. But if the original value of RR is .7, the increase in LRR is .1. The latter case is the opposite of the former case. The change in LRR

BRAND I

	RR	SBR	#T (000)	S(T)$_i$ YEAR t					MARKET SHARE OF TRIERS, YEAR t		
				0	1	3	6	10	0	1	3
	.4	.2	200	0	40.0	54.3	55.5	55.6	.0	.20	.27
	.4	.2	200	100	68.0	56.5	55.5	55.6	.45	.34	.28
	.4	.2	600	0	120.0	163.0	166.6	166.7	.0	.20	.27
	.4	.2	600	100	148.0	165.2	166.6	166.7	.15	.25	.28
	.1	.3	200	0	60.0	51.5	51.3	51.3	.0	.30	.26
	.1	.3	200	100	43.0	51.0	51.3	51.3	.49	.22	.26
	.1	.3	600	0	180.0	154.6	153.8	153.8	.0	.30	.26
	.1	.3	600	100	163.0	154.1	153.8	153.8	.16	.27	.26

LONG-RUN RETENTION RATE

Repeat Rate	SWITCHBACK RATE				
	.1	.2	.3	.4	.5
.1	.100	.182	.250	.308	.357
.2	.111	.200	.273	.333	.385
.3	.125	.222	.300	.364	.417
.4	.143	.250	.333	.400	.455
.5	.167	.286	.375	.444	.500
.6	.200	.333	.429	.500	.557
.7	.250	.400	.500	.572	.625
.8	.333	.500	.600	.667	.714

	Switchback Rate			
	.6	.7	.8	.9
.1	.400	.438	.471	.500
.2	.429	.467	.500	.529
.3	.462	.500	.533	.563
.4	.500	.539	.571	.600
.5	.546	.583	.615	.643
.6	.600	.636	.667	.692
.7	.667	.700	.727	.750
.8	.750	.778	.800	.818

produced by an incremental change in either RR or SBR depends on the value of the other variable.

For the above reasons, it will become progressively "easier" to improve the long-run retention rate by improving the repeat rate as the level of the repeat rate increases. On the other hand, it will be progressively "more difficult" to improve the long-run retention rate by improving the switchback rate as the switchback rate improves. The problem is complicated by the fact that many marketing actions improve both variables and that the cost of gaining an incremental improvement in each variable may differ between variables, by the variable's level and by the level of the other variable. Nonetheless, the relationships which have been discussed can have an important bearing on marketing efficiency and the results produced by a budget. It is especially important to monitor satisfaction or

postpurchase P among triers, and product availability, D.

A, D and P as components of CTR Since CTR is usually modeled as the serial product of the three underlying variables, A, D, and P, it is immediately apparent that the effect of changing one of the variables depends on the size of the product of the other two variables. For example, if $A = .1$ and $D = .1$ and P is increased from .4 to .5, CTR will increase from .004 to .005. However, if $A = .9$ and $D = .9$, the same change in P will increase CTR from .324 to .405. Even so, the percentage increase is 25 percent in both cases. For all multiplicative model elements, this relationship must be kept in mind.

Targeting markets and concentrating spending Although it may be impossible for a manager to aim a marketing program at just those consumers who are most likely to prefer his or her product, doing so can greatly increase marketing efficiency by increasing P, the proportion of individuals who will buy the product if they are aware of it and can find it. Not only will P be larger, but selective targeting reduces the number of individuals who must be made aware and possibly the extent of the needed distribution. In this case, the share of consideration sets can be increased among the most purchase-prone segment of the market, thereby increasing trial and/or repeat purchases for a given level of marketing spending. The share of consideration sets attainable for a given budget can also be increased by narrowing the market covered by confining marketing to a particular geographic region. However, the larger A and D will apply to a smaller number of individuals.

A catalog seller of apparel who is planning a price promotion on men's wool shirts illustrates how the above factors can increase efficiency. This retailer will use a selective mailing list that excludes former customers who live in warm climates and customers who have purchased exclusively women's apparel. This mailing piece is likely to be read by a high percentage of all recipients, all readers can order by mail or telephone, and the average level of preference is expected to be high. In other words, the marketing expenditure is likely to produce a high level of the triple product, $P \times A \times D$. If the mailing is expanded to cover the firm's entire mailing list, some additional sales can be made but at a greatly reduced rate per marketing dollar.

Similar effects can be observed for industrial goods. As an illustration, a producer of heavy equipment can concentrate sales calls promoting a new machine among customers who have well-worn equipment or customers who are planning to expand or relocate their plants. Efficiency can be enhanced further by eliminating sales calls on small firms that can be better served by industrial equipment middlemen.

The above approaches depend heavily on a firm's capacity to identify and classify potential customers. An important example is the costly effort of tobacco companies to obtain the names, addresses and brand use of about 28 million smokers (*Business Week*, 1992). These lists have been used to deliver coupons, samples, and advertising directly to each company's prime prospects, avoiding the high waste of reaching non smokers. Nevertheless, if trial sales are viewed as important, an expanded target market would be required.

Decay coefficients   Awareness and distribution rates are increased by marketing actions, but in the absence of such support both rates will decrease over time. The more rapidly one or both rates decay, the more marketing effort will be required to sustain or increase the share of potential customers who will have a product in their consideration set. In Chapter 12, a model is presented that makes due allowance for the decay dynamics while aiding a manager to choose an efficient size and strategic allocation for each year's marketing budget.

The complex effects of variables on profits
Many of the topics that have been covered point

out the complex causal chains with which a marketing manager must deal. A way to get a better overall view of this complexity is to remember that actions occur in two principal domains: those that affect the nature of the offer and those that define the marketing support for the offer. The objectives of these actions find their final expression in marketing outcomes such as market share and economic outcomes such as net contribution to profit.

Therefore, one must trace the effects of decisions concerning the offer and marketing support through the intermediate variables displayed in Figure 10-1, then trace the effects through the further linkages shown in Figure 11-1 to see the final economic effects. These lengthy causal links emphasize the power of an easy-to-visualize spreadsheet model described in Chapter 11. It efficiently carries each change through from managerial action to estimates or empirical evidence about changes in key model inputs to the final managerially relevant measures of effectiveness.

The principal missing elements in these models are precise transformations of one variable into another. For example, managers have only a rough idea about how spending on advertising will change awareness or repeat purchase behavior. Progress is being made on some of these matters, but market dynamics will always limit the precision with which analysis can reduce uncertainty about how actions will translate into results.

Price effects   Price analysis in the present context requires careful consideration. Price changes that have a lasting, nonpromotional character are modifications in the offer and should be handled as such. Difficulties arise when numerous price promotions are used. They strongly affect the average price paid by customers and can have an important effect on the brand's image. For these reasons, they should be treated as a price reduction or price level decision related to the offer and not simply a promotional pricing action. On the other hand, occasional promotional price reductions that have clear-cut short-term objectives can logically be included as part of a brand's marketing support. An additional complication may be the differential manner in which market segments respond to promotional prices and to changes in the offer price.

A related problem concerns the degree to which pricing actions have an important additional effect on primary demand. The average rate at which a market segment purchases the product may be increased or decreased, and in a few cases the composition of the market segment or the total market may change. When large price changes are being contemplated, sensitivity analyses should be directed toward exploring the effect on all phases of demand.

Retailer and distributor support Another complication surrounds retailer and distributor support that is a proxy for the brand seller's direct marketing effort. In some product classes a brand manufacturer passes large sums on to retailers and/or distributors in the form of cooperative marketing funds. These moneys must be spent in specific ways to support the brand. In this case, the push and pull objectives of the expenditures may become significantly blurred. Nevertheless, it is desirable to keep track of the share of the effort going to enhance awareness and associated results, and the share of effort devoted to improving the width and forcefulness of distribution support.

VALUE PRODUCED BY MARKETING

Although many aspects of price making were treated in Chapter 6, more complete coverage appears elsewhere (for example, Nagle, 1987). Direct coverage of other major mix elements is not presented in this text. Two important reasons can be cited: First, detailed discussions of advertising, personal selling, distribution, and logistics appear in the marketing literature, and second, a great deal of the material is necessarily specific to a product class, firm, or market.

Instead, this section deals briefly with three topics that are closely associated with the design of a strategy and budget and their constituent mix elements.

The first concerns the value added by marketing support and the *scope* and *roles* that are implied for marketing. The second covers the tasks that marketing must perform and the *tools* that are available to do the job. The third concerns the cost and quality differences in marketing tools that serve similar functions. When these perspectives are joined to a detailed knowledge of the specific product, market, and firm, a great deal is known about what spending patterns will constitute efficient, effective marketing strategies.

Value Added—The Scope and Role of Marketing Support

The distinction between analyzable and unitary objects has already been developed. This distinction can serve as a starting point for a discussion of the *scope* of marketing support spending and the *role* of various support activities in relationship to the value received by the buyer and user. A related construct is the degree to which the product is ego-intensive. Consider the following diagram, where the extremes have been labeled A through D.

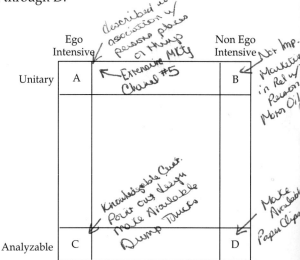

A. These products must be described in terms of their association with persons, places, and things, since there are few physical product attributes that can be used to describe them or by which consumers can judge them. The producer and/or distributor provides much of the value through advertising, packaging, and distribution. To build consumer preference, it is necessary to have the product favorably presented by distribution or a field sales force, and favorably associated by its advertising. This extensive marketing task requires that a large percentage of the sale price to the final buyer be devoted to marketing activities. The location, decor, service, and advertising that support the sale of Chanel No 5 perfume is a prime example.

B. These products are not viewed as important by consumers. They must be marketed largely in terms of their relationship to favored persons, places, and things. Motor oil that is associated with a famous race car driver is illustrative.

C. These products are important to the customer's welfare but their benefits are conveyed principally by the product's physical attributes. Most customers will be fairly knowledgeable and fairly well equipped to judge a product's ability to satisfy their needs. Marketing's job is to point out the relative advantage of the product's design and make the product available. High loaders and dump trucks are illustrative.

D. These products contribute modestly to the consumer's welfare but their need satisfying attributes are easily examined and judged. Ready availability is the dominant concern. Paper clips are illustrative.

The marketing task can be described in a similar manner for products that occupy intermediate positions on the two attribute continuums used in the above diagram. Many other product attributes could have been used to define the marketing task more fully .

The above classification scheme can help a manager appraise the size and nature of the marketing task and to judge what part of the utility received by the consumer is due to the product's physical design and what part is due to its marketing support. It also helps one judge what part of the value delivered by marketing support can be attributed to the awareness and image developed by pull spending, and how much is due to push spending. The contribution to value made by the producer's marketing support is paid for principally from manufacturing margin, and the distributor's contribution is principally paid for out of the reseller's margins. The bigger the value creation task assumed by marketing, the smaller will be the share of the price paid by the final buyer that will go to pay production costs.

Producers and resellers must understand their contribution to value creation for each type of product they market. The manufacturer can develop a marketing and pricing policy by deciding on the *scope* of required marketing activities and the *role* that will be played by the manufacturer and the reseller in the value chain that extends to the final buyer.

A partial list of additional *product-specific* factors bearing on the *scope* of marketing and the *role* assumed by various activities includes:

Width of the seller's product line

Producer's cost advantage/disadvantage

Product's performance advantage/disadvantage

Influence of potential substitutes

Life-cycle position

Extent of demand

Price level

Degree of innovativeness or newness

Required maintenance

Required instructions or training

Durability

Rate of consumption

Size

Weight

Shelf life

Storage requirements

Number of buyers

Processing required after production but before use

Complexity

Manufacturing margin, percent

Consumer/industrial

These and other characteristics define a multidimensional space that represents the *product specific* influences on *marketing scope*, the *actors*, and their *roles* or activities. They indicate much about the contribution that must be made by the producer, distributor(s), reseller(s), personal selling by the producer and resellers, and so forth.

A partial list of the influences of *buyer behavior* on the *scope* and *role* of marketing support includes:

Purchase rate

Intensity of shopping

Ego involvement

Degree of buyer knowledge

Value of exclusivity

Value of variety

Presence of a third-party specifier

Size of the average purchase

Sensitivity to nonprice incentives

Sensitivity to price

Use contexts

Organizational or family influences

Single or multiple types of items purchased at one time

Rapid or deliberate purchase behavior

Preference for single or multiple sources

The above multidimensional descriptions of the product and buyer behavior influences do not exhaust the possibilities. Although they will not be reviewed here, the components of the market environment, the competitive environment, the reseller environment, the media environment, and the firm's resources could be examined separately. They all influence the amount that must be spent on marketing support to satisfy customers, as well as the allocation of these funds to the various activities or elements that make up the marketing mix.

The Tasks and Tools of Marketing Support

Defining marketing's tasks involves such matters as defining the target market, examining the positioning to be established, determining the communications message, appraising the reach, frequency, and cost associated with various patterns of advertising, deciding what promotional incentives may be required to produce the needed levels of trial, and so on. In this manner, management develops the specific actions required to efficiently generate the relevant levels of awareness.

In a similar manner, defining marketing's tasks involves estimating the structure of distribution and the kinds of functions that resellers should perform to produce the needed levels of product availability. Doing so leads to judgments about the required field sales effort, discount schedules to various classes of resellers, training and sales support for distributors, and the like. Again, an appraisal of these matters should indicate the efficient marketing actions that will be needed to reach various desired levels of distribution and the cost of these actions.

Developing marketing support in the above manner allows one to see the overall size and nature of the task. It also lets management predict the levels of awareness, A, and availability, D, that progressively larger levels of marketing spending can generate. These intervening variables drive trial and long-term retention, *and* the sales volume achieved by marketing spending. A manager hopes to enhance consumer (and reseller) value in a manner that not only satisfies these participants in the process but also provides the manager with the desired level of profit.

A table displaying the tasks as column headings and the tools as row stubs can help a manager rough out an intermediate level of detail for one or more marketing strategies. Illustrative tasks/tools tables are Table 10-1 for an industrial product (or product line) and Table 10-2 for a consumer product (or product line). Once the format of a tasks/tools table has been developed for the manager's situation, text entries can be made in each active cell. In turn, these descriptions help define the mix elements that will enter the strategy and budget and something

about the likely cost of execution. The table can be further elaborated by preparing a different one for each year and/or major market segment, such as heavy and light users of the product class.

Cost and Quality Differences in Mix Elements
Moriarity and Moran (1990, p. 147) report that the full cost of delivering a message about an industrial good varies greatly from method to method.

Per-hour face-to-face contact by a national account manager	$500
Per-hour face-to-face contact by a direct sales representative	$300
Per-hour telemarketing contact	$17
Direct mail contact	$1

The efficiency of each method or tool can only be judged in terms of their efficiency in creating awareness and preference. Negotiating a sale to a national account cannot be handled by direct mail, but direct mail can pave the way for a successful sales contact. More importantly, direct mail and telemarketing can greatly increase the

TABLE 10-1   INDUSTRIAL PRODUCT TASKS/TOOLS TABLE

Support Tools	\multicolumn{6}{c}{SUPPORT TASKS}
	Leads	Prospects	Building Interest	Making the Sale	Postsale Service	Acct. Mgt.
Sales: National Accounts						
Direct						
Distributors						
VARs						
Telemarketing						
Direct Mail						
⋰						

TABLE 10-2 CONSUMER PRODUCT TASK/TOOLS TABLE

| Support Tools | SUPPORT TASKS | | | | | PURCHASING INCENTIVES | | | |
	Identify Target Buyers	Create Buyer Awareness	Build Product Acceptance	Identify Target Resellers	Create Favorable Availability	Trial	Repeat	Switch-back	Postsale Activties
M/R and Planning									
PULL: Advertising									
Media 1									
Media 2									
• • •									
Label Allowance									
Sampling									
Coupons									
• • •									
PUSH: Display Allowance									
Label Alowance									
Case Allowance									
Display Material									
• • •									

efficiency of a salesperson in finding and screening prospects, as well as handling routine inquiries, reorders, and the like.

In every case, marketing managers have to be alert to both the cost and effectiveness of the available marketing tools when applied to their specific marketing tasks. Clearly, one must understand the scope of the task, but it takes know-how and imagination to deploy the right mix of tools. Discovering the right balance between pull and push and between keeping current customers and regaining former customers goes a long way toward defining a winning strategy/budget.

CONCLUDING REMARKS

In this chapter, a model has been described that uses essential and readily obtainable market measures to examine the economic effectiveness of strategies planned on behalf of a new or modified product. It is clearly possible to perform the same general type of analysis by relying directly on estimates of sales and market share, bypassing the intermediate variables such as awareness and distribution. In this case, management would be buying simplicity at the cost

of reduced understanding of the forces that drive the sales of the product. In turn, this reduced understanding is very likely to limit management's capacity to develop effective strategies and to monitor their performance in the marketplace. For these reasons, a purely sales- and share-based model was not developed for new or modified products. In these cases, knowledge about the status of awareness and distribution is too important. Instead, the discussion of such a model will be deferred to the chapters that deal with established products.

An illustrative application of the model presented above will be made to a consumer product in Chapter 11. Appendix 11-1 provides instruction for building the associated spreadsheet. Given an understanding of the model and the details of the illustration, a manager and his or her technical staff should be able to develop the data and modeling tools required to make practical applications. Although the illustration is specific to a single brand, the approach is applicable to a wide variety of both consumer and industrial products. Chapter 12 presents a model and computer program that allow one to go directly from a spending pattern to an efficient budget, estimates of the intervening variables, and the resulting sales and profits.

REFERENCES

Bass, Frank M.: "A New Product Growth Model for Consumer Durables," *Management Science*, 15, January 1969, 215–227.

Blattberg, Robert and John Golanty: "TRACKER: An Early Test Market Forecasting and Diagnostic Model for New Product Planning," *Journal of Marketing Research*, 15, May 1978, 192–202.

Business Week, March 16, 1992, p. 62.

Clarke, Darral G.: *Marketing Analysis and Decision Making*, The Scientific Press, Redwood City, CA, 1987, pp. 111–133.

Claycamp, Henry J., and L. E. Liddy: "Prediction of New Product Performance: An Analytical Approach," *Journal of Marketing Research*, 6, November 1969, 414-420.

Eskin, Gerald J.: "Dynamic Forecasts of New Product Demand Using a Depth of Repeat Model," *Journal of Marketing Research*, 10, May 1973, 115–129.

Farris, Paul, James Olver, and Kees de Kluyver: "The Relationship Between Distribution and Market Share," *Marketing Science*, 8, Spring 1989, 107–132.

Fisher, J. C., and R. H. Pry: "A Simple Substitution Model for Technological Change," *Technological Forecasting and Social Change*, 2, May 1971, 75–88.

Fourt, L. A., and J. W. Woodlock: "Early Prediction of Market Success for New Grocery Products," *Journal of Marketing*, 25, October 1960, 31–38.

Horsky, Dan, and Leonard S. Simon: "Advertising and the Diffusion of New Products," *Marketing Science*, 2, Winter 1982, 1–17.

Lawrence, K. D., and W. H. Lawton: "Applications of Diffusion Models: Some Empirical Results," in *New Product Forecasting*, Y. Wind, V. Mahajan, and R. Cardozo (eds.), Lexington, Mass.: Lexington Books, 1981, pp. 529–541.

Luce, Duncan R.: *Individual Choice Behavior*, New York: John Wiley and Sons, 1959.

Maffei, R. B.: "Brand Preference and Simple Markov Processes," *Operations Research*, 8, 1960, 210–218.

Moore, William L.: "Concept Testing," *Journal of Business Research*, 10, 1982, 279–294.

Moriarity, Rowland, and Ursula Moran: "Managing Hybrid Marketing Systems," *Harvard Business Review*, 68, November–December 1990, 146–155.

Nagle, Thomas T.: *The Strategy and Tactics of Pricing*, Englewood Cliffs, N.J.: Prentice-Hall, 1987.

Parfitt, J. H., and B. J. K. Collins: "Use of Consumer Panels for Brand Share Predictions, *Journal of Marketing Research*, 5, May 1968, 131–145.

Pringle, Lewis G., R. Dale Wilson, and Edward I. Brody: "NEWS: A Decision-Oriented Model for New Product Analysis and Forecasting," *Marketing Science*, 1, Winter 1982, 1–29.

Pessemier, E. A.: "Varied Individual Behavior: Some Theories, Measurement Methods and Models," *Multivariate Behavioral Research*, 20, January 1985, 69–94.

———: *Product Management: Strategy and Organization*, 2d ed., New York: John Wiley and Sons; reprinted by Krieger, Malabas, Fl., 1988, pp. 170–174.

Rogers, Everett M.: *Diffusion of Innovations*, 3rd ed., New York: Free Press, 1982.

Silk, A. J., and G. L. Urban: "Pretest Market Evaluation of New Package Goods: A Model and Measurement Method," *Journal of Marketing Research*, 15 (2), May 1978, 171–191.

APPENDIX 10-1 TRIAL CURVE ANALYSIS

In the text of this chapter, LAUNCH and TAKEOVER amounts were discussed as they apply to a curve plotting cumulative number of triers. The LAUNCH quantity is the amount of cumulative marketing spending (or the amount of time) needed to attain 10 percent of the maximum potential trial sales. The TAKEOVER quantity is the amount of the same independent variable required to attain 90 percent of the maximum potential trial sales, $\#T_{max}$. If a manager can estimate these two quantities, the TRIAL (or TRIALS) program can fit a suitable curve over the entire range that may be assumed by the independent variable, usually cumulative marketing spending or time.

Another way to obtain the same result is to enter the two parameters of the curve, the shape and scale parameters. This latter option is useful only in the case of analyses that reflect a nearly identical set of conditions as a prior analysis that produced estimates of these parameters.

Where adequate historical records of trial purchases are available, records covering the firm's and/or its competitors' products, they can also fit a formal trial curve. Using both elapsed time and total marketing dollars as independent variables will permit a manager to see how much of the trial rate can be explained by these two variables and to see the degree of commonality across similar products of the shape of the trial curve. Each analysis produces an estimate of the curve's parameters and a measure of how well the curve fits.

If a manager has a reasonable degree of confidence in his or her estimates of the maximum number of people who will try the product and the parameters of the curve, the same computer program produces a useful set of predicted trial sales for each planned level of cumulative marketing spending (or possibly for each time period). However, the program does not permit one to examine possible negative trial.

Whether or not the above prior analysis of sales data has been completed, observed trial following a product's introduction can be used to fit the model. Usually, five or more observations are used to predict future levels of trial. The larger the number of observations, the more confidence can be placed in the model and its predictions. Unfortunately, the longer the stream of observations, the less useful the shorter set of predictions that is based on them will be. Furthermore, in a dynamic environment, larger numbers of observations tend to include progressively less relevant data.

The model requires three primary types of input data:

1. The shape and scale parameters of the model, estimates of LAUNCH and TAKEOVER amounts, or a long enough stream of observations of the dependent variable to estimate the model.

2. An estimate of the maximum number of triers.

3. A stream of independent variable values.

Each stream of independent variables has an associated stream of dependent variables. Some or all of the dependent variables may be recorded as zeros, but these zeros must be contiguous and follow whatever positive values are entered. When the program encounters a zero dependent variable, it produces a forecast using the associated independent variable.

The program outputs are estimates of the model parameters, if these were not part of the input data. Estimates of the dependent variable are provided as called for by the model inputs. As appropriate, the output also includes a measure of how well the model fits the observed data. In addition, for each decile of the trial curve the program provides an associated value of the independent variable. The following illustration uses five observed variable pairs to estimate the dependent variable for the next five independent variables.

The second part of the output uses time as the independent variable and forecasts levels of the dependent variable just as it did in the original analysis. Note, however, that this analysis changes the model parameters. If this type of secondary analysis is desired when entering LAUNCH and TAKEOVER levels or when entering model parameters, a separate run of the program must be made for each case, using cumulative spending or time as required.

TRIAL CURVE ANALYSIS

by

Edgar A. Pessemier

Copyright © 1988 By Edgar Pessemier, Seattle, WA.

Problem: TEST PROBLEM 1   07–09–1988   08:55:53

The independent variable is Cum. Mktg. and its units are Dollars

The units of the sales variable are Units

The maximum number of potential trial sales is 129300
The number of observations is 10

Observation Number	Dependent Variable	Independent Variable	Share of Trial
1	42,800.000	8,800.000	0.331
2	65,700.000	16,800.000	0.508
3	110,500.000	23,900.000	0.855
4	113,800.000	30,100.000	0.880
5	122,300.000	35,400.000	0.946
6	0.000	40,200.000	0.000
7	0.000	44,600.000	0.000
8	0.000	48,600.000	0.000
9	0.000	52,300.000	0.000
10	0.000	55,900.000	0.000

Scale Parameter   17,497.6875
Shape Parameter   1.4736

UNIT VALUE

Dependent Variable	Estimate of Dependent Variable	Residual
42,800.00	39,376.93	3,423.07
65,700.00	78,882.67	−13,182.67
110,500.00	102,754.43	7,745.57
113,800.00	115,315.25	−1,515.25
122,300.00	121,628.76	671.24

Average Relative Absolute Error   0.0739

FORECAST VALUES

Independent Variable	Estimates of Dependent Variable	Estimated Share of Trial
40,200.00	125,013.984	0.967
44,600.00	126,860.273	0.981
48,600.00	127,872.133	0.989
52,300.00	128,446.438	0.993
55,900.00	128,791.242	0.996

Deciles of Cum. Trial	Associated Independent Variable Level
.10	3,800
.20	6,323
.30	8,693
.40	11,092
.50	13,645
.60	16,490
.70	19,847
.80	24,167
.90	30,816
.99	49,324

Observation Number	Dependent Variable	Independent Variable	Share of Trial
1	42,800.000	1.000	0.331
2	65,700.000	2.000	0.508
3	110,500.000	3.000	0.855
4	113,800.000	4.000	0.880
5	122,300.000	5.000	0.946
6	0.000	6.000	0.000
7	0.000	7.000	0.000
8	0.000	8.000	0.000
9	0.000	9.000	0.000
10	0.000	10.000	0.000

Scale Parameter   2.1532
Shape Parameter   1.2852

UNIT VALUE

Dependent Variable	Estimate of Dependent Variable	Residual
42,800.00	40,272.44	2,527.56
65,700.00	77,228.14	−11,528.14
110,500.00	101,343.92	9,156.08
113,800.00	115,208.94	−1,408.94
122,300.00	122,551.37	−251.37

Average Relative Absolute Error 0.0664

FORECAST VALUES

Independent Variable	Estimates of Dependent Variable	Estimated Share of Trial
6.000	126,205.367	0.976
7.000	127,933.992	0.989
8.000	128,717.242	0.995
9.000	129,058.977	0.998
10.000	129,203.117	0.999

Deciles of Cum. Trial	Associated Independent Variable Level
.10	0
.20	1
.30	1
.40	1
.50	2
.60	2
.70	2
.80	3
.90	4
.99	7

REVIEW QUESTIONS

Q10-1 Discuss marketing support's lost trial, how it might be measured, and one or more target levels against which it might be judged.

Q10-2 What drives trial purchases? What drives repeat purchases? (See Figure 10-1.) To what conditions do comparative product preferences apply and what do they mean?

Q10-3 What influences the percentage of people who are aware? What drives the percentage of distribution that supports a product? What does the temporal model of awareness tell you? What does the "share of choice set" mean?

Q10-4 Why might one perform a segmentation or subsegmentation analysis of potential demand? Trial purchases of our product? Repeat purchases of our product?

Q10-5 What can one do when interpurchase times are long? Can LRR be used?

Q10-6 What standards should be used when choosing or defining support spending (mix) elements?

Q10-7 Why should one bother to compute multiple measures of a strategy/budget's economic effectiveness?

COMPUTER EXERCISES

TRIAL CURVE ASSIGNMENTS

1. Use the TRIAL program to fit an adoption/trial curve to the air conditioner data. (Because you do not have expenditure data, use time as your independent variable.) What is your evaluation of the results? For what period (if any) would your cumulative trial curve estimates be useful?

2. Instead of fitting the trial curve to data, as was done in the illustration in Appendix 10-1, enter

ROOM AIR CONDITIONER DATA

Date	Cost of Last Unit Produced	Added	Cum. Added	Scrapped
1947			28	0
1948		48	76	0
1949		58	134	0
1950		130	264	0
1951	$220	155	419	0
1952		235	654	0
1953		708	1,362	1
1954		1,004	2,366	5
1955		844	3,210	17
1956		1,160	4,370	37
1957		1,000	5,370	61
1958	160	1,037	6,407	98
1959		1,187	7,594	154
1960		908	8,502	270
1961		709	9,211	520
1962		800	10,011	761

(Units (000))

Adopted from Carrier Corporation (A), (1964), Harvard Business School Case, 9M84, M99, p. 16.

LAUNCH and TAKEOVER cumulative marketing spending levels of 4,000 and 30,000, respectively. Enter the independent variable sequence shown in the illustrative problem output, but enter all zeros for the associated dependent variables. Compare the results to those found in the illustrative problem. (Note that to compute results for time as an independent variable, appropriate new values must be entered for the LAUNCH and TAKEOVER amounts.)

3. Estimate the LAUNCH and TAKEOVER times and rerun the illustrative problem with these inputs. Compare the results for time and for the above results for cumulative marketing spending.

4. Reenter the data after the units of measure for the dependent variable (trial purchases) and the maximum number of potential triers have been changed from units to thousands. Rerun the analysis and discuss the results.

5. Reenter the data after the units of measure have been changed to thousands as in 4 and also in thousands for the independent variable (cumulative marketing dollars). Rerun the analysis and discuss the results.

6. Increase the maximum number of potential triers to 142,000 and rerun the analysis. Decrease the maximum number of potential triers to 115,000 and rerun the analysis. Discuss the effect of these changes on the forecast levels of trial and the parameter.

7. If you put in estimates of the two parameters of the curve instead of deriving them from input data, what effect would you expect this action to have on the average relative absolute error of the forecasts?

8. In the illustrative analysis in Appendix 10-1, why is the average relative absolute error less when elapsed time is the independent variable instead of cumulative marketing spending? Does it make sense for the model's shape parameter to change when the independent variable is changed?

11

AN ILLUSTRATIVE MARKETING PLAN FOR A NEW PRODUCT: A Spreadsheet Model

The foregoing chapter described a model for assessing the worth of alternative marketing strategies, a model that is most applicable to new or modified products. In this chapter an illustrative application is presented to help potential users appraise the implementation task; describing the market and a set of marketing strategies, evaluating the worth of each strategy, exploring potential improvements in the selected strategy, and setting up the procedures needed to monitor market results.

A lengthy Appendix 11-1 contains detailed instructions for the construction of a spreadsheet model like the one used to analyze the problem described below. Some readers may want to read this material before moving on, others may want to refer to the appendix from time to time, but most can appreciate the illustration without reference to the computational details. The principal purpose of the appendix is to help the person who wants to build a new spreadsheet application.

AN ILLUSTRATIVE APPLICATION

Product ↙

This discussion concerns the possible introduction of a premium/superpremium Canadian whiskey. Since the data used to develop this illustration are fragmentary, the illustration should *not* be considered a serious analysis of the product class or the new product. Instead, the data provide an appreciation of the inputs one must use, the computations that are required, and the final results that one obtains.

The General Problem Statement

In this illustrative case, a manager has been asked by his company to appraise a potential new product in the premium/superpremium segment of the Canadian whiskey category. The company is a large producer and blender of distilled spirits that sells one or more brands in the medium- and high-price levels in each of several product categories.

Issue: appraise potential new product in premium/superpremium segment

In late 1982, the firm marketed two brands of Canadian: a moderately successful medium-priced brand and a popular high-priced brand. The potential new product being considered would give the company a Canadian whiskey product strategy that is similar to the premium brand strategy being used by some distillers in the Scotch whiskey category. Chivas Regal®, a leading superpremium Scotch brand, sells at a substantially higher price than regular premium brands.

Prestige products like superpremium spirits not only require that buyers be aware of the product, they usually require that their peers be aware of the product's status. For example, serving a premium Scotch, Canadian, or gin may impress all of one's guests, even though only a small share of these people consume any particular brand. Media schedules that reach beyond the pool of potential triers may not constitute wasted circulation. Favorable attitudes of non-users can add value to a product.

Many of the better-known brands in the medium and higher price ranges of all categories of distilled spirits were heavily advertised, with spending on individual brands occasionally exceeding $10 million annually. No brand held a large share of total liquor sales, but brands often held large shares in a given category. For example, Bacardi® rum and Smirnoff® vodka held important shares in their respective categories. Among Canadian whiskeys in 1982, Black Velvet® held about a 10 percent share and Canadian Club® held about a 16 percent share. In the same year, Black Velvet spent about $5 million and Canadian Club spent about $12 million on advertising. These figures led management to estimate that at least $800,000 must be spent to sustain a share point in the high-priced end of the Canadian whiskey category.

One of the rationales for considering a new Canadian product entry was the growing popularity of the lighter whiskeys. The volume of all spirits and Canadian's share of spirits sales for selected years appear above along with the projections for 1990.

		YEAR		
	1960	1970	1980	1990
Millions of Gallons, All Types	—	405	430	460
Canadian Percentage of Sales	5	9	12	15

In 1983, a 1 percent share of the total spirits market would yield sales of about 4.31 million gallons, but a 1 percent share of the Canadian category would produce sales of only 540,000 gallons. Therefore, $1.48 per gallon or $.39 per liter for advertising would be needed for an established brand per desired share point of the Canadian whiskey market. At a superpremium price, advertising cost per liter might be higher.

If the premium end of the Canadian category is 25 percent of all Canadian sales, or 13.5 million gallons, a 1 percent share of these sales produces just 135,000 gallons, or 510,000 one-liter bottles. To enter the high-priced end of this market, management decided to look at the $17.50 and $21.50 prices for a one-liter bottle (with comparable prices for other sizes).

Management also believed that after federal and state taxes were paid, retailers and wholesalers received their margins, and the variable cost of production of about $2.80 was deducted, the $17.50 price would leave about $5.60 and the $21.50 price would leave about $7.52 per liter to cover marketing costs and general overhead and provide a profit.

To help think about the target market for the proposed brand, management decided to divide the market into two major segments: males 20–39 with 1982 incomes greater than $25,000, and males 40–64 with incomes greater than $35,000. The younger group included about 15.5 million people and the older group included about 7 million people. Although using only males in the selected age and income brackets was a great simplification, the two primary segments made it easier to position the product and to target the two audiences. Since bar sales and sales to women and elderly males for their personal use were ignored, the forecast of results would be conservative.

Management experienced some difficulty in estimating the number of potential buyers of the new product to be used in the analysis. The 22.5 million males in the target market were first reduced to the number of people who from time to time would purchase premium Canadian whiskey. Ten percent of the younger segment (1,550,000) and 15 percent of the older segment (1,050,000) were expected to fall into this category. In turn, management estimated that 500,000 younger customers and 350,000 older customers were the constituent elements of the 850,000 individuals viewed as potential buyers of a superpremium whiskey. Long term, $4 million was the maximum annual marketing spending contemplated at a 5 percent share of the relevant market.

Going from the target market to a market of potential triers involved evaluating the characteristics of the target market, the demand characteristics of the relevant classes of products, the new product's characteristics, and how the product would be supported with marketing effort. During the planning period, it was believed that 850,000 people were prepared to make one or more purchases of superpremium Canadian whiskey. Besides considering these matters, management estimated that the potential rate of superpremium purchases per capita among older customers was about 50 percent higher than it was among younger customers. A more detailed disaggregate analysis of this market appears at a later point.

It is useful to recall that the analysis of relative brand preference should be confined to brands that are possible substitutes in one or more of the use contexts when potential buyers are willing to consider a superpremium product. The volume of sales for this collection of products is the current market of interest. When the available classifications of sales do not fully satisfy the above conditions, adjusted estimates should be used.

Upscale media were considered appropriate for both younger and older potential buyers, but more athletic, "swinging" copy appeals were planned for the younger segment. Among older buyers, the higher-priced alternative was expected to be popular, principally as a gift item and as a Canadian whiskey to be served to guests. The lower-priced alternative was likely to be more popular among younger buyers as an item of consumption in a social setting. The two prices were expected to produce about the same total sales volume, but the marketing programs would differ in size and emphasis. The higher price would call for a somewhat higher budget and more emphasis on the older segment. These facts are reflected in the market analysis and the proposed patterns of marketing spending.

Cannibalization of the firm's premium Canadian brand was expected to be negligible if the new product were priced at $21.50. At the $17.50 price, the established brand might lose as much as 5 percent of its sales to the new brand.

Actions and the Market Environment

In this and the two following major sections, the order and content reflect the organization of the spreadsheet described in Appendix 11-1. Each subsection discusses the entries required by the illustrative problem for years 1, 3, 6, and 10 in the 10-year planning horizon.

The offer The unit of measure is the 1-liter bottle. Here it is assumed that the 1-liter bottle is representative of the entire mix of sizes that may be sold. If this is not the case, adjustments are needed.

The two alternative prices being analyzed are $17.50 and $21.50 per 1-liter bottle. Prices and costs of all sizes are expected to increase moderately over the years after the planned introduction in 1983. In this illustration, however, no adjustments are made for temporal trends in the cost, demand, or price.

The proposed new product will be a 12-year-old whiskey that can satisfy the most discriminating Canadian drinker. In addition, it will be packaged in a distinctive, aesthetically appealing bottle. During the Christmas season the bottles will come in a high-quality gift wrap suitable for direct giving.

The product's positioning depends in part on the market segment and use occasion. Among older customers, the principal appeal is prestige in social settings and as a gift, with a rare taste treat serving as an added appeal for personal consumption. Among younger customers, moving up and belonging appeals encourage these potential customers to enjoy an affordable luxury. Settings and occasions that are especially attractive to active, socially mobile younger males are planned for this segment. Copy and media selection also support the above positioning strategy.

The question of product name remained open. Serious attention had been given to using some version of the name of the firm's premium Canadian brand but for the moment management plans to use a new name. Whatever name is ultimately used, management thought that the name should convey an image that falls somewhere between the images suggested by the contemporary Black Velvet and the traditional Canadian Club brand names.

Target, product class and potential trier markets   In the introduction to this illustration, the target market was described in some detail. Management chose 22.5 million males in the 20–64 age bracket with middle to upper incomes and then divided this group into two age segments, 20–39 and 40–64. Of these target markets, 10 percent of the younger segment and 15 percent of the older segment were assumed to purchase premium Canadian whiskey. A smaller number were expected to be potential purchasers of superpremium Canadian whiskey.

The per-capita consumption data were calculated by estimating that the latent 1983 demand for premium Canadian brands was 51 million

NUMBER OF MALE CUSTOMERS

	Younger	Older
Target Market	15,500,000	7,000,000
Premium Canadian Buyers	1,550,000	1,050,000
Superpremium Canadian Buyers	500,000	350,000

liters and for superpremium brands, 5.1 million liters. It was further estimated that about the same total quantity would be consumed by the younger and older customers.

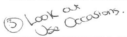

1983 TOTAL PURCHASES IN LITERS
(000,000)

	Younger	Older
Premium Canadian	25.5	25.5
Superpremium Canadian	2.55	2.55

1983 PER-CAPITA CONSUMPTION IN LITERS

	Younger	Older
Premium Canadian	16.45	24.29
Superpremium Canadian	5.10	7.28

Each of these segments was divided into three use contexts: personal use, social use, and gift giving. The distribution of demand across subsegments and each subsegment's estimated liter sales are summarized below.

DISTRIBUTION OF SUPERPREMIUM SALES

Use Contexts	YOUNGER		OLDER	
	%	Liter (000,000)	%	Liter (000,000)
Self	45	1.15	60	1.53
Social	50	1.27	25	.64
Gift Giving	5	.13	15	.38
Total	100	2.55	100	2.55

④ Set Share Objective.

Since the firm hopes to realize at least a 3 percent share of the premium Canadian sales, or 1.53 million liters, the final market share objective is 33 percent of the undeveloped superpremium market. To better judge the reasonableness of the firm's market share objective, management turned to an analysis of the forces that drive the attainment of sales and market share. In doing so, it is necessary to evaluate what share of the 500,000 younger potential superpremium buyers and 350,000 older potential superpremium buyers will eventually purchase the firm's new brand and the rate at which these people will repurchase it.

Comparative preference and share of choice
The central question here is the extent to which the analysis should recognize different degrees of preference (and trial purchase) across the two market segments and the three use contexts for each segment. Management decided to test the impact of the alternative prices and their positioning strategies on product preference in both segments and under the three use contexts. A research design was worked out in which a sample of 300 respondents was drawn from premium Canadian customers in each segment. These people expressed their relative preference for the proposed product at a given price when it was being supported by its associated positioning. Each respondent made choices from a suitable assortment of whiskey brands and under each of the three use contexts. In addition, each respondent estimated his rate of purchase and the percentage of his purchases that are made for consumption in each use context.

In developing these data, it was not clear what products and brands to include in the set from which respondents made choices. Since management believed that at least initially competition (substitution) would take place principally within higher-priced Canadian whiskeys, choices were limited to the upper half of the premium Canadian price range. From this relatively complicated analysis, management obtained the following values of $P(j,k)$, the relative product preference (and trial purchase) for segment j (1 = younger and 2 = older) and subsegment k (1 = personal use, 2 = social use, and 3 = gift giving).

Product Preference

PREDICTED SHARE OF TRIAL CHOICES

Alternative: $17.50	Alternative: $21.50
$P(1,1)= .27$	$P(1,1)= .09$
$P(1,2)= .48$	$P(1,2)= .18$
$P(1,3)= .12$	$P(1,3)= .06$
$P(2,1)= .45$	$P(2,1)= .42$
$P(2,2)= .54$	$P(2,2)= .60$
$P(2,3)= .60$	$P(2,3)= .84$

– older higher.

Market objectives The firm wanted to expand its role in the growing market for Canadian whiskey by establishing itself in the undeveloped superpremium part of the market. Company executives hoped to achieve at least a 3 percent share of the premium market and a major share in the latent superpremium market. Sales of at least 1,530,000 liters in terms of 1983 demand would be required. Initially, media advertising of about $.50 per liter was expected to produce about one share point in the superpremium Canadian product class. No objectives had been stated for the other elements in the marketing mix. Overhead ran about 20 percent of company sales (or about 10 percent of retail sales). After deducting this allocated amount from net contribution profit, management hoped that a brand would earn before-tax profits equal to 20 percent of company sales.

Mix or expenditure categories Management settled on seven budget categories for marketing support spending. Each category is briefly described below.

$M(1) *Local Newspaper:* Introductory and brand awareness advertising run in the sports and business sections of the paper.

$M(2) *National Magazines:* Predominantly prestige copy in upscale magazines like the *New Yorker* and *Gourmet.*

$M(3) *"Swinger" Magazines:* Predominantly socializing, belonging appeals in upscale active settings run in magazines such as *Playboy, Esquire,* and *Sports Illustrated.*

$M(4) *Billboards:* Mainly upscale name recognition copy on painted, lighted boards in major upscale, urban traffic arteries.

$M(5) *Missionary Sales:* Where permitted to improve the percentage of distribution support.

$M(6) *Wholesale Sales:* To obtain wholesale and state liquor commission store distribution and support. Both $M(5) and $M(6) involve a reallocation of sales effort by the firm's sales force.

$M(7) *Christmas Gift Wraps.*

$M(5) to $M(7) include incentives to open accounts and obtain reseller cooperation. The spending levels planned for the two prices are noted below for the four benchmark years in the planning period.

Competitive response   Management believes that one major competitive product entry might appear, but that the product category is too small and too marketing intensive to attract much additional competition. Nevertheless, competitive activities could be strongly influenced by the new product's market success. Finally, a new brand must fight for shelf space. Makers of all brands in the Canadian premium market and many retailers are likely to resist the shelf demands made by the new product.

Market Results

Percentage aware   The awareness measure that management decided to use was based on answers to the question "What brands come to mind when you think about liquor?" The results were then normalized to apply to the Canadian

	MARKETING BUDGET $000,000			
	1983	1985	1988	1992
ALTERNATIVE: $17.50				
Local Newspapers	2.0	2.0	1.4	1.1
National Magazines	2.4	1.5	1.0	.75
"Swinger" Magazines	2.8	2.5	2.05	1.25
Billboards	.6	.5	.35	.25
Missionary Sales	1.2	1.0	.45	.40
Wholesale Sales	2.4	2.0	1.4	1.0
Christmas Gift Wrap	.6	.6	.35	.35
Total	12.0	10.1	7.0	5.1
ALTERNATIVE: $21.50				
Local Newspapers	2.0	1.8	1.25	.95
National Magazines	4.75	3.6	2.4	1.8
"Swinger" Magazines	1.8	1.2	.8	.6
Billboards	.75	.6	.35	.25
Missionary Sales	1.2	1.2	.8	.6
Wholesale Sales	3.0	2.4	1.6	1.2
Christmas Gift Wrap	.75	.6	.4	.3
Total	14.25	11.4	7.6	5.7

CATEGORIES

product class. After this had been done for 1982 data, the percentages for Black Velvet and Canadian Club were 54 and 30, respectively. This top-of-the-mind awareness measure ran in a range from 10.8 percent to 2.4 percent per million dollars of annual advertising.

These data were useful in making subsequent awareness estimates for the new product, but management was conscious of their weaknesses. There was a significant measurement problem that is not easily solved. (See the discussion in Chapter 10). Furthermore, management needed to apply whatever measure is adopted to the level of awareness that can be obtained by advertising designed to influence specific segments of the superpremium Canadian whiskey market, not just potential buyers of Canadian whiskey. For example, some of the spending targeted at one segment may not reach the other segment or leave a lasting impression. Finally, all raw awareness measures tend to make advertising in the early years appear to be less effective, since in later years growing purchases and availability contribute to awareness.

To be conservative, management assumed that early in the product's life, about five to nine percentage points in awareness would be produced by $1 million in advertising. For year 4, ten percentage points in awareness per million dollars of advertising was adopted. The lower expenditures on advertising in years 5 through 10 were considered to be large enough to sustain the awareness rate obtained by the end of year 4. The awareness data at the top of the next column were adopted for potential buyers of superpremium brands under the two prices and marketing budgets noted in the foregoing section.

Percentage distribution Management had fairly good data on the distribution of premium Canadian, but a superpremium might be more like the distribution of superpremium Scotch. After consulting with the firm's sales force and making a careful review of the distribution of both Scotch and Canadian brands in relation to the forcefulness of their marketing programs, man-

	AWARENESS RATE			
	1983	1985	1988	1992
Alternative: $17.50				
Younger Segment	45	64	65	65
Older Segment	33	53	59	59
Alternative: $21.50				
Younger Segment	42	58	59	59
Older Segment	51	71	72	72

agement adopted the percentages of volume-weighted distribution for the new product noted below. Due to changes in shopping habits over time, exposure to the new product was expected to grow some even after the share of outlets stabilized. Some recognition of that fact influenced management's judgments about the components of the trial rate.

	SHARE OF DISTRIBUTION			
	1983	1985	1988	1992
Alternative: $17.50				
% Distribution	40	70	80	80
Alternative: $21.50				
% Distribution	35	65	75	75

Share of choice sets, $f(A,D)$ The percentage of potential buyers of the new product who will know about the new product and have it available at the time of purchase can be estimated by multiplying the percentage of distribution (availability) by the percentage who are aware. Management performed these calculations and then made a small upward adjustment to account for the fact that distribution created its own increment of awareness. The final results for the four key years appear on page 336.

Cumulative trial rate, CTR = $P \times f(A,D)$ Having estimated P and $f(A,D)$, it is a simple matter of multiplication to obtain the table on page 336.

Independent of these computed figures,

A*O

	SHARE OF CHOICE SETS			
	1983	1985	1988	1992
Alternative: $17.50				
Younger Segment	.180	.448	.520	.520
Older Segment	.132	.371	.472	.472
Alternative: $21.50				
Younger Segment	.147	.377	.443	.443
Older Segment	.179	.462	.540	.540

management had made two types of graphs of the cumulative trial curves for each of the segments at each of the two price levels. One graph used time on the horizontal axis and one used cumulative spending on the horizontal axis. These analyses helped management choose cumulative spending levels that could efficiently produce a satisfactory cumulative trial rate by the end of the introductory period. Aggregation of the segment graphs provided an estimate of the time path of the trial rate and the marketing spending needed to produce these results. The

latter plot influenced the data used to compute the above rates. In turn, these rates were used to derive the trial figures that appear on the top of page 337.

Note that the analysis of trial data by use contexts could not be carried forward, because a single person typically made purchases for all three use contexts. Therefore, consumption weighted $P(j,k)$ values from the prior table were used for each of the two primary segments. In turn, the aggregate $P(j)$ data were used to compute the cumulative trial rates. The cumulative number of triers for each segment and price level were obtained by multiplying the aggregate rate by 500,000 for the younger segment and by 350,000 for the older segment.

The components of the repeat purchase rates were analyzed with care, but the details are not presented. It is sufficient to note that at the $17.50 price, the long-run repeat rate is .17 for the younger segment and .09 for the older segment. At the $21.50 price, the rate for the younger segment is .27 and for the older segment, .44.

P*A*O

		CUMULATIVE TRIAL RATE			
Segment	Subsegment	1983	1985	1988	1992
PRICE: $17.50					
1	1	.049	.121	.140	.140
1	2	.086	.215	.250	.250
1	3	.022	.054	.062	.062
2	1	.059	.167	.212	.212
2	2	.071	200	.255	.255
2	3	.079	.223	.283	.283
PRICE: $21.50					
1	1	.013	.034	.040	.040
1	2	.026	.068	.080	.080
1	3	.009	.023	.027	.027
2	1	.075	.194	.227	.227
2	2	.107	.277	.324	.324
2	3	.150	.388	.454	.454

ANNUAL AND CUMULATIVE TRIAL				
	1983	1985	1988	1992
PRICE: $17.50				
Younger Segment				
Annual New Triers	33,075	30,778	4,777	0
Older Segment				
Annual New Triers	22,869	26,161	5,405	0
Cumulative Total Trial	55,944	146,596	177,324	177,324
PRICE: $21.50				
Younger Segment				
Annual New Triers	9,812	10,146	1,662	0
Older Segment				
Annual New Triers	32,987	34,558	5,322	0
Cumulative Total Trial	42,799	110,450	129,329	129,329

[handwritten margin notes: "Aggregation of Segment graphs × 500,000 and 350,0"]

The first analysis The result of analyzing the above data was very disappointing. Some important output measures are shown below. If the below figures are credible, the proposed new product must be rejected or a dramatically more effective strategy must be developed.

Management was somewhat surprised that the sales at the lower price were not larger. Two principal explanations were suggested by the study that had been made of relative product preference: First, at the $17.50 price many premium-priced brands were possible substitutes but at the $21.50 price no substitute brands were available, and second, for those motivated principally by the prestige value of a superpremium, preference increased at the higher price. Nevertheless, management recognized that the research was limited and subject to error, and that there was little relevant experience to rely upon.

A revised strategy After extended discussions, management recognized two major problem areas. First, the assortment of brands used in the preference analysis included many brands that could not be logically included in a separate superpremium category or in the volume esti-

	1983	1985	1988	1992
$17.50 Price				
Annual Unit Sales	85,089	181,122	192,924	188,282
Market Share (5.1)[1]	.0167	.0355	.0378	.0369
Net Contrib. ($000)	(11,824)	(9,568)	(6,670)	(4,797)
$21.50 Price				
Annual Unit Sales	82,370	207,673	239,760	239,216
Market Share (5.1)[1]	.0162	.0407	.0470	.0469
Net Contrib. ($000)	(13,631)	(9,838)	(5,797)	(3,901)

[1]Base: 5.1 million liters.

[handwritten notes: "Issues — Assortment of Brands — Effect of Brand Name"]

mate of 5.1 million liters for that product category. Because relative preference had been measured against this larger set of brands, the effective volume data should have included the sales of all the test brands. When adjusted in this manner, the 5.1 million-liter figure became 20.0 million liters. This raised the per-capita consumption in liters from 5.10 to 20.0 for the younger segment and from 7.28 to 28.85 for the older segment.

Second, management was prepared to rethink the question of brand name since the choice of a name could strongly influence four important elements: the product's relative preference rating, the effort required to reach any level of awareness, the effort required to reach any level of distribution, and the cannibalization that might be experienced. Awareness and, to a lesser degree, distribution would be favorably influenced by the use of some version of the firm's premium Canadian brand name. Call the latter old premium brand name OPB, and the new name NSPB, or new superpremium brand. OPB was priced at $11.50 retail per liter and had a 13 percent market share. The brand was available in 87 percent of all outlets and the level of brand awareness was about 46 percent. By displaying both brands in some of the advertising and by letting OPB create a good part of the awareness needed by NSPB, advertising costs could be reduced. Management believed that somewhat more than half of the level of advertising and personal selling originally planned would produce results for an OPB named superpremium that are equal to the results attainable under the original planned budget for an NSPB-named product.

Although brands like Johnny Walker® Scotch sold both a premium and a superpremium under the same general brand name, it was unclear what effect the use of the OPB name would have on relative preference for the superpremium brand. After much discussion, it was assumed that the effect would be negligible at the proposed $21.50 price. The preference among

current buyers of OPB might increase, but some loss of prestige could occur among buyers of other brands of premium Canadian. Finally, about 5 percent of the sales of the firm's established premium brand was expected to be cannibalized if the OPB name were used.

In response to all of the rethinking outlined above, the larger 20-million-liter market base and the OPB name were adopted. In response to the latter decision, awareness levels were expected to increase by 10 percent of the currently projected unaware when spending 40 percent less on advertising and personal selling. Distribution was expected to increase by 5 percent of the distributors not carrying the new product when sold under a different brand name. The relative levels of product preference were left unchanged and the cannibalization rate was set at 5 percent of the established brand's sales.

Given the new assumptions and estimates, management proceeded to an analysis of repurchase behavior. To estimate LRR for each market segment, management first computed a context-weighted preference score for each segment. The results were .134 for the younger segment and .528 for the older segment. Using these data and the new estimates of distribution, management developed the following estimates of the long-run retention rate under the revised marketing strategy.

	Younger	Older
SBR = Switchback rate	.3	.4
RR = Repeat rate	.2	.5
LRR = SBR/(1 + SBR − RR)	.273	.444

Although these estimates were based on fragmentary data, it is clear that scanner and other types of panel data can be obtained that are relevant both to making prior estimates and to monitoring the progress of a new product's introduction. Since little is known in the present case about how LRR may vary over time, especially as it may be influenced by a changing competitive climate, no direct adjustments are made. It should be remembered, however, that all estimates apply to people who have tried the product and are among the 850,000 who were considered to be possible buyers of the new product and the existing products against which it was tested.

The above repurchase rates apply to people who have tried the new product by the beginning of a year and to half of the people who tried the product during the year. (Alternatively, half the rate could be applied to all new triers during a year.) Using this base of triers gives management an estimate of the number of people to whom the rate of unit purchase and LRR can be applied. Completing these multiplications yields estimates of annual unit sales.

Tables 11-1a to 11-1e show the spreadsheet used to complete the analysis of the new marketing strategy that was based on the above data.

Economic Results

Numerical input rows are marked with an asterisk and text input rows are marked with a T in column 3. The entire spreadsheet will not be reviewed row by row, but a few items will be noted that strongly influenced management's decision to launch the new superpremium using the revised strategy. For each of these items and in the following discussion, the spreadsheet row numbers in question are recorded in square brackets to simplify cross-referencing.

For the analysis of the new marketing strategy, the key output appears in Tables 11-1d and e. By year 5, annual contribution profit [134] had become positive and was likely to stabilize at an annual rate of about $3.5 million. The cumulative net cash flow became positive by year 10. Although the present worth and ROI figures [143 and 145] are unattractive, manage-

ment recognized that the short ten-year planning time horizon contributed to this result. Given the long (indefinite) market life that management believed will follow a successful introduction, the new strategy is deemed to be acceptable. The use of conservative market data that excluded demand from bars, women, and people over 65 further supported approval of the new superpremium Canadian whiskey.

Because the $21.50 price was at the extreme limit of the price per liter, some members of management argued that the analysis should be completed for a $19.50 price as well as the $21.50 price. Others pointed out that it would always be easier to reduce the price than to increase it so they did not want to consider starting with a $19.50 price.

In situations in which significant disagreement arises, results can be computed under each competing set of assumptions. Working up new data sets can be inconvenient but recomputing results is not time consuming. In fact, the capacity to structure and quickly update an analysis is one of the principal strengths of a computerized spreadsheet model. In most situations, a series of different scenarios and inputs can be examined and some assessment can be made of the likelihood that each one represents the true future state of affairs.

In some cases, weighted sums should be produced to estimate an expected outcome for the proposed strategy. For example, one may redo the analysis for a strategy under each of the competitive climates that may occur. Doing so may involve reestimating the preference, awareness, and distribution input data. The recomputations can be completed quickly, and the expected outcome and the range of possible outcomes can be presented to the responsible executive(s). These exercises will not be completed here. Instead, the discussion will turn to the use of graphic output. Graphs are produced as part of the spreadsheet and are updated, as are any other parts of the results when any changes are made in the numerical input.

Just for reference

TABLE 11-1a SPREADSHEET ANALYSIS—ILLUSTRATIVE NEW CONSUMER PRODUCT

	Description/Year		1983	1984	1985	1986	1987	1988	1989	1990	1991	1992
1	SPREADSHEET TEMPLATE—SUPERPREMIUM CANADIAN WHISKEY											
2	Alternative: Higher retail price, $21.50; Limited Premium Market											
3												
4	**Description/Year**											
5												
6	**Offer:**											
7	Units: One liter bottle											
8	Unit Retail Price											
9	(Our Net Yield), $UP:	*	$10.32	$10.32	$10.32	$10.32	$10.32	$10.32	$10.32	$10.32	$10.32	$10.32
10	Unit Variable Cost, $UVC:	*	$2.80	$2.80	$2.80	$2.80	$2.80	$2.80	$2.80	$2.80	$2.80	$2.80
11	Unit Contribution, $UC		$7.52	$7.52	$7.52	$7.52	$7.52	$7.52	$7.52	$7.52	$7.52	$7.52
12	Features: A 12 Year Old Superpremium Canadian	T										
13	Whiskey, Established Brand Name	T										
14	Positioning: The best. An affordable luxury.	T										
15	A taste treat.An outstanding gift.	T										
16												
17	**Target Market and Subseg. Share of Seg. Spending:**											
18	**Segment 1: Males 20-39, Income>$25,000**	*	500000	500000	500000	500000	500000	500000	500000	500000	500000	500000
19	Subsegment 1: personal use, %(1,1)	*	0.450	0.450	0.450	0.450	0.450	0.450	0.450	0.450	0.450	0.450
20	Subsegment 2: social use, %(1,2)	*	0.500	0.500	0.500	0.500	0.500	0.500	0.500	0.500	0.500	0.500
21	Subsegment 3: gift giving, %(1,3)	*	0.050	0.050	0.050	0.050	0.050	0.050	0.050	0.050	0.050	0.050
22	**Segment 2: Males 40-65, Income>$35,000**	*	350000	350000	350000	350000	350000	350000	350000	350000	350000	350000
23	Subsegment 1: personal use, %(2,1)	*	0.600	0.600	0.600	0.600	0.600	0.600	0.600	0.600	0.600	0.600
24	Subsegment 2: social use, %(2,2)	*	0.250	0.250	0.250	0.250	0.250	0.250	0.250	0.250	0.250	0.250
25	Subsegment 3: gift giving, %(2,3)	*	0.150	0.150	0.150	0.150	0.150	0.150	0.150	0.150	0.150	0.150
26												
27	**Preference Share (Share of Informed Choice):**											
28	Seg. 1, Subseg. 1, P(1,1)	*	0.090	0.090	0.090	0.090	0.090	0.090	0.090	0.090	0.090	0.090
29	Seg. 1, Subseg. 2, P(1,2)	*	0.180	0.180	0.180	0.180	0.180	0.180	0.180	0.180	0.180	0.180
30	Seg. 1, Subseg. 3, P(1,3)		0.060	0.060	0.060	0.060	0.060	0.060	0.060	0.060	0.060	0.060
31	**Segment 1, P(1)**		0.134	0.134	0.134	0.134	0.134	0.134	0.134	0.134	0.134	0.134
32	Seg. 2, Subseg. 1, P(2,1)	*	0.420	0.420	0.420	0.420	0.420	0.420	0.420	0.420	0.420	0.420
33	Seg. 2, Subseg. 2, P(2,2)	*	0.600	0.600	0.600	0.600	0.600	0.600	0.600	0.600	0.600	0.600
34	Seg. 2, Subseg. 3, P(2,3)		0.840	0.840	0.840	0.840	0.840	0.840	0.840	0.840	0.840	0.840
35	**Segment 2, P(2)**		0.528	0.528	0.528	0.528	0.528	0.528	0.528	0.528	0.528	0.528
36												

(handwritten annotations: "nod?"; "Dist. of Spend p.332"; "p.333"; "Preferred"; "Preferred")

TABLE 11-1b SPREADSHEET ANALYSIS—ILLUSTRATIVE NEW CONSUMER PRODUCT

1 *SPREADSHEET TEMPLATE—SUPERPREMIUM CANADIAN WHISKEY*
2 **Alternative: Higher retail price, $21.50; Limited Premium Market**

#	Description/Year	1983	1984	1985	1986	1987	1988	1989	1990	1991	1992
37	**Marketing Objectives:** T										
38	Establish a preeminent share T										
39	of the undeveloped T										
40	superpremium market.										
41	**Supporting Spending:**										
42	Local Newspapers, $M(1) *	$1,200,000	$1,100,000	$1,080,000	$950,000	$850,000	$750,000	$700,000	$600,000	$580,000	$570,000
43	National Magazines, $M(2) *	$2,850,000	$2,500,000	$2,160,000	$1,900,000	$1,600,000	$1,440,000	$1,300,000	$1,200,000	$1,100,000	$1,080,000
44	"Swinger" Magazines, $M(3) *	$1,080,000	$900,000	$720,000	$650,000	$550,000	$480,000	$450,000	$420,000	$390,000	$360,000
45	Billboards, $M(4) *	$450,000	$400,000	$360,000	$300,000	$250,000	$210,000	$190,000	$170,000	$160,000	$150,000
46	Total "Pull" Spending	$5,580,000	$4,900,000	$4,320,000	$3,800,000	$3,250,000	$2,880,000	$2,640,000	$2,390,000	$2,230,000	$2,160,000
47	Cum. "Pull" Spending	$5,580,000	$10,480,000	$14,800,000	$18,600,000	$21,850,000	$24,730,000	$27,370,000	$29,760,000	$31,990,000	$34,150,000
48	Missionary Sales, $M(5) *	$720,000	$720,000	$720,000	$600,000	$600,000	$480,000	$450,000	$420,000	$390,000	$360,000
49	Wholesale Sales, $M(6) *	$1,800,000	$1,600,000	$1,440,000	$1,200,000	$1,100,000	$960,000	$910,000	$840,000	$790,000	$720,000
50	Christmas Wrap, $M(7) *	$750,000	$700,000	$600,000	$600,000	$500,000	$400,000	$400,000	$400,000	$300,000	$300,000
51	Total "Push" Spreading	$3,270,000	$3,020,000	$2,760,000	$2,400,000	$2,130,000	$1,840,000	$1,760,000	$1,660,000	$1,480,000	$1,380,000
52	Cum. "Push" Spreading	$3,270,000	$6,290,000	$9,050,000	$11,450,000	$13,580,000	$15,420,000	$17,180,000	$18,840,000	$20,320,000	$21,700,000
53	Total Marketing Spending, $TM	$8,850,000	$7,920,000	$7,080,000	$6,200,000	$5,380,000	$4,720,000	$4,400,000	$4,050,000	$3,710,000	$3,540,000
54	Cooperative Marketing Funds, $CM *	$0	$0	$0	$0	$0	$0	$0	$0	$0	$0
55	Net Marketing, $NTM	$8,850,000	$7,920,000	$7,080,000	$6,200,000	$5,380,000	$4,720,000	$4,400,000	$4,050,000	$3,710,000	$3,540,000
56											
57	**Competitive Response:** T										
58	Not more than one major T										
	competitive entry during the										
	planning period.										
59											
60	**Percent Aware (Adj. A):**										
61	Segment 1, A(1) *	0.420	0.50	0.58	0.58	0.58	0.59	0.59	0.59	0.59	0.59
62	Segment 2, A(2) *	0.510	0.61	0.71	0.71	0.71	0.72	0.72	0.72	0.72	0.72
63	Aggregate Awareness	0.457	0.545	0.634	0.634	0.634	0.644	0.644	0.644	0.644	0.644
64											
65	**Percent Distribution:**										
66	Segment 1, D(1) *	0.350	0.45	0.65	0.67	0.72	0.75	0.75	0.75	0.75	0.75
67	Segment 2, D(2) *	0.350	0.45	0.65	0.67	0.72	0.75	0.75	0.75	0.75	0.75
68	Aggregate Distribution	0.350	0.450	0.650	0.670	0.720	0.750	0.750	0.750	0.750	0.750
69											

Handwritten annotations:

- (top right, with arrow) "Est. Should actually compute from $"
- (near rows 57–58) "No, because — category is too small + too mktg intensive to attract... new... entrants — much higher than industry average"
- (near row 60) "Based on Black Velvet + Canadian Club... — Est."
- (near row 65) "Based on Seagrams + Reserve + Canadian + Scotch + ... of blend of Canadian Club... Begins to lag Pioneer"
- (left margin) "Q8G", "Modified", "by Based on 9/c", "?35c"

341

TABLE 11-1c   SPREADSHEET ANALYSIS—ILLUSTRATIVE NEW CONSUMER PRODUCT

1 SPREADSHEET TEMPLATE—SUPERPREMIUM CANADIAN WHISKEY
2 Alternative: Higher retail price, $21.50; Limited Premium Market

	Description/Year	1983	1984	1985	1986	1987	1988	1989	1990	1991	1992
70	Share of Choice Sets: f(A(j),D(j))										
71	Segment 1, (A(1)*D(1))	0.147	0.225	0.377	0.389	0.418	0.443	0.443	0.443	0.443	0.443
72	Segment 2, (A(1)*D(2))	0.179	0.275	0.461	0.476	0.511	0.540	0.540	0.540	0.540	0.540
73											
74	Cum. Trial Rate: CTR = (a + b*P(j,k)*f(A(j),D(j))										
75	Seg. 1, Subseg. 1, CTR(1,1)	0.013	0.020	0.034	0.035	0.038	0.040	0.040	0.040	0.040	0.040
76	Seg. 1, Subseg. 2, CTR(1,2)	0.026	0.041	0.068	0.070	0.075	0.080	0.080	0.080	0.080	0.080
77	Seg. 1, Subseg. 3, CTR(1,3)	0.009	0.014	0.023	0.023	0.025	0.027	0.027	0.027	0.027	0.027
78	**Segment 1, CTR(1)**	0.020	0.030	0.050	0.052	0.056	0.059	0.059	0.059	0.059	0.059
79	Seg. 2, Subseg. 1, CTR(2,1)	0.075	0.115	0.194	0.200	0.215	0.227	0.227	0.227	0.227	0.227
80	Seg. 2, Subseg. 2, CTR(2,2)	0.107	0.165	0.277	0.285	0.307	0.324	0.324	0.324	0.324	0.324
81	Seg. 2, Subseg. 3, CTR(2,3)	0.150	0.231	0.388	0.400	0.429	0.454	0.454	0.454	0.454	0.454
82	**Segment 2, CTR(2)**	0.094	0.145	0.244	0.251	0.270	0.285	0.285	0.285	0.285	0.285
83											
84	**Potential Demand**										
85	Segment 1, S#(1)	500,000	500,000	500,000	500,000	500,000	500,000	500,000	500,000	500,000	500,000
86	Rate of Purchase, RUP(1) *	20.00	20.00	20.00	20.00	20.00	20.00	20.00	20.00	20.00	20.00
87	**Segment 1 Purchases, SUP(1)**	10,000,000	10,000,000	10,000,000	10,000,000	10,000,000	10,000,000	10,000,000	10,000,000	10,000,000	10,000,000
88	Subseg. 1 Purchases, SUP(1,1)	4,500,000	4,500,000	4,500,000	4,500,000	4,500,000	4,500,000	4,500,000	4,500,000	4,500,000	4,500,000
89	Subseg. 2 Purchases, SUP(1,2)	5,000,000	5,000,000	5,000,000	5,000,000	5,000,000	5,000,000	5,000,000	5,000,000	5,000,000	5,000,000
90	Subseg. 3 Purchases, SUP(1,3)	500,000	500,000	500,000	500,000	500,000	500,000	500,000	500,000	500,000	500,000
91	Segment 2, S#(2)	350,000	350,000	350,000	350,000	350,000	350,000	350,000	350,000	350,000	350,000
92	Rate of Purchase, RUP(2) *	28.85	28.85	28.85	28.85	28.85	28.85	28.85	28.85	28.85	28.85
93	**Segment 2 Purchases, SUP(2)**	10,097,500	10,097,500	10,097,500	10,097,500	10,097,500	10,097,500	10,097,500	10,097,500	10,097,500	10,097,500
94	Subseg. 1 Purchases, SUP(2,1)	6,058,500	6,058,500	6,058,500	6,058,500	6,058,500	6,058,500	6,058,500	6,058,500	6,058,500	6,058,500
95	Subseg. 2 Purchases, SUP(2,2)	2,524,375	2,524,375	2,524,375	2,524,375	2,524,375	2,524,375	2,524,375	2,524,375	2,524,375	2,524,375
96	Subseg. 3 Purchases, SUP(2,3)	1,514,625	1,514,625	1,514,625	1,514,625	1,514,625	1,514,625	1,514,625	1,514,625	1,514,625	1,514,625
97	Total No. of Purchasers, T#P	850,000	850,000	850,000	850,000	850,000	850,000	850,000	850,000	850,000	850,000
98	Total Unit Purchases, TUP	20,097,500	20,097,500	20,097,500	20,097,500	20,097,500	20,097,500	20,097,500	20,097,500	20,097,500	20,097,500
99											

[handwritten annotations: "Demand * Share of Spend" at bottom; annotation near CTR row]

TABLE 11-1d   SPREADSHEET ANALYSIS—ILLUSTRATIVE NEW CONSUMER PRODUCT

1 SPREADSHEET TEMPLATE—SUPERPREMIUM CANADIAN WHISKEY
2 Alternative: Higher retail price, $21.50; Limited Premium Market

	Description/Year	1983	1984	1985	1986	1987	1988	1989	1990	1991	1992
100	**Trial and Repeat**										
101	Aggregate Cumulative Trail Rate, CTR → $P_i f_i \lambda D$.	0.0504	0.0773	0.1299	0.1339	0.1439	0.1522	0.1522	0.1522	0.1522	0.1522
102	Incremental Trial Rate, Seg. 1, ITR(1)	0.0196	0.0104	0.0203	0.0015	0.0039	0.0033	0.0000	0.0000	0.0000	0.0000
103	Incremental Trial Rate, Seg. 2, ITR(2)	0.0942	0.0507	0.0987	0.0075	0.0187	0.0152	0.0000	0.0000	0.0000	0.0000
104	**Switchback Rate**										
105	Segment 1, SBR(1) *	0.3000	0.3000	0.3000	0.3000	0.3000	0.3000	0.3000	0.3000	0.3000	0.3000
106	Segment 2, SBR(2) *	0.4000	0.4000	0.4000	0.4000	0.4000	0.4000	0.4000	0.4000	0.4000	0.4000
107	**Repeat Rate**										
108	Segment 1, RR(1) *	0.2000	0.2000	0.2000	0.2000	0.2000	0.2000	0.2000	0.2000	0.2000	0.2000
109	Segment 2, RR(2) *	0.5000	0.5000	0.5000	0.5000	0.5000	0.5000	0.5000	0.5000	0.5000	0.5000
110	**Longrun Repeat Rate**										
111	Segment 1, LRR(1)	0.2727	0.2727	0.2727	0.2727	0.2727	0.2727	0.2727	0.2727	0.2727	0.2727
112	Segment 2, LRR(2)	0.4444	0.4444	0.4444	0.4444	0.4444	0.4444	0.4444	0.4444	0.4444	0.4444
113	**Aggregate Repeat Rate**	0.3434	0.3434	0.3434	0.3434	0.3434	0.3434	0.3434	0.3434	0.3434	0.3434
114											
115	**Trial of Our Product:**										
116	Segment 1, TP(1)	9,812	5,207	10,146	774	1,936	1,662	0	0	0	0
117	Segment 2, TP(2)	32,987	17,741	34,558	2,624	6,560	5,322	0	0	0	0
118	Total Trial of Our Product, TTP	42,799	22,947	44,704	3,398	8,496	6,984	0	0	0	0
119	Cumulative Trial	42,799	65,746	110,450	113,848	122,345	129,329	129,329	129,329	129,329	129,329
120											
121	**Repeat Purchases of Our Product:**										
122	Segment 1, RP(1)	2661	67721	109591	139374	146765	156577	161110	161110	161110	161110
123	Segment 2, RP(2)	129773	329340	533087	681363	717496	764243	785182	785182	785182	785182
124	Total Repeat Purchases, TRP	156534	397061	644678	820737	864261	920821	946292	946292	946292	946292
125											
126	Total Unit Sales per Period, TUS	199333	420008	689382	824136	872757	927805	946292	946292	946292	946292
127	Cumulative Total Unit Sales, CTUS	199333	619341	1308723	2132858	3005616	3933421	4879712	5826004	6772296	7718588
128	Market Share per Period, MS	0.0099	0.0209	0.0343	0.0410	0.0434	0.0462	0.0471	0.0471	0.0471	0.0471
129											
130	Total Dollar Sales, $S	$2,057,115	$4,334,485	$7,114,419	$8,505,079	$9,006,855	$9,574,948	$9,765,732	$9,765,732	$9,765,732	$9,765,732
131	Gross Margin, $GM	$1,498,983	$3,158,462	$5,184,150	$6,197,500	$6,563,134	$6,977,094	$7,116,115	$7,116,115	$7,116,115	$7,116,115
132	Gross Contribution, $GC	($7,351,017)	($4,761,538)	($1,895,850)	($2,500)	$1,183,134	$2,257,094	$2,716,115	$3,066,115	$3,406,115	$3,576,115
133	Loss to Cannibalization, $CC *	$0	$0	$0	$0	$0	$0	$0	$0	$0	$0
134	Net Contribution, $NC	($7,351,017)	($4,761,538)	($1,895,850)	($2,500)	$1,183,134	$2,257,094	$2,716,115	$3,066,115	$3,406,115	$3,576,115
135											

TABLE 11-1e   SPREADSHEET ANALYSIS—ILLUSTRATIVE NEW CONSUMER PRODUCT

1 SPREADSHEET TEMPLATE—SUPERPREMIUM CANADIAN WHISKEY
2 Alternative: Higher retail price, $21.50; Limited Premium Market

	Description/Year	1983	1984	1985	1986	1987	1988	1989	1990	1991	1992
136	Plant and Equipment	$1,000,000 *									
137	Working Capital, % Sales	$411,423	$866,897	$1,422,884	$1,701,016	$1,801,371	$1,914,990	$1,953,146	$1,953,146	$1,953,146	$0
138	Investment Cash Flow per Period	$1,411,423	$455,474	$555,987	$278,132	$100,355	$113,619	$38,157	$0	$0	($1,953,146)
139											
140	Net Cash Flow per Period	($8,762,440)	($5,217,012)	($2,451,836)	($280,632)	$1,082,779	$2,143,475	$2,677,958	$3,066,115	$3,406,115	$5,529,261
141	Cumulative Net Cash Flow	($8,762,440)	($13,979,452)	($16,431,289)	($16,711,921)	($15,629,142)	($13,485,666)	($10,807,709)	($7,741,594)	($4,335,480)	$1,193,781
142											
143	**Present Value:**	($7,527,841)									
144											
145	**R.O.I.:**	0.011									
146											
147											
148											
149	Model Coefficients										
150											
151	CTR Intercept = a	0									
152	CTR Slope = b	1									
153	Working Capital										
	Fraction of Sales	0.2									
154	Cost of Capital (xxx)	0.15									
155											

(handwritten annotations: "where did these come from" pointing to the model coefficients; "Terminal Value?"; "Tax effects"; "— Tom")

344

USING GRAPHIC RESULTS

An examination of Table 11-1 convinces most people that a less confusing way is needed to present the most important finding of an analysis, and to let the relevant executives grasp the underlying characteristics of a market, especially the way that marketing actions can drive the performance of a product or product line. Graphic summaries are an important route to the more efficient use of spreadsheets that are as detailed as the ones needed to appraise the marketing strategy for a new or improved product.

To indicate some of the uses and benefits of graphic summaries, a substantial number of graphs will be discussed that were developed directly from the data presented in Table 11-1. Although these graphs do not exhaust the possibilities or the breadth of the analysis that can be derived from each one, the advantages gained from the use of graphic data should become clear. To simplify the process, we will concentrate on the more critical first half of the ten-year planning horizon.

Patterns of Marketing Spending

The general strategic thinking that went into the development of the marketing mixes for the strategies that have been examined are described in the foregoing text and do not need to be repeated. It is useful, however, for management to review the expenditure patterns over time to be sure that they are suitable and that the components of both the "pull" and "push" parts of these expenditures are appropriate. Figure 11-1 shows the components of the "pull" parts of marketing spending, media expenditures in the current case. Figure 11-2 shows the components of the "push" segment of marketing spending, principally personal selling and retail promotions.

The "pull" segment is almost twice as large as the "push" segment and both parts decline gradually over the five-year period displayed in

FIGURE 11-1 Media "pull" spending—illustrative new consumer product.

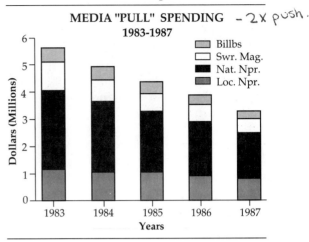

these two graphs. Furthermore, the proportions of the budgets devoted to the various mix elements do not change greatly over the five-year period.

Management put together the mixes it believed would most efficiently yield the target levels of "pull" and "push" results. Analytical

FIGURE 11-2 Distribution "push" spending—illustrative new consumer product.

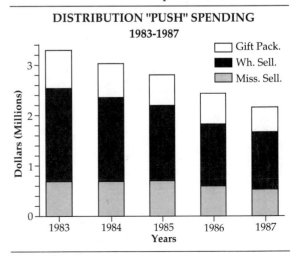

aids to performing this budgeting task are available (see Chapters 12, 13, and 14) but in this illustration it is assumed that the work was performed judgmentally with the aid of historical records of how well various spending patterns had performed.

The Direct Results of Pull and Push Spending

The clear and immediate objective of pull spending is to increase awareness among potential purchasers. The relationship between media expenditures and awareness was explored in Chapter 10. Figure 11-3 shows the relationship which was assumed for the input data used in the spreadsheet analysis. The first-year expenditure of $5.6 million produces the largest increment of awareness. Slowly declining spending levels during the following two years produce further sizable increases in awareness. (These facts might have been clearer if the zero origin had been included.) Expenditures after year 3 only sustain the relatively high level of awareness that will be reached with the aid of cumulative pull spending of about $15 million.

FIGURE 11-3   "Pull" spending versus awareness—illustrative new consumer product.

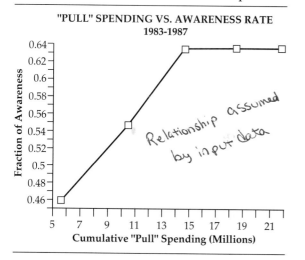

FIGURE 11-4   "Push" spending versus distribution share—illustrative new consumer product.

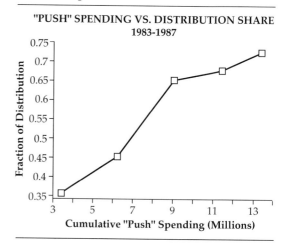

The relationship of cumulative pull spending to the awareness rate lets management deal with direct, measurable results of a major spending component of the product's marketing strategy. Historical records can be developed to produce useful estimates of this response pattern. These data should be used to establish that the input data used to develop Figure 11-3 are reasonable. When the data are accepted, they become benchmarks against which the strategy's actual performance can be measured. Departures of the observed market behavior from these estimates have great diagnostic value, permitting dynamic adjustment of the marketing strategy.

The push component of spending is concerned principally with the work of the field sales organization and with retail promotions. The effect of these expenditures on the share of distribution is shown in Figure 11-4.

The largest increase is obtained during the first year, with the share of distribution starting to level off by year 5. The smaller increase estimated for year 2 reflected management's belief that many distributors would delay stocking the product until the product had proven itself. As in the case of pull spending, the market performance can easily be monitored in relationship to the estimates, simplifying diagnosis and adjustment.

Although the figures are not shown in Figures 11-3 and 11-4, management believes that annual spending of about $2.0 million on pull elements and $1.3 million on push elements will be needed to sustain the levels of awareness and distribution that will produce unit sales of about 950,000 liters. A lower marketing support program would result in a decline in the trial rate and negative annual increments of trial. In other words, spending less than $3.3 million annually on marketing would be a policy of harvesting the brand, seeking increased profits at the expense of declining sales.

Analysis of Demand and Sales

In reviewing the reasonableness of both the size and the distribution of marketing spending, careful attention must be given to who the potential triers are and how trial takes place over time. Figures 11-5 and 11-6 display the cumulative trail rates by segment and subsegment. Trial rates are much lower among the larger but younger segment than they are

FIGURE 11-6 Cumulative trial rate, older segment 2—illustrative new consumer product.

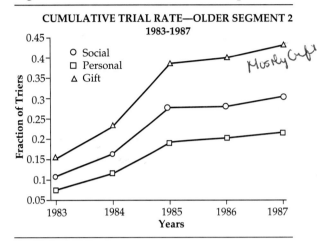

among the smaller but older segment. The younger segment's trial purchases are predominately for social use, with gift-giving motives running a weak third. On the other hand, gift giving is the predominate motive for trial among the older segment. (Note that within each market segment the trial due to each use context was assumed to be a constant percentage over time.)

It is assumed that the marketing mix that was adopted is well suited to these trial rates. In other words, spending efficiently takes advantage of latent opportunities rather than inefficient spending producing a desired rate of trial. Monitoring market results against these predictions permits management to adjust the marketing mix to take advantage of conditions as they are observed.

Figure 11-7 summarizes the temporal changes in the aggregate trial rate. The curve has an S-shaped form often found for relatively new products. The estimated curve in Figure 11-7 met management's prior judgments about the acceptance of new brands of premium whiskeys. It must be observed, however, that both the height and the shape of the curve can be changed by a number of managerial actions. For

FIGURE 11-5 Cumulative trial rate, younger segment 1—illustrative consumer product.

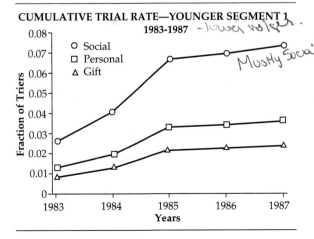

FIGURE 11-7   Cumulative trial rate, all segments—illustrative new consumer product.

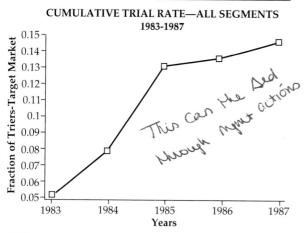

FIGURE 11-8   Units purchased by all segments—illustrative new consumer product.

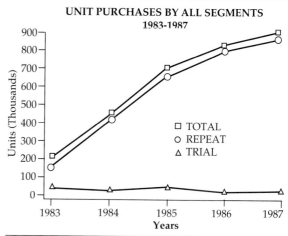

example, the offer can be made more attractive or more can be spent to increase awareness or distribution.

When management examined the kinds of curves shown in Figures 8-2 and 8-3, it was considering how the market would behave under varying degrees of marketing pressure. This analysis led to selecting a level of marketing support that would produce an attractive level of trial in relationship to the spending needed to achieve that level. Overspending involves increasing trial by spending increments that are uneconomically large, and underspending involves failing to increase trial when it is economically attractive to do so. The discussion will return to this topic.

Turning from trial to total unit purchases, it is important to see how unit sales grow over time, and what part of annual unit sales are due to trial purchases and what part are due to repeat purchases. The estimated results for the revised strategy appear in Figure 11-8. The long-run significance of repeat purchasers is clear. They depend to an important degree on the product's desirability (relative preference). It is equally clear that repeat purchases can be made only by people who have made a trial purchase (and are

satisfied with the product). Naturally, management will be very concerned about trial purchases during the first several years of the new product's market life. This focus will shift to repeat purchases as the product becomes better established.

Segment demand is shown in Figure 11-9. Since the analysis reported in this figure was

FIGURE 11-9   Segment unit demand—illustrative new consumer product.

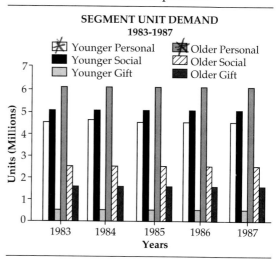

based on the assumption of no temporal change in the structure of potential customers, segment and subsegment differences are the only subject of interest in this graph. It is clear that the largest source of potential unit demand is personal use (10.5 million liters), the second largest demand is social use (7.5 million liters), and the third largest is gift giving (2.0 million liters). These data provide direction for a product's copy platform and media plan. In the common situation in which potential demand is temporally dynamic, these data would also guide changes over time in a marketing strategy.

Market Share Analysis

It is very common for managers to set objectives in terms of market share and to think about various resource commitments in terms of their capacity to produce share gains. There are several problems associated with this perspective. First, it is far from clear what base should be used to compute market share. In the case at hand, the potential sales base of 20 million liters is used, yielding a 4.7 percent share for the product at the end of year 10. If computed on the

basis of the potential purchases of just super-premium products (5.1 million liters), the share would be 18.6 percent. If computed on the basis of all premium Canadian products (51 million liters), the share would be 1.86 percent. Figure 11-10 shows the estimated temporal growth in market share during the first five years after introduction.

Second, connecting resource inputs to share results is complicated by the fact that share does not measure the size of the sales results, but only its size relative to some base. Furthermore, share is influenced by more than one mix element and how (if at all) each interacts with other mix elements. Nevertheless, market share is a useful index when used in conjunction with other measures, because it measures the relative effectiveness of a program and it measures results in a way that is unconfounded with the effect of growth or shrinkage in the product category.

Figure 11-11 shows the relationship of marketing spending to market share and net contribution to profit. Over time, marketing spending declines in relation to market share. The effect of buying market share in the early years is clearly visible. So is the favorable effect of reduced mar-

FIGURE 11-10 Market share—illustrative new consumer product.

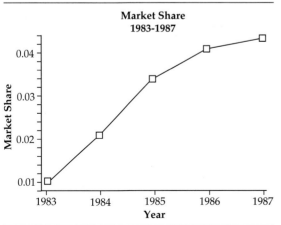

FIGURE 11-11 Market share relationships—illustrative new consumer product.

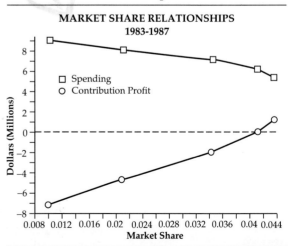

FIGURE 11-12   Dollar sales and net contribution—illustrative new consumer product.

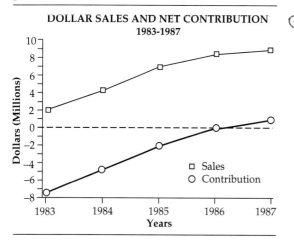

DOLLAR SALES AND NET CONTRIBUTION
1983-1987

keting effort on contribution to profit during later years. The reduced year-to-year changes in sales and profit are also visible. The above effects should be examined for all prior new product entries to help management make estimates for the spreadsheet analyses.

To round out the sales-based analysis of profits, annual dollar sales and net contribution to profits can be placed on the same graph. See Figure 11-12. Four years are expected to pass before annual contribution to profit becomes positive. Both sales and profits increase over the entire five-year period but at a declining rate. As indicated earlier, long-run annual net contribution is estimated to run about $3.5 million. Long-run dollar sales will run about $9.8 million.

SENSITIVITY ANALYSIS

Purpose

Once a market model has been constructed, it can be used for a variety of purposes. First and foremost, it is a test device that forecasts the results of taking a particular set of marketing

actions. Second, it makes explicit the kind of data that must be available, and records the beliefs about the nature of the market held by one or more members of management. Third, it can be used as an educational tool, communicating the beliefs of one or more people to others in the organization. Fourth, it can be used to enhance a person's or group's understanding of how each of a wide variety of marketing actions, changes in market structure, or estimates about market response will affect important intermediate results and final measures of economic effectiveness. In the two following sections, the first and fourth purposes will be explored in some detail.

Test strategies   At several earlier points, it was observed that one of the important advantages of spreadsheet software is its capacity to recompute model results rapidly and accurately after changes have been made in model inputs. In the present case, model inputs can be divided into three major classes: actions that are the direct product of a marketing strategy, estimates about the structure of the market, and estimates about market behavior that are related to the first two items.

Most sensitivity analyses are concerned with examining the effects of alternative marketing actions and estimates of market behavior. Although these items can be tested with the aid of a series of basic spreadsheet models, they do not display the old and new inputs or the old and new results in a convenient form. By using a three-dimensional spreadsheet program, one can easily compare the results of changes with the original results or with other alternatives. Each new spreadsheet is stacked in the third dimension so alternatives can be compared across the stacked spreadsheets. Typically, all spreadsheets will have the same row labels, even though some of the entries may be zeros, and the same column labels.

Hierarchical model structures   Figure 10-1 presented a flow diagram of the effects of mar-

FIGURE 11-13 Economic flow model for marketing planning.

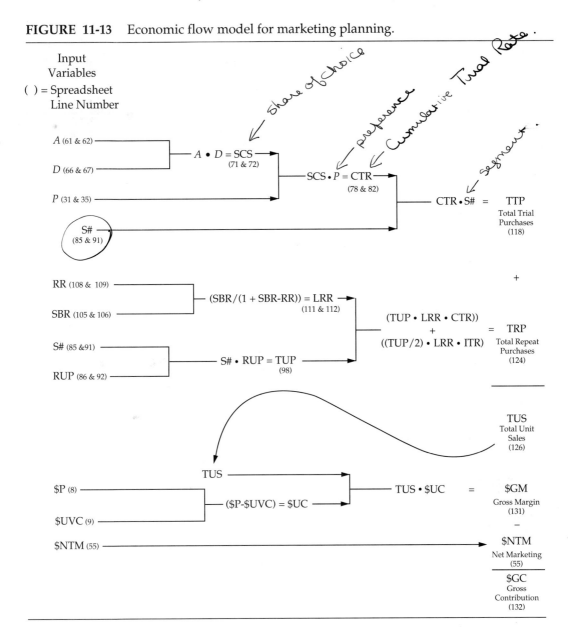

keting actions on trial and repeat purchases. Figure 11-13 extends these relationships, carrying the flow of effects down to the level of economic effectiveness.

In most sensitivity analyses, the focus is on how changes in one or more input variables change the economic effectiveness of an alternative. It is usually desirable to carefully examine the entire flow of causality shown in Table 11-1 and Figure 11-13, noting how changing an input variable changes each successive affected variable. An understanding of these hierarchical relationships can help a manager formulate more effective alternative strategies, which can be tested by the spreadsheet methods that are outlined here.

Illustrative Sensitivity Analyses

Two analyses are presented below. The first one is a sensitivity analysis that analyzed the lower-priced strategy for the illustrative Canadian whiskey. The second analysis discusses the overall effect of simultaneous changes in two variables.

Lower priced alternatives   In the foregoing whiskey illustration, management had concluded that the high-priced strategy was the best. Nevertheless, at least one person believed that a price between the two prices that had been examined would be a better choice. This position was based on the assumption that a retail price in the range from $18.95 and $19.50 would be much more appealing to the younger market segment and would do little or nothing to reduce the appeal of the brand to the older market segment. In an attempt to assess the attractiveness of this alternative and the assumptions on which it was based, the concerned individuals first used a supplemental spreadsheet analysis in which the retail price was reduced to $19.35 and the annual unit price (revenue) was reduced by 10 percent to $9.29. The preference for the brand among younger potential buyers

was increased by 20 percent of the feasible increase (1 minus the current level of preference).

A second, more aggressive approach was also examined. In this case, the same price and preference changes were employed but it was further assumed the media expenditures in "swinger" magazines would be increased by $1 million in each of the first two years. The expected effect of this spending increase was to increase the brand awareness of the younger segment and the brand's availability to this group of potential buyers. The latter assumptions were included in the analysis by increasing the awareness rates and the distribution rates for the younger segment by 10 percent of the feasible increase. A few summary results from the analyses of the two pricing alternatives are noted in the table below.

Both of the reduced price alternatives produced improved measures of effectiveness. The question is, is the gain large enough to outweigh the loss of pricing flexibility? Clearly, it would be easier to reduce the price after some market experience had accumulated than it would be to raise the price.

Some unresolved issues   The question raised in the above paragraph and a number of related questions remained unanswered at this point. Some of them might be answered by further analysis and additional marketing research. Chapter 12 describes an analytical approach determining an efficient set of annual budgets

SENSITIVITY ANALYSIS—YEAR 10

Description		Unit Sales	Mkt. Share	Net Contr. (000)	Cum. Net Cash Flow (000)
Alternative 1	Prior	946,292	.0471	$3,576	$1,194
	New	1,155,433	.0575	$3,786	$3,956
Alternative 2	Prior	946,292	.0471	$3,576	$1,194
	New	1,194,362	.0594	$4,209	$6,428

and the distribution of each budget to various strategic objectives. Nevertheless, it is important to recognize that the cost in time and money may not justify the effort. There will always be unanswered questions and residual doubt at the point at which a final decision must be made.

In addition, there are some unresolved modeling issues that should be recognized. A price change is certain to have an effect on the brand preferences of potential buyers. This effect was accounted for in the illustrative analyses. The possible effect of a price change on primary demand, either increasing the purchases made by a current potential customer or increasing the number of potential customers, was not recognized. These and related modeling questions are addressed in Chapter 12.

CONCLUDING REMARKS

In the foregoing chapter and in this chapter, a model of the market has been presented and the process of developing a marketing plan for a new or improved product has been reviewed. The basic steps are briefly reviewed below.

Choose a Model of the Market

The market model presented here uses a series of natural intervening variables and the concepts of push and pull to classify support spending. A spreadsheet could have been developed that focused on a single measure of marketing support effectiveness, such as market share or unit sales. For a new or improved product where trial is important to the product's success, a more disaggregate approach that employs direct measures of effectiveness is recommended. The next chapter presents a formal model that allows a manager to go from planned expenditure levels directly to forecasts of intervening variables and economic outcomes. Furthermore, the model lets one confidently select the best division of efforts between pull

and push as well as between retaining buyers and attracting former buyers.

Chapters 13 to 15 discuss a model that does use changes in market share as a principal measure of the results produced by marketing action. The latter model is applied to the problem of determining the best size of an established brand's annual budget, and how these funds should be divided among the various mix elements or spending categories.

Regardless of the specific model one chooses to use, several important matters must be attended to. The model user needs to have a clear definition of the model's structure and the individual input variables that enter the model, a capacity to obtain the data that the model demands, and a firm understanding of how model inputs influence forecast results.

Defining Marketing Alternatives

The second key step in the planning process is to develop a set of promising marketing alternatives. Doing so is principally a managerial art that is based on a detailed knowledge of the market. Furthermore, it is not sufficient to loosely describe the alternatives. Each one must be stated in terms of the model's required inputs to make direct analysis possible. Additional information must be provided to help those responsible to estimate the values of the input variables and the effects that these variables will produce.

Examining Model Results

Once the data are in hand for the alternatives and the model has been run for each one, it is time to review the model's various intermediate and final measures of effectiveness. This examination may lead to a revision of the inputs, particularly if the results appear to be inconsistent or unreasonably large or small. Next, it is useful to discard the clearly dominated strategies and perform sensitivity analyses on selected variables in the remaining strategies. This alternative-narrowing, alternative-improvement process should continue until several marketing plans emerge. These plans may be individually attractive but have competing advantages and disadvantages that are not fully accounted for in the final measures of effectiveness. The Canadian whiskey illustration involved the kind of process that has just been described. It should be noted, however, that a simple illustration necessarily lacks the richness of detail that is typically encountered in a natural setting.

Postdecision Actions

Once a strategy has been selected, management must settle on the measures of effectiveness that will be used to track the success or failure of the plan, establish the review points that will be used, and authorize the collection and analysis of data. As market results accumulate, management must revise the inputs to the model, recompute the forecast, and make such revisions in the marketing plan as may be called for by the emerging situation.

When a marketing plan is revised, the usual cycles of formulating alternatives, developing forecasts, and performing sensitivity analyses should be followed that were used during the original planning process. Until the product matures and the market approaches equilibrium, these review and adjustment efforts assume a key role in determining the success or failure of a new market entry.

Communicating the Marketing Plan

As soon as a plan or plan revision takes shape, a good deal of thought should be given to the written form the plan will be given. Long and short forms may prove to be useful. If only a long form is employed, it should have a short summary as its first section. In most cases, an approved plan should be rewritten in several forms to serve as implementation instructions for the various people and organizational elements who will be responsible for putting the plan into effect.

REFERENCES

Pessemier, Edgar: *Product Management: Strategy and Organization*, 2d ed., New York: John Wiley and Sons, 1982; reprinted by Krieger, Malabar, FL, 1988.

APPENDIX 11-1 GENERAL SPREADSHEET LAYOUT FOR THE ANALYSIS OF A STRATEGY

Here, the discussion turns to the format a manager can use to appraise the desirability of each strategy and budget alternative. It is assumed that the general characteristics of each strategy are well defined, but the analysis process can lead to redefining part or all of each strategy and budget alternative.

In performing the analysis, it is further assumed that a spreadsheet program similar to Lotus 123®, SuperCalc®, or Excel® will be used to store the relevant data and perform the computations that are required. The *dominant layout* of a spreadsheet is one that uses one sheet to represent a single strategy/budget. The columns define each year (or period) in the planning horizon. The rows define the actions, marketing responses, and economic consequences. If several different strategies and budgets are being considered and a three-dimensional spreadsheet program is being used, alternatives can be stacked in the third dimension for easy comparison.

To simplify the work, a manager may initially analyze only a few years and fill in the intervening years' data and results at a later time. For example, if a ten-year planning period is employed, only the columns for years 1, 3, 6, and 10 may be used initially. Doing so may permit the elimination of some dominated strategies/budgets before all the years have been analyzed and complete comparative results have been computed for the surviving strategies/budgets.

Turning to the row definitions, a natural order of analysis starts with the *actions* taken *and* the associated market *environment*. The actions include the offer and the marketing support given to the offer. The environment is principally concerned with the competitive climate and the market's perceptions of and preferences for the manager's offer. When these elements have been developed, the *market results* of the strategy/budget should be laid out in enough detail to permit a full analysis of their *economic consequences*.

We now turn to a detailed description of the spreadsheet: row descriptors, the data required, and how the required computations are made for each year in the planning period. *In this example, it is assumed that the product modeled is a frequently purchased product and that repeat sales are a function of the switchback and repeat rates.* When reading this section, it is helpful to have a copy of Figures 11-1Aa, 11-1Ab and 11-1Ac available. The first section deals with Figure 11-1Aa.

Actions and Market Environment

Offer   *Price, variable cost, and contribution margin* Price per unit, $UP, usually refers to the average price per unit that the product will yield. Any convenient unit of measure, such as packages, cases, or pounds, can be used but it should be clearly stated and used throughout the analysis. The price per unit should be net of all reductions except those made purely for promotional purposes. The cost of promotional price reductions should appear at a later point in the spreadsheet as marketing expenses since the reductions are often used to achieve some short-term push or pull marketing objective. On the other hand, if quantity discount schedules apply and customers are given discounts for prompt payment, the unit price should be the predicted average unit net yield.

The analysis should recognize the expected year-to-year changes in average unit price caused by strategic changes, customer learning, changes in competitive pressure, and other evolving influences.

If price refers to a product line instead of a single product, price is the average net yield (as defined above) from a unit of sales. In this case, the unit is made up of the expected mix for the constituent products. For example, if the net yield from a unit of A is $1.00 and from a unit of B is $2.00 and two units of A sell for every unit of B, the unit price of the new artificial (analytical) unit of 2A and 1B used in the analysis will be $4.00. In forecasting sales and comparing contribution margin, the artificial unit is used. At any

point, however, artificial units can always be converted back into the natural units of the constituent products. Note especially that the composition of an artificial unit and therefore the price used can vary from year to year and from one strategy and budget to another.

Unit variable costs, $UVC, are average unit variable costs per period and should be stated in the same bases as unit prices. If price refers to a product line, then so should costs. Generally, unit variable costs will change over time because of experience curve effects.

The unit contribution margin, $UC, is the difference between price and variable cost per unit, $UC = $UP − $UVC.

Features and positioning   The specific features and planned changes over time should be stated in order to lessen possible confusion about the product definition and required changes. The positioning strategy should be clearly stated and planned changes should be noted. These are textual entries.

Size of market   *Total number of purchasers*   T#P is the total number of purchasers in the BASE of analysis. (In this example, a consumer product is assumed and T#P refers to people rather than organizations.) T#P will be equal to either #TM, the number of people in the target market, or #PCB, the total number of product class buyers. In this example, T#P = #PCB.

If final customers differ to an important degree in terms of their rate of unit purchase or their responsiveness to various types of marketing actions a manager may take, segmentation analysis is needed. If the market is segmented, a separate row needs to be reserved for each class of final customers. If subsegments exist, they should be represented hierarchically with subsegments under segments.

In this example, it is assumed that it is possible to segment the market into J segments. In this case, S#(j) is the number of purchasers in segment j. The total number of purchasers is equal to the sum of the purchasers in each of the segments:

$$T\#P = \sum_{j=1}^{J} S\#(j) \qquad (11\text{-}1A)$$

FIGURE 11-1Aa   Spreadsheet template for marketing planning.

Layout of a Spreadsheet Template

Alternative ————————————————————

Time Periods: ————————————

Descriptions	1	2	3	...
Offer: Units Unit Price (our sales price) $UP Unit Variable Cost, $UVC Unit Contribution, $UC Features:	Text: ———————— ...			
Positioning:	Text: ———————— ...			
Target Market: Segment, Subsegments, and Share of Segment Spending	Text: ———————— ... % (j, k)			
Comparative Preference Share: Segment 1, P(1) Subsegment 1, P(1, 1) Subsegment 2, P(1, 2) Segment 2, P(2)	= SUM all k (P(j, k)* % (j, k), where % (j, k) = share of segment j's purchases in subsegment k.			
Market Objectives:	Text: ———————— ...			
Supporting Spending: Mix Element 1, $M(1) Mix Element 2, $M(2) Mix Element N, $M(N) Total Mktg, $TM Cooperative Mktg Funds, $CM Net Mktg $NTM	= SUM all i($M(i)) = $TM - $CM			
Competitive Response:	Text: ———————— ...			

(Left margin labels: ACTIONS & MARKET ENVIRONMENT)

Furthermore, the j segments may be broken into K_j subsegments. If the subsegments are purchase units instead of subsegments like purchase occasions for each purchase unit, the total number of purchasers is the sum of all the purchasers in each of the subsegments [where the percentage of the jth segment that is in the kth subsegment is $\%(j,k)$]:

$$T\#P = \sum_{j=1}^{J}\sum_{k=1}^{Kj} S\#(j)\%(j,k) \qquad (11\text{-}2A)$$

FIGURE 11-1Ab Spreadsheet template for marketing planning.

Layout of a Spreadsheet Template

Alternative ______________________________

Time Periods: ____________

	Descriptions	1	2	3	…
MARKET RESULTS	Percent Awareness: *A* Segment 1, *A*(1) Segment 2, *A*(2)				…
	Percent Distribution: *D* Segment 1, *D*(1) Segment 2, *D*(2)				…
	Share of Choice Sets: f(*A*, *D*) Segment 1, f[*A*(1), *D*(1)] Segment 2, f[*A*(2), *D*(2)]				…
	Cumulative Trial Rate: CTR = a + b[*P*(j, k)* f(*A*(j), *D*(j))] Segment 1, CTR (1) Subsegment 1, CTR (1, 1) Subsegment 2, CTR (1, 2)	= SUM all j[CTR(j, k)* %(j, k)], or direct estimate			…
	Potential Demand Segment 1, S # (1) Rate of Purchase, RUP (1) Segment 1 Purchase, SUP(1) = S # (1)* RUP (1) Subsegment 1 Purchase, SUP (1, 1) = SUP (1)* % (1, 1) .... Segment 2, S # (2) Rate of Purchase, RUP (1) Segment 2 Purchase, SUP(2) = S # (2)* RUP (2) Subsegment 1 Purchase, SUP (2, 1) = SUP (2)* % (2, 1) .... Total Number of Purchasers: T # P = SUM all j[S # (j)] Total Unit Purchases: TUP = SUM all j[Sum all k(SUP (j, k))], or SUM all j(SUP (j))				…

When the period of analysis is several years long, it is likely that the total number of purchasers, T#P, will change. In this case T#P should have a temporal subscript. Usually, it is assumed that marketing actions by any company will not change the overall size of the market, but that they will shift market shares.

Total number of units purchased The total number of units purchased of all competing brands during a period is TUP. As with T#P, it is usually assumed that actions of individual firms do not influence the total number of units purchased, just which brands are purchased. RUP is the rate of unit purchase or the average number of units purchased per period by

FIGURE 11-1Ac Spreadsheet template for marketing planning.

Layout of a Spreadsheet Template

Alternative _____

Time Periods: _____

Descriptions	1	2	3	...
				...
Trial of Our Product				
Segment 1, TP (1)	= ITR (1)* S # (1) ⎰ a trial cannot be			
Subsegment 1, TP (1, 1)	= TP (1)* % (1, 1) ⎱ distributed but aggregate trials can.			
Total Trial of Our Product, ~~TPP~~ TTP	= Sum all j(SUM all k (TP(j,k))), or SUM all j (TP(j))			...
Repeat Purchase of Our Product				
Segment 1, Subsegment 1, RP (1, 1)	= SUP (1, 1)* CTR (1, 1) $_{t-1}$ * LRR + (SUP(1, 1)/2)* ITR(1, 1)$_t$ * LRR			
Segment 1, Subsegment 2, RP (1, 2)	= SUP (1, 2)* CTR (1, 2) $_{t-1}$ * LRR + (SUP(1, 2)/2)* ITR(1, 2)$_t$ * LRR			
Total Repeat Purchases, TRP	= SUM all j (sum all k (RP(j, k)))			...
Total Unit Sales in Period t, TUS	= TTP + TRP			
Cumulative Total Unit Sales, CTUS	= SUM all t (TUS(t))			
Market Share in Period t, MS	= TUS/TUP			...
Total Dollar Sales, $S	= TUS* $ UP			
Gross Margin, $ GM	= TUS* $ UC			
Gross Contribution, $ GC	= $ GM - $ NTM			
Net Contribution, $ NC	= $ GC - $ CC			...
Plant and Equipment				
Working Capital (___ % Sales)				
Investment Cash Flow				
Net Cash Flow in Period t				
Cumulative Net Cash Flow				
Present Worth: _____				
(Discount Rate: _____)				
ROI: _____				...

(Left margin vertical label: ECONOMIC RESULTS)

each of the potential purchasers. Therefore, the total units purchased is the product of the number of purchasers times the average quantity purchased:

$$TUP = T\#P \times RUP \qquad (11\text{-}3A)$$

When the market is segmented, each segment, j,

may have a different average purchasing rate, RUP(j). Here, the total units purchased is a weighted sum of the average units purchased by each segment:

$$TUP = \sum_{j=1}^{J} S\#\ (j) \times RUP(j) \qquad (11\text{-}4A)$$

In this example, it is assumed that each of the sub-segments in the *j*th segment has the same purchase rate RUP(*j*). The total number of purchases in the *k*th subsegment of the *j*th segment is SUP(*j,k*). Notationally,

$$SUP(j,k) = S\#(j) \times RUP(j) \times \%(j,k) \quad (11\text{-}5A)$$

Comparative share of preference   Because the product, price, positioning, and competitive offers tend to change over the planning period, *P* must also change. Therefore, *P* needs to be stated for each year. Customer knowledge and beliefs usually change slowly, so dramatic short-run shifts are uncommon.

As with the total number of purchases and total number of purchasers, the share of preference can be analyzed either by segment or by subsegment if large differences occur across these groups. If preference differs by segment, the relative preference for the product in the *j*th segment is *P(j)*. Similarly, the preference in the *k*th subsegment of the *j*th segment is denoted by *P(j,k)*. The average preference of the *j*th segment is

$$P(j) = \sum_{k=1}^{Kj} \%(j,k) \times P(j,k) \quad (11\text{-}6A)$$

Similarly, the average preference across all segments is a weighted average of the segment preferences:

$$P = \sum_{j=1}^{J} (S\#(j)/T\#P) \times P(j) \quad (11\text{-}7A)$$

If these segments have greatly differing purchase rates, the relevant weighting should be by number of purchases per segment rather than by people.

Marketing objectives   Next, the objectives of the strategy/budget should be stated in operational terms. For example, annual goals can be stated both for direct results such as levels of awareness and distribution as well as indirect results such as cumulative trial, repeat purchase rates, and sales. If the objectives are well founded, the failure of an alternative to meet them means that it is unattractive. On the other hand,

developing a strategy and budget which exceed the stated objectives provides encouragement.

Some of the objectives may be general ones that apply to all of the firm's new product opportunities. Others may be specific to a market or a current situation. In any case, they should include key elements that a manager's superiors will examine when approving or rejecting a strategy/budget, and that they will use to measure the success of a new product program. An absence of such a set of objectives can lead to confusion, misunderstandings, and the adoption of weak strategies and budgets.

Support spending   *Defining the mix elements and their measures of effectiveness*   Here, the total amount spent on each of the previously defined support elements is recorded. This should include all major marketing support spending regardless of the source of the funds. Only categories that are directly related to outputs should be included.

Spending by element   The way spending is expressed may vary from category to category. When sales commissions are used, sales compensation is frequently budgeted as a percentage of sales. Other marketing expenses may be expressed in a similar manner, but the majority of marketing spending is budgeted in dollar amounts. The total expenditure on the *i*th of the *I* marketing support elements is recorded as $M(*i*). The total marketing spending, $TM, is the sum of the expenditures on each of the *i* mix elements:

$$\$TM = \sum_{i=1}^{I} \$M(i) \quad (11\text{-}8A)$$

A second consideration is the degree to which marketing costs are borne by others, especially suppliers. In soft drink bottling, a large part of a bottler's marketing expenditures may be borne by Coca-Cola, Pepsico, and other providers of extract. Similar arrangements are found elsewhere. These externally provided funds can be an important part of a firm's marketing expenditures but they must be excluded when computing contribution to profit. The cooperative marketing expenditures are denoted as $CM.

Total spending—gross and net   The presence of various kinds of cooperative marketing funds and discount structures makes it necessary to recognize both gross and net marketing spending. *Gross spending is a measure of marketing effort, whereas net spending measures the cost of the marketing effort.* Therefore, net marketing spending, $NTM, is total spending minus cooperative expenditures:

$$\$NTM = \$TM - \$CM \qquad (11\text{-}9A)$$

Competitive responses   This is a textual entry detailing expected current and future competitive moves in terms of both the offer and level and type of marketing support.

Market Results

Four market responses have to be included in the spreadsheet: awareness, distribution, trial sales, and repeat purchases. In turn, trial and repeat sales are summed to obtain total sales.

Awareness   The awareness rate, A, in each time period should be linked to the level of marketing support. For example, an equation similar to Equation (10-10) could be used to estimate awareness in each period based on advertising expenditures. Alternatively, the awareness rate can be set directly. In either case, one needs to think about the level of awareness that can be achieved with different levels of support.

If the analysis is carried out at the segment level, it is possible to estimate different levels of awareness for each of the J segments, $A(j)$.

Distribution   Similarly, the percentage of distribution coverage can either be directly estimated for each period or it can be made a function of marketing support expenditures. If desired, different distribution levels can be reported for various segments, $D(j)$.

Trial   The cumulative trial rate, CTR_t, is estimated for each period with one of the following functions:

$$CTR_t = P_t \times f(A_t, D_t) \qquad (11\text{-}10Aa)$$

or

$$CTR_t = a + b \times (P_t \times f(A_t, D_t)) \qquad (11\text{-}10Ab)$$

where the function $f(A_t, D_t)$ may be equal to the product of A_t and D_t or some more complicated function.

The incremental trial rate in the tth period, ITR_t, is calculated using Equation (10-2):

$$ITR_t = CTR_t - CTR_{t-1}$$

If either P, A, or D differs by segment and subsegments, then CTR and ITR will be segment or subsegment rates and will be denoted by $CTR(j,k)_t$ and $ITR(j,k)_t$. The segment trial rates will then be given by:

$$CTR(j)_t = \sum_{k=1}^{K} CTR(j,k)_t \times \%(j,k) \qquad (11\text{-}11Aa)$$

and

$$ITR(j)_t = \sum_{k=1}^{K} ITR(j,k)_t \times \%(j,k) \qquad (11\text{-}11Ab)$$

The total number of people who have tried the product by period t, $\#T_t$, is calculated by multiplying the cumulative trial rate, CTR_t, by the total number of purchasers in period t, $T\#P_t$:

$$\#T_t = CTR_t \times T\#P_t$$

and the corresponding number of people that try the product in period t, TP_t, is

$$TP_t = ITR_t \times T\#P_t \qquad (11\text{-}12A)$$

Similarly, the total number of people in segment j who have tried the product by period t, $\#T(j)_t$, is

$$\#T(j)_t = CTR(j)_t \times S\#(j) \qquad (11\text{-}13A)$$

and the number of people in segment j that try the product in period t, $TP(j)_t$, is

$$TP(j)_t = ITR(j)_t \times S\#(j) \qquad (11\text{-}14A)$$

Repeat purchases   Because this example deals with a frequently purchased product, there are two formulas for repeat purchases. One is for repeat purchases made during the same year as the trial purchase and the second is for repeat purchases made in the years after the trial purchase. (This analysis is not broken down by segment in the manner shown in Figure 11-1Ac. The number of repeat purchases made by people who made their trial purchase in the same period, RFP_t, is given by Equation (10-4):

$$RFP_t = ITR_t \times (TUP_t/2) \times LRR$$

The number of repeat purchases made by people who made their trial purchase in a previous period, RBP_t, is given by Equation (10-5):

$$RBP_t = CTR_{t-1} \times TUP_t \times LRR$$

The total number of repeat purchases, TRP_t, is the sum of these two as given in Equation (10-6):

$$TRP_t = RFP_t + RBP_t$$

Sales   Total unit sales of this product in period t, TUS_t, is the sum of trial and repeat sales in this period:

$$TUS_t = TTP_t + TRP_t \qquad (11\text{-}15A)$$

Market share   Dividing the product's projected unit sales, TUS, by the market's projected unit purchases, TUP, yields an estimate of the product's market share, MS. This share applies to a market made up of potential triers of the product class and not some broader, less relevant group of final customers. However, share can be computed on any meaningful base.

Economic Results

Computations dealing with the economic results for a new product begin in the middle of Figure 11-1Ac, the third page of the illustrative spreadsheet. Starting with a period's total dollar sales, the economic results have their principal summary expressions in the net contribution to profit, the investment needs, and the net cash flow. The sequence of calculations that starts with unit sales and ends with the net cash flow is described below.

Dollar sales   Total dollar sales, $\$S_t$, is given by:

$$\$S_t = TUS_t \times \$UP \qquad (11\text{-}16A)$$

If price varies across market segments and it is necessary to account for these differences, dollar sales must be developed at the segment level and summed to get total dollar sales.

Gross margin   Due to changes in unit sales, unit price, and unit variable cost, gross margin also may change from period to period. Each period's gross margin is equal to total unit sales times unit contribution margin:

$$\begin{aligned}\$GM &= TUS \times \$UC \\ &= TUS \times (\$UP - \$UVC)\end{aligned} \qquad (11\text{-}17A)$$

This relationship suggests a variety of ways to improve gross margin before considering direct marketing costs.

Gross contribution   Gross contribution is gross margin less the firm's or business unit's marketing expenditures on behalf of the new or revised product. The net marketing spending is total marketing spending less any cooperative funds received from outside sources in support of the firm's marketing effort on behalf of the new product.

$$\$GC = \$GM - \$NTM \qquad (11\text{-}18A)$$

Net contribution   If the new product does not cannibalize existing products, gross and net contribution are equal. Cannibalization can reduce the contribution to profit that a new product will yield. In turn, the losses in sales of other products must be converted into losses in annual contribution which are labeled cannibalized contribution, $\$CC$:

$$\begin{aligned}\$CC = &\ TUS \times (\%TUS \text{ from Cannibalization}) \\ &\times (\$UC \text{ of Cannibalized Product(s)})\end{aligned} \qquad (11\text{-}19A)$$

$\$CC$ is deducted from gross contribution to arrive at the net contribution for the period, $\$NC$:

$$\$NC = \$GC - \$CC \qquad (11\text{-}20A)$$

Investment   In the present analysis of a new product's strategy/budget, items like test marketing and buy-in marketing costs are considered ordinary expenses and are recognized in the period in which they are incurred. On the other hand, plant and equipment costs and working capital needs are recognized as investment cash flows. (If after-tax cash flows are considered, depreciation and other noncash expenses must be recognized in tax computations and added back to obtain net cash flows.) The recoverable value of the investments includes working capital and is treated as a cash inflow at the end of the final period in the analysis. Although the definition of investments used here is somewhat arbitrary, it provides a clear separation of marketing and nonmarketing commitments called for by the new product.

Measures of strategy effectiveness over a stated economic life So far the analysis has focused on the events that take place within a year or other time period. To judge the worth of a strategy/budget, a longer perspective is needed. Although the economic life of plant and equipment will generally exceed ten years, the latter period is usually long enough to complete a suitable analysis. If it is not, a period as long as twenty years can be considered. The longer period, however, necessarily incorporates "iffier" estimates. If the success of a project is strongly contingent on results in the ten- to twenty-year interval, the proposed new product carries considerable risk.

Although not all of the following measures are displayed on Figure 11-1Ac, they all can be of some value in appraising the acceptability of an alternative strategy/budget and in making comparisons between opportunities outside a single product class or business unit.

Present value One of the more widely used measures of a proposal's desirability is its present value. This index is computed by summing the discounted annual net cash flows over the planning horizon (or economic life) for the strategy/budget. The discount rate used is usually the firm's risk-adjusted cost of capital. The larger the positive present value of an alternative strategy/budget, the more preferred the alternative.

"Payback" period Managers are usually interested in how long an alternative strategy/budget will have a negative cumulative cash flow. Until a new product

pays back its up-front negative cash requirements, any adverse change that precipitates termination of the product's sales will result in an out-of-pocket loss. It is during this period that the proposed product is particularly vulnerable to unexpected adverse developments. For this reason, alternatives with long payback periods are riskier than alternatives with short payback periods.

Unit sales to payback This measure is similar to the temporally based payback period described above. It is simply cumulative unit sales through the period required for cumulative cash flow to turn positive. This number may be more meaningful than the payback period is to marketing personnel as a way to judge the riskiness of alternative strategies/budgets.

Expected annual market share The market share that must be achieved each year is also a hurdle that has important meaning to marketing personnel. In some product classes and some markets, management can easily gauge what is an attainable or unattainable market share given the marketing program being contemplated and the likely competitive response.

Expected final market share per cumulative net marketing dollar In many cases, the market development effort for a new product is designed to reach a certain market share objective by the end of the planning period. For this reason, it is useful to see how efficiently that objective can be obtained. By dividing the expected final market share by the cumulative net marketing spending, one obtains a convenient index for use in comparing alternative strategies/budgets.

Expected cumulative net contribution per cumulative net marketing dollar A financially oriented measure of marketing efficiency is obtained by dividing the cumulative net contribution by the cumulative net marketing spending. Alternatives that return a relatively large contribution per marketing dollar make better use of marketing resources. This type of marketing efficiency can be especially important when marketing dollars must be rationed across a set of opportunities.

REVIEW QUESTIONS

Q11-1 Review the spreadsheet formulas to see if any are in error or need simplification.

Q11-2 In the Canadian whiskey illustration, can you think of a better demand analysis and segmentation scheme than the one used?

Q11-3 How would you predict the required comparative preference, share-of-choice values for an offer? Should one monitor these data? If so, how?

Q11-4 How would you estimate awareness as a function of support spending? Should one monitor these data? If so, how?

Q11-5 Do one or more perceptual mapping studies, joint space analyses, or conjoint studies have a role to play in the illustration?

Q11-6 How, if at all, would you change the support spending (mix) categories used by management?

Q11-7 Were the right prices tested? Test another price, making any needed changes in other data.

Q11-8 Try some alternative values of SBR and RR to see how LRR responds and how profits are affected.

Q11-9 Considering the relationships in Figure 11-13, do some sensitivity analyses on the spreadsheet in Tables 11-1a through 11-1e.

Q11-10 When faced with a new problem, describe how you would change the number and definition of the market segments and the number and definition of the support spending elements needed to create a spreadsheet template.

Q11-11 Did management make a good choice of the data to graph? What graphs would you add or drop?

COMPUTER EXERCISES SPREADSHEET EXERCISES

ASSIGNMENT I

Activate Lotus 123® and retrieve CANSPR.WK1 from the CAMP directory on the C: drive.

Go to line 8 in column D (1983). Change the price realized by the brand seller to $11.75, implying a retail price of $24.95. Copy the price to columns E (1984) through M (1992).

Go to lines 28 through 30 and lines 32 through 34 in column D and make these entries:

Seg. 1, Subseg.	1	.08
	2	.15
	3	.05
Seg. 2, Subseg.	1	.45
	2	.65
	3	.85

As each entry is made, copy it to columns E through M.

Recalculate the spreadsheet and review the financial results on lines 128 through 145, comparing them with those shown in Table 11-1c. Discuss the effects of the changes that you made.

If you save this spreadsheet, name it CANSPR1.WK1 or use some other previously unused file name.

ASSIGNMENT II

Retrieve a fresh copy of CANSPR.WK1 from the CAMP directory on the C: drive.

Go to lines 61 and 62 and lines 66 and 67. Add .05 to each of the entries in columns D through M.

Recalculate the spreadsheet and review the intermediate results on lines 71, 72, 78, 82, 102, and 103. Also, review the financial results in lines 128 through 145. Discuss the effects of the changes that you made.

If you save this spreadsheet, name it CANSPR1.WK1 or use some other unused name.

ASSIGNMENT III

Retrieve a copy of CAN0.WK1 from the CAMP directory on the C: drive.

Reorganize the worksheet so it will apply to the machine tool illustration that was discussed in Chapter 7. In particular, use five mix elements of your own choosing and organize the market into two major industry segments and a third "All Other" segment. Under each segment, include three subsegments; small, medium, and large customers.

Test the new spreadsheet by entering sample data in years 1983 and 1984. Are the totals correct?

If you save this spreadsheet, name it TOOL.WK1 or use some other unused file name.

ASSIGNMENT IV

For the machine tool illustration in Chapter 7, describe how you would estimate the product preference, awareness, and distribution entries required to complete an analysis like the one that is outlined in the spreadsheet that you developed in Assignment III. Also describe how you would monitor these variables after the product was introduced. Will it be easier or harder to monitor trial and repeat purchases? Explain.

ASSIGNMENT V

Load the CAN083.WK1 spreadsheet from the CAMP directory into your Lotus 123® program. This file has a substantial amount of missing data for the year 1983. See lines 18 and 22 concerning the size of the market segments; lines 42–45 and 48–50 concerning support spending; lines 61–62 and 66–67 dealing with awareness and distribution; and lines 105–106 and 108–109 dealing with the components of repeat purchasing.

Since the offer is unchanged, choose a new level of 1983 support spending and its distribution to the mix elements. Record these figures and, as needed, adjust the levels for years 1984–1992. Make new entries for the size of the market, accounting for any change in size that may be due to the new spending levels. Adjust the subsequent years' market size as necessary. Make new estimates of the levels of awareness and distribution related to your new levels of support spending, and adjust subsequent years as necessary. Enter new estimates of the components of the 1983 repeat purchase rate and all of the affected following years.

When the spreadsheet has been recalculated, look at the results, commenting on the effectiveness of your new pattern of marketing support spending. If you save the spreadsheet, save it with a new name, say CAN084A.WK1.

12

DIRECT FORMULATION OF MULTIPERIOD PLANS AND BUDGETS: NEW OR MODIFIED PRODUCTS

The causal relationships that operate when a new or modified product is marketed were discussed in Chapter 10. Particular attention was given to the division of sales between trial purchases and subsequent repeat and switchback purchases. In addition, emphasis was given to the roles of awareness and distribution, and to how these elements are driven by the pull and push components in a product's marketing budget. Chapter 11 illustrated the application of a spreadsheet model that incorporated all of the elements that were outlined in Chapter 10.

The approach that was presented relied on the manager or the marketing research staff to estimate the levels of intervening variables, like rates of awareness and distribution and repeat and switchback purchases. Although these variables are functions of the spending patterns adopted by a manager, methods were not provided that allowed one to go from spending patterns to intervening variables, or to key results like the cumulative trial rate and the long-run retention rate.

This chapter is devoted to remedying that limitation by formally specifying the process by which marketing actions produce changes in A, D, RR, and SBR. Doing so extends rather than re-creates the basic model presented in the two foregoing chapters. Although the extended model could be presented in a spreadsheet format (see Appendix 12-1, the section on Forecasting Market Results), *a simpler representation is built into the NEWSTRAT computer program. A version of the Canadian whiskey data is used to illustrate the use of this program.*

The discussion is conducted at two levels. The body of the chapter text de-emphasizes the technical features of the model by focusing principally on the managerial issues. Although a good deal of notation is employed, the bulk of it was introduced in Chapters 8–11. Appendix 12-1 is devoted to additional discussion about model components, how one can estimate the coefficients from data, how to use this chapter's results to enhance the spreadsheet model, and some thoughts about coefficient validity and model behavior.

CUMULATIVE TRIAL RATES

In the case of a new or modified product, initially a marketing program focuses on generating trial. The trial rate is a function of three variables: P, product preference; A, product awareness; and D, product distribution. Their relationship is shown in the following equation:

$$CTR_t = a + b[P \times f(A_t, D_t)]$$

or

$$CTR_t = a + b[P \times (A_t \times D_t)] \qquad (12\text{-}1)$$

The latter form is used here. When P is fixed and A_t and D_t are measured at regular intervals, a simple regression will produce estimates of the coefficients a and b. As long as these coefficients are applied to products with properties that are similar to those used in the regression analysis, they can be used to predict the cumulative trial rate. The offer is fixed, so P is fixed for the analysis, but A_t and D_t are driven by the manager's marketing expenditures.

Together A_t and D_t determine the brand or product's *Share of Consideration Sets* at time t, SCS_t. It is the share of the potential buyers who will be aware of the product and have it available at the time of purchase. SCS_t is related to A_t and D_t in the following manner:

$$SCS_t = A_t \times D_t \qquad (12\text{-}2)$$

The above definition applies to market aggregates and the current model. A common alternative definition concerns the number of brands that someone considers on a given purchase occasion without reference to availability; see Roberts and Lattin (1991).

Given the above structure, a manager may find it desirable to examine how the cumulative trial rate is influenced by differing annual levels of total marketing spending that are efficiently allocated to push and pull activities. Both historical evidence and the perceived urgency to establish the product's market position guide the establishment of the total spending levels. In turn, these decisions affect the cumulative trial rate, CTR_t, for each year and the share of consideration sets among potential buyers. If A_t and D_t are unknown, SCS_t can be estimated for a target level of CTR_t.

$$SCS_t = (CTR_t - a)/(b \times P) \qquad (12\text{-}3)$$

As Equation (12-2) shows, the share of consideration sets grows as awareness and/or distribution increases. Awareness is directly increased by pull spending that is designed to influence final buyers. Distribution is directly increased by push spending that is designed to influence resellers. If a method can be found to link PULL$\$_t$ and PUSH$\$_t$ spending to levels of awareness and distribution, a manager can compute the levels of CTR_t that a given set of budget allocations will produce.

Linking PULL$\$_t$ to Awareness

Before a product is introduced, no one is aware of it. At the end of the first period following introduction, awareness is increased by PULL$\$_1$ spending and exposure of the product by resellers. At the end of the second period, some of those who were aware during period 1 will forget about the product. These people and the people who did not become aware during period 1 can be made aware by period 2's spending, PULL$\$_2$, and exposure of the product by resellers. These relationships can be generalized and stated symbolically for the awareness rate:

$$A_t = \alpha A_{t-1} + \beta(1 - \alpha A_{t-1})\text{PULL}\$_t^{\#} + \sigma(1 - \alpha A_{t-1})D_t$$

Share remaining aware	Share that can become aware	Pull spending per target customer	Share that can become aware	Rate of distribution (12-4)

| | Direct effect of pull$ on awareness | | Indirect effect of distribution | |

The first term on the right of the equal sign is particularly significant because it defines the rate of awareness that remains after forgetting eliminates some people who were previously aware. Therefore, α is a decay (or carryover) coefficient that can be estimated experimentally, from panel data or from a regression using data for similar products. In this discussion and in the associated illustration, it is assumed that $\alpha = .8$.

The term $(1 - \alpha A_{t-1})$ measures the percentage of people who are available to become aware in the tth time period. It is this rate that is affected by PULL$\$_t$ spending. But because the amount spent is spread over the number of people who are potential customers, T#P, pull spending is converted to dollars per potential buyer, PULL$\$_t^\# = $ (PULL$\$_t$/T#P).[1] The β coefficient determines the effect that pull spending will have on the period's rate of awareness.

The last term in the equation deals with the contribution made by distribution to awareness. Once again, the percentage unaware in period t is $(1 - \alpha A_t)$. Unlike pull spending, however, D_t is the fraction of all commodity volume (AVC)(ACV) distribution that the product has during period t, usually a year. The σ coefficient determines the effect that distribution has on increasing awareness, playing the same role for distribution that β plays for pull spending.

Equation (12-4) allows one to go from PULL$\$_t$ spending (and knowledge of the effect of PUSH spending on distribution) to an estimate of awareness provided that the β and σ coefficients can be estimated. Appendix 12-1 demonstrates how these estimates can be made with the aid of a regression program like the one included in Lotus 123®. In the absence of adequate historical data, a manager can develop estimates of the model's coefficients from subjective estimates

---

[1] It might be informative to use #TM in place of T#P as a normalizing constant. Even if this change is made, some spillover of pull activities to a broader group is likely to occur. In any case, the efficiency of reaching *any* group greater than T#P is reflected in the higher pull costs associated with reaching it.

about market responsiveness. This latter procedure is used in a following illustrative application of the NEWSTRAT computer program.

Linking PUSH$\$_t$ to Distribution

Before a product is introduced, distribution is zero, but by the end of the first period the product has gained some fraction of the available distribution support as measured by its share of all commodity volume of distribution. The fraction gained, D_1, must be attributed to push spending on behalf of the product, PUSH$\$_1^\#$, and the product's value to resellers. The former variable is measured in terms of dollars spent per potential customer, and the latter variable is measured by the product of the product's relative desirability to consumers, P, and the relative amount the firm will spend to support the product, TM$\$^* = $ TM$\$_t$/CTM$\$_t$. When the product of these two variables grows, so does the ease with which resellers can sell the product—a larger fraction of potential buyers know about the product and like it. In the second time period, the above influences on distribution remain at work. In addition, most of the distribution attracted during period 1 is expected to continue in period 2. Therefore, the equation for D_t has a similar structure to the one that was developed for A_t.

$$D_t = \Gamma D_{t-1} + \delta(1-\Gamma D_{t-1})\text{PUSH}\$_t^\# + \epsilon(1-\Gamma D_{t-1})(P \times \text{TM}\$_t^*)$$

Retained distribution	Dist. that can be affected	Push spending per target customer		Dist. that can be affected	Product appeal to resellers

Direct effect of ~~PULL$~~ PUSH$ on awareness

Indirect effect of the product's appeal on ~~awareness~~ distribution   (12-5)

The term ΓD_{t-1} is the carried-over distribution and Γ is the decay parameter. Like the α parameter in Equation (12-4), it is greater than zero and less than one. Here, it is assumed that it is .8, but the value of Γ can be estimated by the methods outlined in Appendix 12-1. A regression procedure can be used to estimate δ and ϵ, the coefficients that respectively determine the contribution of PUSH\$$_t^{\#}$ per potential customer and the contribution of the product's commercial desirability to the rate of distribution.

With the aid of Equation (12-5) and the estimated coefficients, push spending (and the contribution of the product's relative desirability to resellers) can be used to estimate the rate of distribution, D_t, in future periods. This rate is a major component of the product's share of consideration sets, SCS_t, and the associated cumulative trial rate; see Equations (12-1) and (12-2).

Dynamics of Push Spending

In some cases, there is a distinct trend in push activities as a product becomes established. Initially, push effort is devoted to opening reseller accounts. The order and characteristics of the target resellers to whom this account opening activity is directed can modify the pattern, but normally it gets off to a vigorous start and then declines over time. Equation (12-5) can be modified to allow for this temporal effect.

Push dollars are also spent to gain cooperation in a firm's promotions, cooperative advertising, and the like. Unlike the push dollars spent to open accounts, spending on reseller marketing effort produces short-term results and less carryforward effect. Furthermore, the number of resellers to whom this activity is directed grows as more of them carry the firm's product. Therefore, spending on these activities becomes a larger share of push spending as a product becomes better established. An equation can be written for this separate form of push. Doing so would allow one to combine an equation for resellers gained with an equation for cooperation gained.

The above elaboration of the model is seldom warranted because most of the differences in the effects of the two kinds of spending can be rec-

ognized by the choice of Γ, the distribution decay coefficient. If push is predominantly devoted to opening accounts and little subsequent effort is needed to encourage cooperation, Γ will be relatively large, as will the carryover effect. On the other hand, if the accounts that are opened require high levels of effort to maintain cooperation, Γ will be smaller and distribution must be sustained by continued push expenditures. In the latter case, the coefficients might be made time dependent, but expanding the model to this degree will seldom be feasible.

Declining Effectiveness of Spending on Awareness, Distribution, and Trial

The term $(1 - \alpha A_{t-1})$ appears in the expression that accounts for the effect on awareness of pull spending. This term becomes smaller as awareness grows. Therefore, the increase in awareness that a given pull expenditure will produce declines as the prior rate of awareness increases. [Similar statements can be made about the analogous term's effect on distribution in Equation (12-5).] Because awareness initially grows, the amount lost each period by decay also increases. With the effectiveness of pull dollars tending to decrease and the amount of the decay loss tending to increase, uniform substantial amounts of pull spending per period will eventually lead to an equilibrium level of awareness. At this point, the gains made will just offset the decay losses.

As the above discussion implied, the term $(1 - \Gamma D_{t-1})$ in the equation for distribution has the same effect that the $(1 - \alpha A_{t-1})$ term in Equation (12-4) had on awareness. The more distribution one gains, the less that remains to be gained. As distribution tends to increase over time, the effect of push spending tends to decline, and the decay losses tend to grow. Here again, if uniform amounts of push spending are employed each period, an equilibrium level of distribution will be reached. At this level, the distribution lost is just offset by that gained.

It is important to recognize the shifting efficiency of a budget. In the period during which a product establishes its place in the market, a manager should spend more heavily because efficiency is high. Later efficiency decreases so less will be spent and sales maintenance becomes a principal objective. The manager's problem is to choose the right sales targets, given the resources that are required to reach these targets. The model equations that have been presented form the basis for choosing the most profitable trial sales targets and the budgets needed to reach them.

Some Empirical Observations Concerning Equations (12-4) and (12-5)

Several analyses have been completed to illustrate some of the behavior implied by Equations (12-4) and (12-5). A simplified version of the TEST PROBLEM data for the NEWSTRAT program was used (see Figures 12-1A–12-1C), but annual spending on marketing was set at a uniform $9,000,000, 40 percent allocated to pull and 60 percent to push. The level of awareness, distribution, and the share of choice sets were computed for each of ten years, along with the annual contribution of the retrained, direct, and indirect components to awareness and distribution.

The above analyses were completed under two basic conditions; a) starting with year one estimates of the awareness (.457) and distribution (.35) rates provided by management, and b) using only the model parameters derived from managerial judgments to compute the first year levels of awareness and distribution. Except for year one of CASE A, all estimates were made using TEST PROBLEM parameters and data[2] in Equations (12-4) and (12-5). The following details cover selected distribution and awareness rates *and* the components of these rates; the

[2]Alpha = .8, Gamma = .8, Beta = .0343, Sigma = .1885, Delta = .0443, Epsilon = .8695, TNP = 850,000, CTMD = 25,000,000, P = .3.

	CONTRIBUTION TO THE RATE	
	CASE A	CASE B
Distribution (Computed using (12-5))		
Year 1 Retained		.000
Direct PUSH$		.275
Indirect		.094
Total D_1	.350	.369
Year 2 Retained	.280	.295
Direct PUSH$	.198	.194
Indirect	.068	.066
Total D_2	.546	.555
Year 10 Retained	.595	.595
Direct PUSH$	.111	.111
Indirect	.038	.038
Total D_{10}	.744	.744
Awareness (Computed using (12-4))		
Year 1 Retained		.000
Direct PULL$		.145
Indirect		.070
Total A_1	.457	.215
Year 2 Retained	.366	.172
Direct PULL$	.092	.120
Indirect	.065	.087
Total A_2	.523	.379
Year 10 Retained	.530	.527
Direct PULL$	.068	.069
Indirect	.066	.066
Total A_{10}	.664	.662

retrained (carryover) rate from the prior year, the rate increase that was directly due to current spending on either pull or push, and the rate increase that was due to the indirect effect of other current influences.

The conclusions that can be drawn from these analyses are:

In any *given period*, the rate of awareness or distribution may depend more on the retained effect and indirect effect than on current direct spending.

Indirect contributions to both awareness and distribution are relatively large and can be equal to direct contributions later in a product's market life. See especially year ten.

Differential responsiveness per dollar leads to the relatively efficient 60–40 allocation of marketing spending in favor of push activities. The resulting rates of distribution are higher than the rates of awareness.

Although the details are not shown in the above table, these expected results were observed: 1) the retained effect becomes larger before it reaches a steady state, 2) it becomes a predominant component of both the rate of distribution and awareness, and 3) the annual contribution from marketing spending to these two rates declines as the retained rates increase.

These analyses also permit one to see how the annual share of consideration sets, $SCS_t = A_t \times D_t$, behaves over time.

SHARE OF CONSIDERATION SETS, SCS_t

YEAR	CASE A RATE	CASE B RATE
1	.160	.079
2	.285	.210
3	.370	.318
4	.422	.390
5	.455	.435
6	.472	.461
7	.483	.476
8	.489	.485
9	.492	.490
10	.494	.493

Several important market characteristics are illustrated by the above data:

Early results strongly depends on what management assumes can be achieved by a first year budget. Contrast CASE A with CASE B.

Later year results, however, may not be strongly influenced by what has been achieved by first year marketing spending. See the share of consideration sets in years five through ten.

If a less efficient allocation of the marketing budget is employed, lower levels of SCS_t are observed. For example, if 20 percent and 60 percent allocations to pull are used, the year ten results for CASE A are .477 and .472 respectively, and for CASE B are .474 and .471.

In considering the above analyses, one must remember that the same annual budget and budget allocation were used for all ten years. Also, the model parameters came from the TEST PROBLEM and no constraints were employed. Other inputs will produce different computed values.

Restating the Influences on Awareness and Distribution

A useful way to simplify Equations (12-4) and (12-5) is to change the dependent variable in each case from a simple rate for the period to the change in the rate expressed as a fraction of the largest possible change. The changes in awareness and distribution are, respectively, $(A_t - \alpha A_{t-1})$ and $(D_t - \Gamma D_{t-1})$. The largest possible changes in the awareness and distribution rates are, respectively, $(1 - \alpha A_{t-1})$ and $(1 - \Gamma D_{t-1})$. Therefore,

Relative change in awareness rate
$$= RCA_t = (A_t - \alpha A_{t-1})/(1 - \alpha A_{t-1})$$

and

Relative change in distribution rate
$$= RCD_t = (D_t - \Gamma D_{t-1})/(1 - \Gamma D_{t-1})$$

Using the above dependent variables, the two basic equations simplify to

$$RCA_t = \underset{\substack{\text{Change} \\ \text{contrib. by} \\ \text{direct PULL\$} \\ \text{per capita}}}{\beta PULL\$_t^{\#}} + \underset{\substack{\text{Change indirectly} \\ \text{contrib. by} \\ \text{PUSH\$}}}{\sigma D_t} \qquad (12\text{-}6)$$

and

$$RCD_t = \underset{\substack{\text{Change} \\ \text{contrib. by} \\ \text{direct PUSH\$} \\ \text{per capita}}}{\delta PUSH\$_t^{\#}} + \underset{\substack{\text{Change indirectly} \\ \text{contrib. by the} \\ \text{appeal to resellers}}}{\epsilon (P \times TM\$_t^{*})} \qquad (12\text{-}7)$$

In each equation, just two elements contribute to the relative change, one directly driven by either pull or push spending and one that is the indirect effect of the other factors. If the relative importance of the effect of direct spending is known or can be estimated in each case, one can easily estimate the β and δ coefficients. The size of the σ and ε coefficients can be determined in the same manner if the values of D_t and $(P \times TM\$_t^{*})$ are available.

Restating Equations (12-4) and (12-5) in the above manner further clarifies the meaning of the coefficients and simplifies calculating the coefficients either from historical data or, in the absence of usable historical data, from managerial judgments. The latter approach is employed in a following illustrative application of the NEWSTRAT program to the Canadian whiskey problem.

Dividing the Budget

If meeting trial sales targets is a reasonable goal during the early years of a new product's market life, how should these targets be met? Because the offer and P are fixed in the analysis, one must obtain a suitable share of the buyers' consideration sets. Efficiently doing so requires spending the right amount on marketing effort and choosing the right division of the effort between pull spending directed to final buyers

and push spending directed toward resellers. Here, the discussion is confined to a general examination of the right division of TM$_t$, the product's total marketing budget for period t. Ways to determine the right size of TM$_t$ will be examined at a later point.

The easiest way to see how a budget should be divided is to observe that *if* it is equally costly to add increments to the awareness rate and the distribution rate, the two rates should be equal. A demostration is helpful.

$A_t + D_t$	$A_t \times D_t = SCS_t$
.2	$.1 \times .1 = .01$
.3	$.2 \times .1 = .02$
.4	$.3 \times .1 = .03$
but	
.4	$.2 \times .2 = .04$
.5	$.3 \times .2 = .06$
.6	$.4 \times .2 = .08$
but	
.6	$.3 \times .3 = .09$
	. . .

In the last case above, if the total of the rates were distributed in an extreme fashion, say $A_t = .5$ and $D_t = .1$, the product would be .05 instead of .09. When costs are equal, the "best" results are obtained when $A_t = D_t = (SCS_t)^{1/2}$.

Unfortunately, the cost of an increment in the awareness rate does not in general equal the cost of the same size increment in the distribution rate. Instead of trying to directly compute ideal levels of PULL$_t$ and PUSH$_t$ in any given year, various spending allocations are examined that span the feasible range. This approach allows a manager to find an efficient allocation *and* to see the relative disadvantage of adopting a less efficient allocation. The NEWSTRAT computer program that will be demonstrated later in this chapter can be used to complete this computational task. As it completes the analysis for each year, the program recommends an efficient allocation of the annual budget. This budget accounts for both the desirable balancing noted above and the cost effectiveness of spending on the two budget categories.

Pull Versus Push Activities

If spending is to be assigned to one of two mutually exclusive categories, a manager must be convinced that the division is both feasible and desirable. Two main points make the affirmative case. First, the audiences or targets of the spending categories are wholly distinct, as are the principal means of reaching each. Mass media reach the final buyers of consumer goods, whereas personal selling, trade shows, and trade magazines reach wholesalers and retailers of these goods. Selective personal selling, trade shows, and trade magazines reach the final buyers of industrial goods. Different selective personal selling reaches resellers but some overlap occurs with trade shows and trade magazines. On the whole, it is not difficult either to assign directly or reasonably allocate the marketing spending to the category that will influence final buyers in contrast to the category that will influence resellers.

Second, the information and incentives that are delivered to final buyers tend to differ sharply from the information and incentives delivered to resellers. Final buyers are interested in personal consumption benefits. By way of contrast, resellers are interested in the sales and profit potential of a product. To the extent that appeals to final buyers help a reseller realize a product's potential, the reseller may be interested in the product's special consumption appeals. Nevertheless, one will seldom confuse the copy directed to consumers with the copy directed to resellers.

Given the distinctive purposes, audiences and content of pull versus push marketing activities, it makes sense to separate them for both strategy and budget development. To formalize this process, two added lines should appear in the spending section of a product's analysis spreadsheet. These lines record the amounts allocated to accomplish pull objectives and the amounts allocated to accomplish push objectives. Allocations to these two categories can be made analytically with the help of the NEWSTRAT computer program.

LONG-RUN RETENTION RATE

If the time between purchases is long enough, repeat and switchback purchases become irrelevant. All purchases in the planning period are trial purchases. Here, less extreme repurchase behavior is examined. As the rate of trial grows, attention should shift to the long-run retention rate, LRR. This rate is a key intermediate variable because it accounts for the rate at which last-time buyers rebuy the product, RR, and the rate at which former triers who are the last-time buyers of competing products will switch to the manager's product, SBR. Furthermore, it predicts the long-run market share *among customers who have tried the product*. The size and changing level of LRR_t as RR_t and SBR_t change over time are excellent predictors of a product's health. Furthermore, all three of the above rates have important diagnostic value and can be used to positively influence the formulation of a product's strategy/budget.

In Chapter 10, two aspects of the long-run retention rate were discussed in detail. One aspect concerned how rapidly it converged to its long-term value for constant repeat and switchback rates. Usually, three repurchase cycles are adequate, but longer times are required when SBR is small.[3] If RR is equal to one, a brand will eventually take over the entire market among triers, regardless of the size of SBR. As a result, care must be taken to assign a reasonable upper bound to RR. This bound will be determined by consumer variety seeking, the product's salience,

---

[3]Equation (10-15) can be used to avoid the convergence problem associated with LRR, but it requires an estimate of the total number of triers each period.

and other forces that influence the variability of purchasing behavior. The NEWSTRAT program deals directly with this issue through an externally imposed constraint.

The second aspect of the long-run retention rate discussed in Chapter 10 concerned values of the repeat and switchback rates that can lead to a given long-run retention rate. Recall Equation (8-9),

$$LRR = SBR / (1 + SBR - RR)$$

Therefore,

$$RR = 1 + SBR - (SBR/LRR) \qquad (12\text{-}8)$$

and

$$SBR = [LRR(1-RR)]/(1-LRR) \qquad (12\text{-}9)$$

All three of the above variables must be greater than zero and less than one.

Also note that if one sets a target long-run retention rate, either Equation (12-8) or (12-9) can be used to compute the feasible combinations of RR and SBR. For example,

GIVEN LRR = .1		GIVEN LRR = .3	
If RR =	Then SBR =	If RR =	Then SBR =
.1	.100	.1	.386
.2	.088	.2	.343
.3	.077	.3	.300
.4	.066	.4	.257

By emphasizing or de-emphasizing the retention of customers versus gaining former buyers, a manager can influence the levels for RR, SBR,

and subsequently LRR. Managers should make this choice in a manner that will efficiently lead to the desired long-run retention rate. In turn, achieving the selected rates depends on annual marketing budgets, the efficiency with which they are spent, and the characteristics of the product and market.

Increasing Repeat and Switchback Rates

In Chapter 10 a table was presented that displayed the forces that determined the size of the repeat rate and the switchback rate. The table at the foot of the page expands the discussion by identifying how each of these forces can be measured. The notation that is employed will be used in two equations that predict the repeat and switchback rates implied by the manager's and the competitors' spending patterns.

D_t and P were defined earlier. CD_t and CP are the same variables for competitors. S is the percentage of the product's last-time buyers who are satisfied, and CS is the percentage satisfied after using the competitors' products. In the absence of S and SC, the P and CP values from a conjoint analysis can be used. All of the data are readily measurable or should have been measured as part of the planning activities.

The two remaining variables in the first row of the table below are important allocations of the firm's total marketing effort, spending to increase repurchase, and spending to induce switching. The last variable in the second row, total marketing expenditures by competitors, is recognized but not allocated. The spending to increase repeat purchases is directed toward last-time buyers. Initially this pool of people is very small, but it grows as the product's market share grows. For this reason, efforts to encour-

			$ SPENDING	
Source	Availability	Satisfaction	Repurchase	Switchback
Our	D_t	P or S	$OR\$_t$	$OS\$_t$
Competitors	CD_t	CP or CS		$CTM\$_t$

age repeat buying must start at a modest level, usually beginning in the second period of the product's life.

During any period, no more should be spent on gaining a repeat purchase than the contribution generated by the purchase. The computer model imposes this limitation on spending to encourage repeat buying. Also, it was noted that retention spending must be limited so that it will not produce a repeat rate that is larger than the manager's specified maximum. This limit recognizes the fact that some level of brand switching will occur for reasons that cannot be successfully influenced by the product's marketing program.

The spending on retaining customers as well as the spending to switch customers are each divided by total competitive marketing spending. (The resulting quantities are called $OR\$_t^*$ and $OS\$_t^*$.)[4] The effect of this adjustment is similar to the effect of expressing push and pull spending on a per-capita basis. Using per-capita push and pull makes allowance for differing market sizes, and using the competitive adjustment to retention and switchback spending makes an allowance for different marketing intensities across product categories.

Spending to switch back buyers of other products to the manager's product is directed to the buyers of all competing products. In most cases, this large pool of purchasers changes little as the manager's product matures. For this reason, dynamic limits do not have to be imposed on switchback spending. Furthermore, no particular upper limit needs to be set on the switchback rate as may have been required for the repeat rate. In both cases, however, the logical upper limit is 1.0.

Predicting the Repeat and Switchback Rates

With the above preliminary subjects out of the way, the forces driving repeat and switchback rates can be examined. The primary direct influ-

ence on each rate is the adjusted spending level described above. The indirect influence in each case is the relative preference and availability of the product. This latter quantity is

$$PD_t = \quad (P/CP) \quad \times \quad (D_t/CD_t) \qquad (12\text{-}10)$$

Relative product preference	Relative availability

Because the relative product preference is a constant and the relative distribution component will change slowly following a product's introductory phase, PD_t becomes quite stable. When it is an important influence on RR_t and SBR_t, it tends to prevent wide annual swings in the two latter rates.

The equation for the *repeat rate* is

$$RR_t = (c \times PD_t) \quad + \quad (d \times OR\$_t^*) \qquad (12\text{-}11)$$

Indirect influence on the repeat rate	Direct effect of spending on the repeat rate

and the equation for the *switchback rate* is

$$SBR_t = (g \times PD_t) \quad + \quad (h \times OS\$_t^*) \qquad (12\text{-}12)$$

Indirect influence on the switchback rate	Direct effect of spending on the switchback rate

If estimates can be made of the relative importance of the direct effect of each type of spending on the above rates, the c, d, g, and h coefficients of the model can easily be computed.

Target Levels of LRR or MS

Once a new product has achieved a substantial level of trial, repurchase behavior becomes an increasingly dominant force in driving sales and

---

[4]Because the model states these and other variables relative to competitive spending, it is assumed that competitive spending is greater than or equal to the product's spending.

market share. The more frequently a product is purchased and the higher the rate of brand switching, the stronger the effect will be.

Overall market share and profit prospects are usually appraised prior to approval of a product's introduction and its associated strategies and budgets. A manager is likely to set long-run sales and market share targets for the posttrial period and estimate the size of the total marketing budgets required to achieve these goals.

To find efficient relationships between spending, long-run retention rate, and market share, the manager must adopt a strategy that dynamically allocates the budget to retaining last-time buyers versus attracting triers who purchased a competing product on the last purchase occasion. The question is, what rule should one use to make the division of total marketing spending, TM$_t$, between retaining buyers and attracting the buyers of other brands?

Once most trial purchases have been made, a simple but effective rule is to let the percentage spent on retention equal the product's last-period market share among triers, and the percentage spent on gaining switchback sales equal to one minus the product's last-period market share among this group.[5] This means that the effort in each case will be proportional to the size of the two groups of prospective buyers. When adopted, this rule provides an easy way to obtain tentative values of OR$_t$ and OS$_t$.

The cost of inducing a retention sale usually differs from the cost of inducing a switchback sale. For example, the last-time buyer may be individually contacted while much waste may be involved in reaching potential switchback buyers. In such cases, some trial and error allocations must be made of TM$_t$. In turn, the resulting estimates of RR$_t$, SBR$_t$, and LRR$_t$ can be used to examine the economic consequences of each allocation. The latter analysis may suggest

a larger or smaller total budget. The NEW-STRAT computer program can be used to reduce the effort needed to complete the analyses.

Efforts to Retain Versus Switch Last-Time Buyers

A single marketing activity can produce both repeat and switchback effects, but because the audiences are distinct, the share of the effect serving each purpose can be estimated with reasonable accuracy. Furthermore, the division is subject to managerial control, just as the division between push and pull is subject to managerial action.

A cents-off promotion can be part pull and part push in its effect, but it may also be partially effective in retaining last-time buyers and partially effective in attracting the last-time buyers of other brands. On the other hand, a cents-off coupon placed in the product's package will be almost entirely directed toward push and repurchase. In contrast, advertising to consumers that offers a factory rebate for trading in a competitive product will be very strongly pull and switchback in orientation. Some spending will have little direction in terms of repeat and switchback among final buyers. For example, a push campaign might promote the firm's prompt delivery and liberal credit policies. In such cases, the repeat to switchback allocation would be in proportion to the size of the potential repeat and switchback groups served by resellers. Finally, when trial purchases are being sought, this spending is classified as switchback dollars.

Normally, the emphasis on retaining customers increases over time as the product's market share increases. If one considers what happens when a monopoly is terminated, the reverse situation develops. Following divestiture, AT&T's marketing activities on behalf of its long-distance business was devoted entirely to retaining its pool of former monopoly customers. As competition made serious inroads,

---

[5]The rate of overall brand switching influences the difficulty of retaining last-time buyers. This complication is ignored, since this behavior will tend to be reflected in the size of the coefficients in both Equations (12-11) and (12-12)

AT&T shifted to a forceful effort to recapture its former customers. The main appeals were service reliability, competitive rates, and no charge to switch back to AT&T.

Ways to encourage other forms of repeat and switchback behavior are not hard to find. For example, a catalog sales operation can send catalogs to people who have made prior purchases from the firm and/or send catalogs to a list of potential new customers. Although purchases made by former customers seldom become strictly repeat purchases of items, they constitute continuing patronage. In a similar manner, although purchases made by people on the new mailing list may not be strictly switchback purchases, they do represent new patrons. For these reasons, many of the strategic issues discussed for individual products and services carry over to sales from a product line or to broader patronage questions.

In any case, a manager has to think through the effects of support spending on purchase behavior, allocating it to push versus pull and repurchase versus switchback. The results should be recorded on lines that can be provided on the product's analysis spreadsheet. No strategy is complete without this breakdown because it strongly influences the further assignment of support dollars to expense categories for media, personal selling, and so on. This division also gives direction to the product's positioning and the contents of its marketing communications.

The Role of Market Segmentation

The narrower or more specialized a product's appeal, the smaller the number of people who are expected to try the product will be. Generally, the more focused the product's appeal and the smaller the number of potential triers, the more brand loyal these people will be. They will have fewer ready substitutes for the brand so that once they have tried the product, little effort may be required to gain repeat purchases. Alter-

natively, it can mean that this small group of loyal buyers deserves special attention to ensure their continued loyalty because it is difficult to attract brand switchers. The larger the proportion of last-time buyers to possible brand switchers (larger market share of the narrow market), the less important it is to influence the latter group.

The narrower or more specialized a product's appeal, the smaller the set of brands against which it will naturally compete will be, but this degree of focus may have little influence on the size of the target market. In the Canadian whiskey illustration, the original target market included 22,500,000 people. This is the group that was reached by key media and distribution. Of this group, only 2,600,000 people were expected to drink any kind of Canadian whiskey, and just 850,000 people were viewed as possible buyers of a superpremium Canadian whiskey. The 200,000 trial purchase limit is reached after an allowance is made for the forcefulness of the firm's marketing program and the possible entry of one or more competitive products. It is important to recognize the characteristics of these different *BASES* and how they enter and influence the economic analysis.

SOME ADDITIONAL CONSIDERATIONS

The Role of the Offer

The offer is fixed for a given analysis but it need not be fixed for other purposes. As Equation (12-1) emphasizes, the desirability of the product, P, determines the probability that people who have the product in their consideration set will try the product. P also plays a role in attracting distribution, Equation (12-5), and in determining the long-run retention rate and the market share; see Equations (12-10), (12-11), and (12-12). Finally, the product's price and design affect unit costs and margins. All of these facts should encourage a manager to examine how sensitive sales and profits are to changing levels of product preference. The more sales and profits respond to price changes and changes in the product's design and positioning, the more important it becomes that these effects be recognized. At a minimum, sensitivity analyses should be conducted for alternative levels of price, preference, and unit cost. The results should guide the manager's actions and the actions of others, particularly influential people in research and development and manufacturing.

First-Year Strategies and Budgets

In the foregoing parts of this chapter, a model was presented that can materially assist a manager in planning the size and allocation of the annual budgets for a new or improved product. A serious question arises, however, as to whether the introductory year is so unique that it must receive separate treatment. Several important reasons support the case for separate handling. First, nearly all of the firm's efforts are devoted to generating trial purchases and to placing the product with effective resellers. Second, management is eager to develop an integrated, unified program. Such programs offer little opportunity to reallocate effort. The alternatives that are considered usually constitute distinct marketing programs, each one requiring different levels of total marketing effort and different fixed components. Finally, a model that predicts the relative success of such programs is unlikely to be helpful in examining the kinds of ongoing strategic issues that the model presented in this chapter is best equipped to handle.

Because of these considerations, the computer model that is discussed in the following section accepts the results estimated by management for the proposed first-year program. It is assumed, however, that no direct effort will be made to produce repeat purchases during this period. The first-year results become the baseline used to model effects of the second and subsequent

years' strategies and budgets. In the latter years, alternative levels and budget allocations to pull and push and retain and switchback activities are considered with the objective of selecting efficiently deployed annual budgets. Because a model is necessarily a simplification of reality, the user should seek opportunities to make improvements in the model's recommendations.

Overruling Model Recommendations

In two instances, the model provides the user with a way to constrain the model's operations. One such opportunity concerns setting an upper limit on the repeat rate. The rationale for doing so has already been discussed. The second opportunity allows the user to set minimum and maximum limits on the percentage of the total budget that can be allocated to pull activities (and therefore to push activities). These constraints may be needed to prevent excessive oscillation in the share of annual budgets allocated to pull and push efforts.

A policy of spending heavily on pull one period and spending heavily on push the next period may be desirable, especially if it creates critical mass for marketing directed toward customers one period and critical mass for efforts to influence distribution during the next period. On the other hand, the hidden costs of major shifts in the allocation of marketing resources may be high enough to require a much steadier approach. An extensive review of the literature dealing with pulsing appears in Hahn and Hyum (1991). Their analysis of advertising concludes that the ratio of pulsing costs to fixed costs is the principal determinant of the desirability of pulsing. When the ratio is small, pulsing is the preferred policy. This result should also apply to pull and push spending. In short, specific details of the manager's situation that cannot be reasonably incorporated into the model can dictate how much oscillation is desirable. More will be said about this subject in connection with the following test problem output.

DEVELOPING A STRATEGY AND BUDGETS WITH THE AID OF THE NEWSTRAT COMPUTER PROGRAM

The NEWSTRAT program can be implemented in two distinct ways. First, appropriate historical data can be analyzed by regression methods and the model coefficients can be entered directly into the program. Doing so can remove a large part of the errors and biases frequently found in managerial judgments. Nevertheless, suitable data bases are seldom available. Attempts to perform regression analysis typically must make do with observations on products that differ in important ways from the current product, and that were obtained under market conditions that are not sufficiently similar to those that the current product will face. In addition, the number of observations can be small and they may contain serious measurement errors. For these reasons and the suspicion that many managers harbor for analyses performed by methods that they do not fully understand, one is often led to reject an analytical procedure. When conditions are right, however, basing the NEWSTRAT model on prior analytical efforts can be a highly valuable approach. Even if some subsequent adjustment in the model's coefficients are called for, one should seriously consider using formal analysis as an initial stage in strategy development. Readers interested in this approach will find further discussion in the section on Computing Model Coefficients of Appendix 12-1.

A second approach to using the model and program is to make judgments about the important intervening variables. These inputs can be used by the program to compute the required model coefficients. The two particularly relevant sets of questions taken from the NEWSTRAT data form appear below. Responses to these questions are conditioned on the other inputs entered on the form. Question Q6 concerns several first-year outcomes and the expected second-year results. The latter data are needed to model the awareness and distribution rates.

The responses to questions Q15 perform a similar function for the repeat and switchback rates.

Q6 Given your planned spending during years 1 and 2 (recorded in Q5), what outcomes do you expect (.###)?

> (Answer only year 1 for a regression-based model.)

Year

1 Fraction spent on PULL activities .____
   Expected awareness rate .____
   Expected distribution rate .____

2 Fraction spent on PULL activities .____
   Expected awareness rate .____
      Fraction of relative change due to PULL .____
   Expected distribution rate .____
      Fraction of relative change due to PUSH .____

Q15 (Answer only year 1 for the regression-based model.)

Year

1 Fraction of total spending that will be devoted to RETAINING last-time buyers .____
   Expected repeat rate .____
   Expected switchback rate .____

2 Fraction of total spending that will be devoted to RETAINING last-time buyers .____
   Expected repeat rate .____
      Fraction of the rate due to retention spending (as contrasted to relative availability and product preference.) .____

   Expected switchback rate .____
      Fraction of the rate due to switchback spending (as contrasted to relative availability and product preference.) .____

With the exception of answers to the queries about the relative importance of direct spending on pull and retention activities, answers to the remaining parts of the above two questions can be taken directly from a spreadsheet analysis like the ones discussed in Chapter 11. The meaning of the two importance (fraction of effect) questions was discussed in relation to Equations (12-6), (12-7), (12-11), and (12-12). These questions deal with simple marketing effects and should pose little difficulty for a manager.

FIGURE 12-1A   NEWSTRAT data form—low spending case.

*DATA FORM FOR NEWSTRAT**

Completed by_____   Date:_____

Q1 Problem   Descripton__CANADIAN WHISKEY   –   Reanalysis_____

_____File No.___1_____

Q2 The cumulative trial function coefficients:

"a"_____0.0_____. "b"_____1.051_____.

Q3 The awareness decay rate is __.__8____

       The distribution decay rate is __.__8____

Q4 Years in the planning horizon (1 < PH < = 10) ___10____

Q5 Target total marketing spending (000), TM$ (T)

Year	1	8850	Year	6	4720
	2	7920		7	4440
	3	7080		8	4050
	4	6200		9	3710
	5	5380		10	3540

Q6 Given your planned spending during years 1 and 2, what outcomes do you expect (.###)?

Year   (Answer only year 1 for regression-based model.)

1   Fraction spent on PULL activities ._63___
          Expected awareness rate ._457___
          Expected distribution rate ._35___

2   Fraction of spending on PULL activities ._62___
          Expected awareness rate ._545___
            Fraction of relative change due to PULL ._7___
          Expected distribution rate ._45___
            Fraction of relative change due to PUSH ._65___

handwritten: If Close—direct spending effect is low/high / If wide

---

*Simplified input; e.g., using P in place of $S_{(T-1)}$ and using a single average variable unit cost.

If the year-1 and year-2 answers to the Q6 awareness rate questions are close to one another, the level of direct spending on awareness in year 2 has less effect than if the answers were more widely separated. Similar remarks apply to the responses concerning the rate of distribution for the same question. In both cases, the second year's rate compared to its value in year 1 is influenced by the money directly allocated to pull (or push) and the appropriate indirect influences. The fraction of the relative change in the rate due to direct effects is also recorded in Q6. Naturally, the size of the annual budget is a strong influence. (See Q5 in Figure 12-1.) The larger the budget that can be allocated one way or the other, the larger the relative change in the rate will be.

The response to Q15 does not have a base level in the prior year since direct decay and carryover are not a factor in determining the size of the repeat or switchback rates. See Equations (12-11) and (12-12). Therefore, the estimated rates

FIGURE 12-1B NEWSTRAT data form—low spending case.

Q7 Preference level for our product (.###), P: _._3___

Q8 Average preference level for competitors' products, (.###), CP: _._35___

For competitors as a group

Year	Q9: Total Spending (000), CTM$(T)	Q10: Average Rate of distribution (.###), CD(T)
1	25000	_._70
2	25000	_._69
3	25000	_._68
4	25000	_._67
5	25000	_._66
6	25000	_._65
7	25000	_._65
8	25000	_._65
9	25000	_._65
10	25000	_._65

Q11 The total number or purchasers, T#P _____850000_____

Q12 Purchaser's annual unit purchases, RUP __23.64_____

Q13 Our product's average annual price, UP(T):

Year 1 _____10.32_____   Year 6 _____10.32_____

2 _____10.32_____   7 _____10.32_____

3 _____10.32_____   8 _____10.32_____

4 _____10.32_____   9 _____10.32_____

5 _____10.32_____   10 _____10.32_____

Q14 The product's average variable unit cost, VUC: ___2.80____.

are based on the results produced by annual spending to retain or switch buyers. The more one spends for each purpose in year 2, the larger the respective repeat rates and the switchback rates will be. One expects the repeat rate to be in the neighborhood of the product's market share among last-time buyers. The switchback rate usually is in the neighborhood of the product's overall market share among all competitors in the prior year, unless the product's total expenditures are much higher or lower.

The above two questions and the other, simpler questions used to generate model inputs are shown on the data form in Figure 12-1. Most of

these inputs are straightforward and have been discussed at length. In the case of the recently introduced decay coefficients for awareness and distribution, additional comments are in order. These coefficients are entered in response to Q3. The entries are usually based on managerial judgment or historical records. In particular, recall that the smaller each coefficient becomes (greater decay), the larger the budget must be to sustain a given market share.

Each decay coefficient indicates how much of the prior awareness rate or distribution rate will remain if all marketing spending is terminated for a year but orders for the product are accept-

FIGURE 12-1C   NEWSTRAT data form—low spending case.

Q15 (Answer only year 1 for the regression-based model.)

Year
   1   Fraction of planned total spending that will be devoted to RETAINING last-time buyers. _._0_____

         Expected retention (repeat) rate. _._3_____
         Expected switchback rate. _._15_____

   2   Fraction of planned total spending that will be devoted to RETAINING last-time buyers. _._2_____

         Expected retention (repeat) rate _._35_____
            Fraction of the rate due to retention spending (as contrasted to relative availability and product
               preference. _._4_____

         Expected switchback rate _._25_____
            Fraction of the rate due to switchback spending (as contrasted to relative availability and product
               preference). _._45_____

Q16 Constraints on PULL spending:

         Minimum fraction of the annual budget (#.##) _._2_____
         Maximum fraction of the annual budget (#.##) _._7_____

      Constraint on the REPEAT (retention) rate:

         Maximum rate._._85_____

ALTERNATIVE REGRESSION-BASED MODEL COEFFICIENTS

Q17 Coefficients of the awareness equation:

      Beta ____._0343____,   Sigma ____._1885____

Q18 Coefficients of the distribution equation:

      Delta ____._0433____,   Epsilon ____._.8695____

Q19 Coefficients of the retain equation:

      c____._3757____, d ____._2.2096____

Q20 Coefficients of the switchback equation

      g ____._2460____, h ____._4439____

---

ed and processed in the usual manner. No pull activities are undertaken and no push activities like missionary selling or dealer promotions are employed. For this reason, the decay coefficients may lie well below their upper limit of one. If the decay coefficient is .7, only about 3 percent of the initial rate will remain at the end of ten years of simple order taking, but if the decay coefficient is .9, about 30 percent will remain.

The values that the coefficients assume are strongly contingent on the nature of the product and its distribution. Low-salience products that are seldom purchased are easily forgotten, but highly salient products may be easily remembered by most buyers. Since the model deals with new products, one seldom can profit from customers' prior experience with the brand helping to fix its name and properties in buyers' minds.

Similar differences can be found in the degree to which distributors will continue to handle the product if they are given little support. If the product is well liked and well known, the drop-off in distribution and distributor support may be very slow. If the product is an important profit producer for the distributor, it may be hard to replace in the short run. All of these illustrations suggest that careful attention be given to specifying the decay coefficients, particularly since they are important determinants of the efficiency of the marketing dollars spent on behalf of a product.

The NEWSTRAT computer program has two built-in checks on the validity of the estimates submitted to the model. First, the model checks to see if any of the coefficients are negative. If one or more are, the program terminates after recommending that this chapter be consulted for possible clues concerning the cause of the problem. Second, the program examines the computed values of the awareness, distribution, repeat, and switchback rates that are computed each year for the budget submitted to the program. If any of these rates is too large (1.0 or larger), the program reports this fact, recommends a review of the data, and stops without completing the final summary output table. Additional ways to examine the model's behavior and validity are discussed in the section on Coefficient Validity in Appendix 12-1.

As a reference point for the above discussion, a completed NEWSTRAT data form is shown in Figure 12-1. These data and the associated estimates are loosely based on the Canadian whiskey illustration that was described in Chapter 11. The coefficient entries to Q17–Q20 came from the NEWSTRAT analysis and are recorded just for the reader's information.[6]

---

[6]If an identical model and coefficients are needed for subsequent analyses, the user should select the externally entered coefficients option. In this case, just enter new year-1 values for Q6 and Q15 and the desired prior model coefficients for Q17–Q20. Other entries are recorded in the usual manner.

A REVIEW OF SEVERAL NEWSTRAT ANALYSES OF THE CANADIAN WHISKEY ILLUSTRATION

With modest alterations, the entries in Figure 12-1 are taken from Table 11-1. Table 12-1 displays some key results produced by the NEWSTRAT program for two budget levels and three sets of decay coefficients. The lower budget levels are the same ones used in the spreadsheet analysis. The higher levels were used to meet two objectives: to obtain a larger market share and to sustain this share.

A number of characteristics of the Canadian whiskey illustration and of the model's operations are noteworthy. First, the lower budget proposed in Chapter 11 does not yield the stable market share management originally expected. Second, market share and profits are strongly influenced by the levels of the decay coefficients. Given the lower budget, if the true decay coefficients are .7, the product will be unprofitable, but if the coefficients are .9, profits are available during the planning period. Even in the latter case, however, the market share continues to decline in the face of the planned lower levels of total spending. Third, the higher budget will sustain a larger market share into the foreseeable future, but shares and profits are responsive to the speed of decay. Given the more attractive outcomes attainable at higher spending levels, an upward revision of the original spending plan should be made.

The awareness and distribution rates produced by the lower and higher budgets are of interest. These rates and the associated cumulative trial rates appear in Table 12-2. As expected, the lower budget can not sustain the maximum rates that are reached in years 4 and 5. On the other hand, not only does the high budget realize higher rates, but also the maximum trial rate reached in year 6 is maintained for the balance of the planning period.

Table 12-3 shows the allocations of the higher budget to pull and push and repeat and switch-

TABLE 12-1   REANALYSIS OF THE CANADIAN WHISKEY
ILLUSTRATION INPUTS EXCEPT NEW BUDGETS, DECAY
COEFFICIENTS, AND THE HIGH BUDGET PARTS OF Q6
APPEAR IN FIGURE 12-1.

Alpha =	.7	.8	.9	.7	.8	.9
Gamma =	.7	.8	.9	.7	.8	.9
Year	**Budgets in ($000)[1]**					
1	8,850	8,850	8,850	10,000	10,000	10,000
2	7,920	7,920	7,920	9,000	9,000	9,000
3	7,080	7,080	7,080	8,000	8,000	8,000
4	6,200	6,200	6,200	8,000	8,000	8,000
5	5,380	5,380	5,380	8,000	8,000	8,000
6	4,720	4,720	4,720	8,000	8,000	8,000
7	4,400	4,400	4,400	8,000	8,000	8,000
8	4,050	4,050	4,050	8,000	8,000	8,000
9	3,710	3,710	3,710	8,000	8,000	8,000
10	3,540	3,540	3,540	8,000	8,000	8,000
Total Net Contribution to Profit (000)	(12,882)	(2,958)	15,878	17,864	26,580	44,416
Year	**Market Share**					
1	.007	.007	.007	.010	.010	.010
2	.024	.023	.022	.036	.034	.033
3	.037	.038	.039	.053	.054	.056
4	.049	.055	.064	.078	.083	.087
5	.044	.053	.066	.077	.085	.099
6	.035	.045	.062	.084	.091	.105
7	.029	.040	.059	.079	.090	.120
8	.024	.034	.055	.085	.093	.122
9	.020	.030	.051	.080	.092	.125
10	.016	.026	.049	.085	.094	.125

[1]Increasing the budget may require adjustments to the awareness and distribution levels
recorded in Q6 and Q15 in Figure 12-1.

back activities. The long-run retention rate among the triers is also displayed. In years 2 through 10, where allocations were developed by the model, about one-third of the total budget is assigned to pull activities and the remaining two-thirds is devoted to push activities. In addition, a good deal of oscillation is evident, pulsing distribution efforts and then pulsing pull efforts. The allocation pattern for repeat and switchback spending shows an early effort to develop switchers (predominantly triers) and then a steady shift to heavy emphasis on encouraging brand loyalty. The split in years 4 through 10 is 90 percent retention and 10 percent switchback spending. From year 4 to the end of the planning period, the long-run retention rate lies between .5 and .6.

Although the higher budget is appealing, at least two issues remain to be considered. The first is the desirable degree of oscillation between

TABLE 12-2 REANALYSIS OF THE CANADIAN WHISKEY ILLUSTRATION

See Figure 12-1 for inputs other than the budgets and Q6 update. Alpha = gamma = .8.

	Low Budget			High Budget		
Total Net Contribution to Profit ($000)	(2,958)				26,580	
			RATE			
Year	Aware	Dist.	Trial[1]	Aware	Dist.	Trial[2]
1	.46	.35	.05	.56	.45	.08
2	.48	.57	.09	.57	.69	.12
3	.51	.64	.10	.62	.70	.14
4	.54	.63	.12	.62	.75	.15
5	.52	.64	.12	.67	.72	.15
6	.52	.62	.10	.64	.77	.16
7	.50	.61	.10	.68	.73	.16
8	.49	.59	.09	.65	.77	.16
9	.48	.58	.09	.68	.74	.16
10	.46	.56	.08	.65	.78	.16

(handwritten margin note: lower budget can not sustain the maximum rates that are reached in years 4 & 5)

[1]Declining cumulative trial, years 6–10.
[2]Steady-state cumulative trial, years 6–10.

TABLE 12-3 ANNUAL BUDGET ALLOCATIONS AND LONG-RUN RETENTION RATE FOR THE HIGH BUDGET. ALPHA = GAMMA = .8.

	($000)				Long-Run
Year	Pull	Push	Repeat	Switchback	Retention Rate
1	6,300	3,700	0	10,000	.176
2	1,800	7,200	1,567	7,433	.318
3	3,600	4,400	5,155	2,845	.405
4	2,000	6,000	7,200	800	.578
5	4,400	3,600	7,200	800	.567
6	1,600	6,400	7,200	800	.590
7	4,400	3,600	7,200	800	.578
8	1,600	6,400	7,200	800	.592
9	4,000	4,000	7,200	800	.582
10	1,600	6,400	7,200	800	.583
Aver. (last 9 years)					
	2,778	5,333	6,347	1,764	
Aver. as a % of the Total (last 9 years)					
	.34	.66	.78	.22	

(handwritten margin note: 90% retention, 10% Sw.)

(handwritten margin notes: 1/3 pull, 2/3 push — lots of oscillation — early effort to develop Sw, rather than switch to loyalty)

Issues
- *desirable level of oscillation*
- *attainability of rates*

pull and push. The second is the degree to which various rates are attainable, especially the repeat and switchback rates. To investigate these matters, the model was rerun with the upper and lower percentage allocations to pull set at .3 and .4. The summary output of the analysis appears in Figure 12-2. Little change occurred in the overall allocation of effort to pull activities but the amount of year-to-year variation is greatly reduced. The adverse effect of this smoothing on profits is modest; a decline of less than $1 million, or about 3 percent. If marketing spending is more efficient with less pulsing (which it may not be), steadier spending is called for.

Without historical data and/or a solid knowledge of the product class, little can be said about how reasonable the projected awareness, distribution, and switchback rates may be. One does know, however, that in years 4 through 10, the levels of spending to encourage repeat purchasing pushes the repeat rate up to the limit imposed by management. Somewhat lower annual budgets or reduced spending on repeat activities may be in order. Any possible changes that may improve the marketing strategy and budget can be examined with the aid of the NEWSTRAT program, but these extended analyses will not be carried out here. Instead, various features of the program will be described.

ADDITIONAL NEWSTRAT CHARACTERISTICS

The foregoing section concentrated on illustrating the main features of the NEWSTRAT program by applying it to the Canadian whiskey problem. The way that the program was used in the above illustrations provided few clues about how sensitive the key intermediate variables and profits were to the annual spending levels and allocation decisions. The first part of the section looks at the effect of allocation decisions on the annual levels of intervening variables. The sec-

ond part extends these remarks to an analysis of the oscillating behavior of push and pull allocations. The third part reviews the properties of repeat and switchback allocations. The fourth part describes a program option that lets one adjust total spending during the analysis of each year to achieve a target level of trial or market share. The fifth and final part discusses an option that can be used to fine-tune the annual allocations.

Sensitivity Profiles of the Allocation Process

As Figure 12-2 shows, the basic summary output of the program simply displays the consequences of the best annual allocations found by the search process. For each year, the allocations to pull and push and to retain and switchback are displayed along with the resulting intervening variables and the critical economic measures. In the absence of more details about each year, a manager cannot easily estimate the adverse effects of departing from the recommended allocations.

Because the model simplifies reality, some departure from the recommended levels of spending can be expected. Questions about smoothing the oscillation in pull and push spending, shifting overall budget levels, or transferring spending between years can be expected to arise. A program option that displays details about the annual analyses is a good place to start when such questions must be answered. The results that are shown in Figure 12-3 are based on the high spending alternative whose outcomes appear in Figure 12-2. However, the pull minimum and maximum are set at the original .2 and .7. (Also, the final pull and repeat budgets for years 2 and 5 have been set at the levels noted on the output.) The two panels are shown for year 2. Each one displays the intermediate variables produced by eleven test alloca-

Higher pull constraints

FIGURE 12-2   Summary budget—high spending case.

Year	Total Budget	Pull	Spending Push	Spending Repeat	Switchback
1	$10,000,000	$6,300,000	$3,700,000	$0	$10,000,000
2	$9,000,000	$2,700,000	$6,300,000	$1,567,259	$7,432,742
3	$8,000,000	$2,400,000	$5,600,000	$4,939,954	$3,060,046
4	$8,000,000	$3,200,000	$4,800,000	$7,200,000	$800,000
5	$8,000,000	$2,720,000	$5,280,000	$7,200,000	$800,000
6	$8,000,000	$3,200,000	$4,800,000	$7,200,000	$800,000
7	$8,000,000	$2,400,000	$5,600,000	$7,200,000	$800,000
8	$8,000,000	$3,200,000	$4,800,000	$7,200,000	$800,000
9	$8,000,000	$2,560,000	$5,440,000	$7,200,000	$800,000
10	$8,000,000	$3,200,000	$4,800,000	$7,200,000	$800,000
Nine-Year Average		$2,842,222	$5,268,889	$6,323,024	$1,788,087
Percentage of Total		.350	.650	.780	.220

—modest $ ↓
—if spending is more efficient smoothing is called for

Year	Aware Rate	Dist. Rate	Share of Choice S.	Cum. Trial Rate	Repeat Rate	Switchback Rate	Long-run Ret. Rate
1	0.560	0.450	0.252	0.079	0.300	0.150	0.176
2	0.588	0.654	0.385	0.121	0.372	0.280	0.308
3	0.605	0.718	0.434	0.137	0.662	0.230	0.405
4	0.635	0.729	0.463	0.146	0.847	0.200	0.566
5	0.643	0.746	0.479	0.151	0.850	0.207	0.580
6	0.658	0.743	0.489	0.154	0.850	0.210	0.583
7	0.650	0.760	0.494	0.156	0.850	0.214	0.588
8	0.662	0.750	0.497	0.157	0.850	0.212	0.585
9	0.657	0.760	0.499	0.157	0.850	0.214	0.588
10	0.666	0.750	0.500	0.158	0.850	0.212	0.585

Year	Dollar Budget	Avail. Triers	Unit Sales	Dollar Sales	Market Share	Net Contrib. to Profit
1	10,000,000	67,537	208,412	2,150,813	.010	−8,432,741
2	9,000,000	103,146	656,909	6,779,299	.033	−4,060,046
3	8,000,000	116,387	1,064,436	10,984,982	.053	4,560
4	8,000,000	124,018	1,616,468	16,681,953	.080	4,155,842
5	8,000,000	128,443	1,736,213	17,917,716	.086	5,056,321
6	8,000,000	130,960	1,790,112	18,473,952	.089	5,461,639
7	8,000,000	132,443	1,832,662	18,913,070	.091	5,781,617
8	8,000,000	133,239	1,838,641	18,974,778	.092	5,826,583
9	8,000,000	133,710	1,856,150	19,155,468	.092	5,958,249
10	8,000,000	133,943	1,851,632	19,108,844	.092	5,924,274

Total Net Contribution Profit 25,676,296

not very responsive

FIGURE 12-3   Annual test budget results—high spending case, year 2.

Year:	2	Total Spending	$9,000,000			
Test	Cum. Trial Rate	Share Choice Set	Aware Rate	Distrib. Rate	PULL$ ($000)	PUSH$ ($000)
1	0.123	0.391	0.569	0.687	1,800	7,200
2	0.122	0.388	0.579	0.670	2,250	6,750
3	0.121	0.385	0.588	0.654	2,700	6,300
4	0.120	0.381	0.598	0.638	3,150	5,850
5	0.119	0.378	0.608	0.622	3,600	5,400
6	0.118	0.374	0.617	0.605	4,050	4,950
7	0.116	0.369	0.627	0.589	4,500	4,500
8	0.115	0.365	0.637	0.573	4,950	4,050
9	0.113	0.360	0.646	0.557	5,400	3,600
10	0.112	0.354	0.656	0.540	5,850	3,150
11	0.110	0.349	0.665	0.524	6,300	2,700

The best pull and push strategy is

1	0.123	0.391	0.569	0.687	1,800	7,200

Year's final pull budget $3,000,000 *responsive*

Test	Retain ($000)	Switchback ($000)	Retain Rate	Switchback Rate	Long-run Ret. Rate	Market Share
1	0	9,000	0.246	0.301	0.285	.030
2	157	8,843	0.258	0.299	0.287	.030
3	313	8,687	0.270	0.297	0.289	.031
4	470	8,530	0.282	0.294	0.291	.031
5	627	8,373	0.294	0.292	0.292	.031
6	784	8,216	0.307	0.289	0.294	.031
7	940	8,060	0.319	0.287	0.296	.031
8	1,097	7,903	0.331	0.284	0.298	.032
9	1,254	7,746	0.343	0.282	0.300	.032
10	1,411	7,589	0.355	0.279	0.302	.032
11	1,567	7,433	0.367	0.277	0.304	.032

The best retain and gain strategy is

11	1,567	7,433	0.367	0.277	0.304	.032

The final switchback budget is $7,930,000

tions. For the pull and push allocations in year 2, the best allocation is the lowest pull level that was tested. For the retain and switchback allocations in year 2, the highest tested allocation to switchback is best.

The first thing to observe about this particular illustrative problem is that the share of choice sets and the cumulative trial rates are not very responsive to the pull and push allocations during this year. This is true because both awareness and distribution levels are above .5, and increasing one reduces the other one. Second, the repeat rate is sensitive to spending allocations, but the switchback rate is much less so. As a result, the long-run retention rate is not very responsive and the market share is even less responsive. Management made the choices of the final pull and switchback budgets.

Moving to the two panels for year 5, the above comments hold for pull and push spending but do not for the allocations to retain and switchback spending. See Figure 12-4. The repeat rate is very responsive. Because the rate is high and reaches the high upper limit imposed by management, the long-run retention rate also increases sharply. Similar statements can be made about market share. By studying the response profiles and type of allocation for each year, management can appraise the leeway that exists to alter the program's recommended allocations. Efficiency issues, the need to cooperate with other marketing programs of the firm, and

FIGURE 12-4 Annual test budget results—high spending case, year 5.

Year:	5	Total Spending			$8,000,000		

Test	Cum. Trial Rate	Share Choice Set	Aware Rate	Distrib. Rate	PULL$ ($000)	PUSH$ ($000)
1	0.152	0.483	0.636	0.760	1,600	6,400
2	0.152	0.483	0.644	0.750	2,000	6,000
3	0.152	0.482	0.651	0.740	2,400	5,600
4	0.152	0.481	0.659	0.730	2,800	5,200
5	0.151	0.480	0.667	0.720	3,200	4,800
6	0.151	0.479	0.674	0.710	3,600	4,400
7	0.151	0.478	0.682	0.700	4,000	4,000
8	0.150	0.476	0.690	0.690	4,400	3,600
9	0.150	0.474	0.698	0.680	4,800	3,200
10	0.149	0.473	0.705	0.670	5,200	2,800
11	0.148	0.471	0.713	0.660	5,600	2,400

The best pull and push strategy is

1	0.152	0.483	0.636	0.760	1,600	6,400

Year's final pull budget				$3,000,000		

Test	Retain ($000)	Switchback ($000)	Retain Rate	Switchback Rate	Long-run Ret. Rate	Market Share
1	0	8,000	0.289	0.314	0.307	.046
2	800	7,200	0.352	0.302	0.318	.048
3	1,600	6,400	0.414	0.289	0.331	.049
4	2,400	5,600	0.476	0.277	0.346	.052
5	3,200	4,800	0.538	0.264	0.364	.054
6	4,000	4,000	0.600	0.252	0.387	.058
7	4,800	3,200	0.663	0.239	0.415	.062
8	5,600	2,400	0.725	0.227	0.452	.068
9	6,400	1,600	0.787	0.214	0.502	.075
10	7,200	800	0.849	0.202	0.573	.086
11	8,000	0	0.850	0.189	0.558	.083

The best retain and gain strategy is

10	7,200	800	0.849	0.202	0.573	.086

The final switchback budget is					$800,000	

a desire to produce a unified, well-integrated program are the kinds of considerations that can lead one to depart from the program's recommendations.

Oscillating Pull and Push Allocations

Awareness, A_t, and distribution, D_t, compete for a share of total marketing spending. As one increases pull spending, push spending is necessarily decreased as $PUSH\$_t = TM\$_t - PULL\$_t$. This fact means that increasing $PULL\$_t$ increases the rate of awareness carried forward relative to the rate of distribution carried forward. During the next time period, this change makes pull spending relatively less attractive and push spending relatively more attractive than they otherwise would have been.

If $PULL_{t+1}$ is reduced and $PUSH\$_{t+1}$ is increased in response to the new set of circumstances, the reverse conditions result. In time period $t + 2$, pull spending becomes more attractive than it otherwise would have been without the spending changes in period $t + 1$. For these reasons, the division of spending between pull and push can oscillate in the manner that is observed in Table 12-3. Further perspectives on the instabilities that can arise in lag structures are presented by Gleick (1987, pp. 59–77); Hanssens, Parsons, and Schultz (1990, pp. 109–153); and Morrison (1991).

A more detailed view of the model's behavior can be developed by algebraically simplifying the equations for A_t and D_t for a *given time period*. Both equations become linear functions of the percentage of the budget devoted to pull spending, Ω_t. Specifically, $D_t = K_{1,t} + K_{2,t}\,\Omega_t$ and $A_t = K_{3,t} + K_{4,t}\,\Omega_t$, and the share of choice sets, SCS_t, becomes a quadratic function of Ω_t. The SCS_t function is normally concave downward, but its height, curvature, and location change each time period because the coefficients $K_{i,t}$ are functions of the last period's changing rates of awareness and/or distribution as well as the model's other elements.

These relationships can be illustrated by

FIGURE 12-5   Response of SCS_t to pull and push allocations.

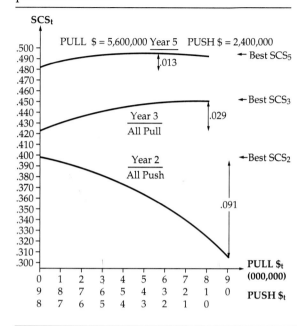

rerunning the Canadian whiskey test problem without imposing constraints on the allocation of the total budget to its pull and push components. See Figure 12-5. Several important features of the model can be observed:

1. The SCS_t functions are concave downward.

2. The level of the SCS_t function tends to increase and its range tends to decline as cumulative spending increases. Therefore, spending in each successive time period tends to produce fewer gains per dollar, but contributes more to sustaining higher levels of awareness and distribution.

3. At higher levels of cumulative spending, the SCS_t function becomes flatter because its level depends more on past spending than on current spending.

4. In early periods when past spending is less influential, errors in allocating funds to pull

and push can seriously reduce marketing effectiveness. Potential buyers who have the product available will be unaware or aware people will be unable to find the product.

5. The model evolves over time. In one period it may recommend allocating all spending to pull and the next period it may recommend all spending be allocated to push activities. As year 5 in the above graph shows, allocating part of the budget to pull and part to push can be the best decision. As the earlier discussion pointed out, pulsing spending can be a wise decision, *but* the model does not directly include the usual rationales for this behavior. Similarly, the model does not include any cost penalty for volatile spending patterns. The user must implement a decision to reduce volatility by imposing constraints during the analysis or by adjusting the model's recommendations.

6. Since the model evolves over time in the manner illustrated in Figure 12-5, a user is advised to examine the year-by-year details. (See Figures 12-3 and 12-4 for constrained results for years 2 and 5.) Doing so will increase a user's appreciation of the way a market is likely to respond to allocations to pull and push activities.

Repeat and Switchback Allocations

Just as SCS_t for a given year and budget is a function of the budget, LRR_t for a given year and budget is a function of the division of the budget between repeat and switchback efforts. Except for the contribution of the distribution rate, the repeat and switchback rates for each year are independent of prior years' results. After the initial introduction of a product, the distribution rate usually changes slowly, and it is but one element in the indirect forces that influence repurchase behavior. Therefore, independence for a given year and budget is assumed so that the long-run retention rate can be written as a function of Φ_t, the percentage of

the budget spent to encourage switchbacks. In this case, $LRR_t = (X_1 + X_2 \times \Phi_t) / (X_3 + X_4 \times \Phi_t)$ where $X_1, \ldots, X_4$ are functions of the components of Equations (12-11) and (12-12)[7].

When the data for years 2 and 10 from the Canadian whiskey illustration are inserted in the above equation, the results are the curves shown in Figure 12-6.

Figure 12-6 points out a number of interesting features of spending to keep or regain triers.

1. The illustrative functions are concave upward and decreasing. The functions can also be concave downward. In either case, LRR_t can increase or decrease as more is spent on switching back triers. The levels of the coefficients for a given year determine the function's shape and level.

---

[7] $X_1 = g \times (P/CP) \times D_t/CD_t)$
$X_2 = h \times (TM\$_t/CTM\$_t)$
$X_5 = c \times (P/CP) \times (D_t/CD_t)$
$X_6 = d \times (TM\$_t/CTM\$_t)$
$X_3 = 1 + X_1 - X_5 - X_6$
$X_4 = X_6 + X_2$

FIGURE 12-6 Long-run retention rate as a function of the percentage spent on switchbacks.

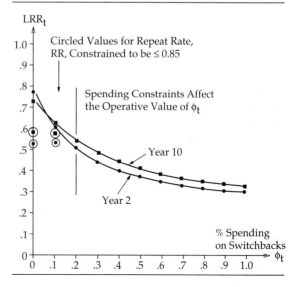

2. In the unconstrained case, the best result is obtained by choosing the highest or lowest percentage allocation to switchback activities that produces results in the feasible range of LRR_t.

3. When the repeat rate is externally constrained to lie below some limit, it may be wasteful to choose an allocation that leads to a higher repeat rate. In Figure 12-6, the constrained results for $\Phi_t = 0$ and .1 remain above those for $\Phi_t = .2$ but show a declining trend. When the limit on RR_t is reduced, the best value of Φ_t will tend to lie between 0 and 1 rather than at one of the extremes. Also, the share of spending devoted to inducing switchbacks is increased when the number of triers who can be retained is uneconomically small.

4. Increasing total spending will increase the level of the function and the importance of the allocation decision.

5. As the rate of distribution increases [see PD_t in Equations (12-11) and (12-12)], the indirect influences on repeat and switchback behavior grow and the relative importance of the allocation decision decreases.

6. When one chooses $\Phi_t = 1$ or 0, the RR_t or SBR_t element of LRR_t that does not receive spending support must be maintained solely by the indirect elements. The year 2 and year 10 indirect contributions to the repeat and switchback rates are given below.

THE ILLUSTRATIVE PROBLEM

		INDIRECT CONTRIBUTION TO THE RATE FROM PD_t	
Year	Total Spending (000)	RR	SBR
2	9,000	.250	.162
10	8,000	.304	.200

Achieving Target Levels of Trial or Market Share

When detailed annual output is being produced by NEWSTRAT, a program option permits the user to change total annual spending and obtain revised estimates of the results. This capacity lets one start with a set of unproven annual marketing budgets and target levels of trial or market share. If the second year's analysis fails to produce the target results, that year's total spending can be adjusted up or down and the analysis repeated until the desired level has been obtained. The user can repeat this process for each of the following years, producing a series of budgets and budget allocations that meet the targets for trial or market share.

Fine-tuning Allocations

As noted earlier, upper and lower limits on the percentage of an annual budget that can be allocated to pull spending are set by the entries to Q16 in Figure 12-1. By varying these limits and rerunning the program (as they were varied to produce the results in Figure 12-2), the adverse effects of departing from the program's unrestrained recommendations can be examined. A systematic use of this feature, comparing the results to the unconstrained output, is a quick way to study one common class of potential change.

Once the general level of annual spending on pull and push and retain and switchback activities is established, a manager may want to look at more finely divided expenditure patterns than those produced by the standard program output like the ones shown in Figures 12-2 and 12-3. A NEWSTRAT option lets the user specify a new, narrower range for a year's budget analysis. In turn the program produces a new table using the narrowed range, testing eleven budgets in this interval. This extended analysis can lead management to choose allocations that call for spending levels lying between those shown in Figures 12-2 and 12-3.

MAKING A STRATEGY WORK

At this point what one wants to accomplish may be clear but what actions will produce the desired results may be far less clear. Here only three areas of managerial control are examined, but they point toward a wider range of positive actions.

Increasing the Effective Life of Marketing Spending

The sales and profit importance of the decay coefficients has received a good deal of attention. What remains to be considered is what a marketing manager can do to reduce the speed with which the effects of pull and push expenditures dissipate over time. As far as customer awareness is concerned, all aspects of the offer and the marketing program should be made more memorable. The choice of a name, logo, package, and message can contribute. Orville Redenbacher's popcorn and Smucker's jams and jellies have made a virtue of necessity by emphasizing the name. In the fast food area, McDonald's uses a large array of methods to make consumers favorably recall its menu items and recognize its outlets. Repeated use of the golden arches, Ronald McDonald, and the Mc prefix for the names of menu items are examples. To make its PC and PS/2 desk-top computers readily and favorably recognized, IBM used its established logo, unified product colors and design features, a Charlie Chaplin look-alike, and a set of MASH spokespersons. All such approaches extend the time during which prospective customers are affected by any period's marketing effort. The simple conclusions are that the awareness decay coefficient is important, it is the product of many forces outside of management's control, but it can be favorably influenced by strategic decisions that increase the coefficient and the sales and profits produced by marketing.

A similar situation exists with respect to dis-

tribution. Distributor loyalty and cooperation vary from product to product and from one line of trade to another, but marketing managers are far from helpless. Resellers want to carry products that are easy to sell, absorb few resources, and yield attractive margins. The product's attractiveness to final buyers and the strength of the marketing program that supports it are key elements in influencing distributors. In particular, the more success a product has in developing a loyal clientele (large repeat rate), the more difficult it will be for a reseller to drop or neglect the product.

Other simple steps can increase coverage and build distributor cooperation. For example, distributor loyalty can be increased by supplying computer links to simplify and speed reorders, by providing prompt delivery and claim adjustment, and by providing advance notice about important market developments. Loyal resellers will continue to carry the product and support it with positive sales programs. When all the influences on a reseller work for the marketing manager, the decay coefficient increases, extending the effectiveness of the marketing strategy and budget.

Choosing a Desirable Mix of Pull and Push

In the foregoing Canadian whiskey illustration, the model suggested using about one-third of the budget to directly increase customer awareness and about two-thirds to widen distribution and increase distributor support. The mix may be efficient for this product type, but quite different allocations should be employed for other product classes. The balance one chooses between pull and push depends on shopping and buying behavior and the nature of the product.

A marketing manager has to size up these pressures when deciding on the mix of pull and push to use in support of the product. Competitive practices must also be examined. If competitors appear to be using an inefficient mix, a dif-

Influences Increasing Pull	**Influences Increasing Push**
No reseller sales effort needed beyond providing efficient, convenient availability	Needed sales effort cannot be provided by the mfgr. of the product
No postsale service	Need postsale service
Reliance on mfgr. for product assurance	Reliance on reseller for product assurance
National market	Segmented market
Media reaches intended audience	No efficient media
Few large mfgrs./providers	Many small mfgrs./providers
Low pull costs	Low push costs

. . .   . . .

ferent strategy has special appeal. On the other hand, if competitors appear to be using an efficient mix, departures from this mix are likely to be risky. Nevertheless, niche strategies exist in the pull and push domain as well as in the kind of offer a manager chooses and the level of marketing support that he or she adopts.

If pull and push have unequal strategic importance in determining the size of SCS_t, a more complicated function, $f(A_t, D_t)$ can replace the simple $A_t \times D_t$ function in Equation (12-1). As the foregoing illustration has pointed out, however, differences in the effectiveness and cost of each of these two variables are captured by the model's parameters, and they are principal determinants of the recommended allocations.

Choosing the Right Retain and Switchback Mix

Having expended a good deal of effort to make initial sales, management is naturally eager to have buyers' continued patronage. The product has had a chance to demonstrate its merits and the buyers' brand awareness is high. These people make preferred targets and should be the base on which future sales are built. Nevertheless, efforts to retain customers can be seriously limited by management's ability to identify and reach these people. The problem is most pro-

nounced for moderately priced, frequently purchased products that move through lengthy channels of distribution.

A manager should consider the wide range of options that are available to learn who purchased—name, address, and phone number—and whether buyers can be reached by direct purchase–repurchase incentives. The latter are incentives that are delivered at the time of purchase. Mail-order companies and other direct sellers have a natural advantage and often include repurchase incentives when shipping the order. The billing lists of credit extenders can serve the same purpose. Warranty and service records can be helpful marketing tools when resellers make the final sale. Practices in the automobile field provide examples. Finally, if contact with the final buyers is important in making repeat sales (and in keeping in touch with market development), forward integration may be called for.

When resellers are a key element in a marketing program, a substantial part of the push spending should be devoted to helping resellers encourage repeat purchases. Numerous methods are available. Label and display allowances partially serve this purpose, and coupons packed with the product are directly effective in fostering repurchase. Manufacturers of frequently purchased consumer goods have offered towels, glassware, and certificates for items of silver plate. These incentives are packed in successive shipments of the merchandise to encourage repeat purchases. Premiums offered in exchange for collected labels can have a similar effect.

Patronage allowances offered to resellers and possibly to final buyers also encourage repurchase. Airline mileage clubs, quantity discounts, and patronage premiums offered to order placers for industrial products are examples. Supermarkets have offered computers to schools for collections of cash register tapes. In addition, they have promoted sets of encyclopedias and stainless steel cookware at discounted prices, offering just one new unit each week. Trading stamps, games, and proprietary credit programs have also been widely used by retailers to encourage continued patronage. Marketing managers have been fairly inventive in identifying potential repurchasers and inducing larger repurchases. The range of managerial actions is broad and deserves careful consideration.

The problem of reaching potential switchers is much less severe if they are all viewed as buyers who did not buy the last time (instead of just people who have tried the product but did not buy it last time). This large group includes many unaware people and people who do not favor the manager's product. Effort at market segmentation may reduce the number of ill-disposed people, but in any case the message and the media used to reach those who did not buy the product last time usually differ from the approach used to attract last-time buyers. These contrasting characteristics of attracting repeaters rather than brand switchers indicate that for most products it is more efficient to influence last-time buyers. However, the effectiveness of doing so is greatly reduced by the relatively small number of potential repeaters.

CONCLUDING REMARKS

Chapters 10, 11, and 12 were devoted to structuring market behavior in a manner that can help a marketing manager develop a marketing strategy for a new or improved product. Build-

ing a long-range plan in this manner serves two main purposes: It measures the product's economic potential and it provides an efficient strategy for marketing to enhance and deliver value.

It is highly unlikely that a long-range marketing plan will be executed in its entirety. Markets change and competitive products and competitive marketing actions evolve in ways that were not anticipated. Costs are more or less than forecast. These and other developments force a marketing manager to continually reevaluate the plan that was originally set in motion. When replanning is required, the same structure that was originally used can help to update the plan. New information is taken into account and the parts of the plan that need revision are brought up to date.

It is important to observe, however, that the kind of plan that is used to approve or reject a new or improved product and to guide a long-run marketing strategy is not entirely suitable for constructing a detailed marketing plan. This is particularly true of the annual plan for a mature product. In this latter case, the trade-offs between spending on the individual elements of an annual plan become more important. Deciding what specific spending elements should make up the plan, how much should be spent on each one, and the degree to which these elements should stand alone or depend on one another become important considerations.

Chapters 13 to 15 deal directly with building the annual marketing plan and integrating it with the plans for the firm's related products. This task calls for a perspective that is principally concerned with how marketing actions affect market share and is less concerned with trial sales. Although the rates of awareness, distribution, repeat, and switchback have important diagnostic value, the close link of market share to key economic measures like dollar sales and profits makes the latter index more valuable. In terms of earlier remarks about the effect of spending, the focus changes from direct results to the indirect market share results of the marketing strategy and budget.

REFERENCES

Gleick, James: *Chaos: Making a New Science*, New York: Penguin, 1987.

Hahn, Minki, and Jin-sak Hyum: "Advertising Cost Interactions and Optimal Pulsing," *Management Science*, 37 (2), February 1991, 157–169.

Hanssens, Dominique, Leonard Parsons, and Randall Schultz: *Market Response Models: Econometric and Time Series Analysis*, Boston: Kluwer Academic Publishers, 1990.

Morrison, Foster: *The Art of Modeling Dynamic Systems*, New York: John Wiley & Sons, 1991.

Roberts, John H., and James M. Lattin: "Development and Testing of a Model of Consideration Set Composition," *Journal of Marketing Research*, 28, November 1991, 429–440.

APPENDIX 12-1 ESTIMATING NEWSTRAT PARAMETERS

COMPUTING MODEL COEFFICIENTS

The following preliminary steps are taken just once for a reasonably stable product class if varied data are available covering a set of similar products. Because a number of preliminary transformations are needed, for example RCA_t, RCD_t, and PD_t, a Lotus 123® spreadsheet should be set up to complete the process. If this is done, Lotus 123® can also be used to compute the model coefficients.

1. Historical data for similar products are used to compute the a and b coefficients that appear in Equation (12-1) for the cumulative trial rate.

   Compute SCS_t, and $P \times SCS_t$ to obtain the independent variable. CTR_t is the dependent variable.

   Use regression analysis with an intercept.

2. Prior knowledge about the decay coefficient α and historical data for similar products are used to compute the coefficients β and σ that appear in Equation (12-4) for the awareness rate.

   Compute $(1 - \alpha A_{t-1})$ and $(A_t - \alpha A_{t-1})/(1 - \alpha A_{t-1})$ to obtain the dependent variable. Compute $PULL\$_t^{\#}$ and record D_t as the independent variables.

   Use regression analysis with a zero intercept.

3. Prior knowledge about the decay coefficient Γ and historical data for similar products are used to

compute the coefficients δ and ε that appear in Equation (12-5) for the distribution rate.

Compute $(1 - \Gamma D_{t-1})$ and $(D_t - \Gamma D_{t-1})/(1 - \Gamma D_{t-1})$ to obtain the dependent variable. Compute PUSH$\$_t^{\#}$ and $P \times$ TM$\$_t^{*}$ as the independent variables.

Use regression analysis with a zero intercept.

4. If doubt exists about the proper values for α and Γ, steps 2 and 3 can be repeated with new trial values. The trials with the highest R^2 point to the best value of the decay coefficient.

5. Historical data for similar products are used to compute the coefficients c and d that appear in Equation (12-11) for the product's repeat purchase rate.

Compute PD_t, and OR$\$_t^{*}$ as the independent variables. RR_t is the dependent variable.

Use regression analysis with a zero intercept.

6. Historical data for similar products are used to compute the coefficients g and h that appear in Equation (12-12) for the product's switchback rate.

Compute PD_t and OS$\$_t^{*}$ as independent variables. SBR_t is the dependent variable.

Use regression analysis with a zero intercept.

Once in hand, the coefficients can be used directly as inputs to the NEWSTRAT program. See the last section of Figure 12-1 for a set of coefficients computed by the NEWSTRAT program from judgmental inputs in the Canadian whiskey illustration.

Direct Forecasts of Cumulative Trial Rates

When target trial levels are chosen in advance to reflect management's interest in a particular outcome, the TRIAL program discussed in Chapter 10 is a convenient tool for producing annual estimates. As an illustration, a set of new target trial levels was computed for the superpremium Canadian whiskey. The previous aggregate trial levels and the new proposed trial levels for the trial growth years are:

Year	1	2	3	4	5
Old CTR$_t$	.051	.077	.130	.134	.144
New CTR$_t$	.085	.143	.179	.201	.215

Both rates apply to the 850,000 potential buyers of the products against which the new product is assumed to compete. Although a subsequent NEWSTRAT analysis indicated that the new levels were too ambitious, Table 12-1A shows how these ambitious levels were generated using quarterly time periods as the independent variable. Alternative targets could be produced in the same manner. Table 12-1A also shows the target levels of A_t and D_t, assuming that the cost of attaining the level of one equals the cost of attaining the level of the other.

Forecasting Market Results from Planned Marketing Spending

If the coefficients of the NEWSTRAT program are available, the spreadsheet approach can be expanded to predict the intervening variables and the economic outcomes of marketing expenditures. This extension integrates Equations (12-4), (12-5), (12-11), and (12-12) into the spreadsheet. Then the following relationships are invoked for period t.

The cumulative trial rate is

$$CTR_t = a + b(P \times (A_t \times D_t))$$

The number of trial purchases is

$$TP_t = (CTR_t - CTR_{t-1}) \times T\#P$$

The number of nontrial purchases is approximately

$$RP_t = CTR_t \times T\#P \times RUP \times LRR_t$$

Therefore, the total unit purchases are

$$TUS_t = TP_t + RP_t$$

When A_t, D_t, RR_t, and SBR_t are predicted from marketing expenditures using the equations developed in this chapter, the sales results of marketing spending can be directly produced by the spreadsheet analysis. Doing so allows one to go from planned

TABLE 12-1A MODEL TRIAL DATA:

Input Data Generated with the Aid of the TRIAL Program

TRIAL Input
    Independent Variable: Time
    Units of Time: Quarters
    Maximum Number of Trial Sales: 200,000
    Number of Quarters: 20
    Launch Time: 1
    Takeover Time: 19
    (BASE of CRT_t = 850,000)
    TRIAL Output

SEPARATELY COMPUTED

Time (Qtr)	Share of Trial (200,000 Base)	Share of Trial (850,000 Base)	Share of Consideration Sets, SCS_t	$(SCS_t)^{1/2}$ (Target $A_t = D_t$)
4	.362	.085	.270	.520
8	.606	.143	.453	.673
12	.759	.179	.566	.753
16	.854	.201	.637	.798
20	.912	.215	.681	.825

expenditures to economic results. The following spreadsheet changes are required:

1. Rows for recording the percentage of push and the percentage of repeat must be added.

2. Ten additional coefficients are added to the bottom of the spreadsheet.

3. The rows that were used for inputs of A_t, D_t, SBR_t, and RR_t are computed by formula with the aid of planned levels of marketing expenditures. D_t must be computed before A_t is computed.

4. The sales, profits, and other measures of effectiveness become direct functions of the product offer and the effect of the marketing support.

Some Possible Refinements of the Model

In Equations (12-5) and (12-10), P (or S if it is used), along with the equivalent variable for competitors, does not carry a time subscript. In some cases, this

simplification can be a serious limitation, particularly if competitive product introductions or withdrawals are expected or if important product improvements are likely to occur. At the price of increased complexity, the model can be extended to remedy this deficiency.

It is also worth noting that the second and third terms in the equation for A_t are negatively correlated. The more one allocates to $PULL\$_t$, the less that can be allocated to $PUSH\$_t$. The latter variable indirectly contributes to awareness. The effect can be reduced by replacing D_t with lagged distribution, D_{t-1}. However, doing so lessens the physical association of the rate of distribution to the rate of awareness.

When D_{t-1} replaces D_t in Equation (12-4), a simpler approach is available for determining the best share of $TM\$_t^*$ going to PULL (and PUSH) during a given year. Although the algebra is messy, this share is equal to the simple ratio of two constants, each of which is computed from expressions from Equations (12-4) and (12-5). This fact is of some interest, but a manager is better off knowing the effects of a full range of allocations, not just the best allocation.

Finding the Best Annual Budget

In the current NEWSTRAT program, the problem of determining the best level of each year's marketing budget is left to a relatively crude trial-and-error process controlled by the user. A more sophisticated version of NEWSTRAT can be developed to locate a "best" annual budget and efficient allocation to push and pull and repeat and switchback. The added steps would be:

1. Define the largest and smallest acceptable total marketing expenditures for each year.

2. For the associated feasible range of the total budget during the planning period, select some equally spaced budget levels.

3. Randomly select a spending level for each year in its feasible range that sums to one of the levels defined in step 2 above.

4. Complete the analysis for each year using the budgets developed in step 3.

5. Compute the overall results using the best within-year allocations developed in step 4.

6. If the total contribution to profit (or some other measure of effectiveness) is the largest one found for the total budget level, save the results.

7. Repeat steps 3 through 6 a large number of times for each budget level and subsequently for all the budget levels.

The result is a response function that relates profit to total marketing spending, given that the spending is efficiently allocated to the constituent years and within each year. Some possible elaborations of this approach are suggested by the discussion of the MARMIX model that appears in Chapters 13 through 15.

Coefficient Validity and Model Behavior

Something can be learned about the behavior of the equations for awareness and distribution by fixing the amount spent on PULL\$ and PUSH\$. Rearranging Equations (12-4) and (12-5), one can write

$$D_t = (1 - \Gamma D_{t-1}) Q_2 + \Gamma D_{t-1} \quad \text{and} \quad A_t = (1 - \alpha A_{t-1}) Q_4 + \alpha A_{t-1}$$

| The rate that can be gained this period | The rate that is left from last period | | The rate that can be gained this period | The rate that is left from last period |

$$Q_2 = \delta \text{PUSH\$}^{\#} + \epsilon(P \times \text{TM\$}_t^*) \quad \text{and} \quad Q_4 = \beta \text{PULL\$}^{\#} + \sigma D_t$$

| Contribution from PUSH\$ | Contribution from appeal of product to resellers | | Contribution from PULL\$ | Contribution from distribution |

This period's rate of capture of the available rate of distribution

This period's rate of capture of the available rate of awareness

These intuitively appealing equations for D_t and A_t can be restated as

$$D_t = D_{t-1} [\Gamma(1 - Q_2)] + Q_2 \quad \text{and} \quad A_t = A_{t-1} [\alpha(1 - Q_4)] + Q_4$$

Letting $Q_1 = \Gamma(1 - Q_2)$ and $Q_3 = \alpha(1 - Q_4)$ yields

$$D_t = D_{t-1} Q_1 + Q_2 \quad \text{and} \quad A_t = A_{t-1} Q_3 + Q_4$$

which are linear first-order difference equations in standard form. Because Q_2 and Q_4 are expected to be between 0 and 1, Q_1 and Q_3 must also fall within this range. When the conversant value of D_t is computed first, A_t monotonically converges to $Q_4/(1 - Q_3) = Q_4/(1 - \alpha + \alpha Q_4)$. D_t monotonically converges to $Q_2/(1 - Q_1) = Q_2/(1 - \Gamma + \Gamma Q_2)$.

The above properties provide insight into the model's behavior and a test of the validity of the model's coefficients. Unfortunately, these results cannot be applied directly to the oscillation issue because PULL\$ and PUSH\$ can vary over time. The NEWSTRAT model's allocation of total annual marketing dollars to pull and push is based on maximizing $A_t \times D_t$ and not on the two component variables.

REVIEW QUESTIONS

Q12-1 How does the approach used in this chapter build on the model presented in the two foregoing chapters?

Q12-2 How does the approach used in this chapter differ from the one used in the two foregoing chapters?

Q12-3 Discuss the meaning and importance of SCS_t.

Q12-4 Why do the awareness terms on the right-hand side of Equation (12-4) disappear in the first period?

Q12-5 Apply your response to Q12-4 to Equation (12-5) for distribution.

Q12-6 Discuss the meaning of RCA_t and RCD_t.

Q12-7 How can you directly estimate the coefficients in Equations (12-6) and (12-7)?

Q12-8 Discuss the dynamics of pull and push spending.

Q12-9 Discuss the rationale used to efficiently divide the total budget for a period into pull and push components.

Q12-10 In your own words, describe the meaning of the right-hand side of Equation (12-8). Do the same thing for Equation (12-9).

Q12-11 On purely operational and applied grounds, justify the division of the total budget into efforts to retain current buyers and to gain brand-switching buyers.

Q12-12 Discuss the role of the offer in this analysis.

Q12-13 Why might a first-year strategy require separate analysis?

Q12-14 When and why might one overrule the recommendations of the model?

Q12-15 Explain the basic operations of the NEW-STRAT program.

Q12-16 Discuss the difficulty one might experience answering questions Q6 and Q15 in Figure 12-1.

Q12-17 Why do the NEWSTRAT results for the Canadian whiskey problem differ so much from the results displayed in the spreadsheet in Table 11-1?

Q12-18 Discuss the effect of various levels of the decay coefficients on the results expected from a strategy/budget.

Q12-19 Discuss the issues surrounding smoothing of year-to-year allocations to pull and push activities.

Q12-20 What can be learned from a detailed study of the trial budgets examined during the analysis of each year's strategy?

Q12-21 What did you learn from Figures 12-3 and 12-4?

Q12-22 Discuss the ways in which one can make a strategy work better.

Q12-23 Discuss the conclusions one can draw from Figure 12-5.

Q12-24 If the response curves for years 6–10 were plotted on Figure 12-5, what would they look like? What is the maximum level attained by SCS_t?

Q12-25 Show that the limit of A_t and D_t defined in the section on Coefficient Validity of Appendix 12-1 for constant expenditures has the same form as the definition of LRR. Is this reasonable?

COMPUTER EXERCISES MULTIPERIOD PLANS AND BUDGETS: THE NEWSTRAT PROGRAM

1. Rerun the NEWSTRAT data in NEWZ1 (file 1) using the three annual (000) levels of total marketing spending (Q5):

Year	(1)	(2)	(3)
1	10000	10000	8000
2	9000	9000	8000
3	8500	7500	8000
4	8500	7500	8000
5	8500	7500	8000
6	8500	7500	8000
7	8500	7500	8000
8	8500	7500	8000
9	8500	7500	8000
10	8500	7500	8000

Before making a computer run for each case, make whatever changes in the inputs to Q6 and

Q15 that you believe are needed to reflect the new spending levels. During each run, save the resulting data in file 2, labeling it BUDGET TRIALS.

a. Did you use externally generated coefficients (based on the Test Problem) or did you let the model compute new coefficients in each case? If new coefficients were produced, how much did they change the model?

b. What did you learn from comparing the results from (1) and (2) with the high budget results displayed in Tables 12-1, 12-2, and 12-3 and Figure 12-2?

c. What effect did the less aggressive introduction in case (3) have on the performance measures?

d. Are any other analyses needed before the marketing manager makes a final decision on this product?

2. Assume that the model coefficients have been estimated and will be used in a modified version of the spreadsheet in Figure 12-1.

a. Describe the changes that will be required to allow one to go from planned annual expenditures directly to computed estimates of the intermediate variables (A_t, D_t, RR_t, SBR_t . . .).

b. Write the equations for A_t, D_t, RR_t, and SBR_t in Lotus 123® format after indicating the new line arrangement (if any) that your spreadsheet will have.

3. Using the input data in Q1–Q6 of Figure 12-1, compute the values of β, δ, c and g. Compare your results with the values recorded in Q18–Q21.

PART 5

MARKETING DELIVERS VALUE: PLANNING AN ANNUAL STRATEGY/BUDGET

ONE-PERIOD MARKETING PLANS AND BUDGETS: ESTABLISHED PRODUCTS

USING THE MARMIX PLANNING AND BUDGETING MODEL

MORE TOPICS IN PLANNING AND BUDGET ANALYSIS

13

ONE-PERIOD MARKETING PLANS AND BUDGETS: ESTABLISHED PRODUCTS

The last section of Chapter 10 discussed the scope of marketing and the tasks and tools that are appropriate to a particular product and market. These remarks were made in the context of developing a marketing plan for a new or improved product. With modest modifications, they apply to mature products as well. As a product class develops over time, product designs and manufacturing methods tend to change more slowly, distribution stabilizes, and customers need less new product knowledge. Buying and selling become more routine. These conditions reduce the capacity for marketing to add value and tend to lower the share of the purchase price devoted to marketing effort. Nevertheless, the model developed in the last chapter emphasized the fact that substantial ongoing marketing effort is required to sustain or expand product's sales and profits during the period following market introduction.

Potential buyers and users of new and improved products have less than adequate information about these products. In addition, distributors are uncertain about the product's likely market performance. The marketing program which supports such a product must educate customers and resellers about the offer's virtues. Time is required to complete this process. Marketing support spending carries this burden, and the results need to be assessed by examining direct measures such as share of awareness and distribution as well as sales over time.

An established product presents the marketing manager with a different strategy and budgeting problem. Although some market dynamics are normal, such products have achieved a degree of market stability. It is hard to generate a great deal of excitement about an established product because it is no longer new and its formerly distinctive characteristics may have been copied. In this situation, the task is more likely to be to provide incentives for renewed or repeat brand purchases and to encourage distributors to give the brand an advantageous share of the push they give to the product class. Awareness and distribution levels will tend to change slowly. Experience on the part of all the actors makes it easier to predict the outcome of marketing effort in terms of changes in sales and market share.

Still, efforts to improve market share continue to be divisible into changes in the offer and changes in the level and allocation of marketing support. Since the problem of analyzing ways to improve the offer has already been discussed in Chapters 5 and 6, the focus here will be on how many dollars should be spent in support of the offer during the coming planning period. The use of a single period that is rarely longer than a year is due to the predominately tactical characteristics of such marketing programs.

A perspective on marketing planning for established products and the associated MARMIX model are discussed in the following sections. A number of related items will be deferred to later chapters. Chapter 14 includes detailed instructions for using the model, an illustrative application, and some notes on the interpretation of the program output. Chapter 15 extends the model to include such matters as the distribution of a fixed budget to mix elements, the use of awareness and distribution as intervening model variables, and the analysis of decentralized strategies and budgets which become components in an overall division or company marketing budget.

MARKETING PLANS FOR AN ESTABLISHED PRODUCT

A marketing budget is prepared for two principal purposes: planning and control. From a planning perspective, a budget assigns resources to a strategy and work to the various parts of the marketing organization and outside suppliers. From a control perspective, however, a budget is more than a financial forecast; it is a commitment to make an agreed-upon outcome happen.

In practice, most companies use a "goals down, plans up" approach. Top management reviews the company's long-term strategic opportunities and requirements, usually once a year, and sets goals for the coming twelve months (Kotler, 1988). Next, each unit of the organization develops proposals that support this long-term strategy. These plans, once approved by top management, become the official plan and budget.

Whatever the form of the process and scope of the budgeting effort, it is important to realize that the principal purpose of the budget is to facilitate the implementation of a strategy through planning and control. This means that an overarching strategy statement must be available before an effective budget can be drawn up. Experience indicates that this fact is often overlooked and can lead to substantial problems (de Kluyver and Pessemier 1986). A bad strategy is hard to implement—it is considerably more difficult than a good strategy. Yet rarely are budget shortfalls attributed to strategic deficiencies. More commonly, the execution of the strategy is called into question.

For these reasons, the MARMIX decision support model cannot be employed until two essential sets of decisions have been made. The *first* set of decisions are those required by the strategic plan for a product or product line. Typically this longer-term plan will include consideration of matters not properly part of an annual marketing budget, such as construction plans and long-run product development. The *second* set of decisions that falls outside the scope of the annual marketing budget concerns the nature of the offer. How a product is positioned in terms of advertising copy and how the product will be priced influence demand and revenue, but unlike marketing support spending, they do not directly result in marketing expenditures. Nevertheless, the nature of the offer is an essential fact that a manager must have when planning the supporting marketing budget.

As shown in Figure 13-1, MARMIX helps marketing management to determine the appropriate size of the budget and the best way to distribute the budget across the expense categories

FIGURE 13-1   The marketing planning process.

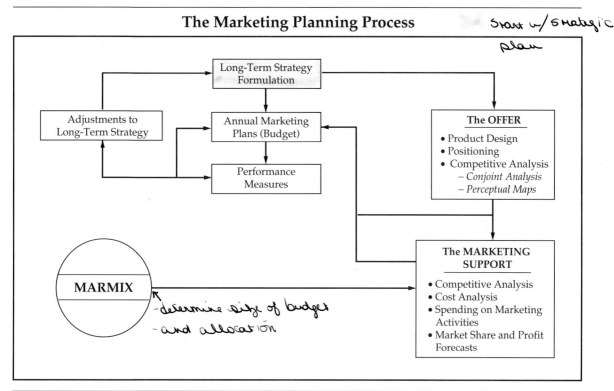

[handwritten: Start w/ strategic plan]

[handwritten near MARMIX: – determine size of budget – and allocation]

[handwritten in text: historical data to explain]

or mix elements that make up the annual marketing budget. Nevertheless, the process starts at the top of the diagram with a strategic plan. The current year in this plan provides the immediate background required to formulate current decisions concerning both *the offer* and *the marketing support* for the offer. The left side of the flow chart shows the feedback from marketing performance. If performance is not in line with the plan, adjustments must be made in the strategic plan and in the two major elements in the annual marketing plan.

Over the past decade or two, a number of useful methods, such as conjoint analysis and joint-space analysis, have been developed to help formulate the best offer. Another group of modeling approaches has also appeared that deals principally with the marketing support

given to the offer. Two examples of this group are BRANDAID (Little, 1970) and MARMIX (Pessemier, 1982). When detailed sales and marketing data are available, analytical methods can be used to help a manager understand the forces driving market results. Cooper and Nakinishi (1988) have applied this modeling approach to grocery products, and Rangaswamy and Krishnamruthi (1991) have fitted a multiplicative model to pharmaceutical prescriptions.

This text cannot fully cover the advantages and limitations of various formal models that use historical data directly to explain market behavior. It is sufficient to note that they can be useful, often powerful adjuncts to the various approaches outlined here. One must recognize, however, the limitations of analyzing market observations. *First,* changing conditions can render the past either irrelevant or positively misleading. *Second,* the range covered by the recorded independent variables may be too narrow to provide valid indications of their effects. For example, a model may include a variable that measures price differences between competing brands. If these differences are very small, most models correctly indicate that these price differences were unimportant determinants of sales. Nevertheless, this analysis is silent about the possibly large effect that a big sustainable price difference would have on sales. *Third,* because models must simplify reality, omitted variables frequently lead to incorrect conclusions about the causes of market behavior.

The limitations noted above become particularly troublesome when the analysis focuses on fewer aggregate units. When a single product or single geographic area is examined, degrees of freedom may become a problem. More importantly, it is often impossible to observe enough variation in measured variables or to obtain measures of all key variables. For example, if all competitors in an area are either doing or not doing something of potential importance, the effects of this marketing action must be examined by direct experimentation or by reference to other areas that have less limited experience (but may also differ in other important ways). In most cases, managers must rely on broader theoretical or experimental knowledge rather than causal or econometric models.

We believe that the MARMIX model is a powerful, understandable approach that managers can tailor to their special circumstances. After a MARMIX model has been constructed, it represents a *manager's* beliefs about the market rather than the model builder's beliefs about the market.

MARMIX Objectives

The objectives of MARMIX are highlighted in Figure 13-2. The model is built to take advantage of the accumulated wisdom of the marketing

FIGURE 13-2   MARMIX objectives.

MARMIX Objectives

- Mirror management's understanding of the market in a formal model.

- Use the formal model to predict the market share and profit results of any marketing budget.

- Use the model's predictive power to find the best level of total spending and the best distribution of this amount across the different kinds of marketing activities or mix elements.

organization, the personal judgments of its experienced leaders, and any external evidence relevant to the product, product class, and market. Nevertheless, it is parsimonious, as managers must provide information that is limited to essentials and concerns easily understood matters. Only twenty-three questions must be answered when completing the MARMIX data requirements.

Once the model has been built and management gains confidence in its validity, MARMIX can be used to predict the market share and profit results that are implied by any marketing budget. The model allows a manager to see how sensitive market share and profits are to changes in the organization's long-term strategy, the offer, the chosen spending pattern, market conditions, and competitive actions. In addition to being an aid to making current decisions, the modeling activity also enhances management's understanding of the product's market and financial behavior.

The end result of this process is a model that helps a manager determine how much to spend during the next period and how to spend it. MARMIX performs this task in a way that lets the manager know how a full range of total budgets would perform if each budget were efficiently allocated. In short, the model will help the manager to choose the best overall spending level and the best distribution of these dollars to the separate marketing activities.

The Frame of Marketing Effectiveness

A convenient way to represent the relationship between expenditures in an expense category, or mix element, and marketplace results is with the frame of marketing effectiveness shown in Figure 13-3. The horizontal axis represents spending on a single mix element that ranges from its minimum to maximum level. In most cases, the minimum expenditure level will be zero, but in some instances, a nonzero minimum may exist

because of constraints such as an existing contractual agreement covering media. The upper limit can be a spending level beyond which additional spending is expected to have little or no positive results or it can be any other limit imposed by management. This axis is usually scaled in terms of the dollars spent on that mix element or activity, but can also be scaled as a percentage of sales for some categories such as sales force commission.

The vertical axis shows the *percentage* of the potential market share change that spending a given amount on this mix element can have. These two axes of a *frame of marketing effectiveness* appear in Figure 13-3, along with a variety of response function forms.

As spending ranges from the minimum level

FIGURE 13-3   The frame of marketing effectiveness.

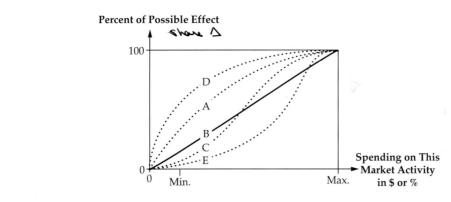

**Frame of Marketing Effectiveness:
An Essential Building Block**

Percent of Possible Effect

share Δ

Max = The Largest Allowable Level of Spending

A = A Concave Formal Response Function
B = A Linear Formal Response Function   } • Formal Response Functions Are Built In
C = An S-shaped Formal Response Function

D & E = Illustrative Direct Response Function   • Direct Response Functions Are Defined by the User

Min = Lowest Allowable Level of Spending   • Response Functions Assume a Normal Competitive Spending Response to Your Spending Level to a maximum, it is expected to produce increasingly favorable sales results, but not necessarily at a uniform rate per dollar spent. Furthermore, there is little reason to believe that the pattern of results, as spending goes from zero to its maximum level, will be the same for all marketing activities. To accommodate these differences, MARMIX provides two options: A manager or analyst can select either one of three preprogrammed functions or can directly define the shape of the function.

The three MARMIX preprogrammed functions are displayed in Figure 13-3: concave downward (A), linear (B), and S-shaped (C). The *concave* function represents the case in which the first dollars spent produce the greatest effect per dollar; as spending increases the efficiency of each dollar decreases. The *S-shaped* function produces little effect per dollar at low spending levels. In the mid-spending range, efficiency increases rapidly. As spending approaches the maximum, efficiency declines. The *linear* function produces the same effect per dollar at all expenditure levels.

Alternatively, the manager can directly define any monotonically increasing response function that represents how spending levels on a marketing activity are expected to translate into market results. The upper and lower (D and E) dashed functions in Figure 13-3 are examples of directly defined functions. The shape is strictly up to the responsible manager and his or her analysts.

The expected share effect of spending will vary from one category or mix element to another. For some products, the maximum effect of advertising may be small, but for other products, large spending will produce relatively large results. At a later point, *the frame of marketing effectiveness for each mix element will be rescaled in recognition of its unique effectiveness.*

Mode of Operation

The user of MARMIX has to provide the four classes of inputs shown in Figure 13-4a. The *first* class of inputs concerns the basic economics of the market and the product, such as the level of primary demand and the product's unit price and variable cost. The *second* set contains the descriptions of the separate market mix ele-

FIGURE 13-4a & b How MARMIX works.

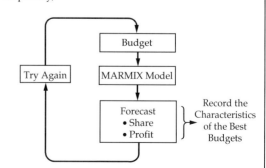

How MARMIX Works

Usen provides these 4 inputs:

- Management provides basic data about the size of the market, unit price and cost, etc.

- Marketing activities are organized into meaningful expense categories or mix elements.

- Management judges how spending on each mix element influences market share.

- Management judges how the market results produced by spending on one mix element may be related to spending on other mix elements.

The above data let MARMIX build a model that incorporates available knowledge and managerial judgments.

This model enables repeated forecasts using trial budgets. Graphically,

Budget → MARMIX Model → Forecast • Share • Profit → Record the Characteristics of the Best Budgets; Try Again

ments or activities. The *third* class of data concerns defining the characteristics of each mix element's *frame of marketing effectiveness*. The *fourth* class specifies how the frames of marketing effectiveness for the separate mix elements should be combined to produce the overall result.

With all of the inputs in place, the MARMIX model builds a mathematical representation that mirrors management's beliefs about the market and that forecasts the market share and profit consequences of any budget. As shown in Figure 13-4b, by repeating the process of choosing a trial budget, computing the results, and keeping a record of the best budget allocation at each of ten total spending levels, the model can guide the selection of a very efficient total budget and an efficient distribution of the budget to individual expense categories.

MARMIX Benefits

An important and easily overlooked benefit of using a model like MARMIX is that it requires a fresh, often revealing look at the marketing activities conducted on behalf of a product or product line. Too often marketing expenditures are placed in convenient accounting categories that have little to do with explicit strategic objectives. For example, all sales salaries may be aggregated even though some sales activities may be directed toward wholesalers and others may be directed toward retailers. Similarly, some advertising may be designed to raise consumer awareness and other advertising may try to influence the ordering behavior of selected wholesalers. Any important marketing activity with a separate set of objectives, measures of effectiveness, and spending requirements should be analyzed separately. The MARMIX model encourages this kind of thoughtful analysis.

Once the spending categories or marketing mix elements have been properly described, a *frame of marketing effectiveness* is defined for each mix element. The frame provides a disciplined,

common perspective for a marketing manager and his or her associates to represent their beliefs about how the market will respond to marketing spending on each important activity. Furthermore, the standard marketing effectiveness frame reminds management to consider the degree of confidence it has in the essential data about each activity, and may suggest opportunities to collect additional information. This deeper understanding of the marketing process can enhance management's capacity to communicate the bases of its budget request and allocation decision to upper levels of management.

Besides considering the effect of spending on one mix element or activity while all other activities are at a given level, MARMIX also requires one to think about the degree to which the effectiveness of spending in one area depends on the level of spending in other areas. In most markets, the effect of spending on one activity will depend on the spending in one or more other activities or mix elements. A benefit of the MARMIX model is that management's beliefs about these matters are directly represented by the structure of the model and are used to predict the results of any expenditure pattern. The model's structure is determined by the model user, not the creator of the decision aid.

In addition to the expanded knowledge and communication capacity one gains from using the MARMIX model, it also has the capacity to locate a best level of total spending on behalf of the product or product line and the best allocation of these dollars to the various marketing mix elements. Not only does the model locate the single superior spending pattern, but it also offers a range of efficient budgets which helps management better appreciate how the market responds to marketing actions.

Another model benefit grows out of MARMIX's capacity to easily construct alternative models, each of which may represent competing beliefs. This allows each participant in the budgeting process to have his or her own model and predictions of the results of adopting any particular budget. In this case, each of these models can predict the results of whatever budget is adopted and the actual market outcome can be compared to these forecasts.

A related model benefit is its capacity to employ several estimates of a given input. By using different levels of an input about which one is uncertain, the separate derivative forecasts will indicate how sensitive the predicted outcomes are to possible errors in the assumptions going into the model. If results and the budgets that the model recommends are very sensitive to an input about which there is a great deal of uncertainty, management should consider ways to improve confidence in the inputs used in the final model.

A further aspect of the model's flexibility is its capacity to look at the effects of possible future changes in the market and the firm's offer. If a price, design, or positioning change is being considered, the effect on the supporting marketing program and the product's profitability can easily be examined. This same kind of analysis can be conducted to study the effects of external matters such as changes in competitors' behavior. Figure 13-5 summarizes the benefits MARMIX can deliver to the individual manager and the organization.

How to Select and View Mix Elements

Since the selection of appropriate expense categories is so important, the four basic criteria for defining marketing mix elements must be kept in mind. The *first* one is market *responsiveness.* This means that explicit favorable marketing results must flow from spending on the activity in question. *Second* is *controllability.* If a manager has no control over the level of spending on an element, it should not be included. This matter is significant in organizations in which responsibility for a product or product line is diffuse. It can indicate the need for joint budgeting activities, reorganization, or some other mechanism to prevent the division of authority from creating

FIGURE 13-5   The ways that MARMIX can help you.

Ways MARMIX Can Help You

- Help you identify and describe your marketing actions in analytically useful terms.

- Help you think through how spending on each marketing activity affects share and profit results.

- Help you see how the effects of the separate marketing activities combine to produce overall share and profit results.

... MOST IMPORTANTLY,

- Help you find the "best" total budget and distribution of the budget to each marketing activity (or mix element), and let you examine a wide range of attractive alternatives.

- Provide one or more models that can be used to forecast the effect of marketing budgets–past, present, and future.

- Provide a way to test how sensitive a budget's expected performance is to errors in the model's inputs.

- Provide a way to explore the share and profit effect of change in the relative desirability of your product (the offer), and external events such as more aggressive competition.

---

inefficient marketing budgets. The *third* criterion is *separability.* If it is impractical to separately account for significant marketing activities, it will become difficult to understand how allocated resources produce results. The *fourth* criterion is *simplicity.* Generally speaking, managers should ignore or pool unimportant activities to make the task of model construction simpler and the results easier to communicate.

The question of market responsiveness is fundamental to effective thinking about a marketing budget and, more generally, to the formulation of a marketing strategy. Spending on marketing activities is undertaken for one of three purposes:

1. To change the perceptions or knowledge levels of consumers, distributors, or even competitors in some favorable manner;

2. To favorably change their preferences or dispositions to act; or

3. To change their behavior in some favorable way.

The expected market results of spending need to be identified and measures of these outcomes need to be available so that management can tell how well spending is achieving the desired results. The above selection criteria for mix elements are summarized in Figure 13-6.

Sample Frames of Marketing Effectiveness

Share effects of response function forms   As Figure 13-7a shows, a linear response function returns the same size increment of market results for each equal size increment of spending. The value of each additional dollar of spending is constant. For example, when spending money to add stores to a consumer in-store sampling campaign, each added store might be expected to yield about the same added sales volume. In Figure 13-7b, a concave downward response function produces the greatest return per dollar at low levels of spending and progressively smaller returns per dollar as spending approaches the maximum practical level. This effect might occur in the in-store sampling example if one is able to choose the largest stores first, then move on to progressively smaller stores. The S-shaped response function shown in Figure 13-7c produces little in the way of results per dollar at low levels of expenditure, but in the mid-range the return per dollar is

FIGURE 13-6   Criteria for selecting mix elements.

Criteria for Selecting Mix Elements
(Categories of Marketing Action)

- MARKET RESPONSIVENESS – results must results
- Controllability – do they oversee
- Separability (internal records)
- Simplicity (amount spent) – is it important?

- RESPONSIVENESS concerns the degree to which expenditures favorably change...
  - Knowledge
  - Disposition and/or
  - Behavior
  among key actors (consumers, distributors, competitors, etc.)

FIGURE 13-7a   Frame of marketing effectiveness—linear element.

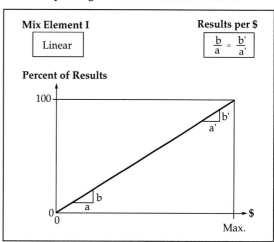

Frame of Marketing Effectiveness:
Spending—Percent of Attainable Results

much improved. At higher levels of spending the return per dollar declines to progressively lower levels. For example, the potential effect of modest media spending can be limited by the clutter of competing messages, and high levels of media spending can induce wearout among an increasing percentage of the audience.

One should also consider the relationship between the overall amount of share gained and the change in expenditure that is required to achieve it. A very small maximum expenditure in relation to the share gain produced by that activity tells management that whatever can be gained is available for a modest commitment of marketing dollars. On the other hand, if the maximum spending level for a mix element is very large in relation to the share gain it can produce, it is far more costly to gain any proportion of the possible marketing results. *As the maximum expenditure level increases, the percentage of the results attained at any spending level will decline.* The opposite effects are observed when a maximum is decreased. In short, the maximum level of spending in relationship to the associated

FIGURE 13-7c   Frame of marketing effectiveness—S-shaped element.

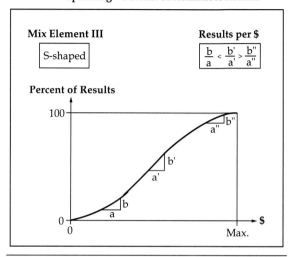

FIGURE 13-7b   Frame of marketing effectiveness—concave element.

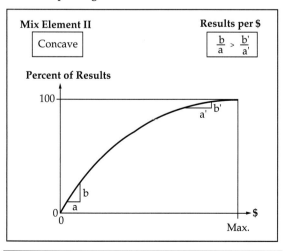

share results is a strong determinant of the marketing activity's efficiency.

Efficiency of mix elements   The frame of marketing effectiveness lets a manager see the degree to which a marketing activity or mix element produces marketing results. *This is done by specifying how market share changes as marketing expenditures on the mix element range from their lowest to their highest level.* These data are used to rescale the vertical results axis so that results are stated in terms of market share points instead of in terms of the percentage of possible results. The top graph in Figure 13-8 shows a mix element that has the potential of producing five share points, whereas the bottom graph shows a mix element that has a potential for producing three share points.

If two mix elements have the same shape and potential for changing market share but do not have the same maximum spending levels, the mix element with the lower maximum level will be the more efficient mix element. This is illustrated in Figure 13-9.

FIGURE 13-8 Frame of marketing effectiveness—additive mix element—differing effect.

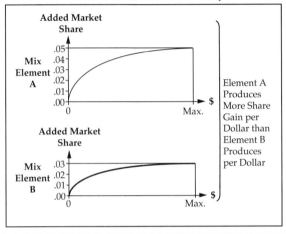

Frame of Marketing Effectiveness:
Additive Mix Elements–
Potential Results and Efficiency

Element A Produces More Share Gain per Dollar than Element B Produces per Dollar

FIGURE 13-9 Frame of marketing effectiveness—differing costs of additive mix elements.

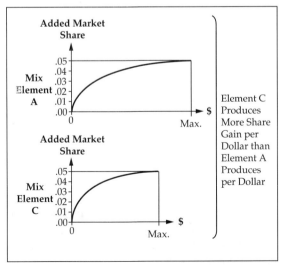

Frame of Marketing Effectiveness:
Additive Mix Elements–
Potential Results and Efficiency

Element C Produces More Share Gain per Dollar than Element A Produces per Dollar

Figure 13-10 shows how the effectiveness of all the mix elements can be displayed on a common graph to facilitate the comparison of the share contribution and cost efficiency of each mix element. The admissible range of spending and the share change caused by going from the minimum level to the maximum level is readily observable. For example, assume that spending on TV advertising can decrease from the normal level of $300,000 to a minimum of $200,000 or increase to a maximum of $900,000. When moving over this range, the sales effect is eight share points, the difference between the 20 and the 28 percent shares. Since the share change of 8 percent is obtained by spending $700,000 over the minimum, this overall expenditure produces 1.14 share points per $100,000 in advertising spending. Computing this index for each of the mix elements provides a rough basis for comparing their overall efficiency. The real efficiency of each element, however, often depends on the interactions among mix elements as well as the shape of the response function. This is the subject of a later discussion.

Additive and multiplicative effects All of the frames of marketing effectiveness that have been displayed so far have shown mix elements that are represented as being independent of other mix elements. In this case, a spending level indicates the change in the number of share points that a mix element contributes. This is called an additive model. When the sum is computed across all mix elements, one has an estimate of the market share that a given budget will produce.

If some of the mix elements interact with other mix elements in making their contribution, the vertical axis of the frame of marketing effectiveness must be scaled in a different manner. Figure 13-11 shows a multiplicative (interactive) mix element with the vertical scale arranged such that at the normal level of spending on

FIGURE 13-10   Market share effect of mix element spending.

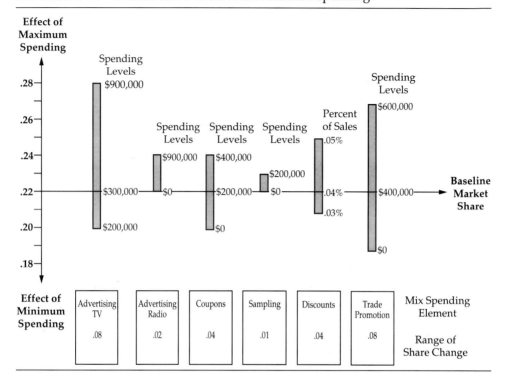

the mix element the mix element's contribution to sales will not change the product's normal market share. As expenditures are cut below the normal level, an appropriate percentage reduction is made in the normal market share to reflect the lower support level. When expenditures on a mix element rise above the normal level, the normal market share is increased to reflect these effects of the increased support.

Using Frames to Build a Model

The additive case   In the foregoing text, the basic desirability of the offer was represented by *P*, the share of choices that the product would receive from informed customers who had all competing products available. Here a somewhat different approach is used in which the market share achieved at the normal or baseline rate of support spending is adjusted downward to allow for the share contribution made by normal support spending. The remaining share is the share that can be attributed solely to the offer. The expected market share result from a given budget will be the simple sum of all the elements in the additive model; the share contributed by the offer and the share contributed by the marketing support. See Figure 13-12.

The multiplicative case   The all-multiplicative model is one in which the market share effects of spending on any one element depend on the spending levels for all the other marketing mix elements. It differs in formal structure

FIGURE 13-11   Frame of marketing effectiveness—multiplicative mix element.

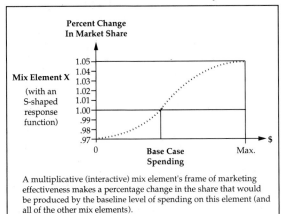

Frame of Marketing Effectiveness:
Multiplicative Mix Elements—
Potential Results and Efficiency

A multiplicative (interactive) mix element's frame of marketing effectiveness makes a percentage change in the share that would be produced by the baseline level of spending on this element (and all of the other mix elements).

from the additive model. In common with the additive model, the baseline market share is that which is expected when all mix elements are at their normal level of spending. The spending levels in any proposed new budget can produce *percentage* increases or decreases in the normal share. Furthermore, this percentage is multiplied by the percentage changes caused by other elements. Figure 13-13 shows the structure of the all-multiplicative or fully interactive model.

The mixed model case   It is also possible that some mix elements make an independent (additive) contribution and other mix elements interact or depend of the level of spending of other mix elements for their effect (multiplicative). MARMIX can also handle this situation. Here, one must specify the dependencies that must be accounted for. The model that the program develops will take these relationships into account. As Figure 13-14 indicates, the formal structure gets a little messy, but all the user has to do is specify the relevant relationships.

As Figures 13-12 through 13-14 imply, for any

model structure one can appraise the share of revenue that is due to the value of the offer and the share that is due to the value created by marketing effort. For details supporting this assertion, see Appendix 14-1.

Origin of the Effects of Spending

An issue that arises in connection with the minimum level of spending concerns where the starting value or origin of the response function should be located. It might be that a firm cannot hire sales personnel for a commission rate of less than 3 percent. In this case, the origin of the response function is at 3 percent even if quality requirements may dictate a 4.5 percent minimum. See for example, Figure 13-15. On the other hand, a firm may have a contract that requires management to spend a minimum amount on a particular type of media. Spending levels below the latter minimum would produce results, so the origin of the response function

FIGURE 13-12   Using effectiveness frames to build a model—the additive case.

Using Effectiveness Frames to Build a Model

THE OFFER is the basic product element in the model. It is the share that is attributable solely to the product's design, price and positioning. It is the base case's (or any period's) market share less the share attributable to marketing expenditures.

ADDITIVE MIX ELEMENTS define what spending on a mix element can independently add to the share produced by the offer. A pure (simple) additive model could be:

Market Share = Market Share + Market Share
                        Due to   Due to
                     THE OFFER   One or More
                                        MIX ELEMENTS

These contributions to market share
are all independent of each other.

FIGURE 13-13   Using effectiveness frames to build a model—the multiplicative case.

Using Effectiveness Frames to Build a Model

MULTIPLICATIVE MIX ELEMENTS define the percentage of change a spending level for the mix element will make in the product's bases case market share. (Recall the base case share is influenced by the offer AND the base case spending on all mix elements). In a pure multiplicative model, each element's effect on market share depends on the contribution of all other elements. Here,

$$\text{Market Share} = \begin{pmatrix} \text{Normal or} \\ \text{Base Case} \\ \text{Market Share} \end{pmatrix} \times \begin{pmatrix} \text{Share Change} \\ \text{Due to} \\ \text{Spending on} \\ \text{Mix Element} \\ \text{A} \end{pmatrix} \times \begin{pmatrix} \text{Share Change} \\ \text{Due to} \\ \text{Product of Other} \\ \text{Mix Element's} \\ \text{Contributions} \end{pmatrix}$$

All elements affect each other.

should be zero and the minimum expenditure level would be the mandated minimum. MARMIX provides the option of using either type of origin (beginning level) of the response function for each frame of marketing effectiveness.

Finally, the fixed cost of initiating a marketing action can be modeled by using the minimum. For example, to solicit orders by phone, a firm may have to equip a facility before it hires operators. The fixed cost could be treated as

FIGURE 13-14   Using effectiveness frames to build a model—both additive and multiplicative elements.

Using Effectiveness Frames and Multiplicative Elements

MIXED MODEL WITH BOTH ADDITIVE AND MULTIPLICATIVE ELEMENTS

Most marketing programs have activities or mix elements that make independent contributions and other mix elements that interact with one or more other mix elements. For a seven mix element case, one might have

$$\text{Market Share} = \begin{pmatrix} \text{Additive} \\ \text{Element} \\ \#6 \end{pmatrix} + \begin{pmatrix} \text{Additive} \\ \text{Element} \\ \#2 \end{pmatrix} + \left\{ \left[\begin{pmatrix} \text{Multi} \\ \text{Element} \\ \#1 \end{pmatrix} \times \begin{pmatrix} \text{Multi} \\ \text{Element} \\ \#4 \end{pmatrix} \times \begin{pmatrix} \text{Multi} \\ \text{Element} \\ \#7 \end{pmatrix} \right] \right.$$

$$\left. + \left[\begin{pmatrix} \text{Multi} \\ \text{Element} \\ \#3 \end{pmatrix} \times \begin{pmatrix} \text{Multi} \\ \text{Element} \\ \#5 \end{pmatrix} \right] \right\} \times \begin{pmatrix} \text{Offer's} \\ \text{Relative} \\ \text{Desirability} \end{pmatrix}$$

[handwritten annotations: ⊗, "Base Case Mkt Share", "Cont of Offer.", ✳]

Fortunately, the user of MARMIX does not have to be concerned with how these more complicated structures are developed. The program does it for the user.

FIGURE 13-15 Review of the effects of marketing spending.

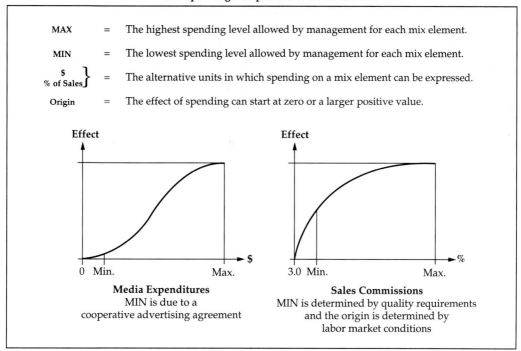

Review of the Effects of Spending
The Spending Components of a Mix Element

MAX   =   The highest spending level allowed by management for each mix element.

MIN   =   The lowest spending level allowed by management for each mix element.

$ \left.\begin{matrix} \$ \\ \% \text{ of Sales} \end{matrix}\right\} $ = The alternative units in which spending on a mix element can be expressed.

Origin   =   The effect of spending can start at zero or a larger positive value.

Media Expenditures
MIN is due to a
cooperative advertising agreement

Sales Commissions
MIN is determined by quality requirements
and the origin is determined by
labor market conditions

both a minimum and the origin, but any contemplated spending below this level is automatically treated as zero spending.

How the MARMIX Model Makes Recommendations

Once the minimum and maximum spending levels have been specified, the model selects a total budget from one of the eight evenly spaced budget levels within the range of possible total expenditures. Next, it randomly assigns the available total budget to the separate marketing activities. In making this assignment, the model takes the limits that have been imposed on spending for each mix element into account. The model then forecasts the market share, sales,

and profit consequences of this budget allocation. This part of the program has the same structural features that have been described above: a set of frames of marketing effectiveness combined in an additive, multiplicative, or mixed manner.

The program draws repeated sample budgets and budget allocations, predicts their consequences, and keeps track of the best results. After testing thousands of sample budgets, the program can give a manager a very good picture of how market share and profits are likely to respond to various size budgets that have been efficiently distributed to the separate mix elements.

Once this task has been completed, the program makes further improvements in the best allocation found at each of the eight out of the ten total budget levels. (The two extreme budget levels cannot be reallocated.) The final result is the most attractive budget found for each of the ten budget levels spread across the feasible range of spending. Finally, a substantial amount of descriptive detail is presented about each of these ten budgets. Figure 13-16 summarizes the process.

Figures 13-17 and 13-18 display some of the most important types of program output. Figure 13-17 summarizes the contribution to profit and market share results of an analysis. Contribution to profit and share results are displayed for the best budget at each spending level. These data give management a good overview of how share and profit (both in absolute terms and in terms of the productivity per marketing dollar[1]) change

across the entire feasible range of marketing spending.

In this illustration, the contribution to profit does not vary greatly, as the total marketing budget ranges from $1.4 million to $2.0 million. Nevertheless, the expected market share at the lower budget is 32 percent and at the higher budget 36 percent. (The above contribution figures include an adjustment for the future value of a share gain or loss from the current or normal share.)

If marketing dollars are not rationed, a manager will tend to choose the budget with the highest total contribution to profit. When a fixed total marketing budget is allocated across two or more products or product classes, a manager will choose the set of budgets which jointly will yield the largest contribution to profit given the fixed total budget. Chapter 15 explains an analytical approach to this broader budgeting problem.

---

[1]This figure can be negative becasue it is the change from the minimum spending level and excludes co-op spending.

FIGURE 13-16   How MARMIX makes budget recommendations.

- Choose one of ten total budgets spread across the range from the smallest to the largest total budget.

- Randomly allocate the total budget to the separate mix elements.

- Compute the share and profit results and see if this is the best profit showing of any budget at this budget's total spending level. If it is, file the budget's characteristics for future reference.

REPEAT THE PROCESS MANY TIMES

- Choose the ten best budgets, one for each total spending level and try to improve the performance by making additions and deletions to the mix spending levels.

- Display the characteristics of these improved budgets. For each budget, display

  - Total Profit
  - Market Share
  - Total Marketing Spending and Its Distribution
  - The Amount of Cooperative Funding
  - The Weight Given Future Effects
  - The Market Share per Dollar Spent
  - The Profit per Dollar Spent

FIGURE 13-17 Best total marketing budgets for ten equally spaced budgets from minimum to maximum spending.

**Best Total Marketing Budgets from
10 Equal Size Intervals from Minimum to Maximum Spending**

Trial Budget Number	Total Marketing Budget	Contribution		Marketing Share	
		Dollars	Per Marketing Dollar	Units	Per (000000) Marketing
1	261,281	470,564	0.00	0.106	0.000
2	602,277	623,965	0.44	0.157	0.145
3	953,759	757,009	0.41	0.205	0.142
4	1,384,832	1,522,306	0.94	0.324	0.195
5	1,724,674	1,400,053	0.64	0.346	0.165
6	2,056,063	1,189,221	0.40	0.358	0.141
7	2,388,201	924,051	0.23	0.367	0.123
8	2,717,527	695,615	0.09	0.374	0.110
9	3,042,240	417,998	−.02	0.378	0.099
10	3,364,800	126,698	−.10	0.380	0.083

The next output form is somewhat more complex but helps management to understand some important additional features of each of the budgets that was summarized in Figure 13-17. Figure 13-18 separates contribution to profit into the amount attributable to the coming planning period and the amount that is due to the effects that the budget's share gain or loss will have on the results in subsequent planning periods. In a similar manner, total spending is separated into the amount spent by the organization and the amount covered by cooperative allowances. Next, the program displays the allocation of the total budget to each mix element. Finally, dollar sales and share statistics are reported. The contribution to profit per marketing dollar and the market share per million dollars of marketing spending are also reported.

Developing MARMIX Inputs

The mix element worksheet   The mix element worksheet form is a convenient place for each participant in the budgeting process to record his or her beliefs about the essential characteristics of each mix element's frame of marketing effectiveness. Although most of the elements shown in Figure 13-19 have been discussed, nothing has been said about estimates of competitive spending. These should be recorded for three levels of spending on the firm's product since these levels can influence competitors' spending. In any event, the amount that is recorded should cover all competitors' spending on the mix element but exclude the firm's spending. (Competitive spending levels are not directly used in MARMIX's calculations, but they are included to remind the manager to consider them when making judgments.)

Once all the participants in the budget process have recorded their judgments on a mix element worksheet, their judgments can be compared. If disagreements are pronounced, a formal effort should be made to resolve the differences and to develop common data set. If necessary, separate models can be run using the different assumptions.

FIGURE 13-18 Summary of Economic Results Before Using the Improvement Routine.

Before Attempting Improvements

	1	2	3	4	5
Contribution To Profit					
Total	470,564	623,965	757,009	1,522,306	1,400,053
Current	647,052	722,413	780,529	1,360,137	1,204,520
Future	−176,488	−98,449	−23,521	162,169	195,533
Cont. per $	0.00	0.44	0.41	0.94	0.64
Total Marketing Spending					
Total	261,281	602,277	953,759	1,384,832	1,724,674
Ours	246,625	593,247	940,288	1,364,756	1,700,786
Coop.	14,656	9,030	13,471	20,077	23,887
Mix Element Spending					
Adv-TV	200,000	217,892	266,160	276,402	428,130
Adv-Radio	0	4,758	30,811	33,988	15,974
Coupons	0	148,452	158,804	205,774	338,210
Sampling	0	16,301	33,830	41,032	113,829
Discounts	0.030	0.037	0.048	0.048	0.048
Trade Prom.	0	103,805	275,321	527,399	509,884
Sales Performance					
Our $ Sales	2,042,691	3,007,223	3,933,297	6,228,326	6,640,699
Our Share	0.160	0.157	0.205	0.324	0.346
Share per $1,000,000 Mktg.	0.000	0.145	0.142	0.195	0.165

FIGURE 13-18 *(Continued)* Summary of Economic Results Before Using the Improvement Routine.

Before Attempting Improvements

	6	7	8	9	10
Contribution To Profit					
Total	1,189,221	954,051	695,615	417,998	126,698
Current	975,425	725,667	456,701	172,254	−121,856
Future	213,797	228,384	238,914	245,744	248,553
Cont. per $	0.40	0.23	0.09	−0.02	−0.10
Total Marketing Spending					
Total	2,056,063	2,388,201	2,717,527	3,042,240	3,364,800
Ours	2,028,636	2,357,272	2,683,175	3,004,556	3,313,856
Coop.	27,427	30,929	34,352	37,684	50,944
Mix Element Spending					
Adv-TV	561,263	721,433	722,234	814,841	900,000
Adv-Radio	234,650	347,809	550,120	796,931	900,000
Coupons	368,035	376,258	390,251	387,804	400,000
Sampling	30,555	76,167	129,223	177,070	200,000
Discounts	0.048	0.049	0.050	0.050	0.050
Trade Prom.	531,924	520,794	567,636	503,310	600,000
Sales Performance					
Our $ Sales	6,866,424	7,046,717	7,176,859	7,261,279	7,296,000
Our Share	0.358	0.367	0.374	0.378	0.380
Share per $1,000,000 Mktg.	0.141	0.123	0.110	0.099	0.083

FIGURE 13-19   Mix element worksheet.

Date: _____

By: _____

MIX ELEMENT WORKSHEET

Marketing Activity or Mix Element

- Element No. _____ Name: _____

- Description and objectives: _____

_____

- Measure(s) of effectiveness: _____

_____

- Inputs expressed in: $ _____, % of sales _____ .

Market
Share

- Our zero spending level _____   _____

- Our normal or baseline spending level _____   _____

- Our minimum allowable spending level _____   _____

- Our maximum practical spending level _____   _____

- Competitors' spending at our spending levels

Minimum	Normal	Maximum
_____	_____	_____

Characteristics of responses to our spending

- Origin of response to spending _____

- Response function shape and rationale

Spending % of Maximum	% Results		
0	.00	Use	Data at the left _____
1/6	.__		Formal function below _____
2/6	.__		If formal function, check one
3/6	.__		concave _____ ; s-shaped _____ ; linear _____
4/6	.__		Comments: _____
5/6	.__		_____
1	1.00		_____

- Record the number of the mix elements, if any, that this mix element interacts with _____ , _____ ,

_____ , _____ , _____ , _____ , _____ , _____ , _____ , _____

- Comments: _____

_____

_____

The MARMIX data form   The consolidated input form fills two sides of an 8.5- × 11-inch sheet of paper. One side covers general information about the market and brief descriptions of the mix elements that will be used. See Figure 13-20. It is important to define the market carefully and have a good estimate of primary demand. Typically, these are not simple matters. One input on this side of the form that has not been discussed is the sensitivity of market share at normal baseline spending levels to changes in the product's unit price. In addition to estimating market share at the baseline price level, management needs to estimate market share at three higher and three lower price levels. These data are not used directly by the model, but they are used in a final section of the analysis to suggest possible opportunities for favorably repricing the product.

The second side of the input form calls for an estimate about the frame of marketing effectiveness for each mix element (expense category) and how each mix element fits into the structure of the model. See Figure 13-21. Three other items appear on this form that have not been discussed. The first one concerns the degree to which a gain or loss of market share produced by a proposed budget will carry over into subsequent periods. See questions Q22–Q22B. The second matter concerns the degree to which suppliers and others may provide some financial support for the marketing effort. See questions Q23–Q23C. If available, this help should be recognized when assessing the desirability of any marketing budget. Third, management can record a variety of intermediate variables at the three primary spending levels: minimum, baseline, and maximum. Q24A–Q24F cover these optional background inputs.

Finally, the program offers a number of options during the progress of the analyses. These matters need not influence the basic input data, but response to these on-screen queries determine the types of analyses that will be performed.

MARMIX APPLICATIONS[2]

During the development of the MARMIX model and the associated computer program, both industrial and consumer applications were initiated. Some of the more instructive features of three industrial and three consumer product cases are described briefly below. These cases deal more with organizational and strategic questions than with technical matters. Important aspects of these latter matters will be dealt with in Chapter 14.

Industrial Products

Case 1   An early implementation of the model took place at a large (Fortune 500) company for an industrial product. The application involved the development of a marketing plan for sheets of entangled fibers that are used in the manufacture of disposable surgical gowns and drapes marketed to hospitals. The total market for surgical gowns and drapes was relatively static. The disposable segment, however (as opposed to the segment composed of reusable materials such as cotton), was growing at an annual rate of 8 percent.

The relationships among the various companies in the disposable segment were extremely complex. Some companies only manufactured the basic fabric and sold it to a second group of firms, the gown and drape makers who manufactured the end product and sold it to hospitals. Others were fully integrated. It was not uncommon, however, for fully integrated suppliers to buy some of their raw material from producers. The company for which this analysis was performed belonged to the first category: It concentrated on the manufacture of a branded, patented fabric which it sold to the two leading gown

[2]Parts of this section are based on materials originally written by Cornelis de Kluyver.

FIGURE 13-20   MARMIX data form—page 1.

DATA FORM FOR MARMIX

Completed by _____   Date _____

Date of Analysis (mm/dd/yy) _____ : I.D. Number of Data File _____

Q1: Problem description _____
_____
_____
_____

Q2: Number of months in the analysis _____

Q3: Number of mix elements _____

Q4: Names of the mix elements (12 spaces or less for each one)

1.
2.
3.
4.
5.
6.
7.
8.
9.
10.

Q5: Define the sales unit (units, gallons, dozens, etc.) _____

Q6: Primary demand (000 units) _____

Describe the components of primary demand _____
_____
_____

Q7: Baseline unit price in dollars and cents _____

Describe the components of average unit price _____
_____
_____

Q8: Unit variable cost in dollars and cents _____

Describe the components of unit variable cost _____
_____
_____

Q9: Given normal marketing expenditures, the market share at each of the
following unit prices (relative to the baseline unit price) is:

Price: −30%   −20%   −10%   Baseline   +10%   +20%   +30%
Share: . ___   . ___   . ___   . ___   . ___   . ___   . ___

① actually used by the model

FIGURE 13-21 MARMIX data form—page 2.

Mix Elements	Q10 Spend Units (Circle one) $ F	($000) Our Spending — Q11A Base Line	Q12A Min.	Q13A Max.	Competitive Spending — Q11B Base Line	Q12B Min.	Q13B Max.	Indep 0	Q14 Possible Interaction Group (one check per row) Group 1	2	3	4	5	6
1.	0 1													
2.	0 1													
3.	0 1													
4.	0 1													
5.	0 1													
6.	0 1													
7.	0 1													
8.	0 1													
9.	0 1													
10.	0 1													

Optional Intermediate Variable Questions
- Q15 Mkt share at min. spending.
- Q16 Mkt share at max. spending.
- Q24A Budget's percentage PULL effect.
- Q24B Expected percentage AWARE.
- Q24C Expected percentage DISTRIBUTION.
- Q24D Expected percentage TRIAL purchase.
- Q24E Purchase REPEAT rates.
- Q24F Purchase SWITCHBACK rates.

Mix Elements	Q17 A Funct. Form F D	B Origin (000 or .###)	Answer Q18 or Q19 only Q18: Enter the Fraction of the Largest Attainable Effect At Fraction of Maximum Effect 0/6	1/6	2/6	3/6	4/6	5/6	6/6	Q19 Funct. Shape (Circle one) C S L	Q20 Zero Spend. Share	Q21 Max. Spend. Share
1.	0 1		.00	.	.	.	.	.	1.00	1 2 3	.	.
2.	0 1		.00	.	.	.	.	.	1.00	1 2 3	.	.
3.	0 1		.00	.	.	.	.	.	1.00	1 2 3	.	.
4.	0 1		.00	.	.	.	.	.	1.00	1 2 3	.	.
5.	0 1		.00	.	.	.	.	.	1.00	1 2 3	.	.
6.	0 1		.00	.	.	.	.	.	1.00	1 2 3	.	.
7.	0 1		.00	.	.	.	.	.	1.00	1 2 3	.	.
8.	0 1		.00	.	.	.	.	.	1.00	1 2 3	.	.
9.	0 1		.00	.	.	.	.	.	1.00	1 2 3	.	.
10.	0 1		.00	.	.	.	.	.	1.00	1 2 3	.	.

Q22 What fraction (decimal) of the sales gained or lost this period will continue next period? _____
Q22A If non-zero answer, for how many periods beyond the current period will the effect last? _____
Q22B If one or more periods, what is the firm cost of capital (a decimal > 0)? _____
Q23 Is part of your marketing spending paid by entities outside your firm? Y = 1 or N = 0
Q23A If yes and a fixed amount is received, enter the amount (000) $_____
Q23B If yes and a percentage of product sales is received, enter the fraction __.__
Q23C If yes and a percentage of marketing expenses is received, enter the fraction __.__
Q24C Do you want to enter optional estimates of the intermediate effect of marketing spending? (Y = 1, N = 0)__
       If, yes, go to Q24A-Q24F above.

COMMENTS: _____
_____
_____
_____

and drape makers, one of which was a fully integrated supplier.

Intense price competition had eroded the profit margins of the gown and drape makers. In addition, a leading competitor had begun to consolidate its position as a fully integrated supplier to the medical apparel market by adding production capacity, expanding its sales force, and intensifying its R&D into lower-cost production methods.

In formulating its annual plan, the company faced other problems. First, because of the intense price competition, R&D was important to lower unit costs. Second, end-user awareness of the product was relatively low, primarily because the gown and drape makers never identified the material by name in their end product and their marketing to the hospitals. Third, the hospitals, under government pressure to reduce costs, were becoming more price sensitive, and purchase decisions were increasingly being made by administrators rather than by operating room nurses who understood the product's value. Fourth, since every hospital had its own accounting system, it was difficult to prove the long-term cost effectiveness of the product. Fifth, because hospitals would rarely admit to incidences of postoperative infection, it was difficult to prove the product's ability to reduce such infections. Sixth, disposables threatened to become commodities as more hospitals switched from reusable to disposable products. Finally, the company faced potentially severe capacity limitations which impeded its ability to compete aggressively.

Despite these problems, management saw opportunities, because

1. Preference for disposable products was increasing

2. Professional groups like the Association for Operating Room Nurses favored the use of disposables

3. More clinical proof of the product's effectiveness had become available, and

4. New uses for the product, such as for scrub suits, were under development.

In view of these circumstances, the company's two main strategy objectives were to (1) at least maintain market share for the next two years, with minimal price erosion until the capacity problems would be solved, and (2) convince the garment makers that the company could support them in promoting the product to end users and that it would remain a dominant force in the disposable fabric business.

The previous year's budget consisted of large expenditures for a sales force and smaller expenditures for advertising and promotion. Advertising and promotion were principally directed toward operating room nurses who traditionally decided what garments to buy. At issue was whether a similar allocation would meet the revised strategy objectives or whether significant changes should be made.

The product manager responsible for the budget described the previous year's budget as primarily push oriented with approximately 75 percent of the budget directed toward the garment makers. He felt that in view of the revised circumstances an increased emphasis on pull might be appropriate and he was interested to learn whether a MARMIX analysis would shed additional light on the issue. He also felt unsure about the total amount spent on marketing support for the product. If the emphasis on push were maintained, he saw little justification for increasing the budget. If, on the other hand, increased pull were used, he felt that additional spending might be indicated.

The MARMIX analysis began with distinguishing between marketing effort aimed at intermediaries (the gown and drape makers) and that directed toward end users (the hospitals). Six mix elements were identified, three at each level: sales force activity, trade support, and advertising and promotion. Because of clear evidence of interaction patterns, a multiplicative model was used.

Concave response functions were chosen for

marketing effort directed at garment makers; S-shaped functions for end user efforts. In scaling and calibrating the response functions, the curves targeted toward intermediaries were most easily specified. The various missionary activities were less easily modeled, in part because of the "distance" between the company and the end users. Setting the maximum effective spending levels, in particular, generated considerable debate.

Value added by marketing was another concept that made model specification more difficult than anticipated. Management tended to underestimate the share contributed by marketing activity, reflecting extreme confidence in the technological superiority of the product. Only after several analysis runs designed to check the validity of the input estimates did the real extent of value added by marketing effort become apparent.

In the final analysis, an "optimal" budget emerged that was substantially higher than the baseline allocation. All mix elements had been increased and some had been set at their maximum values. The directions of these changes were plausible and their implications clear; the changing nature of the industry combined with the relatively high prevailing margins and low expenditure levels made it profitable to invest in market share. The magnitude of the proposed allocations, however, was somewhat suspect, particularly in view of the company's capacity limitations. Several reasons can be cited. First, management could not confidently make the input estimates for maximum spending. Second, the difficulties with estimating the value added by marketing cited above may have been a contributing factor. Finally, this case study illustrates the phenomenon that judgment-based decision models are most valid in a range that does not represent a radical departure from the baseline input. The proper conclusion, therefore, was to take a careful look at increasing the budget and reallocating some of these expenditures toward end users. On the basis of this analysis, the company decided to increase its marketing

budget by 25 percent, begin end-user missionary selling, and increase end-user advertising and promotion.

Is this new? Should they be using New Star?

Case 2   An application that is similar to the foregoing case concerns another innovative synthetic sheet product. The product had many uses, but the relatively small home construction market was management's immediate problem. When applied during the construction of a residence or other frame structure, the product served as an air barrier that improved the efficiency of the building's insulation. Although it was invisible in the finished structure, it could save a home buyer about 30 and 10 percent, respectively, on heating and cooling.

From the builder's point of view, the product cost less to apply than the traditional but inferior material. Although no special skill was required to understand and apply the product, complex distribution and communication requirements stood in the way of rapid adoption. In addition to these obstacles before management, timing of the marketing effort was important because in the near future the firm's current monopoly position was likely to be challenged by three or four major producers.

The links between the consuming home *Audiences* buyer and the firm ran through distributors; *Distrib* building supply retailers, and contractors. The *Retailers* contractor had to be informed about the product's value to the home buyer and its favorable *Contractors* cost comparison to traditional methods. If contractors continue to realize sufficient savings in construction costs and enhanced values to home buyers, the product's early sales growth should continue. (At the time of the reported MARMIX analysis, sales were in the $2 million to $4 million range.) In the educational process of both contractors and home buyers, distributors and retailers have exerted an important influence. Other influentials have been members of the architectural community and government bodies that control building codes.

The annual marketing budget for the product

was in the $500,000 to $1 million range, with about one-third of the budget allocated to the sales force. The remainder went to numerous advertising and promotional activities. Only a small proportion of the latter activities were directed to the home buyer. The bulk of the effort went to cooperative advertising with distributors, retailers, and builders, to advertising in trade magazines, and to producing press releases.

The main strategic objective of the marketing program over the next several years was to grow the market principally by increasing trial, and to establish a commanding position for the firm's air barrier sheet before significant competitive capacity comes on line. In the latter regard, there was some uncertainty about the value that marketing could add during the early part of the product's life cycle, and how to allocate the effort between push at various levels of distribution and pull exerted among both builders and home buyers. Management believed that currently about 40 percent of the product's value was attributable to marketing spending. Management also believed that it was wise to rely more heavily on push early in the product's market life and then introduce strong pull elements later in the market development process. As sales grow and brand competition becomes a serious factor, pull spending would be designed to build brand preference rather than product class acceptance.

Seven mix elements were chosen for analysis of the next annual budget; sales force, advertising to end users, advertising to intermediaries, builder support, dealer support, distributor support, and publicity. Concave response functions were assigned to all mix elements except advertising to end users, which was assigned an S-shaped curve. Since the degree to which mix elements were interactive or independent was in doubt, several alternative structures were explored before a fully multiplicative model was adopted.

Baseline spending was distributed in the following manner; 26 percent to sales force, 0 percent to advertising to end users, 24 percent to advertising to intermediaries, 4 percent to builder support, 23 percent to retailer support, 20 percent to distributor support, and 3 percent to publicity. The specified maximum levels that were adopted represented highly varied percentage increases over the baseline levels. For example, advertising to end users was zero in the baseline budget and was assigned a maximum of more than $1 million, while the publicity maximum was set at only $5,000 above the baseline level. The total maximum levels, however, were somewhat more than three times the total spending at the baseline level. Finally, the share effect of spending on sales force, advertising to end users, advertising to intermediaries, and support to retailers and distributors was judged to be substantial, while support to builders and funds for publicity were judged to have much less effect on market share.

The MARMIX analysis indicated that a total budget of about two and one half times the baseline level would maximize total contribution to profit (an increase of about $2 million), and would increase market share by about 50 percent (at the expense of the currently inferior competitive products). The large recommended increase was due principally to the large new spending on advertising to end users. The decision to move ahead in this new direction for strategy and spending hinged on management's judgments about the effectiveness of the added pull component in the marketing program for the coming year. To test the effect of eliminating advertising to end users, the model was rerun. The results indicated that the baseline spending on other mix elements could be improved, but that including advertising to end users increased profits.

Case 3   Although this case did not get beyond the preliminary discussion phase, it raises some interesting data and modeling issues that are worth considering. The company in question has several major divisions, each making fairly distinct major types of industrial machinery. Some of these goods went to a small number of final users—for example, the military services—whereas other goods were sold to numerous original equipment manufacturers who incorporated the goods in their products. Finally, some goods were sold to a wide range of industrial supply firms and final users.

In discussing the application of MARMIX with this organization, it was quickly apparent that marketing or, more broadly, business-generating activities are scattered throughout the organization. For example, one of the best ways for a sales representative to develop new business is to find a way for one of the company's development engineers to cooperate with the prospect's engineering group when the latter group is working on a new or redesigned product. The development engineer can suggest numerous cost-saving, value-enhancing design modifications, many of which involve the firm's products. Since the development engineering group is not under the sales manager's direct control, and since the group usually has much current work on orders already booked as well as on the company's regular product line, it may be difficult or impossible for a sales representative to get the design engineering support required to make a sale.

An analogous problem occurred with respect to the estimating group's operation. Customers frequently need very prompt price information. Work loads among the engineers who make the requisite estimates can seriously delay bids and result in the loss of sales. The need for improved management methods is as great in this case as it is for development engineering. The remainder of the marketing activities are less complex, consisting of such items as trade shows and customer educational programs, media advertising, direct mail advertising, telemarketing, and field selling. These latter activities are easily accounted for and are under the direct control of the marketing manager.

The problem encountered in this company was that some key marketing activities were not separated into analytically useful categories that could be influenced or controlled by the marketing manager. Most of these activities were lumped into general overhead classifications which the accounting procedures tended to allocate only to existing projects and current revenue streams. Sorting these matters out involved organizational changes that extended beyond the division that was contemplating the application of MARMIX to one of its product lines. There is some possibility that reviewing the model's requirements may produce positive long-range changes in administrative and accounting practices, but an immediate application of MARMIX could not easily be made in this case.

The division's product line also presented a few complications. The physical characteristics of the items sold varied markedly from year to year, since many of the items were custom designed or modified for individual customers. This difficulty is more apparent than real, since the size and value of an average order and the functional characteristics of products do not change rapidly. The number of potential orders can vary sharply with economic conditions, but annual forecasts are relatively accurate. The main problem in performing a MARMIX analysis of this kind to product line is segmenting the market by type of buyer. Segmentation analysis requires separation of revenue, costs, and marketing expenditure data so that separate analyses can be performed for each major class of buyer. When this is done, efficient marketing programs can be developed that make due allowance for the different needs of each major market segment.

Consumer Products

Case 1 The basic problem was to establish the "best" size and distribution of next year's marketing budget for a manufacturer that sold a single class of consumer products. The product line can be thought of as a set of multiple offerings in a product class such as soups or snack foods that are sold predominately through supermarkets. The manufacturer's unit sales price was somewhat less than $1 per unit and variable costs represented about 70 percent of this selling price.

In the past few years the products' market share has increased about one percentage point a year and management has insisted that a budget must leave the firm with a market share at least as large as one they could expect from following past policies. Management believed that adequate in-store display and wide distribution were the main determinants of unit sales volume. Advertising was assumed to play a supporting role. Sales to chains and independent wholesalers were made by brokers in much of the country, with the company's own sales force handling the remainder of the country.

Five expense categories were initially used in the computer analyses. They were media advertising, displays, introductory promotions, merchandising, and sales force. Displays included only special display units, end displays, and the like. Introductory promotions included case allowances and permanent display materials offered as a package to induce initial purchases. Merchandising principally covered in-store stock maintenance and allied activities concentrated on new-account servicing. When coupons were used, they were used in conjunction with a display promotion or an introductory promotion. Therefore, coupon costs were included in these latter two categories. Sales force costs covered only direct sales to chains and independent wholesalers. Since brokers' fees were not controllable, their commissions were initially treated as a variable expense deducted from the selling price of each unit in the areas covered by brokers.

In general, management believed that changing one mix element changed the effect achieved from other mix elements. For example, media advertising had a modest effect on selective demand since supermarkets typically carried only one brand in the product class, but it helped brokers and salespeople to open new accounts and obtain cooperation with display and coupon promotions. Advertising also had a modest effect on the results obtained from trade promotions. Due to these and related considerations, management chose a multiplicative model.

Management was unsure about the rate at which the market responded to the expenditures on each mix element as these expenditures ranged from zero to their maximum. The predominant feeling was that small expenditures produced insignificant results, but once you got over a threshold, results improved rapidly until another threshold was reached, when results per dollar of added expenditure began to decline rapidly. In short, the S-shaped function was the preferred choice for each mix element. (It should be noted that if expenditures can be targeted to individual areas to gain critical mass and if the most promising areas are the first to receive these allocations, management might be persuaded to use a concave function for some or all of the mix elements.)

Considerable thought and some speculation was required to estimate the maximum effective spending levels and the potential effect of each mix element. Taking each mix element in order:

Media advertising   Media advertising was seen principally as a support activity. The question was how large a maximum level should be set, given that the main purpose was to help salespeople open new accounts and maintaining favorable displays. The figure which was used was twice the baseline level. The effect of advertising on market share was judged to be small.

Display   Spending to gain favorable display treatment had a fairly direct relationship to improving sales in stores that stocked the product, but stores limited the improved display treatment that they would give to the product class. A spending limit of about four times the baseline level was used here. The market share

why mult products?

effect of display, as well as the effect of introductory promotions and merchandising, were all judged to be moderate.

Introductory promotions Spending to open new accounts was limited by the brokers' and salespeople's available time and by the accounts which were available to open or convert from competitors' brands. A spending limit of two and a half times the baseline level was used.

Merchandising The comments related to introductory promotions apply to this marketing activity.

Sales force This spending category is unusual in that more and/or better salespeople could be used in the territories currently serviced by the firm's own sales force, and company salespeople could be substituted for broker salespeople in other territories. Here, management initially considered only the possibility of changing the level of effort in territories serviced by its own sales force. The ability to change this level during the planning period was considered to be modest, with the maximum about 50 percent more than the baseline level. The market share effect of spending on the sales force was deemed to be potentially greater than spending on other mix elements.

Estimating the unit primary demand for the products involved the analysis of SAMI shipment data (commercially available data on warehouse shipments by brand). All SAMI data were in case units which were converted to consumer sales units (analysis could have been completed in case units if these units had been more easily communicated). A few regions of the country were excluded because they were not currently covered by the firm's distribution network and were unlikely to be covered in the future.

The expected average unit price was based principally on last year's results, adjusted for a slight upward trend that management believed

would continue. Since the several products the firm offered were all sold at the same base price, this input to the program posed no difficulty.

The product's variable cost per unit included all direct labor and material used in the manufacturing process, freight and handling, and broker commissions (adjusted for the percentage of sales made by brokers). Therefore, the average unit price less the variable unit cost represented the average unit contribution available to cover controllable marketing expenses, fixed overhead, and before-tax profits.

Although they will not be discussed in detail, several disaggregate MARMIX analyses were eventually run. One natural step was to look at the profit potential of territories with brokers in comparison to territories with company salespeople. To do so, all revenue, costs, and expenses had to be separated for the two types of territories. In the broker territories, the company had no sales force expense but it suffered a lower gross unit contribution to profit. In the company sales force territories, the gross unit contribution to profit was larger but sales force expenses had to be deducted to get the net contribution to profit. This procedure provided guidance about two important marketing problems: the development of a more efficient distribution policy and the selection of a more efficient approach to managing the form of distribution that was adopted in any type of territory.

Little directly applicable experience or company and industry data were available to help estimate the share effects of minimum and maximum levels of total spending. Nevertheless, management displayed little hesitation in judging the effects of wide changes in marketing expenditures. A useful benchmark was provided by the fact that the difference between the maximum and minimum indicated how the effect of marketing expenditures compared with product design and price in influencing purchase. If raising expenditures from zero to the managerially defined maximum produces only a modest increase in market share, marketing is not judged to be a dominant force. On the other hand, if the same change in spending produces a big increase in market share, marketing is considered likely to be a dominant influence.

Finally, management chose to ignore any future benefits from share gains that might flow from a given budget, since they believed that a share gain would completely disappear in the absence of a sustained marketing effort. With these data, the model produced a relatively flat contribution to profit curve as the total budget increased from its minimum to its maximum level. The maximum contribution to profit occurred at about half the baseline spending level. This small gain in contribution to profit could only be obtained at the cost of losing five percentage points of market share. As already noted, this loss was unacceptable. (This fact tends to call into question management's statement about the irrelevance of a current period's share gain or loss to future performance.)

Given the requirement that the marketing budget should not produce a decline in market share, two possibly acceptable actions were suggested. First, the current budget could be reallocated to increase contribution to profit by about $250,000 and increase market share by three and a half percentage points. Second, a more aggressive stance could be taken, increasing the marketing budget so long as it sustained the previous contribution to profit. In this case, nearly $2 million could be added to marketing spending to increase market share by sixteen percentage points. Management chose a smaller increase in spending, which yielded a small share gain, increased contribution to profit, and imposed fewer management problems. Furthermore, a very aggressive budget and large share increase would have greatly increased the chances of a strong competitive response. An analysis of the effects of competitive responses had not been made in the completed analyses.

Case 2   In the soft drink industry, more than half of the 30 billion retail sales are made in cola-flavored products. In terms of all flavors, Pepsi

Cola and Coca-Cola account for 60 percent of the market. These two companies and other producers of concentrate distribute their brands through food stores, fast food chains, vending machines, and a variety of other outlets. In nearly all cases, franchised bottlers are a key element in the marketing and delivery system. The bottler discussed here has annual sales volume in the $100 million to $700 million sales range and represented one of the two major cola brands. The four operating components of the firm are marketing to food services and vending outlets, marketing to food stores, manufacturing, and delivery systems. The budget analysis work reported below was completed on behalf of food store marketing personnel.

Due to the turmoil that surrounded Coca-Cola's reformulation of Coke®, brands in this category were viewed as inappropriate candidates for a test of MARMIX, so the firm chose to study a brand it represented in one of the secondary flavor categories; e.g., lemon-lime, orange, root beer, or mixer flavors. The flavor in question represented about 5 percent of food store soft drink sales in the bottler's franchise area, and the firm's brand held about 20 percent of this amount. Each of the major competing brands held somewhat larger shares. One of these latter brands was a chain store private brand.

The private brand sales were included in the product class despite their lower prices and restricted distribution, but the proprietary nature of the brand made it difficult to measure the magnitude and trend of its sales. The fact that the franchise area did not match the areas used by government and private agencies to produce relevant population and sales statistics also complicated the process of estimating future primary demand for the entire product class. The unit of demand was a case of 12-ounce cans. All products not sold in this form were converted to this unit.

Developing information about the marketing mix elements proved to be as difficult as developing information on demand. Not all potential marketing elements were being used at the time of the analysis, and internal accounting classifications did not always reflect strategically meaningful expense classifications. After some discussion by the concerned marketing personnel, TV advertising, radio advertising, coupons, discounts, sampling, sales incentives, and trade promotions were adopted.

Considerable discussion was also required to decide how market share responded to spending on each mix element. The forms adopted for response functions were S-shaped except in the case of sampling, which was defined to be linear. (Each new store added to the sampling plan was assumed to produce the same effect as each store previously included in the plan.) The simple multiplicative model form was selected to account for what was assumed to be a complex pattern of interactions.

The first computer run of MARMIX immediately suggested that the input data were incorrect, since the most profitable policy would be to withdraw all marketing support and allow the sales to rapidly approach zero. This outcome was due to two errors in input. *First,* the food service and vending channels sales had been omitted and one baseline spending category had been moderately understated. These understatements occurred because marketing personnel making the initial estimates did not have direct responsibility for sales and expenses unrelated to food stores. Nevertheless, any marketing on behalf of the brand supported sales in all channels, making these sales and expenses relevant. *Second,* the carryover effect of share gains (or losses) had been underestimated. When these errors in input were corrected, the model produced satisfactory forecasts of market share and profits, indicating that the brand could be very profitable if it were supported by a somewhat more aggressive marketing budget.

Once the revised data and analyses were in hand, a second group marketing meeting was held, during which the data revisions were discussed and the essential features of the final model were explained. Since a computer had been set up in the conference room, it was possible to examine the effects of changes in the inputs on model forecasts and to produce forecasts for several alternative budgets suggested by the managers and analysts who were present.

In addition to improving the brand's budget, the process had several organizational benefits. First, the model and process improved the food stores marketing group's understanding of the market and the brand's strategy. Second, the model provided a vehicle to help them communicate with two important elements within the firm: the senior marketing executive who would review and approve the final budget, and the food service and vending group whose cooperation was valued.

Case 3 A medium-size greeting card company completes this set of case examples. It illustrates some important aspects of defining marketing mix elements, a topic treated elsewhere in this text. First, however, the nature of the industry must be outlined. The greeting card industry is heavily influenced by a few major firms, most notably Hallmark and American Greeting Card. These full-line producers and marketers offer cards for all occasions in all major styles and at various price levels. Their distribution is very wide and can include proprietary outlets and a range of non-greeting card products. The smaller firms, including the one for whom the reported MARMIX analysis was completed, tend to be niche strategists to one degree or another. These companies may offer cards that have special design orientations or are targeted to particular market segments. To some extent, these firms provide design leadership.

The retailers of greeting cards want up-to-date lines that appeal to their particular clientele, offer attractive margins, and do not duplicate cards offered by competing retailers. For these reasons, a very wide variety of cards is available at any time, and the designs turn over rapidly. To an important extent, turnover is driven by the seasonal nature of cards; e.g., Christmas, Valentine's Day, and Mother's Day.

As a result, inventory and assortment management are important factors at all levels.

Card designs can be produced in house by card companies, but medium and small card firms depend predominantly on free-lance designers. When the design skills of an individual and the card company's requirements are a good fit, positive long-term relationships can develop. The MARMIX analysis firm described here depended predominantly on free-lance designers. Their designs produced sales volume in the $2 million to $4 million category. The firm's sales program was executed through broker representatives who tended to sell noncompeting lines to several segments of the retail trade.

Except for the very large card firms, marketing programs were devoted almost entirely to push elements. Motivating representatives and helping them to locate prospects, open new accounts, and keep established accounts were the dominant concerns. Diverse tools were used for these purposes. Commissions and related incentives were important to representatives, but so were the flow of new products, sales support, and sales training activities. Lead generation was accomplished primarily through trade shows and trade advertising. Account opening was assisted by telemarketing, direct mail, and deals on display racks for cards. Point-of-purchase materials, telemarketing, direct mail, and cooperative advertising helped maintain accounts. Promotional discounts and allowances were important in opening new accounts and maintaining current accounts. There was a question about whether these price concessions should be analyzed separately and whether efforts directed toward primary and special accounts should be separated for purposes of budgetary analysis.

After detailed consideration of the pros and cons of various mix categories, nine entered the final analyses; representative compensation, representative support, representative product development, leads—primary trade, leads—special trade, account opening—primary trade, account opening—special accounts, account maintenance—primary trade, and account maintenance—special trade.

The role assigned to product development and to promotional pricing needs explanation. Management believed that a sizable amount of line expansion served little purpose other than to motivate representatives by giving them fresh designs to present. As a result, one-third of the product development costs were allocated to the marketing budget and treated as a sales force expense. The question about discounts and allowances concerned whether they should be treated as a marketing cost or as a more general reduction in the average price of the offer. Management concluded that discounts and allowances were less connected to the lines' overall price level than they were to marketing objectives for specific market segments. Therefore, the components of these reductions that could be linked directly to marketing efforts were included in the costs of opening and maintaining accounts.

The discussions held by management while it was trying to resolve the above issues materially improved marketing objectives and management's capacity to connect spending to concrete outcomes. Of particular interest was the fact that the selected mix categories suggested how to balance spending with specific tasks and market segments, and indicated relatively straightforward ways to connect measurable results to the expected outcomes. For example, it was easy to see the relative emphasis given to primary and special accounts and to measure how the account-opening activity was performing by keeping appropriate account records.

There are numerous other interesting aspects of the case. For example, decisions to adopt a mixed additive and multiplicative model structure and to examine the effects of price elasticity further increased the usefulness of the MARMIX exercise. Nevertheless, it is sufficient to conclude by observing that the analyses improved the size and allocation of the firm's marketing budget.

Some Generalizations

Problem structure Applications of MARMIX emphasized the valuable problem-structuring aspects of the modeling process. Although there are other questions that could be used to parameterize a model, the questions that are used produced a constructive examination of the problem by requiring judgments that a manager should be able to make. Although it is always somewhat painful to record one's judgments, doing so creates a suitable degree of care and provides a useful record for future reference.

Organizational impact It is clearly the case that MARMIX helps the members of a decision-making group share know-how and build a consensus about what marketing strategy will be most appropriate. In this structured environment, group thinking about the problem helps develop a common set of assumptions before data are submitted to the model.

The accessibility of the rationale for the recommended strategy can improve communication to higher management and to contiguous elements in the organization. In a similar manner, the standardized format is an important aid to making period-to-period comparisons of strategies and budgets, to producing future budgets, and to making postmortem evaluations of the budget's performance. MARMIX can generate an improved decision-making environment in which the quality of the inputs and accuracy of the outputs should grow with experience.

Forecasting accuracy We would like to present a large body of budgets and forecasts produced by MARMIX and by several competing approaches, showing that MARMIX was a clear-cut winner. We cannot produce this kind of evidence and, unfortunately, we doubt that it can be produced for any similar decision-support system.

It is impossible to implement several budgets in identical environments and it is very difficult to find sufficiently similar environments to permit meaningful tests. In most of the cases that have been collected, share and profit results could be compared to the forecasts, but the sample size is too small to be meaningful. Furthermore, comparisons were occasionally complicated by changes in the environment, requiring changes in the model.

If forecasting accuracy is the only issue, knowledgeable "friends of the firm" might make independent forecasts of the outcome for the adopted MARMIX budget. These forecasts could be compared to market results. No doubt this approach carries its own set of practical problems. In short, one cannot be very optimistic about providing short-run measures of predictive validity for models of the type that have been discussed here any more than similar tests can be made of results obtained from unaided managerial judgments. The best test will be long-run performance and managerial acceptance.

CONCLUDING REMARKS

This chapter has covered two important aspects of the MARMIX approach to planning the marketing budget for an established product class. The first half of the chapter covered the essential features of this budgetary aid from a managerial perspective. Principal attention was given to the nature of the required inputs, the structural features of the model, and the general nature of the output. The second half of the chapter reviewed some application experiences. A few barriers to successful application were noted, but more importantly the substantial individual and organizational benefits of the approach were discussed.

A marketing manager or analyst with budgetary responsibilities should be willing to state his or her beliefs about the product's market and its economic characteristics. Furthermore, these judgments should be recorded in an analytically traceable form and submitted to a program like

MARMIX. Only in this way can the quality and the consequences of one's judgments be examined before they are tested in the marketplace. When this view is accepted by the organization, the process of developing the model becomes a central vehicle for pooling knowledge and achieving the level of consensus needed for a budget to become an organizational commitment to produce the forecasted results.

REFERENCES

Cooper, Lee G., and Masao Nakanishi: *Market-Share Analysis,* Nowell, Mass: Kluwer Academic Press, 1988.

de Kluyver, Cornelis, and Edgar Pessemier: "Benefits of a Marketing Budgeting Model: Two Case Studies," *Sloan Management Review,* 27, Fall 1986, 27–38.

Kotler, Philip: *Marketing Management: Analysis, Planning and Control,* 6th ed., Englewood Cliffs, N.J.: Prentice-Hall, 1988.

Little, John D. C.: "Models and Managers: The Concept of Decision Calculus," *Management Science,* 16, 1970, B466–485.

Pessemier, Edgar A.: *Product Management: Strategy and Organization,* 2d ed., New York: John Wiley and Sons, 1982.

Rangaswamy, Arvid, and Lakshman Krishnamurthi: "Response Function Estimation Using Equity Estimators," *Journal of Marketing Research,* 28, February 1991, 72–83.

APPENDIX 13-1 SIZE OF THE SIMULATION SAMPLE AND CONFIDENCE IN THE RESULTS

The MARMIX program uses a series of randomly allocated budgets at each of eight evenly spaced intervals between the previously defined minimum and maximum budgets. In a standard MARMIX analysis, a user has to make a decision about how many samples will be examined for each of the eight (extremes excluded) total spending levels. The answer should be determined by the number of mix elements in the plan and how confident the user needs to be about the goodness or near optimality of the best allocation found for each budget level.

As an aid to making this decision, the program suggests a number of samples for each budget level. This number grows rapidly as the number of mix ele-

ments increases since it is related to how many ways any one of three levels of spending for any mix element can be combined with the same number of levels for the other spending elements. The extent to which the best per-budget contribution profit grows as the number of samples per budget level increases is illustrated below.

The average fraction increase after invoking the improvement routine is 1.19, indicating the potential value of this program segment. However, the improvement routine takes advantage of its capacity to shift the levels of total spending as well as to allocate these budgets. Increasing the sample size used in the basic analysis (before improvement) produces a important positive effect, but the results are subject to the random nature of the process. Also in the above case, the improvement routine does not increase the profit levels for samples larger than 1,100 per budget level.

Another perspective on the confidence that one can place in model results can be obtained by looking at the variability of total contribution profit across independent samples of the same size. As an illustration, ten independent analyses with 1,000 sample budget allocations in each one were completed for the test problem. A $1.5 million fixed level of total spending was used in each analysis. Following the program's improvement routine, the average absolute deviation of the observed maximum contribution profit levels from the average level was less than 2.5 percent of the latter average. In light of the data below, one must assume that the MARMIX model will provide reasonably stable results if samples as large as those suggested by the program are used. If the user wants to increase his or her confidence in a

MEAN RESULTS OVER EIGHT BUDGET LEVELS FOR A PROBLEM WITH SEVEN MIX ELEMENTS

No. of Samples Per Budget Level	Frac. Chg.	BEFORE IMPROVEMENT		AFTER IMPROVEMENT	
		Best Contr. Profit (000)	Frac. Chg.	Best Contr. Profit (000)	Frac. Chg.
225	—	7,957	—	9,374	—
550	2.0	8,026	1.0087	9,508	1.0143
1100	2.0	8,225	1.0248	9,948	1.0463
2200	2.0	8,230	1.0006	9,809	.9860
4400	2.0	8,317	1.0106	9,807	.9998

given set of input data, the random number generator's seed can be changed for one or more additional large-sample analyses.

Several other aspects of the sampling process are noteworthy. First, occasionally larger budgets can produce a smaller market share than a smaller budget. Second, on equally infrequent occasions, a larger sample of budgets can produce less desirable results than a smaller sample of budgets. The first sample drawn may produce a near-optimal allocation or a large sample may fail to uncover any near-optimal allocations. It is also worth observing that the minimum and maximum budget allocations are unaffected by the sampling process and may have very inefficient distributions to individual mix elements. The fixed allocation of the maximum budget may prove to be so inefficient that its contribution to profit is less than those produced by a smaller budget.

REVIEW QUESTIONS

Q13-1 How does a one-period analysis for an established product differ from a multiperiod analysis of the strategy/budgets for a prospective new but not strongly innovative product?

Q13-2 Discuss the frame of marketing effectiveness for two distinctively different categories of support spending.

Q13-3 Discuss the criteria for selecting mix elements and how they may differ from standard accounting expense categories.

Q13-4 Describe two expense categories, one that you believe has a naturally concave response function and one that you believe has a naturally S-shaped response function. Justify your choice of these categories.

Q13-5 Discuss the vertical axis of the frame of marketing effectiveness before and after it has been rescaled.

Q13-6 Discuss the information displayed in Figure 13-10.

Q13-7 How do additive and multiplicative (rescaled) response functions differ in the way that they affect predicted market share?

Q13-8 Discuss how one should use the worksheet shown in Figure 13-19.

Q13-9 What answers to questions in Figure 13-20 and Figure 13-21 are not required by the model's computations? What purpose do they serve?

Q13-10 In a few sentences each, describe the central messages in each of the six case summaries that appear at the end of the chapter.

14

USING THE MARMIX PLANNING AND BUDGETING MODEL

This chapter builds directly on the material in the foregoing chapter. The first two sections very briefly describe criteria for choosing the marketing strategies and the budget categories (mix elements) to be analyzed. The third section contains a detailed treatment of the program inputs. The fourth section displays and discusses the output from an illustrative test problem. The final section presents some general observations about the managerial uses of the output. The chapter concludes with an Appendix which discusses several technical characteristics of the MARMIX model.

CHOOSING STRATEGIES FOR ANALYSIS

The first question that must be dealt with is whether more than one definition of the offer will be examined. If one is considering several pricing and/or positioning strategies, it is useful to examine the market support and the expected profit potential associated with each one.

Furthermore, each offer can usually be combined with several unique patterns of marketing support. For example, a manager may want to see how a program of sales through brokers only compares with a program of sales made exclusively by the firm's own sales force, how a marketing program using a TV advertising pull component compares with one that does not use this component, or how a market environment in which competitors introduce new product designs compares with one in which only current product offerings are available. All such comparisons require modified inputs and additional MARMIX analyses.

In any case, a manager must think these matters through in light of his or her need to know and the time and effort required to complete the computer analyses. The MARMIX program makes provision for storing forty separate sets of input data. This number is adequate for almost any set of concurrent analyses or for subsequently consolidating a hierarchical budget structure that includes multiple budgets for products and sales areas. Parsimony is as important in the choice of alternative strategies for analysis as it is in the choice of mix elements for use in each strategic alternative.

CHOOSING MIX ELEMENTS—ORGANIZATIONAL AND STRATEGIC ISSUES

A basic set of criteria for choosing the mix elements was noted in Chapter 13:

1. The expected size of the expenditures covering the activity,

2. The separability of the activity for purposes of accounting and control,

3. The degree to which sales are responsive to changes in expenditures on the activity,

4. Controllability by the responsible manager, and

5. The need to keep it simple.

Also, it is recommended that one use mix elements that can be linked directly to marketing objectives.

In addition to traditional mix elements, there are several other ways to divide the total level of support into categories. One other possibility that is often in sympathy with the above observations is first to allocate funds to projects that can be treated like ordinary mix elements in an analysis even though each project may be made up of many natural expense items. For example, decisions can be made about the levels of marketing support spending that will be allocated to projects like a spring machine tool builders show or a full-line promotional event. Measurable outcomes can be developed as readily for such activities as they can be for the more traditional mix elements.

When projects are used as the basis for budgeting, resource allocations must be made at two levels: first to the projects and then within the project to the advertising, personal selling, and other components that might make up a project. Only when the latter spending allocations have been summed across all projects does management have a total budget for personal selling, promotional discounts, and the like. One way to approach this problem is to initially lay out the components of a set of projects by substituting projects for tasks in a tools and task table like the one shown in Table 10-1 and 10-2.

Another primary division of spending focuses on expanding distribution coverage and support (push) versus increasing buyer awareness (pull), or on market objectives like opening new accounts (switchback) and maintaining old accounts (repeat). In the former case budgeted dollars are initially assigned to these push and pull tasks and subsequently within-task allocations are made among the more traditional spending categories, such as consumer coupons, display allowances, and advertising. Similarly, efforts can be directed first toward market segments like national, regional, and local chains. The funds allocated to each segment are subsequently allocated to natural accounting categories. Typically, the allocations will vary markedly from segment to segment. A table similar to the ones in Table 10-1 and 10-2 can aid preliminary analysis.

Finally, one might *build up* a total budget from budgets that are first developed for separate elements such as geographic regions, projects, market segments, or organizational units. As a first step, each of these elements is analyzed separately, and use may be made of any of the strategies for defining budgetary categories or mix elements that have been described above. At a second stage, management must choose the best level of total support for each unit of analysis—say a geographic area—including the most efficient within-unit allocation to the associated mix elements. Finally, the spending levels are summed across the component units for the common mix elements. Doing so yields the total spending level for each natural budget category.

As Chapter 15 points out, the above approach creates a budgetary hierarchy in which the output of one set of analyses becomes the input to one or more higher-level analyses.

This chapter's text and the associated illustration concentrate on a simple set of focused natural mix elements, but a manager must remain aware that this decision about the way the budget categories are defined can have an important effect on the effectiveness of the adopted strategy/budget. If any doubt exists about how to proceed, it may be advisable to complete the MARMIX analysis for each of several approaches to defining mix elements.

A USER'S PERSPECTIVE ON PROGRAM INPUTS

This section discusses the entire data input process for MARMIX by examining the program's on-screen input queries. To facilitate this effort, it is useful to have a mix element worksheet and the two-page data form available. A blank mix element worksheet appears in Figure 13-19 and a blank data form appears in Figures 13-20 and 13-21. The mix element worksheets may be used as a convenient place to work up the data relevant to each mix element. A completed data form for the test problem appears in Figures 14-25a and 14-25b. A reader who wants to start a computer analysis after completing this chapter will find it helpful to fill in a blank data form while going through the instructions that follow.

General Layout of the Data Form and the Program

The front of the data form is used to record:

1. The date of the analysis, the computer data file number, a description of the problem, the time unit of analysis, and the number and names of the marketing activities or mix elements which will be analyzed, and

2. The basic unit price, cost, and demand data.

The back of the form has space to record:

1. Spending levels, share effects, various characteristics of each mix element, and how the mix elements will enter the model,

2. The overall effects of large changes in spending,

3. Optional estimates of intermediate variables,

4. The effect, if any, of the planned budget on future results, and

5. The nature of any cooperative marketing support.

These inputs determine the main features of the model. Once the data have been entered, the program generates some summary statistics and performs the core analyses. Figure 14-1 contains a flow diagram of the process.

Two forms of the program are provided: one that produces printed output and one that produces output only on the computer screen. The first time data are entered, it is advisable to use the latter screen output version. It offers added flexibility in correcting inputs as they are entered (on-screen instructions are provided), and it allows a user to try several versions of the input before producing a permanent printed record. When printed results are desired, the data file saved by the screen version can be read by the printer version. New data entry is not required and changes can still be made (although in a somewhat less convenient manner).

Starting to Use MARMIX

MARMIX should be run on an IBM/AT or PS/2 computer with a fixed disk drive, 640,000 RAM, and a coprocessor chip, or on a fast compatible machine. The MARMIX program is provided on 3 1/2-inch high-density removable disks. See Appendix 15-1 for details about these disks: how

FIGURE 14-1   Flow diagram of the MARMIX program.

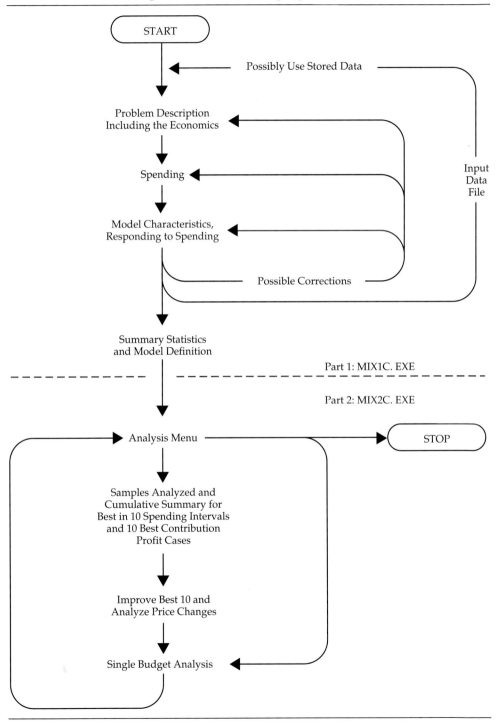

to load them onto a fixed disk, and how to start the program.

Program Characteristics

The version of MARMIX discussed here is the one that appears in the CAMP LEARN program set. (See Appendix 15-1.) This program consists of two program segments. The first segment includes a program, a variable number of data files, and some supporting elements. When the program is started for the first time, only the included TEST PROBLEM file is available. After a user enters data, they are saved in one or more data files. The data files can be called up by the first program segment, modified as necessary, resaved by the program, or removed.

The first program segment is designed to record the required input, summarize the input, develop the MARMIX model, and indicate its predictive characteristics. The necessary data and model parameters are recorded in a form that can be read by the second program segment. When the first segment is no longer needed, the second segment can be started. When the second segment has been loaded and started, it reads the required data and parameters and is ready to perform whatever analysis is called for.

The second program segment performs the basic sampling analyses. It recommends a sample size but will use any size greater than 100 per budget level that a user specifies. For problems with six mix elements (the largest number permitted by the text's companion program), several minutes may be needed to analyze 1,000 samples for each of the eight nonextreme budget levels that are examined. Once the sample results are available, the program can make incremental changes in the budgets to improve the total contribution profit for the best budget found at each spending level. The improvement process typically takes less than a minute of computing time. Finally, a number of descriptors and measures of effectiveness are printed for ten good budgets, a price change analysis is

run for each budget, and the user can examine the effect of any alternative budgets that appear to be interesting.

Steps in Completing the Input Requirements

As the text covers the questions that appear on the data form, a prospective user should carefully consider the issues involved and record answers *before* starting a data entry session at the computer. The essential marketing questions that the program asks and that must be answered during the computer session are outlined below.

The initial procedural questions ask if a color monitor is being used, and if printed output is called for, what print style is desired. Next, the monitor asks whether stored data will be used or original data will be entered. The program allows a user to store the data for up to forty problems. In the material that follows, original data will be entered for a test problem. If stored data are used, the questions below need not be answered, but the old stored data can be modified before they are passed on to the analysis segment of the program.

Q1:   General description of the problem (three lines only)?

       The answer to this question should clearly identify the budget problem and separate it from other, potentially similar problems.

Q2:   Number of months in the analysis?

       Normally, the entry is twelve to specify an annual budget. Shorter or longer periods can be used.

Q3:   The number of mix elements (excluding price)?

       This number is ten or less (six or less in the student version). The answer must be compatible with the answer to the next question.

Q4:   Enter the names of the mix elements using twelve or fewer characters for each one.

As previously discussed, marketing dollars should be budgeted to a modest number of expense categories that are closely associated with the responses of buyers and consumers and that serve specific strategic objectives. In general, marketing expenditures should be identified with favorable changes in the knowledge, disposition, and/or behavior of key actors. These changes are best understood in terms of the benefits delivered to clients or prospective clients.

Q5:   Definition of the sales unit?

The unit of sales is usually a physical measure common to all competitors. For example, square yards for fabrics, pounds or cases of a particular size for food products, thousands of board feet for lumber, and volumes for publishers. Once stated, the unit defined here must be used throughout the analysis.

Q6:   Primary demand (000 units)?

Primary demand is the number of units (in thousands) of sales available for division among all competitors during the period covered by the analysis. The unit of measure and the size of the market control the entry. For this reason, a subsidiary question is included so there will be no confusion about the market definition.

Q6*:   If demand is an amalgam of market segments and/or product types, briefly describe the contents of your estimate.

The answer to this subsidiary question should clarify such matters as what geographic or other market boundaries may apply, what types of buyer or consumer are included, and what products were considered.

Q7:   Baseline unit price (dollars and cents)?

This is the (average) price at which the firm sells the product(s). If the sale is *not* made to a final buyer, the price paid by the first intermediary is recorded.

Q7*:   If the baseline unit price is an average covering various products and/or price levels, briefly describe the components of the average.

The answer to this subsidiary question should clarify how the price entered in response to Q7 was determined. Price can vary seasonally, by class of buyer, by grade, and so forth. People who read or act on an analysis need to know the basis of the inputs that were employed.

Q8:   Unit variable cost (dollars and cents)?

Unit variable costs are costs that change directly with the number of units produced and sold. If total sales double, total variable costs will double. These costs *exclude* "fixed" general and administrative expenses *and* all the marketing budget items that are the subject of the MARMIX analysis.

Q8*:   Briefly describe the components of variable unit cost.

The components of unit cost should be described in enough detail to make the content of these costs clear to another reader of the budget analysis.

Q9:   Given normal marketing expenditures, the market share at each of the following unit prices (relative to the baseline price) are (.###)?

The baseline market share is the share that is expected from the budget which would have been used before completing the MARMIX analysis. This market share should be expressed as a decimal fraction (.###). If the product or product-class momentum is to be maintained, this share will normally be close to a simple projection of the past trend.

In addition, this question asks for an estimate of the market share under the same baseline budget but at six additional price levels, ±30 percent, ±20 percent, and ±10 percent.

Q10: How should the spending level for each mix element be expressed? If indirectly as a fraction of dollar sales enter a 1, but if spending is expressed directly in dollars, enter a 0.

Normally, expenses are budgeted directly in dollars, but for items like sales commissions it may be more convenient and realistic to budget them indirectly as a percentage of sales (.###). The spending inputs and outputs can be expressed in terms of whatever budgeting basis is most appropriate for each mix element.

Q11: The *baseline* and the associated competitive spending by mix elements (000 or .###)?

The expenditures recorded here should be just large enough to sustain the baseline market share recorded for Q9. Note that not all mix items need to have nonzero spending levels. Mix elements may be included for which no spending is currently planned but about which management wants MARMIX to make a recommendation. In this case, the program may recommend spending on mix elements that are not currently being utilized.

The total competitive spending levels that are recorded should be the levels that are expected given the firm's baseline spending levels.

Once the program develops a model, it will make a market share forecast for the baseline pattern of expenditures and check this forecast against the answer to Q9, making such adjustments as may be required to improve the model's predictive validity.

Q12: The *minimum* spending allowed and the associated competitive spending by mix element (000 or .###)?

The minimum spending level for a mix element is normally zero, but there are numerous reasons a positive minimum may be required. For example, key media may have minimum requirements, an existing contract for marketing services may call for some minimum level of spending during the next period, or management may impose a minimum as a matter of policy.

The total competitive spending levels that are recorded should be the levels that are expected given the firm's minimum spending levels.

Q13: The *maximum* spending allowed and the associated competitive spending by mix element (000 or .###)?

This maximum spending level for each mix element is the largest amount management is willing to consider. This practical upper bound, along with the effect that can be attained as spending goes from its minimum to its maximum, defines the general marketing efficiency of each mix element.

The total competitive spending levels that are recorded should be the levels that are expected given the firm's maximum spending levels.

Q14: How does each mix element enter the model structure? (0 means an independent element and 1 through 6 can identify distinct group(s) of interactive elements.)

If all elements are independent, all 0s are entered, and if all elements are interactive, all 1s are entered. In other cases, a 0 is entered for each independent element and a separate common integer is entered for the elements in each group of interactive elements. (A 1 is used for the first such group, a 2 for the second such group and so on).

Q15:   At the baseline price, the market share produced by *zero* spending on *all* mix elements?

The answer to this question indicates the respondent's beliefs about the degree to which the product or product line's market performance depends solely on the relative appeal of the product at its current price. For some products like mature industrial materials, marketing effort may play a relatively small role. For other products like beer or cosmetics, a large part of the delivered value is contributed by marketing activities. This estimate, like the one required by Q16, may take a manager outside the range of his or her normal experience. However, careful consideration of where the product falls along this continuum of marketing's importance will help one judge how much the product's market share would decline if the firm resorted to simple order taking during the planning period.

Q16:   At the baseline price, the market share produced by *maximum* spending on *all* mix elements?

The comments made about Q15 apply to the effect of maximum spending. The question calls for a judgment about a level of spending which may be beyond management's experience. The degree of increase that is recorded helps define how responsive market share is to a broad increase in marketing support. The estimate applies to the planning period during which the increases in expenditures are assumed to be in effect.

Q17:   *Formal* response function = 0, *direct* response function = 1: And on a separate line, *origin:* (000 or .###), usually 0.

A response function can be thought of as a prescription for converting expenditures into effects on market share. The model assumes that increasing expenditures increase market share but allows a user to specify how this increase in share occurs as spending on a mix element goes from zero or a nonzero origin to its maximum.

A response function usually has its origin at zero, but in some cases no response will be observed until after some positive spending threshold has been passed. For example, levels of compensation might require a nonzero origin.

Since no results are produced by expenditures from zero through and including an origin greater than zero, any expenditures in this range must be reduced to zero. For the sake of completeness, the lowest analyzed level of spending is zero for all mix elements. Following this step, all other trial levels of spending observe the minimum spending limits imposed by the user.

The simplest way to define the shape of a response function is to select from among three preprogrammed functions, one concave, one S-shaped, and one linear. The *formal* forms are shown in Figure 14-2 along with a fourth function that was *directly* specified by a manager.

As long as it increases steadily, a DIRECT function can have any shape that reflects how dollars are converted into share effects. Question 18 is used to define the shape of a DIRECT function. The user enters the percentage of the maximum effect that is realized at five equally spaced spending levels falling between the origin and the maximum.

FIGURE 14-2 Three formal and one direct response functions.

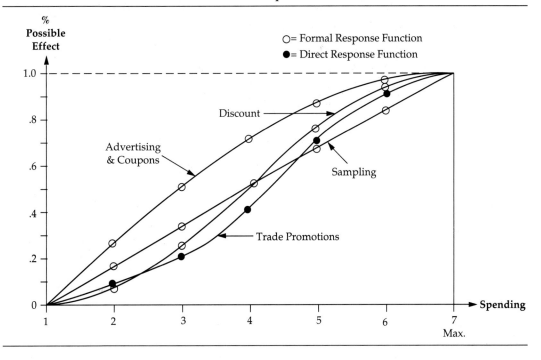

Figure 14-3 provides more details, this time focusing on an additive, directly defined concave function.

Q18: For each directly defined mix element and spending level, enter the percentage (decimal) of the maximum response that will be attained.

This question must be answered for each *directly defined* response function. Five equally spaced spending levels across the feasible range are presented and the user is asked to enter the percentage of the maximum effect that would result at each level.

Q19: For each formally defined mix element, enter the defining number: 1 = concave function, 2 = S-shaped function, and 3 = linear function.

This question must be answered for each *formally* defined mix element. See Q17.

Q20: If a mix element's spending is cut to ZERO, the effect on market share will be?

The baseline spending, the new reduced spending, and the baseline market share are displayed for each mix element. The user is asked to estimate the new share appropriate to the new reduced spending. These estimates, along with the similar upside estimates provided in response to Q21, record how responsive sales and market share are to spending levels for each expense category or mix element.

Q21: If a mix element's spending is raised to the MAXIMUM, the effect on market share will be?

FIGURE 14-3   Some properties of an additive direct concave response function.

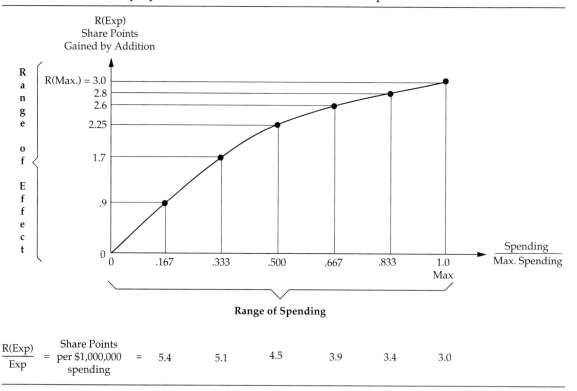

The format of this question is like the one used for Q20. The only difference is that spending is raised to its limit instead of being lowered to its limit for each spending category.

The characteristics of the estimates made in response to Q20 and Q21 are displayed in Figure 14-4. The baseline budget is shown along the horizontal line through the test problem's baseline market share (.22). The maximum budget figures appear at the top of the bar showing the share effect. The minimum budget is shown at the bottom of each effect bar. The length of the effect bar in share units is recorded at the bottom of the chart. Trade promotions and TV advertising are most influential and radio

advertising and sampling are least influential.

It is useful to think of each vertical effect bar in Figure 14-4 as the vertical effect axis of a response function. Figure 14-5 displays two such functions, one for TV advertising and one for sampling. A $200,000 minimum level of spending on TV is indicated. This minimum could be policy determined or contractually required. TV advertising can produce a large increase in market share, adding eight share points at maximum spending. Maximum spending on sampling (in store) produces a much smaller increase in market share.

As noted earlier, the linear functions have a special property when they ap-

FIGURE 14-4　Summary of estimated effects of spending on changes in market share.

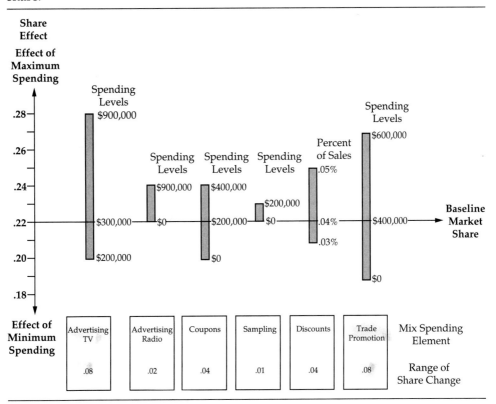

pear as additive elements. In this case, if it pays to spend anything on the mix element, it pays to spend up to the maximum. This is a convenient way to include items that management believes should be done at a specific level if they are done at all. For this property to be operational, the element must be an additive element whose effects are independent of other elements' effects on market share.

Q22:　What fraction (decimal) of a sales gain or loss during this planning period will continue in the next period?

　　If the answer is 0, the user goes on to question Q23. If the answer is a positive number (less than or equal to 1), two additional subquestions must be answered.

Q22A:　How many periods beyond the planning period will this effect be observed?

　　Say a manager enters .3 to Question 22 and a 4 to Question 22A. This means that an increment of sales and contribution equal to .3 of those realized in the planning period will occur in the following period. A .3 × .3 = .09 increment will occur in the period after that, and similar declining effects will be felt in the two following periods. These future increments to contribution profit are due to the current marketing budget and can

FIGURE 14-5   Comparison of the efficiency of expenditures on two mix elements.

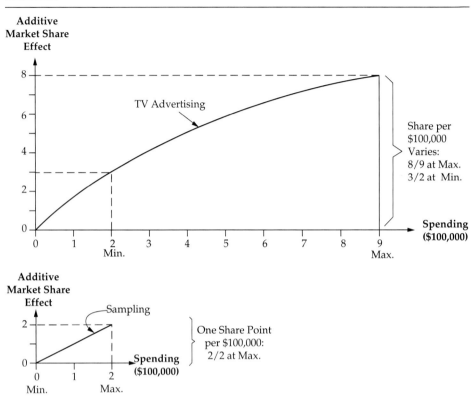

be converted to their present value. To do so, the model needs a discount rate, usually the applicable cost of capital.

Q22B: The firm's annual cost of capital (.### > 0)?

When the present value of the future contributions has been computed, this amount is reported separately in the summary data on superior budgets along with the current contribution and total of the two contribution figures. The total contribution is the criterion used to judge the effectiveness of a total budget and its distribution to the separate marketing activities (mix elements).

Q23: If suppliers, franchisers, or others provide part of your marketing funds, enter a 1. Otherwise enter a 0.

If 0 is entered, the program's required inputs are complete. If not, Q23A–Q23C must be answered.

Q23A: If a fixed amount is provided, enter the dollar amount (000). Otherwise enter a zero.

Q23B: If the amount that is provided is a fraction of sales, enter the fraction (.###). Otherwise enter a zero.

Q23C: If the amount that is provided is a fraction of marketing expenditures, enter the fraction (.###). Otherwise enter a zero.

Occasionally, cooperative funds will be a percentage of the spending on one or more mix elements. Since the model does not accommodate this level of detail, approximate the cooperative allowance by entering an adjusted fraction in response to Q23C and/or adjust the final contribution profit figures.

Q24: Do you want to enter optional estimates of the intermediate effects of marketing spending ($Y = 1, N = 0$)?

If the answer is yes, estimates should be entered for six variables at each of three levels of spending, minimum, baseline, and maximum. (See Q24A–Q24F on the data form.) The six intermediate variables are (a) the percentage of all spending devoted to pull objectives, (b) the expected percentage of prospective buyers who will be aware of the product, (c) the expected percentage distribution (volume weighted) among resellers who will stock the product, (d) the percentage of sales that are expected to be trial purchases, (e) the expected repeat purchase rate, and (f) the expected switchback purchase rate. The program echoes these assumptions and for each spending level it prints the percentage of buyers' choice sets that include the product and the long-run retention rate. The use of these data is discussed in Chapters 10, 11, 12, and 15.

Revising Program Inputs

As the user enters responses to the program's on-screen queries, the printer version of the program echoes most of the inputs to the printer. This printed list of inputs should be reviewed carefully and any required corrections should be made. At the conclusion of an input session

using either version of the program, whether it is a session during which the user made original entries or recalled previously recorded data from the program disk, the user is given a chance to correct or modify the inputs which the program will use. Changes in the data cannot be made after analysis has begun since the new data could affect the model's structure. Instead, one must restart the program by choosing STOP from a menu or keying Ctrl/Break. When C> appears enter LMIXMENU and push the Enter key.

As noted earlier, the screen version of the program provides a way to correct input errors as they occur. When using this program, on-screen instructions appear near the beginning of the work session.

Input Requirements for the Second Program Segment

The second segment of the program makes some on-screen queries that need additional explanation. *First*, the program asks if a fixed budget will be analyzed. If so, the user must enter the budget total in (000)s. In this case, the basic sample analysis will allocate this amount, ignoring any other levels. *Second*, if a basic analysis is being conducted, the user must specify the number of samples that will be examined at each of the eight nonextreme budget levels. Although using the number recommended by the program can lead to an extended computing delay if the problem has more than six mix elements, a user can be confident that the results will lead to a near-optimal total budget and allocation to the spending categories. A more detailed discussion of the effects of the number of samples on results is included in Appendix 13-1. *Third*, the program asks if a new sequence of random numbers is desired for the analysis. In most applied work the answer will be no, but starting a new sequence typically has little effect on the final budget.

During the two sampling and search phases of this program segment, the program continuously reports on the percentage of the total sample that has been completed. About six minutes are required to complete 1,000 (the standard number in this case) sample observations for each of the eight budget levels for the test problem when the program is run on an IBM/AT with a coprocessor.

A TEST PROBLEM PERSPECTIVE ON PROGRAM OUTPUT

The test problem reported below has many of the characteristics of the applied problems described in Chapter 13 but it also uses all the available input options. A reader may find it useful to fill in a blank data form by recording the echoed input shown in the output section for the first part of the MARMIX program. Doing so will clarify the relationship of the input data recorded on the data form to the printed echo of the data entry. When the form is completed it can be compared to the one that appears in Figure 14-25 at the end of the illustrative output. The output pages in Figure 14-6 are sequentially numbered in the upper right-hand corner.[1]

---

[1]The response function graphs for advertising—radio and for coupons are omitted since they are similar to the response function for advertising—TV (Figure 14-7).

FIGURE 14-6   Test problem output of MARMIX program, part 1.

MARKETING MIX MODEL BUILDER

by

Edgar Pessemier

Copyright © 1986, 1993 by Edgar Pessemier, Seattle, Washington. All rights reserved

---

```
MARKETING MIX MODEL OUTPUT                          VERSION 4.0


      Status of Data Files
No.              Date            Time
 1            09/09/88        10:20:22
  TEST PROBLEM
 2
 3
 4
 5


The data file identifier being used is:  1
DATA RETRIEVED.

Today's date:   10-06-1989       Present time:    10:16:31
Q1:  A General Description of the Problem: TEST PROBLEM
Q2:  Number of months in the analysis.    12
```

FIGURE 14-6 (Continued)   Test problem output of MARMIX program, part 1.

Q3: Number of mix elements.   6

Q4: Names of the mix elements

  Mix element   1
    Adv-TV
  Mix element   2
    Adv-Radio
  Mix element   3
    Coupons
  Mix element   4
    Sampling
  Mix element   5
    Discounts
  Mix element   6
    Trade Prom.

Q5: Definition of sales unit.   Dozens

Q6: Primary unit demand   8,000,000

  Excludes sales to employees and charitable gifts.

Q7: Unit price. $ 2.40

Average of regular prices, excluding trade promotion reductions. Volume weighted
 average.

Q8: Unit variable cost. $ 1.35

Labor, materials, etc. in manufacturing and distribution that change in total as
 units produced change.

Q9: At normal (baseline) marketing expenditures, your market
share estimate at each of the following unit prices is:

	-30%	-20%	-10%	Base-line	+10%	+20%	+30%
PRICE:	-30%	-20%	-10%	line	+10%	+20%	+30%
SHARE:	.300	.250	.230	.220	.210	.190	.140

FIGURE 14-6 (Continued)   Test problem output of MARMIX program, part 1.

Q10: Spending units-of-measure: 1=fraction of $ sales, 0=dollars.
  Adv-TV
        0
  Adv-Radio
        0
  Coupons
        0
  Sampling
        0
  Discounts
        1
  Trade Prom.
        0

Q11: Baseline spending by mix element, ours and competitors.

	Our Spending	Competitors' Spending Given Our Spending
Adv-TV		
	300000.000	2000000.000
Adv-Radio		
	0.000	1200000.000
Coupons		
	200000.000	1000000.000
Sampling		
	0.000	1000000.000
Discounts		
	0.040	0.040
Trade Prom.		
	400000.000	1500000.000

Q12: Our minimum spending (less than or equal to baseline spending), and competitors' responses.

	Our Spending	Competitors' Spending Given Our Spending
Adv-TV		
	200000.000	1700000.000
Adv-Radio		
	0.000	1000000.000
Coupons		
	0.000	950000.000
Sampling		
	0.000	500000.000
Discounts		
	0.030	0.039
Trade Prom.		
	0.000	1200000.000

FIGURE 14-6 (Continued)   Test problem output of MARMIX program, part 1.

```
                                                         Page   4
Q13: Our maximum spending (greater than or equal to baseline spending) and
competitors' responses.
                       Our               Competitors' Spending
                     Spending              Given Our Spending
Adv-TV
                   900000.000                 3000000.000
Adv-Radio
                   900000.000                 2000000.000
Coupons
                   400000.000                 1300000.000
Sampling
                   200000.000                  600000.000
Discounts
                        0.050                       0.042
Trade Prom.
                   600000.000                 1550000.000


Q14: Specification of the model's structure.

Group Assignments of Interactive Mix Elements.
                             Interactive Groups
Adv-Radio                        1
Coupons                          1
Sampling                          2
Discounts                         2
Trade Prom.                       2

Q15: Market share produced by all element spending at ZERO.            .1

Q16: Market share produced by all element spending at their MAXIMUMS. .38

                                                         Page   5

Q17: FORMAL response function = 0, DIRECT response function = 1.
      ORIGIN: (000 or .###), usually 0.

     Funct.               Origin
Adv-TV
        0                    0
Adv-Radio
        0                    0
Coupons
        0                    0
Sampling
        0                    0
Discounts
        0                   .03
Trade Prom.
        1                    0
```

FIGURE 14-6 (Continued)   Test problem output of MARMIX program, part 1.

```
Q18: Response by mix element and spending level.
                Spending Levels     Percent Response
Trade Prom.
                  100,000.000
                                       0.100
                  200,000.000
                                       0.200
                  300,000.000
                                       0.400
                  400,000.000
                                       0.700
                  500,000.000
                                       0.850

Q19: Response function form: 1=concave, 2=s-shaped, 3=linear.
  Adv-TV
      1
  Adv-Radio
      1
  Coupons
      1
  Sampling
      3
  Discounts
      2
```

```
Shape of the Response Functions
                        Spending Levels
     1        2        3        4        5        6        7
Adv-TV
   0.0000   0.2588   0.5000   0.7071   0.8660   0.9659   1.0000
Adv-Radio
   0.0000   0.2588   0.5000   0.7071   0.8660   0.9659   1.0000
Coupons
   0.0000   0.2588   0.5000   0.7071   0.8660   0.9659   1.0000
Sampling
   0.0000   0.1667   0.3333   0.5000   0.6667   0.8333   1.0000
Discounts
   0.0000   0.0670   0.2500   0.5000   0.7500   0.9330   1.0000
Trade Prom.
   0.0000   0.1000   0.2000   0.4000   0.7000   0.8500   1.0000
```

FIGURE 14-6 (Continued)   Test problem output of MARMIX program, part 1.

```
Q20: Market share effect of ZERO spending for a mix element.
                    Spending              Market Share
             Normal        New        Normal        New
Adv-TV
            300,000.00     0.00        0.22
   New market share                                  .2
Adv-Radio
              0.00         0.00        0.22
   New market share                                  .22
Coupons
            200,000.00     0.00        0.22
   New market share                                  .2
Sampling
              0.00         0.00        0.22
   New market share                                  .22
Discounts
              0.04         0.00        0.22
   New market share                                  .21
Trade Prom.
            400,000.00     0.00        0.22
   New market share                                  .19
```

```
Q21: If a mix element's spending is raised to the MAXIMUM, the
effect on market share will be:
                    Spending              Market Share
             Normal        New        Normal        New
 Adv-TV
            300,000.00  900,000.00     0.22
   New market share                                  .28
 Adv-Radio
              0.00     900,000.00      0.22
   New market share                                  .24
Coupons
            200,000.00  400,000.00     0.22
   New market share                                  .24
Sampling
              0.00     200,000.00      0.22
   New market share                                  .23
Discounts
              0.04        0.05         0.22
   New market share                                  .25
Trade Prom.
            400,000.00  600,000.00     0.22
   New market share                                  .27
```

FIGURE 14-6 (Continued)   Test problem output of MARMIX program, part 1.

```
Q22: Future effects of strategy
   Percent of share gain      Period's share gain         Annual
      carried forward          remains effective      cost of capital
          0.30                        4                    0.10


Q23: Cooperative Marketing Funds

Fixed coop. funds.
   10000
Coop funds as a fraction of sales.
   .0010
Coop funds as a fraction of market spending.
   .010


DATA SAVED.
```

| | Our Base | Competitor's | Our Spending Fract. Total |
Mix Elements	Spending	Spending	Spending
Adv-TV			
	300,000.000	2,000,000.000	0.130
Adv-Radio			
	0.000	1,200,000.000	0.000
Coupons			
	200,000.000	1,000,000.000	0.167
Sampling			
	0.000	1,000,000.000	0.000
Discounts			
	0.040	0.040	0.000
Trade Prom.			
	400,000.000	1,500,000.000	0.211
Total	$ 1,068,960	$ 7,299,040	

FIGURE 14-6 (Continued) Test problem output of MARMIX program, part 1.

Baseline Economics

	Per Unit	Total Dollars
Sales	2.40	4,224,000.00
Variable Cost	1.35	2,376,000.00
Before Mktg. Contribution	1.05	1,848,000.13
Variable Mktg. Cost	0.61	1,068,960.00
Final Contrib. Margin	0.44	779,040.13

Model Format

	Spending Unit 0:Dollars	Specifi-cation 0:Formal	Shape 1:Concave 2:S-shaped 3:Linear	Func. Orig. (000)	Model Effect 0:Addit.
Mix Element	1:Fract.S.	1:Direct		(.##)	+:Multi.
Adv-TV	0.00	0.00	1.00	0.00	0.00
Adv-Radio	0.00	0.00	1.00	0.00	1.00
Coupons	0.00	0.00	1.00	0.00	1.00
Sampling	0.00	0.00	3.00	0.00	2.00
Discounts	1.00	0.00	2.00	0.03	2.00
Trade Prom.	0.00	1.00	0.00	0.00	2.00

**** Function ****

Page 9

Intermediate Market Effects
at Given Spending Levels

Marketing Elements	Minimum	Baseline	Maximum
Percent PULL	0.750	0.700	0.650
Percent AWARE	0.700	0.800	0.900
Percent DISTRIBUTION	0.500	0.600	0.800
Share of CONSID. SETS	0.350	0.480	0.720
Percent TRIAL Purch.	0.005	0.010	0.015
Purch. REPEAT Rate	0.150	0.200	0.250
Purch. SWITCHBACK Rate	0.150	0.250	0.400
Long-run REPEAT. Rate	0.150	0.238	0.348

FIGURE 14-6 (Continued)   Test problem output of MARMIX program, part 1.

```
Test of Model's Predictive Validity
                          Expected       Model's Computed
                        Market Share       Market Share
      Maximum
                            0.380              0.380
      Baseline
                            0.220              0.220
      Origin
                            0.100              0.100

      Fraction Baseline Adjustment    0.111

      Fraction Maximum Adjustment     0.163
```

Page   10

```
ANALYSES OF THE FIRST EIGHT SAMPLE BUDGETS

Sample No. Mktg. dollars  Total cont. profit  Market share    Dollar sales

    1      $  1,068,960      $    803,954         .220       $  4,224,000
Mix element spending levels
    1    300,000.000     2          0.000    3   200,000.000   4        0.000
    5          0.040     6   400,000.000

    2      $          0      $    665,505         .100       $  1,920,000
Mix element spending levels
    1          0.000     2          0.000    3         0.000   4        0.000
    5          0.000     6          0.000

    3      $    763,048      $    414,657         .151       $  2,891,428
Mix element spending levels
    1    316,666.656     2   150,000.000    3    66,666.664   4   33,333.332
    5          0.033     6   100,000.000

    4      $  1,264,015      $    268,063         .186       $  3,564,046
Mix element spending levels
    1    433,333.313     2   300,000.000    3   133,333.328   4   66,666.664
    5          0.037     6   200,000.000
```

FIGURE 14-6 (Continued)   Test problem output of MARMIX program, part 1.

```
    5      $  1,777,089      $      208,465        .231        $   4,427,229

Mix element spending levels
    1     550,000.000      2    450,000.000    3   200,0000.000   4   100,000.000
    5           0.040      6    300,000.000

    6      $  2,309,033      $      287,383        .291        $   5,593,058
Mix element spending levels
    1     666,666.625      2    600,000.000    3   266,666.656   4   133,333.328
    5           0.043      6    400,000.000

    7      $  2,839,962      $      269,518        .342        $   6,570,620
Mix element spending levels
    1     783,333.313      2    750,000.000    3   333,333.313   4   166,666.656
    5           0.047      6    500,000.000

    8      $  3,364,800      $      126,697        .380        $   7,296,000
Mix clement spending levels
    1     900,000.000      2    900,000.000    3   400,000.000   4   200,000.000
    5           0.050      6    600,000.000
```

Several sections of the output deserve special attention.

1. On the top of output page 6 of Figure 14-6, the shape of each element's response function is defined. The percentage of the possible response produced by each mix element is shown as spending increases in uniform increments from the origin (zero or nonzero origin) to the element's maximum spending level. These shapes should all be in line with management's beliefs about market share responsiveness to spending. The difference between responses to Q20 and Q21 indicates how the vertical axis of each response function will be scaled to allow for its impact on market share. See the discussion of Figures 14-4 and 14-5. The graphic output display of the response functions and the hangbar graph and its associated table should be reviewed carefully to be sure they reflect the manager's best judgments. These graphs (Figures 14-7 to 14-12) follow output page 10 in Figure 14-6.

2. The top of output page 8 provides a summary of the baseline input spending pattern as a percentage of the spending by all brands, including the firm's brand. (Zero percentages are shown where a base level cannot be established; for example, for entries shown as a percentage of sales.)

FIGURE 14-7   Response function—TV advertising.

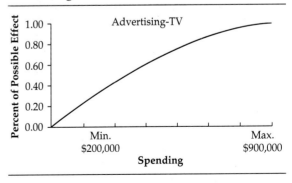

FIGURE 14-8   Response function—sampling.

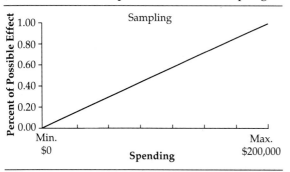

FIGURE 14-9   Response function—discounts.

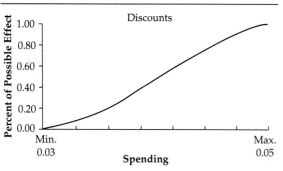

FIGURE 14-10   Response function—trade promotions.

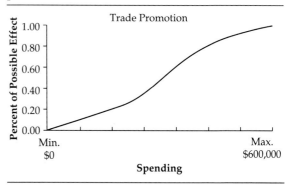

3. The bottom two tables on output page 8 summarize, respectively, some of the economics at baseline spending and the structural features of the model. Again, these data should be reviewed to confirm that the model matches the manager's beliefs about the behavior of the market and how it responds to marketing activities.

4. The optional section on validation appears on output pages 9 and 10 of Figure 14-6. Page 9 shows how well the model's rescaled inputs and its outputs match a manager's subjective estimates of the shares that would be obtained at minimum, baseline, and maximum spending. The size of the adjustments needed to produce a perfect fit of the model forecasts to baseline and maximum spending share inputs is noted.

5. On output page 10, forecasts appear for market share and total contribution to profits for various evenly spaced spending patterns (over the feasible range for each mix element). The forecasts should closely match a manager's expectations. If all of the above conditions are met, the user can be reasonably sure that the model's output will be compatible with his or her best judgments.

FIGURE 14-11   Summary of estimated effects of spending on changes in market share.

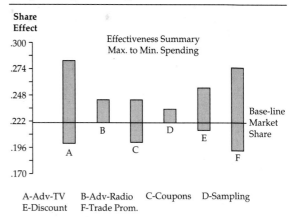

FIGURE 14-12 Numerical data associated with Figure 14-11.

Page   12

Element Name	% $	Orig. (000)	Min (000)	Base- Line (000)	Max (000)	Spending Range	Share Range
Adv—TV	$	0	200	300	900	700	0.08
Adv—Radio	$	0	0	0	900	900	0.02
Coupons	$	0	0	200	400	400	0.04
Sampling	$	0	0	0	200	200	0.01
Discounts	%	0.03	0.03	0.04	0.05	0.02	0.04
Trade Prom.	$	0	0	400	600	600	0.08

Data Saved for Budget Analysis Segment.

In this case, one can confidently proceed to the analysis in Part 2 of the MARMIX program. The output of the latter analysis appears in Figures 14-13–14-24.

The top of output page 13 (Figure 14-13) shows the results of analyzing 1,000 random sample budgets and saving the best one at each of the eight nonextreme total expenditure levels (evenly spaced levels across the feasible range). The graph following page 13 (Figure 14-14) shows the changing distribution of spending across mix elements as the size of the total budget changes. On output pages 14 and 15 (Figures 14-15 and 14-16), details are displayed for the best budget found at each expenditure level. The graph following page 15 (Figure 14-17) summarizes the way a market and the product's economics respond to various sizes of efficiently allocated marketing budgets. Pages 16–18 (Figures 14-18, 14-20, and 14-21) and the associated graphs (Figures 14-19 and 14-22) show the same kind of data for these budgets after attempts were made to improve each budget selected during the sampling process.

Several computational details should be noted. On output pages 13 and 16, the column labeled

contribution per marketing dollar is the contribution at the indicated spending level less the contribution at the minimum level subsequently divided by the firm's incremental marketing spending (not total spending). The column labeled market share per (000,000) marketing spending is calculated in a similar manner, with the share figures replacing contribution figures. Finally, total dollar spending figures on output pages 14–15 and 17–18 include expenses expressed as a percentage of sales after the spending levels have been converted to dollar amounts.

Note that some trade-offs may be called for when choosing a final budget. Current contribution to profit may be traded off against future contribution to profit, total contribution may have to be traded off against market share, and in some cases maximizing contribution per dollar of marketing spending may override other considerations. Furthermore, final choice of a budget may very well be dictated by factors that were not included in the model's computations. Page 19 (Figure 14-23) shows the sensitivity of results to alternative price levels and a graph of the fifth budget level results appear in Figure 14-24. Figure 15-9 in the next

FIGURE 14-13   Test problem output—MARMIX, Part 2: "Before improvement" summary results and budget allocations.

Page   13

A sample of 1000
per budget level were analyzed and improvements have or will be attempted for the best budgets found at each of ten expenditure levels

Best total marketing budgets from 10 equal size intervals from 0 to maximum spending.

incremental

Summary of Sampling

Trial Budget Number	Total Marketing Budget	Contribution Dollars	Per Mktg Dollar	Market Share Dollars	Per (000000) Marketing
1	0	665,505	9,999.99	0.100	1.000
2	650,278	700,918	0.05	0.169	0.106
3	1,007,982	739,687	0.07	0.209	0.108
4	1,369,617	1,114,618	0.33	0.282	0.134
5	1,699,639	1,173,660	0.30	0.321	0.131
6	2,003,880	1,056,330	0.20	0.339	0.120
7	2,329,406	893,852	0.10	0.355	0.110
8	2,666,513	663,121	-0.00	0.365	0.100
9	2,960,125	432,778	-0.08	0.372	0.093
10	3,364,800	126,698	-0.16	0.380	0.084

Each Mix Element's Share of Budget

	Budget Levels									
	1	2	3	4	5	6	7	8	9	10
Adv-TV	0.000	0.485	0.278	0.207	0.390	0.340	0.315	0.245	0.268	0.267
Adv-Radio	0.000	0.066	0.050	0.033	0.005	0.086	0.143	0.223	0.225	0.267
Coupons	0.000	0.181	0.163	0.152	0.090	0.120	0.126	0.130	0.129	0.119
Sampling	0.000	0.026	0.037	0.031	0.003	0.015	0.026	0.047	0.061	0.059
Discounts	0.000	0.196	0.191	0.191	0.178	0.149	0.134	0.131	0.119	0.108
Trade Prom.	0.000	0.045	0.280	0.386	0.335	0.290	0.255	0.223	0.198	0.178

FIGURE 14-14   Graph of "before improvement" share of marketing spending of six marketing mix elements for each of four budget levels.

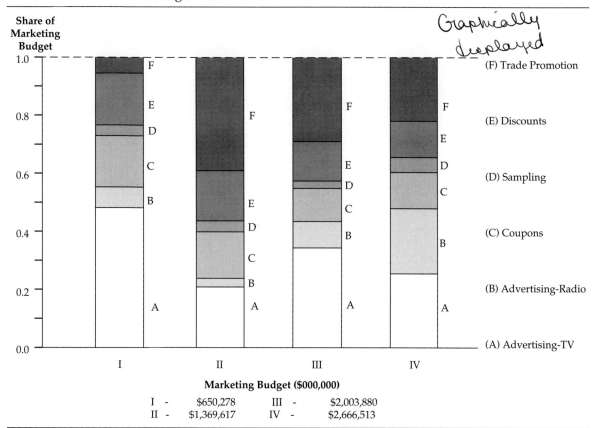

Marketing Budget ($000,000)

| I | - | $650,278 | III | - | $2,003,880 |
| II | - | $1,369,617 | IV | - | $2,666,513 |

chapter shows the optional forecasts for a revised budget and price that management was considering.

The Effects of Input Errors

Input errors can affect key model output like market share and contribution to profit. These effects are potentially interesting, especially when management is very uncertain about the correct input value. Sensitivity analysis and additional information collection may be needed. Input-output relationships are also of interest when there is an opportunity to favorably

influence the true value of an input. For example, the product's desirability may be improved by a design change or by lowering its price. Some of the more straightforward connections are summarized in Table 14-1.

Other input errors such as misspecifying the structure of the model or the shape of the response functions are not as simple in their effects. Naturally, the principal defense against input errors is careful initial analysis of the problem.

Some input errors have no effect on the model's output. For example, the maximum competitive spending on sampling should have been 1,600 instead of 600. Since competitive

FIGURE 14-15 Summary of the best "before improvement" results for the five lowest test budgets.

Page   14

Detail of best budget at each level ...

BEFORE Attempting Improvements

	1	2	3	4	5
CONTRIBUTION PROFIT					
Total	665,505	700,918	739,687	1,114,618	1,173,660
Current	851,920	779,977	757,544	1,018,302	1,017,253
Future	-186,415	-79,059	-17,857	96,316	156,407
Cont.per $	9999.99	0.05	0.07	0.33	0.30
TOTAL MARKETING SPENDING					
Total	0	650,278	1,007,982	1,369,617	1,699,639
Ours	-11,920	640,529	993,899	1,350,506	1,676,485
Coop.	11,920	9,750	14,083	19,111	23,153
MIX ELEMENT SPENDING					
Adv-TV	0	315,433	280,533	284,183	662,107
Adv-Radio	0	42,953	50,520	44,793	8,339
Coupons	0	117,985	164,273	208,197	152,415
Sampling	0	16,991	37,598	43,015	5,039
Discounts	0.000	0.039	0.048	0.048	0.049
Trade Prom.	0	29,385	282,684	528,305	568,920
SALES PERFORMANCE					
Our $ Sales	1,920,000	3,246,871	4,003,299	5,414,419	6,157,114
Our Share	0.100	0.169	0.209	0.282	0.321
Share per $1,000,000 Mktg.	1.000	0.106	0.108	0.134	0.131

FIGURE 14-16 Summary of the best "before improvement" results for the five highest test budgets.

Page   15

BEFORE Attempting Improvements

	6	7	8	9	10
CONTRIBUTION PROFIT					
Total					
	1,056,330	893,852	663,121	432,778	126,698
Current					
	871,282	683,912	437,136	197,395	-121,856
Future					
	185,049	209,940	225,985	235,383	248,553
Cont.per $					
	0.20	0.10	-0.00	-0.08	-0.16
TOTAL MARKETING SPENDING					
Total					
	2,003,880	2,329,406	2,666,513	2,960,125	3,364,800
Ours					
	1,977,330	2,299,293	2,632,831	2,923,391	3,313,856
Coop.					
	26,550	30,113	33,682	36,734	50,944
MIX ELEMENT SPENDING					
Adv-TV					
	681,993	734,104	654,123	792,425	900,000
Adv-Radio					
	171,691	333,629	595,829	666,898	900,000
Coupons					
	240,670	293,364	347,155	381,245	400,000
Sampling					
	29,961	60,775	125,881	179,281	200,000
Discounts					
	0.046	0.046	0.050	0.049	0.050
Trade Prom.					
	581,723	595,027	595,429	587,276	600,000
SALES PERFORMANCE					
Our $ Sales					
	6,511,113	6,818,754	7,017,067	7,133,223	7,296,000
Our Share					
	0.339	0.355	0.365	0.372	0.380
Share per $1,000.000 Mktg.					
	0.120	0.110	0.100	0.093	0.084

FIGURE 14-17   Graphic summary of market share, total contribution, and future contribution. Data from Figures 14-15 and 14-16.

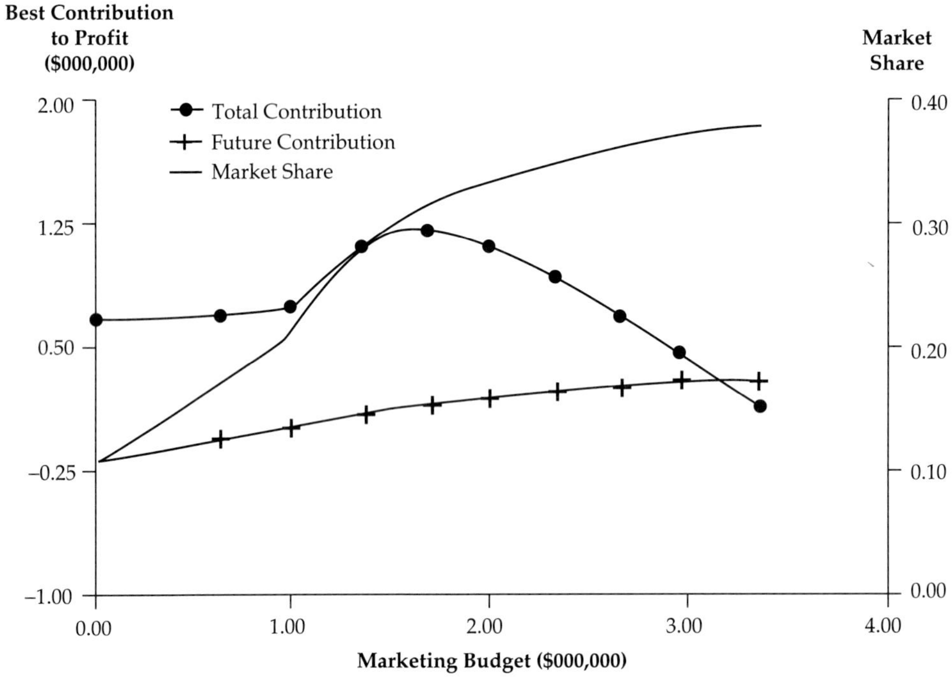

SOME APPLICATIONS OF THE MARMIX RESULTS[2]

Total Spending

Figure 14-26 shows the distribution of total contribution to profit and its current and future components over a full range of spending levels. In this illustration, attempts to buy share face a rapid decline in current contribution to profit and a slow gain in future contribution. This is a general phenomenon that forces a manager to con-

sider the adverse effect on current profit of attempts to increase market share and the adverse future effects of gaining current profits by a harvesting strategy. The S-shaped market share curve commonly results from the difficulty of balancing the mix with a limited budget and from the declining productivity as spending approaches the limit for each mix element. As this example shows and numerous other analyses confirm, it is *highly unlikely that budgeting total marketing effort as a fixed percentage of expected sales is an effective decision rule.* Its only merit is simplicity. Similar computer plots produced by the MARMIX program for the TEST PROBLEM appear in Figures 14-17 and 14-22.

Although the numerical results are not shown, total spending also shows considerable sensitivity to unit variable cost and cooperative marketing effort. A reduction in unit variable cost increases unit contribution, and therefore

spending levels constitute only assumptions, this error did not enter into the model's computations.

---

[2]Much of this and the next section first appeared in a paper by Edgar Pessemier and Cornelis de Kluyver.

FIGURE 14-18 "After improvement" summary results and budget allocations.

Page 16

Best total marketing budgets from 10 equal size intervals from 0 to maximum spending.

Trial Budget Number	Total Marketing Budget	Contribution Dollars	Per Mktg Dollar	Market Share Dollars	Per (000000) Marketing
1	0	751,150	9,999.99	0.109	1.000
2	755,649	849,160	0.25	0.193	0.125
3	1,399,304	1,142,329	0.35	0.287	0.135
4	1,610,512	1,241,720	0.36	0.318	0.137
5	1,561,229	1,315,179	0.42	0.320	0.143
6	1,726,374	1,226,139	0.33	0.328	0.134
7	1,920,919	1,174,630	0.27	0.342	0.127
8	2,091,037	1,099,302	0.21	0.351	0.122
9	2,216,611	980,235	0.14	0.352	0.115
10	2,408,307	892,499	0.10	0.362	0.110

Each Mix Element's Share of Budget

	Budget Levels									
	1	2	3	4	5	6	7	8	9	10
Adv-TV	0.000	0.399	0.223	0.280	0.290	0.305	0.307	0.286	0.272	0.275
Adv-Radio	0.000	0.046	0.036	0.026	0.005	0.031	0.051	0.066	0.091	0.110
Coupons	0.000	0.264	0.142	0.129	0.131	0.139	0.141	0.150	0.147	0.139
Sampling	0.000	0.022	0.027	0.022	0.003	0.017	0.032	0.053	0.075	0.083
Discounts	0.000	0.229	0.189	0.183	0.194	0.170	0.159	0.160	0.151	0.144
Trade Prom.	0.000	0.039	0.384	0.360	0.377	0.337	0.310	0.285	0.265	0.249

total contribution to profit at any level of expenditures. This makes it easier to justify large expenditures to increase market share. Similarly, cooperative marketing efforts raise expected profitability by lowering the firm's cost of achieving any level of marketing effort.

Efficiency

The efficiency of dollars spent is illustrated in Figure 14-27. Due to the interactive effects of spending on various mix elements, the total contribution to profit and contribution per market-

FIGURE 14-19   Graph of "after improvement" share of marketing spending for six marketing mix elements for each of four budget levels.

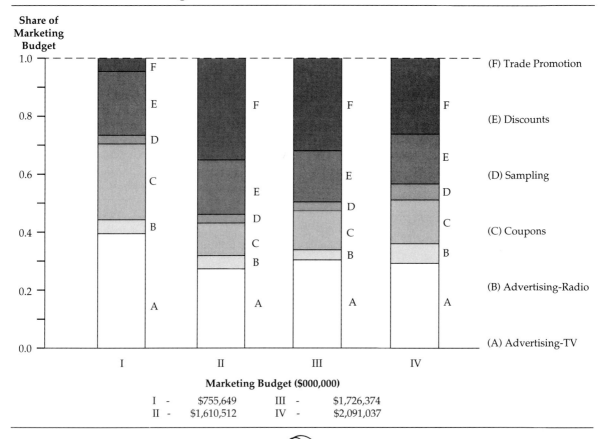

ing dollar curves rarely are steadily increasing or decreasing.

The more complex relationships substantially complicate finding optimal total spending levels and budget allocations. If one is solely concerned with maximizing total contribution to profit, total spending of $1.6 million would be a good choice. If, however, total spending is limited, say because of allocations to other products or product lines, *the opportunity effect of allocating funds to the other products must be taken into account.* A solution to this constrained optimization problem is presented in Chapter 15.

The behavior of individual mix element allocations also deserves careful attention. Since the efficiency of funds allocated to any mix element changes as total spending is varied *one must question any budget rule that calls for allocating a fixed percentage of the total budget to each mix element.* This variance in the efficient allocation to different mix elements is illustrated for four different budget levels in the share-of-spending plots shown in Figure 14-14 and Figure 14-19.

These figures show that the shape of the response functions and the model's structure significantly affect the distribution of spending as the total budget increases. It is difficult to generalize about the direction of this change because of the complex process by which spending generates profit, but the use of a program

FIGURE 14-20 Summary of the best "after improvement" results for the five lowest test budgets.

Page 17

AFTER Attempting Improvements

	1	2	3	4	5
CONTRIBUTION PROFIT					
Total	751,150	849,160	1,142,329	1,241,720	1,315,179
Current	924,224	890,435	1,038,676	1,090,014	1,159,630
Future	-173,074	-41,275	103,653	151,707	155,549
Cont.per $	9999.99	0.25	0.35	0.36	0.42
TOTAL MARKETING SPENDING					
Total	0	755,649	1,399,304	1,610,512	1,561,229
Ours	-12,085	734,379	1,369,806	1,578,308	1,529,470
Coop.	12,085	21,270	29,498	32,204	31,759
MIX ELEMENT SPENDING					
Adv-TV	90,000	301,641	311,506	451,069	452,745
Adv-Radio	0	35,031	50,520	42,581	8,339
Coupons	0	199,551	198,454	208,197	204,470
Sampling	0	16,991	37,598	35,082	5,039
Discounts	0.000	0.047	0.048	0.048	0.049
Trade Prom.	0	29,385	536,685	579,441	588,339
SALES PERFORMANCE					
Our $ Sales	2,084,889	3,713,860	5,505,102	6,099,021	6,146,514
Our Share	0.109	0.193	0.287	0.318	0.320
Share per $1,000,000 Mktg.	1.000	0.125	0.135	0.137	0.143

FIGURE 14-21 Summary of the best "after improvement" results for the five highest test budgets.

```
                                                          Page   18

AFTER Attempting Improvements

                 6            7            8            9            10
CONTRIBUTION PROFIT

  Total
             1,226,139    1,174,630    1,099,302      980,235      892,499
  Current
             1,058,992      985,505      895,676      775,792      672,160
  Future
               167,147      189,125      203,625      204,443      220,339
  Cont.per $
                  0.33         0.27         0.21         0.14         0.10

TOTAL MARKETING SPENDING

  Total
             1,726,374    1,920,919    2,091,037    2,216,611    2,408,307
  Ours
             1,692,820    1,885,149    2,053,386    2,177,694    2,367,277
  Coop.
                33,554       35,771       37,651       38,917       41,030

MIX ELEMENT SPENDING

  Adv-TV
               526,793      589,362      598,493      602,252      662,433
  Adv-Radio
                53,335       98,251      138,301      200,873      264,134
  Coupons
               240,670      271,728      313,514      325,964      334,376
  Sampling
                29,961       60,775      110,913      166,168      200,000
  Discounts
                 0.047        0.047        0.050        0.049        0.050
  Trade Prom.
               581,723      595,027      595,429      587,276      600,000

SALES PERFORMANCE

  Our  $ Sales
             6,289,857    6,561,494    6,740,714    6,750,823    6,947,284
  Our Share
                 0.328        0.342        0.351        0.352        0.362
  Share per $1,000.000 Mktg.
                 0.134        0.127        0.122        0.115        0.110
```

FIGURE 14-22 Graphic summary of market share, total contribution, and future contribution. Data from Figures 14-20 and 14-21.

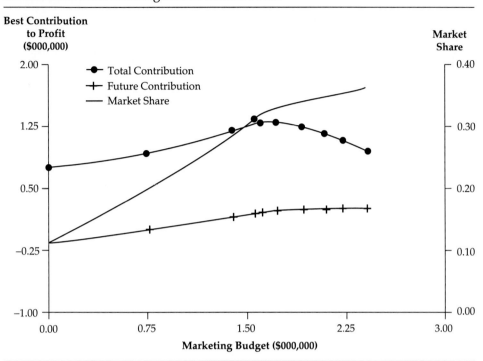

such as MARMIX can help avoid decidedly sub-optimal spending levels and allocations.

Price Changes

Earlier, it was argued that price is inherently part of the offer and therefore should be analyzed prior to the formulation of a support budget. Nevertheless, price sensitivity affects market performance and the budget-setting process. MARMIX provides two output measures which help a manager to assess the potential desirability of a price change. For each budget level and allocation, the program displays (1) the market share needed to sustain the budget level's contribution to profit at each of a set of different price levels and (2) the estimated market share at each of these price points.

When the "share-needed" curve lies below the "share-estimated" curve, price changes can have a positive effect on total profits. Referring to Figure 14-28, for an illustrative $1.4 million budget, a price increase of as much as 75 cents per unit would increase total contribution. A price reduction is not profitable. At higher levels of total spending, the share needed to sustain the original profit level is higher at the new price levels. For lower budget levels, a lesser share preserves profitability. See Figure 14-23. These estimates of the share needed at each price level to sustain total contribution are computed on the basis of management's subjective inputs about price elasticity.

If a manager wants to compute total contribution to profit for a new promising price level, say $2.65, at a somewhat higher level of spending, say $1.73 million, a MARMIX option will

FIGURE 14-23   Price and share sensitivity analysis.

```
PRICE/SHARE SENSITIVITY ANALYSIS

Given the price/share relationship estimated at baseline spending AND holding total con-
tribution profit fixed:

Total Budget        0
Unit Price     1.68   1.92   2.16   2.40   2.64   2.88   3.12
'Est.' Share   0.210  0.144  0.120  0.109  0.104  0.094  0.069
Needed Share   0.286  0.166  0.116  0.090  0.073  0.062  0.053

Total Budget   755,649
Unit Price     1.68   1.92   2.16   2.40   2.64   2.88   3.12
'Est.' Share   0.286  0.226  0.204  0.193  0.185  0.167  0.123
Needed Share   0.595  0.344  0.242  0.187  0.152  0.128  0.111

Total Budget 1,399,304
Unit Price     1.68   1.92   2.16   2.40   2.64   2.88   3.12
'Est.' Share   0.368  0.315  0.296  0.287  0.274  0.248  0.182
Needed Share   0.913  0.529  0.372  0.287  0.234  0.197  0.170

Total Budget 1,610,512
Unit Price     1.68   1.92   2.16   2.40   2.64   2.88   3.12
'Est.' Share   0.396  0.345  0.327  0.318  0.303  0.274  0.202
Needed Share   1.019  0.590  0.415  0.320  0.261  0.220  0.190

Total Budget 1,561,229
Unit Price     1.68   1.92   2.16   2.40   2.64   2.88   3.12
'Est.' Share   0.398  0.347  0.329  0.320  0.306  0.276  0.204
Needed Share   1.020  0.590  0.415  0.320  0.261  0.220  0.190

Total Budget 1,726,374
Unit Price     1.68   1.92   2.16   2.40   2.64   2.88   3.12
'Est.' Share   0.404  0.354  0.336  0.328  0.313  0.283  0.208
Needed Share   1.058  0.613  0.431  0.333  0.271  0.228  0.197

Total Budget 1,920,919
Unit Price     1.68   1.92   2.16   2.40   2.64   2.88   3.12
'Est.' Share   0.417  0.368  0.350  0.342  0.326  0.295  0.217
Needed Share   1.117  0.647  0.455  0.351  0.286  0.241  0.208

Total Budget 2,091,037
Unit Price     1.68   1.92   2.16   2.40   2.64   2.88   3.12
'Est.' Share   0.425  0.377  0.360  0.351  0.335  0.303  0.223
Needed Share   1.161  0.672  0.473  0.365  0.297  0.250  0.216

Total Budget 2,216,611
Unit Price     1.68   1.92   2.16   2.40   2.64   2.88   3.12
'Est.' Share   0.426  0.378  0.360  0.352  0.336  0.304  0.224
Needed Share   1.176  0.681  0.479  0.370  0.301  0.254  0.219

Total Budget 2,408,307
Unit Price     1.68   1.92   2.16   2.40   2.64   2.88   3.12
'Est.' Share   0.435  0.387  0.370  0.362  0.345  0.312  0.230
Needed Share   1.225  0.709  0.499  0.385  0.313  0.264  0.228
```

TABLE 14-1   SOME EFFECTS OF INPUT ERRORS

	EFFECT ON OUTPUT	
Input "Too High"[1] for	Share	Contribution to Profit
Primary demand	0	+
Unit variable cost	0	−
Max. spending for a mix element	−	−
Share result from max. spending on a mix element	+	+
Share at max. total spending	+	+
Share from min. total spending	+	+
Share at baseline total spending	+	+
Share or time of carry forward	+	+

[1]If the words "Too High" are changed to "Too Low," the signs of the output effects are reversed.

provide the desired estimate. In this case, a total predicted profit of $1.36 million is shown in Figure 15-9, a very modest increase over the original estimate of $1.32 million when spending $1.56 million. Market share at the new spending level is .285 compared with the prior .320. Although this repricing analysis can be valuable,

caution should be exercised in its use. When prices are changed, adjustments in the frames of marketing effectiveness are usually called for. As a result, if any change in the offer is seriously being considered, the decision-maker should return to the input portion of the program, make the necessary adjustments, and repeat the budget analysis.

FIGURE 14-24   Graph of and share sensitivity analysis for the fifth budget level in Figure 14-23.

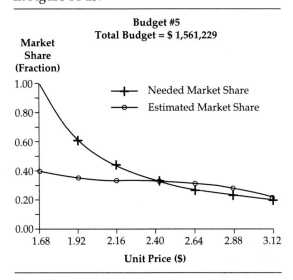

Aggregate (Single Mix Element) Analysis

A simple but useful form of preliminary MARMIX analysis is to specify a single mix element, total marketing spending. This single response function defines how market shares relate to overall budgets that are efficiently employed. These budgets can range from a zero or other minimum level to a maximum level in the same manner that they do in ordinary mix elements.

The main purpose of making such preliminary MARMIX runs is to gain insight into how responsive sales and profits are to variable levels of important inputs. Primary unit demand, unit price, unit variable cost, and marketing efficiency as expressed by maximum spending and the height and the shape of the aggregate response function are candidates for this form of exploratory analysis.

FIGURE 14-25a   Data form for MARMIX (Front).

DATA FORM FOR MARMIX (Front).

Completed by _____ Date ___*1 Jan 89*___

Date of Analysis (mm/dd/yy) _____ :   I.D. Number of Data file ___*1*___

Q1: Problem description: ___*Test problem*___

Q2: Number of months in the analyses ___*12*___

Q3: Number of mix elements ___*6*___

Q4: Names of the mix elements (12 spaces or less for each one)

1. *AdV-TV*
2. *AdV-Radio*
3. *Coupons*
4. *Sampling*
5. *Discounts*
6. *Trade Prom.*
7.
8.
9.
10.

Q5: Define the sales unit (units, gallons, dozens, etc.) ___*Dozens*___

Q6: Primary demand (000 units) ___*8000*___

Describe the components of primary demand ___*Excludes sales to employees and Charitable gifts*___

Q7: Baseline unit price in dollars and cents ___*2.40*___

Describe the components of average unit price *Average of "regular" prices, excluding trade promotions reductions. Volume weighted average*

Q8: Unit variable cost in dollars and cents ___*1.35*___

Describe the components of unit variable cost *Labor, materials, etc. used in manufacturing and distrubution that changes in total as the number of units produced changes*

Q9: Given normal marketing expenditures, the market share at each of the following unit prices (relative to the baseline unit price) are:

Price:	−30%	−20%	−10%	Baseline	+10%	+20%	+30%
Share:	.30	.25	.23	.22	.21	.19	.14

FIGURE 14-25b Data form for MARMIX (Back).

Mix Elements	Q10 Spend Units (Circle one) $	F	($000) Our Spending Q11A Base Line	Q12A Min.	Q13A Max.	Competitive Spending Q11B Base Line	Q12B Min.	Q13B Max.	Indep 0	Q14 Possible Interaction Group (one check per row) 0	1	2	3	4	5	6
1. Adv-TV	Ⓞ	1	300	200	900	2000	1700	3000	✓							
2. Adv-Radio	Ⓞ	1	0	0	900	1200	1000	2000			✓					
3. Coupons	Ⓞ	1	200	0	400	1000	950	1300			✓					
4. Sampling	Ⓞ	1	0	0	200	1000	500	600				✓				
5. Discounts	0	①	.04	.03	.05	.04	.039	.042				✓				
6. Trade prom.	Ⓞ	1	400	0	600	1500	1200	1550				✓				
7.	0	1														
8.	0	1														
9.	0	1														
10.	0	1														

Optional Intermediate Variable Questions:

		.10		Q15 Mkt share at min. spending.
			38	Q16 Mkt share at max. spending.
	.75	.70	.65	Q24A Budget's percentage PULL effect.
	.70	.80	.90	Q24B Expected percent AWARE.
	.50	.60	.80	Q24C Expected percent DISTRIBUTION.
	.005	.010	.015	Q24D Expected percent TRIAL purchase.
	.15	.20	.25	Q24E Purchase REPEAT rates.
	.15	.25	.40	Q24F Purchase SWITCHBACK rates.

Mix Elements	Q17 A Funct. Form F	D	Q17 B Origin (000 or .###)	Q18: At Fraction of Maximum Spending 0/6	1/6	2/6	3/6	4/6	5/6	6/6	Q19 Funct. Shape (Circle one) C S L	Q20 Zero Spend. Share	Q21 Max. Spend. Share
1. Adv-TV	Ⓞ	1	0	.00	.	.	.	.	.	1.00	① 2 3	.20	.28
2. Adv-Radio	Ⓞ	1	0	.00	.	.	.	.	.	1.00	① 2 3	.22	.24
3. Coupons	Ⓞ	1	0	.00	.	.	.	.	.	1.00	① 2 3	.20	.24
4. Sampling	Ⓞ	1	0	.00	.	.	.	.	.	1.00	1 2 ③	.22	.23
5. Discounts	Ⓞ	1	.03	.00	.	.	.	.	.	1.00	1 ② 3	.21	.25
6. Trade prom.	0	①	0	.00	.1	.2	.4	.7	.85	1.00	1 2 3	.19	.27
7.	0	1		.00	.	.	.	.	.	1.00	1 2 3	.	.
8.	0	1		.00	.	.	.	.	.	1.00	1 2 3	.	.
9.	0	1		.00	.	.	.	.	.	1.00	1 2 3	.	.
10.	0	1		.00	.	.	.	.	.	1.00	1 2 3	.	.

Q22   What fraction (decimal) of the sales gained or lost this period will continue next period? __.3__

Q22A   If non-zero answer, for how many periods beyond the current period will the effect last? __4__

Q22B   If one or more periods, what is the firm cost of capital (a decimal > 0)? __.1__

Q23   If part of your marketing spending is paid by entities outside your firm? (Y = 1) or N = 0

Q23A   If yes and a fixed amount is received, enter the amount (000) $ __10__

Q23B   If yes and a percent of product sales is received, enter the fraction __.001__

Q23C   If yes and a percentage of marketing expenses is received, enter the fraction __.01__

Q24   Do you want to enter optional estimates of the intermediate effect of marketing spending (Y = 1) N = 0) __1__

  If, yes, go to Q24A - Q24F above.

COMMENTS: _____

FIGURE 14-26   Total, current, and future contribution to profit and market share.

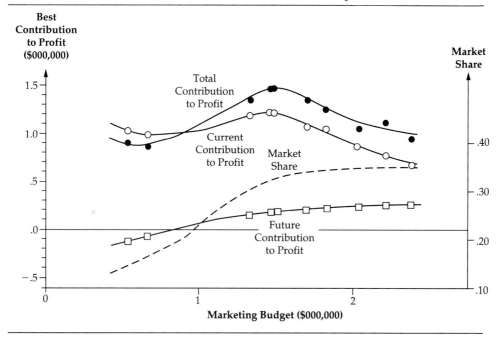

FIGURE 14-27   Total contribution and contribution per marketing dollar.

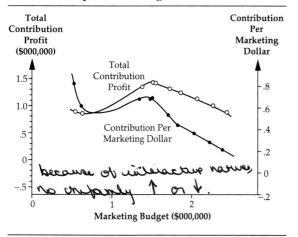

FIGURE 14-28   Price analysis: Base, $1,399,304 total budget and $2.40 unit price.

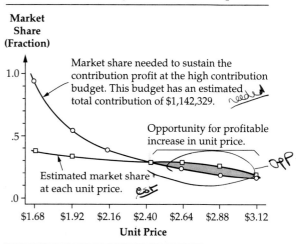

As an illustration, a set of analyses based on the TEST PROBLEM was completed. A single response function was used that roughly approximated the S-shaped results shown in Figure 14-22. In addition to the $2.40 unit price used in the original problem, prices of $2.15 and $2.65 were examined. The $2.15 price was assumed to produce a .28 baseline market share and the $2.65 price was assumed to produce a .18 market share. The response function was anchored at a $2.5 million maximum, producing a .28 larger market share than the share that was expected at zero spending. At the $2.65 unit price, zero spending was assumed to yield a .08 market share, and at the $2.15 price, zero spending was assumed to yield a .12 market share. The results of the analyses follow.

Price	Maximum Contrib. Spending (000)	Market Share	Expected Contrib. to Profit (000)
$2.15	1,033	.284	802
2.40	2,011	.356	1,232[1]
2.65	2,011	.333	1,799

[1]The results on this line vary from the allocated budget illustration since the single mix element response function used here (a formal S-shaped function) did not closely match the output share function shown in Figure 14-22.

Contribution to profit is sensitive to a $.25 reduction or a $.25 increase in unit price and the associated effects on market share at various levels of spending.

More complicated test strategies are common. For example, the manager of a consumer product might consider sales through brokers as a replacement for the firm's own sales force. This action would substitute variable brokers' commissions for the variable cost of sales commissions paid to the firm's salespeople. In addition, it would change the fixed costs of recruiting, training, and managing the product's sales representatives. Finally, using brokers may change the effectiveness of the sales effort. A single mix element analysis may be a simple way to make a rough appraisal of the alternative. In this case, however, a postanalysis adjustment in the contribution to profit must be made to account for the new level of fixed cost.

Fixed Costs of a Mix Element

In the above example, the fixed cost of a sales force had been treated as part of the fixed general marketing overhead. In a number of cases, a discretionary marketing action involves both fixed and variable costs. This problem is easily illustrated with a mailing designed to produce direct orders that can be sent to part or all of a 10,000-name mailing list. The fixed cost of acquiring the list, preparing the art, and making the printing plates is $5,000. The variable cost of printing a mailing piece, addressing it, and attaching the required postage is $.60 per piece mailed. A response function in this case, Case A, is the solid line shown in Figure 14-29.

The dotted line in the graph shows a second case, Case B, in which the names on the mailing list were ordered by their sales potential at a cost of $.10 per name. This $1,000 is an added fixed cost of acquiring the list, raising the origin and the maximum spending levels by this amount. It also changes the shape of the response function from linear to concave downward.

Usually, it is desirable to convert a linear or S-shaped response function for an independent element to a concave function, the more concave the better. If the mix element is dependent, more analysis is required to determine the best functional shape and location. The main point is that a manager should think through how he or she can favorably redefine each mix element's response function and then complete alternative MARMIX analyses if a direct choice cannot be made of the more efficient functional form.

FIGURE 14-29   Response function for a mix element with a fixed-cost component—two alternative approaches to a direct mail program.

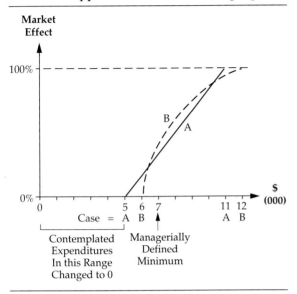

CONCLUDING REMARKS

Reducing the budgeting question to a tractable, quantitative problem has been the focus of marketing researchers for years. The issue is succinctly summarized by Chakravarti, Mitchell, and Staelin (1981):

> While model-based approaches have great potential for improving decision making in these situations, it is also difficult to construct and operationalize valid models of these environments. The models tend to be either too simple so they are not valid representations of the real world or so complex that the manager does not understand the models and, consequently, does not use them.

The development and implementation of MARMIX were designed to bridge this gap by allowing managers to both *construct* and *calibrate* models of their budgeting situation. Experience with the simple but realistic MARMIX models built by managers has shown that they can become comfortable with the program's scope, design, and structure.

Brief case studies on the implementation of the program were reported in Chapter 13. These applications show that the program can help produce a more efficient and effective budget. A number of other benefits accrue from this type of approach. First, the implementation process forces managers to carefully frame a model of their own product and market. Assumptions about how the market views the company's product, its positioning, and its competitive strengths, which are seldom stated or questioned, now have to be made explicit. This produces a deeper understanding of the forces that affect market share and the relationship between them. Strategy formulation is improved and made more responsive to market forces.

A greater appreciation of what information is needed, in what form, and bearing what value, is a second benefit. Market size and growth estimates, share data, and conclusions about which elements to include in the budget are generally relatively easy to come by. Defining suitable maximum spending limits, the impact of competitive activity on market share, and value added by marketing rank among the more difficult tasks. This realization sharpens marketing research efforts and thereby increases their effectiveness.

Finally, better communication with third parties—managers of other product lines, research personnel, manufacturing, accounting, and so on—stands out as a third type of benefit. The structure imposed by a decision support model standardizes the terminology and concepts used, forces more timely responses, and increases coordination within the organization.

REFERENCES

Chakravarti, D., Mitchell, A., and R. Staelin: "Judgment-Based Marketing Decision Models: Problems and Possible Solutions," *Journal of Marketing*, 45, 1981, 13–23.

APPENDIX 14-1
MATHEMATICAL PROPERTIES OF THE MARMIX MODEL

In a simple additive model, market share is the sum of the effects produced by each marketing mix element and the effect contributed by the offer. In the sense that it is used here, the offer includes the entire constellation of the product's design and physical features, the image it has already registered on potential buyers and users, and its current price per unit. Symbolically, in an all-additive case:

Marketing's Contribution to Market Share	Contribution from Spending on Mix Element 1	Contribution from Spending on the nth (Last) Mix Element
$MCMS^+$ =	$R_1^+(EX_1)$ + $\cdots$ +	$R_n^+(EX_n)$

where $R_i^+(EX_i)$ is an additive response function that converts expenditures on mix element i, EX_i, into market share effects. Finally,

Expected Market Share	Marketing's Contribution to Marketing Share	Contribution from the Product at its Proposed Price
EMS^+ =	$MCMS^+$ +	$PCMS$

PCMS is the product's relative desirability at its planned price compared with that of competing products before value is added by marketing spending. It can be expressed as PI $\times$ BMS, where PI is the relative importance of the product to buyers and users (compared to the value added by marketing expenditures), and BMS is the baseline market share.

In a simple multiplicative model, the product's baseline market share is subject to percentage increases and decreases contributed by spending on each mix element, Symbolically,

$$\text{EMS}^* = R_1^*(\text{EX}_1) \times \cdots \times R_n^*(\text{EX}_n) \times \text{BMS}$$

where $R_i^*(\text{EX}_i)$ is a response function that converts expenditures on mix element i into the percentage change in the baseline market share *after* it has been adjusted for any changes contributed by the spending pattern for the other mix elements.

If all spending is terminated, the joint percentage effect of the reductions yields a market share equal to PCMS, the share that cannot be attributed to marketing spending during the planning period. This share must be due to buyers' and users' desire for the product, given its image and its price. The share contributed by the marketing effort is

$$\text{MCMS}^* = \text{EMS}^* - \text{EMS}^*(0)$$

where

$$\text{EMS}^*(0) = \underbrace{R_1^*(0) \times \cdots \times R_n^*(0) \times \text{BMS}}_{= \text{PI}} = \text{PCMS}$$

Given the above relationships, it is easy to define a mixed model, one with some multiplicative and some additive elements. This can be done by including a zero spending element and a positive spending element in each spending category, one additive and one multiplicative. In this manner, each mix element makes a contribution to market share in either an additive or a multiplicative manner. The final result can be expressed symbolically if we first let

TA = the sum of all the additive elements

TM = the share contribution from all the multiplicative elements

Then,

$$\text{EMS} = \text{TA} + \text{TM} + \text{PCMS} \qquad (14\text{-}1\text{A})$$

The model is even more flexible than Equation (14-1A) indicates, since several groups of multiplicative elements may be present such that each group contributes an additive increment to market share.

Expanding Equation (14-1A) for K multiplicative subsets of mix elements,

$$\text{EMS} = \text{TA} + ((\text{TM}_1 + \text{TM}_2 + \cdots + \text{TM}_k) \times \text{BMS} + \text{PCMS})$$

where

$$\text{TM}_k = \left(\prod_{j \in J_k} R_j^*\left(\text{EX}_j\right) - \prod_{j \in J_k} R_j^*(0) \right)$$

Total contribution profit is the criterion used by MARMIX to evaluate the worth of each budget. Next period's contribution profit is:

$$\text{CP} = \left((\text{PUD} \times \text{EMS}) \times \text{UC}\right) - \sum_{i=1}^{N}\left(\text{EX}_i\right)$$

where

PUD = primary unit demand

and

UC = unit contribution or unit price less unit variable cost.

In the above computation of contribution profit, any externally supplied marketing support such as cooperative advertising dollars has been accounted for. Furthermore, total contribution profit is CP plus the future contribution profit which may be due to any carryover gain or loss in market share during future periods (discounted to present value).

RESCALING THE RESPONSE FUNCTIONS

At this point, it is helpful to recall several points about scaling response functions.

1. For an additive element, the vertical axis is scaled so that as spending goes from its baseline value to a maximum, the baseline market share will rise by the amount the user specifies. Also, when spending decreases from its baseline value to zero, the baseline market share will decrease by the amount the user specifies. The vertical market share axis begins at zero. The horizontal spending axis begins at zero or a nonzero origin and termi-

nates at the maximum spending level specified by the user.

2. For multiplicative elements, the vertical axis equals one when an element's spending is at the baseline level. This scaling is accomplished under a constraint on the minimum value for the vertical axis. This minimum must be such that the product of the minimum values for *all* mix elements *and* the product's baseline market share will equal the estimates of market share when all spending levels are at their minimums. (A similar constraint could be imposed on maximum spending.) For the multiplicative case, the estimated minimum market share is

$$\text{MMS}^* = \underbrace{R_i^*(0) \times \cdots \times R_n^*(0)}_{= \text{PI}} \times \text{BMS} = \text{PI} \times \text{BMS} = \text{PCMS}$$

The minimum result is the same for the additive model because $R_i^+(0) = 0$ for all i.

$$\text{MMS}^* = \underbrace{R_i^+(0) + \cdots + R_n^+(0)}_{= 0} + (\text{PI} \times \text{BMS}) = \text{PCMS}$$

In the case of a mixed model with some additive and some multiplicative elements, positive spending has an effect in only the appropriate part of the model. In the other part of the model, the response function value for the ith element becomes either $R_i^+(0)$ or $R_i^*(0)$. If all active additive elements contribute TA share points and all active multiplicative elements change the share by increments determined by the separate TM_k multiplicative groups, Equation (14-1A) above is the result.

Because of the way the response functions are scaled and of potential inconsistencies in the input data and the model's structure, a percentage adjustment may be required to fit the model's share forecasts to the manager's share forecasts. In any case, errors tend to be greatest at maximum spending, the level of spending that is usually furthest removed from a manager's experience. If a review of the model's forecasts at various spending levels proves to be unsatisfactory, a manager must reject the model.

REVIEW QUESTIONS

Q14-1 Write an explantion of the model structures described in Appendix 14-1. Describe PCMS in your own words.

Q14-2 Describe several mix elements whose effect you expect to be independent of each other and several mix elements whose effect you expect to depend on the levels of the other mix elements in the same group.

Q14-3 Describe the difference between a formally defined and a directly defined response function.

Q14-4 Read the output of the sample TEST PROBLEM, relating it to the data form (Figures 14-25a and 14-25b).

What, if anything, don't you understand?

What errors, if any, did you find?

What conclusions should a responsible manager draw?

What additional analyses, if any, would you complete?

Q14-5 What are the pros and cons of considering the future effects of a strategy/budget?

Q14-6 Explain why pricing decisions cannot be made directly from the final output of a regular MARMIX analysis?

Q14-7 Why is it unwise to make allocations to mix elements as a fixed percentage of sales?

Q14-8 Develop a MARMIX mix element set that could be useful for each of the following products:

a. A machine tool

b. A planned vacation and residential community

c. An over-the-counter analgesic

d. A chain of computer stores

e. A metropolitan university

Q14-9 In each of the above cases, propose a model structure and present arguments in favor of each of your choices.

Q14-10 Using the TEST PROBLEM as background, perform a single mix element analysis to examine the effect of increasing the product's appeal by 15 percent at the expense of a 10 percent increase in the product's variable cost. In addition, try to do the analysis with a paper and pencil.

COMPUTER EXERCISES MARMIX EXERCISES

1. Consult the output from the MARMIX test problem that appears in Chapter 14. See especially the input data in Figures 14-25a and 14-25b, and the output response functions in Figure 14-17. Fill in a blank MARMIX data form like the one shown in Figures 13-20 and 13-21, but aggregate all mix elements into a single mix element called total marketing. Note that the discount spending levels must be converted from percentages to dollars before the entries in Q11A, Q12A, and Q14A can be summed. Ignore the entries in columns Q11B, Q12B, and Q14B. Next, convert the market share curve in Figure 14-17 to a percentage of potential effect curve for spending levels that run from $0 to $3 million in increments of $500,000. Doing so will give you a rough approximation of the response function required by Q18 on the MARMIX data form. Enter .1 in Q20 and .38 in Q21. Complete the rest of the relevant questions but ignore the intermediate variables. Save the file under a new name and complete the analysis. Comment on the results.

2. Assume the test problem is a health care item that is used by both men and women. Increase the unit price in Q7 from $2.40 to $2.65. To the extent that it is desirable to do so, revise the entries in Q6, Q9, Q15, Q16, Q20, and Q21. Save your file under a new name and number, and rerun the analysis. Compare your results with those recorded in Figures 14-6 and 14-24, and comment on the desirability of the price change.

3. Using the input form shown in Figures 13-20 and 13-21, set up and run a MARMIX analysis. Build

on the background data from the Canadian whiskey illustration presented in Chapter 11 and assume that at the end of 1984 you are planning marketing spending for 1985. The 1983 and 1984 results were close to those shown in Figures 11-1a through 11-1c. However, the pattern of marketing spending did not necessarily follow the pattern that appears in the plan.

In completing this work, ask for all of the available graphic and tabular output. Examine these items to evaluate the validity and effectiveness of your strategy/budget.

a. If you revised and reran your analysis one or more times, describe the process and the results.

b. How does your final strategy and budget differ from the original plan?

c. How will you "sell" your new strategy/budget to senior marketing management?

4. Run the test problem using 200 samples per budget level instead of 1,000. Compare the results with those in Figure 14-13.

15

ADDITIONAL TOPICS IN PLANNING AND BUDGET ANALYSIS

A major portion of this chapter describes three aspects of MARMIX modeling that are not fully covered in prior chapters: allocating effort when the product's total budget is fixed; allocating a global budget to products, product lines, sales territories, or other independent components; and the role of assumptions in shaping model inputs and results. The latter part of the chapter discusses the degree to which managerial actions determine how a market responds, how a model is defined, how more favorable results can be obtained, and how a manager can improve the predictive validity of the marketing model. The chapter closes with outlines for a market and product fact book and a marketing plan. Appendix 15-1 contains instructions for installing and using all the computer programs that are associated with the text.

EFFICIENT ALLOCATION OF A FIXED BUDGET

The Basic Problem

Frequently, senior executives provide a fixed total budget that a marketing manager must allocate. In this case, a manager should take two distinct actions. The first step is to run a standard unconstrained MARMIX analysis to examine the full range of budget levels, each one efficiently allocated to the mix elements. These data provide a good idea of the sacrifice in sales and profits implied by the constraint on marketing spending. Although the spending limitation may be well founded, the analysis of alternatives can lay the groundwork for a constructive adjustment of the budget.

The second step that should be taken is to ensure that the adopted distribution of the fixed total budget to individual mix elements is efficient. Using a large number of sample allocations at the fixed total budget level will accomplish this purpose. The part of the MARMIX program that performs budget analysis asks the user whether a single budget will be analyzed and if so, the amount of the budget. The user always specifies the sample size for a single budget level. At least 5,000 observations should be chosen for a fixed budget to increase one's confidence about the reported budget allocation.

The program output for a fixed budget is like the output produced by a standard analysis, except that the results are limited to the minimum, fixed budget, and maximum levels. The illustrative test problem displayed in Figures 14-6 through 14-23 was rerun using 5,000 samples for a fixed budget of $1 million. The essential results appear in Figures 15-1a and 15-1b. Reducing the best $1.5 million level of spending to about $1 million sacrificed more than $300,000 in contribution to profit (after accounting for the $500,000 reduction in marketing spending) and

about .08 in market share. A small benefit from running the larger sample was a new allocation that provided a modest improvement in the expected profit from a $1 million budget.[1]

The Groups of Components Problem

A similar problem arises when a fixed budget must be distributed across products, sales areas, or other independent components. In this case, the input response functions become versions of the output produced by the separate MARMIX analyses for the component problems. This more complex task requires a separate program, which is discussed in the next section.

---

[1]The fixed-budget option must be run as part of an initial analysis and not as an extension of an initial analysis.

FIGURE 15-1a Basic sampling summary output—test problem at $1 million fixed budget.

```
                                                    Page 10

INPUT RECEIVED BY THE BUDGET ANALYSIS SEGMENT


A sample of 5,000
per budget level was analyzed and improvements have or will be attempted for the best bud-
gets found at each of ten expenditure levels.

Best total marketing budgets from 10 equal size intervals from 0 to maximum spending.
```

Trial Budget Number	Total Marketing Budget	Contribution Dollars	Per Mktg Dollar	Market Share Dollars	Per (000000) Marketing
1	261,281	470,564	0.00	0.106	0.000
2	0	0	0.00	0.000	0.000
3	1,014,438	1,008,022	0.71	0.236	0.172
4	0	0	0.00	0.000	0.000
5	3,364,800	126,698	-0.10	0.380	0.083
6	0	0	0.00	0.000	0.000
7	0	0	0.00	0.000	0.000
8	0	0	0.00	0.000	0.000
9	0	0	0.00	0.000	0.000
10	0	0	0.00	0.000	0.000

FIGURE 15-1b   Basic sampling summary output—test problem at $1 million fixed budget.

Page 11

BEFORE Attempting Improvements

	1	2	3	4	5
CONTRIBUTION PROFIT					
Total	470,564	0	1,008,022	0	126,698
Current	647,052	0	983,084	0	-121,856
Future	-176,488	0	24,938	0	248,553
Cont.per $	0.00	0.00	0.71	0.00	-0.10
TOTAL MARKETING SPENDING					
Total	261,281	0	1,014,438	0	3,364,800
Ours	246,625	0	999,761	0	3,313,856
Coop.	14,656	0	14,677	0	50,944
MIX ELEMENT SPENDING					
Adv-TV	200,000	0	227,149	0	900,000
Adv-Radio	0	0	42,657	0	900,000
Coupons	0	0	35,114	0	400,000
Sampling	0	0	37,830	0	200,000
Discounts	0.030	0.000	0.047	0.000	0.050
Trade Prom.	0	0	459,389	0	600,000
SALES PERFORMANCE					
Our $ Sales	2,042,691	0	4,532,217	0	7,296,000
Our Share	0.106	0.000	0.236	0.000	0.380
Share per $1,000,000 Mktg.	0.000	0.000	0.172	0.000	0.083

BUDGET ALLOCATIONS ACROSS SALES DISTRICTS, PRODUCT LINES, AND OTHER INDEPENDENT COMPONENTS

Often a set of independent marketing strategies must be combined into an overall marketing strategy for a business unit. For example, when internal and external information is sufficient, a manager will want to tailor-make the marketing strategy for each product in a product line or each sales area. Competitors making a major push in one or more geographic areas or against one or more of the firm's products may call for selective responses. In addition, these competitive actions may require the use of a specific market model for each area and product. When it does, separate MARMIX analyses should be made of the strategies required for these distinct situations.

Even in the absence of strong competitive targeting, products, sales areas, and the like can be different enough to require a separate MARMIX model and/or strategy for each one. In such cases management must have a way to combine individual results into an efficient overall strategy that makes allowance for the existence of any overall budget constraint. These matters are handled by the CONSOLIDATION program, the subject of this section.

The capacity to take advantage of individual differences depends on the differences being large and actionable enough to be worth the cost of analysis and administration. In addition, the model described below assumes that the separate components can be treated as being independent of each other. This is true for most products, sales areas, and other components. If it is not the case, a more complex model structure is required or a single budget must be developed to cover all of the linked component elements, with adjustments made informally.

An example of a linked or dependent situation is a mobile sales force that is supported by national advertising and sells a full line of prod-

ucts. If one product or area is emphasized during a given time period, doing so will automatically reduce the attention that otherwise could be given to the other products and areas. In these kinds of situations, a set of alternative strategies can be formulated and separately analyzed, but the allocation problem cannot be solved by the methods described below.

Recent moves by Procter and Gamble and other consumer goods companies (*Business Week*, 1988) have enhanced the value of a budget consolidation program. These firms have placed a product-line or category manager between brand managers and marketing or general management. The purpose of this move is to coordinate the brand strategy/budgets for all brands in a product line. Since interbrand differences are usually large, this coordination activity requires careful resource allocations to each brand. For this purpose, the product-line manager needs a formal procedure that accounts for the responsiveness of each brand to the full range of possible allocations. The same can be said for other schemes that impose a decision hierarchy like having division marketing managers who guide the work of district marketing managers.

In any case, decentralized analyses should be completed and communicated up the hierarchy before top-down allocations are made. For category or product-line managers, the brand managers' individual response functions are consolidated and a response function is estimated for the overall product line. The latter budget assumes that each brand's budget will be efficiently allocated across the mix elements. In turn, an overall response function is estimated for all potential allocations to each of the product lines. The senior marketing manager uses the latter response function to choose the overall spending level and to assign budgets to the individual product lines. Finally, the category or product-line manager allocates the budget to the individual brands within each product line and each brand manager allocates the brand budget to the mix elements.

Output as Input

The final output of each MARMIX analysis shows the contribution to profit expected from a series of marketing budgets. When adjusted, the MARMIX *output* functions become the *input* functions to the CONSOLIDATION program. MARMIX contribution to profit output for a brand or area does not necessarily increase as spending increases, and a manager may want a spending range that is smaller than the one defined by the range of the total underlying mix elements. Organizational needs may define spending limits, or a range may be chosen to eliminate higher spending levels that promise lower returns. For these and other reasons, a manager is given an opportunity to redefine every MARMIX *output* response function before it is used as an *input* response function in a CONSOLIDATION analysis.

An illustrative redefinition of a component (zone one in the East group of components) appears in the CONSOLIDATION program output shown in Figure 15-2. The top panel of this figure shows the spending levels and associated profit levels read from MARMIX-created computer files. The absolute minimum and maximum lines are from the before-improvement output and the remaining numbered lines are from the after-improvement output. (The former data are unaffected by the changes in total spending that can be made by the improvement routine.) The two lines that follow these data echo the user's decision concerning the spending range that will be used in the analysis, $0 to $1.3 million for the current illustration.

The left-hand column of the bottom panel in Figure 15-2 contains the chosen minimum and maximum spending levels. Here, the minimum is at zero spending and the maximum is at the absolute maximum. The latter spending level is expected to produce the highest contribution to profit displayed in the right-hand column of the top panel. The remaining five spending levels are developed by the computer to be evenly distributed between the two extremes. The contribution to profit figures in the right-hand column

are also computer generated. They are contribution forecasts for the spending levels that appear in the left-hand column. If the user wants to adjust these forecasts, the program provides an opportunity to do so.

The final entries in the bottom panel define a seven-level response function for the zone one component. This function is used in the CONSOLIDATION analysis in a manner that is similar to the way that MARMIX uses a response function for a marketing mix element. If a MARMIX analysis has *not* been completed for the component problem, the bottom panel can be completed using unaided judgment, but this procedure is not recommended. In any case, one response function of each component in the overall set for which a consolidated budget is being developed is needed. Finally, if components are divided into groups for which intermediate budget allocations must be computed, group response functions are also developed during the course of the analysis.

Grouping Components

Component budgets for products or sales areas may be assigned to one of several groups. In some instances, these groups form natural product or geographic divisions. In other cases, the groups may be formed for analytical convenience. The largest total number of components is forty and the largest number of groups is eight. When a group is analyzed, the output is a group result or output function similar to the one produced by a standard MARMIX analysis, with each component taking on the role of a mix element. *The budget allocation to any component is assumed to be efficiently allocated to the underlying mix elements.* The CONSOLIDATION program prints the results, which are treated as input to the final stage. They are subject to the same kind of adjustments made above to the input response functions based on MARMIX output for a component.

A final analysis is produced by substituting adjusted group response functions for the com-

FIGURE 15-2   Echoed input for a CONSOLIDATION analysis—zone one in the East division.

```
Previously recorded data will be used in this analysis

PROBLEM STRUCTURE

      Group No.:1   Group Name:  EAST
               No. of Components in the Group: 3

      Group No.:2   Group Name:  WEST
               No. of Components in the Group: 3


Analysis will be in terms of TOTAL CONTRIBUTION TO PROFIT

DATA RECEIVED

REDEFINED INPUT DATA

Group,  1  :  East          Component,  1  :  ZONE ONE

Level No.    Our Spending      Contribution Profit
Abs. Min.              0.          4,222,937.
    1            463,144.         27,204,710.
    2            519,103.         29,504,360.
    3            581,439.         31,010,250.
    4            661,086.         34,661,488.
    5            707,800.         36,566,060.
    6            904,706.         37,635,620.
    7          1,017,094.         40,809,920.
    8          1,156,855.         42,281,120.
    9          1,213,314.         42,933,632.
   10          1,300,000.         43,265,420.
Abs. Max.      1,300,000.         43,265,420.

Level No. of Desired Minimum 0

Level No. of Desired Maximum 10

Level No.    Our Spending    Contribution Profit
    1                0.           4,222,937.
    2          216,667.          14,775,068.
    3          433,333.          25,327,198.
    4          650,000.          34,153,280.
    5          866,667.          37,429,000.
    6        1,083,333.          41,507,192.
    7        1,300,000.          43,265,420.
```

Before improvement?

ponent-adjusted response functions and rerunning the CONSOLIDATION program. The output forecasts the effect of using various spending levels for the overall budget and indicates what share of each of these budgets should be assigned to each group of components. In turn, the group budgets are efficiently allocated to the components of each group. Finally, the amounts assigned to each component are efficiently allocated to the mix elements by reference to the original MARMIX output. This sequential process assures management that all of the budget-setting actions will promise excellent overall profit.

Input Data and Analysis at the Group Level

The iterative process starts with a MARMIX analysis of the strategy/budget for each component. The number of component analyses should be no larger than the number of marketing strategies that can differ significantly and have an important effect on the firm or business unit's overall performance. Similar components should be pooled, and unimportant components can be handled by less formal methods.

First, the components, such as brands or sales areas, are identified and analyzed. The MARMIX program creates computer files that define the response function output for each problem. These files are subsequently read by the CONSOLIDATION program. Second, if the number of component problems is greater than eight or if the components can be subdivided into groups that have important common features, groups should be formed. Next, data like those shown in Figure 15-2 should be prepared for each component in each group by using the CONSOLIDATION program and entering the required data through the computer keyboard. Once the data have been prepared for all groups, the group-by-group analyses are undertaken. When this work is completed, the same process is followed with the group output replacing the component output as input to the final analysis.

Group Response Functions and the Final Analysis

The output produced for each group is similar to the output obtained from a standard MARMIX analysis. These output files are stored by the computer just as the standard MARMIX outputs are stored. Once this work is complete, a final overall analysis is performed that is like the one used for each group. The output is normally a series of expenditure levels and the contribution profit for one or a series of possible overall budgets. If a fixed budget is specified by the user, only the minimum, fixed, and maximum budget levels are reported. Otherwise, ten budget levels are reported. In any case, these data are developed under the assumption that a budget assigned to a group will be efficiently allocated to the underlying component budgets and in turn the component budgets will be efficiently allocated to the underlying marketing mix elements.

The allocations that are finally made to components (possibly through one or more groups) may not be the same amounts as the expenditure levels that were originally used by MARMIX. If they are not, the allocations at each level can be more fully defined by performing a MARMIX fixed-budget analysis for each final component budget. The following illustration should clarify these steps.

The Overall Marketing Mix

Once the budget-determination process has been played out, a manager may want to examine the characteristics of the overall budget. If the mix elements used in the component strategy/budgets are defined in the same way, the spending levels for a mix element can be summmed across the components and each mix element's share of the overall budget can be computed. When mix element definitions are not compatible or the component budgets do not have a common set of objectives and market environments, great care should be taken in using these data to describe the overall strategy.

Overall Sales, Total Marketing Spending, and Profit Projections

Overall sales, spending, and profits are easily computed as the sums of the underlying

MARMIX results produced by the final budgets. Since the homogeneity issue does not arise here, the meaning of the sums is clear. The sums can be formed in a hierarchical fashion starting with the components within a group to get group totals and then across groups to obtain the overall total. This process is shown graphically in Figure 15-3.

An Illustrative Problem

Figure 15-2 shows the type of printed output that is produced by the CONSOLIDATION program from the saved MARMIX computer files and the associated user input. In the illustration that will be described, six sets of MARMIX output are used. The component budget analyses are conducted for the three components assigned to each of two groups. It is helpful to think of each component as a sales zone with its own sales force, regional competitors, and clients.

These geographic units face sufficiently different circumstances to require separate strategies and budgets.

The zone one sales area is located in the East geographic division. It has a major concentration of high-volume users of the company's product. A new plant had recently come on line to serve this zone, which produced a very high grade form of the product. Since this grade commanded a premium price, the margins are generous, but so are fixed costs. Competition is expected to narrow margins in the foreseeable future. The remaining five zones cover large geographic areas with widely scattered, smaller-volume consumers. Most of these customers are not very quality sensitive.

Each division oversees the marketing activities of its assigned zones. This problem structure is noted at the top of Figure 15-2. Printed input summaries in the format shown in this figure for zone one are also provided (but not shown here) for zones two and three of the EAST divi-

FIGURE 15-3   A hierarchical representation of a CONSOLIDATION analysis.

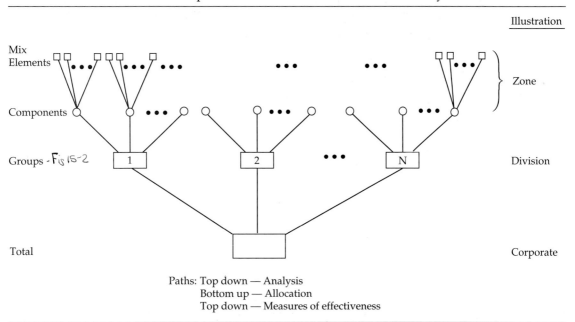

Paths: Top down — Analysis
Bottom up — Allocation
Top down — Measures of effectiveness

sion and zones A, B, and C of the WEST division. Once these data have been adjusted and echoed to the printer, the CONSOLIDATION program searches for the best budget allocations for each division (group). Basic sampling results for the EAST division are shown in Figure 15-4.

The EAST division is by far the most profitable, principally due to the large sales and profit potential of its New England sales area, zone one. The input data for both the EAST and WEST divisions used in the final overall analyses are displayed in Figure 15-5. The data used for both illustrative divisions were primarily

FIGURE 15-4   Basic sampling CONSOLIDATION analysis output—East division.

```
The number of samples per budget level for the EAST Group is 1,000


                                                              Page 1
EAST Group:     BASIC SAMPLING Results
                      1           2           3          4          5
CONTRIBUTION TO PROFIT

                5,364,617   27,643,236   38,515,652   44,185,892   45,584,808

TOTAL MARKETING SPENDING

                  385,704      877,652    1,369,600    1,861,547    2,353,496

COMPONENT SPENDING ALLOCATIONS

ZONE 1
                        0      461,211      854,333    1,207,113    1,274,313
ZONE 2
                  114,704      141,798      183,914      293,136      625,022
ZONE 3
                  271,000      274,642      331,353      361,299      454,161


                      6           7           8          9          10
CONTRIBUTION TO PROFIT

               45,918,404   46,151,192   46,441,212   46,541,216   46,614,708

TOTAL MARKETING SPENDING

                2,845,444    3,337,392    3,829,340    4,321,288    4,813,236

COMPONENT SPENDING ALLOCATIONS

ZONE 1
                1,293,878    1,291,483    1,299,554    1,298,728    1,300,00
ZONE 2
                  522,845      592,504      698,274      724,491      739,053
ZONE 3
                1,028,721    1,453,405    1,831,512    2,298,069    2,774,183
```

FIGURE 15-5 Echoed input for a CONSOLIDATION analysis—East and West divisions for an overall analysis.

Group, 9 : OVERALL   Component, 1 : EAST

Level No.	Our Spending	Contribution to Profit
Ads. Min.	385,704.	5,364,617.
1	385,704.	5,364,617.
2	877,652.	27,643,240.
3	1,369,600.	38,515,648.
4	1,861,547.	44,185,888.
5	2,353,496.	45,584,808.
6	2,845,444.	45,918,400.
7	3,337,392.	46,151,192.
8	3,829,340.	46,441,208.
9	4,321,288.	46,541,220.
10	4,813,236.	46,614,712.
Abs. Max.	4,813,236.	46,614,712.

Level No. of Desired Minimum 1

Level No. of Desired Maximum 10

Level No.	Our Spending	Contribution to Profit
1	385,704.	5,364,617.
2	1,123,626.	33,079,438.
3	1,861,548.	44,185,888.
4	2,599,470.	45,751,604.
5	3,337,392.	46,151,192.
6	4,075,314.	46,491,212.
7	4,813,236.	46,614,712.

Group, 9 : OVERALL   Component, 2 : WEST

Level No.	Our Spending	Contribution to Profit
Abs. Min.	246,625.	3,410,815.
1	246,625.	3,410,815.
2	1,004,657.	6,270,897.
3	1,762,690.	9,240,470.
4	2,520,723.	11,405,410.
5	3,278,755.	12,463,510.
6	4,036,786.	13,107,750.
7	4,794,819.	13,097,850.
8	5,552,852.	12,706,420.
9	6,310,884.	12,091,390.
10	7,068,916.	10,745,760.
Abs. Max.	7,068,916.	10,745,760.

Level No. of Desired Minimum 1

Level No. of Desired Maximum 10

Level No.	Our Spending	Contribution to Profit
1	246,625.	3,410,815.
2	1,383,674.	7,755,685.
3	2,520,722.	11,405,408.
4	3,657,771.	12,785,630.
5	4,794,819.	13,097,850.
6	5,931,868.	12,398,905.
7	7,068,916.	10,745,760.

drawn from real analyses. It is hard to say whether the generally flat divisional (group) response functions that were reported are typical results.

Finally, the overall allocation of a fixed $5 million budget to the two divisions is shown in Figure 15-6a and the overall unrestricted allocation is shown in Figure 15-6b. A convenient summary of the overall-to-groups and group-to-components allocation process is displayed in Figure 15-7. The initial component input data were the output response functions from six MARMIX analyses *after* each one had been redefined to span a seven-point spending continuum. The first output of the CONSOLIDATION program is a response function for each group (division in the present illustration). In turn, these data are redefined, as were the components' data, to serve as input to group analysis. The output of the group analysis is another response function and a set of budget allocations (or more limited output if a fixed-budget limit is specified).

At this point a budget is chosen for the overall marketing activities and it is allocated to the West and East divisions (groups). The division

budgets are allocated to the individual zones (components). At the component level, the assigned (allocated) budget is further allocated to the mix elements employed by each zone for the original MARMIX analyses. Using the output of each zone's MARMIX analysis, an estimate is made of the zones' contribution to profit and dollar sales. These data have been entered in Figure 15-7.

Although the above process is not easily described, in most cases it is easily executed. If the number of components is large, a large number of MARMIX runs will be needed, but normally they will have been completed in the absence of a hierarchical budgeting procedure. Given a large number of components and groups, the computations required to make allocations to mix elements and the forecasts of profits and sales at the component level may be tedious enough to justify the construction of a spreadsheet model to perform this work. These complications are due not to the use of the CONSOLIDATION program but to the complex budgetary task associated with a hierarchy that has many separate budgets at the lowest level.

FIGURE 15-6a   Final output of overall CONSOLIDATION analysis—$5 million fixed budget.

	1	2	3	4	5
OVERALL Group: BASIC SAMPLING Results			Page 3		
CONTRIBUTION TO PROFIT					
	8,775,432	0	56,899,716	0	57,360,472
TOTAL MARKETING SPENDING					
	632,329	0	5,000,000	0	11,882,152
COMPONENT SPENDING ALLOCATIONS					
EAST					
	385,704	0	2,481,366	0	4,813,236
WEST					
	246,625	0	2,518,634	0	7,068,916

FIGURE 15-6b Final output of overall CONSOLIDATION analysis—no fixed budget.

The number of samples per budget level for the OVERALL Group is 1,000

Page 3

OVERALL Group: BASIC SAMPLING Results

	1	2	3	4	5
CONTRIBUTION TO PROFIT					
	8,775,432	44,141,572	51,508,908	55,588,348	57,777,972
TOTAL MARKETING SPENDING					
	632,329	1,882,309	3,132,290	4,382,270	5,632,250
COMPONENT SPENDING ALLOCATIONS					
EAST					
	385,704	1,630,727	1,862,212	1,861,335	2,598,796
WEST					
	246,625	251,582	1,270,078	2,520,935	3,033,454

	6	7	8	9	10
CONTRIBUTION TO PROFIT					
	58,875,076	59,386,416	59,674,624	59,080,908	57,360,472
TOTAL MARKETING SPENDING					
	6,882,231	8,132,211	9,382,191	10,632,172	11,882,152
COMPONENT SPENDING ALLOCATIONS					
EAST					
	3,222,242	4,075,492	4,588,684	4,810,514	4,813,236
WEST					
	3,659,989	4,056,719	4,793,508	5,821,658	7,068,916

THE ASSUMPTION SET, INCLUDING INTERMEDIATE VARIABLES

The MARMIX data forms (see Figures 14-25a and 14-25b) have space in which one can record two types of assumptions—central and supple-

mental. The central assumptions concern price elasticity and competitive spending. The elasticity assumptions are recorded as part of the response to Question 9. The baseline estimate is an essential part of the model inputs, but the other price and share estimates are used only to compute the price and share sensitivity analysis

FIGURE 15-7   Summary budget tree for CONSOLIDATION analysis.

	Spending Allocations[1]	Contribution Profit[2]	Dollar Sales[3]
Zone A	$ 370,000	$ 500,000	$ 3,200,000
West $2,520,000 — Zone B	2,127,000	9,800,000	17,500,000
Zone C	23,000	450,000	2,200,000
Total	$2,520,000	$10,800,000	$22,900,000
Overall Limit $5,000,000 (Input) — Zone 1	$1,265,000	$43,000,000	$67,000,000
East $2,480,000 — Zone 2	596,000	1,800,000	4,750,000
Zone 3	619,000	700,000	2,400,000
Total	$2,480,000	$45,500,000	$74,150,000
Total	$5,000,000	$56,300,000	$97,050,000

[1] CONSOLIDATION output; [2] Estimated from CONSOLIDATION output;
[3] Estimated from MARMIX output

that appears in Figure 14-23. Similarly, competitive spending data entered in response to Questions 11B, 12B, and 13B serve solely as assumptions underlying the spending and response function estimates used by the model. Stated another way, competitive action at three levels of company spending specifies an essential aspect of the market to which the other input estimates relate. If these market conditions are not clearly stated, a manager might have trouble making consistent estimates, remembering the basis on which his or her judgments were made, or communicating the reasonableness of the MARMIX input to people who might make other assumptions about competitive responses.

The supplemental assumptions concern the intermediate variables that were discussed in Chapters 10, 11, and 12. To the extent that it is possible to do so, these variables should be estimated for the minimum, baseline, and maximum spending levels. The optional input on the second page of the test problem's MARMIX data form appears on p. 501, along with the echoed data and related computed results.

The baseline percentage pull effect is simply an assessment of the way current spending is being targeted—the relative emphasis being given to favorably influencing final buyers as compared with favorably influencing distribution. If the budget is substantially reduced or substantially increased, the relative emphasis on pull versus push may change. Management's assumptions in this regard should be recorded for the minimum and the maximum spending levels.

Next, the estimated levels of awareness and distribution are entered for the three spending

INTERMEDIATE VARIABLE INPUT TO THE TEST PROBLEM

OUR SPENDING			
Min.	Baseline	Max.	Questions
.75	.7	.65	Q24A Budget's percentage pull effect
.7	.8	.9	Q24B Expected percentage aware
.5	.6	.8	Q24C Expected percentage distribution
.005	.01	.015	Q24D Expected percentage trial purchase
.15	.2	.25	Q24E Purchase repeat rate
.15	.25	.4	Q24F Purchase switchback rate

INTERMEDIATE VARIABLE OUTPUT FROM THE TEST PROBLEM

Marketing Elements	INTERMEDIATE MARKETING EFFECTS AT GIVEN SPENDING LEVELS		
	Minimum	Baseline	Maximum
Percentage pull	.750	.700	.650
Percentage aware	.700	.800	.900
Percentage distribution	.500	.600	.800
Share of consideration set	.350	.480	.720
Percentage trial purchase	.005	.010	.015
Purchase repeat rate	.150	.200	.250
Purchase switchback rate	.150	.250	.400
Long-run retention rate	.150	.238	.348

levels. In this case, the figures should increase as the level of spending increases. With these data in hand, the MARMIX program computes the associated share of the target market that will have the product in its consideration set at the time a purchase is made from the product class. Since awareness and distribution are easily monitored, a forecast of these intermediate variables should be made for the budget that is finally adopted.

The next recorded intermediate variable is the percentage trial, the share of sales that is expected from first-time buyers of the product. For a mature product, these figures will be small but they will increase as a function of spending. In addition, they depend on strategic decisions concerning such matters as the choice of advertising media and the content of sales programs. Whatever the particular forces are that drive trial share, this figure clearly indicates how much sales will depend on attracting new customers. The share used here is the expected number of triers divided by the expected total unit sales. This figure *cannot* be compared with the trial rate used in Chapters 10, 11, and 12, which is the percentage of product-class buyers who are expected to make a trial purchase.

The estimates of the repeat rate and the switchback rate permit the program to compute the important long-run retention rate. The latter rate is an important indicator of how well the product is able to attract purchases from those who have tried the product. In addition to making estimates at the three input spending levels, these data should be predicted and monitored for the budget that is finally adopted.

POINTS OF CONTROL—A WIDER PERSPECTIVE

Changing the Shape and Range of the Response Functions

A user of MARMIX should recognize that a great deal of freedom can be exercised in defining the upper and lower spending limits for any mix element. In the absence of some external constraint, the minimum level will be zero. External constraints can include such matters as contractual requirements or policies concerning the degree to which various mix elements must be employed. In the absence of external considerations, the maximum spending level is set at the lowest level beyond which no noticeable positive effects will be observed. Alternatively, the minimum and maximum allowable levels for a mix element can be set purely at the pleasure of the user. For example, a manager may feel that he or she cannot estimate the effect of spending less than x or more than y. In this case, x is the minimum and y is the maximum even though noticeable effects on share can be observed when spending less than x and more than y. Although MARMIX permits the use of limits like x and y, the effect that these limits

have on the results produced by MARMIX response functions should be understood.

In Figure 15-8, two response functions are shown, one concave downward and one S-shaped. A number of possible xs and ys appear along the spending axis. When a straight line connects the adjacent upper and lower limits (x_i, y_i), closely spaced limits tend to produce a linear slope (the rate at which dollars produce results) that is similar to one appropriate for a smooth curve. If the range of spending increases, say to (x_i, y_{i+1}), a number of piecewise linear segments may be needed to approximate a smooth response function. Whatever limits a user employs, MARMIX breaks up the range into six equal intervals. Narrowing or shifting the spending range does not change the effect of a given level of spending on market share; it simply constrains spending. The closer the limits become, however, the better chance there will be that optimal spending will be outside the range.

A manager can influence the model's behavior in other ways by changing the response function input for a mix element. For example, suppose the original chosen value of x_1 is 0 and y_6 is $500,000 for the direct-mail mix element. By negotiating a favorable contract for printing and artwork, the same maximum effect may be obtained at $y_6 = \$400,000$. As a result, the final budget may contain a larger physical quantity of this more efficient marketing activity or the same quantity at a lower cost.

Another possible efficiency enhancement might be selecting a better advertising agency. Improved copy and artwork might increase the sales that a given mailing produces. The effect is to favorably rescale the response function's vertical effect axis. *Every aspect of a marketing program should be reviewed to reduce the cost of a program and to increase the effectiveness of each dollar spent.*

If one assumes that the shape of the above-mentioned response function for direct mail is linear, management may find a way to sequence a mailing list so that for any expenditure the most promising potential customers will receive

FIGURE 15-8   Two illustrative response functions—basic input format.

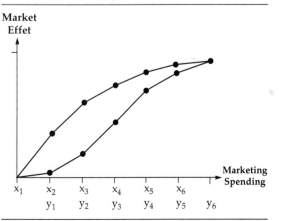

mailings. This action changes the shape of the response function from linear to concave downward. If there is a great deal of diversity in the potential of the names on the list, the curve may rise sharply before it flattens at higher spending levels.

Four kinds of response function manipulations have been noted: spending range selection, cost reductions, effectiveness enhancements, and direct shape changes. The desirable effect of the last three actions is clear. If the spending range is too narrow, the best budget allocation may be excluded. Spending allocations near the minimum or maximum may indicate that this is the case. For this reason, it is desirable to have spending limits near the response function's "physical" limits.

Influencing the Model's Structure

The degree to which mix elements have independent or dependent effects on sales is determined largely by the nature of the product, market, and mix elements. Nevertheless, *management has a degree of control.* Continuing with the direct mail example used above, this activity can be designed to produce mail order sales without the assistance of other parts of the marketing mix. In this case, it is an independent element. On the other hand, direct mail may be used to produce inquiries that are followed up by a field sales force or by telemarketing. In this case, sales are produced by the joint effect of direct mail and personal selling.

Usually management will find little reason to manipulate the model structure directly, but there is ample reason to consider the best ways to direct the spending on each mix element. Given the overall objectives of a marketing strategy, it can make sense to have some independent elements and others that are strongly dependent. This is the place where the art of marketing management has a strong role to play. *The objective is to find appropriate points at which the results will exceed the simple sum of the parts but not allow an element's effectiveness to be limited by dependence on an ineffective element.* If it is more effective to let salespeople do their own prospecting, direct mail can be used for other, more productive independent purposes.

Influencing Contribution to Profit and Performing Sensitivity Analyses

Product characteristics as an influence on demand and cost In formulating a strategy /budget, it was assumed that the offer is fixed. The product's design and price were not manipulated as decision variables in Chapters 10 through 14 or in the early parts of this chapter. It was argued that a manager should separately analyze alternative offers, completing a strategy /budget analysis for each of the competing offers. The final choice is between complete alternatives, alternatives that include both the offer and its supporting marketing program.

In the process of following this format for analysis and decision-making, it is important to recognize how the essential properties of different offers influence the final marketing program that is adopted. Two of the simplest properties of an offer are its unit price and its variable cost per unit. In general, a lower price expands unit demand and reduces the unit contribution profit, whereas a higher price produces the opposite effect. The effect of the product's price on its total contribution to profit is determined by three elements: the unit contribution (unit price minus variable cost), the product's baseline market share (which is related to the product's appeal as estimated by a conjoint or similar analysis), and the primary demand for the product class. Also, it indirectly involves *all* of the mix elements.

If a unit of sales produces more contribution, it pays to spend more to sustain or increase demand and/or market share. If a sales unit yields less contribution, potential demand and/or market share must increase or spending must be cut to maintain or increase total contribution to profit. Similar statements can be made about changes in product features. Offering a more appealing, more costly product must increase demand or market share or reduce marketing expenses enough to compensate for the loss in unit contribution because of the increased product cost. *In short, the appeal of a product and its unit contribution are powerful forces that help shape the size and to a lesser degree the distribution of a marketing budget.*

To examine how profits respond to changes in a product's characteristics, it is frequently worth performing a sensitivity analysis before approving product changes or costly efforts to redesign a product. It may also be worthwhile to determine how much the bottom line will be affected by various changes in the product's appeal and cost structure as a way to motivate manufacturing and product development groups to contribute to more successful marketing strategies.

Efficiency in marketing and manufacturing
A number of issues concerning marketing efficiency have been discussed in this section. A remaining issue that has received little emphasis in marketing but a great deal of attention in the manufacturing sector is the importance of being the high-quality, low-cost producer. These conditions provide the capacity to price competitively while preserving the margins needed to support a sound marketing strategy and provide an adequate profit. If a product is poorly made or overpriced, there is little that a marketing strategy can do to salvage the situation. For an informative discussion, see Magaziner and Patinkin (1989).

Even less attention has been given to the development of cost-effective, well-managed marketing programs. For many products, marketing expenses are an important share of the product's price to the final buyer, and it usually makes an important contribution to the value received by the user. Since an efficient marketing program can do a great deal to create a suc-

cessful product, this book has devoted much attention to planning an efficient marketing strategy and budget. Once a good plan has been developed, attention must focus on implementation. *Although we have had very little to say about the subject, good execution is essential to success.* Marketing managers must stay on top of their plans, monitor progress, make needed corrections, and motivate all concerned to turn the planned results into the desired bottom-line outcomes.

Shifting expenses between fixed and variable categories   Given the key role played by expenses, the advantages and limitations of various kinds of expenses deserve attention, as does the opportunity to shift some expenses between fixed and variable categories. Fixed expenses are known in advance and decrease as a percentage of sales as sales increase. This type of expense increases the rewards of success and the costs of failure. Variable expenses increase in total as sales increase but remain constant per unit of sales. Relatively high fixed expenses and volatile sales lead to large fluctuations in profits. High variable costs relative to fixed costs reduce the effects of sales fluctuations. In addition, fixed costs often involve extended commitments such as the purchase of assets or long-term contractual arrangements.

For any or all of the above reasons, a marketing manager may want to influence the fixed or variable composition of the spending on marketing. Opportunities to do so are not uncommon. For example, an in-house marketing research function (a largely fixed expense) may be discontinued in favor of buying research services from outside providers (usually a variable expense). *With respect to a MARMIX analysis, recall that only total variable and controllable marketing expenses are considered.* Fixed marketing expenses that are not otherwise assigned to overhead must be accounted for separately.

A marketing manager may have limited interest in the fixed versus variable mix of manufacturing costs unless relatively high fixed-costs increase unit margins during periods of higher sales and decrease unit margins in periods of lower sales. Furthermore, a high fixed-cost structure may lead upper management to emphasize short-term sales increases at the expense of more profitable longer-run objectives. For these reasons, the structure of manufacturing costs can lead to unstable marketing budgets and profits.

A related topic concerns cost reductions that may flow from accumulated experience or learning. For most mature products this phenomenon has little effect on annual marketing budgets and is not considered. The subject is covered in Chapter 6 in connection with the EXPER program.

Analysis of Significantly Changed Strategies

Output in Figure 15-9 illustrates the use of MARMIX to forecast the result of a price and spending increase for the test problem that was initially analyzed in Chapter 14. This feature of the program allows one to evaluate any number of spending patterns and unit prices. Three primary purposes are served. The first is to forecast the results from the budget that is adopted. Rounding off expenditures and making allowances for such matters as media discount schedules usually produce a final budget that is somewhat at odds with the best output recorded in the final MARMIX summary. In the above illustration, a joint change in the expenditure pattern and the unit price was explored. If the price change does not require modifying the model's parameters, the change may be desirable, slightly increasing total contribution to profit, but at a sacrifice of market share.

The last remark leads to a second use of the single budget analysis option: the exploration of substantially different strategies from the one used in the basic analysis. The existing model is usually similar to one that could be developed for the new strategy. When this is the case, the

old model can be used to screen new alternatives. The previous section on Influencing Contribution to Profit discusses this kind of analysis for a revised offer. Out of this screening process the user hopes to find one or more new strategies/budgets that are promising enough to justify additional analysis. The latter analyses normally require changes in the MARMIX inputs beyond those used in the single budget option. In this manner a new set of outputs can be generated for each new competing strategy.

A third important use of the single budget option is to produce forecasts for alternative budgets proposed by people who are active in the strategy/budget process. By completing a single budget analysis for each competing budget, a quick forecast can be made of the effect of adopting each one. This process is effective only to the extent that there is substantial agreement about the validity of the original model inputs. If this kind of agreement has not been achieved, a complete MARMIX analysis will be needed for each dissenting individual.

The single budget analysis segment of the program may surprise an analyst by producing market shares above or below those produced by a prior budget with the same total spending level. These results are due to two types of effects: the effects of a price change (if any) on the test budget's market share and the differences in efficiency of the two budgets' distributions to their mix elements. Referring to Figure 15-9, the single budget spending level is close to the level 6 budget shown in Figure 14-20. The level 6 budget produced a market share of about .33, while the new single budget yields a share of only .285. Note that the single budget has sharply increased spending on sampling over the level 6 budget, but includes a price increase that is expected to depress share (.955 of the level at the lower price used for the level 6 analysis). In spite of the loss of share the net effect of the changes is positive, since the modified budget is expected to produce additional contribution to profit.

FIGURE 15-9   Forecast of results produced by a trial price, budget, and budget allocation.

```
                                               Page 20

NEW BUDGET AND/OR UNIT PRICE: TEST   1

Mix spending levels for new budget   1
                   Expenditures
Adv-TV
                    350000
Adv-Radio
                    90000
Coupons
                    220000
Sampling
                    300000
Discounts
                    .045
Trad Prom.
                    520000
Unit Price          2.65

Given the new price, the new market share as a fraction of the old market share
is .955

RESULTS OF TEST 1

    Total Contribution to Profit
                        $  1,359,201.
    Market Share
                             .285.
    Total Spending
                        $  1,726,064.
Current Contribution to Profit
                             $  1,258,543.
Future Contribution to Profit
                             $    100,658.
Share/(000,000 Spend.)                        .108
```

THE PLACE OF INFORMATION SYSTEMS AND MODELS IN MARKETING PLANNING AND CONTROL

Marketing Information

The growth of detailed, up-to-date marketing data has been documented by McCann (1986). Some areas like consumer package goods have been most dramatically affected, but scanner inputs, buyer identification with individual items purchased, and computerized records and file matching can be found in most large marketing data bases. The growing sophistication of independent marketing information and research providers has added a large body of syndicated and custom research to the data that is being generated in-house by aggressive marketing organizations.

At the 1991 TIMS Marketing Science Conference, McCann outlined some ways in which large disaggregate data bases can be efficiently turned into guidance for marketing actions. One computer program described by McCann suggests appropriate content for sales calls made on a chain store buyer. The salesperson may ask for more shelf space, a wider representation of the firm's product line, more aggressive pricing for one or more brands, or some other appropriate action that can be supported by the facts. The firm's data base should contain information about performance elements of the buyer's stores, as well as the targets or norms that the seller's firm uses to judge performance. The program quickly accesses these facts and summarizes its analysis in verbal and/or graphic form for the salesperson. Emphasis is given to actions that will enhance the competitive position of the salesperson's firm and that will convince the buyer that a change in behavior is in his or her best interest.

A second level of decision support of the kind described above uses the output of analyses completed for individual current and/or prospective customers. The extent to which each customer is likely to be responsive to an action is recorded. When these results are summed across customers, marketing management has a strong indication of the need for and effects of an action. For example, if 70 percent of all stores have failed to give a brand as much shelf space as its sales volume warrants, marketwide actions designed to improve the brand's shelf space may be called for. On the other hand, if only 15 percent of all stores have underallocated space, either selective action or no action is indicated. Additionally, the individual level analyses can be examined in a hierarchical manner. First, opportunities are examined for a narrow class of retailers or small geographic areas. Subsequently, the outputs are analyzed for larger groups or markets. When performed efficiently, the basic questions are examined only once at the disaggregate level and the results are passed on to successively higher levels of aggregate analysis.

It is particularly interesting to note that the kind of computer program(s) described above can be built with no more than spreadsheet and word processing software if the programs are integrated with readily available marketing data-base software. Also, it is important to observe that the know-how needed to ask the right questions and perform the right analyses appears just at the most disaggregate level where data and analysis methods are typically simple. At higher levels of aggregation, the procedures are equally simple. The principal problems one encounters arise from the size of the data bases and the cost of data collection.

The problem for marketing management is to effectively convert data into information. A good start can be made by taking seriously Drucker's (1988) remark that "Information is data endowed with relevance and purpose," and McCann's warning about the serious problems associated with the rapid growth of raw and semianalyzed data. If data are not demonstrably relevant, a manager should ignore or eliminate them. If data are relevant, ways must be found to discover their meaning rapidly and put them to work. Increasingly, diagnostic work is being done by computer screening methods. These methods allow a manager to concentrate on the application of the analytical results rather than on the analysis of data.

In the planning activities and models presented in this text, a small set of essential variables has been emphasized. Most marketing information systems provide some of these data. Few if any systems provide all of the essentials. This observation can be checked against the outlines of the market and product fact book and the marketing plan that appear in the next two major sections.

Marketing Models

Marketing models that can help a marketing manager plan more effectively have been discussed at a number of points. These models should *not* be thought of as a substitute for managerial judgment. Instead, they are aids: efficient, consistent structures for problem solving and for completing onerous computations. They take advantage of the large, growing, and widely available power of the computer, but they impose some burdens. To use a model efficiently, marketing managers must understand the model's rationale, develop the requisite inputs, and be familiar enough with its operating characteristics to appreciate the model's strengths and weaknesses. This book was written in the hope of accomplishing these tasks for a limited number of general-purpose models.

A wide range of models have *not* been covered here that may prove to be useful in selected circumstances. Although such models can be very useful, they deal with matters not treated in this book or are principally applicable to a limited class of products or situations. In addition to these applied models, there is a large collection of models that have been developed for scholarly purposes. The findings produced by these models frequently provide helpful managerial insights into the operation of markets, but they are seldom applicable to the kinds of strategy/budget formulation processes that are the principal focus of this discussion.

Improving Management's Marketing Model

In earlier chapters as well as in the foregoing discussion, we have noted that management decision-making has a surprising degree of control over *how* markets respond to various levels of spending on individual mix elements, and on *how* spending on various mix elements relates to spending on other mix elements in producing overall results. In short, *a marketing model cannot be specified until one knows a good deal about the particulars of a manager's strategic plan*. This fact and the fact that the marketing environment is continuously changing

mean that one cannot develop a single model that will be effective over an extended period of time. Therefore, managers should not rely heavily on models with a fixed structure and fixed parameter values. A more dynamic approach such as an annually developed MARMIX model is needed to assist managers to identify an effective strategy/budget for a product. In contrast to many traditional approaches that involve the analysis of a long series of historical data, this process relies more on current information and managerial inputs.

When considering how to improve management's modeling capability, you need to divide the inputs to MARMIX into those that are largely factual and/or internally oriented and those that are estimates of market responses. Inputs to questions Q1–Q8, Q10–Q13, and Q23 fall into the first category. The accuracy of these inputs must be checked carefully, but the model's structure is not strongly affected by errors. The MARMIX model's structure and behavior are much more sensitive to the inputs to questions Q9 and Q15–Q22. Since these inputs are principally the product of managerial judgment, they should be scrutinized carefully.

We subscribe to the philosophy stated by Cooper and Nakanishi (1988, p. 9):

> A model is merely one approximation of the reality of the market and competition . . . the analyst will have to choose consciously among several alternative representations (i.e., models) of the market and competition which fits best the specific conditions he/she faces.

Dependence on managerial judgment, however, requires careful monitoring of how well the operant marketing model is performing and a continuous search for ways to improve the model. A procedure for doing so includes these steps:

1. For each decision period, *independently* generate a set of competing models.

2. Using each independently produced model, forecast the market results of employing the adopted budget.

3. Using independent judges, evaluate each model's performance in light of the market conditions which prevailed.

4. Preserve the results in 3 as indicators of preferred model characteristics.

5. Review the findings in 4 as part of the next period's planning process.

This view of marketing planning models is closely related to the genetic algorithm discussed by Walbridge (1989). It accepts the inevitability of imperfect responses to a dynamic environment, but it uses accumulated experience to weed out poor performing models and to improve the performance of succeeding models. In Walbridge's world, "blind variation, good record keeping and retaining the best solutions" have produced marvelous genetic results, but marketing managers do not have the luxury or 3.5 billion years of field tests. The model adopted by marketing planners and managers must be based on a sound understanding of the market and the likely effects of their actions. MARMIX provides an easy-to-use way to employ the knowledge of the decision-maker and supporting staff.

THE MARKET AND PRODUCT FACT BOOK

The fact book is a body of data needed to develop a marketing plan. In spite of the title given to this background information, it is usually too extensive to reside between the covers of a single volume. Where applicable, these records span at least five years and cover such essential matters as general product and industry information, internal company sales and cost data, and an array of research findings. The research results come from both syndicated external sources and proprietary studies.

AN OUTLINE OF A MARKET AND PRODUCT FACT BOOK

A. The Market

1. *Definitions* Product class and potential customers.

2. *Overall Size* Units and dollars.

3. *Sales and Distribution* Our product(s) and competitive products (if any) by geographic area in both units and dollars.

4. *Consumption* By customer characteristics, season, and geographic area.

5. *Definition of Segments* By characteristics of the offer and the customer.

6. *Consumption and Sales by Segment*

7. *Relevant Social, Economic, and Political Developments*

B. Marketing Operations

1. *The Offer* Our product(s) and competitive products (if any).

   a. Product characteristics

   b. Positionings

   c. Price (and relevant price promotions)

   d. Evaluation of each offer's strategy

   e. Backup analyses such as conjoint and perceptual studies, and comparative preference shares

2. *The Support* Our product(s) and competitive products (if any).

   a. Support spending by expense category and allocations to push and pull and repeat and switchback objectives.

   b. Spending targets: directional and qualitative evaluation of each spending category

c. Overall evaluation of each product's marketing program, including attained levels of A_t, D_t, RR_t, and SBR_t.

d. Backup analyses including prior spreadsheet and/or MARMIX analyses for our product.

C. Economic and Technical Developments

1. Technical Developments

   a. Product

   b. Process or manufacturing

   c. Communications

   d. Distribution

2. Economic Developments

   a. Product sourcing and cost

   b. Marketing costs

   c. Competition and market structure

   d. Profitability

D. Legal and Organizational

1. Legal and Tax

   a. Legislation

   b. Litigation

2. Organization

   a. Our marketing organization and individual responsibilities

   b. Competitors' marketing organizations

E. Our Detailed Marketing Data

1. Weekly/Monthly Sales and Costs
2. Sales Breakdowns

   a. Geographic areas and/or sales territories

   b. Market segments or classes of customers

   c. Product sizes and/or models

3. Weekly/Monthly Unit Prices

4. Weekly/Monthly Personal Selling Support

5. Weekly/Monthly Advertising Media and Copy

6. Weekly/Monthly Promotions

7. Public Relations

8. Distribution Patterns and Rates

9. Awareness Patterns and Rates

10. Comparative Preference Shares

11. Summaries of Relevant Marketing Research Studies

The items in the fact book outline are largely self-explanatory or have already been covered in detail. For a given market or product, a few items might be deleted and some specialized items might be added. In any case, data should be compatible across the years covered by the fact book. This requirement means that definitions, research instruments, sampling plans, and the like should be carefully thought out and changed as little as possible. If the fact book is not properly designed and maintained, each successive manager will be ignorant about vital aspects of the market and the product. Learning time will increase and strategic errors will become more common and more serious.

Many of the items appearing in a historical fact book are the by-product of ongoing internal record-keeping activities, and other items are regularly acquired from external sources. The frequency and the form of these data are not easily changed. Other internally and externally developed data can be acquired at a time and in a form that are controlled by marketing management. These discretionary data should be designed to fill gaps in the less controllable data and be scheduled to identify important changes in the market promptly.

THE MARKETING PLAN

The following outline can help a manager to organize a written marketing plan that uses the computer aids which have been discussed in this book. The plan should be based on the data contained in a fact book, the analysis of several promising offers, and the analysis of one or more marketing support programs for each of these offers. The associated market and financial forecasts can be drawn from spreadsheet/NEWSTRAT or MARMIX work and supporting analyses. A spreadsheet/NEWSTRAT approach is best suited to the evaluation of potential new or modified products, and the MARMIX approach is best suited to finding the best strategy and budget in the next planning period for a mature product.

When the product is established and the planning period is short—say two years or less—written marketing plans can follow a simplified version of the outline, and spreadsheet analyses can be dropped or limited to a single planning period. On the other hand, important new markets or products call for greater care and more risk-reducing information. In this case, contingency plans assume greater importance, techniques like market tests and regional rollouts come into play, and the outline appearing below should be expanded to cover these details.

AN OUTLINE FOR A MARKETING PLAN

A. An Executive Summary

A brief (about two-page) statement of the key conclusions and recommended actions.

B. The Market and Its Development

1. Market Definition
2. Market Size and Growth
3. Behavioral Features

    a. Customer patterns of purchase and use
    b. Distributor purchases and sales practices
    c. Analysis of push and pull effectiveness

4. Our and Competitive Offerings

    a. Design
    b. Positioning
    c. Price
    d. Comparative shares of preference
    e. Expected product development

5. Our and Competitive Shares of Choice Sets

    a. Awareness
    b. Distribution
    c. Share of choice sets

6. Our and Competitive Support Spending

    a. Total spending by brand
    b. Push and pull and repeat and switchback spending by brand
    c. Overall strategic posture of each brand

7. Our Sales and Brand Switching

    a. Brand sales in units and dollars by suitable breakdowns
    b. Brand market shares
    c. Characteristics of heavy, light, and non-buyers of each brand
    d. Repeat and switchback rates by brand

C. Marketing Objectives and Alternatives

1. Objectives
2. Alternatives Explored

    a. Alternative 1
    b. Alternative 2

D. The Marketing Strategy and Budget

1. Choice of a Strategic Alternative

2. The Chosen Strategy and Budget

  a. The offer
    a.1 Features and packaging
    a.2 Positioning
    a.3 Price structure, including functional and geographic differentials

  b. The support and the push and pull and repeat and switchback emphasis

  c. Detailed discussion of each expenditure category
    c.1 Personal selling
      c.1.1 (Major) final buyers
      c.1.2 Intermediaries
    c.2 Advertising
      c.2.1 Campaigns
      c.2.2 Media
      c.2.3 Copy
    c.3 Sales promotion
      c.3.1 Final buyers
      c.3.2 Intermediaries

    . . .

  d. Timing and marketing events

3. Forecasts of Key Measures of Effectiveness

  a. Direct market measures

  b. Indirect market measures

  c. Economic measures

E. Implementation and Monitoring

1. Assigned Managerial Responsibilities

2. Milestones and Monitored Measures

3. Review Procedures

F. Appendices

1. Conjoint, Perceptual, and Related Study Results

2. Spreadsheet/NEWSTRAT Analyses

3. MARMIX Analyses

4. Marketing Research Studies

5. Abstracts of Historical Data

6. Abstracts of Relevant Parts of Prior Plans

G. Separate Supporting Facts and Analyses

As needed, provide one or more supporting volumes containing information that might be required by a critical reader. Here, more detail is presented directly or by citation than can be presented in the fact book or in the main marketing plan.

Note: An outline for a marketing plan that does not make allowance for the computer aids discussed here can be found in a text by Lehmann and Winer. (1988, pp. 14–18).

The above outline recognizes that a marketing plan will be read by several audiences, each with different needs. Senior managers will read the executive summary and perhaps scan selected sections of special interest. The responsible marketing manager will be knowledgeable about the entire plan. The manager's staff will be expected to be well informed about most of the plan and to be expert in selected areas. These same staff members and selected personnel in the firm's marketing research department and the outside advertising agency will be well informed about selected topics and frequently will have contributed to important sections of the plan.

The historical value of the plan should not be overlooked. It is a road map with milestones. Whether the trip is successful or unsuccessful, one should be able to ascertain why by referring to the plan *and* an annotated history of its implementation. The latter point is important. The plan provides a basis for monitoring performance, but it also provides a opportunity to examine changing circumstances that may have influenced the results. Unless the evolving conditions and management's responses are recorded, it is difficult or impossible to associate marketing actions to outcomes. If reviews are held at regular intervals, the documents produced by these marketing audits can represent the kinds of annotation management should append to each plan.

CONCLUDING REMARKS

As the title states, this text is about the analyses and plans marketing managers need to effectively create value. It covered the conceptual and technical essentials that a product or marketing manager must know to effectively carry out his or her duties. Perhaps a greater advantage of the modeling perspective presented here is that it helps a manager to find promising alternative products and marketing strategies and budgets, and to choose the best ones. To perform the latter task, a manager must;

Understand what he or she needs to know,

Know how to find out,

Know how to analyze the data and accumulated knowledge, and

Know what actions should follow from the analyses.

In serving these ends, the text chapters focused on the following issues:

Chapter	Focus
1	Understanding planning and setting overall objectives
2	Understanding product and market evolution
3	Understanding the development process
4	Searching for new products
5	Designing the offer
6	Pricing the offer
7	Illustrations of offer development
8	Appraising buyer acceptance
9	Forecasting market performance
10–12	Delivering marketing value during a product introduction
	The tasks and tools of marketing support
	Trial purchases
	Awareness and distribution
	Pull versus push spending
	The role of decay coefficients
	Repeat and switchback spending
13–15	Delivering marketing value for mature products
	Frames of marketing effectiveness and response functions
	Independent and interactive effects of spending
	Accounting for future effects
	Evaluating the effects of a set of feasible spending levels
	Allocating a global budget to the components
	Making marketing more efficient
	Writing a marketing plan and creating a marketing fact book

The reader must look to the marketing literature for detailed coverage of such matters as managing distribution, advertising, and a sales force. It is the authors' hope that the integrative planning approach presented here will help a manager to choose and direct these elements in a way that produces satisfying results.

Finally, the emphasis that has been placed on the creation and delivery of value has been strictly intentional. Any manager who loses sight of the customers' needs and the social role of marketing is not likely to produce the most favorable results for the company's customers or the company.

In dealing with the above topics, repeated use has been made of three fundamental marketing variables: P, A, and D, or simply PAD. Their principal features appear below.

The first variable, P, is predominantly a function of the offer. The latter two variables, A and D, are predominantly functions of marketing support. The text has explained their meaning, how they are measured, and how they can be used as inputs to a range of decision aids. Less fundamental but nonetheless important are the repeat rate RR, the switchback rate SBR, and the decay rates. They shape the character of marketing support.

FUNDAMENTAL MARKETING VARIABLES

Marketing Variables	Individual: Consumer	Market: Aggregate
Preference: P (and postpurchase satisfaction)	Value or utility of the choice object, Levels (None, . . . Max.)	*Share* of choice, given awareness and availability
Awareness: A	Extent of awareness or knowledge, Levels (None, . . ., Complete)	*Share* of people who attain a level of awareness
	Resellers	
Distribution: D	Extent of distribution *support*, Levels (None, . . . , Complete)	*Share* of reseller support reaching a given level
	Continuous or ordered categories	Binary categorization of individual data to compute a share or rate

REFERENCES

Business Week, July 25, 1988, 72 ff.

Cooper, Lee J., and Masao Nakanishi: *Market Share Analysis,* Boston, Mass.: Kluwer Academic Publishers, 1988.

Drucker, Peter: "The Coming of the New Organization," *Harvard Business Review,* January–February, 1988, 45–53.

Lehmann, Donald R., and Russell S. Winer: *Analysis for Marketing Planning,* Plano, Tex.: Business Publications, Inc., 1988.

McCann, John: *The Marketing Workbench: Using Computers for Better Performance,* Homewood, Ill.: Dow Jones-Irwin, 1986.

Magaziner, Ira, and Mark Patinkin: *The Silent War,* New York: Random House, 1989.

Walbridge, Charles: "Genetic Algorithms: What Computers Can Learn from Darwin," *Technology Review,* January 1989, 47–53.

REVIEW QUESTIONS

Q15-1 Discuss when and why one might want to find the best allocation of a single marketing budget rather than the best allocations for a series of budgets spanning the feasible range. What is the disadvantage of this approach?

Q15-2 Discuss why one might want to complete a MARMIX analysis for each of a series of sub-problems and then determine the proper overall budget and its subsequent allocations to the complete hierarchy of problem levels.

Q15-3 Explain in some detail how a hierarchy of response functions is used to solve a multi-component and/or hierarchical budgeting problem.

Q15-4 Discuss the sampling process used in MARMIX to locate a good budget allocation at any spending level. Why do sample sizes become painfully large when the number of spending (mix) elements grows to ten (or more)? (Someone who is familiar with the literature might consider whether this problem can be solved by using dynamic programming.)

Q15-5 Are the optional intermediate inputs worth entering for a MARMIX analysis? Justify your answer.

Q15-6 Develop a new illustration of how one can change the shape and range of a response function.

Q15-7 Develop a new illustration of how one can change the structure of a MARMIX model.

Q15-8 Develop a new illustration of how one can shift expenses between fixed and variable categories and show how this act can change the size and/or the preferred distribution of a marketing budget.

Q15-9 Assume that you have been appointed brand manager for an established consumer brand. What would you need to know that would not be covered in the market and product fact book and the prior marketing plans if they followed the outlines that appear at the end of Chapter 15?

Q15-10 How would your answer to Q15-9 change if the brand were an industrial product or service?

APPENDIX 15-1 INSTALLING AND OPERATING SELECTED COMPUTER AIDS

NOTICE

The computer programs that are associated with this text are licensed for the sole use of the owner of this text and for use on one computer at a time. They may not be reproduced for any other purpose.

These programs are not warranted to be fit for any purpose. All risks of use and any damage that might result therefrom are the sole responsibility of the user. Use of the programs constitutes acceptance of the above terms.

Installing the CAMP Programs on the Hard Disk

1. While in the C: drive's root directory, enter SET to display the current environment. That environment must include PATH=C:\;C:\DOS. If it does not, see your DOS manual for instructions.

2. Make a backup copy of the CAMP disk. Refer to your DOS manual and the COPY command.

3. Make sure you do not currently have a directory named CAMP on your hard disk.

4. Insert the CAMP program disk in drive A and bring up the A> prompt.

5. Type INSTALL, then press Enter. The INSTALL program does the following:

   a. Creates a directory named CAMP

   b. Copies the programs and related files from the program disk in drive A to your CAMP directory, and

   c. Makes the CAMP directory the current directory

Note: You must be in the CAMP directory to run these programs. Furthermore, the CAMP directory *must* be on the logical C drive.

INTRODUCTORY DESCRIPTIONS

The computer programs and some of the illustrative data are available on a disk designed for use by students. The disk is labeled CAMP (for Computer-Aided Marketing Planning) LEARN PROGRAMS. To start any of the eight programs, the user enters LMIXMENU (after starting DOS 3.0 or higher with the GRAPHICS.COM file in the path noted in 1 above and setting the correct disk drive and/or directory). When the menu appears, the number of the desired program is entered.

There are two versions of each of the main programs, one for printer output and another for output to the screen. The screen-only output versions of the MARMIX programs are valuable as a vehicle for setting up and testing an input data set without generating printed output. The input file saved by the screen-only versions of NEWSTRAT and MARMIX can be read directly into the printer version of the program. In addition, the screen-only MARMIX program includes easy-to-use procedures for correcting inputs as they are entered from the keyboard. The procedures for making corrections are described on-screen at the beginning of the screen-only program. Changes in the keyed-in or read-from-file input data can also be made in both the printer and screen-only programs just before the data set is used in the analysis segment of MARMIX and NEWSTRAT. Files can be erased only in the screen-only versions.

The screen-only versions can also serve as teaching aids. In classrooms that are suitably equipped, an instructor can use these programs to project real-time work on a large screen. In most cases, an applied user

will require a printed record of one or more final analyses.

SYSTEM REQUIREMENTS

To be run effectively, these programs must be installed and run from a hard disk on an IBM AT or 100 percent compatible computer that has a minimum of 640K of memory and uses a 3.0 or higher version of DOS. If graphics are desired, a CGA, EGA, or VGA graphics card is required, and if printed output is desired, an IBM Proprinter or compatible printer is required. To avoid excessive run times on many MARMIX problems, a 12-MHz AT (286) machine with a math coprocessor is the recommended minimum computing power.

The nonexecutable files included on the disk are:

File Name	File Description
CANSPR.WK1	A spreadsheet that includes the basic analysis of the Canadian whiskey illustration. See Figures 11-1a through 11-1c. This file must be loaded into the Lotus 123®, Release 2.01 (or comparable program). In addition, two incomplete spreadsheet files are included: CANO.WK1 and CAN83.WK1.
NEWSTRAT Files	
ZFILES	Files of active data file names
NEWZ1	Test data
MARMIX Files	
PRTSC.COM	Assembler program for screen dumps
BFILES	File of active data file names
DATA1	Test data

Running the CAMP Programs

1. If you are not already in the CAMP directory, make it the current directory (CD\CAMP).

2. Type LMIXMENU, then press Enter.

3. Enter the number from the menu that corresponds to the program you wish to run.

4. When the program is finished, you will be returned to the menu.

Using the Spreadsheet File

1. Bring up your Lotus 123® program.

2. Use the program procedure for loading the CANSPR.WK1 file from the CAMP directory.

Running the Experience Curve Analysis Program

1. From the main menu, enter the number which corresponds to the version you want to run— either screen or printer output.

2. Once the program is loaded, it will ask you whether or not you are using a color monitor. If you are, enter a Y, if not, just press Return.

3. If you are using the printer version, you will then be prompted for a brief identifying name for the analysis.

Note. If you are using the printer output version, every item entered and subsequent output will be echoed to the printer; if not, data entered will be displayed on the screen.

4. Next you will be prompted for the period of analysis. This should consist of no more than six letters and would be something like Month or Year.

5. You will then be prompted for the number of periods to be examined. This number must be fifty-two or less. For example, if you entered Year for the period of analysis, you would enter the number of years in the analysis.

6. Next, for every period of analysis, you will be prompted for the cumulative production to the end of that period. For example, if the period of analysis entered was Year and the number of periods was five, you would enter the cumulative production to the end of the year for years 1 through 5.

7. You will then be asked whether you want to enter parameters directly. Enter a 1 if you want to enter parameters directly; a 0 if not.

If you enter 0, you will be prompted for:

a. The expected unit cost of last unit produced in period 1 and

b. The added units to reduce the cost of the last unit by 10 percent

If you enter 1, you will be prompted for:

a. The slope parameter and

b. The estimated cost of the first unit

The model parameters will now be displayed on the screen and/or the printer.

8. You will now have the option of computing the cost of any unit at any level of cumulative production.

Enter 0 if you don't want to compute one or more such unit costs.

To compute unit costs, enter the cumulative number of units produced that includes this last unit. After printing the estimated unit cost the program will return to this prompt to allow you to compute additional unit costs until you enter 0.

9. The program will now display and/or print for every time period

a. The total cost to date and the average cost to date, as well as

b. The total cost and average unit cost in that period

10. You now have the option of computing the discounted manufacturing margin.

Enter 0 if you don't want to compute the discounted manufacturing margin. The program will then end.

If you enter 1, you will be prompted for

a. The discount rate in decimal form, and

b. For every period, the average unit price in that period

The program will now display and/or print

a. The unit manufacturing margin and the total manufacturing margin for every period, as well as

b. The present worth of the manufacturing margin

The program will now end.

Running the Trial Curve Analysis Program

1. From the main menu, enter the number which corresponds to the version you want to run, either screen or printer output.

2. Once the program is loaded, it will ask you whether or not you are using a color monitor. If you are, enter a Y; if not, just press Return.

3. When using the printer version, you will be prompted for a brief identifying name for the analysis.

Note. If you are using the printer output version, every item entered and subsequent output will be echoed to the printer; if not, echoed input and subsequent output will be displayed only on the screen.

4. Next, you will be prompted for the name of the independent variable (e.g., Cum. Mktg.).

5. You will then be prompted for the units of the independent variable (e.g., Dollars).

6. Next, you will be prompted for the units of the dependent sales variable (e.g., Dozens).

7. You will then be prompted for the maximum number of trial sales.

8. Next, you will be prompted for the number of independent variable observations. This number *must be fifty or less.*

9. You will then be prompted for the type of inputs that you will provide to fit the model.

If you enter 1, you will be ready to input the dependent and independent variables for each observation (step 10).

If you enter 2, you will be prompted for

a. The launch value of the independent variable and

b. The takeover value of the independent variable.

The program will now display the scale parameter and shape parameter calculated from the launch and takeover values entered above. (See Appendix 10-1.)

If you enter 3, you will be prompted for the following model parameters:

a. The scale parameter and

b. The shape parameter.

10. When entering dependent variable observations, for each observation you are prompted for the dependent variable followed by a comma, then the independent variable (e.g. 42800,8800).

Note. When the model is estimated from launch and takeover values (by entering a 2 at step 9 above), or if the model parameters are entered directly (by entering a 3 at step 9 above), enter zeros for all dependent variable (trial sales) values (for which trial sales forecasts are desired).

The program will accept fifty or fewer independent observations. The associated dependent values must be consecutive nonzero observations, if any, followed by as many zero entries as desired.

When the model is fit from trial sales observations (by entering a 1 at step 9), the model is fit using positive pairs. In all cases, the program produces forecasts for the dependent values that have zero entries.

11. After entering the dependent and independent variables for each observation, you will have the opportunity to change an observation. If you want to change an observation, enter the observation number; otherwise, enter 0.

12. The program will now display for each observation:

    a. The dependent variable

    b. The independent variable

    c. The share of trial

If you provided prior trial sales history to fit the model (by entering a 1 at step 9), the program will now display:

    a. The scale parameter

    b. The shape parameter

    c. For each nonzero dependent variable, the estimate of the dependent variable and the residual, and

    d. The average relative absolute error

13. The program will now display:

    forecast values for the observations with a zero dependent variable and the associated independent variables and shares of trial.

14. You will now have the option of viewing a plot of trial forecasts. If you have graphic capabilities and wish to view the plot, enter a Y; otherwise, enter an N or just press Return. Press any key to go on from a graphic image. Then you will be asked if you want a hard copy. Enter Y to print the graph or N to go on.

15. The program will now display:

    deciles of cumulative trial and associated independent variable levels.

16. You will now have the option of viewing a plot of the trial curve form. If you have graphic capabilities and wish to view the plot, enter a Y; otherwise, enter an N or just press Return.

17. You will now be offered three options for continued execution.

If you enter 1 the program will *end*.

If you enter 2 the program will *restart*.

If you enter 3 the program will *repeat the analysis with time as the independent variable*. If this option

is chosen, results are produced without further data entry.

Running the NEWSTRAT Program

1. From the main menu, enter the number that corresponds to the version of NEWSTRAT that you want to use: the printer or the screen-only version.

2. As the printer version of the program starts up, it reminds you to turn on the printer and put it on line.

3. The program header is displayed and you are asked if you want to see all or part of the list of stored data files. Enter the desired list length or zero to continue.

4. A menu appears which asks whether you want to enter data from the keyboard, use stored data, erase a file (if using the screen-only version), or stop.

5. If you choose to enter data, you are asked for the file number that you want to use. You may not use file number 1, which has been reserved for the illustrative data used in Chapter 12. If you choose to use the stored data, you are asked to enter the number of the file. Files can be erased when you are using the screen-only version of the program.

6. If you enter data from the keyboard, you are asked if the data include coefficients based on market estimates of if you will use regression-based estimates. In either case, you will subsequently receive input queries for the questions displayed on the program's data form. (See Figure 12-1.)

    Data entry is greatly simplified if you complete the data form before you start a computer session. In the printed version of the program, all your inputs are echoed to the printer.

7. If you use stored data, the data are loaded, and when the printer version is used, they are echoed to the printer. (The saved files are labeled NEWZ1, NEWZ2, etc.)

8. After the input data are available and the model coefficients have been displayed, a menu appears

that provides three options. Choose *option 1* if you want to make any changes in the data. If you do enter 1, you are asked to enter the question number(s) for the relevant question(s).

When all changes are complete, enter 0 to continue. The new coefficients are displayed and in the printer version all changes are echoed to the printer.

9. After you make an analysis choice as described in 10 and 11 below, but before the analysis process begins, the data are stored. Before storing data, the program asks if you want to use a new file number. If you respond no, the number entered in 5 above is used. If you respond yes, the available empty files are displayed and you are asked to enter your choice of a file number and a description of the file. You may not use file number 1 because it is reserved for the Canadian whiskey data that are discussed in Chapter 12.

10. Next, the above-mentioned menu provides two computing options. Choose *option 2* to print out the year-by-year search for a good division of the budget to push and pull and to retain and gain expense categories. This option provides several suboptions during each year's computations.

Suboption 1 allows you to search for a good division of the budget in more detail by narrowing the spending range that is divided into ten equally spaced divisions. Finally, you must specify your choice of a budget devoted to pull spending (and to switchback spending) for each year.

Suboption 2 allows you to change total annual spending (and thereby the year's attainable cumulative trial rate) and repeat the year's analysis.

Suboption 3 lets you accept the program's recommendation for the division of the budget between pull and push (and between repeat and switchback) without further data entry for the year.

11. *Option 3* lets you skip printing the yearly results. In this case, the program chooses the best budget allocations located for each year and displays these results in three summary tables. The same summary tables are displayed following the analysis performed when option 2 is chosen.

It is frequently useful to use option 3 first to explore the general effects of alternative annual budgets. Once a promising set of annual budgets has been located, a more detailed study of the budgets can be made, possibly making revisions by using the flexibility available in option 2.

RUNNING THE MARMIX PROGRAMS

Input Format Warning

Failure to follow the three rules noted below has produced most of the errors that users have experienced.

> Most sales and spending estimates must be entered in thousands, omitting the last three digits. Usually, the on–screen prompt includes (000).
>
> All market share estimates must be entered in decimal form. Usually, the on–screen prompt includes (.###).
>
> For each mix element (as well as for total spending) the market share at minimum spending must be less than or equal to market share at baseline spending and market share at maximum spending must be greater than or equal to market share at baseline spending. Similarly, the amount spent at the minimum level must be less than or equal to baseline spending and the amount spent at the maximum level must be greater than or equal to baseline spending.

Details about the MARMIX model appear in Chapter 13 and instructions for entering program inputs appear in Chapter 14. Some output capabilities are noted below and the file management capabilities are described. *File erasure capabilities are available just in the screen-only versions.*

FILE MANAGEMENT

The program has a limited set of file-handling capabilities that permit forty input data files to be active at one time. Upon starting the program:

1. *Review* as many file names and numbers as necessary to locate an active file that you want to use,

or to delete one or more files if the screen-only program is being used.

2. *To enter data* from the keyboard, enter 1 for the initial input prompt list and, when prompted to do so, enter the number of the file in which you want to save the data. You may not overwrite file number 1.

3. *To use stored data,* enter 2 from the initial input prompt list, and then enter the number of the stored data file when prompted to do so. The file will be loaded and you will be asked if you want to make any changes in the inputs before the program begins its analysis.

4. *To use a prior model and data for analysis only,* enter 3 in response to the initial prompt and, when prompted to do so, enter the desired file number. The program will load the relevant files and transfer control to the second analysis program segment.

5. *To erase previously used files,* you must *use the screen-only version* of the program. It allows you to enter 4 to the initial prompt to activate the erase option. After a 4 has been entered, you will be prompted for the number of the file that you want to erase. When this number has been entered, the data file and all other files related to the data file will be erased. Next, you are asked if you want to erase another file. If so, enter the file number, and if not, enter 0 to return to the initial menu. At this or any other time you are in this menu in the screen-only version of the program, you can enter 5, which will take you back to the main menu that you used to start the program.

Storing Data Used in Program Segment One

After stored data or key-entered data have been used by the first program segment, you have a chance to choose a new number and name for the files in which the input and intermediate data are stored before control is passed to the second program segment. This feature is particularly useful when you start with a base case and want to test a series of modifications without revising (overwriting) the original file. (The program does not allow you to overwrite file number 1.) This capability can also be used for student assign-

ments when an instructor wants to provide the same set of initial conditions for students who will subsequently test their own modifications to the model.

At the completion of the input section of the first program segment:

1. *To use the original file number and name,* enter N to the prompt that asks if you want to assign a new number and name to the file.

2. *To assign a new number and name,* enter Y to the above prompt. The program will display the numbers of all of the available file numbers.

3. Next, a prompt asks you to enter the available number that you want to use and to enter the new file descriptor.

4. The program saves the data produced during your work session in a DATA# and a TDATA# file with the new number. The latter file along with the TDATAV file are required by the second program segment.

By using the screen-only version, you can erase any feasible DATA# file and remove the file name for the BFILES list of file names. The subsidiary transfer file, TDATA#, is also erased. Alternatively, one or more of these files can be erased from the CAMP directory on the hard disk by using the DOS "erase" command. (See your DOS manual for details.)

Chapter 13 discusses the MARMIX modeling approach and Chapter 14 provides detailed instructions for data entry. You are strongly advised to complete a data form before you enter any data in the computer.

Avoiding Graphic Output

You may avoid all graphic output by entering N (for No) when you are asked if you want to see graphic output. This action is required if your computer does not have a fully IBM AT® or PS/2® compatible graphics cards.

Using a Laser Printer

If an HP Laserjet® or compatible printer is your default printer and you do not choose to print any of the graphic images, the other program output will be printed in the usual manner. If you have a choice of C to continue or P to print a graphic image on your screen, you must always enter C.

Running the CONSOLIDATION Program

As noted in Chapter 15, the input to this program can be either response function output (not permitted by the LEARN version of the programs) from a series of MARMIX analyses *or* a series of response functions entered directly from the keyboard. The first type of input is both usual and preferred. These input func-

tions reflect the contribution to profit promised by each of ten levels of spending on some subsidiary component of a group such as a product, product line, activity, or sales area to which an overall budget will be allocated. The contribution to profit that is input can include the period's results and the future effect of the period's results, or simply a single period's profits.

Because of the complex input requirements, the CONSOL program is not included on the CAMP LEARN disk and its User's Guide is not reproduced in this text.

INDEX